Running Xen:
A Hands-on Guide to the
Art of Virtualization

Running Xen
A Hands-on Guide to the
Art of Virtualization

Jeanna Matthews
Eli M. Dow
Todd Deshane
Wenjin Hu
Jeremy Bongio
Patrick F. Wilbur
Brendan Johnson

PRENTICE
HALL

Prentice Hall
Upper Saddle River, NJ · Boston · Indianapolis · San Francisco
New York · Toronto · Montreal · London · Munich · Paris · Madrid
Cape Town · Sydney · Tokyo · Singapore · Mexico City

The publisher offers excellent discounts on this book when ordered in quantity for bulk purchases or special sales, which may include electronic versions and/or custom covers and content particular to your business, training goals, marketing focus, and branding interests. For more information, please contact:

U.S. Corporate and Government Sales
(800) 382-3419
corpsales@pearsontechgroup.com

For sales outside the United States please contact:

International Sales
international@pearson.com

Visit us on the Web: www.informit.com/ph

Library of Congress Cataloging-in-Publication Data:

Matthews, Jeanna N.

Running Xen : a hands-on guide to the art of virtualization / Jeanna N. Matthews, Eli M. Dow, Todd Deshane, Wenjin Hu, Jeremy Bongio, Patrick F. Wilbur, Brendan Johnson.

p. cm.

ISBN 0-13-234966-3 (pbk. : alk. paper) 1. Xen (Electronic resource) 2. Virtual computer systems. 3. Computer organization. 4. Parallel processing (Electronic computers) I. Title.

QA76.9.V5M38 2008

005.4'3--dc22

2007052439

ISBN-13: 978-0-132-34966-6
ISBN-10: 0-132-34966-3

This product is printed digitally on demand.
Second printing June 2008

Editor-in-Chief
Mark Taub

Acquisitions Editor
Debra Williams Cauley

Development Editor
Michael Thurston

Managing Editor
Gina Kanouse

Project Editor
Chelsey Marti

Copy Editor
Geneil Breeze

Indexer
Erika Millen

Proofreader
Meg Shaw

Technical Reviewers
Jessie Yu
Ken Hess
Jose Renato Santos
Andrew Warfield
Tom "Spot" Callaway
Simon Crosby
Tom Doeppner
Dan Kuebrich
Jim Owens
Zach Shepherd
Keegan M. Lowenstein
Ryan Kornheisl
Igor Hernandez
Alexander M. Polimeni
Erika Gorczyca
Justin Bennett
Joseph Skufca
Mathew S. McCarrell
Krista Gould
Ron Arenas

Publishing Coordinator
Kim Boedigheimer

Cover Designer
Alan Clements

Senior Compositor
Gloria Schurick

This book is dedicated to the Applied Computing Laboratories at Clarkson University and especially to the Clarkson Open Source Institute. May the labs always be a place for contribution, for achievement, for experimentation, and for fun.

Contents

Foreword

The Xen open source hypervisor is changing the world of virtualization. It encourages the broad distribution of a common industry standard hypervisor that runs on a wide range of architectures from super computers to servers to clients to PDAs. By focusing on the hypervisor, the "engine" of virtualization, rather than a specific product embodiment, the Xen open source project enables multiple vendors and the community to combine the common cross platform virtualization features of Xen into exciting new products and service offerings.

To date, the community around the Xen hypervisor has been squarely in the camp of developers and expert users. While the Xen-users mailing list offers a friendly and useful source of advice for those wanting to deploy and manage Xen-based environments, the new user might find herself in need of advice about best practice and step-by-step instructions for the deployment of Xen. *Running Xen: A Hands-on Guide to the Art of Virtualization* speaks directly to this critical need. It provides users with everything they need to know to download, build, deploy, and manage Xen implementations.

To the authors, a set of Xen contributors, practitioners, and researchers, I would like to say thank you on behalf of the broader Xen community for an accessible and immediately useful book. Code might rule, but "know-how" builds the community itself. Clear information, advice, and documentation like this book will allow the Xen project to grow and solidify its user base, to renew its creativity and innovation, to focus itself on a larger set of new virtualization initiatives.

To the readers, I would like to say welcome to the community of Xen users. We look forward to your involvement and contributions! We believe this book will provide you with an excellent introduction to running Xen.

Ian Pratt, Xen Project Leader
VP Advanced Technology, Citrix Systems

Preface

We began using Xen in the fall of 2003 soon after reading the paper "Xen and the Art of Virtualization" published in the Symposium on Operating Systems Principles (SOSP). After attending SOSP and talking to some of the authors, Jeanna Matthews returned excited about Xen. She and her graduate operating systems course at Clarkson University decided to repeat and extend the results reported in that paper. That class included two of the coauthors for this book, Eli Dow (currently at IBM) and Todd Deshane (currently completing his Ph.D.), who were both studying for their Master's degrees at the time. In the process of repeating the results from the 2003 Xen paper, we learned a lot about running Xen—much of it the hard way! Our goal for this book was to write exactly the material we wished was available when we first started using Xen.

In July 2004, we published the paper "Xen and the Art of Repeated Research," describing our experience with Xen and presenting the results we obtained repeating and extending the results. All the authors, in addition to being a part of the Fall 2003 graduate operating systems course, were also members of the Applied Computing Laboratories at Clarkson University, specifically the Clarkson Open Source Institute (COSI) and the Clarkson Internet Teaching Laboratory (ITL). These labs were founded to provide students with hands-on experience with cutting-edge computing technologies and to form a community in which everyone both learns and teaches. Other students in the labs—both graduate and undergraduate—began to use Xen as the basis for both production systems and for research projects. Through the years, we have used Xen as the basis for a number of academic papers as well as the basis of award-winning team projects. In the process, we have learned a lot about running Xen. It is our goal in this book to share this knowledge with you and to make your experience running Xen as smooth and simple as possible.

The book is targeted at individuals and organizations that are deploying Xen systems. It walks the reader through the basics, from installing Xen to using prebuilt guest images. It even tells readers how to experiment with Xen using only a Xen LiveCD. It covers the basics of virtualizations and important elements of all Xen systems like the hypervisor and Domain0. It explains the details of the xm commands for managing guest domains. It helps users deploy custom guest images based on operating systems from Linux to Windows. It covers more advanced topics such as device virtualization, network configuration, security, and live migration. We hope you will find it a good mix of introductory and advanced topics that will prove useful from your first Xen deployment experiment to running production Xen systems.

Chapter 1, "Xen—Background and Virtualization Basics," is a quick introduction to virtualization in general and to Xen in particular. Chapter 2, "A Quick Tour with the Xen LiveCD," provides an overview of Xen's functionalities by exploring the Xen LiveCD. Chapter 3, "The Xen Hypervisor," focuses on the hypervisor that is the core of any Xen system and some other trusted components such as Domain0 and xend. We build on that common understanding of the Xen hypervisor by concretely showing you how to install and configure your own hard-disk-based Xen installation in Chapter 4, "Hardware Requirements and Installation of Xen Domain0." After you have your own hypervisor installation up and running, this book eases you into using guest images by first showing you how to download and use images available from the Internet in Chapter 5, "Using Prebuilt Guest Images." Chapter 6, "Managing Unprivileged Domains," covers the basics of administering the running DomUs or unprivileged guest domains. You are then guided through the various methods of creating your own custom guest images in Chapter 7, "Populating Guest Images." Now that you have all these guests, Chapter 8, "Storing Guest Images," covers a variety of choices for storing guest images for online use as well as backup and sharing.

The second half of this book delves into more advanced system management topics including device management (Chapter 9, "Device Virtualization and Management"), networking (Chapter 10, "Network Configuration"), security (Chapter 11, "Securing a Xen System"), resource distribution (Chapter 12, "Managing Guest Resources"), and migration (Chapter 13, "Guest Save, Restore and Live Migration"). We conclude with a survey of some of the popular administrative tools available for your Xen systems in Chapter 14, "An Overview of Xen Enterprise Management Tools."

Throughout the book, we include listings illustrating relevant commands and their output. We use the command prompt to indicate where the command should be run.

For example, the following would indicate a command to be run as root on the privileged domain, Domain0:

[root@dom0]#

The following would indicate a command to be run as any user in a regular guest domain:

[user@domU]$

Watching these command prompts will help you identify which of the many guests in your Xen system should be used for running any given command.

It is our intention to maintain a website with additional information and materials relevant to the book. We have registered the domain, runningxen.com, for this purpose and are working on assembling materials. We invite you to check on our progress and to send questions or suggestions.

Acknowledgments

We are indebted to the many people who provided feedback and suggestions on the book's content. Simon Crosby provided key feedback on the overall content of the book. Keir Fraser answered a number of technical questions with amazing speed and good humor. Andy Warfield provided feedback for Chapter 9. We thank all the Xen contributors who have released their work to the open source community.

Several of the authors attended the Xen Summit at IBM T.J. Watson Research in April 2007 and we would like to express our gratitude to all the organizers and attendees. Many people provided invaluable feedback and advice in various conversations— short and long. We would especially like to thank Sean Dague, who provided excellent overall Xen advice and feedback throughout this process, and Jose Renato Santos, who provided detailed feedback on the networking material in the book. In general, online materials from all the Xen summits were an invaluable resource for us, as was the Xen Wiki, Xen mailing lists, and other similar resources. We appreciate the efforts of all the individuals who contributed to those materials.

We would like to thank everyone who read early drafts of the book. Jessie Yu in particular went above and beyond the call of duty in reviewing and helping to revise many chapters. Jim Owens provided valuable early feedback for Chapter 13. Tom "Spot" Callaway from Red Hat gave us some excellent suggestions about Chapter 14. (Thanks also to Spot and Máirìn Duffy for several screenshots in that chapter.) Chris Peterman did some early writing on the security chapter and provided valuable comments in the initial phases of organizing the text. Lindsay Hoffman and Barbara Brady provided detailed comments on the writing in Chapter 10. Ryan Kornheisl read a number of chapters and helped test many of the instructions in the book. Anthony Peltz also helped with testing.

We would also like to thank everyone who helped with final revisions. In the last days before the manuscript was submitted, a small army of people volunteered to do a fresh read of many chapters, finding everything from typos to substantial problems. We would like to thank Zach Shepherd, Keegan M. Lowenstein, Igor Hernandez, Alexander M. Polimeni, Erika Gorczyca, Justin Bennett, Joseph Skufca, Mathew S. McCarrell, Krista Gould, and Ron Arenas. We couldn't have done it without you! Tom Doeppner and Dan Kuebrich from Brown University also provided some very helpful feedback on Chapter 3. We would especially like to thank Michael Thurston and Ken Hess for their excellent suggestions. Beside the authors, we believe they are the only ones who have read the entire book!

We would like to thank many members of the Clarkson Open Source Institute and Clarkson Internet Teaching Laboratory who over time added to our understanding and hands-on experience with Xen. Bryan Clark (now at Red Hat), Steven Evanchik (now at VMware), Matt Finlayson, and Jason Herne (both now at IBM) were all co-authors on the 2004 "Xen and the Art of Repeated Research" paper. Jason Herne, Patricia Jablonski, Leslie Cherian, and Michael McCabe were all coauthors on the 2005 "Data Protection and Rapid Recovery From Attack With A Virtual Private File Server and Virtual Machine Appliances" paper, which used Xen for some of the prototypes being tested. Madhu Hapauarachchi, Demetrios Dimatos, Gary Hamilton, Michael McCabe, and Jim Owens were coauthors on the 2007 paper "Quantifying the Performance Isolation Properties of Virtualization Systems." Justin Basinger, Michael McCabe, and Ed Despard were part of the Xenophilia project that won second place in the 2005 Unisys Tuxmaster competition. Cyrus Katrak and Zach Shepherd have been key to the deployment of Xen in our production environment in the Applied CS labs. They have both been a crucial source of advice and feedback.

We would like to thank the OpenSolaris Xen Community Leaders, especially Todd Clayton, Mark Johnson, John Levon, and Christopher Beal, for their quick and helpful responses over e-mail and IRC during our testing of Xen on OpenSolaris. We would like to have included more coverage of Solaris in this book. Additional support in Solaris for Xen beyond what is covered in this book is expected soon.

We would like to thank our editor, Debra Williams Cauley, for her help and encouragement through this entire process. Thanks also to Catherine Nolan who initially contacted us about this project.

Richard A. Wilbur provided access to early HVM-enabled equipment used in testing.

Jeanna Matthews would like to thank her husband Leonard Matthews and children Robert and Abigail Matthews for their patience and love throughout this whole process. She would also like to thank her current and former students—including the six other authors on this book—for all she continues to learn from them.

Eli M. Dow would like to thank his parents, Terry and Mona, as well as his siblings, Ian and Ashley, for everything. He would also like to thank IBM and the Test and Integration Center for Linux for their support during the writing process. Specifically he wishes to acknowledge Frank Lefevre, Duane Beyer, Robert Jay Brenneman, Phil Chan, Scott Loveland, and Kyle Smith for their insightful conversations regarding virtualization and this book in particular. Eli would also like to thank the wonderful faculty and staff at Clarkson University who made his academic career such a wonderful experience. Lastly he would like to thank his significant other, Jessie, for her enduring patience during the writing process.

Todd Deshane would like to thank his significant other, Patty, for her support during the writing of this book.

Wenjin Hu would like to thank his mom, Yajuan Song, and his dad, Hengduo Hu, for their constant support of his study at Clarkson University, and his friend, Liang Zheng, for emotional support.

Patrick F. Wilbur would like to thank his mother, Claudia, his father, Richard, and his significant other, Krista, for their support and patience throughout the development of this book.

About the Authors

Jeanna Matthews is an associate professor of Computer Science at Clarkson University (Potsdam, New York) where she leads several hands-on computing laboratories including the Clarkson Open Source Institute and Clarkson Internet Teaching Laboratory. Students in these labs and in her classes have been winners in a number of prestigious computing contests including the 2001, 2002, and 2004 IBM Linux Challenge, the 2005 IBM North American Grid Scholar's Challenge, the 2005 Unisys Tuxmaster competition, and the 2006 VMware Ultimate Virtual Appliance Challenge. Her research interests include virtualization, operating systems, computer networks, and computer security. She is actively involved in the Association for Computing Machinery as treasurer of the Special Interest Group on Operating Systems, editor of *Operating Systems Review*, and is a member of the Executive Committee ACM's U.S. Public Policy Committee, US-ACM. She is also the author of a computer networking textbook, *Computer Networking: Internet Protocols in Action*, that has been translated into several languages. Jeanna received her Ph.D. in Computer Science from the University of California at Berkeley in 1999.

Eli M. Dow is a software engineer in IBM's Test and Integration Center for Linux in Poughkeepsie, NY. He holds a B.S. degree in Computer Science and Psychology as well as an M.S. in Computer Science from Clarkson University. He is passionate about open source software and is an alumnus and founding member of the Clarkson Open Source Institute. His interests include virtualization, Linux systems programming, the GNOME desktop, and human-computer interaction. He is the author of numerous IBM developerWorks articles focused on Linux and open source software. Additionally, he has coauthored two books on the mainframe hypervisor z/VM, entitled *Introduction to the New Mainframe: z/VM Basics* and *Linux for IBM System z9 and IBM zSeries*. His first published experience with Xen was coauthoring an early academic paper entitled

"Xen and the Art of Repeated Research." Recently he has focused on developing highly available, enterprise customer solutions deployed on virtualized Linux using the z/VM hypervisor.

Todd Deshane expects to obtain a Ph.D. in Engineering Science from Clarkson University in 2008. He also has a Master of Science in Computer Science and a Bachelor of Science in Software Engineering from Clarkson. While at Clarkson University, he has had a variety of research publications—many involving Xen. In 2005, a project that was based on Todd's Master's thesis—an open source collaborative, large database explorer—won first place in the Unisys TuxMaster competition. Todd's primary academic and research interests are in the area of operating system technologies, such as virtual machine monitors, high availability, and file systems. His doctoral dissertation focuses on using these technologies to provide desktop users with an attack-resistant experience, with automatic and autonomic recovery from viruses, worms, and adverse system modifications. During his Ph.D. years, Todd has been a teaching assistant and an IBM Ph.D. Fellowship recipient. At IBM, Todd has worked on internship projects involving Xen and IBM technologies. Todd enjoys teaching, tutoring, and helping people.

Wenjin Hu graduated from Clarkson University in 2007 with a Master's degree of Computer Science and is currently working on his Ph.D. His Masters thesis was "A Study of the Performance Isolation Properties of Virtualization Systems." His research field is applying virtualization techniques to operating systems and security.

Jeremy Bongio is currently a Master's student at Clarkson University. He won second place in the Unisys Tuxmaster competition in 2005 with a project called Xenophilia, an early effort to make Xen more user friendly. He is a current member and former student director of the Clarkson Open Source Institute, where he actively learns and experiments with different kinds of virtualization.

Patrick F. Wilbur is currently pursuing graduate studies in Computer Science at Clarkson University. His interests include operating systems, systems and application security, natural language processing, and home automation. In his spare time, Patrick enjoys composing music, experimenting with amateur radio, storm chasing, and working on various electronics, software, and carpentry projects around the house. He is currently a member of the Clarkson Open Source Institute, a volunteer at the Applied Computer Science Laboratories at Clarkson University, an emergency communications volunteer, and a member of the Association for Computing Machinery.

Brendan Johnson graduated from Clarkson University in 2002 with a Bachelor's degree in Computer Science and a minor in Mathematics. Brendan continued his education at Clarkson University and obtained a Master's of Science in Computer Science with a thesis in quantum computing. Brendan is currently a senior software architect at Mobile Armor, a world leading "Data At Rest" encryption software company.

## Chapter 1

Xen—Background and Virtualization Basics

Xen is a virtual machine monitor (*hypervisor*) that allows you to use one physical computer to run many virtual computers—for example, running a production Web server and a test server on the same physical machine or running Linux and Windows simultaneously. Although not the only virtualization system available, Xen has a combination of features that make it uniquely well suited for many important applications. Xen runs on commodity hardware platforms and is open source. Xen is fast, scalable, and provides server-class features such as live migration. This chapter discusses common uses and types of virtualization, describes the history of virtualization and origins of Xen, provides a brief overview of the Xen architecture, and compares Xen with other virtualization systems.

Common Uses and Benefits of Virtualization

Virtual machine monitors provide a convenient way to use the same physical computer hardware for many different tasks. Operating systems have been doing this for years simply by enabling users to run many different applications at once, such as Web browsers, database servers, and games. However, without virtualization, the act of choosing an operating system and system configuration to run on your physical computer has the unfortunate side effect of closing off many other options. For example, if you run Linux to develop and test programs in that environment, you may not be able to run programs written exclusively for Windows. Also, if you run the newest and fully patched version of Windows, reproducing problems experienced by customers on earlier versions may be difficult. Additionally, if your Web server and database server require different versions of a system library, they may not be able to run on the same system. Without virtualization in each of these examples, you would need to maintain many physical machines, each with a special software configuration, even if the computing resources in one machine are sufficient to run all of your applications at once.

Virtual machine monitors (*hypervisors*) are becoming increasingly important in modern computing because they allow many different operating systems and software configurations to exist on the same physical machine. The hypervisor controls the underlying hardware, allowing it to be used by many guest systems at once, and gives each guest system the illusion that it is running on its own private hardware.

The hypervisor abstracts the physical resources of the host computer into discrete virtual counterparts that can be allocated for use by individual guests. Virtual guests treat their virtual hardware as if it were real, and the hypervisor ensures that this illusion is seamless. Additionally, hypervisors must ensure some level of isolation between guests. In a way, hypervisors act as both magician and traffic cop. Figure 1.1 illustrates the relationship between the physical hardware, the hypervisor, and the guest virtual machines.

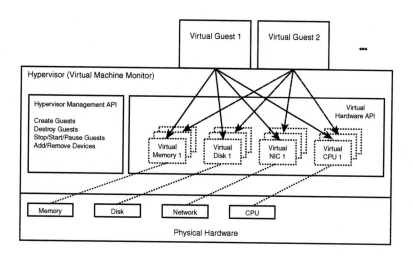

FIGURE 1.1 The hypervisor sits between the guest domains and the physical hardware.

Virtual machine monitors also provide a uniform interface to the hardware. This uniform interface shields guest systems from some lower level details of the physical computing resources and provides portability, which is another key benefit of virtualization. In fact, many modern hypervisors allow guest systems to move from one physical machine to another without interruption. Guest system configurations can easily be developed on one machine and then deployed on many systems. This eases the job of managing or deploying software on a collection of machines with different hardware characteristics. Guest systems can even migrate from one physical computer to another while running. Xen calls this *live migration*. Some benefits of virtualization are as follows.

- Debugging operating systems is time consuming and requires exceptionally skilled programming. Virtualization can ease the burden by allowing a developer to test new operating systems as a guest on a more stable host. This technique has been used for many years and has proven effective. Similarly, security researchers can create guest operating systems that are isolated from one another as well as the host. Such guests allow researchers to study the effects of worms, Trojans, and viruses, without affecting the host system. These isolated guests are colloquially referred to as being "sandboxed." Sandboxed guests can also be used to test updates or cutting-edge software before applying them to production systems.

- Another benefit of virtualization is the ability to recover quickly from software problems caused by deliberate malicious attacks or accidental malfunctions. By maintaining a copy of a stable guest image, recovering from an attack can be as simple as rolling back to this trusted saved point.

- Virtualization can provide higher availability by relocating guests when a server machine is inoperable. Server environments can have many physical machines, each running a number of guest systems. Guest systems can be moved seamlessly between physical machines to balance the load dynamically, thus using the aggregate resources most efficiently. Many enterprise customers have enjoyed these benefits on exotic hardware platforms for many years. Xen now provides these advantages to a wider audience.

- Other benefits of virtualization become especially clear in a server environment. One example is the ability to consolidate many services on one physical machine while still allowing each service to be administered independently. In a multihosting environment, a service provider may run guest systems belonging to many different individuals or businesses on the same physical machine. Each entity could have its own root or administrative access, make its own choices as to what software to run, and administer its own virtual guest autonomously without any need to consult or coordinate with the owners of the other guest systems.

- Most of the advantages of virtualization, especially on commodity platforms such as x86, derive from the abundance of computing power available on a single machine. As the power of the average system has increased, the amount of computing power that goes underutilized is also increasing—especially with multiprocessor and multicore systems. Virtualization provides a way to take advantage of this latent computing power by consolidation onto today's increasingly powerful physical machines.

- Hypervisors can be especially useful for developers, because the developers no longer need to restart physical machines to switch between various operating systems. Multiboot configurations are just not sufficient for these developers any longer. Developers requiring this functionality are becoming more common as more applications are made multiplatform.

- From a business perspective, virtualization can provide a reduced total cost of ownership (TCO). Hardware is utilized more fully when multiple operating systems coexist on a single physical machine. Imagine running just two virtual machines on each server a company owns. This would mean 50 percent of the hardware would be needed for the same computing infrastructure. Now, we do not mean to imply every computer should be running simultaneous virtualized guest operating systems, but often many machines sit practically idle, and these computers are prime candidates for consolidation via virtualization. Training costs for employees can be decreased when using virtualization because it allows several different training configurations (operating systems and applications) to coexist on a single platform, thus fewer computers are needed for training, and reconfiguration is minimized between different training sessions.

- In many business environments, users are afforded the advantage of being able to virtualize legacy operating systems and applications on modern hardware platforms. Typically, migration of these applications to current architectures is too costly. Even if migration was successful, those applications would need debugging for many years to be as robust as the original applications. With a virtual machine, users are free to execute legacy products in a protected virtual environment without the fear of some rogue legacy application bringing the system to a halt.

- The final benefit of virtualization that bears mentioning is decreased power consumption and cooling infrastructure. Servers running virtualized at higher utilization make more efficient use of power than many systems functioning at low capacity. Because smaller space is occupied by the computing infrastructure, there is more room to adequately cool today's very dense and very warm data centers. In some cases a substantial cost savings for air conditioning can be realized.

Types of Virtualization

Many technical details of virtualization are similar, yet various approaches exist to solve problems associated with the different implementations. Four major virtualization architectures in modern computing provide the illusion of complete stand-alone systems: emulation, full virtualization, paravirtualization, and operating system level virtualization. For completeness, we also briefly discuss two other types of virtualization—library and application level virtualization—even though they are not capable of running complete stand-alone systems with full operating systems.

Modern operating systems on personal computers usually provide a weak form of isolation through the use of individual processes, with generous facilities for sharing data between the processes. Most PCs are designed for a single user, so sharing is often given precedence over isolation. A modern PC might have any number of programs running as separate processes. Each has its own unique process identifiers obtained from a global pool but shares a common underlying file system. In contrast, hypervisors have been designed to obtain much stronger isolation between virtual machines. Most hypervisors provide no more sharing support between guest instances than disjointed physical computers on the same network.

Each virtualization technique trades some level of isolation for increased sharing of resources among its guests. Typically, stronger isolation comes at the cost of some performance. This is due to the overhead required to implement strong isolation mechanisms. Conversely, weaker isolation can relax the implementation requirements in ways that can increase performance.

Emulation

In *emulation*, the virtual machine simulates the entire hardware set needed to run unmodified guests for completely different hardware architecture. This is illustrated in Figure 1.2. Typically, emulation is used to create new operating systems or microcode for new hardware designs before that hardware is physically available. Examples include PearPC, Bochs, and the nonaccelerated form of QEMU.

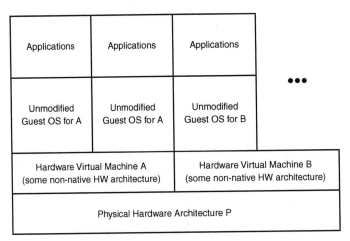

FIGURE 1.2 Emulator virtual machines provide a virtual computing architecture that is not the same as the actual physical architecture of the host machine. Operating systems intended for the emulated hardware are executed unmodified.

Full Virtualization

Full virtualization (also called *native virtualization*) is similar to emulation. As in emulation, unmodified operating systems and applications run inside a virtual machine. Full virtualization differs from emulation in that operating systems and applications are designed to run on the same architecture as the underlying physical machine. This allows a full virtualization system to run many instructions directly on the raw hardware. The hypervisor in this case polices access to the underlying hardware and gives each guest operating system the illusion of having its own copy. It no longer must use software to simulate a different basic architecture. Figure 1.3 illustrates full virtualization.

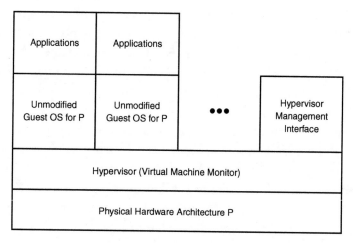

FIGURE 1.3 The full virtualization hypervisor presents the actual physical hardware "P" to each guest so that operating systems intended for the underlying architecture may run unmodified and unaware that they are being run virtualized.

For x86, virtualization systems are often classified as full virtualization if they can run unmodified guest operating system binaries. However, some of these still make some simplifying changes to x86 for easier virtualization and still achieve high performance. The x86 architecture is notoriously difficult to virtualize. Because of this, virtualization specifics (Intel's VT and AMD's AMD-V, discussed in the "Intel VT" and "AMD-V" sections in Chapter 4, "Hardware Requirements and Installation of Xen Domain0") have been added to improve performance and make running an operating system within a Xen virtual machine simpler. They support these changes with clever methods, such as on-the-fly binary translation of instructions that are not desired in their simplified x86 architecture.

Major vendors of full virtualization include VMware Workstation, VMware Server (formerly GSX Server), Parallels Desktop, Win4Lin Pro, and z/VM. Xen supports full virtualization on basic architectures with the previously mentioned hardware support for virtualization.

Paravirtualization

A third common technique for virtualization is referred to as *paravirtualization*. In some instances this technique is also referred to as enlightenment. In paravirtualization, the hypervisor exports a modified version of the underlying physical hardware. The exported virtual machine is of the same architecture, which is not necessarily the case in emulation. Instead, targeted modifications are introduced to make it simpler and faster to support multiple guest operating systems. For example, the guest operating system might be modified to use a special hypercall application binary interface (ABI) instead of using certain architectural features that would normally be used. This means that only small changes are typically required in the guest operating systems, but any such changes make it difficult to support closed-source operating systems that are distributed in binary form only, such as Microsoft Windows. As in full virtualization, applications are typically still run unmodified. Figure 1.4 illustrates paravirtualization.

Major advantages include performance, scalability, and manageability. The two most common examples of this strategy are User-mode Linux (UML) and Xen. The choice of paravirtualization for Xen has been shown to achieve high performance and strong isolation even on typical desktop hardware.

Xen extends this model to device I/O. It exports simplified, generic device interfaces to guest operating systems. This is true of a Xen system even when it uses hardware support for virtualization allowing the guest operating systems to run unmodified. Only device drivers for the generic Xen devices need to be introduced into the system.

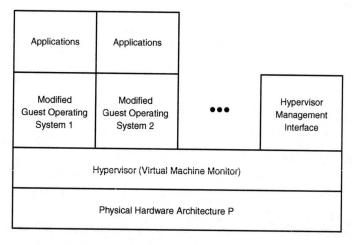

FIGURE 1.4 Paravirtualization hypervisors are similar to full virtualization but use modified guest operating systems to optimize virtual execution.

Operating System Level Virtualization

A fourth technique is *operating system-level virtualization* (also called *paenevirtualization* to reflect that it is "almost virtualization"). In operating system level virtualization there is no virtual machine monitor; instead, the virtualization is done entirely within a traditional single operating system image. Operating systems supporting this type of virtualization are general-purpose, time-shared operating systems with the capability to provide stronger name space and resource isolation. The "guests" created in such a system still look and feel like separate machines with their own file systems, IP addresses, and software configurations. Figure 1.5 illustrates operating system level virtualization.

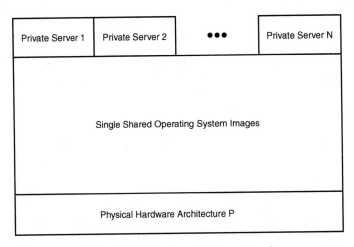

FIGURE 1.5 With operating system level virtualization, all private virtual servers are executed within the context of a single shared operating system image intended for the underlying physical hardware of the host machine.

The advantage of operating system level virtualization is that it requires less duplication of resources. When discussing resources in terms of operating system virtualization, the main architectural idea is to require less physical computer memory for the host system. Guests can often share copies of some user space software programs, libraries, and even stacks of software. At the very least, each of these homogeneous guest instances does not require its own private kernel because they would all be absolutely identical binaries. When operating system virtualization is used, the memory requirements for each new guest can be substantially less. Operating system level virtualization excels in situations that require extreme scalability of concurrently running guests since more of this type of guest can be fit into a given amount of physical RAM. Interestingly, a guest here is something substantially different from guests as we have discussed them so far. In this case a guest is a container of tightly coupled user space processes, and, although typically thought of, not a full-blown operating system instance.

In an environment where each guest wants to run the same operating system, operating system level virtualization can be appropriate. However, for many users, the ability to run different operating system environments on the same machine is the primary reason for virtualization. Operating system level virtualization by definition does not provide those same advantages.

Another weakness of operating system virtualization is that it generally shows weaker isolation across guests. As one guest uses more resources, the performance of all other guests is negatively affected. This is not a fundamental problem. The underlying operating system could be modified to provide stronger isolation, but experience has shown that the complexity and effort required to fully achieve that is high.

In environments where all guests belong to the same administrative domain, weak isolation may be acceptable because the administrator can adjust the allocation of resources to alleviate any problems. This does not work in environments such as multi-hosting environments where guests are owned and operated by different entities with no specific incentive to collaborate fairly.

Implementations of operating system level virtualization include Virtuozzo, Linux VServers, OpenVZ, Solaris Containers, FreeBSD jails, and HP UX 11i Secure Resource Partitions.

Other Types of Virtualization

Two remaining types of virtualization bear mentioning, although unlike the first four we discussed, they are not capable of executing a full operating system. The first is *library virtualization*, which emulates operating systems or subsystems via a special software library. An example of this type of virtualization is the Wine library available on Linux systems. Wine provides a subset of the Win32 API as a library to allow Windows desktop applications to be executed in a Linux environment.

The final type of virtualization discussed in this chapter is *application virtualization (managed runtime)*. Application virtualization is the approach of running applications inside a virtual execution environment. This is different from running a normal application on the hardware. The virtual execution environment provides a standard API for cross-platform execution and manages the application's consumption of local resources. It may also supply resources such as the threading model, environment variables, user interface libraries, and objects that aid in application programming. The most prevalent example of such a virtual execution environment is the Sun Java Virtual Machine. It is important to keep in mind that this technique does not virtualize the full-blown set of hardware necessary for a full operating system.

Overview of Virtualization Types

Table 1.1 contains a summary of the virtualization techniques discussed in this section.

TABLE 1.1 Virtualization Techniques at a Glance

Type	Description	Advantages	Disadvantages
Emulation	The hypervisor presents a complete virtual machine (of a foreign computing architecture to the host) enabling foreign applications to run in the emulated environment.	Simulates hardware that is not physically available.	Low performance and low density.
Full	The hypervisor provides a complete virtual machine (of the same computing architecture as the host) enabling unmodified guests to run in isolation.	Flexibility—run different versions of different operating systems from multiple vendors.	Guest OS does not know that it is being virtualized. Can incur a sizable performance hit on commodity hardware, particularly for I/O intensive applications.
Para	The hypervisor provides a complete but specialized virtual machine (of the same computing architecture as the host) to each guest allowing modified guests to run in isolation.	Lightweight and fast, near native speeds: Demonstrated to operate in the 0.5%–3.0% overhead range. [http://www.cl.cam.ac.uk/research/srg/netos/papers/2003-xensosp.pdf] Allows OS to cooperate with hypervisor—improves IO and resource scheduling. Allows virtualizing architectures that do not support full virtualization.	Requires porting guest OS to use hypercalls instead of sensitive instructions. The main limitation of paravirtualization is the fact that the guest OS must be tailored specifically to run on top of the virtual machine monitor (VMM), the host program that allows a single computer to support multiple, identical execution environments. This especially impacts legacy closed source operating systems that have not yet implemented paravirtualized extensions.

Type	Description	Advantages	Disadvantages
OS level	A single operating system is modified in such a way as to allow various user space server processes to be coalesced into functional units, which are executed in isolation from one another while running on a single hardware platform.	Fast, lightweight virtualization layer. It has the best possible (that is, close to native) performance and density, and features dynamic resource management.	In practice, strong isolation is difficult to implement.
			Requires the same OS and patch level on all virtualized machines (homogeneous computing infrastructure).
Library	Emulates operating systems or subsystems via a special software library. Does not provide the illusion of a stand-alone system with a full operating system.	Provides missing API for application developers.	Often performs more slowly than a native optimized port of the application.
Application	Applications run in a virtual execution environment that provides a standard API for cross-platform execution and manages the application's consumption of local resources.	Manages resources automatically, which eases programmer learning curve. Increases portability of applications.	Execution is slower than native code.
			Overhead of virtual machine incurred when compared to native code.

Virtualization Heritage

Virtualization is certainly an important part of today's computing environments, but many people do not realize virtualization is not a new concept. In fact, virtualization has roots that reach back to the beginning of modern computing. The original implementations still live on in new incarnations, but they are typically used only in niche areas such as the mainframe and generally have gone unnoticed by the personal computer generation. The resurgence of virtualization in modern times has brought the concepts to the general public. Figure 1.6 contains a time line of selected milestones in virtualization. In the next few sections, we explain some of these milestones to help provide a historical context for the Xen hypervisor.

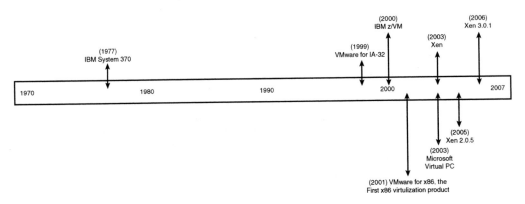

FIGURE 1.6 Time line showing some major events in the history of virtualization

The IBM Mainframe

With the recent commercial interest in commodity virtualization, it is important to look back at the origins of hypervisor technology. Virtualization originated during the 1960s on IBM mainframes. Early computer researchers were interested in the increased robustness and stability offered by hypervisors. Hypervisors allowed multiple operating system guests to run simultaneously, yet ensured that if any one operating system instance crashed, the remaining instances would be isolated. Often, new operating systems and research branches of experimental code would be deployed and debugged alongside stable production instances.

The IBM System/370 was the first commercially available computer system designed for virtualization. With the introduction of the CP/CMS operating system, multiple operating system instances could be run concurrently on the IBM system/370 mainframe hardware. The software implementation was aided by a page translation hardware that enabled efficient support for virtual memory. The cooperation of hardware and software to support virtualization became a staple of the IBM mainframe lineage. In fact, all modern-day IBM mainframes in the System z line continue to provide virtualization support in the hardware. The software that leverages the virtualization hardware most fully is z/VM, which has since superseded the original CP/CMS. The abbreviation VM (virtual machine) is indicative that all the hardware interfaces are virtualized under this operating system. VM/CMS is highly regarded and widely deployed in industry as well as academia. Many modern virtualization approaches owe a great deal to the original mainframe implementations from IBM.

Virtualization on Commodity Hardware

In the 1990s, the Disco project at Stanford led by Mendel Rosemblum used virtual machines to allow commodity operating systems to run on nonuniform memory access (NUMA) computer hardware. However, in this case the commodity operating systems were Silicon Graphics' IRIX, designed to run on the MIPS R10000 processor. This processor, unlike IBM mainframes, was not designed to support complete virtualization. Instead, the Disco project developers used a technique later called paravirtualization to introduce targeted modifications to enable virtualization. The Disco project developers modified and recompiled IRIX to allow it to run on the modified virtual architecture.

The Stanford team turned its attention to modifying another commodity platform not designed for virtualization, x86. This led directly to the founding of VMware and the company's introduction of the first commercial virtualization product for x86. In this case, they enabled running unmodified operating system binaries, such as Microsoft Windows, by performing on-the-fly binary translation for instructions not allowed in their modified x86 architecture. For example, the POPF instruction (which pops from the stack and stores the value into a flags register) must be replaced because when it runs in unprivileged mode it dies silently without making the requested changes to the interrupt-disable flags.

Virtualization Extensions for x86

Since 2005, processor manufacturers such as Intel and AMD have added additional hardware support to their product lines. Intel Virtualization Technology (VT) was developed under the codename Vanderpool and AMD Virtualization (AMD-V) under the codename Pacifica. This hardware furthers the goal of commodity virtualization by adding explicit functionality to enable higher performance hypervisors for full virtualization. With these recent hardware revisions, full virtualization is both easier to implement and has the potential for higher performance. (Recall that Xen uses these extensions to support full virtualization.)

Xen Origins and Time Line

The Xen hypervisor originated at the University of Cambridge Computer Laboratory as part of the ongoing XenoServer project in 2001. The XenoServer project aims to construct a public infrastructure for wide-area distributed computing. The goal of the project is to create a system in which XenoServer execution platforms will be scattered across the globe for use by any member of the public. When the XenoServer infra-structure is completed, its users will submit code for execution and be billed later for any resources consumed during the course of execution. To ensure each physical node is utilized to the fullest extent possible, a high-performance hypervisor for hosting multiple commodity operating systems on a single x86-based server was needed. In that capacity, Xen was created to form the core of each XenoServer node. Xen enables accounting, auditing, and most importantly, the resource management required for the XenoServer infrastructure. For more information on the XenoServer project see `http://www.xenoservers.net/`.

Xen was first publicly unveiled in an academic paper accepted into the 2003 proceedings of the Association for Computing Machinery (ACM) Symposium on Operating Systems Principles (SOSP). The claims of fast virtualization supported on commodity x86 machines garnered wide interest from the academic community. Those claims were independently verified in an academic setting, thus strengthening the claims of performance. Soon after, a growing number of parties became interested in this new take on virtualization. In the years since the initial Xen publication, several major updates to the project have occurred, providing enhanced functionality, reliabil-ity, and performance.

It is noteworthy that during the development of Xen 1.x, Microsoft Research, in collaboration with the University of Cambridge Operating System group, developed a port of Windows XP to Xen. The port was made possible in part by Microsoft's Aca-demic Licensing Program. Unfortunately, due to the terms of that license program, the port was never published, although it is mentioned in the original Xen SOSP paper.

A separate company, XenSource, was founded in 2004 to promote the ubiquitous adoption of an open source Xen hypervisor in the enterprise. XenSource focused its business on supporting the development of the wholly open sourced Xen core, while simultaneously selling enterprise packages and management software to its customers. While XenSource leads and coordinates the development efforts, contributions have been made by a wide array of companies and organizations including IBM, Sun, HP, Red Hat, Intel, AMD, SGI, Novell, the NSA, the US Navy, Samsung, Fujitsu, Qlogic, and many others, including academic researchers from many universities. Together, they produce a standard that all players in the Xen ecosystem can rely on, reducing risk and speeding development for all participants.

During late 2004, Xen 2.0 came on the scene. The new release achieved greater flex-ibility in guest operating system virtual I/O device configuration. At this point in Xen's development, users could configure arbitrary firewall rules, routing, and bridging of guest virtual network interfaces. Additional support was added for copy-on-write LVM volumes as well as loopback files for storing guest operating system disk images. Xen 2.0 included symmetric multiprocessing support, though guest images remained single processor. The most impressive enhancement from a demonstration perspective was the addition of live migration, which allows a running guest operating system instance to be moved across network-connected hardware without perceptible interruption of service. Xen debuted a much touted guest migration function that impressed many casually interested open source hackers.

During 2005, a growing community of interested parties formed around Xen. This trend was evident, both in academia and in industry, and by early 2006 Xen had achieved substantial mindshare in the virtualization space. Major Linux distributors became increasingly interested in leveraging Xen technology for their customers, and Xen-support became standard in many Linux distributions. The Xen 2.0 hypervisor also supported more guest operating systems than ever before, including Linux, Open-Solaris, Plan 9, and several BSD variants.

In 2006, Xen 3.0 introduced an abstraction layer for the hardware virtualization technologies provided by Intel's Vanderpool and AMD's Pacifica implementation. This enabled unmodified guests (called *Hardware Virtual Machine* or *HVM* guests) in addition to the traditional paravirtualized guests. Xen 3.0 also brought support for SMP guest systems (including hot-pluggable virtual CPUs), large memory support, trusted platform module (TPM) support, and a port to the IA64 architecture. Subsequent Xen 3 releases contained a new CPU scheduler with support for weights, caps, and automatic SMP load balancing as well as measurement tools (Xen-oprofile), which will enable Xen developers to optimize code for even greater future performance. Other notable features have included network performance increases from packet segmentation offload, enhanced IA64 support, and the initial port to the Power processor architecture.

In 2007, Citrix acquired XenSource and the XenSource team became the Citrix XenServer Product Group. Also in 2007, Xen 3.1 was released. It has support for the XenAPI, a programmatic interface to Xen commands that allows the integration of third-party management tools, including those based on the Distributed Management Task Force's Common Information Model (DMTF CIM) that is becoming standard for management of heterogeneous clusters. It also enables save/restore/migration capability and dynamic memory control for HVM guests. The current version of Xen is available at http://xen.org/download/. As this book goes to publication, the most recent iteration of Xen, version 3.2, has been released.

Other Virtualization Systems for Commodity Hardware

Xen is not the only virtualization system available, but it has a combination of features that make it uniquely well suited for many important applications. Xen runs on commodity platforms. Xen is open source. Xen is fast, showing near native performance. Xen is scalable. Xen provides server-class features such as live migration. It supports both unmodified guests such as Windows and paravirtualized guests. Many companies are rallying behind Xen as an open source platform in which they can contribute efforts with full assurance that they won't be hidden behind a proprietary platform that could change unexpectedly.

One final distinctive virtualization system feature that we discuss is the installation type. There are two main installation types: *hosted and bare-metal*. Hosted means that the virtualization system is installed and runs on a host operating system. Bare-metal means that the virtualization system is installed and runs directly on the physical hardware, with no host operating system necessary. Xen is a bare-metal virtualization system. Recall also that Xen supports paravirtualization and full virtualization.

This section discusses a variety of commodity virtualization technologies in the marketplace today. We previously discussed different kinds of virtualization from an abstract standpoint. In this section we look at concrete example implementations of each virtualization approach along with their advantages and disadvantages. If you are not interested in these other virtualization technologies, go ahead and skip over this section. Don't worry; there will not be a quiz later.

Emulation

- **Bochs**—An x86 computer simulator available for execution on a variety of platforms, including x86, PowerPC, SPARC, Alpha, and MIPS. Bochs can be configured to emulate many generations of the x86 computing architecture including 386, 486, Pentium, Pentium Pro, and more modern 64-bit implementations. Bochs additionally emulates optional instructions such as MMX, SSE, SSE2, and 3DNow. Bochs has the distinction of simulating not only the processor but also the entire computer system, including the peripherals necessary for ordinary operation. The peripherals include mouse, keyboard, graphics hardware, and networking devices. Bochs is able to run a number of operating systems as guests, including numerous editions of Windows including XP and Vista, DOS, and Linux. It is important to note that Bochs needs a host operating system to operate and does not install on the bare hardware. Bochs is typically hosted on Linux, Windows, or Max OS X.

- **QEMU**—Another example of an emulator, but the ways in which QEMU is unlike Bochs are worth noting. QEMU supports two modes of operation. The first is the Full System Emulation mode, which is similar to Bochs in that it emulates a full personal computer (PC), including peripherals. This mode emulates a number of processor architectures, such as x86, x86_64, ARM, SPARC, PowerPC, and MIPS, with reasonable speed using dynamic translation. Using this mode, you can emulate an environment capable of hosting the Microsoft Windows operating systems (including XP) and Linux guests hosted on Linux, Solaris, and FreeBSD platforms.

  Additional operating system combinations are also supported. The second mode of operation is known as User Mode Emulation. This mode is only available when executing on a Linux host and allows binaries for a different architecture to be executed. For instance, binaries compiled for the MIPS architecture can be executed on Linux executing on x86 architectures. Other architectures supported in this mode include SPARC, PowerPC, and ARM, with more in development. Xen relies on the QEMU device model for HVM guests.

Full Virtualization

- **VMware**—Founded in 1998, was the first company to offer commercial virtualization software for x86 and today offers an extensive product line of virtualization solutions for x86-based servers and desktops. VMware has a bare-metal product, ESX Server. With VMware ESX Server, a hypervisor sits between the guest operating systems and the bare hardware as an abstraction layer. With VMware workstation, the hypervisor runs in hosted mode as an application installed on top of a base operating system such as Windows or Linux. VMware enables the execution of unmodified guest operating systems through on-the-fly translation of x86 instructions that cannot be virtualized. VMware ESX Server and Workstation are commercial products. There is a hosted version of VMWare Server that is freely downloadable as is VMware Player, which allows users to run virtual machines created by VMware Server or Workstation. VMware also hosts an extensive library of free, preconfigured virtual machine appliances. See http://www.vmware.com/appliances/. Note that VMware can run paravirtualized guest's by using VMI (described in the paravirt_ops section later in this chapter).

- **Microsoft**—A relative latecomer to the enterprise virtualization market is set to release Hyper-V, a hypervisor product that will be available both as a stand alone product and as a feature for Windows Server 2008. Microsoft also has a hosted virtualization product that is freely available for Windows called VirtualPC. Virtual PC was initially implemented for the Apple Macintosh by a company called Connectix. The first version was released in the middle of 1997. In 2001 Windows support was released under the moniker Virtual PC for Windows 4.0. Two years later, in 2003, Microsoft realized that virtualization was becoming increasingly pivotal to the enterprise market and purchased Virtual PC and the previously unreleased product called Virtual Server. The software is currently in the marketplace as Microsoft Virtual PC 2007. There is also a version of Virtual PC for Mac that is commercially available. Virtual PC 2004 emulated an Intel Pentium 4 CPU with an Intel 440BX chipset (the chipset that supported Pentium II, Pentium III, and Celeron processors), a standard SVGA Vesa graphics card, audio card, and Ethernet device. Since then, Microsoft has released the Windows version as a free download, while the Mac version remains commercially available. The 2007 edition supports the Windows Vista as guest (32-bit only and without support for the new Aero Glass interface) and host (both 32- and 64-bit). At this time Virtual PC 2007 is available only on the Windows platform. It is interesting to note that both platform implementations use dynamic recompilation to get the job done. Earlier editions of Virtual PC running on the Macintosh platform utilized dynamic recompilation to convert foreign x86 instructions into the native PowerPC instructions. Interestingly, the Virtual PC editions for Windows employ dynamic recompilation for a completely different reason. The Windows edition translates guest kernel mode and real mode x86 code into x86 user mode code. Any guest user mode code is run natively. Guest calls are trapped in some circumstances to increase performance or integration with the host environment.

- **Linux KVM (Kernel Virtual Machine)**—Another newcomer to the virtualization landscape is Linux KVM. KVM is a full virtualization solution that was merged during the 2.6.20 mainline kernel development period. KVM is a modification to the Linux kernel that actually makes Linux into a hypervisor upon insertion of an additional KVM module. The method of KVM operation is rather interesting. Each guest running on KVM is actually executed in user space of the host system. This approach makes each guest instance (a given guest kernel and its associated guest user space) look like a normal process to the underlying host kernel. Thus KVM has weaker isolation than other approaches we have discussed. With KVM, the well-tuned Linux process scheduler performs the hypervisor task of multiplexing across the virtual machines just as it would multiplex across user processes under normal operation. To accomplish this, KVM has introduced a new mode of execution that is distinct from the typical modes (kernel and user) found on a Linux system. This new mode designed for virtualized guests is aptly called guest mode. Guest mode has its own user and kernel modes. Guest mode is used when performing execution of all non-I/O guest code, and KVM falls back to normal user mode to support I/O operations for virtual guests. The KVM module employs a new character device driver to expose virtual hardware to the guest instances through the /dev/kvm entry in the hypervisor file system. KVM guests then access the virtual hardware via a lightly modified QEMU process. When executed on modern hardware with virtualization extensions, Linux (32-and 64-bit) and Windows (32-bit) guests are supported. Although hardware support is needed for Windows guests, KVM is being developed to take advantage of paravirt_ops for Linux guests.

Paravirtualization

- **User-mode Linux**—The paravirtualization implementation known as *User-mode Linux* (*UML*) allows a Linux operating system to execute other Linux operating systems in user space. Each virtual machine instance executes a process of the host Linux operating system. UML is specifically designed to execute Linux guest VMs on a Linux host. UML was merged during the 2.6 kernel development period. UML guests share the usual complement of virtual device types found in modern virtualization implementations. Because UML is a form of paravirtualization, guest kernels must have certain options enabled in the kernel configuration file before compilation. UML kernels can be nested, allowing stacks of guest virtual machines to be executed on one another with a single Linux host instance as the foundation. The major disadvantage of UML is that it is a Linux VM for Linux host solution. Although reasonable, this strategy may not fit today's heterogeneous computing environments that need virtualization benefits.

- **lguest** —Lguest is a another method of virtualization found in the mainline Linux kernel. Lguest is maintained by Rusty Russel and was merged during the 2.6.23 development period. A very interesting detail of lguest is that it is implemented as a kernel module unlike the other virtualization methods which use much different mechanisms described in this book. Though lguest might not be as functional as some other types of virtualization, it is an extremely good tool for learning and experimentation with virtualization implementations due to its relatively small code size. An experimental 64-bit port of lguest is currently being worked on by Red Hat. Though lguest is new, its rapid inclusion into upstream kernel sources makes it worthy of note. You can learn more about lguest at the project homepage: `http://lguest.ozlabs.org/`.

- **A common paravirtualization Interface "paravirt_ops"**—The history of in kernel virtualization shows some early disagreement on how to best implement virtualization in the kernel. There was no standard in kernel interface for implementing paravirtualization. While Xen took one approach, VMWare proposed an alternative cross platform ABI called the Virtual Machine Interface (VMI) in 2005. VMI was merged into the kernel during the 2.6.21 development period. Meanwhile, other implementations of virtualization were taking their own distinct implementation approaches. The Linux kernel developers realized some form of clear implementation solution should be able to underpin each vendor's needs. Thus they used an approach found in other parts of the Linux kernel code. Often in the Linux kernel, if it is known that there will be different implementations of a given function API, an operations structure is used to maintain that single API in a cohesive fashion. The implementation proposed is known as the paravirtual operations structure (also known as the paravirt_ops struct). This method does not enforce any particular ABI, but instead allows runtime selection of the actual implementation of methods in the API. Each virtualization platform may implement their own back-end functions to this common interface. Linux merged patches supporting paravirt_ops during the 2.6.23 mainline kernel development cycle. This recent standardization has occurred in the Linux virtualization space due to the cooperation of many of the virtualization developers and should facilitate faster upstream development of virtualization technologies. With this infrastructure in place, a kernel supporting paravirt_ops should be able to be executed natively, as a Xen guest, or as a VMI guest.

Operating System Virtualization

- **Linux-VServer**—Linux-VServer is an example of operating system virtualization for commodity hardware. Supported by both the 2.4 and 2.6 Linux kernels and operating on a variety of hardware platforms (x86, x86-64, SPARC, PowerPC, MIPS, ARM), Linux-VServer virtualizes a single instance of the Linux kernel such that multiple guests can be instantiated in user space. In VServer terminology, the guests are called virtual private servers (*VPS*). VPSes execute independently with no knowledge of one another. Extra measures are taken to ensure that these VPS processes are isolated via modifications to the Linux kernel's internal data structures and algorithms. Linux-VServer leverages a strict variant of chroot to isolate each VPS's root directory that does not allow the chroot to be escaped. Thus the VPS is isolated to its own portion of the file system and may not peek at its parent or subsequent siblings. The VServer modifications continue with the introduction of an execution context. A context is conceptually the container that groups of VPS processes are coalesced into. Via a context, tools like top or ps only show relevant results for a single VPS. On initial boot, the kernel defines a default context for its own execution. Additionally, VServers use a special spectator context for administration tasks such as viewing every process on the system regardless of which context it is in.

  VServer scheduling is accomplished using a bucket metaphor. A bucket of a fixed capacity is filled with a specified amount of tokens at every specified interval until the bucket is full. Note that any excess tokens are "spilled" out of the bucket. At each timer pop, a process that actually needs (and uses) the CPU consumes exactly one token from the bucket, unless the bucket is empty. Should the bucket be empty, the process is entered into a hold queue until the bucket has been refilled with a minimum M of tokens, at which point the process is rescheduled. This scheduler design is advantageous because tokens may be accumulated in times of quiescence to be cashed in when needed at a later time. Such a context token bucket allows fine-grained control over the processor utilization of all confined processes. A modification of this approach as implemented in VServers is to dynamically modify priority values based on the current fill level of the bucket.

- **OpenVZ**—OpenVZ is another operating system virtualization implementation, similar in spirit to Linux-VServer, but distinct. This implementation also works on a variety of hardware architectures, including x86, x86-64, and PowerPC. OpenVZ is implemented as a modified kernel that supports its own isolated user space virtual environments known as VE's. VEs are also referred to as VPSes, or virtual private servers, as is the case with the Linux-VServer project. VE resources are controlled by constructs called *beancounters*. These beancounters are made up of a number of parameters defining the resource distribution for a VPS instance. The beancounters define the available VE system memory, total available IPC objects, and other system parameters. One implementation distinction worthy of note is in the OpenVZ dual action scheduler. This unique scheduler first selects a VPS instance from the list of virtual servers and then invokes a second level of scheduling to choose which guest user space process should be executed (while respecting standard Linux process priority flags). OpenVZ also supports a notion of a guest operating system checkpoint. A checkpoint occurs when a guest is quiesced and has its state "frozen" and serialized into a file. A checkpointed file can then be transported to another OpenVZ host and resumed. Unfortunately, like many commodity virtualization solutions, OpenVZ comes with yet another set of implementation unique administration tools for virtualization management. Additionally, OpenVZ supports live migration functionality that many system administrators find useful.

Popular Virtualization Products

Table 1.2 contains a list of popular virtualization products along with information about their type and license. Although there are important and subtle differences between them, GPL (GNU General Public License), LGPL (GNU Lesser General Public License), and CDDL (Common Development and Distribution License) are all types of open source licensing. The BSD and MIT licenses are permissive licenses written by the University of California, Berkeley, and Massachusetts Institute of Technology, respectively. Like open source licenses, these licenses permit use of the source code and in fact provide fewer restrictions on use than GPL style licenses. For more information on open source licenses see: http://www.opensource.org/licenses.

TABLE 1.2 Virtualization Products at a Glance

Implementation	Virtualization Type	Installation Type	License
Bochs	Emulation	Hosted	LGPL
QEMU	Emulation	Hosted	LGPL/GPL
VMware	Full Virtualization & Paravirtualization	Hosted and bare-metal	Proprietary
User Mode Linux (UML)	Paravirtualization	Hosted	GPL
Lguest	Paravirtualization	Bare-metal	GPL
Open VZ	OS Level	Bare-metal	GPL
Linux VServer	OS Level	Bare-metal	GPL
Xen	Paravirtualization or Full when using hardware extensions	Bare-metal	GPL
Parallels	Full Virtualization	Hosted	Proprietary
Microsoft	Full Virtualization	Hosted	Proprietary
z/VM	Full Virtualization	Hosted and bare-metal	Proprietary
KVM	Full Virtualization	Bare-metal	GPL
Solaris Containers	OS Level	Hosted	CDDL
BSD Jails	OS Level	Hosted	BSD
Mono	Applications level	Application Layer	Compiler and tools GPL, Runtime libraries LGPL, Class libraries MIT X11
Java Virtual Machine	Applications Level	Application Layer	GPL

Summary

In this chapter we introduced the basic concepts behind virtualization as well as the benefits virtualization can provide. Through the presentation of the various types of virtualization in place today, we provided a solid foundation for you to compare virtualization candidates based on the type of virtualization they implement. We looked at the historical precursors to Xen beginning with specialized hardware from the 1960s and provided discussion of the hardware evolution that enables virtualization like Xen to operate on modern commodity hardware. Your understanding of this material provides the requisite information for you to make informed comparisons between Xen and other virtualization technologies. Because the discussion here has made the case for selecting Xen as a virtualization platform, the remainder of this book focuses exclusively on Xen.

References and Further Reading

"x86 Virtualization." Wikipedia.

http://en.wikipedia.org/wiki/Virtualization_Technology.

"Comparison of Virtual Machines." Wikipedia.

http://en.wikipedia.org/wiki/Comparison_of_virtual_machines.

"Emulation." Wikipedia.

http://en.wikipedia.org/wiki/Emulation.

"Full Virtualization." Wikipedia.

http://en.wikipedia.org/wiki/Full_virtualization.

"Popek and Goldberg Virtualization Requirements." Wikipedia.

http://en.wikipedia.org/wiki/Popek_and_Goldberg_virtualization_
requirements.

"Xen." Wikipedia.

http://en.wikipedia.org/wiki/Xen.

"Xen." Xen.org.

http://xen.org/xen/.

"The Xen Virtual Machine Monitor." University of Cambridge.

http://www.cl.cam.ac.uk/research/srg/netos/xen/.

Xen Project Status and Roadmap from the 2007 Xen Summit.

http://xen.org/xensummit/
http://community.citrix.com/blogs/citrite/barryf/2007/12/14/Xen
+Project+Status+and+Roadmap+from+Xen+Summit

"Relationship between Xen Paravitualization and Microsoft Enlightenment."

http://servervirtualization.blogs.techtarget.com/2007/03/30/
steps-along-the-path-of-enlightenment/

"virtualization.info: News digest and insights about virtual machines and virtualization technologies, products, market trends since 2003."

http://www.virtualization.info/

Chapter 2

A Quick Tour with the Xen LiveCD

If you are interested in trying Xen out for yourself, the quickest method is often the LiveCD provided by the Citrix XenServer Product Group. It allows you to try Xen on your computer without installing Xen or even changing your current system configuration. This chapter walks you through using the LiveCD step-by-step. In the process, you get a taste of starting and managing guest images and other basic Xen commands.

Running the LiveCD

The Xen LiveCD runs entirely within your machine's main memory (RAM) and does not require any installation to a physical hard disk. It can be used to test for hardware compatibility and to familiarize yourself with some of the basic Xen administration commands before committing to a full installation of Xen.

The results in this chapter were obtained on an IBM ThinkPad laptop. Specifically we used a T60p model equipped with an Intel Core Duo processor and 2GB of RAM. Listing 2.1 gives the details of the test system. You might not be able to successfully use the LiveCD yourself because it does not support all hardware configurations. Additionally, the LiveCD has been shown to work with VMware.

LISTING 2.1 Details of the Test System

```
localhost:/ # cat /proc/cpuinfo
processor       : 0
vendor_id       : GenuineIntel
cpu family      : 6
model           : 14
model name      : Genuine Intel(R) CPU        T2600   @ 2.16GHz
stepping        : 8
cpu MHz         : 2161.338
cache size      : 2048 KB
fdiv_bug        : no
hlt_bug         : no
f00f_bug        : no
coma_bug        : no
fpu             : yes
fpu_exception   : yes
cpuid level     : 10
wp              : yes
flags           : fpu tsc msr pae mce cx8 apic mtrr mca cmov ➥
pat clflush dts acpi mmx fxsr sse sse2 ss ht tm pbe nx ➥
constant_tsc pni monitor vmx est tm2 xtpr
bogomips        : 4323.93
```

```
processor        : 1
vendor_id        : GenuineIntel
cpu family       : 6
model            : 14
model name       : Genuine Intel(R) CPU         T2600  @ 2.16GHz
stepping         : 8
cpu MHz          : 2161.338
cache size       : 2048 KB
fdiv_bug         : no
hlt_bug          : no
f00f_bug         : no
coma_bug         : no
fpu              : yes
fpu_exception    : yes
cpuid level      : 10
wp               : yes
flags            : fpu tsc msr pae mce cx8 apic mtrr mca cmov  ➥
     pat clflush dts acpi mmx fxsr sse sse2 ss ht tm pbe nx  ➥
     constant_tsc pni monitor vmx est tm2 xtpr
bogomips         : 4323.93
localhost:/ #
```

Step 1: Downloading the LiveCD Image and Creating the CD

The version used when writing this book was approximately 674MB and was downloaded from http://bits.xensource.com/oss-xen/release/3.0.3-0/iso/livecd-xen-3.0.3-0.iso. We have a mirrored copy of this version on the book Web site (runningxen.com). You can look for a more current Xen LiveCD at http://xen.org/download/.

The LiveCD file is an ISO image and needs to be written to a CD before it can be used. Once downloaded and written to CD, simply insert the disc into your computer's CD-ROM or DVD-ROM drive and reboot the machine. Note that your computer must be set to boot from the CD or DVD-ROM drive in your BIOS settings. The major benefit of the LiveCD is that it does not install Xen, but instead boots a special Xen administrative host (referred to as Domain0) from the CD and not from your local hard disk. The Domain0 is the host platform that the Xen management tools reside on. Guest domains, or guests, other than Domain0 are unprivileged domains, referred to as DomainU or DomU. These guest domains are the running operating system we want to virtualize.

Domain0 and the underlying Xen hypervisor gain a privileged, administrative position in the system during boot. The Xen hypervisor is inserted in the GRUB menu and boots first. The hypervisor then starts Domain0. Finally, configuration files in Domain0 are consulted, which instruct it to start previously created guest domains. These configuration files are discussed in more detail in Chapter 6, "Managing Unprivileged Domains."

The LiveCD contains both the Domain0 and Xen guest images on the same disc. When using the Xen LiveCD, note that it is operating from disc and memory only, thus guests run slower than if they were installed natively on the local hard disk.

Step 2: Choosing a Domain0 Image from the GRUB Menu

The Xen LiveCD contains several Domain0 images. When you first boot the LiveCD you see a GRand Unified Bootloader (GRUB) menu. This menu allows you to select which host environment you want to boot.

In Figure 2.1, seven options are available at the boot loader menu. The first two options are Debian based, the second two options are CentOS (a Red Had Enterprise Linux derivative) based, followed by two OpenSUSE options, and finally a stock (that is, not Xen-aware) Debian kernel.

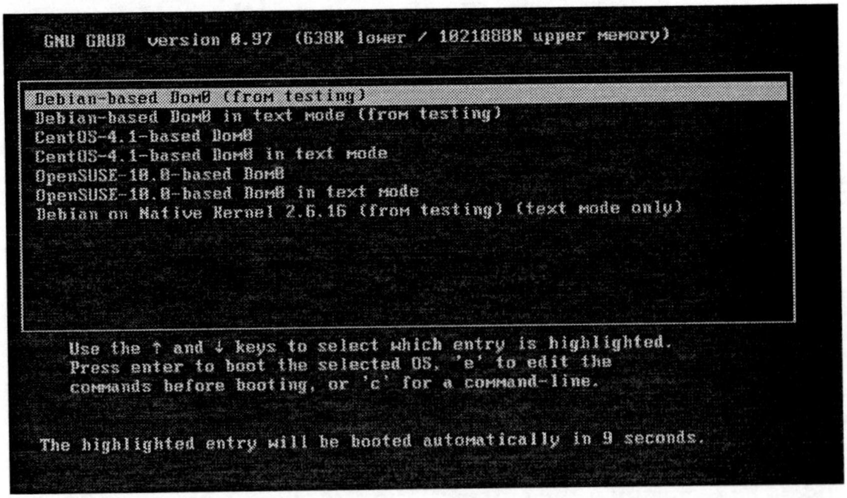

```
 GNU GRUB  version 0.97  (638K lower / 1021888K upper memory)

 Debian-based Dom0 (from testing)
 Debian-based Dom0 in text mode (from testing)
 CentOS-4.1-based Dom0
 CentOS-4.1-based Dom0 in text mode
 OpenSUSE-10.0-based Dom0
 OpenSUSE-10.0-based Dom0 in text mode
 Debian on Native Kernel 2.6.16 (from testing) (text mode only)



 Use the ↑ and ↓ keys to select which entry is highlighted.
 Press enter to boot the selected OS, 'e' to edit the
 commands before booting, or 'c' for a command-line.


 The highlighted entry will be booted automatically in 9 seconds.
```

FIGURE 2.1 LiveCD GRUB menu showing boot choices: Debian-based Dom0 (in text mode or not), CentOS-based Dom0 (in text mode or not), OpenSUSE-based Dom0 (in text mode or not), or Debian on native kernel

Of the six Xen-aware Domain0 kernels located at the top of the list, you will notice that for each distribution listed, there are both graphical and text mode options. If you are operating on a system that has enough resources, you may use a graphical option (any that does not specify "text mode"), which provides many of the amenities expected from a modern computing environment. If your system has limited resources or the graphical environment selections do not work for you, alternatively try the text mode options.

If you are unsure of which image to select, the Debian version is recommended simply because the resulting wallpaper selection is easier on the eyes. After you have made your selection, a bootup sequence similar to most Linux boot procedures rolls by. On the hardware we tested, boot time was under two minutes, and we were presented with a graphical logon screen.

Step 3: Logging In and the Desktop

The login screen shown in Figure 2.2 is the *GNOME Display Manager* (GDM), which describes the login process above the text entry field. The instructions as tested in our environment were for a "root" logon using the password "xensource." If the login is successful, the GDM prompt disappears, and you are presented with a logo for the Xfce Desktop environment.

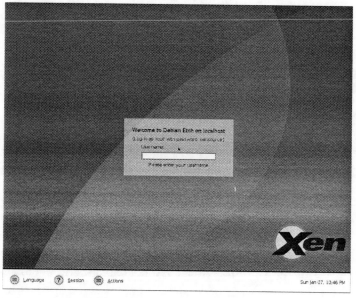

FIGURE 2.2 Logging in to the Debian Domain0 desktop

Xfce is a lightweight graphical desktop environment for various Linux systems. Xfce makes an excellent Xen hosting environment due to its relatively light resource consumption. However, for your own Xen systems, you can choose to deploy GNOME, KDE, or any other windowing environment you prefer.

After Xfce has fully loaded, a panel appears at the top and at the bottom of the desktop. Additionally, two terminal windows open along with an instance of the Firefox Web browser showing some help documentation to get you started. The uppermost terminal defaults to displaying the **xentop** command output. Figure 2.3 shows an example of the full desktop. The xentop utility is a simple console-based application to view virtual guests and their resource allocation/consumption in real time. The second console provides instructions above the prompt on how to create virtual guests using only the command line.

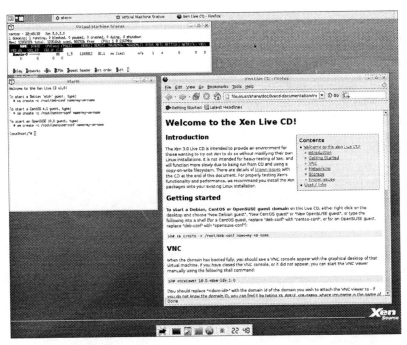

FIGURE 2.3   The desktop automatically displays a "Welcome to the Xen LiveCD!" file, *xentop*, and a
            terminal window

Figure 2.4 shows **xentop** output before the creation of any guests. Note the Domain0 shows up in the output. Later chapters explain the details of the **xentop** output. For now, it is enough to know that each guest started appears in this list.

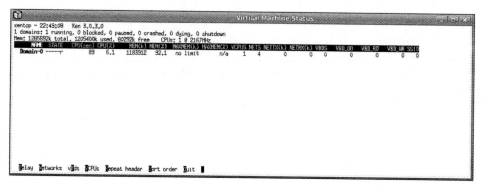

FIGURE 2.4   `xentop` output showing only Domain0

You may also be wondering what other interesting commands and Xen tools come installed on the Xen LiveCD. Listing 2.2 shows a list of Xen commands available on the LiveCD. Though we do not use all these commands in this chapter, they are all available on the LiveCD. Later chapters discuss many of these commands in further detail.

LISTING 2.2 Xen Commands

```
localhost:~# xen<tab>
xen-bugtool       xenstore-chmod      xenstore-write
xenbaked          xenstore-control    xenstored
xencons           xenstore-exists     xentop
xenconsoled       xenstore-list       xentrace
xend              xenstore-ls         xentrace_format
xenmon.py         xenstore-read       xentrace_setmask
xenperf           xenstore-rm         xentrace_setsize
localhost:~#
```

Step 4: Creating Guests

You can follow the instructions in the second console window (shown in Listing 2.3) to create a number of virtual machine guests using the **xm create** command. The -c option specifies to open an intial console to the new virtual machine once the virtual machine creation is completed. The last argument provided is the location of a configuration file that contains all the details about the type of guest to create. You learn more about this later in the book. For now, the LiveCD comes with a number of premade configuration files as shown in Listing 2.3. All you need to do is choose one of these.

If you specify the /root/deb-conf configuration file, you get a new Debian guest. Similarly, the /root/centos-conf file gives you CentOS guest, and /root/opensuse-conf gives you an OpenSUSE guest. These choices should be familiar from the GRUB menu where we have similar choices for Domain0. It is important to recognize that the choice of guest type is completely independent of the Domain0 choice. You can have CentOS and OpenSUSE guests on a Debian Domain0 and vice versa.

LISTING 2.3 Welcome Message with Instructions for Guest Creation

```
Welcome to the Xen Live CD v1.6!
To start a Debian 'etch' guest, type:
  # xm create -c /root/deb-conf name=my-vm-name
To start a CentOS 4.1 guest, type:
  # xm create -c /root/centos-conf name=my-vm-name
To start an OpenSUSE 10.0 guest, type:
  # xm create -c /root/opensuse-conf name=my-vm-name

localhost:~ # xm create -c /root/deb-conf
localhost:~ #
```

You can specify a descriptive name for each virtual guest you create with the **name** parameter. For instance, you may choose to use a scheme as simple as debian_guest1 for the name of your first Debian guest; however, more descriptive schemes may help you in the long run. If you do not specify a name on the command line, **xm create** prompts you for one.

Listing 2.4 shows the result of creating a Debian guest using the **/root/deb-conf** configuration file. (Note: The **xmlib** warning messages can be safely ignored in this case.)

LISTING 2.4 Trace of a Debian-Based Guest Creation

```
Enter name for the domain: debian_guest1
Using config file "/root/deb-conf".
/usr/lib/python2.4/xmllib.py:9: DeprecationWarning:          ➥
    The xmllib module is obsolete.  Use xml.sax instead.     ➥
    warnings.warn("The xmllib module is obsolete.            ➥
    Use xml.sax instead.", DeprecationWarning)
Started domain debian_guest1
i8042.c: No controller found.
Loading, please wait...
INIT: version 2.86 booting
hostname: the specified hostname is invalid
```

```
Starting the hotplug events dispatcher: udevd.
Synthesizing the initial hotplug events...done.
Waiting for /dev to be fully populated...done.
Activating swap...done.
Checking root file system...fsck 1.39 (29-May-2006)

/tmp/rootdev: clean, 34131/125184 files, 133922/250000 blocks
done.
Setting the system clock..
Cleaning up ifupdown....
Loading modules...done.
Setting the system clock again..
Loading device-mapper support.
Checking file systems...fsck 1.39 (29-May-2006)


INIT: version 2.86 booting
hostname: the specified hostname is invalid
Starting the hotplug events dispatcher: udevd.
Synthesizing the initial hotplug events...done.
Waiting for /dev to be fully populated...done.
Activating swap...done.
Checking root file system...fsck 1.39 (29-May-2006)

/tmp/rootdev: clean, 34131/125184 files, 133922/250000 blocks
done.
Setting the system clock..
Cleaning up ifupdown....
Loading modules...done.
Setting the system clock again..
Loading device-mapper support.
Checking file systems...fsck 1.39 (29-May-2006)
done.
Setting kernel variables...done.
Mounting local filesystems...done.
Activating swapfile swap...done.
Setting up networking....
Configuring network interfaces...Internet Systems Consortium ➡
    DHCP Client V3.0.4
Copyright 2004-2006 Internet Systems Consortium.
All rights reserved.
For info, please visit http://www.isc.org/sw/dhcp/
```

```
Setting the system clock again..
Loading device-mapper support.
Checking file systems...fsck 1.39 (29-May-2006)
done.
Setting kernel variables...done.
Mounting local filesystems...done.
Activating swapfile swap...done.
Setting up networking....
Configuring network interfaces...Internet Systems Consortium ➥
    DHCP Client V3.0.4
Copyright 2004-2006 Internet Systems Consortium.
All rights reserved.
For info, please visit http://www.isc.org/sw/dhcp/

Listening on LPF/eth0/00:16:3e:70:c1:a9
Sending on   LPF/eth0/00:16:3e:70:c1:a9
Sending on   Socket/fallback
DHCPDISCOVER on eth0 to 255.255.255.255 port 67 interval 6
DHCPOFFER from 10.0.8.128
DHCPREQUEST on eth0 to 255.255.255.255 port 67
DHCPACK from 10.0.8.128
bound to 10.0.8.1 -- renewal in 16209 seconds.
done.
INIT: Entering runlevel: 3
Starting system log daemon: syslogd.


Listening on LPF/eth0/00:16:3e:70:c1:a9
Sending on   LPF/eth0/00:16:3e:70:c1:a9
Sending on   Socket/fallback
DHCPDISCOVER on eth0 to 255.255.255.255 port 67 interval 6
DHCPOFFER from 10.0.8.128
DHCPREQUEST on eth0 to 255.255.255.255 port 67
DHCPACK from 10.0.8.128
bound to 10.0.8.1 -- renewal in 16209 seconds.
done.
INIT: Entering runlevel: 3
Starting system log daemon: syslogd.
Starting kernel log daemon: klogd.
Starting Name Service Cache Daemon: nscd.
Starting internet superserver: no services enabled,          ➥
    inetd not started.
Starting periodic command scheduler....
Starting GNOME Display Manager: gdm.
```

```
Welcome to the Xen Live CD version 1.6
Debian GNU/Linux Etch debian-guest1 tty1

You can log in as 'root' using password 'xensource'.

debian-guest1 login:
```

Similarly, we could execute the same command once more with a different guest name as shown in Listing 2.5. Provided the system has sufficient resources to facilitate the request, we would then have an identical clone at our disposal.

LISTING 2.5 Creating a Second Debian Guest Using the Name Parameter

```
localhost:~ # xm create -c /root/deb-conf name=debian_guest2

[output omitted]

localhost:~ #
```

You can also create guests without using the command line at all! Simply right-click on the desktop, and a context menu is presented with options to create new virtual guests. Figure 2.5 shows the menu as it is appears on the desktop.

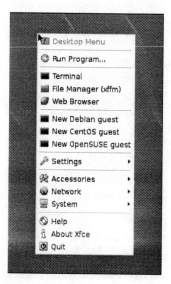

FIGURE 2.5 Graphical menu of guest creation choices

Assuming your host system is equipped with enough RAM, you may make many guests. As each new guest is created, it appears in the **xentop** output.

We recommend creating at least one instance of each of the distributions represented on the LiveCD, creating several guests with the command line method, and creating several guests using the context menu. By the time we were done with our experimentation we had several simultaneous guest operating system instances running concurrently on the guest system described previously in Listing 2.1. As always, depending on hardware, your mileage might vary.

Step 5: Deleting a Guest

If you create more guests than you really want, you can always delete them using the xm destroy command as shown in Listing 2.6. (Note: The **xmlib** warning messages can be safely ignored in this case.)

LISTING 2.6 Deleting a Guest

```
localhost:~ # xm destroy debian-guest1
/usr/lib/python2.4/xmllib.py:9: DeprecationWarning:          ➡
    The xmllib module is obsolete.  Use xml.sax instead.
  warnings.warn("The xmllib module is obsolete.
    Use xml.sax instead.", DeprecationWarning)              ➡
localhost:~ #
```

Notice that the guest has been removed from the **xentop** console, and the resources associated with it have been returned to the Domain0.

Step 6: Interacting with Your Guests

For each guest created, a VNC (Virtual Network Computing) session is automatically created to the guest. VNC is software that allows you to remotely control, and interact with, a computer (the "server" in VNC terminology) by executing a local program (called the "viewer").

One major benefit of VNC is that the server and viewer do not need to be the same architecture or operating system. This capability makes VNC a logical choice for viewing virtualized graphical environments. VNC is widely used and is both freely and publicly available. After the VNC session is operational, you see a normal GDM logon for the individual guest you are attached to. In fact, VNC allows you to use the viewer built into the Domain0 LiveCD, or you could even choose to access the VNC server of one of your DomainU guests from a viewer on a completely different remote machine over a network connection.

If at any time you want to close your VNC session to the guest, you may do so. Reconnecting later is as simple as opening a new console on the Domain0 and typing **vnc <ipaddress>** with the IP address of your guest.

Figures 2.6, 2.7, and 2.8 show the various GDM prompts for each of the DomainU guests we created. Note that the login credentials for the root account are presented on the upper-left corner of the GDM greeter. In this set of experiments, we started an OpenSUSE guest, followed by a CentOS guest, and then a Debian guest. Figure 2.9 shows all three of our virtual machines' VNC windows along with the **xentop** terminal window running on Domain0.

Log into each DomainU using the same username and password as for Domain0 ("root" and "xensource," respectively). Notice that each guest has a distinct look and feel based on the supporting distribution. The default OpenSUSE DomainU desktop is Xfce with a green color scheme. As with other DomainU guests running Xfce, there is a complement of utilities on the panel. The default CentOS color scheme is dark blue. It has practically the same panel configuration as the OpenSUSE guest. Finally, the default Debian DomU guest desktop has a light blue color scheme. It has a slightly different panel configuration as the other types of guests.

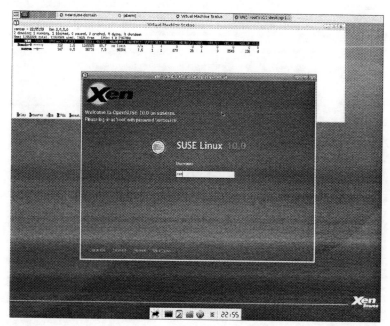

FIGURE 2.6 VNC session showing the login screen of our newly created OpenSUSE Linux 10.0 guest

FIGURE 2.7 VNC session showing the login screen of our newly created CentOS guest

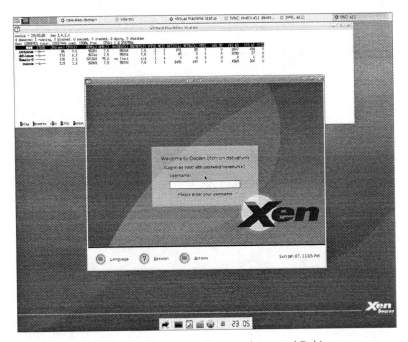

FIGURE 2.8 VNC session showing the login screen of our newly created Debian guest

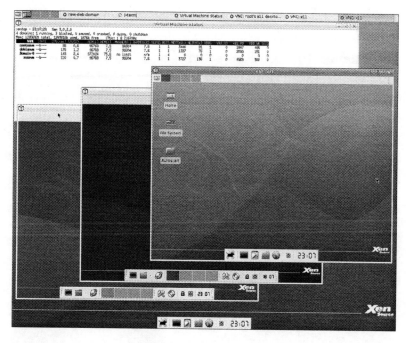

FIGURE 2.9 All three of our virtual machines' VNC windows along with the *xentop* terminal executing on our LiveCD Debian Domain0

Step 7: Testing Your Networking

Networking should be functional on each DomU. To test this, open a Web browser within a guest connected via VNC and attempt to visit Internet Web sites. A good one to try is http://runningxen.com. One quirk observed with the LiveCD is that some of the guests have links to the Mozilla Web browser on their lower panel. It seems that the LiveCD guests have the Firefox Web browser installed instead. If you get a message stating that the Mozilla browser cannot be found, simply launch Firefox from a command prompt with the command **firefox**.

Additionally, guests may connect to each other. For the LiveCD environment, each guest is given a 10.0.*.1 IP address, where the * varies depending on the guest.

Note that our use of the LiveCD involved wired Ethernet connections. Wireless connectivity was not found to be supported on any of our systems.

Figure 2.10 is our Debian-based DomU, showing the network interface with IP address 10.0.1.1. Figure 2.11 is our OpenSUSE virtual machine, showing the network interface with IP address 10.0.3.1. Figure 2.12 is our CentOS virtual machine, showing the network interface with IP address 10.0.2.1.

Note the IP address (prefixed with "inet addr:") shown in the terminal. Each has an ethernet device, namely eth0, eth1, and eth2. Figure 2.12 demonstrates not only the interface, but an execution of the **ping** command that sends packets from the CentOS virtual machine to the Debian-based virtual machine. The important part of the output of the **ping** command is the zero percent packet loss.

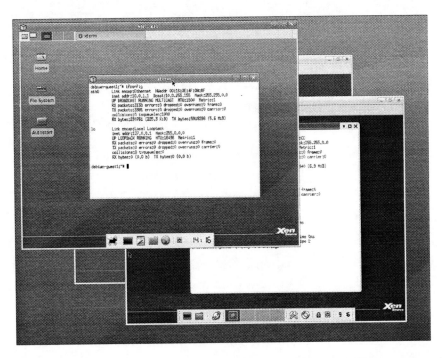

FIGURE 2.10   **ipconfig** run in the Debian guest to illustrate its IP address and other network settings

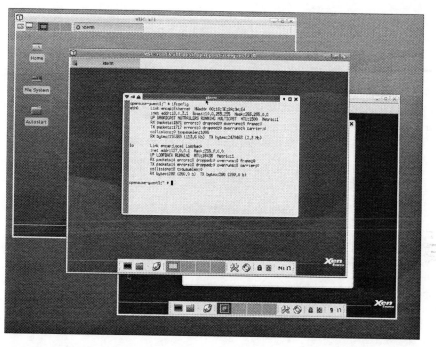

FIGURE 2.11   *ipconfig* run in the OpenSUSE guest to illustrate its IP address and other network settings

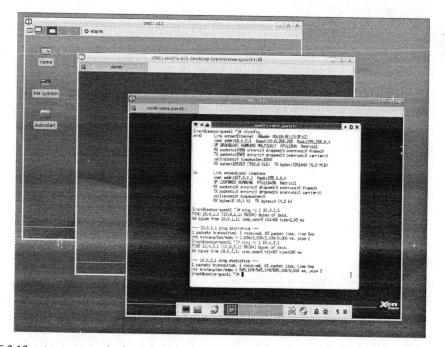

FIGURE 2.12   *ipconfig* run in the CentOS guest to illustrate its IP address and other network settings

Too Many Guests

You might be wondering how you would determine whether you have too many guests. In our testing we created numerous guests that were mostly idle. For our experimentation, we were limited only by memory consumption of the guests and not by CPU consumption. We continued to ask the Xen hypervisor to create more guests until we received the following message shown in Listing 2.7.

LISTING 2.7 Insufficient Memory Warning

```
Enter name for the domain: debian_guest9
Using config file "/root/deb-conf".
Error: I need 98304 KiB, but dom0_min_mem is 262144 and    ➡
shrinking to 262144 KiB would leave only 32412 KiB free.
Console exited - returning to dom0 shell.
Welcome to the Xen Live CD v1.6!

To start a Debian 'etch' guest, type:
  # xm create -c /root/deb-conf name=my-vm-name

To start a CentOS 4.1 guest, type:
  # xm create -c /root/centos-conf name=my-vm-name

To start an OpenSUSE 10.0 guest, type:
  # xm create -c /root/opensuse-conf name=my-vm-name
```

As you can see, Domain0 simply failed to create the guest as we requested. Domain0 prevented us from allocating more memory than would be physically available. If you encounter a message like this and need to enable another guest instance, fear not. It is often possible to squeeze out even more guests using some tuning along with some of the advanced management tools that come with Xen. We cover many of the management commands necessary to overcome this error later in this book.

Summary

Now that you have experimented with the LiveCD, you should be familiar with the basic concepts and functionality of the Xen hypervisor. You saw how easy it can be to create and destroy virtual guests along with monitoring them in real time. We showed that Xen supports multiple types of guests, such as OpenSUSE, CentOS, and Debian Linux, and how Xen DomUs are managed from the special privileged guest known as Domain0. From your Domain0 guest, you saw how easy it is to create and destroy networked virtual machines. Now that you have seen some of the fundamental Xen commands in use, we will explain Domain0, Xen commands, and the Xen system in greater detail.

References and Further Reading

Kumar, Ravi. "Testing out the Xen LiveCD." LWN.net.
   `http://lwn.net/Articles/166330/`.

LiveCD used in this chapter (also see book Web site runningxen.com).
   `http://bits.xensource.com/oss-xen/release/3.0.3-0/iso/`
   `livecd-xen-3.0.3-0.iso`.

Xenoppix.
   `http://unit.aist.go.jp/itri/knoppix/xen/index-en.html`.

Chapter 3

The Xen Hypervisor

The Xen hypervisor is the heart of Xen. It sits between the guest domains and the physical hardware, allocating and controlling resources, enforcing protection and isolation. It literally defines the virtual machine interfaces seen by guest domains. In this chapter, we describe the Xen hypervisor and how it interacts with guest domains. We discuss a special privileged domain, called Domain0, that is used to administer normal guest domains and to control the physical hardware. We also discuss the Xen management daemon, known as xend, that passes control requests to the Xen hypervisor. Finally, we describe XenStore, a database of configuration information used to communicate between domains.

Xen Hypervisor

The Xen hypervisor sits above the physical hardware and presents guest domains with a virtual hardware interface. In this way, it defines the virtual machine that guest domains see instead of the physical hardware. The Xen hypervisor runs on any Xen system, including when running the Xen LiveCD as described in Chapter 2, "A Quick Tour with the Xen LiveCD." Figure 3.1 illustrates the relationship between the hypervisor, the virtual guests, and the physical hardware.

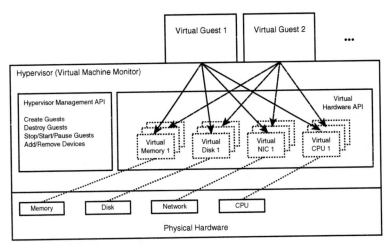

FIGURE 3.1 The relationship of the hypervisor to the physical hardware and guest domains

To minimize modifications to guest operating systems and user level applications running inside guest domains, it is important that the virtual machine look as much like the underlying physical machine as possible. Exposing a completely different virtual machine would mean that none of the standard application level software would run. However, the hypervisor does make some changes in the machine interface it exposes to guest domains.

The following list summarizes the role of the hypervisor:

- **The hypervisor gives each guest domain a portion of the full physical machine resources.** Multiple guests running on the same physical machine must share the available resources. Therefore, the hypervisor does not generally expose the full power of the underlying machine to any one guest. Instead, it allocates a portion of the resources to each guest domain. It can either attempt to partition resources evenly or in a biased fashion to favor some guests over others. It grants each guest a limited amount of memory and allows each guest only its fair share of the CPU. Similarly, it may not want all guests to have access to every physical device in the system and thus it only exposes the devices it wants each guest to see. Sometimes, it may even create virtual devices that have no corresponding underlying physical device—for example, a virtual network interface.

- **The hypervisor exports simplified devices to guest domains.** Rather than emulating the actual physical devices exactly, the hypervisor exposes idealized devices. For example, it doesn't matter whether the network interface card is a 3Com Etherlink or a Linksys wireless card; it can be exposed to guest domains as a generic network class device. Similarly, storage devices are exposed to guest operating systems as generic block devices. This makes it much easier to move guests between physical systems. It also makes it much easier to develop a new operating system or port an existing operating system to a new platform because the operating system running inside a guest VM only needs to support a device driver for each generic class of devices rather than all the possible physical devices. A device driver for the actual physical device need only be running in one domain, such as Domain0.

- **The hypervisor can modify portions of the physical architecture that are difficult to fully virtualize.** The x86 architecture has been notoriously hard to virtualize. Xen exposes a slightly simplified version of the x86 architecture to guest operating systems to make it easier to virtualize efficiently. Care was taken to make sure that these changes only affected the operating systems running in the guest domains and not the user level applications. Operating systems had to be "ported" to the modified virtual machine architecture.

> **NOTE**
> Current versions of Xen have another option. Although they can continue to run guest operating systems that are ported to run on a paravirtualized architecture, they can also take advantage of special hardware support for virtualization that has recently been added to the x86 architecture to run fully virtualized guests. Such hardware support is essential for running closed source operating systems such as Windows, or legacy operating systems that cannot or will not be ported by their owners.

A Privileged Position

The hypervisor's job is to allocate resources to guest domains, to protect guest domains from each other, to provide clean, portable device interfaces, and, if necessary, to provide a virtual machine that can be efficiently virtualized. To do all this it must occupy a privileged position on the system.

In a traditional, nonvirtualized system, the operating system must occupy a privileged position relative to user level applications. Much like a police officer, it uses this privileged position to protect user level applications from each other. To enable this, most processor architectures have at least two privilege levels. The operating system then runs at a higher priority level than user level code, allowing it to force user level applications to "follow the rules."

Protection Rings

In a virtualized system, we have the hypervisor as well as guest operating systems and user level applications. Just as an operating system arbitrates between multiple user level applications, the Xen hypervisor arbitrates between guest operating systems. Thus the Xen hypervisor must run at a higher privilege level than the guest operating systems. However, within the guest domains, we still want the operating system to run at a higher privilege level than the user level applications.

Fortunately, the x86 architecture provides more than two privilege levels. In fact, the x86 architecture has four privilege levels called *protection rings*. Ring 0 is the most privileged, and ring 3 is the least privileged. In a traditional, nonvirtualized system, the operating system executes in ring 0 and the user level applications in ring 3 with rings 1 and 2 typically going unused. In a Xen system, the hypervisor executes in ring 0, guest operating systems in ring 1, and user level applications remain in ring 3.

These protection rings give the hypervisor the leverage it needs to enforce resource sharing and isolation among guest domains. In ring 0, the hypervisor has full control of the physical hardware. Guest domains access the physical hardware only as allowed and coordinated by the hypervisor. All resources needed by guest domains are granted by the hypervisor.

Guest domains make requests of the hypervisor through a set of hypercalls much like user level applications make requests to the operating system with a set of system calls. On x86, system calls are typically done with a software interrupt instruction, int 0x80. Similarly, hypercalls are done with the instruction int 0x82. The hypervisor responds to requests by sending the domain an asynchronous event much like a UNIX signal or an interrupt on real hardware. Here is what an example hypercall might look like in C code:

```
hypercall_ret = xen_op(operation, arg1, arg2, arg3, arg4);
```

Listing 3.1 shows the resulting assembly language for the xen_op routine that sets up the parameters for the Xen hypercall and then actually fires the Xen interrupt.

LISTING 3.1 Assembly for a Xen Hypercall

```
_xen_op:
    mov     eax,  4(esp)
    mov     ebx,  8(esp)
    mov     ecx,  12(esp)
    mov     edx,  16(esp)
    mov     esi,  20(esp)
    int     0x82
    ret
```

With hardware support for virtualization such as Intel's VT-x and AMD's AMD-V extensions, these additional protection rings become less critical. These extensions provide root and nonroot modes that each have rings 0 through 3. The Xen hypervisor can run in root mode while the guest OS runs in nonroot mode in the ring for which it was originally intended.

Domain0

The hypervisor is not alone in its task of administering the guest domains on the system. A special privileged domain called Domain0 serves as an administrative interface to Xen. In a Xen system, Domain0 actually implements some of the functionality we described as being logically a function of the hypervisor. This allows the Xen hypervisor to be a thin layer.

Domain0 is the first domain launched when the system is booted, and it can be used to create and configure all other regular guest domains. Domain0 is also called Dom0 and, similarly, a regular guest domain is called a DomU or unprivileged domain.

Domain0 has direct physical access to all hardware, and it exports the simplified generic class devices to each DomU. Rather than emulating the actual physical devices exactly, the hypervisor exposes idealized devices. For example, the guest domain views the network card as a generic network class device or the disk as a generic block class device. Domain0 runs a device driver specific to each actual physical device and then communicates with other guest domains through an asynchronous shared memory transport.

Domain0 can also delegate responsibility for a particular device to another domain. A driver domain is a DomU that runs a minimal kernel and the backend for a particular device. This has the advantage of moving the complexity and risk of device management out of the Domain0. Moving device management to driver domains can make the system more stable because hardware drivers are notoriously the most error-prone code in an operating system. A driver domain could be stopped and restarted to recover from an error, while stopping and restarting Domain0 can disrupt the entire system.

The physical device driver running in Domain0 or a driver domain is called a backend, and each guest with access to the device runs a generic device frontend driver. The backends provide each frontend with the illusion of a generic device that is dedicated to that domain. The backend understands the details of the real physical device and packages the generic device requests from each frontend into the appropriate form for forwarding to the hardware. Backends also implement the sharing and multiple accesses required to give multiple guest domains the illusion of their own dedicated copy of the device. In general, a smaller and simpler Domain0 is better for the security and stability of the system. Moving device management into driver domains is just one example of this. Although Domain0 typically runs a general purpose operating system, it is wise to use Domain0 strictly for the administration of virtual machines on the system. It is highly recommended that you limit the user level code installed and running in Domain0 to only those applications that are essential to administration of the virtual machines on the system. All other applications can be run in a guest domain. Similarly, it is best to close all unnecessary network ports in Domain0. Overall, a barebones Domain0 is less vulnerable to attack or accidental software fault.

We summarize this comparison of Domain0, driver domains and regular guest domains in Table 3.1.

TABLE 3.1 Comparing Domain0, Driver Domains, and Regular Guest Domains

Type	Privilege Level	Software	Purpose
Domain0, Dom0	Privileged domain	Bare-bones OS	Controls physical hardware.
		Applications to create and configure other domains only or physical device access	Used to create and configure other domains to other domains.
		Physical device drivers	
		Interface to allow other guests to access physical devices controlled	
Driver domain	Privileged domain	Bare-bones OS	Guest domain that is given physical access to a device for the purpose of sharing that device among other domains.
		Physical device drivers	
		Interface to allow other guests to access physical devices controlled	
			Throughout this book, we use the term Driver Domain to refer to a guest with physical access to the device hardware. Domain0 is often used for this purpose. Running device drivers in Domain0 is typically the simplest and most straight-forward configuration.
Regular guest domain, DomU	Unprivileged (by default)	General-purpose OS	Typically virtual device.
			User level applications access only; must run a frontend driver for multiplexed drivers shared with other domains.
			May be granted direct physical access to a device, but best to avoid if possible.

Xen Boot Options

The Xen hypervisor and Domain0 actually gain their privileged position in the system during boot. At system boot time, a bootloader such as GRUB—the GNU GRand Unified Bootloader, is used to choose the software that will control the machine. Because it is the first software "introduced" to the hardware, the Xen hypervisor now has the power to grant control to or withhold control from any other software.

The Xen hypervisor is inserted in the GRUB menu and boots first. The hypervisor then starts Domain0. If other guest domains have been previously created, Domain0 can automatically start them by consulting configuration files that specify the proper settings. These configuration files are discussed in more detail in Chapter 6, "Managing Unprivileged Domains."

Listing 3.2 shows some excerpts from the GRUB configuration file on the LiveCD used in Chapter 2. On the Xen LiveCD, it is /boot/grub/menu.1st, but on some systems it may be in other locations such as /boot/grub/grub.conf or /etc/grub.conf. For the Debian, CentOS, and OpenSUSE Domain0 sections, notice that the same kernel and modules are loaded (/boot/xen-3.0.3.0.gz, /boot/vmlinuz-2.6.16.29-xen, and /boot/initrd-2.6.16-xen.img). This is the equivalent of booting the Xen hypervisor. However, the image passed in the first module line differs. For the Debian Domain0, it is rootfs.img; for the CentOS Domain0, it is centos.img; and for the OpenSUSE Domain0, it is opensuse.img. Also notice that in the last section for the Native Non-Xen kernel, the Xen hypervisor is not booted. Instead, the non-Xen kernel and modules, /boot/vmlinuz-2.6.16-2-686-smp and /boot/initrd-2.6.16-2-686-smp.img, are specified. Of course, in all cases, the kernel and modules are coming from the CD as the root rather than the hard drive.

LISTING 3.2 Excerpt from the GRUB Configuration File on the Xen LiveCD

```
terminal console
timeout   10
default   0

title  Debian-based Dom0 (from testing)
root   (cd)
kernel /boot/xen-3.0.3.0.gz watchdog
module /boot/vmlinuz-2.6.16.29-xen  ro selinux=0
       ramdisk_size=32758 image=rootfs.img boot=cow quiet
module /boot/initrd-2.6.16-xen.img
```

```
title   CentOS-4.1-based Dom0
root    (cd)
kernel /boot/xen-3.0.3.0.gz watchdog
module /boot/vmlinuz-2.6.16.29-xen  ro selinux=0
       ramdisk_size=32758 image=centos.img boot=cow
       hotplug=/sbin/hotplug quiet
module /boot/initrd-2.6.16-xen.img


title   OpenSUSE-10.0-based Dom0
root    (cd)
kernel /boot/xen-3.0.3.0.gz watchdog
module /boot/vmlinuz-2.6.16.29-xen  ro selinux=0
       ramdisk_size=32758 image=opensuse.img boot=cow mkdevfd
       quiet
module /boot/initrd-2.6.16-xen.img


title   Debian on Native Kernel 2.6.16 (from testing)
       (text mode only)
root    (cd)
kernel /boot/vmlinuz-2.6.16-2-686-smp ro 2 selinux=0
       ramdisk_size=32758 image=rootfs.img boot=cow
initrd /boot/initrd-2.6.16-2-686-smp.img
```

Table 3.2 describes a number of additional options that can be used to configure Xen's behavior at boot. They are added directly to the Xen command line in the GRUB configuration file. One of the most important options is how much memory to allocate to Domain0. Domain0 specifies to the hypervisor how much memory is allocated to all other guest domains, but the Xen hypervisor can be told the amount of memory to allocate to Domain0 directly. Because Domain0 should be simple (running the Xen daemon and not much else), it shouldn't need as much memory as a normal guest domain would. Chapter 4, "Hardware Requirements and Installation of Xen Domain0," explains the installation and configuration of Domain0 in detail.

Many of the hypervisor's configuration options control logging, such as the kind of output produced. You can request that the hypervisor produce a substantial amount of debugging information in the form of log messages or even traces of its activity. This output can be sent directly to the screen and/or to one of the serial ports in the system. This is most useful in diagnosing problems at boot. See the Debugging category of options in Table 3.2.

Another configuration option of note specifies what scheduling policy the hypervisor uses. Xen makes changing the scheduling policy easy. A number of different scheduling policies are currently available, including CREDIT and SEDF. SEDF provides weighted CPU sharing and includes real-time algorithms to ensure time guarantees. The CREDIT scheduler is a proportional fair share scheduler.

The CREDIT scheduler was implemented last but is generally recommended. It load balances virtual CPUs of the guest domains across all available physical CPUs. It is a work-conserving scheduler, meaning that physical devices will be idle only when there is no work to do. In contrast, a non-work-conserving scheduler may allow physical devices to be idle even when there is work to do if the idleness helps make the system more predictable.

The CREDIT scheduler allows each domain to be assigned both a weight and a cap. Domains with higher weights get more physical CPU time. Caps are used to limit the amount of CPU a domain can consume.

Other advanced configuration options include whether Symmetric Multiprocessing (nosmp) is supported, whether software IRQ balancing should be done (noirqbalance), and how the Advanced Programmable Interrupt Controller should be handled (apic). There are also some options to override the APIC settings in your BIOS settings. As you might imagine, not all of these options are applicable to every machine. Table 3.2 summarizes the available configuration options.

TABLE 3.2 Xen Boot Options

Option	Category	Description
dom0_mem=X	Standard Configuration	Amount of memory to be allocated to Domain0.
Example: dom0_mem=64M		Units can be specified as B for bytes, K for kilobytes, M for megabytes, or G for gigabytes. If no units are specified, kilobytes is assumed.
lapic	Advanced Configuration	Forces use of the local APIC even if disabled by the uniprocessor BIOS.
nolapic	Advanced Configuration	Do not use the local APIC in a uniprocessor system even if enabled by the BIOS.
apic=default apic=bigsmp apic=es7000 apic=summit	Advanced Configuration	Specifies the APIC platform. This is usually determined automatically.

Option	Category	Description

`console=vga`
`console=com1`
`console=com2H`
`console=com2L`
 	
Default is
`console=com1,vga`
	Advanced Configuration	Specify where Xen console I/O should be sent. More than one destination may be chosen.
		For vga, use regular console for output and keyboard for input.
		For com1, use serial port com1. com2H and com2L allow a single port to be used for both console and debugging. For com2H, characters must have most significant bit (MSB) set. For com2L, characters must have MSB cleared.

`conswitch=Cx`
`conswitch=C`
 	
Example:
 	
`conswitch=a`
 	
`conswitch=ax`
	Advanced Configuration	Used to specify a different character sequence to indicate that serial-console input should be switched between Xen and Domain0. C specifies the "switch character." To actually switch, press Ctrl+C three times for the specified C.
		
		The default switch character is a.
		
		This also controls whether input is automatically switched to Domain0 when Domain0 boots. If the switch character is followed by an x, autoswitching is disabled. Any other value or omitting the x entirely enables autoswitching.

`nosmp`	Advanced Configuration	Disable SMP support.
`sched=credit` `sched=sedf`	Advanced Configuration	Choose a CPU scheduler for Xen to use. Because Xen offers an API for new schedulers to be added, more scheduling choices may appear in the future. The credit scheduler is currently recommended.

`badpage=X,Y,…`
 	
Example:
`badpage= 0x111, 0x222,0x333`
	Advanced Configuration	You can specify a list of physical memory pages not to use because they contain bad bytes. Of course, you could also replace the bad memory!

`noirqbalance`	Advanced Configuration	Disable software IRQ balancing and affinity. Can be used for systems that have hardware for IRQ-routing issues—why do the job twice in hardware and software?

TABLE 3.2 continued

Option	Category	Description
com1=<BAUD>,<DPS>,<IOBASE>, <IRQ> com2=<BAUD>,<DPS>,<IOBASE>, <IRQ> Example: com1=auto, 8n1, 0x408, 5 com2=9600, 8n1	Advanced Configuration/ Debugging	Xen output can be sent to the serial ports, com1 and com2. Typically, this is done for debugging purposes. BAUD = the baud rate. DPS = Data, parity, and stop bits. IOBASE = I/0 port base. IRQ = Interrupt Request Line. If some configuration options are standard, the configuration string can be abbreviated.
mem=X	Debugging/Testing	Limit the amount of physical memory used in the system. Other than debugging/testing, you generally want to use all the memory you have in your system! Units can be specified as B for bytes, K for kilobytes, M for megabytes, or G for gigabytes. If no units are specified, kilobytes is assumed.
tbuf_size=X	Debugging	Request X pages of per-cpu trace buffer space. Traces will be generated in debug builds only.
noreboot	Debugging	Requests that the machine not be automatically rebooted in the case of fatal errors.
sync_console	Debugging	Requests that all console output be sent immediately rather than buffered. Useful for reliably catching the last output generated by a fatal error.
watchdog	Debugging	Enable the Non-Maskable Interrupt (NMI) watchdog timer, which can be helpful in reporting certain failures.
nmi=fatal nmi=dom0 nmi=ignore	Debugging	Specify what to do with an Non-Maskable Interrupt (NMI), parity, or I/O error. For fatal, prints a diagnostic message and hangs. For Dom0, informs Domain0 of the error. For ignore, ignores the error.
apic_verbosity=debug apic_verbosity=verbose	Debugging	Requests that information about the local APIC and IOAPIC be printed.

Table 3.3 contains options that, when specified on the Xen command line in the grub.conf file, will also be propagated to Domain0's command line when it boots. These options have the same syntax as a regular Linux kernel command line. Domain0's kernel is also modified to support one additional nonstandard boot option (xencons or Xen consoles), which is also described in Table 3.3.

TABLE 3.3 Xen-Related Linux Kernel Command Line Options

Linux Option	Description
acpi=off,force,strict,ht,noirq,…	Specify how the Xen hypervisor and Domain0 should parse the BIOC ACPI tables.
acpi_skip_timer_override	Specify that Xen and Domain0 should ignore the timer-interrupt override instructions specified in the BIOS ACPI tables.
noapic	Specify that Xen and Domain0 should use the legacy PIC and ignore any IOAPICs present in the system.
xencons=off xencons=tty xencons=ttyS	Enable or disable the Xen virtual console. If enabled, specify the device node to which it is attached. For tty, attach to /dev/tty1; tty0 at boot time. For ttyS, attach to /dev/ttyS0. The default is ttyS for Domain0 and tty for DomUs.

The GRUB configuration file from the Xen LiveCD did not use many of the options described in Tables 3.2 and 3.3 (only the watchdog option). In Listing 3.3, we show how the Debian-based Domain0 section of the GRUB configuration file shown in Listing 3.2 could be modified to use the dom0_mem and xencons options.

LISTING 3.3 GRUB Configuration File Illustrating Use of Additional Boot Options

```
title Debian-based Dom0 (from testing)
root (cd)
kernel /boot/xen-3.0.3.0.gz dom0_mem=65536 watchdog
module /boot/vmlinuz-2.6.16.29-xen ro selinux=0
    ramdisk_size=32758 xencons=off image=rootfs.img
    boot=cow quiet
module /boot/initrd-2.6.16-xen.img
```

Choosing an OS for Domain0

With hardware support for virtualization, there are few limitations on what operating systems can run in a regular guest domain (without hardware support, operating systems must be ported to run in a guest domain). Even with hardware support for virtualization, there are some special requirements for Domain0, primarily to support sharing of devices among guest domains. Linux and NetBSD have both been fitted with the necessary hooks and tools. Work is in progress for OpenSolaris, and more operating systems are likely to follow suit.

When choosing an OS for Domain0, it is best to stick with an OS with which you are already comfortable. If you currently run NetBSD, using NetBSD as Domain0 would be a natural first step. If you have no particular preference for an OS, we recommend that you start with Linux as Domain0 initially. Currently, selecting Linux as the choice of Domain0 provides the system operator with the most documentation, driver support, and information about possible problems. Linux is the default and most widely used choice for Domain0.

Guest virtual machines run equally well on any type of Domain0. Thus, experimenting with a new Domain0 installation can be as simple as installing the new Domain0 on a second machine and moving over copies of your existing guest domains.

xend

xend, the Xen Daemon, is a special process that runs as root in Domain0. It is a critical part of every Xen system. Users typically interface with xend via the Xen Management (xm) commands. xm commands to start, stop, and manage guest domains actually send requests to the xend daemon first, which are in turn relayed to the Xen hypervisor via a hypercall.

xend and xm are actually both Python applications. The xend daemon listens for requests on an open network port. The xm commands typically send requests to the listening xend daemon on the same machine, but features such as live migration involve sending requests to a xend daemon running on another machine.

xm is in the user interface. xend handles the validation and sequencing of requests from multiple sources. The Xen hypervisor actually carries out the requests.

Controlling xend

The start argument to the xend daemon is used to start xend if it is not already running. No output is produced by this command.

```
[root@dom0]# xend start
```

The stop argument to the xend daemon is used to stop an instance of xend that is currently running.

```
[root@dom0]# xend stop
```

When the restart argument is used, if an instance of the xend daemon is currently running it will be restarted. If an instance of the xend daemon is not currently running, one will be started. xend restart is often used when changes have been made in its configuration file.

```
[root@dom0]# xend restart
```

After you have started xend, you can use the ps command to list running processes and verify that it is running. You actually see a number of Xen related processes/daemons in a typical ps listing. Listing 3.4 includes portions of the ps output from the Xen LiveCD. In this listing, xend is actually listed as python /usr/sbin/xend start because in the automated script that started xend, that is the command line used. Interestingly, there appear to be two copies of xend started by the LiveCD. You can also see the Xen Console daemon (xenconsoled) and the XenStore daemon (xenstored). In addition, you see xenwatch, a utility to monitor Xen domains, and XenBus, a per-guest driver that provides an API for interactions with XenStore. We discuss XenStore in more detail later in this section.

LISTING 3.4 List of Xen-Related Running Processes

```
USER    PID %CPU %MEM VSZ    RSS TTY   STAT START    TIME COMMAND
root      8 0.0  0.0    0      0 ?     S<    13:36    0:00 [xenwatch]
root      9 0.0  0.0    0      0 ?     S<    13:36    0:00 [xenbus]
root   3869 0.1  0.0 1988    924 ?     S     13:37    0:00 ➥
       xenstored --pid-file /var/run/xenstore.pid
root   3874 0.0  0.3 8688   4040 ?     S     13:37    0:00 ➥
       python /usr/sbin/xend start
root   3875 0.0  0.4 49860  5024 ?     Sl    13:37    0:00 ➥
       python /usr/sbin/xend start
root   3877 0.0  0.0 10028   464 ?     Sl    13:37    0:00 ➥
       xenconsoled
```

It is good to be aware of the other Xen-related daemons running on the system. For example, if an attempt to stop or restart the xend daemon fails, it may also be necessary to kill all instances of the XenStore daemon and the XenConsole daemon and sometimes even remove the contents of the xenstored directory.

```
[root@dom0]# killall xenstored xenconsoled
```

```
[root@dom0]# rm -rf /var/lib/xenstored/*
```

While xend is running, it can be useful to query its current condition by using the status argument.

```
[root@dom0]# xend status
```

xend Logs

xend produces a number of logs as it runs. These logs are another important way to gain insight into the status of a running xend instance. The logs are typically kept in /var/log or /var/log/xen.

xend sends its runtime log output to a rotating log file called xend.log. As log files grow too large, they are moved to xend.log.1, xend.log.2, and so forth, until deleted. Similarly, xend logs events (less frequently) to xend-debug.log. If tracing is enabled, xend logs function calls and exceptions to xend.trace.

Listing 3.5 contains a short snippet from xend.log from the Xen LiveCD to illustrate the output. Notice the time and date stamp at the beginning of each log record. Notice also the INFO, DEBUG, and WARNING flags used to indicate the severity of the issue being reported.

Consulting these logs is an important first step in diagnosing any problems you may be having configuring your Xen system. Often, a Web search for the string included in any error message helps you locate postings from others who have encountered and overcome a similar problem.

LISTING 3.5 Sample xend.log

```
[2007-02-24 13:37:41 xend 3875] INFO (__init__:1072)        ➡
     Xend Daemon started
[2007-02-24 13:37:41 xend 3875] INFO (__init__:1072)        ➡
     Xend changeset: Mon Oct 16 11:38:12 2006 +0100          ➡
     11777:a3bc5a7e738c
[2007-02-24 13:37:42 xend.XendDomainInfo 3875] DEBUG )      ➡
     (__init__:1072)
XendDomainInfo.recreate({'paused':0, 'cpu_time':49070788642L,➡
     'ssidref': 0, 'handle': [0, 0, 0, 0, 0, 0, 0, 0, 0, 0,  ➡
     0, 0, 0, 0, 0, 0], 'shutdown_reason': 0, 'dying': 0,     ➡
```

```
        'dom': 0, 'mem_kb': 1183912, 'maxmem_kb': -4,        ➡
        'max_vcpu_id': 0, 'crashed': 0, 'running': 1,         ➡
        'shutdown': 0, 'online_vcpus': 1, 'blocked': 0})      ➡
[2007-02-24 13:37:42 xend.XendDomainInfo 3875] INFO          ➡
        (__init__:1072) Recreating domain 0,                 ➡
        UUID 00000000-0000-0000-0000-000000000000.           ➡
[2007-02-24 13:37:42 xend.XendDomainInfo 3875] WARNING       ➡
        (__init__:1072) No vm path in store for existing     ➡
        domain 0                                              ➡
[2007-02-24 13:37:42 xend.XendDomainInfo 3875] DEBUG         ➡
        (__init__:1072) Storing VM details: {'shadow_memory':➡
        '0', 'uuid': '00000000-0000-0000-0000-000000000000', ➡
        'on_reboot': 'restart', 'on_poweroff': 'destroy',    ➡
        'name': 'Domain-0', 'xend/restart_count': '0',       ➡
        'vcpus': '1', 'vcpu_avail': '1', 'memory': '1157',   ➡
        'on_crash': 'restart', 'maxmem': '1157'}             ➡
[2007-02-24 13:37:42 xend.XendDomainInfo 3875] DEBUG         ➡
        (__init__:1072) Storing domain details:              ➡
        {'cpu/0/availability': 'online',                     ➡
        'memory/target': '1184768', 'name': 'Domain-0',      ➡
        'console/limit': '1048576',                          ➡
        'vm': '/vm/00000000-0000-0000-0000-000000000000',    ➡
        'domid': '0'}                                         ➡
[2007-02-24 13:37:42 xend 3875] DEBUG (__init__:1072)        ➡
        number of vcpus to use is 0
```

xend Configuration

xend has a configuration file, /etc/xen/xend-config.sxp, that can be used to control many aspects of its behavior. This file is consulted whenever xend is started or restarted. After making changes to these values, run xend restart to apply the changes. Table 3.4 summarizes xend's configuration options.

TABLE 3.4 xend Configuration Options

Option	Description	Possible Values	Default
Logging/Debugging			
logfile	Used to change the location of xend's runtime log file.	Filename	/var/log/xen/xend.log

TABLE 3.4   continued

Option	Description	Possible Values	Default
Logging/Debugging			
`loglevel`	Used to filter out logging messages below a specified level.	The five possible levels in order by severity are DEBUG, INFO, WARNING, ERROR, CRITICAL.	DEBUG. This enables all logging.
`enable-dump`	Specifies whether core dumps of guest domains should be saved after a crash.	yes no	no
Management Interfaces			
`xend-http-server`	Specifies whether to start the HTTP management server.	yes no	no
`xend-port`	Used to change the port used by the HTTP management server. Requires the xend-http-server option set to yes.	Port number (0 to 65535). 9000 would be another reasonable choice if it must be changed.	8000
`xend-address`	Specifies the address to which the http management server will bind. Requires the xend-http-server option set to yes.	IP address, localhost, or other network address designator. Specifying localhost prevents remote connections.	'' (two single quotes) This indicates all interfaces.
`xend-unix-server`	Specifies whether to start the UNIX domain socket management interface. This is required for the CLI tools to operate.	yes no	yes
`xend-unix-path`	Used to change the location of the UNIX domain socket used to communicate with the management tools. Requires the xend-unix-server option set to yes.	Filename	/var/lib/xend/xend-socket
`xend-tcp-xmlrpc-server`	Specifies whether to start the TCP XML-RPC management interface.	yes no	no
`xend-unix-xmlrpc-server`	Specifies whether to start the UNIX XML-RPC management interface.	yes no	yes

Option	Description	Possible Values	Default
Management Interfaces			
`xend-relocation-server`	Specifies whether to start the relocation server. This is require for cross-machine live migrations. Relocation is not currently well-secured, so it is best left disabled unless needed.	yes no	no
`xend-relocation-port`	Used to change the port used by the relocation server. Requires the xend-relocation-server option set to yes.	Port number (0 to 65535).	8002
`xend-relocation-address`	Specifies the address to which the relocation server will bind. Requires the xend-relocation-server option set to yes.	IP address, localhost, or other network address designator.	" (two single quotes) This indicates all interfaces.
`xend-relocation-hosts-allow`	Specifies the hosts allowed to send requests to the relocation server. Be aware that spoofing of requests is possible so this is still relatively insecure.	Space separated sequence of regular expressions describing allowed hosts. To be allowed, a host must match one of the listed expressions. e.g., `'^localhost$ ^.*\.foo\.org$'`	" (two single quotes) This indicates that connections from all hosts are allowed.
`external-migration-tool`	Used to specify an application or script to handle external device migration.	/etc/xen/scripts/external-device-migrate	None
Domain0 Configuration			
`dom0-min-mem`	If Domain0's memory can be reduced to free memory for other guests, this specifies the lowest memory level that Domain0 will ever reach in megabytes.	0-Physical Memory Size If 0, Domain0's memory will never be allowed to be reduced.	None
`dom0-cpus`	Specifies the number of CPUs that Domain0 will be allowed to use.	0-Number of Physical CPUs If 0, Domain0 may use all available CPUs.	None

TABLE 3.4   continued

Option	Description	Possible Values	Default
Virtual Device Configuration and Limits			
`console-limit`	Specifies the buffer limit enforced by the console server on each domain in kilobytes. Used to prevent a single domain from overwhelming the console server.	Reasonable buffer size >0	1024
`network-script`	Used to specify a file in `/etc/xen/scripts` containing a script to set up the networking environment.	Filename Often `network-bridge`, `network-route`, `network-nat`, `<customscript>`	None
`vif-script`	Used to specify a file in `/etc/xen/scripts` containing a script to set up the virtual interface when it is created or destroyed.	Filename Often `vif-bridge`, `vif-route`, `vif-nat`, `<customscript>`	None

In the `xend-config.sxp` file, these options are listed one per line in the format, (OPTION SETTING). Individual lines may be commented out by beginning the line with a #. Listing 3.6 shows a sample `xend-config.sxp` file, similar to the one on the Xen LiveCD.

LISTING 3.6 A Sample `xend-config.sxp`

```
#
# Xend configuration file with default configuration lines
# shown commented out.
#

#(logfile /var/log/xend.log)
#(loglevel DEBUG)
#(enable-dump no)

#(xend-http-server no)
#(xend-port            8000)
#(xend-address '')
# Or consider localhost to disable remote administration
#(xend-address localhost)
```

```
#(xend-unix-server no)
#(xend-unix-path /var/lib/xend/xend-socket)

#(xend-tcp-xmlrpc-server no)
#(xend-unix-xmlrpc-server yes)

#(xend-relocation-server no)
#(xend-relocation-port 8002)
#(xend-relocation-address '')
#(xend-relocation-hosts-allow '')
# Or consider restricting hosts that can connect
#(xend-relocation-hosts-allow '^localhost$ ^.*\.foo\.org$')


(dom0-min-mem 196)
(dom0-cpus 0)


#(console-limit 1024)

#(network-script network-bridge)
#(vif-script vif-bridge)


## Or consider routed or NAT options instead of bridged
#(network-script network-route)
#(vif-script     vif-route)
 (network-script 'network-nat dhcp=yes')
 (vif-script 'vif-nat dhcp=yes')
```

XenStore

Another important part of the administrative architecture for a Xen system is XenStore. Earlier in this chapter, we saw the XenStore daemon, xenstored, in the process listing of a running Xen system. In this section, we discuss XenStore in more detail.

XenStore is a database of configuration information shared between domains. Domains read and write the XenStore database to communicate with each other. This database is maintained by Domain0 on behalf of all the domains. XenStore supports atomic operations such as reading a key or writing a key. When new values are written into XenStore, the affected domains are notified.

XenStore is often used as a mechanism for controlling devices in guest domains. XenStore can be accessed in a number of different ways, such as a UNIX socket in Domain0, a kernel-level API, or an ioctl interface. Device drivers write request or completion information into XenStore. Although drivers can write anything they want, XenStore is designed for small pieces of information, such as configuration information or status, and not for large pieces of information, such as in bulk data transfer.

XenStore is actually located in a single file, `/var/lib/xenstored/tdb`, on Domain0. (`tdb` stands for Tree Database.) Listing 3.7 shows the tdb file located in the `/var/lib/xenstored` directory on Domain0 and some attributes of this file.

LISTING 3.7 Contents of `/var/lib/xenstored/`

```
[root@dom0]:/var/lib/xenstored# ls -lah
total 112K
drwxr-xr-x  2 root root 4.0K Feb 24 13:38 .
drwxr-xr-x 25 root root 4.0K Oct 16 11:40 ..
-rw-r-----  1 root root  40K Feb 24 13:38 tdb
root@dom0]:/var/lib/xenstored#
[root@dom0]:/var/lib/xenstored# file tdb
tdb: TDB database version 6, little-endian hash size 7919 bytes
root@dom0]:/var/lib/xenstored#
```

Viewed another way, XenStore is similar in flavor to the /proc or sysfs virtual file system in Linux and some UNIX variants. Internal to the XenStore database file is a logical file system tree with three main paths: `/vm`, `/local/domain`, and `/tool`. The `/vm` and `/local/domain  directory` paths have subareas dedicated to individual domains, while the `/tool` path stores general information about various tools and is not indexed by domain. The second directory level in `/local/domain` might seem somewhat unnecessary given that `/local` contains only the domain subdirectory.

Each domain has two identification numbers. The universal unique identifier (UUID) is an identifying number that remains the same even if the guest is migrated to another machine. The domain identifier (DOMID) is an identifying number that refers to a particular running instance. The DOMID typically changes when the guest is migrated to another machine.

The `/vm` path is indexed by the UUID of each domain and stores configuration information such as the number of virtual CPUs and the amount of memory allocated to the domain. For each domain, there is a `/vm/<uuid>` directory. Table 3.5 explains the contents of the `/vm/<uuid>` directory.

TABLE 3.5 Contents of the /vm/<uuid> Directory

Entry	Description
uuid	UUID of the domain. The UUID of a domain does not change during migration, but the domainId does. Because the /vm directory is indexed by UUID, this entry is somewhat redundant.
ssidref	SSID reference for the domain.
on_reboot	Specifies whether to destroy or restart the domain in response to a domain reboot request.
on_poweroff	Specifies whether to destroy or restart the domain in response to a domain halt request.
on_crash	Specifies whether to destroy or restart the domain in response to a domain crash.
vcpus	Number of virtual CPUs allocated to this domain.
vcpu_avail	Number of active virtual CPUs for this domain. Note: Number of disabled virtual CPUs is given by vcpus minus vcpu_avail.
memory	Amount of memory in megabytes allocated to the domain.
name	Name of the domain.

Regular guest domains (DomUs) also have a /vm/<uuid>/image directory. Table 3.6 explains the contents of the /vm/<uuid>/image directory.

TABLE 3.6 Contents of the /vm/<uuid>/image Directory

Entry	Description
ostype	linux or vmx to identify the builder type
kernel	Filename path on Domain0 to the kernel for this domain
cmdline	Command line to pass to the kernel for this domain when booting
ramdisk	Filename path on Domain0 to the ramdisk for this domain

The /local/domain is indexed by the DOMID and contains information about the running domain such as the current CPU the domain is pinned to or the current tty on which the console data from this domain is exposed. For each domain, there is a /local/domain/<domId> directory. Note that the UUID used when indexing in the /vm directory is not the same as the DOMID used when indexing in the /local/domain directory. The UUID does not change during migration, but the

DOMID does. This enables localhost-to-localhost migration. Some of the information in
`/local/domain` is also found in `/vm`, but `/local/domain` contains significantly more
information, and the version in `/vm` does not change. The `/local/domain` directory
for a domain also contains a pointer to the `/vm` directory for the same domain. Table
3.7 explains the contents of the `/local/domain/<domId>` directory.

TABLE 3.7 Contents of the `/local/domain/<domId>` Directory

Entry	Description
domId	Domain identifier of the domain. The domain ID changes during migration, but the UUID does not. Because the `/local/domain` directory is indexed by domId, this entry is somewhat redundant.
/vm Related Entries	
on_reboot	Refer to Table 3.5.
on_poweroff	Refer to Table 3.5.
on_crash	Refer to Table 3.5.
name	Refer to Table 3.5.
vm	Pathname of the VM directory for this same domain.
Scheduling Related Entries	
running	If present, indicates that the domain is currently running.
cpu	Current CPU to which this domain is pinned.
cpu_weight	The weight assigned to this domain for scheduling purposes. Domains with higher weights use the physical CPUs more often.
xend **Related Entries**	
cpu_time	You might think this would be related to the cpu and cpu_weight entries, but it actually refers to the xend start time. Used for Domain0 only.
handle	Private handle for xend.
image	Private xend information.

Under `/local/domain/<domId>` for each domain, there are also several subdirectories including memory, console, and store. Table 3.8 describes the contents of these
subdirectories.

TABLE 3.8 Subdirectories of the `/local/domain/<domId>` Directory

Entry	Description
/local/domain/<domId>/console	
ring-ref	Grant table entry of the console ring queue.
port	Event channel used for the console ring queue.
tty	tty on which the console data is currently being exposed.
limit	Limit in bytes of console data to be buffered.
/local/domain/<domId>/store	
ring-ref	Grant table entry of the store ring queue.
port	Event channel used for the store ring queue.
/local/domain/<domId>/memory	
target	Target memory size in kilobytes for this domain.

Three additional subdirectories under `/local/domain/<domId>` are related to device management—`backend`, `device`, and `device-misc`. These all have subdirectories of their own.

Earlier in this chapter, we discussed how device management in Xen is divided into backend drivers running in privileged domains with direct access to the physical hardware and frontend drivers that give unprivileged domains the illusion of a generic and dedicated version of that resource. The backend subdirectory provides information about all physical devices managed by this domain and exported to other domains. The device subdirectory provides information about all frontend devices used by this domain. Finally, the `device-misc` directory provides information for other devices. In each case, there can be a `vif` and `vbd` subdirectory. Virtual Interface (`vif`) devices are for network interfaces, and Virtual Block Devices (`vbd`) are for block devices such as disks or CD-ROMs. In Chapter 9, "Device Virtualization and Management," we discuss in more detail how XenStore enables communication between backend and frontend drivers.

Table 3.9 describes a number of tools that can be used to explore and manipulate XenStore. They are often located in `/usr/bin`. These commands allow the XenStore database, which is stored as a file (`/var/lib/xenstored/tdb`), to be viewed as a logical file system.

TABLE 3.9 XenStore Commands

Command	Description
`xenstore-read <Path to XenStore Entry>`	Displays the value of a XenStore entry
`xenstore-exists <XenStore Path>`	Reports whether a particular XenStore Path exists
`xenstore-list <XenStore Path>` `xenstore-ls <XenStore Path>`	Shows all the children entries or directories of a specific XenStore path
`xenstore-write <Path to XenStore Entry> <value>`	Updates the value of a XenStore entry
`xenstore-rm <XenStore Path>`	Removes XenStore entry or directory
`xenstore-chmod <XenStore Path> <mode>`	Updates the permission on a XenStore entry to allow read or write
`xenstore-control`	Sends commands to xenstored, such as check to trigger an integrity check.
`xsls <Xenstore path>`	Recursively shows the contents of a specified XenStore path; equivalent of a recursive xenstore-list plus a xenstore-read to display the values

For example, Listing 3.8 shows an example of a `xenstore-list` on `/local/domain/0`.

LISTING 3.8 `xenstore-list`

```
[user@dom0]#xenstore-list /local/domain/0
cpu
memory
name
console
vm
domid
backend
[user@dom0]
```

Listing 3.9 shows a shell script from the XenWiki used to dump the entire contents of XenStore. Notice the calls to `xenstore-list` and `xenstore-read`. This would be similar to an `xsls` on the XenStore root.

LISTING 3.9 Shell Script for Dumping the Contents of XenStore from `http://wiki.xensource.`
`com/xenwiki/XenStore`

```sh
#!/bin/sh

function dumpkey() {
    local param=${1}
    local key
    local result
    result=$(xenstore-list ${param})
    if [ "${result}" != "" ] ; then
       for key in ${result} ; do dumpkey ${param}/${key} ; done
     else
       echo -n ${param}'='
       xenstore-read ${param}
    fi
}


for key in /vm /local/domain /tool ; do dumpkey ${key} ; done
```

Summary

In this chapter, we discussed the major architectural components of the Xen system. The Xen hypervisor sits between the guest domains and the physical hardware, allocating and controlling resources, enforcing protection and isolation. Domain0 is a special privileged domain used to administer normal guest domains and to control the physical hardware. The Xen management daemon, xend, passes control requests to the Xen hypervisor. XenStore is a database of configuration information used to communicate between domains.

References and Further Reading

"Credit-Based CPU Scheduler." Xen Wiki. Xen.org.
    `http://wiki.xensource.com/xenwiki/CreditScheduler`.
"Dom0." Xen Wiki. Xen.org.
    `http://wiki.xensource.com/xenwiki/Dom0`.
"DriverDomains." Xen Wiki. Xen.org.
    `http://wiki.xensource.com/xenwiki/DriverDomain`.

"DomU." Xen Wiki. Xen.org.
  `http://wiki.xensource.com/xenwiki/DomU`.

"x86 Virtualization." Wikipedia.
  `http://en.wikipedia.org/wiki/Virtualization_Technology`.

"xend-config.sxp (5) – Linux Man page." die.net.
  `http://www.die.net/doc/linux/man/man5/xend-config.sxp.5.html`.

"Xen Disk I/O Benchmarking: NetBSD Dom0 vs Linux Dom0."
  `http://users.piuha.net/martti/comp/xendom0/xendom0.html`.

"XenStoreReference." Xen Wiki. Xen.org.
  `http://wiki.xensource.com/xenwiki/XenStoreReference`.

Xen Users' Manual Xen v3.0.
  `http://www.cl.cam.ac.uk/research/srg/netos/xen/readmes/user/user.html`.

"Xend/XML-RPC." Xen Wiki. Xen.org.
  `http://wiki.xensource.com/xenwiki/Xend/XML-RPC`.

## Chapter 4

Hardware Requirements and Installation of Xen Domain0

Like any software product, Xen has a set of requirements that must be satisfied for proper execution. You may be approaching the question of supported hardware from the perspective of "Will Xen run on a spare, older system I already have?" or "What should I buy if I want a new system to run Xen?" In either case, this chapter is designed to help you choose supported hardware. After addressing hardware configuration issues, we move on to a discussion of both commercial and free/open source methods of Xen installation. Finally, we expand on the free/open source methods by taking you through the installation of Domain0 on a variety of software platforms including several common Linux distributions and XenExpress from XenSource.

Xen Domain0 Processor Requirements

Xen currently runs best on the x86 host architecture. There are ports of Xen to IA64 and Power architectures in progress, but x86 is by far the safest bet for a new Xen installation. Xen requires a Pentium class or newer processor. This requirement includes but is not limited to the Pentium Pro, Celeron, Pentium II, Pentium III, Pentium IV, and Xeon chips from Intel corporation. Additionally, the processor requirements can be satisfied by Advanced Micro Devices (AMD) Athlon and Duron product offerings. If you are lucky enough to own a multicore or hyperthreaded version of any mentioned processors, you will be glad to know Xen supports those too. Xen supports the x86-64 CPUs. Additionally, Xen supports up to 32-way SMP guests. Table 4.1 provides a list of x86 processors suitable for Xen.

TABLE 4.1 x86 Processors Suitable for Xen

INTEL	
Xeon	71xx, 7041, 7040, 7030, 7020, 5100, 5080, 5063, 5060, 5050.
Pentium D	920, 930, 940, 950
Pentium 4	662, 672
Core Duo	T2600, T2500, T2400, T2300, L2400, L2300
Core 2 Duo	E6700, E6600, E6400, E6300, T7600, T7400, T7200, T5600
AMD	
Athlon 64 X2	5200+, 5000+, 4800+, 4600+, 4400+, 4200+, 4000+, 3800+
Athlon 64 FX	FX-62
Sempron	3800+, 3600+, 3500+, 3400+, 3200+, 3000+
Opteron	Everything starting from Rev. F: 22xx and 88xx (base F), 12xx (base AM2)
Turion 64 X2 dual core	TL-50, TL-52, TL-56, TL-60

Note this table is not comprehensive because of the rapid pace of technology. It is quite likely that any newer processors than those shown here are suitable for Xen deployments.

To support unmodified DomU guests such as Windows guests, you need a process with virtualization extensions built in such as Intel VT or AMD SVM support. To accommodate these similar but different technologies, Xen has introduced a generic Hardware Virtual Machine, or HVM, layer.

Intel VT

Intel introduced a new set of hardware extensions called Virtualization Technology (VT), designed specifically to aid in virtualization of other operating systems allowing Xen to run unmodified guests. Intel added this technology to the IA-32 Platform and named it VT-x, and to the IA64 platforms and named it VT-i. With these new technologies, Intel introduced two new operation levels to the processor, for use by a hypervisor such as Xen. Intel maintains a list on its Web site of exactly which processors support this feature. This list is available at `www.intel.com/products/processor_number/index.htm`.

Intel also introduced VT-d, which is Intel's technology for Direct IO. These extensions allow for devices to be assigned to virtual machines safely. VT-d also handles Direct Memory Access (DMA) remapping and the I/O translation lookaside buffer (IOTLB). DMA remapping prevents a direct memory access from escaping the boundaries of the VM. IOTLB is a cache that improves performance. Currently, Xen performs these actions by use of a modified program called QEMU, which has performance drawbacks. As Xen has developed, more of these hardware capabilities have been incorporated into it.

When using Intel VT technology, Xen executes in a new operational state called Virtual Machine Extensions (VMX) root operation mode. The unmodified guest domains execute in the other newly created CPU state, VMX non-root operation mode. Because the DomUs run in non-root operation mode, they are confined to a subset of operations available to the system hardware. Failure to adhere to the restricted subset of instructions causes a VM exit to occur, along with control returning to Xen.

AMD-V

Xen 3.0 also includes support for the AMD-V processor. One of AMD-V's benefits is a tagged *translation lookaside buffer* (*TLB*). Using this tagged TLB, guests get mapped to an address space that can be altogether different from what the VMM sets. The reason it is called a tagged TLB is that the TLB contains additional information known as *address space identifiers* (*ASIDs*). ASIDs ensure that a TLB flush does not need to occur at every context switch.

AMD also introduced a new technology to control access to I/O called *I/O Memory Management Unit* (*IOMMU*), which is analogous to Intel's VT-d technology. IOMMU is in charge of virtual machine I/O, including limiting DMA access to what is valid for the virtual machine, directly assigning real devices to VMs. One way to check if your processor is AMD-V capable from a Linux system is to check the output of the `/proc/cpuinfo` for an svm flag (to check for VT-x, look for the VMX flag).

HVM

Intel VT and AMD's AMD-V architectures are fairly similar and share many things in common conceptually, but their implementations are slightly different. It makes sense to provide a common interface layer to abstract their nuances away. Thus, the HVM interface was born. The original code for the HVM layer was implemented by an IBM Watson Research Center employee named Leendert van Doorn and was contributed to the upstream Xen project. A compatibility listing is located at the Xen Wiki at `http://wiki.xensource.com/xenwiki/HVM_Compatible_Processors`.

The HVM layer is implemented using a function call table (`hvm_function_table`), which contains the functions that are common to both hardware virtualization implementations. These methods, including `initialize_guest_resources()` and `store_cpu_guest_regs()`, are implemented differently for each backend under this unified interface.

Hardware Device Support and Recommendations

The Xen hypervisor offloads the bulk of the hardware support issues necessary for a modern OS to the Domain0 guest OS. This management virtual machine is responsible for most hardware management tasks. The hypervisor is strictly limited to the detection and starting of processors, PCI enumeration, and interrupt routing. The actual device drivers interacting with the hardware are executed within the privileged Domain0 guest. Practically speaking, this implies Xen has hardware compatibility with most of the devices that are in turn supported by the operating system you choose as Domain0. Linux is by far the most common choice for a Xen Domain0 and likely to be the safest bet for wide hardware support.

Disks and Controllers

Xen Domain0s are similar to other operating systems in that they want some form of persistent storage to contain their data. Typically with a home personal computer, workstation, or small to medium business server, the persistent storage comes from a local disk within the machine. Xen, like other operating systems, operates best with a locally attached disk as well.

Some features of Xen, such as live migration, require network-attached storage to work best. However, live migration is for the DomU guests. Because a Domain0 cannot be live migrated, the Domain0 remains on the hardware on which it was installed. Though you may be able to configure a system with a Domain0 to use a network file system, we recommend that at least Domain0 be installed directly on a local disk.

The major thing to focus on when choosing a local disk is that many guests might try to access IO at the same time. Many physical disks will be better if you have the luxury of dedicating each real physical disk and an associated controller to individual machines. Unfortunately, multiple disks with dedicated controllers are a luxury most implementations of Xen will not afford. We certainly do not all have the ability to use high-end RAID units or servers supporting dozens of IDE devices. This becomes an important consideration, because a given Domain0 might support dozens of virtual guests.

It soon becomes clear that no matter what type of disk you use for storage, low latency and high speed will be vital for seamless virtualization. This is not necessarily because of some magic virtualization synergy, but more a reflection that low latency/high speed drives generally result in better performance. For that reason, it is worth considering faster new drives and new interfaces such as serial ATA (SATA). Similarly, local SCSI disks are definitely an option you should consider if you plan on running any kind of serious virtualization server. SCSI disks are often available in high RPM configurations with low seek times.

Some of you might be wondering about the support of Network Attached Storage (NAS) when using Xen. To address this question, we need to remove the ambiguity about what exactly NAS means to Xen. NAS can cover everything from external dedicated network boxes that you plug into your network to a media server you set up yourself with file level protocols. As a rule of thumb, practically anything under the NAS umbrella could be made to work with Xen, but for best performance, it is recommended that you stick to block based protocols between your Xen guests and the storage hardware you plan to use. For example, it is recommended that you select FC, iSCSI, GNBD, or AoE instead of file level protocols such as NFS, SAMBA, or AFS. A study of the performance characteristics of network file systems when used in conjunction with virtual machines can be found in the "References and Further Reading" section of this chapter.

Networking Devices

In general, network device support in Xen is based on the drivers found on your Domain0 guest. In fact the only things to worry about with networking devices are ensuring that your Domain0 kernel contains the necessary normal drivers for your hardware and that the Domain0 kernel also includes the Xen backend devices. If a non-Xen installation of the operating system you choose for Domain0 recognizes a particular network device, you should have no problem using that network device in Xen. Additionally, you may want to ensure that your Domain0 kernel includes support for ethernet bridging and loopback, if you want your DomU kernels to obtain `ethX` devices. If your host kernel doesn't support bridging, or bridging does not work for you, you can select the alternate means of using IP routing in Domain0. This approach can also be useful if you want to isolate your DomU guests from any external networks. Details on advanced network configurations are presented later in Chapter 10, "Network Configuration."

Graphics Devices

Traditionally, virtualization systems have not really bothered with virtualizing graphics adapters. Virtual guests are typically accessed using a network graphics protocol or a remote login protocol from a remote host that acts as the viewer. Older versions of Xen simply offered VGA emulation through a Virtual Network Computing (VNC) protocol backend. This gave users access to graphics environments, but it isn't necessarily the fastest or best method of accessing a guest.

NoMachine NX is an alternative remote display technology that claims near local speed and a high level of application responsiveness. NX is intended to operate well on high-latency, low-bandwidth networks. FreeNX is a GPL implementation of the NX Server.

The Xen developers realized that using these networking protocols for graphics is resource expensive and therefore a weakness. Since Xen 3.0.4, users may experiment with what is called a *virtual frame buffer*. Using these virtual frame buffers, Xen's Domain0 can capture video data written to a specific part of memory and then send it to the display.

Finally, we should mention that it is possible to give a guest complete and sole access to a physical graphics card by hiding it from the Domain0. We cover practical deployment of these visualization tools in more detail in Chapter 9, "Device Virtualization and Management."

Power Management

Currently, there is no form of advanced power management in the hypervisor or Domain0. Executing Xen on a laptop class machine is definitely possible, but it is not recommended due to decreased battery life. In some situations, server systems may see increased CPU temperatures most of the time. Thus, if you are running in a compact chassis or an exceptionally warm system to begin with, Xen may not be ready for your production systems. It should be noted that, with appropriately cooled high density servers such as blades, Xen may provide a great opportunity for power savings by consolidating systems into a single power-efficient chassis.

Help for Unsupported Hardware

If for some reason Xen does not operate on your hardware, your best bet is to provide information directly to the Xen project about it. In fact, Xen developers are working on a list of problematic hardware and need you to help them find things that are broken. If you should ever encounter hardware that works properly with your Domain0 operating system but not when used in conjunction with Xen, they would love to know about it. See more information by visiting `http://wiki.xensource.com/xenwiki/HardwareCompatibilityList`.

Memory Requirements

Keep in mind that the actual memory requirements needed for your particular deployment vary widely based on what you intend to do with your virtual machines. If you want to build custom, extremely minimalist Linux guests, your requirements will be much smaller than if you need to execute 10 Windows guest instances. A good starting point is to envision the number of virtual guests you intend on executing simultaneously, and multiply each guest by its own vendor-specified minimum requirements. Take this partial result and multiply by 1.5 or 2. Finally, do not forget to add in the amount of memory needed for your Domain0 user space and kernel as well. This works well because some systems will be capable of executing stripped down guests, while others might end up using more memory than you had intended. Additionally, it allows for some extra room needed for guest migrations and other advanced management features if you choose to use them. The bottom line is that more memory is always better.

By default, the 32-bit version of Xen supports a maximum of 4GB of memory. Version 3.0 and later releases support Physical Addressing Extensions (PAE), which allows more addressable memory. With PAE-enabled hardware, 32-bit x86 hardware can address up to 64GB of physical memory. Though not all motherboards support such large memory configurations, this is 16 times more address capacity and can definitely be beneficial when running large virtual machines or a large number of virtual machines. When Xen is executing on the supported 64-bit versions of x86 platforms, such as the AMD64 and Intel EM64T systems, up to 1TB of RAM is addressable.

The Domain0 guest itself has been demonstrated to run in 64MB of RAM, but this is certainly not recommended. That specific case can be achieved if you disable practically everything in the Domain0 environment. Domain0 memory consumption is a balance between minimizing Domain0's role (which is good for security reasons) and cutting off too much that can cripple the system for routine maintenance. Additionally, the type of guest networking you choose to deploy can impact the amount of memory your Domain0 guest needs. Keep in mind that each bridged network you build consumes memory on your Domain0, and if you choose to use the Domain0 IP routing method to network your guests, you will incur the overhead of the routing daemon as well as its policies. These firewall and network address translation (NAT) rules can incur memory consumption penalties but may be necessary in your environment. Typically, any installation with more than a few bridges needs more than 64MB of RAM. See the section "Performance of Xen Virtual Network and Real Network" in Appendix E, "Xen Performance Evaluation," for analysis of this overhead. Additionally, if you intend on doing distributed or network block device guests, while retaining an exceptionally small Domain0, you may want to avoid iSCSI, as the memory overhead can be substantial.

It should go without saying that your choice of Domain0 user space operating system can impact the requirements. A stripped down Linux instance for small servers requires fewer resources than the average desktop-oriented Linux distribution. You should plan accordingly. In general, we recommend using 1GB of RAM for your Domain0. This should provide a lot of breathing room for the tools you are familiar with.

Though you should always budget enough memory to meet the minimum requirements for your guest operating system instances, you can cheat a little if the guest will be performing a moderate workload. If you disable unneeded services and execute only command line applications, you will be able to squeeze a lot more guests into the same amount of physical memory. On the contrary, if you plan on running a large application server or database server, you should size it much like you would for individual deployment in a nonvirtualized environment.

One additional consideration you may want to investigate is precisely how much swap space you plan on using with your guests. Linux and other operating systems tend to use swap space when the physical memory is full or close to full. When your guests need more memory resources, inactive pages are migrated to the swap space. Even though swap space may prove helpful in alleviating memory pressures from numerous guests with small amounts of RAM, you should never think of swap as a replacement for more RAM. Swap helps you cheat a little to fit in more virtual machines, but swap is typically on a hard disk, is orders of magnitude slower than RAM, and will adversely affect your performance.

If you are considering running unmodified Windows guests, we recommend using at least 512MB of memory. Microsoft recommends 128 megabytes (MB) of RAM or higher for Windows XP, but you may find you need much more memory depending on your workload. In general, we recommend sizing unmodified Windows guests as if they were running on a stand-alone installation without virtualization.

You need to precalculate the number of expected unmodified guests and multiply by their base requirements to get an idea for your sizing. As always, leave yourself some wiggle room. As with nonvirtualized systems, the best advice is to buy the most memory you can afford and to make sure that the guests you choose to run fit comfortably in that amount of memory.

Choosing and Obtaining a Version of Xen

Most current users of Xen are open source enthusiasts, operating systems enthusiasts, or business customers who appreciate the value of virtualization without feeling quite as affectionate about the price tag that accompanies proprietary commercial systems in the marketplace today. This section of the book shows you where to get the version of Xen that is best suited to your needs.

Open Source Distributions

A common way to obtain Xen is to install a Linux distribution that contains integrated support for Xen. Table 4.2 surveys some of the more popular choices of free/open source Domain0 operating systems.

TABLE 4.2 Summary of Xen-Enabled Free and Open Source Operating System Distributions

Operating System Distribution	Support for Xen
Fedora	Xen 3.X packages included since its Fedora 4 release.
CentOS	Xen 3.X packages since CentOS 5.
OpenSUSE	Includes Xen 3.X support.
Ubuntu	Includes Xen 3.X packages since 6.10 release (Edgy Eft).
Debian	Includes Xen 3.X packages since Debian 4.0 release.
NetBSD	Host support for Xen 3.X is available in the 4.0 release branch
OpenBSD	Support for OpenBSD self-hosting is near complete.
FreeBSD	Support for using FreeBSD as a Xen host is under development.
Gentoo	A Gentoo package exists for Xen in the Gentoo package management system, Portage.
OpenSolaris	OpenSolaris xVM available in OpenSolaris developer version, supported by OpenSolaris on Xen community.

As we mentioned, Linux is currently the most common choice for a Domain0 installation, but there is no "best" operating system distribution for Xen. If you are already familiar with a particular distribution, sticking with the installation process, tools, and package management that you are familiar with is likely to be the best choice. In the long run, most Linux distributions will provide a common subset of Xen functionality. Only a few items pertinent to the average Linux distribution concern Xen compatibility. The bulk of compatibility issues relate to the choice of glibc thread local storage (tls) implementation, or the distribution's choice of a device file system, either devfs or udev. Note that some distributions, such as Fedora and Ubuntu, provide specially built versions of the glibc package to accommodate Xen users. Compatibility is becoming less of an issue as most modern distributions have opted for the Native Posix Thread Library (NPTL) and udev.

Commercially Supported Options

The disadvantage of using a free/open source Xen distribution or even building Xen from the publicly available source code is that you may be at the whim of the developers and community for support. More often than not we have seen communities willing to help one another work through Xen problems as they arise, but sometimes a commercial solution with paid support is more appropriate. A number of companies provide a variety of support, installation, configuration, and management services for Xen. We cover additional information about enterprise Xen support in Chapter 14, "An Overview of Xen Enterprise Management Tools."

Citrix XenServer Product Group and XenSource

XenSource was founded and run by the original Xen development team. In 2007, it was acquired by Citrix and became the Citrix XenServer Product Group. This group leads the open source Xen community, coordinating development efforts, producing and hosting documentation such as the Xen wiki and forums, and organizing summits and workshops. At the same time, the group offers a range of commercial Xen-based solutions and technical support for Xen and combines value-added items along with the open source Xen software for a more complete virtualization solution.

Citrix XenServer Product Group offers a free package, XenServer Express Edition, aimed at developers and enthusiasts. It currently supports up to four guest domains, 4GB of memory, and two physical CPUs. It has support for both Windows and Linux guests and is an excellent alternative to the open source options, especially if you are considering upgrading to commercial support. Citrix also offers two higher-end products, XenServer Standard and XenServer Enterprise. You can read more about their products and offerings at `www.citrixxenserver.com/PRODUCTS/Pages/myproducts.aspx`.

Virtual Iron Software, Inc.

Virtual Iron Software, Inc. was founded in 2003 and provides enterprise-class software solutions for creating and managing virtual infrastructure. Originally Virtual Iron used a different hypervisor technology to underpin its products but switched to Xen in 2006 for its hypervisor infrastructure. The company leverages Xen and hardware-assisted virtualization processors to deliver solutions that are both open and economically attractive when compared to proprietary virtualization solutions. Major products of interest are Virtual Iron Virtualization Manager and Virtualization Services. Virtual Iron's Virtualization Manager provides a central place to control and automate virtual resources and streamlines tasks that are typically laborious and monotonous. Virtual Iron Virtualization Services are deployed automatically on bare-metal, industry-standard servers without requiring software installation or management. These features streamline data center management and reduce operational costs. You can read more about Virtual Iron's products and offerings at `http://virtualiron.com`.

Enterprise Class Linux Support

If you are already an enterprise or business class Linux customer who pays for vendor support, you might already have available support for Xen through your existing Linux vendor. Novell, Inc.'s product, SUSE Linux Enterprise Server (SLES), was the first enterprise platform to include a fully integrated and supported version of Xen 3.0. You can read more about the SUSE Linux Enterprise Server product offering at www. novell.com/products/server/.

A more recent newcomer to the Enterprise Xen support arena has been Red Hat with its release of Red Hat Enterprise Linux 5 (RHEL 5). You can learn more about Red Hat's newest server offering at www.redhat.com/rhel/.

As always, we recommend contacting your distributor through the proper channels to ensure your support contract includes executing the distribution as a Xen Domain0 host or guest. Table 4.3 shows a recap of the commercially supported Xen Domain0 options available for Xen.

TABLE 4.3 Recap of Xen Commercial Support Solutions

Commercial Support Solutions	Notes
Citrix XenServer Product Group	Group founded by the original Xen development team. Acquired by Citrix. Leaders of the open source Xen development effort and also offers commercial packages and support.
Virtual Iron	Company predates Xen. Switched to Xen for its hypervisor infrastructure. Offers commercial virtualization management products.
SUSE Linux Enterprise Server 10	The first commercial implementation of Xen in this form is Novell's SUSE Linux Enterprise Server 10 release, which is broadly supported. Red Hat Enterprise Linux 5, released in early 2007, will also offer Xen.
Red Hat Enterprise Linux 5	RHEL 5 incorporated Xen into the distribution. Though not the first commercial distribution, RHEL 5 provides additional support for tools such as Virtual Machine Manager.

Methods of Installing Domain0 Hosts

If you have made it this far, you are now ready to install a Domain0 for yourself. We will assume that you have some familiarity with installing operating systems and specifically modern Linux distributions. The remainder of this chapter investigates several popular Domain0 operating systems and their Xen installation procedures. Although not comprehensive, this chapter strives to provide a good overview and a variety that spans the most common distributions (from which many other supported configurations are derived or related to).

Installation of the Xen hypervisor is not a fully functional operating environment on its own. It requires a user space to go along with it to provide the facilities for easily constructing and managing virtual machine guests. The choice of user space environment for your Xen Domain0 is important, as it is the foundation on which all your guests will rest. Historically, Linux was the initial candidate for this role. In recent years, some of the BSD families of operating systems as well as OpenSolaris have become viable Domain0 hosts candidates. Each has its own strengths and weaknesses as a host platform for Xen. In this section, we look at each of these options in more detail so that you can choose the Domain0 platform best for your environment.

Common Prerequisite: The Grand Unified Boot Loader (GRUB)

No matter what Domain0 platform of choice you learn about, it is highly recommended that you use the GRUB bootloader. GRUB is a free software bootloader that supports the MultiBoot standard. The bootloader plays an important role in a Xen system because the bootloader is essentially the first software executed after the BIOS. The bootloader is responsible for loading an operating system along with passing control of the hardware to the that operating system; in our case it is a Domain0 kernel. From there, the Domain0 kernel can initialize the rest of the operating system such as the Domain0 user space.

No matter what flavor of Xen you choose to install, at some point during the installation, modification of the bootloader configuration will be necessary by the distribution-provided tools, or manually. If you are already familiar with your bootloader, it is important that you realize that the options accepted by a Xen kernel vary from those passed to a typical Linux kernel

The GRUB configuration file is typically found in `/boot/grub/menu.1st`. Like most things related to computers, there are numerous ways to ensure your configuration file entries are correct. Each distribution uses its own set of tools or conventions when modifying the GRUB configuration file. The common denominator is to edit the file directly using your favorite text editor. We discuss the GRUB entries for each of the Domain0 installations covered later in this chapter.

Linux Distributions

When using any Linux distribution for your choice of Domain0, the installation procedures are fairly consistent from a high level. Typically you need to install the normal operating system as you would for a stand-alone installation; then you add the new

Xen-aware Domain0 kernel, along with a few user space tools used to manage Xen. This method allows you to ensure the distribution works with your hardware before adding the complexities of Xen into the mix. When you are comfortable with the quality of the distribution as compared to your needs, you can then add on the Domain0 virtualization support. In many cases the procedure for doing so is no different from installing any other piece of software using the distribution's supported package management systems.

Keep in mind that each Linux distribution has its own unique strengths and weaknesses as perceived by different types of users. The next few sections present a survey of some of the more common distributions used as a Domain0. If your favorite distribution is discussed in this chapter, feel free to skip to that section. The following sections are intended to augment, but not replace, your distribution's official documentation. By the end of the section, we provide an overview comparison of installation procedures.

OpenSUSE

OpenSUSE is the community supported edition of Novell's commercial SUSE product line. SUSE has the distinction of being the first Linux distribution to ship with Xen support, and thus makes an excellent choice for a Domain0 environment. One advantage of having been supported for some time is that the installation of Xen components is integrated alongside the regular distribution contents and package selection. Xen is integrated nicely into the installer. In this regard, OpenSUSE actually feels as if Xen support was a pivotal feature in the release, and not simply an afterthought like some other distributions.

Installing Xen during a fresh installation of OpenSUSE is simple. When executing the OpenSUSE installer, just before installation commences, you need to enable Xen support during the Installation Settings phase. From this screen, you can view the software packages about to be installed. From the on-screen display, select Software. From the resulting menu, simply check the Xen Virtual Machine Host Server box, shown in Figure 4.1. After selecting the Xen software for installation, click the Accept button in the lower-right corner, and continue your installation of OpenSUSE as normal.

The OpenSUSE community has integrated support for Xen Domain0 and Xen utility installation right into its normal installation process. Though the support is not enabled by default, you need only know where to look to select it for installation.

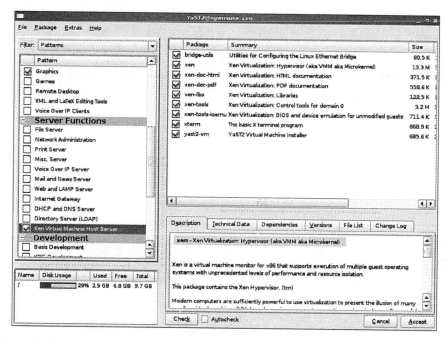

FIGURE 4.1 The OpenSUSE installation process supports Xen natively

Alternatively, you may have installed OpenSUSE without enabling Xen, as it is not selected for installation by default. If you have an existing installation of OpenSUSE, Xen can be added via the normal software installation mechanisms used with this distribution. The easiest method is to use the YaST tool. One way to launch YaST is to click on the Computer menu in the lower-left corner of the default desktop. From there, open the Control Center and select YaST (Yet another Setup Tool).

Using YaST requires you to be logged in as root or have the administrator password. You are prompted for these credentials as needed. On the left of the YaST screen are several categories, one of which is labeled Software. After selecting this entry, you see a display with numerous options on the right-hand panel. From that listing select Online Update. It is important to note that the Online Update selection uses the software repositories you have previously configured. After the Online Update module has loaded, you can choose filters on the left side. Under the Patterns filter, the list on the left looks similar to that of when you're choosing software just before installing OpenSUSE. From here it's just like the fresh install method mentioned previously. Simply navigate to the Server Functions category and place a check mark next to the Xen items as shown in Figure 4.2.

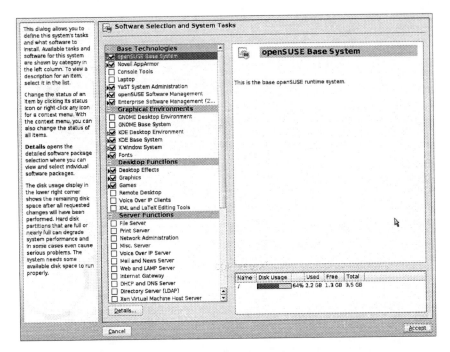

FIGURE 4.2 Drill down into the Xen Virtual Machine Host Server options of YaST.

The OpenSUSE community has also made it easy to add Xen Domain0 and Xen utility support after the initial installation process has completed via its supported software installation system YaST.

When you click Install, the Xen packages are downloaded and installed to your system. Finally, when the installation process has completed, you should ensure your /boot/grub/menu.1st file contains an entry for your new Domain0 kernel. After confirming your that GRUB menu file has the appropriate Domain0 kernel image in place, reboot your machine. Figure 4.3 shows the Domain0 kernel option as shown on our OpenSUSE installation.

The OpenSUSE boot menu contains the Xen kernel option that was automatically added as part of the Xen installation process.

Subjectively, the support in OpenSUSE is top notch and is integrated into the normal means of software installation. If you are unsure of which distribution to use, this makes a very good choice.

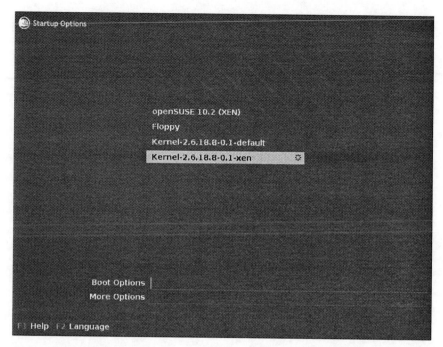

FIGURE 4.3 The OpenSUSE GRUB menu displaying Xen-enabled kernel choices

CentOS

CentOS is an Enterprise-class Linux distribution derived from the source code to Red Hat Enterprise Linux. Because the source code is freely available to the public, it is packaged in as close a fashion to Red Hat's product offering as possible. The material covered in this chapter should apply to both distributions because CentOS aims to be 100 percent binary compatible.

CentOS is a relatively recent release and has followed the lead of SUSE Linux by integrating Xen installation right into the normal distribution installation process. CentOS has integrated a slightly newer set of management utilities into the distribution.

Installing Xen during a fresh installation of CentOS is easy. When running the installer, just before installation commences, you need to enable Xen support during the package selection phase. As shown in Figure 4.4, select the Customize Now radio button. CentOS installation makes it easy to add Xen Domain0 and Xen utility support during the initial installation process. Selecting custom packages is the key.

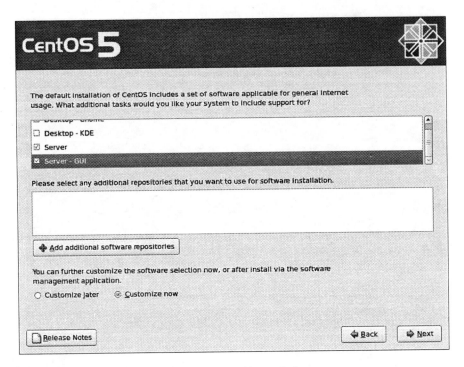

FIGURE 4.4 The CentOS installation process supports Xen natively

From the resulting window, choose Virtualization from the left-hand menu and then make sure there is a check mark next to the Virtualization item on the right side of the screen as shown in Figure 4.5. As you proceed, you are prompted for confirmation of additional virtualization related packages. Ensure that all three items are shown as in Figure 4.6. The selections include gnome-applet-vm, libvirt, and virt-manager. Simply continue your installation as normal, and you are rebooted automatically into your Xen Domain0 kernel.

Selecting Virtualization from the left and right side menus is the key to adding Xen support. Then, as shown in Figure 4.6, one last prompt confirms that the additional packages to support Xen will be installed. Make sure that each of the packages shown has been selected.

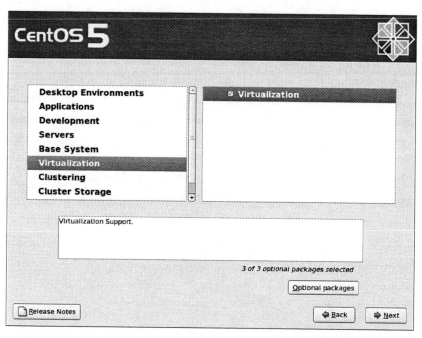

FIGURE 4.5 Choosing virtualization options during the CentOS installation process

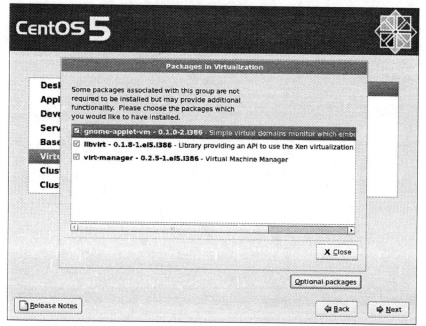

FIGURE 4.6 Selecting all the packages available under the Virtualization option

If you have CentOS installed already and neglected to select the optional packages for Xen support, you can use the tool yum to install it. There are also graphical tools available for this purpose. There are three packages that we would recommend to have a fully functional setup for CentOS. First, the Xen package provides the hypervisor, along with its dependencies. Second, the xen-kernel package provides the Domain0/DomU kernel and dependencies, and updates the GRUB boot menu appropriately. Finally, virt-manager provides a nice GUI interface for creating and managing Xen guests. The virt-manager package contains other tools such as virt-install (a command line, ncurses version of virt-manager) as well. For a more detailed analysis of virt-manager see Chapter 7, "Populating Guest Images." Listing 4.1 shows the full output after doing a default install of Xen on CentOS without Xen support.

LISTING 4.1 Installing Xen on an Existing CentOS System

```
[root@centos]# yum install xen kernel-xen virt-manager
Loading "installonlyn" plugin
Setting up Install Process
Setting up repositories
Reading repository metadata in from local files
Parsing package install arguments
Resolving Dependencies
--> Populating transaction set with selected packages.
    Please wait.
---> Package xen.i386 0:3.0.3-8.el5 set to be updated
---> Downloading header for kernel-xen to pack into
    transaction set.
kernel-xen-2.6.18-1.2747. 100% |===============| 184 kB    00:00
---> Package kernel-xen.i686 0:2.6.18-1.2747.el5 set to be   ➡
    installed
---> Downloading header for virt-manager to pack into        ➡
    transaction set.
virt-manager-0.2.5-1.el5. 100% |===============|  19 kB    00:00
---> Package virt-manager.i386 0:0.2.5-1.el5 set to be updated
--> Running transaction check
--> Processing Dependency: gnome-python2-gnomekeyring >=     ➡
    2.15.4 for package: virt-manager
--> Processing Dependency: xen-libs = 3.0.3-8.el5 for        ➡
    package: xen
--> Processing Dependency: bridge-utils for package: xen
--> Processing Dependency: libvirt-python >= 0.1.4-3 for     ➡
    package: virt-manager
--> Processing Dependency: libxenctrl.so.3.0 for package: xen
```

```
--> Processing Dependency: libblktap.so.3.0 for package: xen
--> Processing Dependency: libxenguest.so.3.0 for package: xen
--> Processing Dependency: python-virtinst for package: xen
--> Processing Dependency: libxenstore.so.3.0 for package: xen
--> Processing Dependency: python-virtinst >= 0.95.0 for    ➡
    package: virt-manager
--> Restarting Dependency Resolution with new changes.
--> Populating transaction set with selected packages.    ➡
    Please wait.
---> Package xen-libs.i386 0:3.0.3-8.el5 set to be updated
---> Package python-virtinst.noarch 0:0.96.0-2.el5 set    ➡
    to be updated
---> Downloading header for gnome-python2-gnomekeyring to    ➡
    pack into transaction set.
gnome-python2-gnomekeyrin 100% |===============| 3.4 kB    00:00
---> Package gnome-python2-gnomekeyring.i386 0:2.16.0-1.fc6 ➡
    set to be updated
---> Package bridge-utils.i386 0:1.1-2 set to be updated
---> Package libvirt-python.i386 0:0.1.8-1.el5 set to be    ➡
    updated
--> Running transaction check
--> Processing Dependency: libvirt.so.0 for package:    ➡
    libvirt-python
--> Processing Dependency: libvirt = 0.1.8 for package:    ➡
    libvirt-python
--> Restarting Dependency Resolution with new changes.
--> Populating transaction set with selected packages.    ➡
    Please wait.
---> Package libvirt.i386 0:0.1.8-1.el5 set to be updated
--> Running transaction check

Dependencies Resolved
```

Package	Arch	Version	Repository	Size
Installing:				
kernel-xen	i686	2.6.18-1.2747.el5	base	14 M
virt-manager	i386	0.2.5-1.el5	base	357 k
xen	i386	3.0.3-8.el5	base	1.7 M
Installing for dependencies:				
bridge-utils	i386	1.1-2	base	27 k

```
gnome-python2-gnomekeyring   i386        2.16.0-1.fc6      base 15 k
libvirt           i386       0.1.8-1.el5        base       119 k
libvirt-python   i386        0.1.8-1.el5        base        43 k
python-virtinst  noarch      0.96.0-2.el5       base        28 k
xen-libs          i386       3.0.3-8.el5        base        83 k

Transaction Summary
==================================================================
Install      9 Package(s)
Update       0 Package(s)
Remove       0 Package(s)

Total download size: 16 M
Is this ok [y/N]:  y
Downloading Packages:
(1/9): xen-libs-3.0.3-8.e 100% |===============|   83 kB    00:00
(2/9): libvirt-0.1.8-1.el 100% |===============|  119 kB    00:00
(3/9): python-virtinst-0. 100% |===============|   28 kB    00:00
(4/9): gnome-python2-gnom 100% |===============|   15 kB    00:00
(5/9): bridge-utils-1.1-2 100% |===============|   27 kB    00:00
(6/9): xen-3.0.3-8.el5.i3 100% |===============|  1.7 MB    00:03
(7/9): kernel-xen-2.6.18- 100% |===============|   14 MB    00:32
(8/9): libvirt-python-0.1 100% |===============|   43 kB    00:00
(9/9): virt-manager-0.2.5 100% |===============|  357 kB    00:00
Running Transaction Test
Finished Transaction Test
Transaction Test Succeeded
Running Transaction
  Installing: xen-libs                       ############## [1/9]
  Installing: bridge-utils                   ############## [2/9]
  Installing: gnome-python2-gnomekeyring     ############### [3/9]
  Installing: kernel-xen                     ############## [4/9]
  Installing: libvirt-python                 ############## [5/9]
  Installing: python-virtinst                ############## [6/9]
  Installing: libvirt                        ############## [7/9]
  Installing: xen                            ############## [8/9]
  Installing: virt-manager                   ############## [9/9]

Installed: kernel-xen.i686 0:2.6.18-1.2747.el5 ➥
     virt-manager.i386 0:0.2.5-1.el5 xen.i386 0:3.0.3-8.el5
Dependency Installed: bridge-utils.i386 0:1.1-2 ➥
     gnome-python2-gnomekeyring.i386 0:2.16.0-1.fc6 ➥
     libvirt.i386 0:0.1.8-1.el5 libvirt-python.i386 ➥
     0:0.1.8-1.el5 python-virtinst.noarch 0:0.96.0-2.el5      ➥
```

```
        xen-libs.i386 0:3.0.3-8.el5
Complete!
[root@centos]#
```

To ensure our Domain0 kernel is ready to be booted, we also edit the contents of the GRUB configuration file. In Listing 4.2, the first entry has "xen" in the kernel name (/xen.gz-2.6.18-1.2747.el5). The two module lines shown in Listing 4.2 are too long to display on a single line. In an actual menu.1st file, the entire module information should appear on a single line.

LISTING 4.2 GRUB Menu

```
[root@centos]# cat /boot/grub/menu.1st
# grub.conf generated by anaconda
#
# Note that you do not have to rerun grub after making changes
# to this file
# NOTICE:  You have a /boot partition.  This means that
#         all kernel and initrd paths are relative to /boot/, eg.
#         root (hd0,0)
#         kernel /vmlinuz-version ro root=/dev/VolGroup00/LogVol00
#         initrd /initrd-version.img
#boot=/dev/sda
default=1
timeout=5
splashimage=(hd0,0)/grub/splash.xpm.gz
hiddenmenu
title CentOS (2.6.18-1.2747.el5xen)
        root (hd0,0)
        kernel /xen.gz-2.6.18-1.2747.el5
        module /vmlinuz-2.6.18-1.2747.el5xen ro              ➧
     root=/dev/VolGroup00/LogVol00 rhgb quiet
        module /initrd-2.6.18-1.2747.el5xen.img
title CentOS (2.6.18-1.2747.el5)
        root (hd0,0)
        kernel /vmlinuz-2.6.18-1.2747.el5 ro                 ➧
     root=/dev/VolGroup00/LogVol00 rhgb quiet
        initrd /initrd-2.6.18-1.2747.el5.img
[root@centos]#
```

After you have rebooted the system, you should ensure your Xen kernel is selected. When the boot process has completed, you can use the uname and xm list commands to ensure you are in fact using your Xen-enabled kernel as shown in Listing 4.3. The output shows a single execution domain, Domain0. In addition, executing uname -a might show our Xen kernel string in the command output; however, this method is not preferred because "xen" might not appear in the kernel name if the name was changed during compilation.

LISTING 4.3 Checking That the Xen Kernel Is Running

```
[root@centos]# xm list
Name                      ID   Mem VCPUs      State   Time(s)
Domain-0                   0  2270     2      r-----  85554.2
[root@centos]#
```

The support for Xen in CentOS is considered to be good—the installation is straightforward, and the addition of Virtualization Manager is an added bonus. CentOS can be a convenient way for beginners to familiarize themselves with Xen. Depending on your needs, it may make sense for you to consider the upstream provider, Red Hat, as many upstream providers have the added benefit of commercial support.

Ubuntu

Ubuntu has quickly become one of the most popular Linux distributions. Ubuntu is a free and open source Linux-based operating system that builds on the Debian distribution. Ubuntu has a regular release cycle, occurring every six months, and a solid focus on usability and default configurations that work with a minimum of user involvement or setup. Ubuntu is a comfortable distribution choice for even novice users and provides both a comfortable desktop experience as well as a solid server platform.

As of Debian 4.0 and Ubuntu 6.10, Xen Debian packages have been available in the respective Debian and Ubuntu repositories.

> **NOTE**
>
> For Ubuntu, the "universe" repository needs to be enabled, if it is not already, because Xen packages are not yet in the "main" Ubuntu repository. Refer to the Ubuntu documentation for more information on managing repositories at https://help.ubuntu.com/community/Repositories. To check on future versions of the Xen packages, and the repository that they fall in, search or browse the Ubuntu packages at http://packages.ubuntu.com/.

In June 2006, Ubuntu 6.06 LTS (Long Term Support) was released. The Ubuntu LTS releases are supported for three years on the desktop version and five years on the server version. The next LTS release is scheduled for April 2008, which would be Ubuntu 8.04.

> **NOTE**
>
> Ubuntu version numbers are based on the release date. The first number corresponds to the year of the release; for example, versions released in 2006 have 6 as the first number. The number after the period corresponds to the month of the release; for example, a release in April, the fourth month, has a second number of 04. Putting them together, if there had been a Ubuntu release in April 2006, which there wasn't, it would have been numbered 6.04.

Although Ubuntu 6.10 had Xen packages available, you needed to choose the proper packages manually. As of Ubuntu 7.04, ubuntu-xen-desktop, ubuntu-xen-server, and ubuntu-xen-desktop-amd64 meta packages, which are packages that depend on all the necessary Xen packages, are available. Listing 4.4 shows the commands and output of installing the Ubuntu Xen packages on Ubuntu 7.10. In the listing we use the apt-get command. Alternatively, you could use a graphical tool such as synaptic.

LISTING 4.4 Using apt-get to Install Ubuntu Xen Packages

```
[root@ubuntu]# apt-get install ubuntu-xen-desktop
Reading package lists... Done
Building dependency tree
Reading state information... Done
The following extra packages will be installed:
  bridge-utils debootstrap libbeecrypt6 libc6 libc6-i686
  libc6-xen libneon25 librpm4 libtext-template-perl
  libxen3.1 linux-image-2.6.22-14-xen linux-image-xen
  linux-restricted-modules-2.6.22-14-xen
  linux-restricted-modules-xen
  linux-ubuntu-modules-2.6.22-14-xen linux-xen python-crypto
  python-dev python-paramiko python-rpm python-xen-3.1
  python2.5-dev xen-docs-3.1 xen-hypervisor-3.1 xen-ioemu-3.1
  xen-tools xen-utils-3.1 xenman
Suggested packages:
  glibc-doc linux-doc-2.6.22 linux-source-2.6.22 nvidia-glx
  nvidia-glx-legacy nvidia-glx-new avm-fritz-firmware-2.6.22-14
  python-crypto-dbg libc6-dev libc-dev xen-hypervisor
```

```
Recommended packages:
  xen-hypervisor-3.1-i386 xen-hypervisor-3.1-i386-pae rpmstrap
The following NEW packages will be installed:
  bridge-utils debootstrap libbeecrypt6 libc6-xen libneon25
  librpm4 libtext-template-perl libxen3.1
  linux-image-2.6.22-14-xen linux-image-xen
  linux-restricted-modules-2.6.22-14-xen
  linux-restricted-modules-xen
  linux-ubuntu-modules-2.6.22-14-xen linux-xen python-crypto
  python-dev python-paramiko python-rpm python-xen-3.1
  python2.5-dev ubuntu-xen-desktop xen-docs-3.1
  xen-hypervisor-3.1 xen-ioemu-3.1 xen-tools xen-utils-3.1
  xenman
The following packages will be upgraded:
  libc6 libc6-i686
2 upgraded, 27 newly installed, 0 to remove and 157 notÂ
upgraded.
Need to get 46.4MB of archives.
After unpacking 123MB of additional disk space will be used.
Do you want to continue [Y/n]? y
Get:1 http://us.archive.ubuntu.com gutsy-updates/main ➥
libc6 2.6.1-1ubuntu10 [4184kB]
Get:2 http://us.archive.ubuntu.com gutsy-updates/main ➥
libc6-i686 2.6.1-1ubuntu10 [1148kB]
Get:3 http://us.archive.ubuntu.com gutsy/universe ➥
linux-image-2.6.22-14-xen 2.6.22-14.46 [17.3MB]

[downloading output omitted]

2ubuntu4 [2200B]
Fetched 46.4MB in 1m20s (580kB/s)

(Reading database ... 92004 files and directories currently ➥
installed.)
Preparing to replace libc6 2.6.1-1ubuntu9 ➥
(using .../libc6_2.6.1-1ubuntu10_i386.deb) ...
Unpacking replacement libc6 ...
Setting up libc6 (2.6.1-1ubuntu10) ...

[setting up of packages output omitted]

Processing triggers for libc6 ... Processing triggers for ➥
libc6 ...
ldconfig deferred processing now taking place
[root@ubuntu]#
```

After the packages are successfully installed, restart your system and make sure you chose the appropriate Xen kernel from the GRUB menu. After you have booted your newly installed Xen kernel, you can test that you are using the correct kernel and that you have a working system by using the uname -a and xm list commands as discussed previously in the CentOS section.

Xen from Binary Packages

In this section, we use Ubuntu 6.06 as the basis to demonstrate how to install Xen from binary packages. This can be applied to other distributions as well.

> **NOTE**
> You could use other distributions as the base for the install. You would just need to get the proper prerequisites for those distributions using the package management tools specific to those distributions. Also, the postinstallation steps will require the appropriate equivalent tools for the other distributions.

To begin, we assume you have performed a successful stand-alone installation of Ubuntu 6.06. This can be done via a direct install or an upgrade to the current supported release. From there we need to install a few extra packages that will make our Ubuntu system a fully functioning Domain0. The iproute and bridge utils programs are required for the xend control tools and enable network connectivity to your guests. The Python scripting language is needed to execute a number of Xen-related utilities.

Listing 4.5 shows the three commands that add support to an Ubuntu distribution. The commands update the list of known packages, update to the current release of all system packages, and install the Xen specific requirements, respectively.

LISTING 4.5 Xen-Related Utilities to Update an Ubuntu System and Install the Necessary Packages

```
[root@ubuntu]# apt-get update

[output omitted]

[root@ubuntu]# apt-get upgrade

[output omitted]

[root@ubuntu]# apt-get install iproute python python-twisted ➥
bridge-utils

[output omitted]
```

Next we need to download the latest prebuilt tar file of Xen. We recommend obtaining the latest supported tarball from XenSource at www.xen.org/download/.

Click the Download link for the latest version of Xen tarballs, and click Binary Download from your choice of either 32-bit SMP, 32-bit SMP PAE, or 64-bit SMP. After downloading the right binary for your environment, extract the archive by running tar xzpvf <the downloaded tarball>.

The tarball extracts to a directory called dist. Familiarize yourself with the contents of the dist directory; in particular, you should focus on the subdirectory named install. The install directory contains binary Xen kernels, modules and hypervisor, configuration files, and all the necessary Xen tools. To begin installing the Xen kernel, hypervisor, and all the Xen-related tools, execute the install.sh script located in the dist directory that we just unpacked. Listing 4.6 shows the commands that we used. Also, notice that the subdirectory 2.6.18-xen of the install/lib/ modules directory corresponds to the <xen kernel version> used in Listings 4.7, 4.8, and 4.9.

> **NOTE**
>
> In our experience, running the install.sh script contained within the Xen binary tarball works without changing the mode to the install.sh file to be executable as its permissions are retained. If, however, you run across an error trying to run the install. sh file, try using the command chmod a+x install.sh.

LISTING 4.6 Running the Install Script

```
[root@ubuntu]# tar xzpf xen-3.1.0-install-x86_32.tgz
[root@ubuntu]# cd dist
[root@ubuntu/dist]# ls install/lib/modules/
2.6.18-xen
[root@ubuntu/dist]#./install.sh

[beginning of output omitted]

Installing Xen from './install' to '/'...
 - installing for udev-based system
 - modifying permissions
All done.
Checking to see whether prerequisite tools are installed...
Xen CHECK-INSTALL  Thu Feb 22 01:18:19 EST 2007
Checking check_brctl: OK
Checking check_crypto_lib: OK
```

```
Checking check_iproute: OK
Checking check_libvncserver: unused, OK
Checking check_python: OK
Checking check_python_xml: OK
Checking check_sdl: unused, OK
Checking check_udev: OK
Checking check_zlib_lib: OK
All done.
[root@ubuntu]#
```

Now we build our `modules.dep` and associated map files. These files are created in the `/lib/modules/<xen kernel version>` directory. You can do this by issuing the command shown in Listing 4.7 in your terminal.

LISTING 4.7 Using depmod

```
[root@ubuntu]# depmod -a <xen kernel version>
```

You may need to increase the number of loopback devices your new Domain0 kernel will support if Domain0 will be managing more than a handful of legacy loopback-configured images. These loopback-configured images still use `file:/` in their disk parameter line and are backed by loopback devices as opposed to blocktap device images that use `tap:aio:/` and are backed by the blktap-based block device backend. We can increase the maximum number of loopback devices by appending `loop max_loop=64` to `/etc/mkinitramfs/modules`.

Then we create our initial ram disk file system (initramfs) image to load modules necessary before accessing the disk by executing the command shown in Listing 4.8.

LISTING 4.8 mkinitramfs

```
[root@ubuntu]# mkinitramfs -o /boot/initrd ➥
    .img-<xen kernel version> <xen kernel version>
```

Finally, with the Domain0 kernel installed, the modules created, and the loopback parameters adjusted, we can create the GRUB entry necessary to boot this new kernel. We recommend prepending to the `Automagic` section of the `/boot/grub/menu.1st` file with an entry tailored to the Domain0 kernel. Listing 4.9 shows an example.

LISTING 4.9 GRUB Menu

```
title Xen 3.0  (Dom0 Based on Linux 2.6 Kernel)
kernel /boot/xen-3.gz
module /boot/vmlinuz-2.6-xen root=<root device> ro
module /boot/initrd.img-<xen kernel version>
```

You don't need to get the xen-utils package because the Xen binary package, the tarball, comes with all the Xen tools as well. Because the utilities are installed, we need to ensure that xend and the guest linked to in /etc/xen/auto, which are started by the xendomains script, are started automatically at boot. This is a straightforward process handled by the update-rc.d command as shown in Listing 4.10.

LISTING 4.10 Starting Xen Services Automatically

```
[root@ubuntu]#  update-rc.d xend defaults
[root@ubuntu]#  update-rc.d xendomains defaults
```

We also need to disable thread local storage as shown in Listing 4.11.

LISTING 4.11 Disabling Thread Local Storage

```
[root@ubuntu]#  mv /lib/tls /lib/tls.disabled
```

If you neglect to disable thread local storage, you will encounter the warning shown in Listing 4.12 at system boot. Functionality will be preserved, but performance will suffer from the additional work imposed on the hypervisor.

LISTING 4.12 Warning Message If Thread Local Storage Not Disabled

```
***************************************************************
***************************************************************
** WARNING: Currently emulating unsupported memory accesses  **
**          in /lib/tls glibc libraries. The emulation is     **
**          slow. To ensure full performance you should       **
**          install a 'xen-friendly' (nosegneg) version of    **
**          the library, or disable tls support by executing **
**          the following as root:                            **
**          mv /lib/tls /lib/tls.disabled                     **
** Offending process: binutils.postin (pid=9521)             **
***************************************************************
***************************************************************
```

Ubuntu provides a Xen-specific glibc that will resolve this issue should you encounter it. If faced with this dialog, issue `sudo apt-get install libc6-xen` for a potential solution.

If you have successfully made it here by following along, it is now time to reboot your Ubuntu system. From the GRUB menu, the topmost item is now our Xen Domain0 kernel. Make sure this item is selected when the GRUB timer runs out. If all goes well, you should see your normal Ubuntu boot procedure, with the exception of starting a few additional Xen-related service daemons.

After your system is completely up, you can verify that your Domain0 is functioning properly by executing the `xm list` command as shown in Listing 4.13. The only domain currently executing is Domain0. This makes sense because we have just rebooted into our Domain0 kernel. If additional DomainU guests were running, they would be visible in the output of this command.

LISTING 4.13 Checking That the Xen Kernel Is Running

```
root@ubuntu_dom0# xm list
Name                      ID    Mem VCPUs     State    Time(s)
Domain-0                   0   2270    2      r-----   85554.2
root@ubuntu_dom0#
```

Overall, Ubuntu is a well supported Xen platform and is a great way to try out the latest binaries directly packaged by XenSource itself, even if it requires a bit of up-front work to get everything installed. The installation is relatively straightforward, and little manual configuration is involved.

If you encounter any problem areas while following along in this section, see the additional resources listed in the "References and Further Reading" section at the end of this chapter.

Gentoo

Compared to those we have explored so far, Gentoo is a different kind of Linux distribution. Gentoo is a source-based Linux distribution, or a metadistribution. This means that all the programs installed in a Gentoo installation are built from source, custom tailored to the build machine as well as to the preferences of the system administrator. This is both Gentoo's greatest strength and its greatest weakness. This also makes Gentoo a more advanced Linux distribution choice, and, as such, we do not recommend this installation for the novice Linux or Xen user.

Some of the distinct advantages of using a source-based distribution such as Gentoo are greater control and knowledge of exactly what packages are installed while being custom compiled for the specific computer. This leads to elaborate knowledge of how Linux itself works because you have to install each component. Due to the minimalistic and tailored installation facilities Gentoo provides, it becomes a strong contender for an optimized, minimal, and security-minded Domain0.

However, the close control of what packages are being installed and compiling from scratch lead to an intensive administrative responsibility and take a great deal of administrative time. This manifests itself in the form of knowing what packages to install, and what versions are stable, to achieve the desired effect. For example, to install a common graphical desktop environment, as many as 290 packages may need to be installed. Luckily, the Gentoo development team has devised a package management system to address the burden of custom building so many packages. This package management system is called Portage. Portage is a system capable of resolving almost any dependencies recursively, thereby limiting the research a system administrator needs to perform before selecting a package for installation. Additionally, Portage "masks" or prevents the installation of software packages not yet fully tested. This section assumes you have completed the initial setup of your Gentoo server with a minimal installation and have logged in for normal use. We explore how to use the powerful Portage package management system to install our Xen Domain0 kernel, as well as the associated user space utilities.

After you have achieved a functioning typical Gentoo installation, it is relatively straightforward to set up a new installation for a Xen Domain0 kernel. At this point, it is important to remember that it is Xen which has to run on the bare hardware (rather than the guest). Some system calls issued by the guests need to be modified because the guest is not running on the bare hardware itself. Typically, without proper guest customization, Xen needs to trap certain operations, mostly related to memory, and replace them with Xen compatible operations. This is expensive, especially when we have an alternative that Gentoo affords us. With Gentoo, we can recompile everything on the system to omit these operations and skip the expensive workaround. To accomplish this, a simple compile time directive, or CFLAG, can be added to the `/etc/make.conf` file.

Open `/etc/make.conf` with a text editor. Locate the beginning of the file where the line starts `CFLAGS= -O2 -march=i686 -pipe` and append the flag `-mno-tls-direct-seg-refs` to it. This command line switch causes all software on the system to be compiled in a fashion compatible with the Xen hypervisor's memory needs in a relatively high performance way. The resulting binaries will not need expensive runtime alterations, and higher performance will be seen overall. Refer to the beginning of this chapter in the thread local storage section and to Listing 4.11 for more information. While we are editing the file, we will add several USE flags that will come into play later. Mainly the flags `sdl vnc sysfs nptlonly` need to be set. If you wish Domain0 to have a graphical user interface (like X Windows), then you should also add X to the USE flag. However, for this guide, we stick to using the terminal. If desired, you can experiment with graphics packages according to the normal Gentoo Handbook.

The final file contents of the `/etc/make.conf` file should look as shown in Listing 4.14.

LISTING 4.14 `/etc/make.conf`

```
CFLAGS="-O2 -march=i686 -pipe  -mno-tls-direct-seg-refs"
CHOST="i686-pc-linux-gnu"
CXXFLAGS="${CFLAGS}"
USE="sdl vnc sysfs nptlonly"
```

The following are additional potential CFLAGs for `/etc/make.conf`:

- **Sdl**—Support for Simple Direct Lay media library, which enables faster DomU console drawing

- **Vnc**—Enables support for VNC as a video device for DomU

- **Nptlonly**—Uses the POSIX thread library to avoid thread local storage problems

- **Sysfs**—Enables sysfs to reflect hypervisor extensions (that is, the `/sys/hypervisor` directory)

- **X**—Enables Domain0 to have a graphical window environment

After this file is configured and saved, the next step is to remake the world, or recompile everything on the system with our new custom settings. This step may take a while, compiling many packages for your platform. To initiate the compilation simply use the `emerge world` command. The `emerge world` command is the universal update command used frequently by Gentoo users.

After the compilation is completed, and subsequent packages are rebuilt, we are ready to move on to something more complex. We need to compile our Xen kernel for

Domain0. Luckily the Portage system has the Domain0 kernel sources readily available. Once again we use the emerge tool. Listing 4.15 shows the two necessary invocations of the emerge command.

LISTING 4.15　Using emerge to Get the Xen Sources

```
[root@gentoo]# emerge -ev world
[root@gentoo]# emerge xen-sources
```

Some xen-source packages may be "masked." Masking a package is Portage's mechanism for protecting inexperienced users from installing certain packages. Packages might be masked because they are simply unstable, or sometimes just not yet tested thoroughly within the context of a Gentoo installation. Using the -p option to pretend to merge allows us to see whether packages will not be installed due to masks.

The output from our call would be like that shown in Listing 4.16. For more information, see the "Masked Packages" section in the emerge man page or refer to the *Gentoo Handbook*. To get around this problem, we need to add these packages to the acceptable list of packages. This is done through a simple echo command to a file. While we are enabling packages, we will also enable xend and the xen-tools; this completes the list of all the required packages for Xen. Now we can rerun our emerge command without the pretend option to see that the kernel sources are the only items Portage is going to install. We now know it is safe to install.

LISTING 4.16　Unmasking the xen-sources Packages

```
[root@gentoo]# emerge -pv xen-sources
Calculating dependencies
!!! All ebuilds that could satisfy "xen-sources" have been ➥
masked.
!!! One of the following masked packages is required toÂ
complete your request:
- sys-kernel/xen-sources-2.6.16.28-r2 (masked by: ~x86 keyword)
- sys-kernel/xen-sources-2.6.16.28 (masked by: ~x86 keyword)
- sys-kernel/xen-sources-2.6.16.28-r1 (masked by: ~x86 keyword)

[root@gentoo]# echo "sys-kernel/xen-source"" >> /etc/portage/package.keywords
[root@gentoo]# echo "app-emulation/xen-tools" >> /etc/portage/package.keywords
[root@gentoo]# echo "app-emulation/xen" >> ➥
/etc/portage/package.keywords
[root@gentoo]# emerge xen-sources
[root@gentoo]#
```

When the xen-sources packages are installed, Portage downloads, decompresses, and patches the kernel. It is up to the system operator to perform the necessary kernel configuration. So let's move to the standard kernel directory /usr/src/linux, where Portage places the kernel, and start the configuration. This directory will be your kernel directory only if you have not had a previous kernel source tree installed. If your Xen kernel sources are somewhere else, adjust accordingly. Listing 4.17 shows the commands used to enter the source directory and start the kernel feature selection menu.

LISTING 4.17 Configuring the Kernel to Support Xen

```
[root@gentoo]# cd /usr/src/linux
[root@gentoo]# make menuconfig
[root@gentoo]#
```

Configure your kernel as normal, paying special attention to building in any of the file systems you used to install the system in the beginning of the guide. To get a jump start on this process you can borrow the kernel configuration used on Gentoo's Live-eCD. All that is required is to copy the file from /proc/config.gz into a temporary directory. Extract the file and then copy it to your new Domain0 kernel source directory. Name the copied configuration file .config.

You might wonder how this kernel configuration option resides in the /proc file system. This proc entry is not just a convenience solely found in Gentoo. In fact, when you have finished configuring a Xen or normal Linux kernel, you should always make sure that you embed the configuration into the kernel image. This can be done easily by selecting the option under General Setup at the kernels menuconfig. For those who choose not to use the menu or graphical configuration tools, simply make sure that CONFIG_IKCONFIG=y and CONFIG_IKCONFIG_PROC=y are set in your .config file.

If you have access to a running kernel configuration for your hardware, you can start your menuconfig for a Xen-enabled kernel based on that working configuration. You will also need to select the Processor type and Features -> Subarchitecture and turn it to Xen-Compatible. This gives us the XEN options we need. To enable Domain0 support, select the new XEN option from the beginning of the kernel menu and select Privileged Guest (Domain 0). Also make sure that all the necessary drivers for your hardware are built, especially the disk driver(s). Then, simply compile the kernel as normal. Listing 4.18 shows the commands used for a typical compile. The last step of copying the kernel binary image to the boot directory allows the new kernel to be booted after the machine has been restarted.

LISTING 4.18 Compiling the Newly Configured Kernel

```
[root@gentoo]# make
[root@gentoo]# make modules_install
[root@gentoo]# cp vmlinuz /boot/
[root@gentoo]#
```

Now we have to tell the GRUB bootloader installation about our new Xen kernel. To accomplish this, we need to edit the `/boot/grub.conf` file with a text editor to look like the example shown in Listing 4.19.

LISTING 4.19 GRUB Menu

```
timeout 10
default 0
splashimage=(hd0,0)/boot/grub/splash.xpm.gz
title Xen Gentoo
root (hd0,0)
kernel /xen-3.0.2.gz
module /vmlinux root=/dev/hda3
```

Now we should have a fully working Domain0 kernel compiled and ready for testing. Before rebooting, we need to install the set of user space xen-tools for interacting with our Domain0 kernel. This package contains the xend and xm family of commands, as well as other related tools for Domain0. These user space utilities are vital for interacting with Domain0 to facilitate guest creation. Listing 4.20 shows the number of packages necessary for your installation and their status with traditional Portage notation. Because we used the -p option, Portage only pretended to install the packages to inform us of the dependencies needed. The output should be similar to what is found in Listing 4.20. This output shows you the relevant USE flags. If the output and package listing look acceptable, it should be safe to install them.

LISTING 4.20 Using emerge to Get the Xen Tools

```
[root@gentoo]# emerge -pv xen-tools

These are the packages that would be merged, in order:

Calculating dependencies
... done!
```

```
[ebuild  N    ] net-misc/bridge-utils-1.2  USE="sysfs" 31 kB
[ebuild  N    ] sys-apps/iproute2-2.6.19.20061214  ➡
USE="berkdb -atm -minimal" 392 kB
[ebuild  N    ] sys-devel/bin86-0.16.17  148 kB
[ebuild  N    ] dev-util/gperf-3.0.2  824 kB
[ebuild  N    ] sys-devel/dev86-0.16.17-r3  686 kB
[ebuild  N    ] app-emulation/xen-3.0.2  USE="-custom-cflags  ➡
-debug -hardened -pae" 4,817 kB
[ebuild  N    ] app-emulation/xen-tools-3.0.2-r4  USE="sdl vnc  ➡
-custom-cflags -debug -doc -pygrub -screen" 0 kB

Total size of downloads: 6,901 kB

[root@gentoo]# emerge xen-tools
[root@gentoo]#
```

Finally, we use the Gentoo `rc-update` utility as shown in Listing 4.21 to add the xend process to the default runlevel. This process starts xend as part of the normal bootup process and prevents you from having to start it manually after each reboot.

LISTING 4.21 Adding the xend Service to the Default Runlevel

```
[root@gentoo]# rc-update add xend default
```

Now we should be ready to reboot and try out our new Xen kernel. After a reboot, you should see your Xen Domain0 kernel selection highlighted as the default. Your Xen Domain0 kernel should load and boot normally (with the addition of a few new startup items such as xend). Figure 4.7 shows the GRUB bootloader option with our Gentoo Domain0 kernel selected.

To easily check whether we are running a Domain0 kernel, we can look for directory /sys/hypervisor. If this directory exists, Xen should be executing properly. Additionally, you may use the uname -n command to look for the name of your kernel. Often, this includes a string about patches applied to the kernel, including whether Xen is enabled.

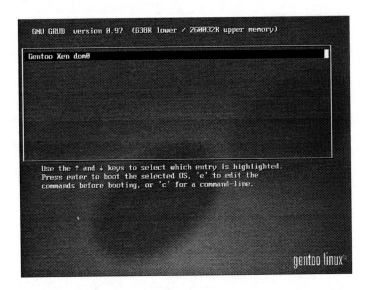

FIGURE 4.7 GRUB menu option for a Gentoo-based Domain0

Gentoo operates well as a Domain0 and provides software optimizations that can
lead to increased performance in virtualized environments. Subjectively, the support in
Gentoo is no different from any other bit of masked software. Experts familiar with the
Gentoo Portage system should have no major difficulty installing a Gentoo-based Do-
main0. Having clarified that point, we would rate the subjective level of support lower
than the previously mentioned binary distributions that provide point-and-click installation. However, for the expert, Gentoo provides a lot of flexibility and customization.

XenExpress

In this section, we use XenExpress, a distribution of Linux provided by XenSource.
(Note that the new Citrix XenServer Express Edition may be somewhat different.)
XenExpress is a derivative of CentOS. The XenExpress installation program assumes
that you intend to install it on a dedicated host to act as a Xen server. The Xen server
is intended to execute the XenExpress operating system on the bare hardware of the
physical host. When selecting XenExpress as your choice of Domain0, keep in mind
there is a minimum requirement of 1GB of memory as well as 16GB of available hard
disk space. Through experimentation we recommend that you double the minimum
required memory and disk for better results.

When installing XenExpress for your Domain0, you are prompted to install some additional software components. The primary disk used for installation contains the essential Domain0 Xen server host, support for Microsoft Windows guests, as well as the Xen administration console. The secondary disk contains all the support needed to create Linux-based virtual machines. As such, we strongly recommend that you install the components from the second CD. Figure 4.8 shows the screen during the XenExpress install that asks whether you want to install the Linux Pack from a second CD. If you want to have quick access to paravirtualized guests, you should answer Yes and insert the Linux Guest Support CD, which is also available for download from the Citrix XenServer site.

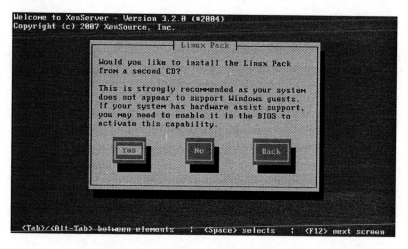

FIGURE 4.8 XenExpress installation prompt for Linux Pack

> **NOTE**
> The install CD has a P2V (Physical to Virtual) option that allows you to convert a physical system to a virtual Xen guest.

One exceptionally interesting feature of the XenExpress Domain0 installation is the addition of special Java client tools used to control your Domain0. These Java tools enable a GUI that can help you with day-to-day administration of your Xen server. Listing 4.22 shows the installation of these tools. The installation RPMs are also found on the Linux Guest Support CD. The Java tools enable any remotely connected operating system that supports Java to act as the graphical display of your Domain0 installation. This feature can be handy because it enables you to deploy, manage, and monitor your virtual machines conveniently. The Java software is supported on any recent workstation or laptop with major operating systems, including most recent Windows operating system variants, as well as properly configured Linux systems. The documentation recommends that you make sure that any machine that will use the client tools has at least 1GB of memory with 100MB of hard disk space available. When in doubt, exercise common sense by making sure that more resources are free, and do not execute the graphical tools on an overloaded host.

XenExpress is not as full featured as some of its non-gratis siblings. XenExpress supports 4GB memory for the host and a maximum of four virtual machine guests operating concurrently. Check the current documentation for supported configurations. For larger numbers of concurrent guests or support for managing multiple physical hosts, you may consider upgrading to the higher-end commercial versions. To launch the tools from a machine you have installed the tools on, simply execute `xenserver-client`, as shown at the end of Listing 4.22. For more information about Citrix XenServer Express Edition, see the following site: `www.citrixxenserver.com/products/Pages/XenExpress.aspx`.

LISTING 4.22 Installing the XenExpress Client Tools

```
[root@externalHost_linux] # rpm -ivh *.rpm
Preparing...                ################################# [100%]
   1:xenserver-client-jre   ########################### [ 20%]
   2:xenserver-client-jars  ########################### [ 40%]
   3:xe-cli                 ########################### [ 60%]
   4:xe-cli-debuginfo       ########################### [ 80%]
   5:xenserver-client       ########################### [100%]
[root@externalHost_linux] # xenserver-client
[root@externalHost_linux] #
```

Non-Linux Domain0 Installations

Currently, development efforts are in progress to enable non-Linux operating systems to act as a Domain0 host. Though there has been progress in FreeBSD and OpenBSD, they do not appear to be as supported as some of the other platforms we have discussed. NetBSD has Xen 3.X support in NetBSD 3.1. OpenSolaris has support for a Xen-based hypervisor, called xVM, in select Solaris Express Community edition builds.

The various BSD derivatives are open source operating systems comparable to Linux with long open source histories. Though support for Xen is not as current, many are trying to make it so, and it is expected that support is only a matter of time.

The OpenSolaris community is a relatively new open source community that develops and supports the continuance of the OpenSolaris project. OpenSolaris is sponsored by Sun Microsystems, Inc. In fact, the code comprising the OpenSolaris project is primarily a subset of the source code for the Sun Microsystems flagship Solaris operating system.

The OpenSolaris source code is pulled from periodically to form the foundation of the commercial Solaris OS product. Because many people enjoy the long list of benefits the Solaris operating system provides, it only makes sense that Xen would be interested in a port to the OpenSolaris platform. In turn, many users of OpenSolaris look forward to the additional features that virtualization can offer them.

As of this writing, the OpenSolaris development community has recently released xVM, the Xen hypervisor for OpenSolaris, which supports Solaris as a Domain0 and as a DomainU, and also offers early support for other Linux and Windows guests.

Table 4.4 summarizes the advantages and disadvantages of the various choices for Domain0 operating system/distribution choices.

TABLE 4.4 Advantages and Disadvantages of Xen Domain0 Platforms

Type	Advantages	Disadvantages
OpenSUSE	Well integrated into the platform. Easy to install and get going.	Xen code is not quite as current. Software isn't necessarily optimized for your hardware and environment.
CentOS	Easy installation with relatively strong integration into the distribution.	Distribution tracks another upstream development process, which causes a short delay in receiving current code, and the support community is not as large as some of the other end user focused distributions.
Ubuntu	A solid performer. Good choice for both package and binary installations. A balance of ease of use and latest release.	Graphical Xen management relies on third party support.
Gentoo	Constantly updated to support newer releases of the Xen Domain0. Software can be optimized for the hardware providing optimal performance.	Increased build complexity. May require additional software development skills as well as more intimate knowledge of your underlying hardware.

TABLE 4.4 continued

Type	Advantages	Disadvantages
Xen Express	Easy installation, excellent additional client tools for remote administration.	DomU images are specifically for XenExpress. Features such as live migration and support for multiple DomUs are not supported for free.

Building from Source

Although we recommend using prebuilt packages for the distribution of your choice for new users, in some situations you may want to compile Xen from source. You may want to develop Xen, or you might simply want to enable some functionality included in Xen that has not been built into your distribution's binary packages, such as the sHype security layer. Also, you may find some of the utilities found only in the Xen source tarball distribution useful.

To obtain a copy of the source code, you can choose either a compressed tarball or a clone from the Xen master mercurial repository. To download a stable version of the Xen code, you may use the Xen download page hosted at `http://xen.org/download`. For those who want to use the Mercurial revision control program via a public repository, it can be found at `http://xenbits.xensource.com`.

After you have the decompressed source code in one form or another, you need to initiate the source code build process. To build Xen, follow the typical Linux source code compilation process using make. The process is governed by a top-level Makefile, which includes a "world" target. When executing the make program using the world target, your system will build Xen proper, build the control utilities such as `xend`, obtain/patch/compile Linux 2.6 source code with Xen support for Domain0, and build a guest DomU kernel for you.

When the build has finished, there will be a top-level directory, `dist/`, containing all resulting build targets. The most pertinent items are the XenLinux kernel images for the Domain0 and DomU in the `dist/install/boot/` directory. The kernel with the `-xen0` extension contains hardware device drivers, and drivers for Xen's virtual devices is intended for your Domain0 usage. Likewise, the kernel with the `-xenU` extension contains only the virtual drivers to talk to your DomU. You may also note the `xen-syms` and `vmlinux-syms` kernel variants, which simply contain the added debugging symbols necessary to debug a crash dump. Finally, in the same directory, you find the configuration files used in the generation of each kernel. Should you want to alter the to alter the set of kernels built, you must simply alter the top-level Makefile line, an example of which is shown in Listing 4.23. Any set of kernels with top-level `build-configs/` directories are eligible for this list.

LISTING 4.23   KERNELS Line in the Top-Level Makefile

```
KERNELS ?= linux-2.6-xen0 linux-2.6-xenU
```

If you want to create a custom Linux kernel supporting Xen, simply follow the typical Linux configuration mechanisms while remembering to specify that the architecture is Xen instead of your usual host CPU architecture. Listing 4.24 shows an example.

LISTING 4.24 Compiling a Custom Xen Kernel

```
[root@linux] # cd linux-2.6.12-xen0
[root@linux] # make ARCH=xen xconfig
[root@linux] # cd ..
[root@linux] # make
[root@linux] # make install
```

As mentioned earlier in the "Gentoo" section, you can also copy an existing configuration file from a running Linux guest to create a Xen version rather easily. Copy the kernel configuration file (normally located in `/usr/src/linux/.config`) into your Xen patched kernel source directory. Then you only need to execute the make old-config command specifying the Xen arch inline (make `ARCH=xen oldconfig`).

Note that you might be prompted with some Xen-specific options. As advised in the Xen documentation, use the defaults unless you really know what you are doing. The kernel images created by the build process can be located in the `dist/install` directory. They can easily be installed by executing the make install command for automatic installation, or manually copied into place for an appropriate custom destination as needed.

After installation has completed, you need to update your GRUB configuration in a fashion consistent with your distribution's documentation. As with any other Xen installation, when your GRUB configuration is complete, you need only to reboot the system and select the corresponding Xen GRUB entry you just created. Note that some users encounter error messages during the XenLinux boot process. Most of these warnings are harmless and can be ignored. If for any reason your kernel boot hangs or panics, you can always reboot your system and select your old kernel to log in to your system as done prior to your Xen installation.

Summary

This chapter began by discussing the hardware requirements for a Xen Domain0 installation. These requirements are vital as the Domain0 allows you to control the other virtual machines on your Xen system. After discussion of hardware, this chapter examined the various choices of Domain0 available to you. We looked at open source and commercially supported distributions and provided an introduction to each. We have tried to objectively describe each, providing hints and insights to the implementation of each as needed.

Finally, we discussed methods of building Xen from source, should none of the packaged distributions be sufficient for your needs. You should now be able to make informed decisions about which Domain0 is best for the needs of your deployment.

Now that you have seen an overview of what a Domain0 is fundamentally, along with what it requires to install and configure, we hope you will continue to experiment with your new Xen system. Right now your Domain0 probably doesn't look much different from a normal installation of the Domain0 host OS with the exception of a few additional packages, but it is very different! You are now ready to move on to the wonderful world of virtual guests. The next chapter delves into this with a practical guide to installing and configuring a variety of these virtual guests yourself as well as demonstrating precisely how to put this infrastructure to work by obtaining preconfigured guest (DomU) instances that will enable you to really put your system to use.

References and Further Reading

Xen Hardware Compatibility List
    `http://wiki.xensource.com/xenwiki/HardwareCompatibilityList`
Fedora
    `http://fedoraproject.org/wiki/Tools/Xen`
CentOS "Installing Xen On CentOS 5.0 (i386)." Howtoforge.
    `http://www.howtoforge.com/centos_5.0_xen`
OpenSUSE
    `http://en.opensuse.org/Installing_Xen3`
Ubuntu
    `http://www.howtoforge.com/perfect_setup_ubuntu_6.10_p3.`
    `https://help.ubuntu.com/community/Xen`

Timme, Falko. "Installing Xen On An Ubuntu 7.10 (Gutsy Gibbon) Server From The Ubuntu Repositories." Howtoforge.

> `http://www.howtoforge.com/ubuntu-7.10-server-install-xen-from-ubuntu-repositories`

Debian

> `http://wiki.debian.org/Xen`

NetBSD

> `http://www.netbsd.org/ports/xen/`

Gentoo Wiki instructions for the installation of Xen on the Gentoo Linux Distribution:

> `http://gentoo-wiki.com/HOWTO_Xen_and_Gentoo`

OpenSolaris

> `http://opensolaris.org/os/community/xen/`

"Compiling Xen from Source"

> `http://www.howtoforge.com/debian_etch_xen_3.1_p5_`

Study of Virtual Machine Performance over Network File Systems

> `http://www.cs.washington.edu/homes/roxana/acads/projects/vmnfs/networkvm06.pdf`

VirtualPower: coordinated power management in virtualized enterprise systems

> `http://www.sosp2007.org/papers/sosp111-nathuji.pdf`

Chapter 5

Using Prebuilt Guest Images

A growing number of prebuilt DomU guest images are available for download from numerous locations. These images provide a quick way to get started running guests on Xen. In this chapter, we demonstrate how to use the three primary prebuilt DomU guest image types: disk images, partition images, and compressed file systems. We consider the relative ease and space requirements of each. Additionally, this chapter demonstrates how to use prebuilt images from non-Xen virtualization systems, such as VMware, and to convert them to be compatible with Xen.

Introduction to DomU Guests

A DomU guest consists of three things:

- A *guest image* that contains a set of files comprising a complete root file system
- An *operating system* kernel possibly with Xen modifications
- A *configuration file* that describes the resources, such as memory, CPUs, and devices granted by the Xen hypervisor to the guest

We begin by looking at each of these three components in detail.

Guest Images

A guest image is any file, physical disk partition, or other storage medium that contains the full installation of an operating system. This includes system configuration files, application binaries, as well as other data files. The simplest and most common example of a guest image is the hard drive of a typical nonvirtualized computer system. In this case, the operating system is installed onto a physical hard drive, and thus the hard drive contains all the files that represent the working system.

For Linux, it is typical to decompose the guest image into two pieces: one for the root file system and one for swap space. You can also choose to configure swap space as part of the root file system in Linux. The advantage of splitting them into separate partitions is beneficial when taking system backups. When backing up an operating system, there is no need to record the fundamentally volatile contents of a swap partition. Similarly, there is no need to represent the contents of swap inside a guest image file that you back up or share with others.

Windows, in contrast, does not typically separate the root file system from the swap area. Instead, the page file (a rough equivalent of Linux swap space) is usually stored on the C drive, the Linux root file system equivalent. After Windows is installed, you can configure it to store its page file on a separate partition or disk. Having the root file system and swap partition on different physical disks can increase overall performance because normal disk accesses and paging (or swapping) accesses can be managed separately.

Operating System Kernels

The guest operating system kernel is a file that contains the operating system executable that manages resources for all user level applications. The kernel file can be stored either within the guest image or in an external file on Domain0. Bootloaders, such as GRUB, provide a choice of kernels to boot. These different kernels might use the same root file system, or guest image. In the case of a guest, the kernel can either be a Xen-compatible kernel (for paravirtualized guests) or an unmodified kernel (for fully virtual guests).

Configuration Files

A configuration file defines the resources that the DomU guest will have using a set of parameters passed to the Xen management tool (xm). In essence, the configuration file specifies whether a virtual machine will be PV or HVM and what type of devices the guest should be granted by the Xen hypervisor. The configuration file is always a file stored external to the guest yet accessible to Domain0. Unlike guest images and the operating system kernel, a configuration file does not have an equivalent file in non-virtualized machines. The most direct comparison in a nonvirtualized environment would be a list of specifications of the physical hardware.

The parameters in the configuration file specify the CPU, memory, disk, and network resources for a guest. For this chapter, we focus mostly on the `disk` parameter of the configuration file and save the more advanced functionality for Chapter 6, "Managing Unprivileged Domains." We need other parameters including the `kernel` (operating system kernel), `ramdisk` (initial RAM disk), `memory`, `vif` (virtual interfaces), and `bootloader` configuration parameters to make working guests, but we cover each of these parameters in more detail in later chapters and Appendix C.

The `disk` parameter is used to export guest images. The general format for the `disk` parameter is an array of three-tuples. (A tuple is an ordered list of items. A three-tuple has three list items). The first item of the three-tuple is for the location of the guest image as seen by Domain0. The second item of the three-tuple is the location of the guest image as seen by the guest, or the device on which the guest image appears to that DomU. The third item of the three-tuple is the access permission that the DomU has to the guest image. An example of how to use the disk parameter in the configuration file is shown in Listing 5.1.

LISTING 5.1 An Example of the Disk Parameter

```
disk = ['phy:hda1,xvda1,w']
```

Listing 5.1 shows an example of the disk parameter line that exports Domain0's physical partition /dev/hda1 to the DomU as /dev/xvda1, with write permissions. The first item of the 3-tuple, the phy: prefix is used to export the physical device, hda1, which is the physical partition on Domain0. Other possible prefixes used to export real or virtual devices are tap:aio, tap:qcow and file:. The second item of the three-tuple is xvda1, which is the virtual partition that appears on the DomU. Other possible values for Domain0 devices are hda1 and sda1. The third item of the three-tuple, w, means that the DomU will have read-write access to the block device. Another possible access permission is r, for read-only.

Block devices are special files (or device nodes) that the operating system uses to move data around. The device nodes are typically backed by a nonvolatile physically addressable device, such as a hard disk, CD or DVD ROM drive, though in some cases even special memory regions can be block devices. Block devices may be read in any order. This is in contrast to character devices which move data to and from user processes. For PV guests that support the Xen virtual block device (xvd) interface (for example, paravirtualized guests such as Linux), it is the recommended way to specify block devices. The xvd interface allows the Xen guest to understand that it has virtual disks instead of native hardware. You can think of xvd as a prefix similar to hd or sd (for example, hda or sda notation used in many systems to denote IDE or SCSI devices respectively), which is used in the same way even though it doesn't truly emulate either of the common disk types, IDE or SCSI, completely. With HVM guests that do not have paravirtual block device drivers installed, you still need to use the hd (IDE) and sd (SCSI) disks for the DomU, because, by default, HVM guests do not have support for xvd block devices.

As we saw in the previous example, Listing 5.1, a physical device node is specified with the phy: prefix and can be any block device found in /dev/, such as /dev/hda1 (the /dev portion is dropped when specifying the device in the disk configuration line). The physical device can be a disk or partition, and it should be exported accordingly to the DomU, using the second element of a three-tuple in the disk parameter. If you export an entire physical disk such as hda or sda, it should be exported as an entire disk—for example, xvda (or similarly sda or hda) to DomU. Similarly, if you export just one partition of physical disk such as hda1 or sda1, it should be exported as a partition—such as `xvda1` (or similarly `sda1` or `hda1`) to the DomU. A good general reference on partitions is The Linux Documentation Project's Linux Partition HOWTO (`http://tldp.org/HOWTO/Partition/intro.html`).

The `phy:` prefix is not the only possible location for the guest image. It can also be a path to a file in which a guest image is stored (for example `tap:aio:`, `file:`, or `tap:qcow:`). In this case the recommended prefix is `tap:aio:`. This tells Domain0 to use the blktap driver with asynchronous I/O (aio). The `tap:aio:` prefix is then followed by the path to the guest image file found within the Domain0 file system. An example usage of `tap:aio` can be found in Listing 5.2. In this example, the `tap:aio:` prefix is used, which means the blktap driver will be used. The file exported is `/xen/images/debian.partition`. DomU will see the image partition as `/dev/xvda1` and it will have write access.

LISTING 5.2 Simple Example of Using `tap:aio:` Prefix in Disk Parameter

```
disk = ['tap:aio:/xen/images/debian.partition,xvda1,w']
```

Notice that the file is exported to DomU as `xvda1` just like in the case of a physical disk. From the DomU's perspective, they are indistinguishable. You can also use the blktap driver with QEMU Copy-On-Write (qcow) file-based image by specifying the `tap:qcow:` prefix. Other image formats such as VMware's Virtual Disk Machine (VMDK) and Microsoft's Virtual Hard Disk (VHD) are not available for use directly with the open source version of Xen due to licensing issues. However, Microsoft's VHD format is available as of XenEnterprise version 3.0, due to licensing agreements by XenSource. Microsoft's VHD format has also been released by Microsoft in its Open Specification Promise, and as a result, support for this format is under development for the open source version of Xen. We describe converting images from other virtualization systems into formats compatible with the open source version of Xen later in this chapter.

There is another, albeit deprecated, way to specify a guest image in the Domain0 file system, using the `file:` prefix, which you are likely to see in older prebuilt images. When the `file:` prefix is specified, the loopback driver is used rather than the blktap driver. The loopback driver makes use of a special variation of a block device backed by an ordinary file called a loopback device. Problems are often associated with using loopback devices. The performance, scalability, and safety properties of the the loopback driver are inferior to the blktap driver. Also, the number of loopback devices is limited by a kernel/initrd option (see the kernel module parameter `CONFIG_BLK_DEV_LOOP` for details), so there is the danger of exceeding that limit when using many file-backed DomU guests. Listing 5.3 shows an example of using the file: prefix, which means the loopback driver will be used. The file exported in this example is /xen/images/ debian.partition. The DomU will see the image partition at run time as /dev/ xvda1, and the DomU will have write access.

LISTING 5.3 Simple Example of Using the Deprecated file: Prefix in Disk Parameter

```
disk = ['file:/xen/images/debian.partition,xvda1,w']
```

> **NOTE**
> Some installations of Xen, including the 3.1 version installed on some Ubuntu-based systems, such as Ubuntu 7.04, have a bug causing tap:aio not to work, so falling back to file: might be necessary in some cases. See the bug report for bug #69389 on Ubuntu's launchpad system at https://bugs.launchpad.net/ubuntu/+source/xen-source-2.6.17/+bug/69389.

Xen DomU guest images can also be imported over the network, as is the case when using NFS (for example, nfs_server, nfs_path, and root parameters as shown later in this chapter and discussed in more detail in Chapter 8, "Storing Guest Images"). Additional methods of importing a guest image over the network, such as iSCSI or ATA over Ethernet (AoE), use the phy: prefix because Domain0 sees the exported network block device in /dev (or a directory within /dev). In these cases, you should also use the phy: prefix and specify the path to the network block device relative to /dev, just as if it were a local disk. For example, when using iSCSI, you should use the device node name that is given to the Domain0 by udev (the automatic device management system used on most modern Linux distributions), because the sd* block device node will not necessarily be consistent each time the iSCSI device is attached (to Domain0). The best way to do this is by using the disk/by-uuid entry, which is actually a symbolic link to the corresponding /dev/sd* entry.

Listing 5.4 shows an example of iSCSI. We examine the details of iSCSI in greater detail in Chapter 8. In this example the exported device will be /dev/disk/by-uuid/ 210936e7-6cc8-401f-980f-d31ec982ffa5, which is actually a symbolic link the corresponding sd* device node found in /dev/. The DomU will see the device as /dev/xvda, and it will have write access to the device. Be advised that the by-uuid support via the kernel and udev was not supported in older Linux distributions, although we have found good support in the more recent distributions that we have tested, such as Fedora and Ubuntu.

LISTING 5.4 An iSCSI Example of a Disk Parameter Line

```
disk = ['phy:disk/by-uuid/210936e7-6cc8-401f-980f-d31ec982 ➨
    ffa5,xvda,w']
```

For AoE, a similar strategy using udev is also possible and has been shown to work equally well. However, AoE block devices found in /dev/etherd/ should be carefully managed in a consistent manner, otherwise multiple guests may use the same device and cause corruption. In Listing 5.5, we demonstrate how you might export an AoE device directly to a DomU. We examine the details of AoE in Chapter 8. In this example, the exported device will be /dev/etherd/e1.1, which is the AoE device found in shelf one and slot one of the physical or logical Ether drive. The DomU will see the device as /dev/hda, and it will have read access to the device.

LISTING 5.5   An AoE Example of a Disk Parameter Line

```
disk = ['phy:etherd/e1.1,hda,r']
```

It is also possible to use an NFS mount as a root file system for your DomU. This method, however, is not recommended due to performance and stability issues under heavy load. According to the Xen user manual, the problems are well known in the Linux NFS implementation and are not specific to Xen.

To configure an NFS server to be used for the root file system of your guest, you need to specify the root configuration parameter as /dev/nfs, specify the nfs_server as the IP address of the server, and nfs_root as the path to the exported file system on the server. Listing 5.6 shows an example of using NFS for the DomU guest image. In this example, DomU uses NFS as its root device with the server and exported path as specified by the nfs_server and nfs_root parameters. You should be aware that nfs_root support also needs to be compiled into the DomU kernel. This support is not typically compiled into the kernel by default.

The NFS root file system method does not require the use of the disk parameter, because the DomU guest is using an NFS mount as its root file system. The disk parameter could still be used to add other virtual drives or partitions as desired. An NFS root example is covered in more detail in Chapter 8.

LISTING 5.6 An NFS Configuration Example

```
root        = '/dev/nfs'
nfs_server  = '2.3.4.5'        # IP address of your NFS server
nfs_root    = '/export/myDomU' # exported root file system on ➥
     the NFS server
```

We use different variations of the disk parameter throughout this and other chapters. For complete usage of the disk configuration option refer to Appendix C, "Xend Configuration Parameter."

Working with Prebuilt Guest Images

A number of types of prebuilt guest images can be downloaded from the Internet. This section describes each image type in detail and shows you how to use them. A growing number of sites provide this service for Xen and other virtualization systems. Some examples of sites performing this service are rpath.com, jailtime.org, virtualappliances. net, and jumpbox.com. It is also increasingly common for Xen system administrators to share special or highly useful guest image files the same way traditional administrators share a useful shell script.

One of the main advantages of using a prebuilt image is the high probability of a successful operation right out of the box. Furthermore, these images are often preconfigured, eliminating time-consuming, and error-prone, configuration time. More often than not, these images have been created and tested by users and/or developers who have a degree of expertise with the operating system or service contained in the image. The main drawbacks of prebuilt images are that they may come with packages that you do not want or need, and they might also have an operating system or installed packages that are unpatched or out of date. This unfortunate downside can mean missing out on features found in newer releases, or in the worst case, missing security patches. Despite these limitations, prebuilt images are a quick and easy way to get started.

Types of Guest Images

Prebuilt guest images come in three distinct formats: a *disk image file*, a *partition image file*, or a *compressed file system image*.

Compressed file systems are one of the best ways to share or back up a guest image because they are compact, but they are often more difficult to deploy as a DomU. The compressed file system images contain the compressed files and directories found in a normal disk image. The compression is typically performed using a utility such as tar or zip. Disk and partition image files are less compact, but they can be used directly as guest images, while compressed file system image files must first be extracted to a physical or virtual disk partition before use.

> **NOTE**
> In theory, compFUSEd (`http://parallel.vub.ac.be/~johan/compFUSEd/`), a compressed overlay file system for Linux based on Filesystem in Userspace (FUSE), could be used to mount a compressed file system image to be used directly as a guest image. This technology is still immature, however, and should be used with care; it is not recommended for production environments yet.

The difference between disk and partition images is that a full disk image may contain multiple partitions (for example, a root partition and a swap partition) as well as a partition table describing how the storage is divided. A partition image contains only one partition and no partition table.

Disk images and partition image files each come in two types: *sparse* and *preallocated*. Sparse image files do not actually take up the space that they can hold until the space is actually used by data. Preallocated image files take up all the space of the image file, even if it does not contain any data. A good way to appreciate the difference between sparse and preallocated image files is to consider what happens if you install a fresh operating disk onto an 80GB hard drive. There may only be 5GB of operating system files and applications being stored, but the file system occupies all 80GB including blank space available for use. A sparse image would only consume the 5GB of actual file data, while a preallocated image would require all 80GB. (Notice that in this case, the compressed file system still takes less space because the actual file data is itself compressed, which is one step more than just not storing the empty space as is done with sparse images. Because it is a compressed file containing the file system that took 5GB to store uncompressed, it will take up some percentage less space depending on the amount of compression that is done.) Figure 5.1 compares partition, disk, and compressed images for ease of use and compact storage relative to each other. We describe in more detail how to use the three types of images in this section, and we discuss how to create your own in Chapter 8.

Technically, it would be possible to have prebuilt images for proprietary operating systems such as Windows, but in practice, most prebuilt images available for download are for open source operating systems such as Linux (the most common), BSD variants, or Plan9. The main reason that you will not find prebuilt images of proprietary operating systems is because of licensing issues.

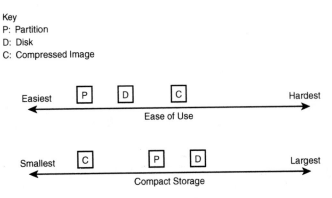

FIGURE 5.1 The Ease of Use line ranges from easiest on the left to hardest on the right, and the Compact Storage line ranges from smallest on the left to largest on the right.

Downloading Prebuilt Guest Images

We now look at some places offering downloadable prebuilt guest images. We use examples from some of these providers later in this chapter.

jailtime.org

The jailtime.org site currently has a small number of Xen guest images prepackaged with a partition image file for the root file system, a partition image file representing the swap partition, and the configuration files for both Xen 2.x and Xen 3.x. According to the jailtime.org administrator, the site is under development and new and improved functionality is planned, including opportunities for user contributed content and downloads. At the time of this writing, you can sign up for an account and contribute comments on the downloadable images, but not upload images that you create. The downloadable images available from jailtime.org include CentOS 4.4, CentOS 5.1, Debian 4.0, Fedora 8, Gentoo 2007.1, Slackware 12.0, and a user-contributed "Clustering Xen" package consisting of a master and some slave nodes. This set of images is only a subset of popular distributions that may be desired, but the releases are relatively current and new versions are updated periodically. Visit www.jailtime.org for more information. To contribute your own images, contact the site administrator.

rpath.com

The rPath company provides software appliances for application distribution and management. The rpath.com site provides many different guest images, not only for Xen, but also for VMware player and ESX Server, Microsoft Virtual Server, QEMU, Parallels, and Virtual Iron. In particular, to download disk images, partition images (referred to as *mountable file systems* on the rPath site), and compressed file system images, the specific page is at `www.rpath.com/rbuilder/`. You can sign up for an account that allows you to start your own project, or join an existing project. Each project can choose the guest image types to make publically available. At the time of this writing, several hundred projects are on rPath's rBuilder system, many of which have images of multiple types that can be used as Xen guest images.

Other Sites

Virtual Appliances (`http://virtualappliances.net/`) is another good place to download virtual appliances that run on VMware platforms, Xen, Virtual Iron, and Microsoft Virtual PC. Finally, JumpBox (`www.jumpbox.com/`) has appliances designed for VMware, Parallels, and Xen.

Mounting and Booting Prebuilt Images

We now describe how to boot prebuilt partition images and prebuilt disk images. Both types of prebuilt images have a lot in common. Disk and partition images may each be used directly as a DomU guest image, and can be either preallocated or sparse files. Partition images and prebuilt disk images both have advantages and disadvantages that go along with being a file—a virtual device that is really a single file does not always behave like a real device. To make modifications to either, they must be mounted. Yet mounting prebuilt disk and partition images involves a different process than typically used when mounting a physical block device such as a physical disk or partition. To complicate things further, the mechanisms to mount a partition image and a disk image differ from one another.

For partition images, standard UNIX tools can be used, while disk images require some nonstandard tools to accomplish a similar task. Each of the tools, both standard and nonstandard, are introduced as needed. We also discuss the creation process for both types of images in Chapter 8.

Boot Methods

There are several different ways to boot DomU images. PV guests can use two methods: one that uses a python-based bootloader, called pygrub, and another that uses a Xen compatible kernel (and optionally an initial RAM disk, such as those typically used to make the Linux boot process more robust) external to the guest, yet accessible by the Domain0. The `kernel` and `ramdisk` parameters are not used with the `bootloader` parameter, because the bootloader is configured to provide the choices for available kernels (with their corresponding initial RAM disks). In this chapter, we focus on pygrub and using a Xen compatible kernel, but we also briefly mention two other options. For HVM guests, there is a special bootloader, called the hvmloader, that is designed specifically to interact with the HVM guest boot process. Refer to the HVM Guest Population section in Chapter 7, "Populating Guest Images," for usage. The final guest boot method that we discuss works over the (real or virtual) network using PXE, and it uses a Python-based loader called pypxeboot. The pypxeboot script is not yet part of an official Xen release (as of Xen 3.2) but could be available soon, so we simply reference the Web site found at www.cs.tcd.ie/Stephen.Childs/pypxeboot/ for more information on it. We now cover using pygrub and also using a Xen compatible kernel and RAM disk.

pygrub

The easiest method to boot a prebuilt image is to use the pygrub bootloader. Pygrub is a Python script that imitates the GRUB bootloader. It is included in Xen and allows you to boot from a kernel that resides within the DomU disk or partition image, thus allowing a DomU guest image to be self-contained, except for its configuration file. To set up the image for pygrub, the disk image itself must contain an appropriate GRUB configuration file that lists a kernel. This GRUB configuration file is contained within the DomU disk image file just like a typical GRUB configuration file resides within the root file system on a nonvirtualized machine. Listing 5.7 shows an example GRUB configuration file. This is the same GRUB configuration file that you would use on a normal system using the first partition of the first hard drive. The pygrub bootloader simply parses a standard GRUB configuration file to boot the kernel contained within the DomU guest.

LISTING 5.7 An Example GRUB `configuration file`

```
default 0
timeout 10
root (hd0,0)
kernel /boot/<kernel>
initrd /boot/<initrd>
```

To use `pygrub` as the bootloader, all you need to do is add the bootloader option to the DomU guest configuration file and point it at the `pygrub` binary, which is stored at `/usr/bin/pygrub`, during a default Xen installation. Listing 5.8 shows a complete working DomU configuration file for the disk image that we downloaded from rPath. We focus on the bootloader and disk parameters in this chapter, but you can note the `memory`, `vif`, and `name` parameters as well. The `bootloader` option specifies the program that Xen will use to boot this guest; in this case it uses `/usr/bin/pygrub`. Notice that we use `xvda` for the disk that the guest will see, because the image that we downloaded was a disk image. This file, as well as other DomU guest configuration files, should be stored in `/etc/xen`.

LISTING 5.8 The Guest Configuration File That Uses *pygrub* for Its Bootloader

```
bootloader = '/usr/bin/pygrub'
disk = ['file:/xen/images/openfiler-2.2-x86.img,xvda,w']
memory = 256
vif = ['']
name = 'openfiler'
```

Next, before we can download and place the disk image from rPath, we recommend creating a more convenient and centralized location to store DomU guest images for future use. If you have not previously created a default location for Xen images, we recommend that you create the directory `/xen/images`. Some distributions might have a location for these images as noted in the official distribution documentation or forums. For instance, Fedora stores Xen DomU images in `/var/lib/xen/images/`. The command to create a directory is `mkdir`, and you can use the `-p` option to create the parent directories as needed.

Specifically for this example, we downloaded the Openfiler NAS/SAN Appliance from www.rpath.org/rbuilder/project/openfiler/releases. Openfiler is a Linux distribution that provides file-based Network Attached Storage and block-based Storage Area Networking in a single framework. You can also find a cached copy available on the Web site for this book. For this example, we choose the x86 Raw Hard Disk Image version of the Xen virtual machine appliance. (Notice that this disk image can also be used by Parallels and QEMU.) Specifically for this example, we obtained version 2.2 and the file openfiler-2.2-x86.img.gz, which we extract with gunzip to openfiler-2.2-x86.img and put it in our /xen/images directory. Listing 5.9 shows the process of extracting the image and putting it in place. The gunzip command is used to extract the file, and the mv command is used to put it in the /xen/images directory.

LISTING 5.9 Extracting and Placing **openfiler** Image Downloaded from rPath

```
[root@dom0]# gunzip openfiler-2.2-x86.img.gz
[root@dom0]# mkdir -p /xen/images
[root@dom0]# mv openfiler-2.2-x86.img /xen/images
[root@dom0]#
```

Finally, with the configuration file and disk image in place, the xm create command, as shown in Listing 5.10, boots the guest using pygrub as the bootloader. Figure 5.2 shows the boot menu with pygrub.

To actually boot the downloaded image, use the command xm create -c name, where name is the filename of the configuration file. Recall from Chapter 2, "A Quick Tour With the Xen LiveCD," that the -c option displays the guest's virtual console in addition to starting the guest. For details on using xm create, refer to Chapter 6 and Appendix B, "The xm Command." The xm create command first looks in the current directory for a DomU guest configuration file specified by name. If a file does not exist in the current directory, it then looks in the /etc/xen directory. You may also pass the full path of the DomU guest configuration file to the xm create command.

LISTING 5.10 Booting the openfiler Guest with xm create

```
[root@dom0]# xm create -c openfiler
Using config file "/etc/xen/openfiler".
```

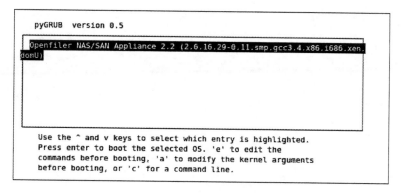

```
pyGRUB  version 0.5

Openfiler NAS/SAN Appliance 2.2 (2.6.16.29-0.11.smp.gcc3.4.x86.i686.xen.
domU)




Use the ^ and v keys to select which entry is highlighted.
Press enter to boot the selected OS. 'e' to edit the
commands before booting, 'a' to modify the kernel arguments
before booting, or 'c' for a command line.
```

FIGURE 5.2 The `pygrub` bootloader menu appears after running the `xm create` command.

After the image boots you should see a message and login similar to the one shown in Listing 5.11. Notice the https (not http) Web address that is given to actually use the Openfiler appliance.

LISTING 5.11 Message and Login Prompt after Successful Boot of Disk Image

```
Openfiler NAS/SAN Appliance
Powered by rPath Linux
To administer this appliance, please use a web browser
from another system to navigate to

https://128.153.18.122:446/

For further information and commercial support, please visit

http://www.openfiler.com

localhost login:
```

After accepting the certificate and agreeing to the GNU public license version 2 (GPLv2), the Openfiler login page appears, as shown in Figure 5.3.

Pygrub can also work equally well with a partition image, again with the requirement that the kernel is found within the image and the GRUB configuration file is set up correctly. The only change you should make is with the disk configuration parameter. Instead of exporting a disk, you are exporting a partition, so you should export xvda1 instead of xvda.

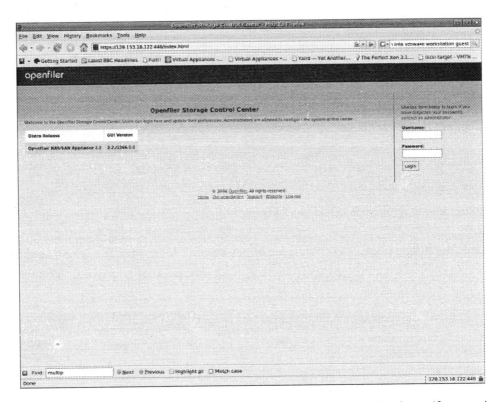

FIGURE 5.3 Going to the https address that precedes the login prompt, accepting the certificate, and agreeing to the license (GPLv2) displays the Openfiler Web login page.

Using an External Xen Compatible Kernel

In the previous example, pygrub was a good option because the disk image that we downloaded contained the kernel and GRUB configuration needed to boot the image; this is not always the case. Some of the prebuilt DomU images that you will find online are meant to be used with a Xen compatible kernel that you have on your Domain0 system. Therefore, they neither contain a kernel nor a GRUB configuration file. They also typically look for an optional initial RAM disk (initrd). Some good examples of DomU guest images that do not have a DomU kernel in them are the images from jailtime.org.

In this case you need to find and use a DomU kernel and RAM disk that are accessible by Domain0 and reference these in the DomU configuration file. Some distributions might still have packages for DomU kernels, but many do not. If your Domain0 and DomU are running the same operating system (for example, Linux), one strategy is to use the Domain0 kernel directly as a DomU kernel. Alternatively, if you have special needs for your DomU guest (for example, you want NFS root file system support in your guest kernel, but not in your Domain0 kernel), you may want to build your own DomU kernel. If you are not in the habit of building kernels, be warned that it is not uncommon to run into roadblocks. The Gentoo Wiki has a good reference for this (see http://gentoo-wiki.com/HOWTO_Xen_and_Gentoo for instructions on building your own DomU kernel). An alternative to building your own DomU kernel, in some cases, is to use loadable kernel modules that can be added into the DomU guest. Be advised that the loadable kernel module approach does not work for all kernel features.

The easiest kernel and RAM disk to choose for the DomU guest is the kernel and RAM disk that the Domain0 uses, because it is both trivially compatible with Domain0 (because it is the Domain0 kernel and RAM disk) and is also therefore already available to the Domain0.

Let's look at a specific example of a prebuilt partition image downloaded from jailtime.org. To follow along with this chapter, head to the jailtime.org Web site and locate an image according to your own preferences. For this example, we used a Linux guest Debian 3.1 image found at http://jailtime.org/download:debian:v3.1. Again, you can see our book Web site for cached copies of the images used in these examples.

The basic idea is to download the compressed package, uncompress it, (optionally) modify it by copying the modules as appropriate, edit the Xen guest configuration file to match your host setup, and boot the guest with xm create. We can optionally modify the image to copy in the appropriate modules if we are working with a PV guest compatible with the Domain0. We do this in this case because we are working with a Linux (specifically Debian) guest.

First, Listing 5.12 shows how to unpack the compressed partition file after it is downloaded. Notice that it contains four files: debian.3-1.img, which is the root file system stored in a partition image file; debian.3-1.xen2.cfg and debian.3.1-xen3.cfg, which are the DomU configuration files for Xen 2.x and Xen 3.x, respectively; and debian.swap, which is the swap space stored in a partition image file.

LISTING 5.12 Extracting Prebuilt Partition Guest Images and Configuration Files from jailtime.org

```
[root@dom0]# tar xjvf debian.3-1.20061221.img.tar.bz2
debian.3-1.img
debian.3-1.xen2.cfg
debian.3-1.xen3.cfg
debian.swap
[root@dom0]#
```

To decide which of the configuration files we need, we must determine what version of Xen we are running. To do this, we run `xm info` and look for the value of `xen_major`, as shown in Listing 5.13. In this case, `xen_major` is 3, and so we know that we will want to use `debian.3-1.xen3.cfg`.

LISTING 5.13 Get Xen Major Version

```
[root@dom0]# xm info | grep major
xen_major            : 3
[root@dom0]#
```

Listing 5.14 then shows how we copy the correct configuration file into place in `/etc/xen`. We use cp to copy the correct configuration file to the `/etc/xen` directory and rename it to a simpler name to type at the same time.

LISTING 5.14 Copy Xen Guest Configuration File into Place

```
[root@dom0]# cp debian.3-1.xen3.cfg /etc/xen/debian_jailtime
[root@dom0]#
```

Next, we put the proper modules inside the partition image (recall that this is an optimization, and not necessarily required in general). To start this we use the uname command, as shown in Listing 5.15. This shows us our running kernel release version is `2.6.16.33-xen`.

LISTING 5.15 Get Kernel Release Version

```
[root@dom0]# uname -r
2.6.16.33-xen
[root@dom0]#
```

Now we can mount the partition image to the loopback device temporarily so that we can copy the modules to it. Listing 5.16 shows the commands to mount the partition image. We use `mkdir` to make a directory for the mount point. Then we use mount with the `-o loop` option to specify the loop option that mounts the source on a loopback device. Notice that we copy the Domain0 modules from the running Domain0 kernel, because that is the kernel that the DomU will use. This is generally only an option when the Domain0 and DomU kernels match exactly. As shown in the listing, we first make a directory to be used as a mount point, and then mount with the option *loop* specified, which is necessary because we are mounting a file that represents a virtual partition.

LISTING 5.16 Mounting the Guest Partition Image

```
[root@dom0]# mkdir /mnt/guest_tmp
[root@dom0]# mount -o loop debian.3-1.img /mnt/guest_tmp
[root@dom0]#
```

Now that we have our partition image mounted at /mnt/guest_tmp, we can check the actual contents by doing a directory listing of the mount point, with the ls command, as shown in Listing 5.17. The content of this directory is the content of the root partition of the guest operating system instance, because the partition was mounted to /mnt/guest_tmp in Listing 5.16.

LISTING 5.17 Using *ls* to List the Contents of the Image

```
[root@dom0]# ls /mnt/guest_tmp
bin   dev  home  lost+found  opt   root  sys  usr
boot  etc  lib   mnt         proc  sbin  tmp  var
[root@dom0]#
```

After we have confirmed our mount is correct, we can copy the correct modules for the current kernel version executing in Domain0 to our DomU image partition that we just mounted and checked. The command we used to do this is shown in Listing 5.18. We use the cp command with the -r option to recursively copy all files and directories from the Domain0 system's module directory for the current running kernel release directory to the modules directory within the DomU partition image file that we have previously mounted to /mnt/guest_tmp. This step might not be necessary prior to booting the image unless some of the modules are necessary for boot. The guest will likely still boot without these additional modules, but having the proper modules in place during the boot process is highly recommended for best results. Unless all the optional kernel components needed for your installation are compiled into your kernel directly, you will need to load these optional modules. Strictly speaking, you will at some point need to manually copy them into the DomU guest. The cp command uses `uname -r` to obtain the release of the current running kernel, because that is the name of the directory within /lib/modules in which the modules associated with the current running kernel should be stored.

LISTING 5.18 Copying Modules from Domain0 to the Guest Partition Image Mount Point

```
[root@dom0]# cp -r /lib/modules/`uname -r` \
/mnt/guest_tmp/lib/modules/
[root@dom0]#
```

Now that we have the modules copied to the partition image file, we can unmount it with the command shown in Listing 5.19. We use the umount command to unmount the partition image file that we have previously mounted to /mnt/guest_tmp. Make sure you are not in the /mnt/guest_tmp directory when trying to perform this command as this command will fail if you are.

LISTING 5.19 Unmounting the Guest Image from the Mount Point

```
[root@dom0]# umount /mnt/guest_tmp
[root@dom0]#
```

Next, we need to choose the kernel that the DomU guest will boot from. In this case, we are going to use the same kernel that the Domain0 is using. We begin with a listing of the /boot directory to find the kernel that matches our running kernel. Recall that we found from the uname -r command, shown previously in Listing 5.15, that the release version of our current running kernel is 2.6.16.33-xen. The running kernel will give a good idea as to the Xen kernel file to look for. Listing 5.20 shows an example of this. We pipe the output of ls to grep to find the possible Xen kernels and recall that our running kernel was 2.6.16.33-xen, so we can suspect the vmlinuz-2.6.16.16.33-xen kernel. Your distribution may name the kernels slightly differently, but there should be a version number indication as well as some token that denotes that it is a Xen-enabled kernel. If necessary, you should be able to check the GRUB configuration file to see which kernel you are using based on which one booted up at startup.

From the listing, we choose vmlinuz-2.6.16.33-xen as the kernel to use in our DomU guest, and specifically we use /boot/vmlinuz-2.6.16.33-xen for our kernel parameters. Similarly, we use /boot/initrd.img-2.6.16.33-xen for the ramdisk parameter.

LISTING 5.20 Find Kernel Image and Initial RAM Disk (initrd)

```
[root@dom0]# ls -l /boot/ | grep xen
-rw-r--r-- 1 root root size date initrd.img-2.6.16.33-xen
-rw-r--r-- 1 root root size date vmlinuz-2.6.16.33-xen
```

```
lrwxrwxrwx 1 root root size date vmlinuz-2.6.16-xen -> ➥
    vmlinuz-2.6.16.33-xen
-rw-r--r-- lrwxrwxrwx 1 root root 4 ... 05:43 xen-3.0.gz -> ➥
    xen-3.0.4-1.gz
[root@dom0]#
```

Listing 5.21 shows the command to actually move the Debian partition images to the directory. We use the `mv` command to move the guest partition images to `/xen/images/`.

LISTING 5.21 Moving the Guest Partition Images Files into Place

```
[root@dom0]# mv debian.3-1.img debian.swap /xen/images/
[root@dom0]#
```

Finally, you can edit the DomU configuration file that we copied into place in Listing 5.14. Use an editor to edit `/etc/xen/debian_jailtime`. For this example, we are working with a PV guest, so the two things you need to change are the kernel, so that it matches the Xen kernel that you are running on (recall that for PV guests, the interface exported by the Xen hypervisor needs to match what the guest is expecting), and the location of the image files. Based on the steps we have taken thus far, the configuration we chose is given in Listing 5.22. The listing includes the changes needed to get the Debian guest to boot and some optimization, such as changing the disk to xvda instead of `sda`. The `tap:aio:` prefix is used for the disk image file instead of the `file:/` prefix that is deprecated. Notice that this time the disk attribute contains a list of two files—one for the root partition image file `debian-3.1.img` and one for the swap partition of the guest `debian.swap`.

LISTING 5.22 The Modified Guest Configuration File for the Debian Guest from jailtime.org

```
kernel = "/boot/vmlinuz-2.6.16-xen"
ramdisk = "/boot/initrd.img-2.6.16.33-xen"
memory = 128
name = "debian"
vif = [ '' ]
dhcp = "dhcp"
disk = ['tap:aio:/xen/images/jailtime/debian/debian.3-1.img, ➥
    xvda1,w', 'tap:aio:/xen/images/jailtime/debian/debian. ➥
    swap,xvda2,w']
root = "/dev/xda1 ro"
```

Finally, we can use the `xm create` command as shown in Listing 5.23 to boot the Debian guest as downloaded from jailtime.org. Recall that we pass the `-c` option to the `xm create` command so that we automatically connect to the guest console to watch the system boot. Notice that `xm create` looks in `/etc/xen/` for the configuration file (after it looks in the current working directory). The default username is `root`, and the default password is `password`. We omit most of the boot process from Listing 5.23 for the sake of brevity.

LISTING 5.23 The **_xm create_** Command Used with the Debian Partition Image from jailtime.org

```
[root@dom0]# xm create -c debian_jailtime
Using config file "/etc/xen/debian_jailtime".
Started domain debian
Linux version 2.6.16.33-xen (shand@endor) (gcc version 3.4.4 ➥
      20050314 (prerelease) (Debian 3.4.3-13)) #1 SMP Mon ➥
      Jan 8 14:39:02 GMT 2007
BIOS-provided physical RAM map:
 Xen: 0000000000000000 - 0000000008800000 (usable)
0MB HIGHMEM available.
136MB LOWMEM available.
ACPI in unprivileged domain disabled
Built 1 zonelists
Kernel command line: ip=:1.2.3.4:::eth0:dhcp root=/dev/xda1 ro

[Output from boot process removed here]

INIT: Entering runlevel: 3
Starting system log daemon: syslogd.
Starting kernel log daemon: klogd.
Starting OpenBSD Secure Shell server: sshd.
Starting deferred execution scheduler: atd.
Starting periodic command scheduler: cron.

Debian GNU/Linux 3.1 debian_pristine tty1

debian_pristine login:
```

Disk Images

In our first example in the previous section, we showed using `pygrub` to boot a disk image. We omitted the details of using `pygrub` with a partition image because the only difference is with the disk parameter (change `xvda` to `xvda1`, for example). In the previous section, we also showed an example of booting a partition image by using a kernel (and RAM disk) that is external to the DomU guest. In this section we show how to boot a disk image with an external kernel and RAM disk. This process is similar to booting the partition image using the Domain0 kernel and RAM disk for the DomU guest, but requires the use of some special commands to access the disk image. Let's take a look at an example of preparing a customized disk image.

The first step is to mount the prebuilt guest disk image in Domain0, and then you can copy the kernel modules into it with the cp command. Recall that one of the biggest differences between disk and partition images is how they are mounted. The main difference is that disk images contain multiple partitions. If using a disk image, we must determine which of its partitions will be the root file system for the guest. To do this, we use the fdisk command with the -l option to list the partitions on the disk (fdisk is discussed in more detail later in this chapter). Listing 5.24 shows the command and output for the Openfiler disk that we previously downloaded from http://rpath.com. This particular choice of disk image has only one partition, so choosing which partition should serve as the root partition is trivially easy. Notice that we are looking for a Linux file system in this case as our guest is a Linux instance, so the choice of root file system must be a Linux compatible file system, such as ext3. If we were looking to boot a Windows guest, we would likely be looking for an NTFS or FAT partition and associated file system. Notice the column header information listed for each partition (in this case there is only one partition, but there can be more). For example, in Listing 5.24, we notice that the value in the Id column is 83, which corresponds to the "Linux" System type.

LISTING 5.24 Using fdisk to List the Partitions within a Disk Image File

```
[root@dom0]# fdisk -l openfiler-2.2-x86-disk.img
You must set cylinders.
You can do this from the extra functions menu.

Disk openfiler-2.2-x86.img: 0 MB, 0 bytes
16 heads, 63 sectors/track, 0 cylinders
Units = cylinders of 1008 * 512 = 516096 bytes

Device              Boot Start  End     Blocks    Id  System
openfiler-2.2-x86.img1  *    1      7120    3588479+  83  Linux
Partition 1 has different physical/logical endings:
    phys=(1023, 15, 63) logical=(7119, 15, 63)
[root@dom0]#
```

We now look at the columns of the fdisk output in more detail.

- **Device**— The first column in the listing is the block device name.
- **Boot**—The second column denotes if the partition is marked bootable; an asterisk (*) denotes bootable, blank if not bootable.
- **Start**—The third column is the starting block on disk where the partition starts.
- **End**—The fourth column is the ending block on disk where the partition ends.
- **Blocks**—The fifth column is the size in blocks of the partition.
- **Id**—The sixth column is the system type ID.
- **System**—The seventh column is the operating system type specified for the partition.

The best tool for mounting the prebuilt disk image in this case is the `lomount` command, which is included as part of the Xen tools. Typically, `lomount` is used to mount a disk image partition to a loopback device; `lomount` is used to make disk images act like real block devices. The one limitation of `lomount` is that it is does not support logical volumes. We look at this problem later when we look at logical volumes in more detail in Chapter 8 and other tools such as kpartx and losetup.

> **NOTE**
> There has been some discussion on the xen-devel mailing list to disable support for tools like lomount in favor of using more robust tools such as kpartx. We discuss the usage of kpartx in Chapter 8. We discussed the disadvantages of loopback devices earlier in this chapter.

The required arguments for `lomount` are `-diskimage` and `-partition`. The `-diskimage` option takes as an argument the actual disk file; the `-partition` option takes the partition number within the disk image that you want to mount. Following these two required arguments, you should put any other options that are required for the `mount` command. Any options that follow the required `lomount` options are simply passed directly through to the `mount` command. For example, the `mount` command typically requires the pathname to the mount point and any other special options that `mount` might need for the situation at hand (for example, file system type or permissions).

A good reference for the mount command and its available options is the Linux man page for mount.

Listing 5.25 demonstrates an example of lomount using the same disk image downloaded from rPath as we used earlier in this chapter. After determining that we need to work with the first partition using the fdisk command in Listing 5.24, we first make a temporary directory to mount the disk image's partition to; then we mount the disk image partition with the lomount command. Recall that before actually doing the lomount command, we used fdisk to determine what partitions are on the disk image.

LISTING 5.25 Using lomount to Mount a Partition within a Disk Image File

```
[root@dom0]# mkdir /mnt/part
[root@dom0]# lomount -diskimage openfiler-2.2-x86-disk.img \
 -partition 1 /mnt/part
[root@dom0]#
```

Once we have the contents of our disk image located at the mount point (/mnt/ part), we can check that it is mounted properly and has the expected contents by using the ls command. The contents in this directory should be the contents normally found in the root partition of your prebuilt guest operating system. Listing 5.26 shows the invocation of the ls command and its output. We use ls to list the files and directories in the mounted disk partition that we mounted with the lomount command in Listing 5.25.

LISTING 5.26 Checking the Contents of the Mounted Partition of the Disk Image

```
[root@dom0]# ls /mnt/part
bin   dev   home   lib          media   opt   root   srv   tmp   var
boot  etc   initrd lost+found   mnt     proc  sbin   sys   usr
[root@dom0]#
```

After we confirm our mount is correct, we next need to obtain and copy the correct modules from the Domain0 to the DomU just as we did with the partition example in Listing 5.18. For completeness, the command is shown again here in Listing 5.27. See the previous example in the chapter with the guest partition image for the details.

LISTING 5.27 Copying Kernel Modules from the Domain0 Host to the Loopback Mounted Guest Disk Image's Partition

```
[root@dom0]# cp -r /lib/modules/`uname -r` /mnt/part/lib/modules
[root@dom0]#
```

Recall that because our guest operating system is mounted via a loopback mechanism, the copy commands we just performed actually placed our Domain0 kernel image, initrd, and modules into the prebuilt guest image. Because we know the Domain0 kernel is executing on our hardware currently, our guest should be fully functional when using the same kernel. We can now unmount the disk image using the umount command.

Once unmounted, we are ready to boot the guest using a configuration that is similar to kernel and RAM disk from the Domain0, as demonstrated in Listing 5.12 through Listing 5.23 containing the partition image case. The subtle difference this time is that we are working with a disk image and not a partition image and therefore the configuration file's disk parameter line reflects this change. The device that the DomU guest sees (the second item of the tuple) is xvda instead of xvda1. Listing 5.28 shows the configuration file for this disk image being used with the kernel and RAM disk.

LISTING 5.28 Modified Guest Configuration File for the openfiler Guest That Uses the Domain0 Kernel and ramdisk

```
kernel = "/boot/vmlinuz-2.6.16-xen"
ramdisk = "/boot/initrd.img-2.6.16.33-xen"
memory = 128
name = "openfiler"
vif = [ '' ]
dhcp = "dhcp"
disk = ['tap:aio:/xen/images/openfiler-2.2-x86.img,xvda,w']
root = "/dev/xda1 ro"
```

This time the guest boots similarly to the Debian guest from the prebuilt Debian jailtime.org partition image without the pygrub menu at the beginning, but the end result should be the same, as we demonstrate for the Openfiler image disk as shown previously in Listing 5.11.

Downloading Compressed File System Images

Another popular method of distribution of guest images is putting the root file system, the files that make up the guest operating system, and applications in a compressed tarball or zip file image. A compressed file system image contains all the files that would be contained in the root ("/") file system of the installed operating system. Compressed file system images are the most compact and also the most flexible for backup or sharing. However, they also require the most manual setup before they can be used.

To use the tar or zip file images, you need to create or identify a spare blank disk, partition, or other storage area that you can use to unpack the files. Alternatively, you could create your own virtual disk or partition image file to store the files.

Compressed file system images are an ideal way for a software vendor to distribute a complete working product installation. This method of software system distribution can be used to illustrate recommendations for proper user configuration. To make a compressed file system image for distribution, a snapshot is made of a properly configured complete installation. The snapshot is then compressed before distribution. As mentioned earlier in this chapter, this method of product distribution is especially popular for open source operating systems and software because then there are fewer restrictions on distribution due to licensing issues.

The Openfiler project distributes its software this way, and we downloaded an Openfiler tarball image from www.rpath.org/rbuilder/downloadImage?fileId=13547 to use in this example. In the example that follows, we describe how we extracted it to an empty partition created with the Gnome Partition Editor (GParted). Alternatively, we could have extracted it to an existing disk or partition image, a logical volume, or to network-based storage.

First, because we don't have existing spare partitions for the root and swap partition, we use GParted to create them. If you already have empty partitions that you can extract the tar file to, you might want to skip this section.

GParted

GParted is the Gnome Partition Editor application. It is used for creating, destroying, resizing, moving, checking, and copying partitions and the file systems on them. GParted uses the GNU libparted library to detect and manipulate devices and partition tables. It also uses optional file system tools that provide support for file systems not included in libparted; these tools are detected at runtime. More information on GParted or downloading GParted may be obtained at http://gparted.source-forge.net. GParted installs and runs in most graphical Linux environments. There is also a LiveCD available at the GParted SourceForge Web site.

GParted has some limitations you should be aware of before you attempt to use it on your own systems. As of this writing, GParted does not support LVM partitions. Also, GParted does not work on a mounted partition. Therefore, if you don't have a non-root or spare partition, or full spare drive, you will need to first use the GParted LiveCD (where the partitions or drives are not mounted) to resize any file systems, even your root file system, that cannot be unmounted normally. Finally, as with any software that makes changes to your disk layout, it is wise to make sure you have backups of any important data. Mistakes can easily be made with a powerful tool like GParted, and the result can be loss of data.

For this example, we work with an extra drive, namely sdb, which already has a partition on it that is formatted ext3 and has some data on it. We backed up the data and unmounted the partition, so we are ready to resize it. Figure 5.4 shows the initial screen when loading GParted.

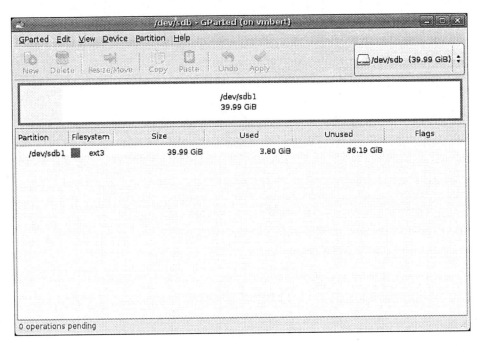

FIGURE 5.4 After selecting the extra drive /dev/sdb from the drop-down in the top-right corner, the partition information for /dev/sdb is displayed.

Next, we select the disk by clicking on it (the drive is represented with a solid outlined rectangle in Figure 5.4), which enables the Resize/Move button on the toolbar. We then click on the Resize/Move button; this brings up a dialog window as shown in Figure 5.5.

We then type in a value for Free Space Following (MiB) that corresponds to the size of the unallocated space we want to create. For this example, we are going to need a 4GB root partition and a 512MB swap partition, so we make the unallocated space the sum of those two, which is 4608MB. After typing in that number and pressing Enter, the Resize button on the dialog is enabled. Figure 5.6 shows the dialog after entering the value.

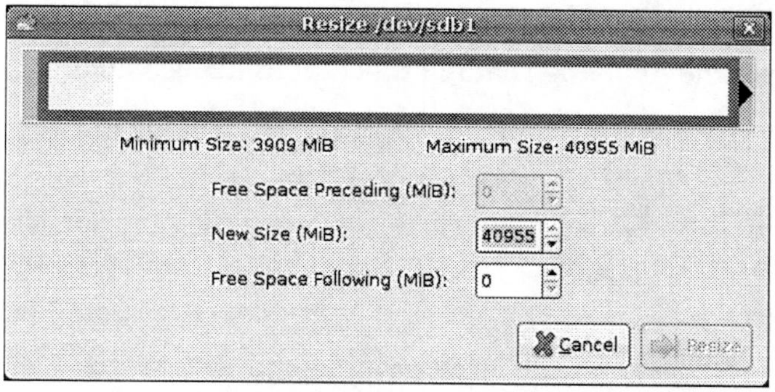

FIGURE 5.5 Clicking the Resize/Move button brings up the GParted Resize dialog.

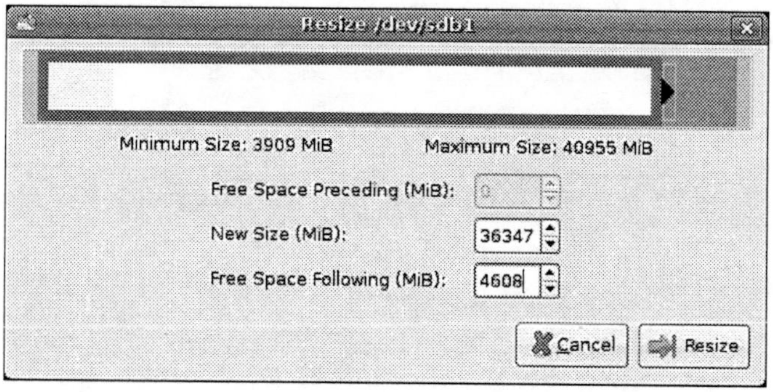

FIGURE 5.6 We type in 4608 and press Enter to enable the Resize button.

After completing the previous step, we click the Resize button, which closes the dialog window and brings us back to the main GParted window. GParted could be used to create the partitions as well, but we use some command line tools to accomplish the partitioning and formatting instead. Because we are finished using GParted, we click the Apply button to actually do the resizing.

Next, we click Apply on the confirmation dialog and the actual resizing operation takes place. This operation does take some time (in our experience it takes approximately 3 to 5 minutes on an 80GB drive on modern hardware), and can take even longer with bigger drives. Figure 5.7 shows the details of the operation after it is complete. To show what is happening, we expand the details by clicking on the triangle next to Details. Each successive operation has a similar triangle next to it that can be expanded to show more. Although not explicitly shown in each case, the results of each command run are shown by clicking the triangle next to the command (we show this explicitly for the second resize command). If you want to see these details yourself, you may need to resize the Applying Pending Operations dialog window.

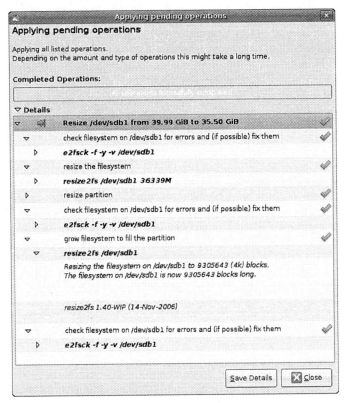

FIGURE 5.7 Clicking Apply brings up the Pending Operation dialog. We have expanded out some of the details you can see the operation and commands that go into doing the actual resize operation.

Finally, when all the operations are complete, you can optionally save the details to an HTML file by clicking the Save Details button, or you can just click the Close button to return to the GParted main window. In Figure 5.8, you see the unallocated space and that there are 0 operations pending in the bottom status box. After confirming your unallocated space you can close GParted.

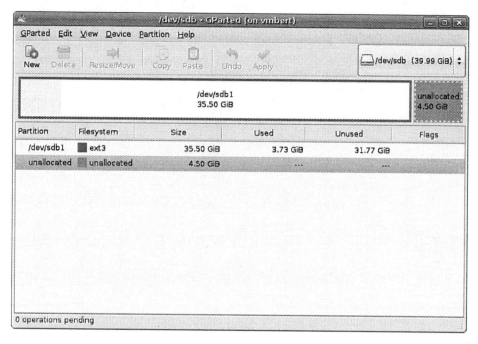

FIGURE 5.8 After the operations have completed, the main GParted window shows the end result with the new unallocated space and no pending operations.

fdisk

We now use fdisk, a partition manipulator for Linux, to create a swap partition and a root partition, as shown in Listing 5.29.

LISTING 5.29 Using fdisk to Create Root and Swap Partitions

```
[root@dom0]# fdisk /dev/sdb
The number of cylinders for this disk is set to 5221.
There is nothing wrong with that, but this is larger than 1024,
and could in certain setups cause problems with:

 1) software that runs at boot time (e.g., old versions of LILO)
 2) booting and partitioning software from other OSs
    (e.g., DOS FDISK, OS/2 FDISK)

Command (m for help): p
```

LISTING 5.29 continued

```
Disk /dev/sdb: 42.9 GB, 42949672960 bytes
255 heads, 63 sectors/track, 5221 cylinders
Units = cylinders of 16065 * 512 = 8225280 bytes
   Device Boot      Start        End       Blocks   Id  System
/dev/sdb1                1       4634      37222573+  83  Linux

Command (m for help): n
Command action
   e    extended
   p    primary partition (1-4)
p
Partition number (1-4): 2
First cylinder (4635-5221, default 4635):
Using default value 4635
Last cylinder or +size or +sizeM or +sizeK (4635-5221, ➡
     default 5221): +512M

Command (m for help): n
Command action
   e    extended
   p    primary partition (1-4)
p
Partition number (1-4): 3
First cylinder (4698-5221, default 4698):
Using default value 4698
Last cylinder or +size or +sizeM or +sizeK (4698-5221, ➡
     default 5221):
Using default value 5221

Command (m for help): p
Disk /dev/sdb: 42.9 GB, 42949672960 bytes
255 heads, 63 sectors/track, 5221 cylinders
Units = cylinders of 16065 * 512 = 8225280 bytes
   Device Boot      Start        End       Blocks   Id  System
/dev/sdb1                1       4634      37222573+  83  Linux
/dev/sdb2             4635       4697        506047+  83  Linux
/dev/sdb3             4698       5221       4209030   83  Linux
```

```
Command (m for help): t
Partition number (1-4): 2

Hex code (type L to list codes): 82
Changed system type of partition 2 to 82 (Linux swap / Solaris)

Command (m for help): p
Disk /dev/sdb: 42.9 GB, 42949672960 bytes
255 heads, 63 sectors/track, 5221 cylinders
Units = cylinders of 16065 * 512 = 8225280 bytes
Device     Boot   Start End         Blocks    Id  System
/dev/sdb1 1        4634  37222573+  83        Linux
/dev/sdb2 4635     4697  506047+    82        Linux swap / Solaris
/dev/sdb3 4698     5221  4209030    83        Linux

Command (m for help): w

The partition table has been altered!

Calling ioctl() to re-read partition table.

Syncing disks.

[root@dom0]#
```

The basic idea is to make a swap partition of 512MB (for this example) and use the rest of the disk for the root partition. For detailed instructions on using fdisk, see The Linux Documentation Project's fdisk section in the partitioning article at: http://tldp.org/HOWTO/Partition/fdisk_partitioning.html. Our commands appear in bold in Listing 5.29. Notice that we use the command p to **p**rint the existing partition table and the command n to create two **n**ew partitions. We specify both partitions as primary partitions, partition numbers 2 and 3, respectively. We use partition 2 as a swap partition and partition 3 as a root partition. We start both partitions at the next available block, the default, by pressing the Enter key. We make the swap partition's end block be 512MB more than its start and use the rest of the drive for the root partition by using the end block as the last available block, the default, again by pressing Enter. We use the t command to explicitly change the **t**ype of the swap partition to 82, which corresponds to Linux (swap). We again print the partition with the p command, to check our work. Finally, we use the w command to **w**rite the partition table changes to disk.

We now have three partitions: /dev/sdb1 we resized to contain the existing data on this disk, and then two blank partitions, /dev/sdb2, which we plan to use for the new guest's swap space, and /dev/sdb3, which we plan to use for the new guest's root file system. To use our new partitions, we first need to format them. To do this, we use the mkfs tool on the root partition and the mkswap tool on the swap partition.

mkfs

The mkfs command is short for *make file system*. mkfs and its family of commands (that is, mkfs.ext2, mkfs.ext3, mkfs.msdos, and so on) are used to build a file system on a device, typically a blank hard drive partition. We use mkfs here to build a file system on our empty disk partition. For this example we use the ext3 file system, which is a robust, journalled file system commonly used as the default file system type for Linux. The command mkfs with the -t ext3 option or equivalently the mkfs. ext3 command formats the virtual disk partition to be an ext3 file system. Listing 5.30 shows the results of running mkfs.ext3 on the root partition (sdb3) we created with fdisk.

LISTING 5.30 Using the mkfs Command to Format the Root Partition to ext3

```
[root@dom0]# mkfs.ext3 /dev/sdb3
mke2fs 1.40-WIP (14-Nov-2006)
Filesystem label=
OS type: Linux
Block size=4096 (log=2)
Fragment size=4096 (log=2)
526944 inodes, 1052257 blocks
52612 blocks (5.00%) reserved for the super user
First data block=0
Maximum filesystem blocks=1077936128
33 block groups
32768 blocks per group, 32768 fragments per group
15968 inodes per group
Superblock backups stored on blocks:
        32768, 98304, 163840, 229376, 294912, 819200, 884736

Writing inode tables: done
Creating journal (32768 blocks): done
Writing superblocks and filesystem accounting information: done
```

```
This filesystem will be automatically checked every 32 mounts or
180 days, whichever comes first.  Use tune2fs -c or -i to ➥
    override.
[root@dom0]#
```

Next, we need to format our swap partition. For this we use the mkswap tool.

mkswap

Swap space is used when programs running in the system want to use more memory than is physically present on the system. Programs or portions of the programs (referred to as *pages*) can be paged or swapped out to disk when they are not in use, thus allowing programs that require more memory to still run.

As discussed in earlier chapters, physical random access memory (RAM) is typically the limiting factor when trying to create additional guests. So, if you can give each guest less real RAM, which is hard allocated to the guest, and use more swap, it means you can make more guests. Using swap space on disk is cheaper than adding more memory, but is also slower. If the pages on swap are rarely accessed, you may get the best of both worlds—as inexpensive as disk space and almost as fast as memory. Fast cheap disks to attach and dedicate to swap means you can try to cram more, smaller actual RAM-consuming guests into a system, because the guests will swap efficiently to the disk, keeping only the working set of each guest in actual RAM. However, if all the pages are used frequently, system performance can slow to a crawl as guests spend all their time moving pages on and off the disk. Finding the right balance often requires some trial and error.

The mkswap command is short for *make swap area* and is used to set up a Linux swap area. The mkswap command takes a device, typically a partition, as an argument. We pass the swap partition (partition number 2 as created previously with fdisk) to mkswap to format the swap space for our example. Listing 5.31 shows the mkswap call and its output.

LISTING 5.31 Using mkswap to Format the Partition as Swap Space

```
[root@dom0]# mkswap /dev/sdb2
Setting up swapspace version 1, size = 518184 kB
no label, UUID=f16b5879-0317-4773-bc24-73efa13c5a22
[root@dom0]#
```

Now that we have both of our new partitions formatted, we can mount the root file system, populate it, and make some customizations for our setup. Listing 5.32 shows the commands to create a temporary directory as a mount point and to mount the root file system to it. We use `mkdir` to make a temporary directory to mount the partition we will use for the guest; then we use the `mount` command to mount the partition to that directory.

LISTING 5.32 Mounting the Root File System

```
[root@dom0#] mkdir /mnt/guest_tmp
[root@dom0#] mount /dev/sdb3 /mnt/guest_tmp
[root@dom0#]
```

Now that we have mounted the root file system we will unpack the contents of the tar file that we downloaded from the rPath Web site. For this example, let's assume we have downloaded the Compressed Tar File version of the Openfiler appliance to `/xen/downloads/`. Listing 5.33 shows how to extract the tar file to the root partition that we created and mounted to `/mnt/guest_tmp`. First we change directory into the mount point; then we use the `tar` command to extract the `tgz` (tar and gunzip'd) file. After the file has been extracted, we list the contents of the mount point and see the familiar Linux directories.

LISTING 5.33 Populate the Root File System

```
[root@dom0]# cd /mnt/guest_tmp/
[root@dom0]# tar xzf /xen/downloads/openfiler-2.2-x86.tgz
[root@dom0]# ls
bin   dev  home   lib          media  opt   root  srv  tmp  var
boot  etc  initrd  lost+found  mnt    proc  sbin  sys  usr
[root@dom0]#
```

Now that we have the root file system populated, we need to take a look at the file system table file (`/etc/fstab`) to find out how the guest expects partitions to be set up, and adjust accordingly. Listing 5.34 shows the contents of the `fstab` file for the Openfiler file system that we unpacked. We use the `cat` command to display the output of the `etc/fstab` file contained within the guest that we have previously mounted.

LISTING 5.34 File System Table File of the Openfiler Guest

```
[root@dom0]# cat /mnt/guest_tmp/etc/fstab
LABEL=/         /               ext3        defaults            1 1
none            /dev/pts        devpts      gid=5,mode=620      0 0
none            /dev/shm        tmpfs       defaults            0 0
none            /proc           proc        defaults            0 0
none            /sys            sysfs       defaults            0 0
/dev/cdrom      /mnt/cdrom      auto        noauto,ro,owner,exec 0 0
/var/swap       swap            swap        defaults            0 0

[root@dom0]#
```

In the `fstab`, we need to pay particularly close attention to the first and last entries—the root partition and the swap partition. This Openfiler appliance happens to be installed on rPath Linux, which is a derivative of Red Hat Linux, and uses a `LABEL=/` line to specify the location of the root partition. This is a common practice for Red Hat Linux based distributions, such as CentOS and Fedora. The alternatives to specifying a `LABEL=/` location are to specify the device, `/dev/hda1`, for example, or to specify the UUID, `UUID=3ab00238-a5cc-4329-9a7b-e9638ffa9a7b`, for example.

We have two options to make our root partition match the root partition that the Openfiler guest expects. We could either modify the `fstab` file to specify the device name or UUID of the root file system we created, or we could label our new root file system with the "/" label that it already specified in the `fstab`. Using the device name (for example, `hda`, `xvda`, and so on) is often more readable but is not as reliable in practice. If BIOS hard drive settings are changed, or the guest configuration file was modified to export a different physical partition but the changes were not reflected in the DomU, then problems may occur and can be tricky to track down. We recommend labeling the partition (using labels or UUID is becoming standard practice for popular distributions, such as Fedora and Ubuntu). Because we are working with an `ext3` partition, we need to use the command `e2label`, which is a command that displays or changes the label on an `ext2` or `ext3` device. Listing 5.35 shows the simple usage of the command.

LISTING 5.35 Basic Usage of `e2label`

```
e2label device [ new-label ]
```

The device argument to e2label that generally refers to a partition is required. The new-label argument is an optional argument.

If no new-label option is specified, e2label displays the current label of the device specified. If the optional new-label is specified, it sets the label of the device to the new label that is specified. There are equivalent commands for other file systems; for example, reiserfs has a reisertune command that accomplishes the same task. Check with the documentation for your file system for the details on how it handles labeling. Another command of note for more advanced functionally is the tune2fs command, which can do labeling and much more.

Listing 5.36 illustrates using the e2label command to label the partition that we are using as our root partition (/dev/sdb3) with the label "/".

LISTING 5.36 Using e2label to Label our Root Partition

```
[root@dom0]# e2label /dev/sdb3 "/"
[root@dom0]#
```

Now, notice that in the fstab from Listing 5.34, the swap space for the guest is specified as /var/swap. This is actually an example of using a file (as Windows uses C:\pagefile.sys) as swap space in Linux. This is why, when we booted the Openfiler guest as a disk image file earlier in this chapter, we did not need to worry about setting up any swap partition for it. However, by placing both the root partition and the swap partition in their own physical partitions, we can get better performance. For the system to use the new partitions, the fstab must point to them. In the case of the root partition, we modified the system to match the fstab, and in the case of the swap partition, we are going to both modify the fstab to match the system and add a label to the swap partition itself. The updated fstab for our guest is shown in Listing 5.37. Use an editor to modify the file /mnt/guest_tmp/etc/fstab and change the swap line as shown. To accomplish this, we first deleted the line pointing to /var/swap and replaced it with a line pointing to a labeled partition. (Recall the original /etc/fstab was shown in Listing 5.34.)

LISTING 5.37 Updated fstab File for the openfiler Guest

LABEL=/	/	ext3	defaults	1 1
none	/dev/pts	devpts	gid=5,mode=620	0 0
none	/dev/shm	tmpfs	defaults	0 0
none	/proc	proc	defaults	0 0

```
none          /sys          sysfs    defaults                    0  0
/dev/cdrom    /mnt/cdrom    auto     noauto,ro,owner,exec        0  0
LABEL=SWAP    swap          swap     defaults                    0  0
```

Because it is no longer needed, we also deleted the swap file that is in the var directory of the guest with the rm command as shown in Listing 5.38. This file was 512MB, so that is why we made our swap partition size to match that size.

LISTING 5.38 Using rm to Delete the Swap File Stored in the Guest

```
[root@dom0]# rm /mnt/guest_tmp/var/swap
[root@dom0]#
```

Finally, we need to update the label on the swap partition to "SWAP", so that the guest will be able to correctly use our swap partition for its swap space. Listing 5.39 shows the command to do this. We use the mkswap command with the -L option to label the swap partition that we previously created.

LISTING 5.39 Using mkswap to Relabel the Swap Partition

```
[root@dom0]# mkswap -L "SWAP" /dev/sdb2
Setting up swapspace version 1, size = 518184 kB
LABEL=SWAP, UUID=62fec7a0-58b1-4aa7-b204-dca701e107ca
[root@dom0]#
```

Now we are ready to make our guest configuration file and boot our guest. However, before we can boot the guest, we need to unmount the partition; let's do that now. Listing 5.40 shows the command to do this. We use umount to unmount the root file system that we had previously mounted at /mnt/guest_tmp. Notice that we first need to change directory (cd) out of the directory before unmounting it so that it is not in use.

LISTING 5.40 Unmount the Root File System

```
[root@dom0]# cd /
[root@dom0]# umount /mnt/guest_tmp
[root@dom0]#
```

Listing 5.41 shows the DomU guest configuration file that we used for this example with the filename saved as /etc/xen/openfiler-tar. Notice that we are using pygrub once more. As described earlier in this chapter, the disk line specifies two partitions—the physical sdb3 visible to Domain0 appears in the guest as xvda1, while the physical sdb2 appears in the guest as xvda2. They are both writable. We use the pygrub bootloader because the openfiler guest does contain a kernel within it, as we saw before. Also, we use physical devices sdb3 as root and sdb2 as swap, assigning them (somewhat arbitrarily) to xvda1 and xvda2, respectively. The guest in this case will not care what the partitions are named because we labeled them appropriately and updated the /etc/fstab to match.

LISTING 5.41 Guest Configuration File Used with the Openfiler Guest Created from the Compressed Tar File

```
bootloader = '/usr/bin/pygrub'
disk = ['phy:sdb3,xvda1,w','phy:sdb2,xvda2,w']
memory = 256
vif = ['']
name = 'openfiler-tar'
```

Finally, we are ready to boot our Openfiler guest that we have created based on the tar file that we downloaded. We boot the guest as shown in Listing 5.42. We use xm create to boot the guest, and the output is omitted because it is identical to booting the Openfiler guest as we did earlier in this chapter with pygrub. The output would be similar to Listing 5.11.

LISTING 5.42 Booting the Guest with xm create

```
[root@dom0]# xm create -c openfiler-tar
[output omitted]
```

Notice that we have now worked with two different files downloaded from rpath.com (a Raw Disk Image and now a Compressed Tar File), both of which were instances of the Openfiler distribution. We also worked with a partition image from jailtime.org. Recall that Figure 5.1 showed the relative ease of use and relative compact size of the three different types. We have shown explicitly the differences in their use. Table 5.1 summarizes some of the advantages and disadvantages of each of the three prebuilt guest image types (disk, partition, and compressed file system).

TABLE 5.1 Comparison of Prebuilt Guest Image Types

File-Based Image Type	Advantages	Disadvantages
Disk	Single file image (root and swap together)	Trickier to work with (i.e., need to work with special commands like lomount).
		Swap partition included in image takes up more space when archiving the image.
Partition	Easy setup, works well with standard file system tools, more efficient archival	Multiple files (root and swap are separate files).
Compressed file system	Flexibility, can be extracted onto any type of image, best for archival, smallest	Existing image, partition, or other storage needed first. More manual work required (i.e., preparing the device—real or virtual—partition and carefully untarring/uncompressing file appropriately).

As you can see, each of the prebuilt image types has its own advantages and disadvantages. Disk files are best if you are looking for a single disk file based solution, but may require special tools to work with and modify it (for example, lomount to mount it). Partition files are easier to work with because you can use the standard UNIX utilities to mount them, and so forth, but require multiple files if you want to have separate root and swap partitions for your guest (and don't want to store swap in a file with the root partition). Finally, compressed file system images are the most flexible, because they can be extracted onto any partition (real or virtual), and are the best and smallest option for archival, but are also the trickiest to work with. They require the most manual labor and setup of a partition ahead of time, and also require extracting of the compressed file before that can be used.

We have only now scratched the surface of partition and disk file images. We show you how to create your own partition and disk images in Chapter 8. At that point, we will also be able to use them in more advanced ways, such as logical volumes.

Converting Images from Other Virtualization Platforms

Many guest images are available for other virtualization platforms, such as VMware and QEMU. Although you could go through the process of manually copying the contents of the running systems to a DomU guest image, often there are tools to convert from one virtualization platform to another. Because the actual disk or partition images are logically the same for each platform, the only real difference between a VMware guest and a Xen DomU guest is the configuration file that tells the underlying platform what disks (and other hardware) it has available to it. To covert a VMware guest to a Xen DomU guest, you need only convert the VMware disk image file, which is a .vmdk file, into something that Xen can understand. QEMU has tools that can convert vmdk files to raw files, which can be used directly by Xen. Listing 5.43 shows an example of converting a VMware vmdk disk file. After converting the disk image file, you must create a DomU guest configuration file that will work with that new disk image. Using pygrub as the bootloader and making the disk image available to the guest is all it takes. Alternatively, you could use a Xen compatible kernel just as we did earlier in this chapter. You could also mount the disk image file and modify it as needed to meet your specific requirements.

LISTING 5.43 Using qemu-img to Convert a VMware Disk to a Xen Compatible Image

```
[root@dom0]# qemu-img convert -f vmdk temporary_image.vmdk \
 -O raw xen_compatible.img
[root@dom0]#
```

VMware workstation can be used to convert the vmdk files from preallocated to sparse files (VMware refers to sparse files as *growable files*) with the vmware-vdis-kmanager. An example usage of this tool is vmware-vdiskmanager -r vmware_image.vmdk -t 0 sparse_image.vmdk.

XenSource has also developed the Virtual Disk Migration Utility, a virtual to virtual (V2V) tool to convert VMware and Microsoft Virtual Server/Virtual PC virtual machines (with Microsoft Windows installed) to the Xen Virtual Appliances (XVA) format. A current limitation of that tool is that it runs only on Windows. See the References and Future Reading section for more information on this utility.

Summary

In this chapter we looked at several ways to download and use prebuilt guest images. We also mentioned many existing sites that offer prebuilt guest images, which you may find useful for your particular needs. Further, we discussed how you can convert disk images from other virtualization systems to images that are compatible with Xen. The tools in this V2V space are likely to continue to grow in number and improve in quality.

This chapter showed you the basics of how to use the `xm create` command to start the guest after all pieces are in place. However, the details of managing DomU guests along with more detailed explanations of some of the xm commands covered so far are in Chapter 6. The details of the DomU guest configuration file and the details of `xm create` are also covered in Chapter 6. For a complete listing of xm commands, see Appendix B. A complete listing of DomU guest configuration options is available in Appendix D, "Guest Configuration Parameter."

In Chapter 7, we describe tools, often distribution-specific ones, that help with the creation of guest images and allow you to populate your guest images so that you do not need to rely on the prebuilt images of others. In Chapter 8, we discuss storage methods for all your guest images, both the ones that you build and the prebuilt ones you download or obtain from others.

References and Further Reading

"Amazon Elastic Compute Cloud (Amazon EC2)." Amazon Web Services.
    `http://www.amazon.com/gp/browse.html?node=201590011.`
"Creating a Swap Space." The Linux Documentation Project: Linux System Administrators Guide.
    `http://tldp.org/LDP/sag/html/swap-space.html.`
Downloadable Images for Xen.
    `Jailtime.org. http://jailtime.org/.`
"Enterprise Virtual Appliances." Virtual Appliances Home.
    `http://virtualappliances.net.`
Examples Using the VMware Virtual Disk Manager.
    `http://www.vmware.com/support/ws45/doc/disks_vdiskmanager _eg_ws.html.`
"Formatting an ext2/3 Partition." The Linux Documentation Project: Linux Partition HOWTO.
    `http://tldp.org/HOWTO/Partition/formatting.html.`
GParted: Gnome Partition Editor.
    `http://gparted.sourceforge.net/.`
    `http://gparted-livecd.tuxfamily.org/`
"HOWTO Xen and Gentoo." Gentoo Wiki.
    `http://gentoo-wiki.com/HOWTO_Xen_and_Gentoo.`
JumpBox Home Page.
    `http://www.jumpbox.com/.`

"Kernel Custom Build." Ubuntu Wiki.
   `https://wiki.ubuntu.com/KernelCustomBuild`.

"Labels." The Linux Documentation Project: Linux Partition HOWTO.
   `http://tldp.org/HOWTO/html_single/Partition/#labels`.

"Partitioning with fdisk." The Linux Documentation Project: Linux Partition
HOWTO.
   `http://tldp.org/HOWTO/Partition/fdisk_partitioning.html`.

pypxeboot: A PXE bootloader for Xen guests.
   `https://www.cs.tcd.ie/Stephen.Childs/pypxeboot/`.

rBuilder Online.
   `http://www.rpath.com/rbuilder/`.

VHD support in open source Xen (initial announcement)
`http://lists.xensource.com/archives/html/xen-devel/2007-06/`
`msg00783.html`

"Xen source browser: lomount." Xen.org.
   `http://lxr.xensource.com/lxr/source/tools/misc/lomount`.

"Xen source browser: pygrub." Xen.org.
   http://lxr.xensource.com/lxr/source/tools/pygrub/.

XenSource Downloads: Virtual Disk Migration Utility:
   `http://tx.downloads.xensource.com/products/v2xva/index.php`
   `http://tx.downloads.xensource.com/products/v2xva/README.txt`

Chapter 6

Managing Unprivileged Domains

The main purpose of virtualization systems like Xen is, of course, running multiple guest domains. To this point, we focused on the prerequisites for guest creation including Domain0 installation, the architecture of the Xen hypervisor, and using prebuilt guest images. In this chapter, we are ready to focus in detail on creating, controlling, and interacting with unprivileged user domains (or DomUs). We describe xm, a command line application used to administer guest domains, and show how to use xm to create, pause, and destroy guest domains. We show how to write configuration scripts that start guest domains automatically at boot. We also cover multiple ways to interact with the guest domains once created, including command line and graphical methods.

Introduction to the xm Utility

The primary tool for administering guest domains is the command line tool, xm, which is actually a Python script that passes requests for domain management to the Xen hypervisor. xm is a wrapper for a multitude of subcommands that can be used to manage devices, activate and deactivate guest domains, and retrieve information on guest configuration and status.

In this chapter, we introduce the most common xm subcommands for managing guest domains. Other xm subcommands are introduced later in relevant chapters. Appendix B, "The xm Command," provides a full list of xm subcommands.

Prerequisites for Running the xm Utility

xm commands are run from inside the Domain0. In fact, one of the primary purposes of the Domain0 is to serve as an administrative interface for creation and management of guest domains. Many xm commands return an error if run outside the Domain0. Within the Domain0, the xm commands should be run with root or administrative privileges.

xm also relies on the Xen daemon (Xend). xm sends requests to Xend, which communicates with the hypervisor. If Xend is not running, the hypervisor and guest domains continue functioning normally, but the administrator will not be able to interact through the xm interface.

You can check whether Xend is running by using the commands in Listing 6.1. An output of 0 would indicate that Xend is currently running, while an output of 3 would indicate that it is not. We illustrate this by running xend status, stopping xend with xend stop, and then rerunning xend status. In this example, we use the echo command to print to the value returned by xend status. (xend status does not print the status value on its own.)

LISTING 6.1 Xend Status

```
[root@dom0]# xend status; echo $?
0
[root@dom0]# xend stop
[root@dom0]# xend status; echo $?
3
```

If Xend is not running, you may see error messages such as those shown in Listing 6.2.

LISTING 6.2 Xend Error Messages

```
[root@dom0]# xm <command>
ERROR: Could not obtain handle on privileged          ➡
    command interface (2 = No such file or directory)
[root@dom0]# xm <command>
Error: Unable to connect to xend: Connection refused.  ➡
    Is xend running?
```

Generic Format of an xm Command

In general, the xm family of commands follows a fairly regular pattern. Listing 6.3 represents the generic command structure.

LISTING 6.3 General Format of an xm Command

```
[root@dom0]# xm <subcommand> [options] [arguments] [variables]
```

Subcommands indicate the specific management operations that you want to invoke (for example, create or pause). Most subcommands accept options, arguments, or variables to modify their behavior. Options are typically specified in the format -x where X indicates the option, and variables in the format var=val where the variable, var, is set to the specified value, val. Arguments tend to simply be placed on the command line directly, in a specified order. Generally, arguments are required, and there is no default value. Variables, on the other hand, tend to be optional and take on a default value if none is specified. Options, variables, and arguments are all specific to the subcommand chosen.

Listing 6.4 shows an example of both an argument and a variable. The name of a configuration file (generic-guest.cfg) is provided as an argument, and the amount of memory, in Megabytes, is specified with the variable string `memory=512`. Note that the command line declarations override any values given in a configuration file. In this case, if `generic-guest.cfg` set the `memory` parameter to 256, the command line `memory` variable setting of 512 would take precedence.

LISTING 6.4 An xm Command Example with Arguments and Variables

```
[root@dom0]# xm create generic-guest.cfg memory=512
[output omitted]
```

Listing 6.5 shows an example of an option. The `-h` option is both an example of the option syntax and a useful tool for exploring the xm subcommands. To see a list of options for any given subcommand, run xm `<subcommand> -h`.

LISTING 6.5 An xm Example with an Option

```
[root@dom0]# xm pause -h
```

Similar to the `-h` option, there is a specific xm subcommand that can be used to explore the xm utility and its syntax. xm `help` can be used to list many commonly used commands. A complete list of possible xm subcommands can be obtained using xm `help --long`. You can also use the `help` subcommand with an argument specifying a subcommand (xm `help <subcommand>`) for more information on that specific subcommand. Listing 6.6 shows several examples of using the xm `help` subcommand.

LISTING 6.6 Using xm `help`

```
[root@dom0]# xm help
<general help menu printed ... >
[root@dom0]# xm destroy -h
<information about the destroy subcommand printed>
```

In the following sections, we describe a number of xm subcommands in detail. In this chapter, we focus on the subcommands related to creating, starting, and stopping guest domains. The complete list of all xm subcommands along with their full options is given in Appendix B.

The xm list **Subcommand**

The first xm subcommand we discuss in detail is xm list. Very simply, it lists all running guest domains, their attributes, and their status. You will frequently check the status of running guests with the xm list command. You can rely on xm list to provide confirmation or feedback on the effects of other xm commands.

Basic List Information

By default, xm list prints a textual table containing a list of all privileged and unprivileged guest domains. The first row contains the characteristics of Domain0. Any further rows contain information about DomUs. For example, Listing 6.7 shows typical output when xm list is run before starting any DomUs. Listing 6.8 shows an example of the output of xm list when many domains are running in the system. The master and slave guest images came from Jailtime.org in an MPI cluster package.

LISTING 6.7 Typical xm list Showing Only Domain0

```
[root@dom0]# xm list
Name                         ID Mem(MiB) VCPUs State   Time(s)
Domain-0                      0     778      1 r-----   2078.8
[root@domO]#
```

LISTING 6.8 Typical xm list Showing Guest Domains in Addition to Domain0

```
[root@dom0]# xm list
Name                         ID Mem(MiB) VCPUs State   Time(s)
Domain-0                      0     778      1 r-----   2243.0
generic-guest                 1     356      1 -b----      6.1
master                        2     128      1 -b----      5.0
slave1                        3      64      1 ------      1.5
slave2                        4      64      1 ------      4.1
slave3                        5      64      1 -b----      3.9
slave4                        6      64      1 -b----      3.5
[rcot@domO]#
```

Now, let's delve into some of the details of each column in the listing.

- **Name**—The first column in the listing contains the unique name given to each guest; Domain-0 is default in the case of the privileged domain. This name is chosen at the creation of a DomU by the user either on the command line or through the guest configuration file.

- **ID**—The second column is the unique domain ID. Domain0 always has the ID 0. This domain ID can change if the domain is migrated to another machine. Each domain also has a universally unique identifier (UUID) that does not change when the domain is migrated. The UUID of a domain can also be designated by the user upon creation, but a UUID will automatically be assigned by default.

- **Memory**—The third column is the amount of main memory granted to that particular domain (in Megabytes). The total amount of memory displayed in this column may be less than the total amount of memory available to the system. This happens if not all memory has been allocated. The default value for the memory variable, if not set otherwise, is 128.

- **Virtual CPUs**—The fourth column contains the number of virtual processors (VCPUs) currently being used. As previously stated, a domain may be given a maximum of 32 VCPUs. The number of VCPUs allocated to a domain might decrease after creation or increase back to a maximum of its original number of VCPUs. The default number of VCPUs for Domain0 is the number of logical CPUs in the machine. The default number of VCPUs for unprivileged guests is one.

- **Domain State**—The fifth column offers domain state information. State information tells you whether a domain is processing something, waiting for more work to do, has been paused by a user, or is down for some reason. Table 6.1 lists the possible states.

  Interestingly, the xm list command always shows Domain0 in the running state. Since xm list runs inside Domain0, Domain0 must be running to use xm list. On a uniprocessor machine, this also means that no other domain should be in the running state.

- **Running Time**—The last column is the amount of time, in seconds, the domain has been using the CPU. Note that this is not wall clock time from when the domain is started, but rather total CPU time that the domain has accumulated. For Domain0, this starts when the system boots. For DomUs, this timer starts when that particular guest is created.

TABLE 6.1 Domain State Abbreviations, Full Names, and Descriptions

Abbreviation	Full Name	Description
r	Running	The domain is currently running on a CPU. At any point in time that you run xm list, there can be no more domains in the running state than there are actual physical CPUs in the system.
b	Blocked	A blocked domain cannot run because it is waiting for a particular action that has not yet completed. For example, the domain may be waiting for an I/O request to complete, or it may have gone to sleep and therefore waiting to be woken up. While in the blocked state, a domain has no need of being scheduled on a CPU.
p	Paused	A domain in the paused state is not eligible to be run on a CPU, much like a domain in the blocked state. However, a paused domain is not waiting for a particular event; instead it has been deliberately paused by the administrator. A paused domain holds allocated resources like memory but will not be eligible for scheduling by the Xen hypervisor. A DomU can be placed into this state, but Domain0 cannot be.
s	Shutdown	The domain has been shut down and is no longer functional, but for some reason the resources allocated to the guest domain have not been deallocated yet. Ordinarily you would see this for a short time frame (split second). If a domain remains in this state too long, there is something wrong.
c	Crashed	The domain has crashed. This state typically occurs when the domain has not been configured during creation to restart on crash.
d	Dying	The domain has begun but not completed the process of shutting down cleanly or crashing.
No State	Scheduled	If no state is shown, the guest is not running on the CPU, but does have work to do. Thus, it is waiting to be given a turn on the CPU.

Listing Information about a Specific Guest

One additional feature of the list subcommand is the ability to list information about only one domain or a few domains at a time by including either the name of the guest or the domain ID. In Listing 6.9, we show an example of each.

LISTING 6.9 Listing Information for a Subset of Guests

```
[root@dom0]# xm list generic-guest generic-guest2
Name                           ID Mem(MiB) VCPUs State   Time(s)
generic-guest                   1      356     1 -b----      6.1
generic-guest2                  3      512     1 -b----      3.6
[root@dom0]# xm list 1
Name                           ID Mem(MiB) VCPUs State   Time(s)
generic-guest                   1      356     1 -b----      6.1
[root@dom0]#
```

This is, of course, a subset of the information printed by xm list when run without any arguments. It can be useful when there are many guests running or in combination with the long option, which is discussed in the next section. It can also be useful if you are writing scripts to manage domains.

If a specified guest does not exist, you receive a straightforward error message, as shown in Listing 6.10. For most xm subcommands, similar easy-to-follow error messages are given when specifying nonexistent guests.

LISTING 6.10 Listing Information of Nonexistent Guests

```
[root@dom0]# xm list blah
Error: the domain 'blah' does not exist.
[root@dom0]#
```

long Option

If run with the long option, the output is in a different, nontabular format with additional information provided, as shown in Listing 6.11. The UUID of each domain is available here as well as CPU weight, shadow memory, maximum amount of memory, features, and some configuration options about what to do when certain signals are sent to the domain. These are variables that can be set in the domain's configuration file or with parameters for the create subcommand.

LISTING 6.11 Using xm list with the long Option

```
[root@dom0]# xm list --long
(domain
    (domid 0)
    (uuid 00000000-0000-0000-0000-000000000000)
    (vcpus 1)
    (cpu_weight 1.0)
    (memory 1131)
    (shadow_memory 0)
    (maxmem 1415)
    (features )
    (name Domain-0)
    (on_poweroff destroy)
    (on_reboot restart)
    (on_crash restart)
    (state r-----)
```

```
   (shutdown_reason poweroff)
   (cpu_time 1169686032.67)
   (online_vcpus 1)
)
[root@dom0]#
```

In Chapter 3, "The Xen Hypervisor," we introduced the XenStore database. You may notice the similarity between the XenStore examples and the data printed by the list subcommand in conjunction with the long option. This similarity is no coincidence. xm list gets most of its data directly from XenStore. However, the exact format of this output is not guaranteed to remain the same for subsequent versions of Xen. One of the functions of the Xen API is to standardize the output of commands so they are more script friendly.

Label Option

The label option to the list subcommand can be used to provide information about security privileges. As shown in Listing 6.12, the output contains a variety of labels created by a user to define the rights and access privileges of certain domains. This is a part of sHype Xen Access Controls, which is another level of security an administrator may use. This is an optional feature of Xen, and in fact must be compiled into a Xen kernel if it is desired. A more detailed discussion of sHype Xen Access Control can be found in Chapter 11, "Securing a Xen System." If sHype was disabled, the label option would display a table where all labels are set to INACTIVE.

LISTING 6.12 Using xm list with the label Option

```
[root@dom0]# xm list --label
Name            ID Mem(MiB) VCPUs State    Time(s) Label
Domain-0         0      778     1 r-----    2243.0 SystemManagement
generic-guest    1      356     1 -b----       6.1 LimitedGuest
master           2      128     1 -b----       5.0 HeadNode
slave1           3       64     1 -b----       1.5 SlaveNode
slave2           4       64     1 -b----       4.1 SlaveNode
slave3           5       64     1 ------       3.9 SlaveNode
slave4           6       64     1 -b----       3.5 SlaveNode
[root@dom0]#
```

The `xm create` Subcommand

`xm create` allows you to boot a new guest domain. The `xm create` command takes a preconfigured image, kernel, and configuration file and starts a running operating system to run in parallel to any other privileged or nonprivileged domains. Before `xm create` can be run, all the necessary components must be in place. After all the necessary elements are in place to bring up a guest domain, using the `create` subcommand is almost as easy as pressing the power button to turn on your computer.

Prerequisites for `xm create`

Before running the `create` subcommand, some essential elements must be in place. Specifically, there must be a guest image, an acceptable operating system kernel, a configuration file to specify parameters for guest creation, and sufficient available resources for new guests. We discuss each of these requirements in more detail in the following list:

- **Guest images**—A guest image includes all programs necessary for a working operating system and any services necessary for the purpose of the guest domain (such as Apache servers). As Chapter 5, "Using Prebuilt Guest Images," discussed in detail, such an image can come in a number of different forms, like a file or an entire disk drive. Whatever form this takes, the image must be accessible from Domain0.

  Typically, there are at least two disk images for a Linux guest image. One for the root file system and one for swap space, though more can be added at the administrator's discretion.

- **Operating system kernel**—The kernel for the new guest domain must also be accessible from Domain0 so that it can be communicated to the Xen hypervisor to run. The kernel can be located directly in a local file system in Domain0 or in some other partition or storage device mounted in Domain0. With the help of `pygrub`, the kernel can also be located inside the guest's image. Chapter 5 discusses how `pygrub` can be used to access a kernel inside a guest's file system image.

- **Domain configuration file**—The guest configuration file contains all information necessary to create the new guest, including pointers to the locations of the guest image and kernel. It also designates many other attributes of the guest domain, including which devices (both virtual or real) the guest should be allowed to access. This includes network devices, hard drives, graphics cards, and other PCI devices. The configuration file also optionally specifies how much memory should be allocated to the guest and the number of virtual CPUs the guest should be granted. We discuss the syntax of guest configuration files in detail later in this chapter.

- **Sufficient resources**—Finally, before actually starting a guest domain, it is important to determine whether all resources specified in the configuration file can be granted.

Deciding how many physical resources to allocate to each guest can be tricky. It is important to consider the total physical resources, what workloads will run inside each guest, possible sources of contention among guests, and the priority of each guest's workload. We discuss other issues related to resource constraints and the sharing of resources among guest domains in Chapter 12, "Managing Guest Resources."

Simple Examples of xm create

In this section, we walk through some simple examples of xm create. We begin our example when Domain0 is the only domain running in the system. Listing 6.13 shows the state of the system.

LISTING 6.13 xm list Showing Domain0 as Sole Guest

```
[root@dom0]# xm list
Name                          ID Mem(MiB) VCPUs State   Time(s)
Domain-0                       0   1154       1 r-----   311.8
[root@dom0]#
```

Next, we create a guest domain using only a configuration file. This may look familiar to you if you followed along using the LiveCD as covered in Chapter 2, "A Quick Tour with the Xen LiveCD." This is essentially how we created all our guests in that chapter, using the preexisting configurations on the LiveCD. Listing 6.14 shows the message given when a guest is created successfully.

LISTING 6.14 Creating a Guest with xm create

```
[root@dom0]# xm create generic-guest.cfg
Using config file "generic-guest.cfg".
Started domain generic-guest
[root@dom0]#
```

Listing 6.15 shows the contents of the configuration script, generic-guest.cfg. Notice that it specifies the kernel (/boot/vmlinuz-2.6-xenU) and two disk images (/xen/generic.img, the root file system for this guest, and /xen/generic.swap, the swap space for this guest). It also specifies a number of other guest attributes including the amount of physical memory, the guest name, and the networking configuration. We discuss these options in more detail in the next section.

LISTING 6.15 Configuration File Used to Create a Guest

```
[root@dom0]# cat /xen/generic-guest.cfg
kernel = "/boot/vmlinuz-2.6-xenU"
memory = 356
name = "generic-guest"
vif = [ 'bridge=xenbr0' ]
disk = ['tap:aio:/xen/debian.img,sda1,w',
        'tap:aio:/xen/debian.swap,sda2,w']
root = "/dev/sda1 ro"
[root@dom0]#
```

At this point, the guest domain has been created and is booting. Listing 6.16 shows the output of xm list, which shows the current status of the Domain0 and the new DomU. Notice that the name and memory attributes match what was specified in the configuration file. Some of these arguments are required, with the exception of memory and name. Variables, on the other hand, tend to be optional and take on a default value if none is specified.

LISTING 6.16 xm list Showing Two Guests Running Now

```
[root@dom0]# xm list
```

Name	ID	Mem(MiB)	VCPUs	State	Time(s)
Domain-0	0	1154	1	r-----	325.1
generic-guest	1	356	1	------	0.2

```
[root@dom0]#
```

Our new domain was given a domain ID of 1. Domain0 always has ID 0, and Domain IDs of newly created domains are picked by incrementing the last Domain ID used, even if the domain with the highest ID is not currently up. Thus, the first DomU created always gets ID 1.

Although most configuration options can also be specified directly on the command line, the create subcommand does require that a configuration file be specified. We could have started our generic guest by specifying an empty file (for example, /dev/null) as the configuration file and then specifying all options on the command line, as shown in Listing 6.17.

LISTING 6.17 Creating a Guest without a Configuration File

```
[root@dom0]# xm create name="generic-guest" \
    memory=356 kernel="/boot/vmlinuz-2.6-xenU" \
    vif="bridge=xenbr0" root="/dev/sda1 ro" \
    disk="tap:aio:/xen/debian.img,sda1,w" \
    disk="tap:aio:/xen/debian.swap,sda2,w" \
    /dev/null
Using config file "/dev/null".
Started domain generic-guest
[root@dom0]#
```

Although this method is valid, the most common and straightforward way to create a guest domain is to have all creation options in the configuration file. Command line options are typically used only to override the default settings in the supplied configuration file. However, as a general rule, we recommend that you fully specify your guest configurations to minimize confusion when you or someone else needs to administer your system later. For example, as shown in Listing 6.18, we could have specified 512MB of memory instead of 356MB with the following command. As mentioned earlier, command line settings always take precedence.

LISTING 6.18 Creating a Guest with a Configuration File as well as Command Line Options

```
[root@dom0]# xm create generic-guest.cfg \
    name="new-generic-guest" memory=512
Using config file "generic-guest.cfg".
Started domain new-generic-guest
[root@dom0]# xm list
Name                        ID Mem(MiB) VCPUs State   Time(s)
Domain-0                     0     1154     1 r-----    325.1
new-generic-guest            1      512     1 ------      0.4
[root@dom0]#
```

One last convenient option is the quiet option, -q. It actively suppresses output from the create command. After you have worked out any problems in your domain creation, you may no longer want to see any status messages printed as a result of the command.

Guest Configuration Files

In the previous section, we showed a sample configuration file for the create sub-command. There are actually two different kinds of configuration files—Python format and SXP or S-expressions. The configuration file in Listing 6.15 was an example of the Python format.

A configuration file in Python format is actually a Python script, meaning it is parsed and executed like a normal Python program. This enables automation of guest creation. A configuration file in SXP format, however, is not interpreted as a script, but is parsed as a file of data.

Guest creation with an SXP file is less flexible than using a Python script, but this can be an advantage. SXP format lets you know exactly what attributes you are passing to a guest and gives you confidence that they will not change upon creation. It is not possible to define variables on the command line when using SXP because the command-line configuration parameters are used to set Python variables

Python Format

Listing 6.19 is an example of a Python configuration script. There are also examples that come with Xen, which should be located in the /etc/xen directory.

LISTING 6.19 Example Python Configuration Script for Guest Creation

```
[root@dom0]# cat another_generic_guest.cfg
kernel = "/boot/vmlinuz-2.6.16-xen"
ramdisk = "/boot/initrd.img-2.6.16-xen"
vif = ['mac=00:16:3e:36:00:05']
disk = ['file:/xen-images/fedora.img,hda1,w',
        'file:/xen-images/fedora-swap.img,hda2,w']
ip = "192.168.0.101"
netmask = "255.255.255.0"
gateway = "192.168.0.1"
hostname = "another generic guest"
root = "/dev/hda1 ro"
extra = "4"
[root@dom0]#
```

Variables are specified first by their name, followed by =, and then their value. Integer values can be written as just a number or can be surrounded by double quotes. String or character values are written surrounded by double quotes. A list of items is written with brackets ([,]) surrounding the entire value with each list item surrounded by single quotes and separated by commas. Thus, the typical formats are VAR=INTEGER, VAR="STRING", and VAR=['STRING', 'STRING', 'STRING'].

Common Configuration Options

Currently more than 50 predefined configuration options are available for use in a configuration file of either format, and additional options are being defined as features are added to Xen. In this section, we discuss some of the most common options. To see a description of all the possible options see Appendix D, "Guest Configuration Parameters."

- **kernel**—This option specifies the location of a kernel the target image will be booted with. A domain cannot be created without a kernel. Either this value has to be set to a valid location or the bootloader option must point to a valid bootloader that knows how to find a kernel. The bootloader option is covered in Chapter 5.

- **ramdisk**—This option specifies the location of an initial RAM disk image to use while booting the kernel. A common mistake is to use initrd as the option's name instead of ramdisk.

- **memory**—This option specifies the amount of memory that should be given to the guest. Too much memory causes an error. The maximum requestable amount of memory is the size of a signed integer or 2,147,483,647MB. There's no reason to request this much yet.

- **name**—This option specifies the unique name of the new guest. If the name is already in use, an error is thrown. The default value is the filename of the Python script.

- **vif**—This option accepts a list containing attributes of a virtual network interface such as ip address, mac address, netmask, vifname, and others. Multiple virtual network cards can be created by adding more entries to the vif list. If the default values of the extra suboptions are acceptable, empty entries, denoted by a pair of single quotes, will suffice.

- **disk**—This option accepts a list containing entries of three parameters. The first parameter is prefixed with the type of device being loaded. `phy:` signifies a physical partition; `file:` is a file mounted through a loopback device; and `tap:aio` is for a blktap device. Blktap devices is mentioned in Chapter 5. After the prefix is the location of the device. The second parameter is what the device should be called on the new guest (for example, `/dev/sda1`). The third parameter decides the mode of access the guest will have, which can be either `w` for read and write access or `r` for read-only access. File images mounted through a loopback device, "file:" has limitations and is deprecated.

- **root**—This option identifies a disk image to use for the root file system of the new guest image. The disk image must come from one of the entries in the disk option, described previously. What literally happens is that the value of root is added to the kernel command line.

- **hostname**—This option adds an entry to the kernel command line that initializes the guest's hostname.

- **extra**—This option accepts a string and is appended to the end of the kernel command line. The kernel command line is the same line used in the GRUB configuration to load the Domain0 for a normal operating system. For Linux guests, once booted, the full arguments passed to the kernel are available in the new guest in `/proc/cmdline`, which is a simple text file. By parsing this file, you can find any arguments passed to the kernel. Listing 6.20 shows the kernel command line arguments produced by Listing 6.19. This can be a useful feature because it allows you to pass arguments to scripts inside the guest. All that a script would have to do is parse that file.

LISTING 6.20 Location of Boot Parameters Used to Boot the Current Working Kernel

```
[user@domU]$ cat /proc/cmdline
ip=192.168.0.101:1.2.3.4:192.168.0.1: ➥
255.255.255.0:pastebin:eth0:off root=/dev/hda1 ro 4
[user@domU]$
```

S-Expression (SXP) Format

SXP is the underlying format of Xen data. When viewing XenStore database entries, running the `list` subcommand with the `--long` option or running the `create` subcommand with the `--dryrun` option, the data is presented in SXP format. Listing 6.21

shows an example SXP format configuration file that creates the same guest domain as the configuration file shown previously in Listing 6.19.

LISTING 6.21 An Example SXP Configuration Script for Creating Guests

```
[root@dom0]# cat another_generic_guest.dryrun.sxp
(vm
    (name another_generic_guest.cfg)
    (memory 128)
    (vcpus 1)
    (image
        (linux
            (kernel /boot/vmlinuz-2.6.16-xen)
            (ramdisk /boot/initrd.img-2.6.16-xen)
            (ip
                192.168.0.101:1.2.3.4:192.168.0.1:
                255.255.255.0:another_generic_guest:eth0:off
            )
            (root '/dev/hda1 ro')
            (args 4)
        )
    )
    (device (vbd (uname file:/xen-images/fedora.img)
                 (dev hda1) (mode w)))
    (device (vbd (uname file:/xen-images/fedora-swap.img)
                 (dev hda2) (mode w)))
    (device (vif (mac 00:16:3e:36:00:05)))
)
[root@dom0]#
```

Path to Configuration Files

Configuration files are typically stored in the /etc/xen directory. However, the path option to xm create allows you to specify another location. You can actually specify a colon-separated list of directories as with the traditional UNIX path environment variable, as shown in Listing 6.22. By default, the path only includes your current directory as well as /etc/xen.

LISTING 6.22 Specifying Multiple Paths to Configuration Files

```
[root@dom0]# xm create generic-guest.cfg \
    --path=/xen/:/etc/xen/auto
[output omitted]
```

xm searched for a file called `generic-guest.cfg` in the `/xen` directory. If we had not specified a filename, xm would have defaulted to looking for a file called `xmdefconfig`.

Diagnosing Problems with Guest Creation

Despite your best efforts, sometimes creation of a new guest will fail. In this section, we discuss some common problems that may occur and the best way to diagnose them.

We describe the use of the `dryrun` option of `xm create` to flush out some errors. We also describe how to view the console output from your guest as it is booting. Finally, we present a list of sample problems and their solutions. Even if you encounter different error messages on your system, we hope these examples give you some ideas about how to approach problems.

Dry Run

An important option for debugging the creation of new guests is the `dryrun` option to `xm create`. The `dryrun` option shows how your configuration file and command configuration options will be parsed by Xen when you execute the `create` subcommand. The guest domain will not actually be created. This allows you to catch syntax errors or other problems in your configuration files or command line parameters. Listing 6.23 shows some sample output. Notice that it is in SXP format.

LISTING 6.23 Translating a Python Configuration File to an SXP Configuration File

```
[root@dom0]# xm create generic-guest.cfg --dryrun
Using config file "/xen/generic-guest.cfg".
(vm
    (name generic-guest)
    (memory 356)
    (vcpus 1)
    (image
        (Linux
            (kernel /boot/vmlinuz-2.6-xenU)
            (root '/dev/sda1 ro')
            (vncunused 1)
            (display :0.0)
            (xauthority /root/.xauthv27eVB)
        )
    )
    (device (tap (uname tap:aio:/xen/generic.img)
```

```
                        (dev sda1) (mode w)))
        (device (tap (uname tap:aio:/xen/generic.swap)
                        (dev sda2) (mode w)))
        (device (vif (bridge xenbr0)))
)
[root@dom0]#
```

The output from a dry run can be saved and used as a configuration script. There are no significant advantages to creating a guest in this way, and most users will not need this functionality.

An SXP style configuration file can be used by specifying it on the command line with the -F option. The same effect is achieved as if the -f option was used; the difference being that configuration options are presented in SXP format with -F rather than as a Python script with -f. When the guest is created in Listing 6.24 the "Using config file ..." message is not printed. This is because with a Python configuration script, xm create will read the variables, form an SXP configuration file, and then create the guest.

LISTING 6.24 Creating a Guest with an SXP Configuration File

```
[root@dom0]# xm create -F sxp-generic-guest.cfg
Started domain generic-guest
[root@dom0]# xm list
Name                     ID Mem(MiB) VCPUs State   Time(s)
Domain-0                  0    1154      1 r-----   4516.5
generic-guest             1     356      1 -b----     25.6
[root@dom0]#
```

Console Output

When creating a guest, it is possible to also gain a terminal (console) to that guest using the -c option on the create subcommand. Listing 6.25 shows how to do this.

LISTING 6.25 Gaining Console Access to a Guest during Creation

```
[root@dom0]# xm create generic-guest.cfg -c
Using config file "/xen/gentoo/generic-guest.cfg".
Started domain generic-guest

<boot sequence not shown>

generic-guest login:
```

Notice we changed from a `[root@dom0]#` prompt to a `generic-guest login:` prompt. We removed the initial boot sequence that displays all the devices and services that are brought up to save space, but it should look like a normal system boot sequence. This new terminal is similar to a serial connection and can accomplish most tasks of a normal console. There is also an `xm console` command to access this console after a domain is already created, which is covered later in this chapter.

The console option, `-c`, is particularly useful for diagnosing problems in guest creation. By connecting to a guest through a serial-like console while booting, you will be able to catch any kernel panic errors should they occur. If, however, you do not use the console option, it is likely that the problematic guest will crash and disappear without you ever knowing why it didn't start. When starting a new guest for the first time, we highly recommend using the `-c` option so you can see errors that may occur if a guest supports a console. However, if the guest doesn't support a console, such as when you run some HVM guests, you might be able to troubleshoot based on log files discussed in Chapter 3.

Sample Problems

Creating a guest can be complicated because there are so many variables to set up, and debugging can be time consuming. Following are common errors that can be encountered during the initial stages of learning how to create configuration files and guests. If you do not find your problem in this list, a simple Web search will often find the answer for you.

Problem 1: String Value Not in Quotes in Configuration File

In Python configuration files, when setting a variable to a string you must surround the value with double quotes. In this case, the error message simply indicates that a syntax error exists and which line the error is on. Listing 6.26 shows the solution.

LISTING 6.26 Incorrect Syntax of Python Configuration File

```
INCORRECT LINE IN CONFIGURATION FILE:
    kernel = /boot/vmlinuz-2.6-xen
ERROR GIVEN BY XM CREATE:
    Error: invalid syntax (generic-guest.cfg, line 1)

CORRECTED LINE IN CONFIGURATION FILE:
    kernel = "/boot/vmlinuz-2.6-xen"
```

Problem 2: Kernel Image Does Not Exist

Another error is thrown when we use the new kernel entry because the /boot/
vmlinuz-2.6-xenFOO file does not exist. As shown in Listing 6.27, the xm create
error indicates that the kernel image does not exist.

LISTING 6.27 Error When Kernel Parameter Points to Nonexistent Kernel

```
INCORRECT LINE IN CONFIGURATION FILE:
    kernel = "/boot/vmlinuz-2.6-xenFOO"
ERROR GIVEN BY XM CREATE:
    Error: Kernel image does not exist: /boot/vmlinuz-2.6-xenFOO
```

Problem 3: Duplicate Guest Name

Similar to domain IDs, guest domain names must be unique. In Listing 6.28, we try to
create a new guest with the same name as a currently running guest.

LISTING 6.28 Reusing Configuration Files without Changing the Name Parameter

```
name = "pastebin"
VM name 'pastebin' already in use by domain 23
```

Often, Xen users add a function to the Python script that dynamically generates a
unique name. Listing 6.29 shows a function from an example configuration script that
is available with the Xen packages from www.xen.org.

LISTING 6.29 Script for Dynamic Naming of Guests

```
def vmid_check(var, val):
    val = int(val)
    if val <= 0:
        raise ValueError
    return val


# Define the 'vmid' variable so that 'xm create' knows about it.
xm_vars.var('vmid',
            use="Virtual machine id. Integer greater than 0.",
            check=vmid_check)


# Check the defined variables have valid values.
```

LISTING 6.29 continued

```
xm_vars.check()

[irrelevant lines of configuration file omitted here]

name = "VM%d" % vmid"
```

The xm_vars.var function defines a new variable to look for on the command line. The first argument is the name of the option. The second argument is a description of the option, which will be printed if used wrong. The third argument is a function to use for checking the value passed to the option. To use the value of this option, name would be defined like in the last line of Listing 6.29 (taken from the same Xen-Source example). Listing 6.30 shows how to use this function and how it would affect the guest's name.

LISTING 6.30 Using a Python Script to Declare Guest Names during Creation

```
[root@dom0]# xm create generic-guest.cfg vmid=23
Using config file "generic-guest.cfg".
Started domain VM23
[root@dom0]# xm list
Name                     ID Mem(MiB) VCPUs State    Time(s)
Domain-0                  0     1154     1 r-----     283.1
VM23                      1      512     1 ------       0.9
[root@dom0]#
```

Problem 4: Insufficient Memory

In Listing 6.31, we allocated 0MB of memory to the new guest. Of course, this means there is no room to load a kernel or programs into.

LISTING 6.31 Memory Parameter Is Set Too Low

```
INCORRECT LINE IN CONFIGURATION FILE:
    memory = 000
ERROR GIVEN BY XM CREATE:
    Error: Invalid memory size
```

A guest must have more than 0MB of RAM. Of course, a guest could also be allocated 1MB of RAM, in which case an "invalid memory size" error would not be thrown, but other errors would probably arise during the creation process similar to

Listing 6.32. The out of memory (OOM) error is printed in an infinite loop during the boot process of the new guest.

LISTING 6.32 Out of Memory Error When a Guest Starts with Too Little Memory

```
[root@dom0]# xm create generic-guest.cfg memory=1
[root@dom0]# xm console generic-guest
Out of Memory: Kill process 2 (ksoftirqd/0) score 0 and children.
<message repeats>
```

On the other hand, the problem could be an attempt to allocate too much memory. This throws another error, as shown in Listing 6.33. Since the host machine only had 1.5GB total, 4GB is overcommitting memory. Notice that the error says even with Domain0's memory, there would not be enough to fill a 4GB request.

LISTING 6.33 Memory Parameter Is Set Too High

```
INCORRECT LINE IN CONFIGURATION FILE:
    memory = 4000
ERROR GIVEN BY XM CREATE:
    Error: I need 4096000 KiB, but dom0_min_mem is 262144 and
    shrinking to 262144 KiB would leave only 1284476 KiB free.
```

Problem 5: Insufficient Loopback Devices

One frequently overlooked item that limits the number of domains is the number of allowed loopback devices. Guest domains often use guest images obtained from the Domain0 file system and access them through a loopback device. If each guest domain has a guest image and a swap image, two loopback devices must be reserved for each guest. This can quickly deplete the pool of loopback devices. As previously mentioned, the use of loopback devices for xen images is deprecated, but some people may still use them.

If you are using loopback devices to access guest file systems and have trouble with the domains not beginning execution when created, the problem could be that you have too few loopback devices available. Typical symptoms of this problem are not an error from xm create, but instead the domain may disappear after creation, or it may start in a paused state for no apparent reason. To diagnose this problem look in /var/log/xen/xen-hotplug.log for XenStore read errors for backend/vbd. Listing 6.34 shows the relevant error messages taken from the log file that would be thrown from a virtual block device not being created because there are too few loopback devices.

LISTING 6.34 Generic Failure Message When the Backend Virtual Block Device Scripts Fail

```
xenstore-read: couldn't read path backend/vbd/12/2050/node
xenstore-read: couldn't read path backend/vbd/12/2049/node
```

Fixing this problem requires increasing the number of loopback devices for the Domain0 kernel.

In the case that loopback support is built into the kernel, a certain number of loopback devices are created on bootup. This sets a limit to the number of devices you are allowed to mount through the loopback interface. To increase this number, just add `max_loop=32` to your Domain0 kernel line of your GRUB entry. Replace `32` with however many devices you want.

In the case that loopback support is built as a module, you can increase the number of loopback devices by passing `max_loop=32` on the command line while loading the loop module with the `modprobe` command.

To see how many loopback devices you currently have available, count the number of loop files you have in your `dev` file system. Listing 6.35 shows a command that can do this for you.

LISTING 6.35 Number of Loopback Devices

```
[root@dom0]# ls /dev/ | grep loop | wc -l
18
[root@dom0]#
```

To see what loopback devices you are currently using, use the `losetup` command as in Listing 6.36.

LISTING 6.36 Number of Loopback Devices in Use

```
[root@dom0]# losetup -a
/dev/loop/0: [0301]:9404422 (/xen-images/gde-swap.img)
/dev/loop1: [0301]:9404421 (/xen-images/gde.img)
/dev/loop10: [0301]:9404433 (/xen-images/ircbot.img)
/dev/loop11: [0301]:9404434 (/xen-images/ircbot-swap.img)
/dev/loop12: [0301]:9404426 (/xen-images/controlcenter.img)
/dev/loop14: [0301]:7766019 (/xen-images/pastebin.img)
[root@dom0]#
```

Problem 6: Unable to Run Networking Script

In the next example, we try to attach the `vif` of the new domain to a nonexistent virtual network bridge. Notice in Listing 6.37 that the error reports that Hotplug scripts are not working. This is because the attachment of a virtual bridge causes a script to run.

LISTING 6.37 Creating a Virtual Interface with a Nonexistent Network Interface Name

```
INCORRECT LINE IN CONFIGURATION FILE:
    vif = [ 'bridge=xnbr0' ]
ERROR GIVEN BY XM CREATE:
    Error: Device 0 (vif) could not be connected. Hotplug scripts
    not working.
CORRECT LINE IN CONFIGURATION FILE:
    vif = [ 'bridge=xenbr0' ]
```

In this case, it was simply a typo in the name of the bridge. Listing 6.38 shows a way to check which virtual bridges are available. In this case, there are two bridges called `xenbr0` and `xenbr1`.

LISTING 6.38 Displaying Virtual Bridges

```
[root@dom0]# brctl show
bridge name       bridge id           STP enabled    interfaces
xenbr0            8000.feffffffffff    no             peth0
                                                      vif0.0
xenbr1            8000.feffffffffff    no             peth1
                                                      vif3.0
[root@dom0]#
```

However, a similar error about Hotplug scripts not working could also be thrown when /bin/sh does not point to bash. Listing 6.39 shows the command to diagnose and fix one example of such a problem. There could be multiple reasons for this error, though, and a Web search will probably be sufficient to resolve the issue.

LISTING 6.39 Fixing /bin/sh to Link to the Correct Shell Program

```
[root@dom0]# ls -l /bin/sh
lrwxrwxrwx 1 root root 4 Dec  6 19:08 /bin/sh -> dash
[root@dom0]# rm -f /bin/sh
[root@dom0]# ln -s /bin/sh /bin/bash
[root@dom0]# ls -l /bin/sh
lrwxrwxrwx 1 root root 4 Dec  6 19:08 /bin/sh -> bash
[root@dom0]#
```

Problem 7: Running the Wrong Kernel in Domain0

Some errors occur that aren't specific to xm functionality. One example is when xm fails to run because you've booted a non-Xen kernel in Domain0. You can check that you are using your Xen kernel by running one of the two following commands shown in Listing 6.40.

LISTING 6.40 Ensuring That a Xen Kernel Is Running in Domain0

```
[root@dom0]# uname -r
2.6.16.29-xen
[root@dom0]# cat /proc/xen/capabilities
control_d

[root@dom0]#
```

The uname command displays the version of your kernel (not necessarily 2.6.16.29). However, Xen-enabled kernels typically have "xen" appended to the end of the version number when they are compiled. If this is not the case, you can also check whether /proc/xen/capabilities exists. This file should only exist when a Xen kernel is booted. If you are not running the Xen kernel, fix the Domain0 kernel line of your GRUB entry to use the Xen kernel. For instructions on how to do this, see Chapter 4, "Hardware Requirements and Installation of Xen Domain0."

Of course, another sign that you are running a non-Xen enabled Domain0 kernel is when an error appears when you start the xend daemon. If you encounter such a message, as in Listing 6.41, you are more than likely not running a Xen enabled kernel in Domain0. You may not even be running the Xen hypervisor. So double-check your GRUB menu file to see whether you started your system with the Xen kernel.

LISTING 6.41 Attempting to Start the Xen Daemon When in a Non-Xen Kernel

```
[root@dom0]# /etc/init.d/xend start
grep: /proc/xen/capabilities: No such file or directory
[root@dom0]#
```

Problem 8: Loading a Kernel Without Modules

Another common set of problems can arise when loading guest kernels that build Xen drivers and other needed drivers as modules instead of directly in the kernel. If you receive errors when booting a guest, double-check whether you are using any modules by searching for .ko files in the /lib/modules/<kernel-version> directory that correlates to the guest kernel version on Domain0. If you find any .ko files, you are using loadable modules, and it's likely you need an initial RAM disk (initrd) image to let the kernel know what modules are available during the boot sequence. You must assign the location of your initrd image to the ramdisk variable. Also, make sure your guest image contains the proper /lib/modules directory. For instructions on how to add the /lib/modules directory to your guest image, see Chapter 5. A good way to diagnose this type of problem is to use the console option (-c) on the create subcommand to catch any kernel panics on boot.

Problem 9: Running the xm Command from a Non-Root Account

The introduction of this chapter mentions that only an account with root privileges can run the command. Listing 6.42 presents the error that would be thrown if accessed without root privileges.

LISTING 6.42 Attempting to Run an xm Command without Root Privileges

```
[user@dom0]$ xm <command>
ERROR: Could not obtain handle on privileged                ➥
     command interface (13 = Permission denied)
Error: Most commands need root access. Please try again as root.
[user@dom0]$
```

The problem is that you are not running the command as a superuser. You must either login as root, su to become root, or use sudo to gain root privileges.

Automatically Starting DomUs

After you have worked all the bugs out of your guest creation, you will likely grow tired of starting guests manually. For example, if you are running ten guests on a single Xen host system, rebooting the entire system and manually starting each one again would be quite a task. The Xen developers realized that such a situation would be burdensome and included an initialization script to start a set of default guests on bootup.

Guest configuration files in /etc/xen/auto/ are started automatically—whenever the xendomains script is started at system boot if the xendomains init script is enabled or after boot. The contents of /etc/xen/auto/ should be symlinks to guest configuration files.

Listing 6.43 shows the environment before we run the script and the configuration files that will be used to boot guests.

LISTING 6.43 List of Configuration Scripts in `/etc/xen/auto` and `xm list` Showing Only Domain0 Running

```
[root@dom0]# xm list
Name                               ID Mem(MiB) VCPUs State   Time(s)
Domain-0                            0     298      2 r-----   4348.8
[root@dom0]# ls -l /etc/xen/auto
total 0
lrwxrwxrwx 1 root  root 12 2007-02-07 23:35 gde -> /etc/xen/gde
lrwxrwxrwx 1 root  root 15 2007-02-07 23:35                     ➥
    ircbot -> /etc/xen/ircbot
lrwxrwxrwx 1 root  root 13 2007-02-07 23:35 ncpr -> /etc/xen/ncpr
lrwxrwxrwx 1 root  root 17 2007-02-07 23:35                     ➥
    pastebin -> /etc/xen/pastebin
lrwxrwxrwx 1 root  root 12 2007-02-07 23:35 rrs -> /etc/xen/rrs
lrwxrwxrwx 1 root  root 12 2007-02-07 23:35 sql -> /etc/xen/sql
[root@dom0]#
```

All the files in this directory are symbolic links to domain creation scripts. They should all be started when we run the initialization script in Listing 6.44. Indeed, the `xm list` output shown in Listing 6.45 indicates that they are all booting.

LISTING 6.44 Starting the `xendomains` Script

```
[root@dom0]# /etc/init.d/xendomains start
Starting auto Xen domains: gde ircbot ncpr pastebin rrs sql *
[root@dom0]#
```

LISTING 6.45 `xendomains` Script Booting Six Guests

```
[root@dom0]# xm list
Name                               ID Mem(MiB) VCPUs State   Time(s)
Domain-0                            0     298      2 r-----   4351.5
gde                                 5     128      1 -b----      6.0
ircbot                              6      64      1 -b----      7.4
ncpr                               24     128      1 ------      4.5
pastebin                           39      64      1 -b----      9.3
rrs                                26     128      1 ------      3.4
sql                                12     128      1 -b----      4.5
[root@dom0]#
```

Shutting Down Guest Domains

After you successfully have guest domains running, you may hate to shut them down, but that is, of course, also a necessary part of administering a Xen system. There are actually three distinctly different methods for shutting down a guest domain: shutdown, reboot, and destroy.

First, we discuss the shutdown subcommand. After a guest is running, all it takes to make it shut down like a normal computer is to send a shutdown signal with this command. The guest safely closes all processes and unmounts virtual devices. Then Domain0 deallocates resources the guest was using. Next, we discuss the reboot subcommand. reboot is roughly the equivalent of a shutdown followed immediately by a create. Like shutdown itself, the reboot command safely shuts down the system. The third option is the destroy subcommand. This is the unsafe way of taking down a guest. No care is taken for running processes. The domain becomes inactive, meaning processes stop executing, and then resources are unallocated. The dangers of destroying a domain outright are discussed later in the "xm destroy" section of this chapter.

Since Domain0 is a privileged domain, commands such as shutdown, reboot, and destroy do not function on Domain0. They simply report an error. This is because all other guest domains depend on Domain0 to execute certain actions on their behalf. Without Domain0 in place, unprivileged domains could not exist.

xm shutdown

The shutdown command is the safest way to bring down a domain. The same signals are sent to the guest domain as if the poweroff or shutdown command were executed while in a guest domain.

When a user is logged in to the guest domain and the xm shutdown command is used, the user sees the normal shutdown process begin as shown in Listing 6.46. Omitted lines consist mostly of normal user programs shutting down.

LISTING 6.46 Guest Shutting Down with the xm shutdown Command

```
[user@domU]$
Broadcast message from root (console) (Wed Mar  7 09:34:03 2007):

The system is going down for system halt NOW!
<shutdown process continues but not shown>
```

We begin our example of xm shutdown with Domain0 and one DomU shown in Listing 6.47.

LISTING 6.47 Domain0 and an Unprivileged Guest Running

```
[root@dom0]# xm list
Name                          ID Mem(MiB) VCPUs State    Time(s)
Domain-0                       0    1154     1 r-----     325.1
generic-guest                  1     356     1 -b----      15.6
[root@dom0]#
```

You run the shutdown command with a guest, by specifying its name or ID. Multiple guests can be specified on the same line with guest IDs or names, separated by a space on the command line. We use the guest ID in Listing 6.48 where we show an example of running the xm shutdown command.

LISTING 6.48 Shutting Down a Guest

```
[root@dom0]# xm shutdown 1
[root@dom0]# xm list
Name                          ID Mem(MiB) VCPUs State    Time(s)
Domain-0                       0    1154     1 r-----     325.1
generic-guest                  1     356     1 ------      18.0
[root@dom0]#
```

Observe the state and time of a guest shutting down. It is going through the normal shutdown process so the guest is using the CPU more. In Listing 6.49, after waiting a bit longer, xm list shows that our domain is no longer running on the hypervisor.

LISTING 6.49 Current Running Guests after a Guest Has Been Shut Down

```
[root@dom0]# xm list
Name                          ID Mem(MiB) VCPUs State    Time(s)
Domain-0                       0    1154     1 r-----     325.1
```

If we had specified a nonexistent domain, we would have received a simple error indicating so, like in Listing 6.50.

LISTING 6.50 Attempting to Shut Down a Nonexistent Guest

```
[root@dom0]# xm shutdown 45
Error: the domain '45' does not exist.
[root@dom0]#
```

When you want to shut down your entire system, it can be a pain to shut down each individual domain separately. The -a option shuts them all down at once. Listing 6.51 shows the results of `xm list` before and after running the `shutdown` command on all guests. Some time had to pass before all guests were down because they went through the usual safe process of shutting down software components in descending order of run levels.

LISTING 6.51 Shutting Down All Guests Currently Running

```
[root@dom0]# xm list
Name                          ID Mem(MiB) VCPUs State   Time(s)
Domain-0                       0     1154     1 r-----    456.2
master                         6      128     1 -b----      6.0
slave1                         8       64     1 -b----      3.2
slave2                         3       64     1 --p---      3.5
slave3                         4       64     1 --p---      3.5
[root@dom0]# xm shutdown -a
< wait about 30 seconds >
[root@dom0]# xm list
Name                          ID Mem(MiB) VCPUs State   Time(s)
Domain-0                       0     1154     1 r-----    456.2
[root@dom0]#
```

In Listing 6.52, the -w option is used to make the command wait until the domain(s) are completely shut down. The `shutdown` command returned in about 30 seconds.

LISTING 6.52 Shutting Down All Guests Currently and Waiting for Processes to Finish

```
[root@dom0]# xm list
Name                          ID Mem(MiB) VCPUs State   Time(s)
Domain-0                       0     1154     1 r-----    456.2
master                         6      128     1 -b----      6.0
slave1                         8       64     1 -b----      3.2
slave2                         3       64     1 -p----      3.5
slave3                         4       64     1 -p----      3.5
[root@dom0]# xm shutdown -wa
Domain slave1 terminated
Domain slave3 terminated
Domain slave2 terminated
Domain master terminated
All domains terminated
[root@dom0]#
```

One important note is that paused domains should not be shut down. It is safest to unpause any paused domains before shutting them down. See the section "Pausing Domains" later in this chapter for more information.

xm reboot

`xm reboot` effectively shuts down a guest domain and then automatically restarts. This means that the new domain will have a different ID, but the same domain name. This command achieves the same results as if the `reboot` command was called in the guest domain itself and not from Domain0.

However, `xm reboot` is more than just a convenience. There is a difference between a reboot and a shutdown followed by a create. PCI Devices and resources such as allocated memory are not reassigned. This decreases the overhead of rebooting a system to a small degree because devices do not have to be remapped to guests, and configuration scripts do not have to be parsed again.

When a user is logged in to the guest domain and the `xm reboot` command is used, the user will see the normal reboot process begin. Listing 6.53 shows the first few lines of this output.

LISTING 6.53 Messages Printed from within a Guest When Guest Is Shut Down from Domain0

```
[user@domU]$
Broadcast message from root (console) (Wed Mar  7 09:34:03 2007):

The system is going down for reboot NOW!
<reboot process continues but not shown>
```

We start our reboot example with Domain0 and one other guest domain running that we reboot in Listing 6.54.

LISTING 6.54 Rebooting a Guest from Domain0

```
[root@dom0]# xm list
Name                         ID Mem(MiB) VCPUs State    Time(s)
Domain-0                      0    1154     1 r-----    325.1
generic-guest                 1     356     1 -b----     15.6
[root@dom0]# xm reboot generic-guest
[root@dom0]#
```

A signal has now been sent to the operating system running in the `generic-guest` domain. The normal reboot process follows like a non-Xen operating system. Listing

6.55 shows what a guest looks like through the xm list command after a reboot. The ID changes, and its time resets, but its memory, VCPUs, and other resources are the same.

LISTING 6.55 State of a Guest after Rebooting

```
[root@dom0]# xm list
Name                      ID Mem(MiB) VCPUs State   Time(s)
Domain-0                   0    1154      1 r-----    325.1
generic-guest              2     356      1 ------      0.7
[root@dom0]#
```

The -a option reboots all guest domains. This of course does not include Domain0. Listing 6.56 shows this option in action.

LISTING 6.56 Rebooting All Currently Running Guests

```
[root@dom0]# xm list
Name                      ID Mem(MiB) VCPUs State   Time(s)
Domain-0                   0    1154      1 r-----    486.2
master                     6     128      1 -b----      6.0
slave1                     8      64      1 -b----      3.2
slave2                     3      64      1 -b----      3.5
slave3                     4      64      1 -b----      3.5
[root@dom0]# xm reboot -a
[root@dom0]# xm list
Name                      ID Mem(MiB) VCPUs State   Time(s)
Domain-0                   0    1154      1 r-----    498.2
master                    11     128      1 -b----      1.0
slave1                    12      64      1 -b----      3.2
slave2                     9      64      1 -b----      2.7
slave3                    10      64      1 -p----      1.3
[root@dom0]#
```

All domains were rebooted and received new domain IDs. All the devices should be the same.

The -w option causes xm to wait until all specified domains have been rebooted. Again, be careful not to shut down paused domains with reboot as this may result in unpredictable behavior. Listing 6.57 shows this command in action.

LISTING 6.57 Rebooting a Guest and Waiting for Processes to Finish

```
[root@dom0]# xm reboot generic-guest -w
Domain generic-guest rebooted
All domains rebooted
[root@dom0]# xm list
Name                    ID Mem(MiB) VCPUs State   Time(s)
Domain-0                 0    1154    1 r-----    325.1
generic-guest            4     356    1 -b----     15.6
[root@dom0]#
```

You can make the shutdown command act exactly like reboot with the -R flag. Listing 6.58 shows how the command would be run, but there is no output, like the xm reboot command.

LISTING 6.58 Reboot with shutdown Command

```
[root@dom0]# xm shutdown -R 4
[root@dom0]#
```

xm destroy

The destroy subcommand is used to instantly and unsafely bring down a domain. The effect of this command is similar to pulling the power cord on a running computer. First, the domain is brought down from being available and taken off the domain list seen from xm list. Then the domain is disconnected from any VIFs, VBDs, and so on. The corresponding VIFs and VBDs are cleaned up, meaning the virtual interfaces are removed, and the file descriptors allowing access to the domain image are removed.

This is very unsafe because no consideration is given for what processes or services are being run on any particular domain and jeopardizes the data integrity of guest images. For example, if one domain is running a network file system server and is taken down, any domain using that file system will lose access to its files leaving any cached IO unresolved and incomplete.

Also, destroying a domain outright unmounts its devices unsafely, including file systems. This could cause IO errors, and on the next creation of that guest a possibly lengthy fsck will probably be forced. If for no other reason than to avoid a nuisance, the shutdown command is preferred.

There are viable reasons for wanting to destroy a guest domain. One reason is if a misbehaving guest will not reboot or shut down properly. Also, if a guest with sensitive data is compromised by a program or hacker, destroying it is a quick way of securing, not necessarily saving, the data.

Once again, we start our example by showing Domain0 and one other guest running in Listing 6.59.

LISTING 6.59 One Guest as well as Domain0 Currently Running

```
[root@dom0]# xm list
Name                    ID Mem(MiB) VCPUs State   Time(s)
Domain-0                 0    1154      1 r-----    325.1
generic-guest            1     356      1 -b----     14.2
[root@dom0]#
```

We now run the destroy subcommand on generic-guest by specifying its name or ID in Listing 6.60.

LISTING 6.60 Destroying a Single Guest

```
[root@dom0]# xm destroy 1
[root@dom0]# xm list
Name                    ID Mem(MiB) VCPUs State   Time(s)
Domain-0                 0    1154      1 r-----    325.1
[root@dom0]#
```

The domain was immediately taken down. This is basic behavior as well as a powerful command. Therefore, it doesn't have options similar to shutdown or reboot.

Pausing Domains

In addition to completely shutting down a domain, it is possible to temporarily pause it. All the settings in the guest domain and all the devices, such as CPUs, network cards, amount of RAM, and so on, are kept the same, but processes of the paused guest domain are no longer scheduled by the Xen hypervisor to be run on any CPU. The new paused state of the guest domain is reflected in xm list by a state of p.

There are advantages to pausing a domain rather than shutting it down with xm destroy and restarting it at a later time. The main advantage is that the state of the guest will be saved while paused. If an important compilation or operation is currently being executed, pausing will not require restarting that operation as long as it doesn't depend on persistent communication with another computer.

Another advantage is that unpausing a guest domain is much faster than booting a guest. Along the same lines, when a guest boots, it puts stress on the system resources available. This overhead is avoided by pausing rather than restarting.

xm pause

Perhaps xm pause is better compared to a system hibernation or standby than anything else. In both cases, pausing a guest domain or hibernating a normal system, the system does not use any CPU cycles but still reserves any RAM it was using along with PCI devices, such as Ethernet cards, graphics cards, and hard drives. Note that if this domain is running a server such as a Web server, it will appear to the clients that the domain has shut down. As with shutdown and destroy, pause cannot be run on Domain0.

First, let's start with a domain already booted and running in Listing 6.61.

LISTING 6.61   One Guest as well as Domain0 Currently Running

```
[root@dom0]# xm list
Name                        ID Mem(MiB) VCPUs State    Time(s)
Domain-0                     0    1154      1 r-----     325.1
generic-guest                1     356      1 ------       0.2
[root@dom0]#
```

Listing 6.62 shows pausing the domain. The domain should now be paused and no longer sending instructions to the CPU. Notice the change in the domain state. It now reads p for paused. Repeated calls to xm list would show no additional time for this domain until it is unpaused.

LISTING 6.62   Pausing a Guest

```
[root@dom0]# xm pause generic-guest
[root@dom0]#
[root@dom0]# xm list
Name                        ID Mem(MiB) VCPUs State    Time(s)
Domain-0                     0    1154      1 r-----     325.1
generic-guest                1     356      1 --p---       0.2
[root@dom0]#
```

xm unpause

To unpause a paused guest domain, simply run the xm unpause command , specifying the domain to unpause, as shown in Listing 6.63.

LISTING 6.63 Unpausing a Guest

```
[root@dom0]# xm unpause generic-guest
[root@dom0]#
```

Listing 6.64 shows that the guest state changes to some other state, which depends on what it was doing at the time it was paused. The state for generic-guest is blank because it's between running and blocking states, which means it is not in a paused state.

LISTING 6.64 State of Guest after Being Unpaused

```
[root@dom0]# xm list
Name                         ID Mem(MiB) VCPUs State   Time(s)
Domain-0                      0    1154      1 r-----    325.1
generic-guest                 1     356      1 ------      0.2
[root@dom0]#
```

You can also create a guest domain in the paused state. Listing 6.65 illustrates the use of the -p option to xm create to start guests in a paused state. This results in the domain not being scheduled on any CPU for execution. Thus, the domain never even starts booting, though it still reserves resources such as main memory, images, and any devices allocated to it. The state of generic-guest is paused. The runtime is 0.0 because it hasn't yet been given the right to use the CPU. To begin executing instructions for the paused domain, we would use the xm unpause command.

LISTING 6.65 Starting a Guest in the Paused State

```
[root@dom0]# xm create generic-guest.cfg -p
[root@dom0]# xm list
Name                         ID Mem(MiB) VCPUs State   Time(s)
Domain-0                      0    1154      1 r-----    325.1
generic-guest                 1     356      1 --p---      0.0
[root@dom0]#
```

Interacting with a Guest Nongraphically

So far we haven't discussed how to interact with your guest. There are two main options here, graphically or nongraphically. In this section, we concentrate on the nongraphical approach, and in the next section, we go into depth on a number of graphical possibilities.

To access a guest domain nongraphically, the `xm` tool offers a serial-like console we introduced previously for the purpose of debugging guest creation. During the `xm create` command , the `-c` option can be used to access this console immediately. Using SSH is also another attractive alternative to `xm console`.

xm console

`xm console` attaches the current console display in Domain0 to the console of the running guest chosen. The effect is similar to an SSH session with a machine. Note, an SSH session is also possible, of course, and is covered in the next section of this chapter. The server and client used in the `console` command act like a serial connection. Programs displayed with `ncurses` or that use pagers will not display properly if viewed with the console. `ncurses` is a pseudo-graphical display tool. An example of an application that uses a pager is the "man" function in Linux.

Another disadvantage to only using `xm console` is that Xen limits you to a single command console. This restricts other users from using the system through `xm console` while you are and can make multitasking more difficult.

Let's say we currently have a guest domain running as shown in Listing 6.66.

LISTING 6.66 One Guest as well as Domain0 Currently Running

```
[root@dom0]# xm list
Name                       ID Mem(MiB) VCPUs State    Time(s)
Domain-0                    0    1154     1 r-----     325.1
generic-guest               1     356     1 ------       6.8
[root@dom0]#
```

We can gain a console to the domain on the current `tty` by specifying which domain we want a console to. Either the domain ID or the domain name shown in Listing 6.66 will be sufficient. In Listing 6.67, we use the domain ID.

LISTING 6.67 Accessing the Xen Console of a Guest with Its Domain ID

```
[root@dom0]# xm console 1
<boot sequence not shown>
generic-guest login:
```

Notice that the prompt changed so you know you are now in the guest domain. We removed the initial boot sequence that displays all the devices and services that are brought up to save space, but it should look like a normal system boot sequence. The initial boot sequence printout is saved in a buffer, so the first time you use the `console` command on a guest, you will receive the full printout.

You can now use the domain *almost* as if you were in a nonvirtualized console. However, try using the man command used for displaying manual pages. The entry will not display properly due to the serial port-like characteristics.

If we had specified an invalid domain ID or domain name, a simple error message would be printed with no consequences. Listing 6.68 shows the error message we would receive.

LISTING 6.68 Using the `console` Command on a Nonexistent Guest

```
[root@dom0]# xm console 34
Error: Domain '34' does not exist.
Usage: xm console <Domain>

Attach to <Domain>'s console.
```

To exit the domain just hold down the right Ctrl button, and press the right bracket (right-Ctrl +]). You should be back to Domain0 after pressing these keys. The prompt looks like Listing 6.69.

LISTING 6.69 Exiting a Guest Console with the Ctrl +] Sequence

```
generic-guest login: [root@dom0]#
```

If you must use man pages or other pager utilities in a Xen console, perhaps piping the output to a temporary file would suffice for now. Try the commands in Listing 6.70. We do not display the whole man page for the sake of saving space.

LISTING 6.70 Viewing Manual Pages in a Xen Console

```
[user@domU]$ man ls > temp_file
[user@domU]$ cat temp_file
LS(1)                                                        LS(1)



NAME
       ls, dir, vdir - list directory contents

SYNOPSIS
       ls [options] [file...]
< man page continues... >
```

SSH

SSH stands for *secure shell*. It is a stable, ubiquitously available application that was built as a replacement for remote login and telnet and includes RSA and DSA encryption. Traffic is encrypted for security. Many SSH sessions can be opened using the same server, which eases multitasking.

To use SSH, you install and run an SSH server on the guest to which you want to connect. The SSH daemon has to be running to listen for connections from SSH clients. Start the server through the init.d script or through an appropriate command.

You must also install and run an SSH client on the computer from which you are remotely connecting. SSH is a default application for most distributions and is probably already installed for you. To connect to the server, simply type ssh followed by the hostname or IP address of the machine you started the server on.

SSH offers an attractive option to running xm console from within Domain0. SSH allows you to connect to your guests directly from an external machine rather than through Domain0. In this way, your virtual guests can be administered just like physical machines in your network. Also, it is wise to eliminate as much direct interaction with Domain0 as possible. A mistake made from Domain0 can not only hurt Domain0, but also hurt all the guest domains. Thus, it is best to avoid using Domain0 as a launching point to access other domains. One disadvantage of SSH relative to xm console is that kernel panics will not be shown by SSH because SSH runs as a process in the guest.

A plethora of documentation about SSH is available online if you want to know more. Also, the man pages for ssh and ssh_config are very thorough.

Interacting with a Guest Graphically

At some point you may want the ability to access a guest through a window manager such as GNOME or KDE. The remainder of this chapter is dedicated to exploring a number of popular methods each with its own advantages and disadvantages. Some of the technologies discussed are well documented on the Internet, so full-length tutorials on the use of each are not given here.

One method of displaying a guest's graphical environment is assigning a PCI device to the guest. This is like taking the graphics card away from Domain0 and giving it to one of the other guests. We do include PCI device assignments as a possible solution in Table 6.2 at the end of this chapter. However, this method is not discussed in detail in this chapter because it is covered in Chapter 9, "Device Virtualization and Management."

X Forwarding with SSH

In the previous section entitled "SSH," we briefly described how to use SSH to gain console access to a guest. However, SSH also has the capability to forward the graphical display of a program running in a guest to a remote machine. This gives the advantage of less overhead than forwarding the entire graphical display from the guest, which we cover later. It's also convenient that you probably already have this application installed on your system.

SSH forwarding of an X graphical display is not entirely necessary, but mainly used for convenience and security. It is possible to change the DISPLAY environment variable to direct the X server to send display information to a particular host, whether local or remote. However, when using SSH to change the destination of a graphical window, many details are hidden from the user. There is also the added benefit of encryption offered by SSH, which the X server does not support on its own.

We now briefly cover some configuration options to be aware of as well as the use of the X forwarding option in SSH.

Configuration of SSH Server and Client

The configuration file for the SSH server on Red Hat and Debian-based distributions should be located in /etc/ssh/sshd_config. Listing 6.71 shows two options essential to X forwarding.

LISTING 6.71 Important Configuration File Lines When Setting Up SSH X Forwarding on Server Side

```
X11Forwarding yes
X11UseLocalhost no
```

The two options in Listing 6.71 as well as two other SSH server configuration parameters that may be of interest are explained in the following list:

- **X11Forwarding**—The main factor in deciding whether X forwarding is allowed over SSH.

- **X11UseLocalhost**—Indicates whether the X server should bind to the local loopback address or accept connections from any address. When set to no, it allows remote connections to the X server. When set to yes, only connections made on the local computer are allowed. However, some earlier versions of the X11 server do not support this option.

- **XauthLocation**—Identifies the full path name of the xauth program, which authenticates an X session with the X server. The default value of XauthLocation is /usr/bin/xauth, which is most likely correct.

- **X11DisplayOffset**—Specifies the X display number that the new X application can be run with. The default value is 10. If this value is set too low, the new X application may interfere with an existing X session. For most purposes, the default value should be fine.

The configuration file for the SSH client on the client's machine should be located in /etc/ssh/ssh_config. Listing 6.72 shows a couple options here that are worth mentioning.

LISTING 6.72 Important Configuration File Lines When Setting Up SSH X Forwarding on Client Side

```
ForwardX11 yes
ForwardX11Trusted yes
```

Both the SSH server and client must support the forwarding of display information. The reason for setting the parameters in Listing 6.72 are explained in the following list:

- **ForwardX11**—Specifies whether the X display of applications will automatically be forwarded over the SSH connection.

- **ForwardX11Trusted**—If this setting is no, there is a time limit to the session and remote users will not be able to use data owned by any existing X application. They will only be able to create new X applications. Saying no here is a bit more secure.

Usage of SSH X Forwarding

Start the server as in the nongraphical section about SSH earlier in this chapter. Making a connection to the server is the same as discussed in the "SSH" section earlier in this chapter except that the -X option is used with the ssh command. Now when you start a program that uses X, the display appears on the client side. For example, running xterm in an SSH session opens a graphical xterm display on the client side.

Sometimes errors can arise when X authentication doesn't work properly. Listing 6.73 shows an error where permissions did not allow the user to change the .Xauthority file.

LISTING 6.73 Error Message with .Xauthority File

```
/usr/bin/xauth:   /home/guest/.Xauthority not writable,      ➡
    changes will be ignored
[user@domU]$ xterm
X11 connection rejected because of wrong authentication.
X connection to localhost:11.0 broken                        ➡
    (explicit kill or server shutdown).
```

All that is necessary to fix this problem is to change the permissions to allow the user to modify the file and then restart the SSH session by logging out of SSH and then logging back in again. Listing 6.74 shows the command we use to fix the permissions.

LISTING 6.74 Fixing Permissions on .Xauthority File

```
[user@domU]$ chmod +wr /home/guest/.Xauthority
[user@domU]$
```

If changing the permissions of the file does not work, try removing the .Xauthority file. When you restart your SSH session, the .Xauthority file will be created again, but with the proper permissions and contents this time.

VNC

Virtual Network Computing (VNC) uses a Remote Framebuffer Protocol to compress and then transfer entire frames of display to a remote computer. Mouse events and keyboard events based on a coordinate system are sent back to the VNC server to interact with the operating system.

The advantage to this approach is that the client machine only has to have a VNC client and a graphical environment to run the client. The graphical environment does not have to be X11. The network bandwidth used to transfer the frames of display will not be a significant burden if the VNC client is on the same machine as the server unless there is a huge number of VNC servers. Over a slow network connection there will be significant lag and Freenx, mentioned later in this chapter, might be a better choice.

A lot of VNC documentation is available online if you want to know more. One thing you might want to investigate is tunneling VNC through SSH. The benefit of doing this is security. It makes it much more difficult for attackers to hijack your session or find the password used to connect to the VNC server. You might also want to consider using TightVNC, which is a GPLed implementation of VNC. TightVNC has more features; for example, SSH is built into it.

Basic Usage

First you need to install a VNC server on the computer you want to remotely connect to and a VNC client from whichever machine(s) you want to access that machine. VNC is supported by most distribution repositories as well as Windows and is trivial to install both server and client.

To run the VNC server, use the `vncserver` command as in Listing 6.75.

LISTING 6.75 Starting a VNC Server

```
[user@domU]$ vncserver :4

New 'localhost.localdomain:4 (username)' desktop is      ➥
    localhost.localdomain:4

Starting applications specified in /home/username/.vnc/xstartup
Log file is /home/username/.vnc/localhost.localdomain:4.log
```

The `:4` just specifies the display number the desktop should be shown on. If the display number isn't specified, the first free number starting from 0 is picked.

To access the display we just started, we execute the `vncviewer` command with the hostname or IP address and the display number included. Listing 6.76 shows an example connection to a guest's running VNC server. Figure 6.1 shows a screenshot of what is displayed.

LISTING 6.76 Accessing a Desktop Remotely through a VNC Client

```
[user@client_side]$ vncviewer 192.168.1.4:4

VNC Viewer Free Edition 4.1.2 for X - built Jan 8 2007 10:03:41
Copyright (C) 2002-2005 RealVNC Ltd.
See http://www.realvnc.com for information on VNC.

Sun Jul 15 19:10:47 2007
 CConn:       connected to host 192.168.1.4 port 5904
 CConnection: Server supports RFB protocol version 3.8
 CConnection: Using RFB protocol version 3.8
```

```
Sun Jul 15 19:10:52 2007
TXImage: Using default colormap and visual, TrueColor, depth 24.
CConn: Using pixel format depth 6 (8bpp) rgb222
CConn: Using ZRLE encoding
CConn: Throughput 20036 kbit/s - changing to hextile encoding
CConn: Throughput 20036 kbit/s - changing to full colour
CConn: Using pixel format depth 24 (32bpp) little-endian rgb888
CConn: Using hextile encoding

Sun Jul 15 19:10:53 2007
CConn:       Throughput 19440 kbit/s - changing to raw encoding
CConn:       Using raw encoding
```

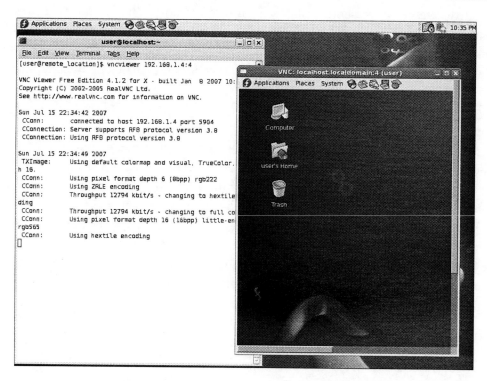

FIGURE 6.1 A VNC connection to a domain

Figure 6.1 shows an example of a VNC server being started and a client view. The window to the left of the screen is a guest being accessed through SSH and running a VNC server. The window to the right is the window created after the client makes a connection to the server.

Virtual Frame Buffer and Integrated VNC/SDL Libraries

A virtual machine's graphical console may be exported using either the VNC or Simple DirectMedia Layer (SDL) graphics libraries that are built into Xen's virtual frame buffer. These libraries operate externally to the guest, and the guest only has to run two device drivers to support the libraries. Use of Xen's integrated VNC or SDL libraries is especially useful when dealing with virtual machines that do not support Xen's virtual text console (xm console), including virtual machines running Microsoft Windows.

There are two Xen device drivers—virtual frame buffer and virtual keyboard—that allow for Domain0 to host graphical access to guests. The virtual frame buffer driver, vfb, is split into a frontend and backend. The frontend allows for a guest to render the frames of the graphical X session into memory. The second driver, vkbd, offers an interface for controlling the mouse and keyboard of the guest's X session. The backend driver allows Domain0 to access these memory locations where guests store frames. Because the memory location of the frame buffers is shared between Domain0 and DomU, there isn't much of a performance impact past running an X session in each guest. However, there is the benefit of running a single VNC or SDL server in Domain0 as opposed to a server in each guest.

A consequence of using a virtual frame buffer is that a virtual console is not established. This means that xm console will not give a terminal, but it will be necessary to use a program like SSH or obtain a terminal through the virtual frame buffer interface. To create a virtual console after a guest has been created, execute the line in Listing 6.77 which appends a line to the /etc/inittab file and evaluates the file again. Some Linux distributions might use a different init daemon that doesn't use the inittab file by default but most main distributions should at least support the file. This makes sure the virtual console is started and remains running even if the tty program is destroyed somehow.

LISTING 6.77 Creating a Virtual Console for Xen

```
[root@dom0]# echo "co:2345:respawn:/sbin/agetty xvc0 9600 vt100-nav" >>
/etc/inittab
[root@dom0]# telinit q
[root@dom0]#
```

If you would like to be able to login to the guest as root, you will also have to add xvc0 to the security file like in Listing 6.78.

LISTING 6.78 Enabling Root Login on a Terminal

```
[root@dom0]# echo "xvc0" >> /etc/securetty
[root@dom0]#
```

Prior to use of its internal VNC library, Xen must be configured to listen on an interface for VNC connections. This configuration option is located in the /etc/xen/xend-config.sxp file, as shown in Listing 6.79.

LISTING 6.79 VNC Related Line in the Xen Daemon Configuration File

```
#(vnc-listen '127.0.0.1')
```

Uncomment, by removing the # symbol, this line to enable listening by the integrated VNC server for local connections only. If you want to allow connections across a different interface, modify the IP address between the single quotes to match the proper interface, or set this address to 0.0.0.0 to listen for VNC connections across all interfaces.

To enable VNC graphics export on a particular guest, edit the vnc=0 line in the guest's configuration file in the /etc/xen directory so that it reads vnc=1, or add the line if it does not exist, as shown in Listing 6.80.

LISTING 6.80 Enabling Xen-Enabled VNC Support through Guest Configuration Files

```
vnc=1
```

You may optionally specify an address to listen for VNC connections if you want it to be different than what is set in /etc/xen/xend-config.sxp, which is done by default. This is done by uncommenting the vnclisten line and setting vnclisten=" 10.0.0.1" (substituting the address for the interface you want to bind VNC with), as shown in Listing 6.81.

LISTING 6.81 Changing the Address a VNC Server Runs on through Guest Configuration Files

```
vnclisten="10.0.0.1"
```

Other optional guest VNC settings include specifying a VNC display to use, enabling the finding of an unused port for the VNC server, and enabling the automatic spawning of vncviewer on the local system for the domain's console. These may be used by uncommenting or modifying the vncdisplay, vncunused, and vncconsole, as shown in Listing 6.82.

LISTING 6.82 Other VNC-Related Variables in Guest Configuration Files

```
#vncdisplay=1  # Defaults to the domain's ID
#vncunused=1  # Find an unused port for the VNC server; default=1
#vncconsole=0  # spawn vncviewer for the domain's
               # console; default=0
```

Xen's SDL graphics library is another way to make a guest's graphical console accessible. To enable SDL, uncomment and set the `sdl` entry to 1 in the virtual machine's configuration file contained in the `/etc/xen/` directory, as shown in Listing 6.83.

LISTING 6.83 Enabling SDL Graphics Library from a Guest Configuration File

```
sdl=1
```

When SDL is used, an X window is created containing the guest's frame buffer as soon as the guest is created. This window is either sent to the active X server on the local system, or piped through SSH to appear on the administrator's system if the administrator is remotely invoking xm create through his or her SSH connection to the Xen system and with SSH X Forwarding enabled (the SSH –X option).

Note that with SDL, as soon as the X window is closed, the virtual machine is immediately killed. This caveat—along with SDL's dependence on an active X server—might make SDL better-suited for temporary use than use on always-up virtual machines, such as for guest installation or brief development and testing work. For instance, SDL can be useful during the installation of Windows guests, prior to configuring remote access services within the Windows. It can then be disabled after a remote access service has been configured; however, SDL may need to be re-enabled should problems with booting the guest occur prior to the starting of services installed on the guest; or VNC should be considered instead.

Freenx

Freenx is similar to VNC but optimized enough to use over low bandwidth networks. Frames of the display are still sent to the remote client. The efficiency is achieved by using heavily optimized compression techniques coupled with caching so that the client remembers portions of the screen, like menus and the desktop that have been displayed. Freenx uses SSH by default to transfer its information. So there is no need to add extra complexity to configure Freenx traffic to be secure unlike VNC. Some extra perks also come with Freenx, such as the capability to suspend and resume sessions so that applications are remembered each time you log in. NoMachine NX is available for both Linux and Windows but Freenx is only available for Linux.

Freenx may not be in your distribution's repository. In that case, you will probably find packages for your distribution on the Freenx (`http://freenx.berlios.de`) download page. After installing, you may have to configure nx for the first time and afterward start the server. Listing 6.84 shows the commands to do this. And that is it; you are now ready to use Freenx.

LISTING 6.84 Configuring and Starting the Freenx Server

```
[root@domU]# nxsetup --install --setup-nomachine-key --clean
[root@domU]# nxserver -start
[root@domU]#
```

To connect to the server, you run the `nxclient` application. This graphical application leads you through the process of identifying where your nx server is running, IP address and such, as well as some simple configuration options such as which window manager you want to use for your Freenx session (GNOME, KDE, and so on). The login credentials are the same as if you are starting an SSH session with the guest. The desktop to the guest that appears looks just like the VNC window.

Remote Desktop

Remote Desktop, also known as Microsoft Terminal Services, is available on virtual machines running certain releases of Microsoft Windows operating systems (including Windows 2000, Windows XP, Windows Vista, and Windows Server Family products). Remote Desktop makes it possible to connect as a Windows user to the Windows installation running on the guest and visually interacts with GUI applications and the desktop.

Remote Desktop may be enabled in Windows XP by going to the Control Panel's System Properties page, and under the Remote tab, checking the allow users to connect remotely to this computer box, as shown in Figure 6.2. Note that, by default, all users who are members of the Administrators group and any that you specify under Select Remote Users, are given remote access after Remote Desktop is enabled. Also note that accounts without passwords set are by default denied remote access to avoid inadvertently risking system security.

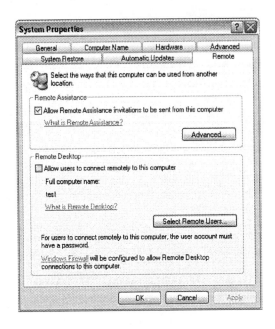

FIGURE 6.2 Remote tab in System Properties where Remote Desktop can be enabled

Remote Desktop provides the capability to remotely access the Windows installation after the boot process has completed, but does not provide remote display of the boot process, the Windows boot options menu that may come up during the boot process when errors are encountered or when manually requested by appropriate keystroke, or the Windows Setup program during the installation process. It is also not useful prior to enabling Remote Desktop in the guest. To view the guest graphically during these stages, either the internal VNC or SDL graphics libraries must be used.

A guest with the Remote Desktop service enabled can be accessed from a Windows system via the Remote Desktop Connection client, Terminal Services Client, or from a Linux/Unix system via your desktop.

Table 6.2 serves as a summary and reference of the pros and cons among different solutions for a graphical interface to guests that have been discussed in this chapter. Be aware that this section is not an exhaustive coverage of all the technologies one could use.

TABLE 6.2 Pros and Cons of Graphical Solutions

Method	Type of Display	Pros	Cons
X forwarding	Single application displayed through SSH	Avoids overhead of transferring entire window	Can't access entire windowing system
			Can't access graphical applications already running
VNC	Full display forwarded	Suggested method with HVM	Inefficient over low bandwidth or heavy traffic networks
		Simple to install and set up	
		Integrated into Xen	
Freenx	Full display forwarded	Efficient over low bandwidth or heavy traffic networks	More complicated to install, though still not very complicated
rdesktop	Full display forwarded	Integrated into some versions of Microsoft Windows	Inefficient over low bandwidth or heavy traffic networks
			Only for connecting to Microsoft Windows guests.
PCI Device Assignment	Full display through hardware support	Offers the best performance for a single guest	Requires a graphics card for every guest running graphical applications
			Can be difficult to set up
			Considered insecure

Summary

This chapter covered the basics of the xm command. You should now be familiar with how to create and run virtual guests, monitor resource utilization, reboot and shut down guests like a normal computer, pause to save the state of a guest, destroy guests unsafely but quickly, and gain console or graphical access to a guest through a number of methods. For a summary of the xm subcommands, see Appendix B.

For the remainder of the book, we assume that you're familiar with these commands because they are the main utilities for interacting and administering guest operating systems.

References and Further Reading

Official Freenx site.
  `http://freenx.berlios.de/info.php`.

Official rdesktop site.
  `www.rdesktop.org/`.

Official VNC site.
  `www.realvnc.com/vnc/index.html`.

X Forwarding over SSH Tutorial.
  `www.vanemery.com/Linux/XoverSSH/X-over-SSH2.html`.

Xen 2.0 and 3.0 User's Manual. University of Cambridge.
  `www.cl.cam.ac.uk/research/srg/netos/xen/documentation.html`.

Chapter 7

Populating Guest Images

In the preceding chapters, we discussed how to use prebuilt guest images and how to manage guests based on existing images. In this chapter, we describe how to create new customized guest images. We first show how to install a Hardware Virtual Machine (HVM) guest such as Windows XP using standard install CD materials. We then describe how to populate paravirtualized guests using several popular Linux distributions. Most methods of populating paravirtualized guests are specific to the operating system or distribution you are installing. We discuss YaST Virtual Machine Management for OpenSUSE, virt-manager for CentOS/ Fedora, debootstrap for Debian/Ubuntu, quickpkg and domi scripts for Gentoo, and XenServer client for Xen Express. Finally, we explain the steps in converting an existing operating system installation into a Xen guest.

Hardware Virtual Machine (HVM) Guest Population

Chapter 1, "Xen—Background and Virtualization Basics," explained the differences between paravirtual (PV) guests and Hardware Virtual Machine (HVM) guests. HVM guests require the hardware extensions provided by Intel VT-x or AMD-V. Xen's HVM layer is a common interface to both Intel's VT and AMD's secure virtual machine (SVM) add-ons to the x86 architecture. This enables HVM guests to be exactly the same as if they are running on bare hardware. PV guests, on the other hand, do not require the hardware extensions, but do require a modified kernel that is aware it is running in a virtual machine rather than directly on the hardware. Because PV guests require modifications to the kernel, creating a PV guest requires access to the operating system source code. As a result, publicly available PV guests are built around open source operating systems. HVM guests can be built around any operating system that runs natively on x86 hardware including open source operating systems such as Linux or Solaris and closed source operating systems such as Windows.

The population of an HVM guest is as simple as installing an operating system from a disc. In this section we present two methods of populating HVM guests—population by manual means and population using the `virt-install` command available on Fedora/RHEL systems. Similarly, we could have used other distributions such as OpenSUSE, Xen Express, and Debian. Because the creating of an HVM guest is similar to a standard operating system install, we cover an example of populating an HVM guest first. Then, later in this chapter, we show the population of a variety of PV guests from within several popular distributions that have Xen support.

Populating a Guest Image from a Disc or Disc Image (Windows XP Example)

First we explore how to manually populate an HVM guest from an installation CD-ROM or disc image. For this example, we use a Windows XP installation disc image. Equivalently, we could have used other operating system installation disc images, such as a Linux or Solaris. To create the image we use the `dd` command as shown in Listing 7.1. It is common for open source operating systems to distribute downloadable ISO image files of their install CDs that could be used from the hard drive.

LISTING 7.1 Using dd to Create an Image of the Windows XP CD

```
[user@linux]# dd if=/dev/cdrom of=winxp.iso
1186640+0 records in
1186640+0 records out
607559680 bytes (608 MB) copied, 125.679 seconds, 4.8 MB/s
[user@linux]#
```

To specifically create an HVM guest, we set the kernel, builder, and device_ model lines in the DomU configuration file as shown in Listing 7.2. For HVM guests we use the path to the hvmloader binary where we would specify a kernel image for a PV guest. Additionally, we set the builder function to be hvm, and we set the device model to the location of the qemu-dm binary. We discuss the device model in more detail in Chapter 9, "Device Virtualization and Management." These settings prepare the HVM environment for our guest to operate.

> **NOTE**
>
> The location of the hvmloader and qemu-dm binaries may be different based on your distribution. In Ubuntu 7.10, for example, the '/usr/' + arch_lib + 'xen/bin/qemu' path is replaced by '/usr'/ + arch_lib + 'xen-ioemu/bin/qemu/'.

LISTING 7.2 The kernel, builder, and device_model HVM Guest Configuration Lines

```
# hvmloader in place of a kernel image
kernel = "/usr/lib/xen/boot/hvmloader"
# guest domain build function (for HVM guests we use 'hvm')
builder='hvm'
# path to the device model binary
device_model = '/usr/' + arch_libdir + '/xen/bin/qemu-dm'
```

The next step is to assign virtual disks for our HVM guest. We first demonstrate installation from an optical disc (CD-ROM or DVD) image file (commonly referred to as an ISO), with an LVM logical volume to be used as the virtual hard disk. Other partition types, such as normal partitions and image files, could be used instead of an LVM logical volume, as well as other storage methods, which are discussed in Chapter 8, "Storing Guest Images." In Listing 7.3 we demonstrate the designation of the installation image as a virtual `hdc:cdrom`. Recall from Chapter 5, "Using Prebuilt Guest Images," the disk parameter is a Python array, which consists of a comma-separated list of three-tuples. Each three-tuple consists of

- A block device path, either physical or virtual device
- Designations, the device as it is attached to the DomU
- Permissions, read or write denoted `r` or `w`, respectively

LISTING 7.3 An Example of an HVM Guest Disk Configuration Line Using a Disc Image

```
disk = ['phy:/dev/XenGuests/hvm1,hda,w','tap:aio:/root/winxp.iso, ➡
    hdc:cdrom,r']
# first device is LVM partition to use as hard disk,
# second device is an image of an installation CD-ROM
```

Using a physical CD-ROM or DVD-ROM drive instead of an image file is accomplished by setting the `hdc:cdrom` device to a physical drive instead of a file. Listing 7.4 shows a similar disk configuration that uses `/dev/cdrom` instead of a disc image file.

LISTING 7.4 An Example of an HVM Guest Disk Configuration Line Using a Physical CD-ROM Drive

```
disk = ['phy:/dev/XenGuests/hvm1,hda,w','phy:/dev/cdrom, ➡
    hdc:cdrom,r']
# first device is LVM partition to use as hard disk,
# second device is a physical CD-ROM drive
```

We simply changed the second tuple by replacing the ISO file with a real CD-ROM device. In our system, `/dev/cdrom` was the physical CD-ROM.

Next, we select a graphics library to use for the HVM guest's display. Xen supports an SDL library and a VNC library. When using the SDL library, executing `xm create` results in a display window appearing within your X server session on Domain0 (assuming you have an active session). The VNC library is convenient when a network-viewable display is needed on an HVM guest (that is, you can then view the output from *any* network connected machine, not just Domain0). Setting `vncconsole` to enabled results in the automatic spawning of `vncviewer` (on Domain0 so you can automatically see the VNC output on the local machine). Listing 7.5 illustrates the enabling of the SDL library for graphics, while disabling the VNC library. The listing also shows many of the other common display-specific options.

LISTING 7.5 HVM Guest Display Configuration

```
sdl=1     # SDL library support for graphics (default=0 disabled)
vnc=0     # VNC library support for graphics (default=0 disabled)

# address for VNC server to listen on
#vnclisten="10.0.0.20"
# default is to use the global 'vnclisten' setting
# global vnclisten is set in /etc/xen/xend-config.sxp

# set the VNC display number (default=domid)
#vncdisplay=1
# find an unused port for the VNC server (default=1 enabled)
#vncunused=1
# spawn vncviewer for domain's console (default=0 disabled)
#vncconsole=0

# no graphics, only serial (do not enable for Windows guests)
#nographic=0

# stdvga (cirrus logic model, default=0 disabled)
# stdvga=0

# start in full screen (default=0 no)
#full-screen=1
```

Finally, population of the guest by an operating system is performed by invoking xm
create on the guest and allowing it to boot from an installation disc or disc image.
Ensuring that the installation disc or disc image is in its proper place, create the guest
to boot the installation. Listing 7.6 and Figure 7.1 illustrate the creation of an HVM
guest domain and the booting of an installer.

LISTING 7.6 Booting an HVM Guest Manually with xm create

```
[root@dom0]# xm create hvmexample1
Using config file "/etc/xen/hvmexample1".
Started domain hvmexample1
[root@dom0]#
```

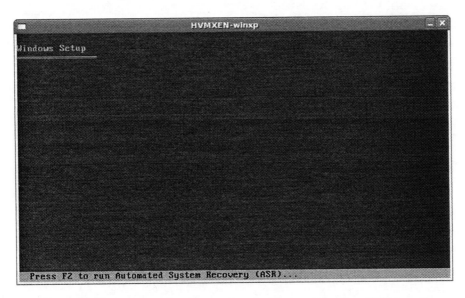

FIGURE 7.1 The Windows XP setup screen loads within the VNC console of our HVM DomU guest.

Listing 7.7 contains a sample guest configuration file for an HVM guest to be populated from a disc image. Listing 7.8 contains a sample configuration for an HVM guest to be built from a physical disc. Most of the configuration file in Listing 7.8 is the same as the ISO Image Configuration in Listing 7.7 (thus this part is omitted), with the exception of the disk parameter, in which we use a physical device (phy:) instead of a disk image file (tap:aio).

LISTING 7.7 A Sample HVM Guest Configuration File (Population from Installation ISO Disc Image)

```
#  -*- mode: python; -*-

arch = os.uname()[4]
if re.search('64', arch):
    arch_libdir = 'lib64'
else:
    arch_libdir = 'lib'


#-----------------------------------------------------------------
# hvmloader in place of a kernel image

kernel = "/usr/lib/xen/boot/hvmloader"

# guest domain build function (for HVM guests we use 'hvm')
builder='hvm'
```

```
device_model = '/usr/' + arch_libdir + '/xen/bin/qemu-dm'

# memory allocation at boot in MB
memory = 128

# shadow pagetable memory,
#should be at least 2KB per MB of memory plus a few MB per vcpu
shadow_memory = 8

name = "hvmexample1"  # name for the domain

# number of CPUs guest has available (default=1)
vcpus=1

# HVM guest PAE support (default=0 disabled)
#pae=0

# HVM guest ACPI support (default=0 disabled)
#acpi=0

# HVM guest APIC support (default=0 disabled)
#apic=0

#----------------------------------------------------------------

# 1 NIC, auto-assigned MAC address
vif = [ 'type=ioemu, bridge=xenbr0' ]

# first device is LVM partition to use as hard disk,
# second device is an image of an installation CD-ROM
disk = ['phy:/dev/XenGuests/hvm1,hda,w', ➥
    'tap:aio:/root/winxp.iso,hdc:cdrom,r']

# boot order (a=floppy, c=hard disk, d=CD-ROM; default=cda)
boot="cda"

# function to execute when guest wishes to power off
#on_poweroff = 'destroy'

# function to execute when guest wishes to reboot
#on_reboot   = 'restart'

# function to execute if guest crashes
#on_crash   = 'restart'
```

```
#----------------------------------------------------------------
# SDL library support for graphics (default=0 disabled)
sdl=1

# VNC library support for graphics (default=0 disabled)
vnc=0

#----------------------VNC----------------------------------------
# address for VNC server to listen on,
# (default is to use the 'vnc-listen'
# setting in /etc/xen/xend-config.sxp)
#vnclisten="10.0.0.20"

# set the VNC display number (default=domid)
#vncdisplay=1

# find an unused port for the VNC server (default=1 enabled)
#vncunused=1

# spawn vncviewer for domain's console (default=0 disabled)
#vncconsole=0

#----------------------VGA----------------------------------------
# no graphics, only serial (do not enable for Windows guests)
#nographic=0

# stdvga (cirrus logic model, default=0 disabled)
stdvga=0

# start in full screen (default=0 no)
#full-screen=1

#----------------------USB----------------------------------------
# USB support
#(devices may be specified through the monitor window)
#usb=1

# normal/relative mouse
#usbdevice='mouse'
```

```
# tablet/absolute mouse
#usbdevice='tablet'


#----------------------MISC------------------------------------
# serial port re-direct to pty device,
# allows xm console or minicom to connect
#serial='pty'


# sound card support (sb16, es1370, all; default none)
#soundhw='sb16'


# set real time clock to local time (default=0 UTC)
localtime=1
```

LISTING 7.8 A Sample HVM Guest Configuration File (Populated from a Physical CD-ROM Drive)

```
[The start of the file is omitted, it is the same as Listing 7.7]

disk = ['phy:/dev/XenGuests/hvm2,hda,w', ➡
     'phy:/dev/cdrom,hdc:cdrom,r']
  # first device is LVM partition to use as hard disk,
  # second device is a physical CD-ROM drive

[The end of the file is omitted, it is the same as Listing 7.7]
```

Automated Population with virt-install

On Fedora/RHEL systems, HVM guests may be easily populated using the included virt-install utility. virt-install asks a series of questions and automatically prepares the guest configuration file according to user input. Listing 7.9 explores how to invoke and use the virt-install utility.

LISTING 7.9 Populating an HVM Guest Using virt-install

```
[root@dom0]# virt-install
Would you like a fully virtualized guest (yes or no)? ➡
This will allow you to run unmodified operating systems. yes
 What is the name of your virtual machine? hvmexample3
 How much RAM should be allocated (in megabytes)? 128
 What would you like to use as the disk (path)? hvmexample3.img
```

```
How large would you like the disk to be (in gigabytes)? 5
Would you like to enable graphics support? (yes or no) yes
What would you like to use for the virtual CD image? ➡
    /root/winxp.iso
Starting install...
```

Assuming you invoke `virt-install` on a system where you have an active X session, `vncviewer` automatically spawns and connects to the display of the HVM guest being created. The installation program included in the virtual disc image is visible in the `vncviewer` window, as shown previously in Figure 7.1. At this point, completing the regular installation process completes the population of the HVM guest.

Recall that if at any time you want to close your VNC session with the guest, you may do so. Reconnecting through VNC is as simple as opening a new console on Domain0 and typing `vncviewer <ipaddress>`, where IP address is the IP of your virtual guest.

Figure 7.2 shows the initial loading of our HVM guest. Figure 7.3 shows the loading of Windows XP, and Figure 7.4 shows Windows XP in use as a guest.

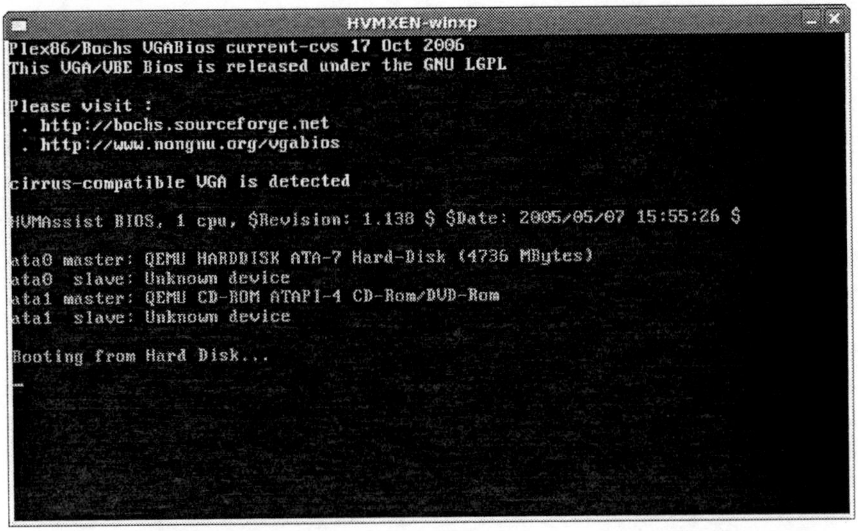

FIGURE 7.2 The HVM BIOS loads within the VNC console of our HVM DomU guest.

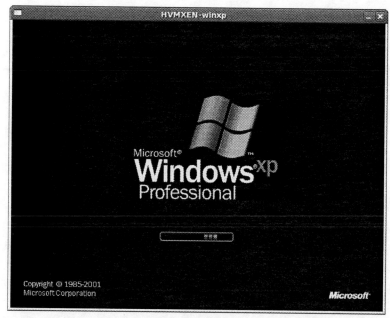

FIGURE 7.3 The Windows XP boot screen loads within the VNC console of our HVM DomU guest.

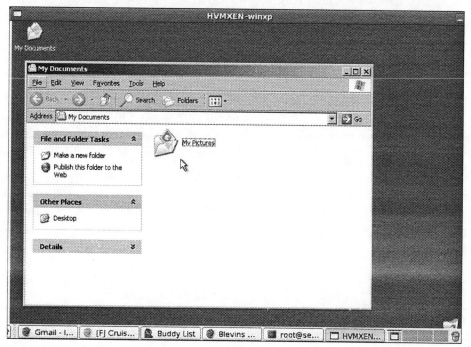

FIGURE 7.4 Windows XP is running as a Xen HVM guest.

HVM population is in many ways the same mechanism used to install an operating system from vendor-supplied media. The variation is that you boot the physical media or ISO into a Xen domU context rather than on the raw hardware, as is done in stand-alone installations. This is accomplished by giving Xen a path to the physical media or ISO, using a special HVM boot loader, and performing the subsequent normal installation. A special VNC-like connection is given instead of a directly attached monitor. Instead of directly writing to the hard disk, as done in a normal installation, the files are written to the virtual disk allocated to the DomU.

Paravirtualized (PV) Guest Population

HVM guests can be easier to use than PV guests while providing support for unmodified guest operating systems. However, PV is the only choice on hardware without HVM support, and there are several other important advantages of PV guests. One of the main advantages to PV is the speed, which was a key to Xen's early success.

Recall that using a PV guest means operating system modifications are necessary to make the guest operating system aware that it is running on top of a hypervisor and virtualized hardware. Of course, PV Windows guests would also be possible with source code. In fact, the initial Xen paper described PV Windows guests created in conjunction with Microsoft Research labs in Cambridge. However, these guests were never generally released.

In general, even for open source operating systems, PV guest support typically lags behind the newest releases due to the time it takes to make modifications. As of Linux version 2.6.23, Xen guest support is available directly in the Linux kernel. This makes the usage of Xen with Linux guests much more manageable (that is, Linux guests with that kernel version or higher would be able to run directly on Linux). PV Windows drivers have also been developed by Novell and can be found at `www.novell.com/products/vmdriverpack/`. These Windows PV drivers have also been integrated into the open source version of Xen. The first release is described on the xen-devel mailing list, found at `http://lists.xensource.com/archives/html/xen-devel/2007-10/msg01035.html`.

We look at a number of tools to support custom installation of PV guests. In general, the tools are all distribution specific. We first look at the YaST Virtual Manager in OpenSUSE Linux, which is a graphical tool used to install an OpenSUSE guest or potentially other guest OSes. We then look at virt-manager on Fedora Linux, which lets you do a Fedora or RHEL install by specifying a mirror containing the install files and packages. Next, we look at debootstrap, which is a command line tool that can be used to bootstrap a Debian/Ubuntu minimal base install into a directory. We also look at quickpkg and domi on Gentoo Linux. quickpkg is the package management system in Gentoo that lets you install into a directory. The domi scripts let you install various guest types. Finally, we look at Xen Express and the tools that it provides to create guests.

> **NOTE**
> This is not intended to be a comprehensive set of Xen guest installation tools. Existing tools are being actively developed, and new tools are being created. Refer to the "References and Further Reading," section at the end of this chapter, as well as the book's Web site for more information.

The examples we cover in this chapter are based on Linux, but Linux is not the only PV guest available. Recent development versions of OpenSolaris can be used as a Domain0 and can run a variety of PV guests. Stable releases of OpenSolaris with Xen support won't be far behind. Other open source operating systems, such as NetBSD, FreeBSD, OpenBSD, and Plan 9, are also known to work as PV guests. Some of these also have Domain0 implementations.

OpenSUSE: YaST Virtual Machine Management

If you installed the Xen tools into OpenSUSE as described in Chapter 4, "Hardware Requirements and Installation of Xen Domain0," you can use the YaST Virtual Machine Management (VMM) module to create and manage Xen DomU guests. To open the VMM module, launch the YaST Control Center, click on System, and select

Virtual Machine Management (Xen). Figure 7.5 shows what the YaST Control Center screen looks like. After clicking on Virtual Machine Management (Xen), a window opens that allows you to manage virtual machines (see Figure 7.6). Finally, after clicking the Add button, a window opens, shown in Figure 7.7, that allows you to create a virtual machine.

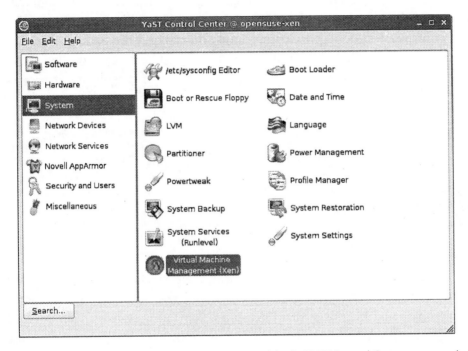

FIGURE 7.5 Clicking on Virtual Machine Management (Xen) in the YaST Control Center opens a window that allows you to manage virtual machines.

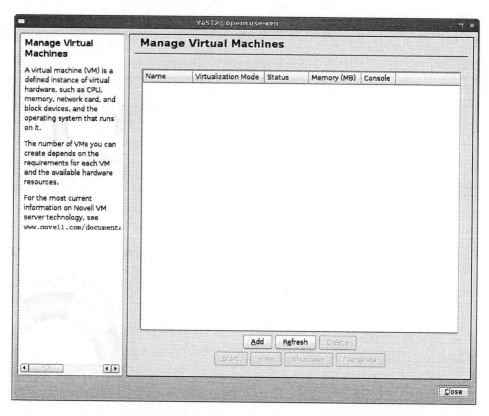

FIGURE 7.6 Clicking the Add button in the Manage Virtual Machines window brings up the Create a Virtual Machine window.

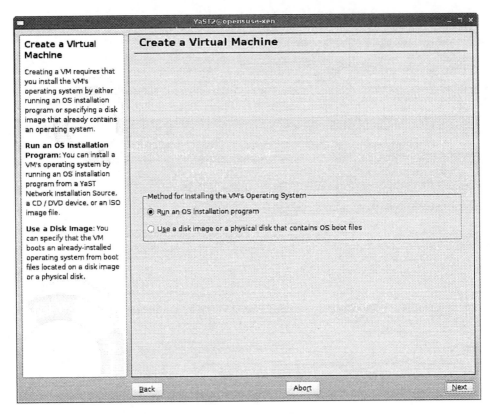

FIGURE 7.7 The Create a Virtual Machine window allows you to choose different methods to install an operating system for your DomU.

The Create a Virtual Machine window offers two choices: You can either run an operating system installation program or use an existing installation. We choose to run the installation program. Select the radio button and click Next button. You get the standard YaST installation process. Follow the installation steps.

Figure 7.8 shows the installation settings window. There are a three installation methods to choose from:

- **Install from CD or ISO Image**—Insert the CD or use an ISO image and follow the install steps.

- **Installing from an Installation Source**—You need to specify the HTTP or FTP source for the installation.

- **Use an Existing Disk or Partition Image**—Click Add and locate the disk image.

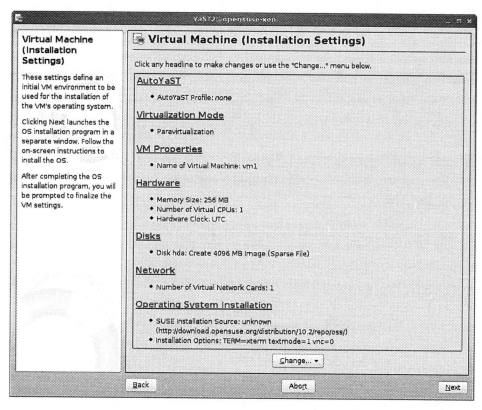

FIGURE 7.8 The Virtual Machine (Installation Settings) window lets you install an operating system just as you would normally install OpenSUSE.

For all installation types, be sure to have at least 512MB of RAM, or configure your guest to have sufficient swap. The YaST installer won't continue without the proper amount of RAM or without being able to activate a swap partition.

NOTE
The details of an OpenSUSE installation are beyond the scope of this book. See the manual at http://en.opensuse.org/INSTALL_Local for documentation on the installation.

CentOS/Fedora: virt-manager

If you installed the Xen tools described in Chapter 4, you can open a tool called Virtual Machine Manager. Virtual Machine Manager is accessible by going to the

Applications menu and clicking on System Tools and then Virtual Machine Manager. (Alternatively, you can run `virt-manager` from the command line.) This opens a window that gives you the option to create a new virtual machine by clicking New. When creating a new virtual machine, Virtual Machine Manager starts a wizard that eases the installation of a DomU guest image. Let's take a closer look at this process.

The first dialog window that you are presented with is named Open Connection. Virtual guests can be connected to the local Domain0, a remote Domain0, or even another virtualization technology. Domain0 facilitates the virtual guest's connection to the Xen hypervisor. For this example, we simply connect to the local Domain0, which is called Local Xen Host as you can see from Figure 7.9.

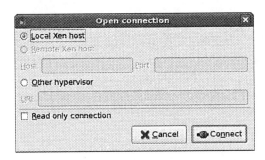

FIGURE 7.9 The Open Connection dialog allows you to connect to local or remote Xen hosts.

After clicking Connect, assuming that Domain0 and xend are running, you see the Virtual Machine Manager main window, shown in Figure 7.10.

Chapter 14, "An Overview of Xen Enterprise Management Tools," touches more on the administration capabilities of Virtual Machine Manager (virt-manager). For this example we focus on using Virtual Machine Manager to create a new DomU guest. To create a new guest, click the New button.

> **NOTE**
> In Fedora 8, the placement of the button to create a new guest has moved to within the main inner frame of Virtual Machine Manager and no longer has a label of "New." Because Fedora is typically used directly as basis for CentOS, this will likely affect the interface for future versions of CentOS as well.

This brings up the Create a New Virtual System window, shown in Figure 7.11, which simply explains the process, from naming your system to setting up install locations and allocating resources to the guest.

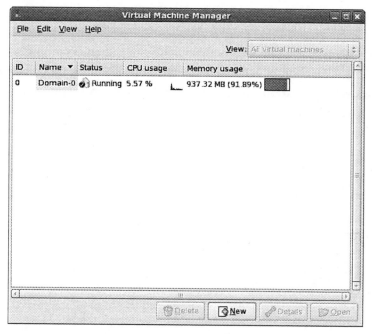

FIGURE 7.10 When first connecting to the local Xen host, the Virtual Machine Manager main window appears.

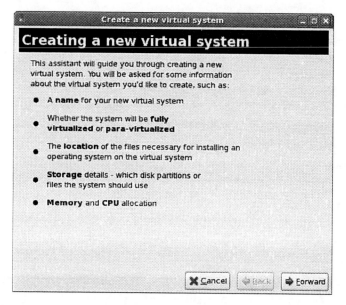

FIGURE 7.11 When creating a DomU, the Create a New Virtual System window appears.

At this window, click the Forward button to bring up a window that allows you to enter a name for your virtual system. We recommend using something descriptive enough to tell the operating system type and function of the virtual machine. Examples of good virtual machine names might be fedora_webserver and windows_gaming, whereas names such as system1 or guest2 are not likely to be descriptive enough to tell what the system is used for without logging in to the guest. Figure 7.12 shows this naming window. After you have chosen a name for your DomU guest, click Forward.

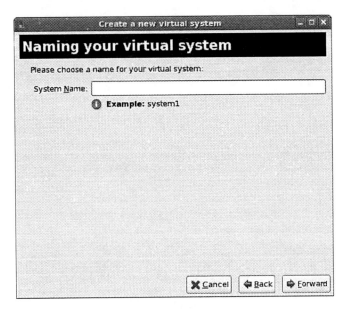

FIGURE 7.12 The Naming Your Virtual System Window allows you to enter a name for your DomU.

Next, you are presented with a window that allows you to enter the installation media. For a paravirtualized system you have two options. The first option is to enter an install media URL, or the path to an online repository containing the installation files. A URL that contains install media for Fedora is `http://download.fedora.redhat.com/pub/fedora/linux/core/6/i386/os`. This is specific to Fedora 6 with i386 architecture. You could browse to a different version of Fedora or a different architecture, such as x86_64. You should use a mirror that is close to you. You can find a list of mirrors for Fedora at `http://mirrors.fedoraproject.org/publiclist` and a list of mirrors for CentOS at `www.centos.org/modules/tinycontent/index.php?id=13`. The Virtual Machine Manager application currently only supports Install Media URLs for Red Hat based distributions, such as Fedora and CentOS, but it is likely to support more by the time you read this.

Alternatively, you can enter the location of a Kickstart file. Kickstart is an automated installation tool designed to allow rapid deployment of systems by reading from the Kickstart configuration file, which provides answers to questions such as which packages to install and other configuration information, such as hostname and user information. For our example, we install a Fedora Core 6 DomU guest using the Install Media URL of `http://download.fedora.redhat.com/pub/fedora/linux/core/6/i386/os`, and we are using a CentOS 5 Domain0 base. You could also choose to use Domain0 systems, such as Fedora, that support virt-manager. After entering your desired install media, click the Forward button. You are now presented with a window, shown in Figure 7.13, that allows you to assign storage space to your DomU guest.

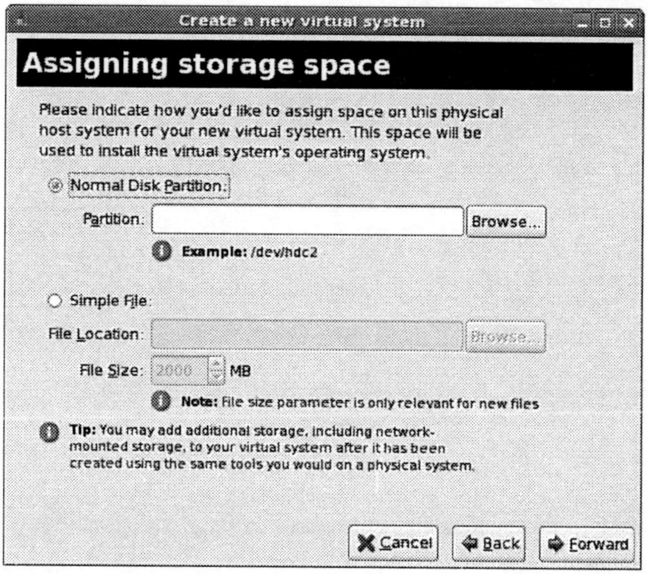

FIGURE 7.13 The Assigning Storage Space window allows you to add a disk to your DomU.

You can choose from a Normal (physical) Disk Partition or a Simple File (it is expected that support for different types of network-based storage could become available in the near future depending on the level of user demand). If you choose a Normal Disk Partition, make sure that it is a partition that either is empty or has content that is disposable, as the installer will erase the data on that partition. Refer to Chapter 5, "Using Prebuilt Guest Images," on using GParted to resize existing partitions in order to make a new blank partition. If you choose Simple File, you should give the name of a file that either does not need to exist or can be created (or used) as your DomU disk. (You should put this file in /xen/images, /var/lib/xen/images, or similar directory, so that you will be able to find it later if you need to work with it.) The more recent versions of virt-manager, such as the ones shipped with Fedora 7 and later, support the ability to create sparse or preallocated images. If you are just making a typical install, we recommend allocating at least 4GB of space for your DomU guest. After you have selected your disk (real or virtual) option and its size (and sparse or preallocated if available), click Forward.

Next, you are presented with a window, shown in Figure 7.14, that allows you to allocate memory and CPU to your guest.

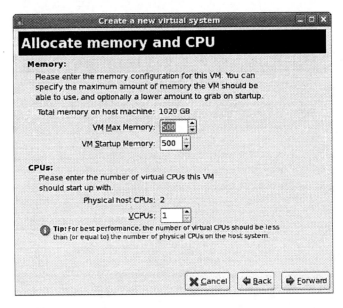

FIGURE 7.14   The Allocate Memory and CPU window lets you specify memory and CPU options for the DomU.

The Fedora and CentOS installation processes usually require at least 256MB of RAM, and sometimes even more, but we recommend that you allocate 512MB or more for the installation process. If you are not able to allocate the recommended amount of RAM, consider creating and activating a swap partition for your guest during the Fedora/CentOS installation process. You can adjust this memory value later for normal usage. VM Max Memory is an upper bound on how much memory the DomU can be allocated, and VM Startup Memory is the requested amount of memory when starting a guest. The tip in Figure 7.14 recommends the number of virtual CPUs be less than (or equal to) the number of physical CPUs on the system. See Chapter 12, "Managing Guest Resources," to learn more about why this is important. After you have entered the memory and CPU values for your DomU, click the Forward button.

Next, you are presented with a summary window, shown in Figure 7.15, that allows you to begin the installation when you click the Finish button.

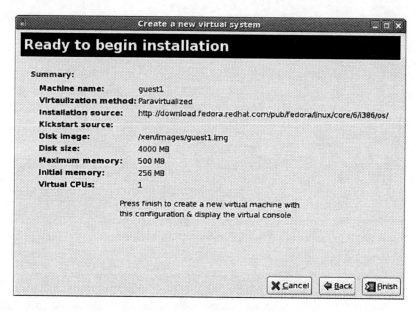

FIGURE 7.15 Finally, the Ready to Begin Installation window shows a summary of the DomU settings.

After you click Finish, a Creating Virtual Machine dialog is presented, as shown in Figure 7.16. This step may take longer than the rest of the steps to load depending on your network connection to the mirror that you are installing from.

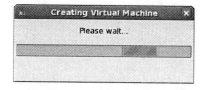

FIGURE 7.16 A progress bar appears after you click Finish on the Ready to Begin Installation window.

After the install images have been downloaded, the system boots in a Virtual Machine Console, shown in Figure 7.17.

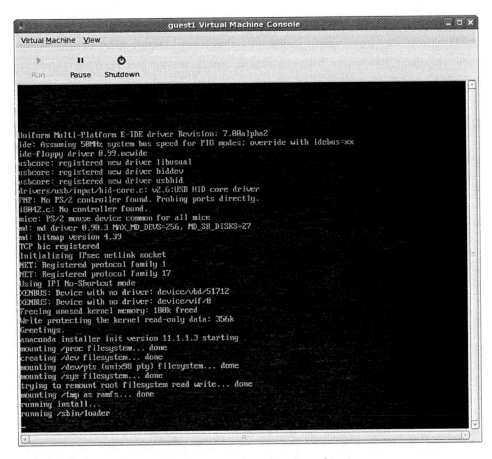

FIGURE 7.17 After the DomU is created, the Virtual Machine Console appears.

At this point, the operating system installation begins, and you can follow the installation procedure as usual. Figure 7.18 shows the beginning screen of the installation process, with the rest of the installation steps omitted.

NOTE

The details of a Fedora installation are beyond the scope of this book. See the manual at www.redhat.com/docs/manuals/enterprise/ for documentation on the installation.

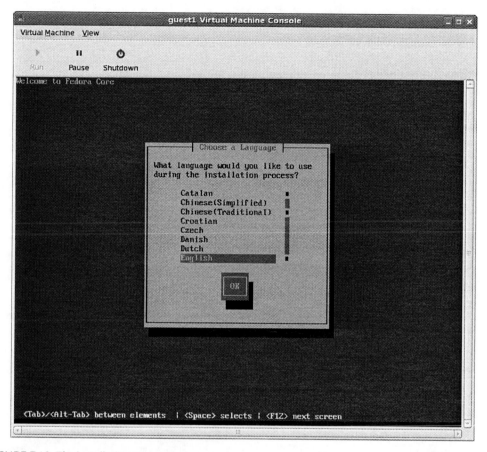

FIGURE 7.18 The installation screen loads next.

Most installations complete without any problems, but sometimes, during a reboot, the Virtual Machine Console will not load. There are two workarounds for this problem. If the DomU guest is running as shown in Figure 7.19, you can console into the guest by double-clicking on the corresponding entry in the list. If it is not running, you can boot it up by running the `xm create` command with the `-c` option and the name of the guest. Listing 7.10 shows this command. You then can console into the guest via Virtual Machine Manager, as described previously, by clicking on the entry in the list, shown in Figure 7.19.

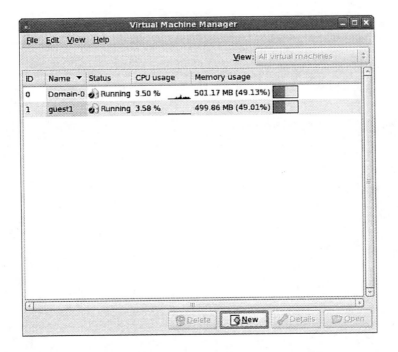

FIGURE 7.19 To get a console into guest1, simply double-click on guest1 in the list.

LISTING 7.10 The xm create Command to Start the Guest Manually

```
[root@dom0]#xm create -c guest1
Using config file "/etc/xen/guest1"
Going to boot Fedora Core (2.6.18-1.2798.fcxen.img)
Started domain guest1
rtc: IRQ 8 is not free
i80042.c: No controller found.
```

Debian/Ubuntu: debootstrap

On Debian-based systems, you can install (if it is not already installed) the package debootstrap with the command apt-get install debootstrap. Once installed, you can run the debootstrap command, which allows you to install basic Debian-based systems into a directory.

The directory where you want the installation should correspond to the root file system of the guest. For this example, we create a partition image to be the root file system, and leave the details of this until Chapter 8. Listing 7.11 shows how to create this file system. The examples of using `debootstrap` assume that your guest's root partition is mounted to /mnt/guest_image, shown in Listing 7.11. You should create partition images for each of the Debian or Ubuntu guests that you want to make.

LISTING 7.11 Creating and Mounting a Partition Image

```
[root@dom0]# dd if=/dev/zero of=/xen/images/sid-example.img \
bs=1024k seek=4000 count=1
[root@dom0]# mkfs.ext3 -F /xen/images/sid-example.img
[root@dom0]# mkdir -p /mnt/guest_image
[root@dom0]# mount -o loop /xen/images/sid-example.img \
/mnt/guest_image
[root@dom0]#
```

First, we need to pick the Debian release to install. If you are on a pure Debian system. you can use `debootstrap` and specify the suite and location, as in Listing 7.12. Suite refers to a specific release of the Debian distribution. In this example, `sid` is the Debian release (or suite), and /mnt/guest_image is the target directory. The /mnt/ guest_image directory is the location that the guest's root partition is mounted.

LISTING 7.12 Using `debootstrap` on a Debian System to Create a Debian Guest Image

```
[root@dom0-debian-based]# debootstrap sid /mnt/guest_image
I: Retrieving Release
I: Retrieving Packages
I: Validating Packages
I: Resolving dependencies of required packages...
I: Resolving dependencies of base packages...
I: Checking component main on http://ftp.debian.org/debian...
I: Retrieving adduser
I: Validating adduser

[Debootstrap output omitted]

I: Configuring sysklogd...
I: Configuring tasksel...
I: Base system installed successfully.
[root@dom0-debian-based]#
```

Similarly if you are on a Ubuntu system, you can use a command, as in Listing 7.13. In this case, Dapper is the suite, or release, of Ubuntu to install to /mnt/guest_image.

LISTING 7.13 Using debootstrap on a Ubuntu System to Create a Ubuntu Guest Image

```
[root@dom0]# debootstrap dapper /mnt/guest_image
I: Retrieving Release
I: Retrieving Packages
I: Validating Packages
I: Resolving dependencies of required packages...
I: Resolving dependencies of base packages...
I: Checking component main on http://archive.ubuntu.com/ubuntu...
I: Retrieving adduser
I: Validating adduser

[Debootstrap output omitted]

I: Configuring gnupg...
I: Configuring ubuntu-keyring...
I: Configuring ubuntu-minimal...
I: Base system installed successfully.
[root@dom0]#
```

The package suites (for example, sid and dapper) are available because the mirrors used are Debian-specific and Ubuntu-specific mirrors, respectively. A CentoOS or OpenSUSE mirror would not work. See the Reference and Future reading section for tools, such as rpmstrap, rinse, yum with the --install-root option, and yast with the dirinstall option, similar to debootstrap that can be used on CentOS and OpenSUSE. The Ubuntu and Debian mirrors and are configured in the standard /etc/apt/sources.list file. If you want to install a Ubuntu release on a Debian system or a Debian release on a Ubuntu system, you need to specify the mirror of the corresponding server on the debootstrap command line. So on Debian you would need to specify a Ubuntu mirror, and you would use a command as shown in Listing 7.14. Similarly, on Ubuntu, you would need to specify a Debian mirror, and you would use a command as shown in Listing 7.15.

The debootstrap command relies on scripts that are suite, or release, specific. For each available release to install, a corresponding script in the /usr/lib/debootstrap/scripts directory specifies how to install that release. If the debootstrap script for the specific release of Debian or Ubuntu that you want to install is not available on the system, you can copy the script from another computer. For example, we had to copy the dapper script from the Ubuntu system to the Debian system between the corresponding `/usr/lib/debootstrap/scripts/` directories to install dapper on the Debian system as shown in Listing 7.14.

LISTING 7.14 Using `debootstrap` on a Debian System to Create a Ubuntu Guest Image

```
[root@debian-dom0]# debootstrap dapper /mnt/guest_image  \
http://archive.ubuntu.com/ubuntu
I: Retrieving Release
I: Retrieving Packages
I: Validating Packages
I: Resolving dependencies of required packages...
I: Resolving dependencies of base packages...
I: Checking component main on http://archive.ubuntu.com/ubuntu...
I: Retrieving adduser
I: Validating adduser

[Debootstrap output omitted]

I: Configuring gnupg...
I: Configuring ubuntu-keyring...
I: Configuring ubuntu-minimal...
I: Base system installed successfully.
[root@debian-dom0]#
```

LISTING 7.15 Using `debootstrap` on a Ubuntu System to Create a Debian Guest Image

```
[root@debian-dom0]# debootstrap sid /mnt/guest_image \
http://ftp.debian.org/debian
I: Retrieving Release
I: Retrieving Packages
I: Validating Packages
I: Resolving dependencies of required packages...
I: Resolving dependencies of base packages...
I: Checking component main on http://ftp.debian.org/debian...
I: Retrieving adduser
I: Validating adduser

[Debootstrap output omitted]
```

```
I: Configuring sysklogd...
I: Configuring tasksel...
I: Base system installed successfully.
[root@debian-dom0]#
```

Gentoo: `quickpkg` and `domi` Scripts

For Gentoo, we cover two options. The first is `quickpkg`, which is similar in concept to `debootstrap`. Both tools install an operating system to a directory. The second option is a `domi` script, which makes use of other package management solutions within a Gentoo system.

quickpkg

Gentoo allows you to compile your system while passing special flags to the compiler. These flags allow you to tailor an installation to your hardware. We've already seen in Chapter 4 the flag `-mno-tls-direct-seg-refs` added to the compilation of Domain0. Often, these same compiler flags are useful in a DomU environment as well. Gentoo has an option that greatly reduces the amount of time needed to set up a DomU system, effectively cutting out the recompilation of packages already built for Domain0. This is done through the use of a Gentoo tool called `quickpkg`. `quickpkg` creates a binary package, similar to an RPM or DEB file, by using the Portage system to know which files belong to that package and then reading those files out of your current file system. This has the previously stated benefit of avoiding the compiling stage but also has a potential pitfall of reading the current file out of your file system. If the file has been modified since it was installed, the new modified file will be picked up and packaged. Due to the source-based nature of Gentoo, some experience with the Gentoo package system and software is recommended. At minimum, users who choose to follow with the creation of custom Gentoo DomU images should have a decent understanding of day to day Gentoo operation. Gentoo has very good online documentation. Refer to the References and Further Reading section of this chapter for more Gentoo resources.

We construct a DomU using the packages already installed in Domain0 as a base. To do this we need the gentools utility suite installed. Listing 7.16 shows the command to do this.

LISTING 7.16 Using emerge to Install gentools

```
[root@dom0]# emerge app-portage/gentoolkit

[Emerge output omitted]

[root@dom0]#
```

Installing the gentools gives us, among other things, the quickpkg tool. Next we need to loop through all the packages currently installed on the system. This can be done from the command line with a simple shell script, as shown in Listing 7.17.

LISTING 7.17 Using a Shell Script to Process All Installed Packages for Use with quickpkg

```
for PKG in $(equery -q list | cut -d ' ' -f 3)
do
  quickpkg =$PKG
done
```

The shell script in Listing 7.17 creates a tarball of every package currently installed and places the tarball into /usr/portage/packages. If you want them to be placed in a different directory, add a line to the /etc/make.conf file of PKGDIR=/some-where/else.

Now that we have a ready supply of packages, a disk must be constructed for our DomU image. We do this by first making a sparse file with dd. Second, we format the file into a file system and mount the file system. Listing 7.18 shows the commands to do this.

LISTING 7.18 Creating and Mounting DomU Image

```
[root@dom0]# dd if=/dev/zero of=/var/xen/domU-Image bs=1M \
seek=8195 count=1
[root@dom0]# mkfs.xfs -f /var/xen/domU-Image

[output omitted]

[root@dom0]# mkdir -p /mnt/domU
[root@dom0]# mount /var/xen/domU-Image /mnt/domU -o loop
[root@dom0]#
```

Now we need a basic Gentoo stage tarball that is far enough along to have the tools we need to deploy the packages, but not too far along or we will simply overwrite everything with our packages. The stage2 tarballs meet both of these requirements. Obtain the standard stage2 tarball from a local Gentoo mirror and extract the tarball to our new image. The process for doing so is well documented in the official Gentoo documentation (again, see the References and Future Reading section for more information). Listing 7.19 shows the commands to do this. You can use a Gentoo mirror of your choice, preferably the fastest one.

LISTING 7.19 Downloading stage2 Tarball

```
[root@dom0]# cd /mnt/domU
[root@dom0]# wget ftp://mirror.iawnet.sandia.gov/pub/gentoo/releases/x86/ ➥
current/stages/stage2-x86-2007.0.tar.bz2

[output omitted]

[root@dom0]# tar -xpjf stage2-x86-2007.0.tar.bz2
[root@dom0]#
```

Now we have a basic Gentoo install from stage2. Next, we need some simple configuration files and a swap space created for our new Gentoo DomU. Listing 7.20 shows the commands to create the swap space and copy the configuration files. The first configuration file, resolv.conf, is the list of the name servers so that DomU can resolve network names. The second configuration file, make.conf, is important. It contains all our special settings, from compiler flags to Gentoo's USE flags. It is important to match these settings from Domain0 because we are going to deploy packages from Domain0. A mismatch can cause a failed emerge later on in the process.

LISTING 7.20 Swap and Configuration Files

```
[root@dom0]# dd if=/dev/zero of=/mnt/domU/swap bs=1M count=256

[output omitted]

[root@dom0]# mkswap /mnt/domU/swap

[output omitted]

[root@dom0]# cp /etc/resolv.conf /mnt/domU/etc/
[root@dom0]# cp /etc/make.conf /mnt/domU/etc/
[root@dom0]#
```

Next, we need to mount some special file systems, just like a normal Gentoo install. Listing 7.21 shows these commands.

LISTING 7.21 Mount `proc` and `dev`

```
[root@dom0]# mount -t proc none /mnt/domU/proc
[root@dom0]# mount -o bind /dev /mnt/domU/dev
[root@dom0]#
```

Now comes an important part of using the Portage system to jumpstart your DomU. We need to copy our current Portage system into the new DomU, as shown in Listing 7.22.

LISTING 7.22 Copying the Gentoo Portage Tree

```
[root@dom0]# cp -R /etc/portage /mnt/domU/etc
[root@dom0]# cp -a /usr/portage /mnt/domU/usr
[root@dom0]#
```

After this step has completed, we have exactly the same Portage tree, profile, and settings in the DomU as in the Domain0. We now use our packages to set up the system on the new DomU. We do this from Domain0 by changing the root directory emerge acts onto our DomU. We must also disable a couple of a safety measures, mainly the collision and configuration protections. Normally this would not be advisable, but because we are installing all the packages from a currently running Gentoo system, we should be fine. Then we simply tell emerge to use our packages and reinstall everything for the "system" target, as shown in Listing 7.23.

LISTING 7.23 Command to Reinstall the System

```
[root@dom0]# ROOT=/mnt/gentoo/ CONFIG_PROTECT=-/etc \
FEATURES=-collision-protect emerge --usepkg --emptytree system

[emerge output omitted]

[root@dom0]#
```

Now, if there are no USE flag mismatches, we are ready to change root into our new DomU. If there are USE flag mismatches, you need to modify the USE flags in the make.conf of the guest, just as you would on a normal Gentoo system, and then rerun the command in Listing 7.23. Listing 7.24 shows the commands to change into the new DomU system.

LISTING 7.24 Using `chroot` to Change Root into the DomU System

```
[root@dom0]# chroot /mnt/domU
[root@domU]# env-update
[root@domU]# source /etc/profile
[root@dom0]#
```

Next we need to install our Gentoolkit in our new environment. This gives us a new tool, `revdep-rebuild`, that reemerges anything that links to something other than our new packages. In other words, it cleans up all the dependencies. We should do the same for the Perl and Python binding. Listing 7.25 shows the commands to do this cleanup.

LISTING 7.25 Cleanup Dependencies

```
[root@domU]# emerge --usepkg gentoolkit

[Emerge output omitted]

[root@domU]# revdep-rebuild --use-pkg

[revdep-rebuild output omitted]

[root@domU]# perl-cleaner all -usepkg

[perl-cleaner output omitted]

[root@domU]# python-updater

[python-updater output omitted]

[root@domU]#
```

Now we are ready to install just as we would install a normal Gentoo system, including various tools for the system. We can continue to use the `--usepkg emerge` flag to save time. If there is a new tool that Domain0 does not have but DomU needs, you can emerge it as normal (without `--usepkg`). Some key items to remember are the file system tools, configuring the DHCP client, setting the root password, and modifying the `fstab` and time zone. Listing 7.26 shows the commands to install these necessary packages and change the root password.

LISTING 7.26 Install Necessary Packages

```
[root@domU]# emerge --usepkg dhcp xfsprogs syslog-ng vixie-cron

[emerge output omitted]

[root@domU]# passwd root

[output omitted]
```

The /etc/fstab for our new DomU should look like Listing 7.27.

LISTING 7.27 A Sample /etc/fstab File

# <fs>	<mountpoint>	<type>	<opts>	<dump/pass>
/dev/xvda	/	xfs	noatime	0 1
/swap	none	swap	sw	0 0
proc	/proc	proc	efaults	0 0
shm	/dev/shm	tmpfs	nodev,nosuid,noexec	0 0

Now we are ready to exit our chroot environment, create our Xen configuration file, and finally boot our new DomU. Listing 7.28 shows the steps to exit the chroot, create the file, and boot the DomU.

LISTING 7.28 Guest Configuration File

```
[root@domU]# exit
[root@dom0]# cat > /etc/xen/gentoo
# general
name    = "gentoo";
memory  = 256;
kernel  = "/boot/xen-domU";
disk = [ "file:/var/xen/domU-gentoo,xvda,w" ];
root = "/dev/xvda ro";
vif = [ "" ];
dhcp = "dhcp";
^D <-- this means to type CTRL+D on the keyboard
[root@dom0]# xm create -c gentoo

[Bootup process output omitted]

login:
```

Gentoo Domi Scripts

The `domi` tool is a script that leverages other distributions' package management systems to quickly and easily build new DomUs. The domi `script` can leverage yum to build Fedora or CentOS DomUs and can use `debootstrap` to construct Debian and SUSE DomUs. Gentoo DomUs can also be built with a `domi` script.

Under Gentoo's Portage system, `domi` is masked. To unmask it, we do the same actions we needed to unmask Xen in Chapter 4. Edit the `/etc/portage/package.keywords` file to include `domi`. The `domi` package also requires several dependencies that are masked, namely multipath-tools, yum and rpm. As always, when unmasking software, understand the ramifications of doing so before proceeding. Listing 7.29 shows the entries that should be added to the `/etc/portage/package.keywords` file.

LISTING 7.29 domi Dependencies

```
app-emulation/domi
sys-fs/multipath-tools
sys-apps/yum
app-arch/rpm
```

Then we can install `domi` by running the `emerge` command as shown in Listing 7.30.

LISTING 7.30 Install domi

```
[root@dom0]# emerge domi

[Emerge output omitted]

[root@dom0]#
```

After emerge finishes, `domi` is installed. The `domi` script requires the use of Device-mapper in the kernel. Device-mapper can be built in to the kernel or built as a module. If Device-mapper is built as a module, make sure the module is installed before running `domi`. Invoke `modpobe` as shown in Listing 7.31.

LISTING 7.31 Load Device-mapper Module

```
[root@dom0]# modprobe dm_mod
[root@dom0]#
```

Now we are ready to configure a new DomU image. For our example, we create a Gentoo DomU. We need to create a configuration file for domi to read. These files are simple and straightforward. Listing 7.32 shows the configuration file used to create a Gentoo guest with domi. The first line of the configuration file tells domi where to create our image file for this DomU. The second line specifies whether we want to use a sparse or preallocated virtual disk. The third line tells domi where to put our Xen configuration for this DomU. The fourth line is the kernel we use to boot the DomU. The fifth line is the type of distribution we want domi to build for us. Current choices of distributions are Debian, Fedora, Gentoo, SUSE, and ttylinux. The sixth line is the name of our new DomU. The seventh line is the type of virtual disk we want to give our new DomU.

LISTING 7.32 A Sample of domi Configuration File for Gentoo Guest

```
DOMI_DISK_FILE="/var/xen/gentoo-domU.img"
DOMI_DISK_SPARSE="yes"
DOMI_XEN_CONF="/etc/xen/gentoo-example"
DOMI_XEN_KERNEL="/boot/xen-domU"
DOMI_DISTRO="gentoo"
DOMI_NAME="gentoo-example"
DOMI_VDISK="hda"
```

To create the DomU guest, we simply invoke domi with the configuration file as an argument, as shown in Listing 7.33.

LISTING 7.33 Build the Gentoo Guest

```
[root@dom0]# domi gentoo-domi.config

[domi output omitted]

[root@dom0]#
```

The domi script then runs to build the new DomU. This may take a while depending on which distribution you selected and your Internet connection speed.

After domi is finished, you are ready to start your new DomU. Listing 7.34 shows the command to start the DomU that we created in Listing 7.33.

LISTING 7.34 Boot the Gentoo Guest

```
[root@dom0]# xm create gentoo-example

[xm create output omitted]

[root@dom0]#
```

Listing 7.35 shows a configuration file used to create a Fedora DomU. Listing 7.36 shows the command to create the Fedora DomU using domi and also shows a snippet of the output of running domi.

LISTING 7.35 A Sample domi Configuration File for a Fedora Guest

```
DOMI_DISK_FILE="/var/xen/fedora-domU.img"
DOMI_DISK_SPARSE="yes"
DOMI_XEN_CONF="/etc/xen/fedora-example"
DOMI_XEN_KERNEL="/boot/xen-domU"
DOMI_DISTRO="fedora"
DOMI_NAME="fedora-example"
DOMI_VDISK="hda"
```

LISTING 7.36 Build a Fedora DomU Guest with domi

```
[root@dom0]# domi fedora_config

##
###fedora-example: initialization (i386)###
###
###fedora-example: initialization (i386)
###
###fedora-example: setup disk
###(sparse file /var/xen/fedora-domU.img)
###
###
###fedora-example:
###setup disk (sparse file /var/xen/fedora-domU.img)
###
1+0 records in
1+0 records out
1048576 bytes (1.0 MB) copied, 0.005433 s, 193 MB/s
```

```
Disk /dev/loop/1: 4295MB
Sector size (logical/physical): 512B/512B
Partition Table: msdos
Number  Start     End      Size     Type       File system   Flags
 1      0.51kB    4026MB   4026MB   primary                   boot
 2      4026MB    4294MB   268MB    primary

add map 1-part1 : 0 7863281 linear /dev/loop/1 1
add map 1-part2 : 0 522648 linear /dev/loop/1 7863282
###fedora-example: setup root fs and swap###
###
### fedora-example: setup root fs and swap
###
Setting up swapspace version 1, size = 267591 kB
Label was truncated.
LABEL=fedora-example-, UUID=b0caa752-158d-49e2-9a32-d6e5a998d969
###fedora-example: copy saved yum cache
### [/var/cache/domi/fedora-pub-fedora-linux-core-4-i386-os]
###
###
### fedora-example: copy saved yum cache
### [/var/cache/domi/fedora-pub-fedora-linux-core-4-i386-os]
###
###fedora-example: fetch and install###
###
### fedora-example: fetch and install
###
# [main]
# reposdir=""
# gpgcheck=0
# debuglevel=2
# installroot=/tmp/domi-12119/mnt
#
# [fedora]
# name=Fedora Core
# baseurl=http://download.fedora.redhat.com/pub/fedora/\
#linux/core/4/i386/os/
#
Warning, could not load sqlite, falling back to pickle
Setting up Group Process
Setting up repositories
fedora                                          [1/1]
```

```
fedora                    100% |===============| 1.1 kB     00:00

[domi output omitted]

### fedora-example: save yum cache
### [/var/cache/domi/fedora-pub-fedora-linux-core-4-i386-os]
###
###fedora-example: cleanup: virtual disk
###
###
### fedora-example: cleanup: virtual disk
###
/dev/mapper/1-part1 umounted
del devmap : 1-part1
del devmap : 1-part2
###fedora-example: cleanup: remove tmp files###
###
### fedora-example: cleanup: remove tmp files
###
```

Xen Express

In Chapter 4, we installed Xen Express as a Domain0 and showed how to install the client packages to administer the Xen Express Server. In this section, we show how to use the Xen Express client to create a guest. We look into the administrative functionality of XenExpress in Chapter 14.

Recall that to start the Xen Express client, you can run the command `xenserver-client`, which loads the XenServer main window as shown in Figure 7.20. By selecting the name that you gave to the Xen server in Chapter 4, you can click the Install XenVM button in the middle toolbar of the window.

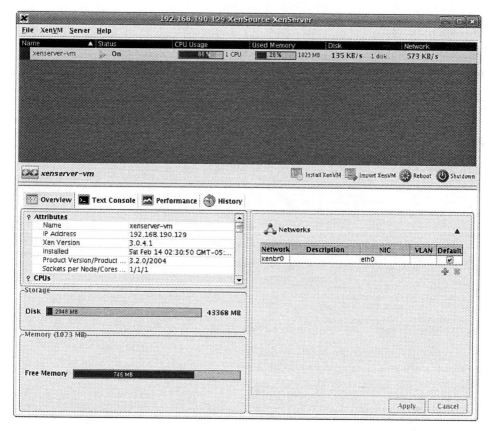

FIGURE 7.20 Clicking on xenserver-vm enables the Install XenVM button.

Clicking on the Install XenVM button brings up a window as shown in Figure 7.21. A number of template guest installations are available to choose from. These are available in the Install From drop-down box and include three PV guest options: Debian Sarge Guest Template, Red Hat Enterprise Linux 4.1 Repository, and Red Hat Enterprise Linux 4.4 Repository. There are five HVM guest options: Red Hat Enterprise 5, SUSE Linux Enterprise 10 Service Pack 1, Windows Server 2003 Standard/Enterprise, Windows 2000 Service Pack 4, and Windows XP Service Pack 2.

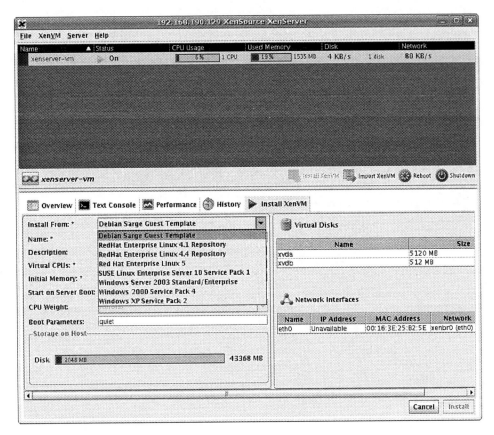

FIGURE 7.21 The Xen Express Install XenVM tab displays the choices for Install From locations.

We use the Debian Sarge Guest Template in the following example. The RHEL 4.1 and RHEL 4.4 repository options bring up a Red Hat Anaconda installer that lets you specify a repository over the network to install from (NFS, HTTP, FTP). This is the same as the CentOS/Fedora install URL media, but in this case we are working with RHEL. The rest of the options are CD/DVD-based installs and therefore require HVM support.

We select the Debian Sarge Guest Template from the Install From drop-down box and also fill in the name, which in this example is called Debian1. The number of Virtual CPUs is set to 1 by default, and the Initial Memory is set to 256 by default. We also check the Start on Server Boot box, so that this guest will start automatically if we reboot our Xen server. The virtual disks and network interfaces have default values as well. The new guest has a 5GB root file system named xvda, a 512MB swap drive for the virtual drives, and a bridged network card, as shown in Figure 7.22.

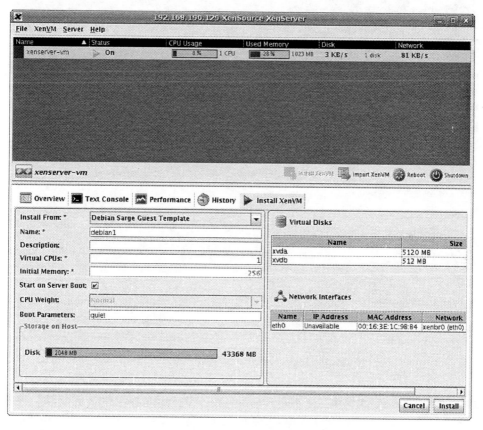

Figure 7.22 The Install XenVM tab with some values filled in for a Debian guest

When you are happy with your settings, click the Install button in the lower right-hand corner. This adds the `debian1` guest to the status window with the status of "* * * Installing," as shown in Figure 7.23.

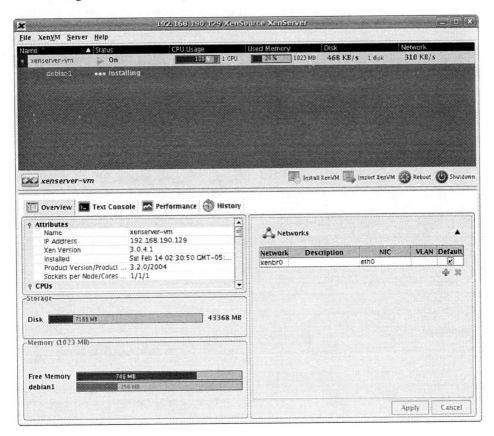

FIGURE 7.23 After clicking Install, the XenExpress main window displays some information.

After the installation has finished, the status changes to "starting," and the History tab opens. This lets you know it was submitted and the elapsed time for the operation. Figure 7.24 shows this window.

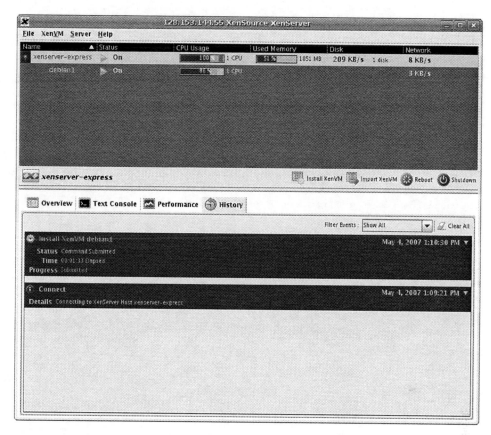

FIGURE 7.24 The History tab shows the submitted and completed events.

After the guest starts automatically, and after being quickly created from the template as shown in Listings 7.22 through 7.24, the status for the debian1 guest changes to On. By clicking on the debian1 guest, the Text Console tab opens, showing the system boot process, as shown in Figure 7.25.

FIGURE 7.25 A standard Debian boot process shows in the Text Console.

At the end of the boot process, a one time configuration of the guest occurs. You are prompted for a root password and a VNC password. Both passwords are typed blind, meaning no characters are echoed to the screen. You are also prompted for a hostname. The ssh server is configured, and some services are started, followed by a login screen, as shown in Figure 7.26.

FIGURE 7.26 During first boot of the Debian guest, a first-time configuration is required.

You now can click on the Graphical Console tab, which prompts you for the VNC password that you just set, and you are greeted with the GDM login as shown in Figure 7.27.

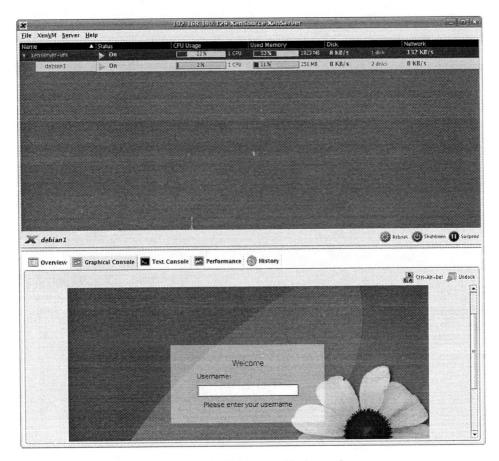

FIGURE 7.27   The login window appears in the Debian graphical console.

You now have a functional Debian Sarge installation that has both text and graphical consoles. Finally, you should notice a button in the top-right corner of the graphical console that allows you to undock the guest so that it is available in its own window. Figure 7.28 shows an example of an undocked window.

NOTE
The default window manager installed is set to XFCE because this takes less space. If you need another desktop environment, such as GNOME or KDE, you can install it just as you would with a normal Debian system.

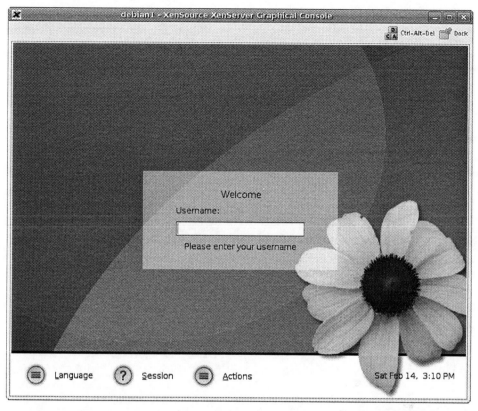

FIGURE 7.28 An undocked Debian graphical console is in a window of its own that you can also put back into the XenExpress main window by clicking the Dock button in the top-right corner.

For more information about Citrix XenServer Express Edition please see the following site: http://www.citrixxenserver.com/products/Pages/XenExpress.aspx.

We have now finished our survey of paravirtual guest population methods. Table 7.1 shows some of the relative advantages and disadvantages of guest installation of each platform along with our subjective experience.

TABLE 7.1 Advantages and Disadvantages of Xen Guest Creation

Type	Advantages	Disadvantages
OpenSUSE	Early adoption of Xen Several good installation options	Some installation methods either are tricky or don't work as well as others.
CentOS	Good mix of command line and graphical tools with the same basic functionality	Some divergence from upstream Xen releases.

TABLE 7.1 continued

Type	Advantages	Disadvantages
Ubuntu	Easy guest installation with distribution tool debootstrap	Support for Xen not in the core (main) packages supported. (However, the community (universe) support is good.)
		Lack of native GUI tools that come with the distribution.
Gentoo	Easiest to install different distributions as guests	Compile flags and options can be confusing. Experience with the Gentoo software build and packaging systems presents a higher barrier to entry
Xen Express	Template-based installations of guests More advanced functionality in GUI interface	Limited support/capability compared to Server/Enterprise versions.
		Compatibility/similarity with other distributions limited.

Guest Image Customization

When making guest images manually or using images downloaded from the Internet, it is often useful to carefully customize the images to distinguish them from one another. This section gives some advice and best practices for customizing Xen images.

Customizing Hostnames

Hostname differentiation is important so that you know what guest you are working with and you don't have any conflicts of guests on the same local network. Making changes to the hostname is often specific to the distribution. Often different automated terminal-based or graphical tools help with this process. When in doubt, refer to the documentation included with your distribution.

However, we can still discuss the most common places to look to make changes and find potential problems. At a minimum, in many distributions the files /etc/hostname and /etc/hosts have a common purpose and format. The /etc/hostname file contains the desired hostname for the system. The /etc/hosts file is used so that the local system tools can look up the system hostname and match it with the localhost and the localhost IP address(es). The /etc/hosts file can vary slightly between distributions, but the general format is demonstrated in Listing 7.37.

LISTING 7.37 A Sample /etc/hosts File

```
#ip address    #hostname    #alias
127.0.0.1      localhost
127.0.1.1      myhostname   myhostname.mydomain.com
```

Another customization is the hostname that gets sent to the Dynamic Host Config-uration Protocol (DHCP) server. On Debian-based systems, the location for sending the hostname is in the file /etc/dhcp3/dhclient.conf. The send host-name line should be uncommented and edited with the desired hostname set. On Red Hat based systems, the DHCP hostname is set by adding the line DHCP_HOSTNAME="desired-hostname" to the file /etc/sysconfig/network/ifcfg-ethX, where "X" is the Eth-ernet device number. The best time to customize these files for the Xen guests are when they are first mounted and populated and before you use xm create to start them; that way when they start up they have the correct hostname set.

Customizing Users

When working with Xen guest domains, it can get cumbersome to deal with local user accounts on each guest. So if you don't already have a network-based authentication solution (such as Kerberos, LDAP, Samba, or Active Directory) in place, setting one up might take some time. An alternative is to use SSH key authentication, which uses a public/private key pair. These keys are used to grant the holder of the private key access to a remote system over SSH, which allow for either the Domain0 or a trusted admin-istrative control point to connect to and administer the guests. SSH key authentication is easy to set up because it requires only a working SSH server and a public key from the connecting host to be appended to the .ssh/authorized_key file. Listing 7.38 shows how to use the commands to create and copy the key to the proper location. See the man pages for ssh-keygen and ssh-copy-id for more information.

LISTING 7.38 Using ssh Tools to Set Up Simple SSH Key Authentication

```
[user@dom0]$ ssh-keygen -t rsa
Generating public/private rsa key pair.
Enter file in which to save the key (/home/user/.ssh/id_rsa):
Enter passphrase (empty for no passphrase):
Enter same passphrase again:
Your identification has been saved in /home/user/.ssh/id_rsa.
Your public key has been saved in /home/deshant/.ssh/id_rsa.pub.
```

LISTING 7.38 Continued

```
The key fingerprint is:
ca:e6:7f:48:be:e6:33:e3:2e:6c:51:4f:84:3f:d8:1e user@dom0
[user@dom0]$ ssh-copy-id -i .ssh/id_rsa.pub domU
[user@dom0]$ ssh domU
Last Login on: <Date>
[user@domU]$ cat .ssh/authorized_keys
ssh-rsa AAAAB3NzaC1yc2EAAAABIwAAAQEA26Z6jyYeprOvOQhpLa6VnLCxKOQk
GVyS5draf5c8JuqNgh6ybERvkcgkuQlY9Yx865bpkhY7HRmunGWyiySOLy0QXx23
Qhf8cW4WfVd1RbMOrvRqVO1sxSZjbfbENkt63sXhaqQsNBc9LI8cg9PWAS0p1FXm
Zwc3QGGnV2sNWakx9bApUZN8okvBncmHuSv7SvTCgjmXuZFrHcK+i3NE5RvOCwCj
ntfaG67hsfMDhhJD9p/h0p+OO+0GaDtVRUI7oXxTYZNKFWe7rxH89UbsNjW7uX5c
zRy8Veq3fSx82vxOyanCUOCJGxJjDxluLi7loQ168a8rj5H2p2P2q1RuCQ==
[user@domU]$
```

Customizing Packages and Services

When building DomU guest images from scratch, you have a lot more control over the packages that get installed. Most Linux distributions' installers or install tools (de-bootstrap, emerge, and so on) allow you to install a minimal, base, or server install. You should start with one of these options for your guest and add more packages only as needed. This has a couple of important benefits. First, it keeps the guest images small, which saves space. Also, having fewer packages installed makes the DomUs that much easier to manage because security updates and version updates need to be applied to each of the DomUs that have a particular software version or release. Finally, services that are not necessary for the guest to perform its role should be disabled at boot or removed altogether.

Customizing the File System Table (/etc/fstab)

In Linux, the /etc/fstab file contains a table that lists block devices, mount points, file system types, and a few other options. The key thing to remember when working with the block devices of a DomU guest is that they will have access only to drives explicitly exported through xm operations. The xm create command reads from the guest configuration file for initial devices, and xm block-attach can attach block devices. The xm create command was covered in Chapter 6. The xm block-attach is covered in Appendix B, "The xm Command."

The advantage to specifying the block devices that the DomU gets allows you to plan accordingly. So when you export a physical partition, sda8 for example, to the guest, you need to specify a partition for the guest. Listing 7.39 shows an example disk line to be used for the guest configuration file. The physical partition sda8 is exported, but the guest sees it as hda2. Listing 7.40 shows an example /etc/fstab file to be used in the guest with the configuration.

LISTING 7.39 Disk Line in Guest Configuration File to Export a File as hda1 and the Local Domain0 /dev/sda8 partition as hda2

```
disk = ['tap:aio:/xen/images/guest_partition.img,hda1,w',  ➡
        'phy:sda8,hda2,w']
```

LISTING 7.40 The /etc/fstab File for Example Guest with Root as hda1 and Swap as hda2

proc	/proc	proc	defaults	0 0
/dev/hda1	/	ext3	defaults,errors=remount-ro	0 1
/dev/hda2	none	swap	sw	0 0

When working with prebuilt guest images, there will likely be an existing /etc/fstab file that may assume that the disk image you are using has a label or UUID defined. For example, when downloading the openfiler tar file, as in Chapter 5, the original /etc/fstab file assumed the root partition was a partition with a label of "/" (the original /etc/fstab can be found in Listing 7.41).

LISTING 7.41 Guest fstab File from Original fstab Tarball

LABEL=/	/	ext3	defaults	1 1
none	/dev/pts	devpts	gid=5,mode=620	0 0
none	/dev/shm	tmpfs	defaults	0 0
none	/proc	proc	defaults	0 0
none	/sys	sysfs	defaults	0 0
/dev/cdrom	/mnt/cdrom	auto	noauto,ro,owner,exec	0 0
/var/swap	swap	swap	defaults	0 0

> **NOTE**
> If your DomU guest is using a kernel and ramdisk from Domain0, you should apply the customization of copying the modules from Domain0 into your guest. We did this in Chapter 5.

Converting Existing Installations

We now look at how to use an existing installation as a guest image. Recall that we already saw one example of using hard drive partitions in Chapter 5, where we used GParted to resize an existing partition. We created new partitions and then unpacked the contents of a compressed tar file. In this chapter, we convert a paravirtual Linux installation. HVM guests are similar. Most differences are with respect to the different operating systems. Windows handles partitions differently than Linux. With Windows, a drive exported as hda shows up as C:, hdb shows up as D:, hdc shows up as E:, and so on. Also, by default, an SCSI sd* device (for example, sda) drive is not supported by Windows without loading drivers during the installation of special drivers at the beginning of the Windows setup process.

In this section, we discuss how you can use an existing nonvirtualized operating system installation as the basis for a Xen DomU guest. If you have an existing OS installation and the proper Xen support for it, you can make that installation into a DomU guest. However, there are some subtle things to be aware of to set it up correctly. It may be tempting to think that because the existing installation on the physical drive works, no modifications are necessary. However, as soon as you make the existing operating system install into a DomU guest, it is confined to the new virtualized world that the Xen hypervisor has exported to it. The DomU guest is limited by the access it was granted in its configuration file. You need to adjust the copied installation to use these virtualized resources rather than the direct physical resources it is expecting.

One important difference when moving to the virtualized world is found in the file system table, /etc/fstab. Recall that we edited the fstab to boot a compressed file system image in Chapter 5. This file tells the kernel how to map the hard drive partitions to the directories in the file system. Listing 7.42 shows a typical fstab file for an operating system installation on a physical machine. This /etc/fstab file was taken from a server running Ubuntu 6.06. For readability, we removed the option errors=remount-ro for the /dev/hda1 partition.

LISTING 7.42 A Basic Example of /etc/fstab

# <file system>	<mount point>	<type>	<options>	<dump>	<pass>
proc	/proc	proc	defaults	0	0
/dev/hda1	/	ext3	defaults	0	1
/dev/hda4	none	swap	sw	0	0
/dev/hdc	/media/cdrom0	udf,iso9660user,noauto	0	0

Notice that the /etc/fstab file for the existing installation refers to actual physical partitions on the local disk(s), including its root partition on /dev/hda1, and its swap partition on /dev/hda4. On a Xen system, Domain0 is typically configured to use these physical resources directly. Other guests may also be granted access to specific partitions on the same drive. It is not generally safe to allow multiple guests to access the same block device (that is, the same partition) unless they are shared read-only. If two guests were to write to the same block device, corruption is inevitable. Each guest image's kernel assumes it has write access to the whole disk or partition, and the file system in each tries to modify the directory structures independently. For example, they may both try to add a file to the / directory at the same time. This can set up a race condition between the competing changes that can result in a corruption of the file system metadata.

Xend actually prevents you from mounting a block device's read/write on more than one guest. There are ways to override this, but it is strongly discouraged. A better way to share the block device is with a network file server (such as NFS) or even a cluster file system (such as the Global File System [GFS]) or the Oracle cluster file system [ocfs2]). We discuss some network-based solutions in more detail in Chapter 8.

So, we need to modify the /etc/fstab file in the existing installation to accurately reflect the actual devices (real or virtual) that will be explicitly exported to it by Domain0. In other words, the guest will only have access to devices in its new virtual world. Listing 7.43 shows an example of the /etc/fstab file for a system installed after the Domain0 installation was in place. This /etc/fstab file was taken from a desktop running Ubuntu 6.10 to be used as a Xen guest. For readability, we removed the option errors=remount-ro for the /dev/hda7 partition and also the options nls=utf8, umask=007, and gid=46 (which is a Windows XP NTFS partition).

LISTING 7.43 An Example /etc/fstab (from Newly Installed System)

# <file system>	<mount point>	<type>	<options>	<dump>	<pass>
Proc	/proc	proc	defaults	0	0
/dev/hda7	/	ext3	defaults	0	1
/dev/hda1	/media/hda1	ntfs	defaults,*	0	1
/dev/hda6	/media/hda6	ext3	defaults	0	2
/dev/hda5	none	swap	sw	0	0
/dev/hdc	/media/cdrom0	udf,iso9660	user,noauto	0	0

For this example, we want the partition /dev/hda7 to be the root partition "/" for the DomU guest install and /dev/hda6 to be the root partition "/" for Domain0. The existing installation we want to boot as a guest was installed after the Xen system. Therefore by default, it believes itself to be the new base system and, without intervention, will attempt to mount Domain0's root partition (/dev/hda6) to /media/hda6 on boot. As we've said, for safety, we do not want to mount any partition mounted by Domain0, especially its root partition, in our new guest. Similarly, any partition mounted in the new guest should not be mounted in Domain0 while that guest is running unless it is mounted read-only. One exception to this rule is that sometimes guest partitions are mounted temporarily writeable in Domain0 to make modifications such as the one we are making to the /etc/fstab. However, this is not done while the guest is running.

To get the system installed on /dev/hda7 to work properly as a DomU guest, some modifications need to be made. First and most importantly, the line referring to the Domain0 root file system (/dev/hda6) needs to be commented out or removed entirely. The minimal amount of changes to the fstab file is found in Listing 7.44. Also, the xm configuration file for the guest needs to be modified to export the partition needed by the guest. This /etc/fstab file was taken from a desktop running Ubuntu 6.10 to be used as a Xen guest. Note that the # sign represents a comment and is ignored by the kernel. For readability, we removed the option errors=remount-ro for the /dev/hda7 partition and also the options nls=utf8, umask=007, and gid=46 (which is a Windows XP NTFS partition).

LISTING 7.44 An Example of a Modified /etc/fstab (from Newly Installed System)

# <file system>	<mount point>	<type>	<options>	<dump>	<pass>
Proc	/proc	proc	defaults	0	0
/dev/hda7	/	ext3	defaults	0	1
#/dev/hda1	/media/hda1	ntfs	defaults,*	0	1
#/dev/hda6	/media/hda6	ext3	defaults	0	2
/dev/hda5	none	swap	sw	0	0
#/dev/hdc	/media/cdrom0	udf,iso9660	user,noauto	0	0

As we saw in Chapter 5, another detail that you may want to take care of is copying kernel modules that are compatible with the Domain0 kernel into the Xen DomU guest. This will soon not be an issue as some Xen DomU support has been added to the Linux kernel as of 2.6.23 using paravirt_ops as described in Chapter 1. It helps if the kernel being booted in the existing installation is already Xen compatible—that is, able to boot as a DomU guest in paravirtualized mode. In this case, we could use pygrub as demonstrated in Chapter 5. However, if the guest kernel is not supported, we will need to boot using an external kernel and RAM disk as demonstrated in Chapter 5. In this case, we should add in the corresponding kernel modules (much like we saw in the example in Chapter 5). Listing 7.45 shows the commands to copy the modules. We first make a temporary directory (with `mkdir`) to mount the guest partition to; then we mount the guest partition (with `mount`), copy the modules (with `cp`), and finally unmount the partition with `umount`.

LISTING 7.45 Copying the Modules for the Domain0 to the Guest Installed on a Partition

```
[root@dom0]# mkdir /mnt/guest_partition
[root@dom0]# mount /dev/hda7  /mnt/guest_partition
[root@dom0]# cp -r /lib/modules/`uname -r` \
/mnt/guest_partition/lib/modules/
[root@dom0]# umount /mnt/guest_partition
[root@dom0]#
```

Next, we need a guest configuration file that grants access to the physical partition that the guest needs to work. For this, we export the physical devices that it is expecting directly. Notice the root parameter in Listing 7.46. It tells the kernel the location of the root file system. As usual, we store the DomU configuration file in /etc/xen; for this example we call it ubuntu-edgy. We use the kernel and RAM disk from Domain0 as our DomU kernel and RAM disk. We export the root file system that the guest expects, /dev/hda7, as well as the swap space the guest expects, /dev/hda5. Be sure to not use the same swap space for the DomU and the Domain0 because that is unsafe.

LISTING 7.46 DomU Guest Configuration File for Existing Installation

```
kernel = "/boot/vmlinuz-2.6.16-xen"
ramdisk = "/boot/initrd.img-2.6.16.33-xen"
memory = 128
name = "ubuntu-edgy"
vif = [ '' ]
dhcp = "dhcp"
disk = ['phy:hda7,hda7,w',hda5,hda5,w']
root = "/dev/hda7 ro"
```

Finally, we can use `xm create` to boot the DomU guest that we have created using our existing installation. Listing 7.47 shows the `xm create` command; its output is omitted because it is similar to the Linux boot processes that we have seen before. We use the xm create command with the -c option so that we can see the guest console as it boots.

LISTING 7.47 Booting the DomU Guest That Was Based on Existing Installation

```
root@dom0 xm create -c ubuntu-edgy
[output omitted]
```

You can now use this guest similarly to how you would it if it were an existing installation, within the constraints of being a Xen guest.

This concludes our examination of how to deploy preexisting stand-alone installations as DomU installations. This method is relatively simple to set up because it allows you to build a working stand-alone system and carefully convert it into a DomU guest. This method also has the obvious requirements that your operating system be Xen compatible and that you have multiple existing installations on your machine or free partitions into which you can do a normal installation to then convert. You should be aware of possible limits on the number of partitions you can create on IDE or SCSI drives, as there are often limits to the number of partitions that can be supported by the operating system. If you are running up against these types of limits, LVM or Network-based storage options might be a better choice for you (see Chapter 8 for details).

Summary

This chapter showed various ways that you can create your own guest images, that can be used as both HVM and PV guests. Additionally, we have demonstrated some things to consider when customizing guest images. Finally, you have been taught how to convert an existing operating system installation into a Xen guest. Chapter 8 shows you more advanced ways to store your guests as well as setup your own custom network and file-based storage solutions.

References and Further Reading

Burdulis, Šarñas. "Xen 3.04 HVM and Debian Etch." Dartmouth College.
http://www.math.dartmouth.edu/~sarunas/xen_304_hvm_etch.html.
"CentOS-4 on Xen."
http://mark.foster.cc/wiki/index.php/Centos-4_on_Xen.

Citrix XenServer Express Edition Download. Citrix.
http://www.xensource.com/Pages/XenExpress.aspx.

"Configuring Gentoo with Xen." Gentoo Linux.
http://www.gentoo.org/doc/en/xen-guide.xml.

"Creating and Installing a CentOS DomU Instance." CentOS Wiki.
http://wiki.centos.org/HowTos/Xen/InstallingCentOSDomU.

"Debian Sarge on Xen."
http://mark.foster.cc/wiki/index.php/Debian_Sarge_on_Xen.

Fedora Xen Quickstart Guide.
http://fedoraproject.org/wiki/FedoraXenQuickstartFC6.

FreeBSD/Xen-Free BSD Wiki
http://wiki.freebsd.org/FreeBSD/Xen

Gentoo Linux Resources
http://www.gentoo.org/doc/en/
http://www.gentoo.org/doc/en/handbook/index.xml
http://gentoo-wiki.com/Official_Gentoo_Documentation

"HOWTO: Virtual Xen Servers and Gentoo." Gentoo Wiki.
http://gentoo-wiki.com/HOWTO_Virtual_Xen_Servers_and_Gentoo.

"HOWTO Xen and Gentoo." Gentoo Wiki.
http://gentoo-wiki.com/HOWTO_Xen_and_Gentoo.

"Installing and Using a Fully-Virtualized Xen Guest." CentOS Wiki.
http://wiki.centos.org/HowTos/Xen/InstallingHVMDomU.

"Installing Xen3 – openSUSE" includes yast dirinstall
http://en.opensuse.org/Installing_Xen3

"Installing Xen on Ubuntu Feisty Fawn – The Complete Newbies Guide."
Redemption in a Blog.
http://blog.codefront.net/2007/06/26/installing-xen-on-ubuntu-feisty-fawn-the-complete-newbies-guide/.

Rosen, Rami. "Virtualization in Xen 3.0." Linux Journal.
http://www.linuxjournal.com/article/8909.

"rpmstrap – Bootstrap a Basic RPM-Based System."
http://rpmstrap.pimpscript.net/.

Timme, Falko. "The Perfect Xen 3.1.0 Setup for Debian Etch (i386)." HowtoForge.
http://www.howtoforge.com/debian_etch_xen_3.1.

"Xen." openSUSE.
http://en.opensuse.org/Xen.

"Xen." Ubuntu Wiki.
https://help.ubuntu.com/community/Xen.

"Xen 3.1 Binary Installation CentOS 5.0 [with HVM support]." Oracle DBA Blog.
http://bderzhavets.blogspot.com/2007/08/xen-3_10.html.

"Xen Tools." Xen guest creation tools for Debian.
http://xen-tools.org/software/xen-tools/.

xen-tools.org rinse
http://xen-tools.org/software/rinse/

Chapter 8

Storing Guest Images

Now that you know how to create and use guest images, the next thing to consider is which storage method is most appropriate for you. In this chapter, we discuss local storage options such as logical volumes; network storage options such as iSCSI, ATA-over-Ethernet (AoE); and network file systems such as NFS. We also discuss the related issue of image archival, including how to create your own file-based disk and partition images.

In Chapter 5, "Using Prebuilt Guest Images," we discussed the use of prebuilt guest images including how to unpack them into a hard drive partition. Physical hard drive partitions performance can be better than using file-based guest images, particularly if you can avoid contention over the same drive, by storing guests on different physical drives than the Domain0. However, there are limits on the number of partitions you can create on a hard drive, and partitioning cannot always be safely preformed. In this chapter, we discuss some additional image storage options related to the issues that arise when partitioning is not an option.

We begin with logical volumes, which offer additional flexibility for local image storage. We then discuss a variety of network-based storage options, including iSCSI and AoE, which both make remote disks accessible directly. We also discuss the role of distributed file systems, such as NFS, in image storage. Finally, we discuss the issue of image archival and sharing. In this context, we describe how to create the same types of prebuilt guest images you used in Chapter 5.

Logical Volumes

A *logical volume manager* (LVM) provides a level of abstraction above the actual block devices (for example, disks). This allows for significant flexibility in managing storage by, among other things, making it easier to group or resize physical partitions. There are logical volume manager implementations for many operating systems, including most UNIX variants and some versions of Windows. The term LVM is often used to refer to the specific implementation of a logical volume manager for the Linux kernel.

An LVM manages *physical volumes* (PVs), block devices such as local or network-attached hard drives or partitions. PVs are broken into smaller units called *physical extents* (PEs), which can be concatenated together or split apart by an LVM to grow or shrink the PVs that they comprise. One or more PVs can be combined to form a *volume group* (VG). From the VG, arbitrary-sized *logical volumes* (LVs) can be created. These LVs can span multiple PVs, allowing them to be any size, as long as the size of all LVs is less than or equal to the total size of the VG. LVMs often support functionality such as various RAID levels for replications, redundancy, or striping. Some support copy-on-write snapshots to facilitate sharing and backup.

After VGs and LVs are created, the underlying PVs are managed behind the scenes. LVs are the unit of storage that is actually mounted and used. The higher level functionality of extending or shrinking the LVs can then be used as needed. Figure 8.1 shows a high-level diagram of a VG—the PVs that it is composed of and the LVs that are made from it.

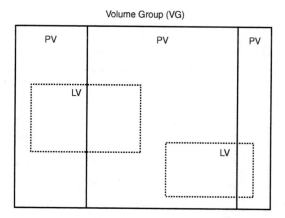

FIGURE 8.1 A volume group (VG) is made up of physical volumes (PVs) and arbitrary logical volumes (LVs) are made out of the VG.

Using an LVM to store your Xen guest system images is an attractive option because it provides useful features such as dynamic resizing of volumes and snapshots. Dynamic resizing of Xen guests is useful because if a guest needs more space, the LV can be resized to give it the additional space required. Similarly if one guest has extra space that would be more useful for another guest, the LVs can be adjusted, rather simply, to accommodate that. The snapshot feature is useful for keeping small point-in-time backups that can be used for recovery or to clone a guest to be used for fail-over, or even to modify it to be used for another purpose. In this chapter, we use LVM2 on Linux as the specific example of an LVM.

Basic LVM Usage

To initialize a partition to support LVM volumes, we use the command pvcreate, or physical volume create. The pvcreate command takes a single argument that can be a whole disk, a metadevice (a logical device that encompasses one or more physical devices), or a loopback file. The pvcreate command itself does not create the VG, but rather initializes the device for later use by LVM. The initialization erases the partition table for the device and creates an LVM-specific metadata area on the device. This step makes any data previously on the drive unavailable. In other words, this command effectively destroys any data previously stored on the disk, so use this command with appropriate caution.

Listing 8.1 illustrates using pvcreate to initialize a spare 10GB partition on /dev/sda9 to be used with LVM.

LISTING 8.1 Using `pvcreate` to Initialize a Partition

```
[root@dom0]# pvcreate /dev/sda9
Physical volume "/dev/sda9" successfully created
[root@dom0]#
```

Now, using the LVM-enabled PV, a VG can be created that uses the PV we just created. (More PVs could have been initialized with the `pvcreate` command and then also used in the VG creation in Listing 8.2.) Next, we use the command `vgcreate`, or volume group create. The `vgcreate` command is used to create a volume by using one or more PVs passed as arguments. The first argument to `vgcreate` is the VG name, and the following arguments are PVs, which were initialized previously with `pvcreate`. The example in Listing 8.2 shows the command for creating a VG named xen_vg using the PV that we initialized in Listing 8.1.

LISTING 8.2 Using `vgcreate` to Create the `xen_vg` Volume Group

```
[root@dom0]# vgcreate xen_vg /dev/sda9
  Volume group "xen_vg" successfully created
[root@dom0]#
```

> **NOTE**
> When creating a volume group with multiple physical volumes, you simply add more devices to the `vgcreate` command line. For example, you could expand Listing 8.2 to be `vgcreate xen_vg /dev/sda9 /dev/sda10` and that would make the `xen_vg` volume group be composed of both `/dev/sda9` and `/dev/sda10`. Also, notice that `/dev/sda10` device would need to have been initialized with `pvcreate`.

After a VG has been created, LVs can be created from it. Recall that LVs are what actually get mounted and used to store a Xen guest's system image. The command used to create an LV is `lvcreate`, or logical volume create. The `lvcreate` command creates a new LV by allocating logical extents from the free logical extent pool of the VG passed as arguments. Listing 8.3 shows the command to create a 4GB LV. The -L option is used to specify the size of the LV, and the -n option is used to specify the name of the LV. The command in the example creates a 4GB LV with the name guest_partition_lvm in the VG xen_vg.

LISTING 8.3 Using `lvcreate` to Create a Logical Volume

```
[root@dom0]# lvcreate -L 4G -n guest_partition_lvm xen_vg
  Logical volume "guest_partition_lvm" created
[root@dom0]#
```

The `lvcreate` command in Listing 8.3 creates a new entry in the `/dev/<volume_group_name>/` directory for the new LV. In this case, it is represented by the entry `/dev/xen_vg/guest_partition_lvm`. A new entry should also be available in `/dev/mapper`, as the entry in `/dev/xen_vg/guest_partition_lvm` is typically a symbolic link to a `/dev/mapper/xen_vg*` device node. The device, `/dev/xen_vg/guest_partition_lvm`, can now be used like a physical partition. Listing 8.4 shows an example of how to format, mount, and populate the drive, as was shown in Chapter 5, with a blank partition. In this example, a compressed file is extracted, but another population method could be used just as easily. Population methods were discussed in Chapter 7, "Populating Guest Images."

LISTING 8.4 Populating the Logical Volume by Extracting Compressed File System into It

```
[root@dom0#] mkfs.ext3 /dev/xen_vg/guest_partition_lvm

[output omitted]

[root@dom0#] e2label /dev/xen_vg/guest_partition_lvm "/"

[output omitted]

[root@dom0#] mkdir /mnt/guest_partition
[root@dom0#] mount /dev/xen_vg/guest_disk_lvm /mnt/guest_partition
[root@dom0#] cd /mnt/guest_partition
[root@dom0#] tar xzf /xen/downloads/openfiler-2.2-x86.tgz
[root@dom0#] umount /mnt/partition
```

Finally, we can create a DomU guest configuration file as shown in Listing 8.5.

LISTING 8.5 DomU Guest Configuration File for Use with LVM

```
/etc/xen/openfiler-lvm
kernel = "/boot/vmlinuz-2.6.16-xen"
ramdisk = "/boot/initrd.img-2.6.16.33-xen"
memory = 128
name = "openfiler-lvm"
vif = [ '' ]
dhcp = "dhcp"
disk = ['phy:xen_vg/guest_disk,xvda1,w']
```

Then, using the xm create command, the guest could be booted as shown in Listing 8.6.

LISTING 8.6 Booting LVM Guest

```
[root@dom0#] xm create -c openfiler-lvm
[output omitted]
```

Resizing Images

The resizing feature of LVM allows guests that are built in an LVM LV to be more flexible. For example, the guest's root file system can be resized if more space is needed. Using LVM to manage the resizing is significantly easier than the process that would be necessary without it. Keep in mind that when growing an LV, after the size of the LV is increased, the size of the file system needs to be increased as well to make use of the new space. Therefore, to truly benefit from this feature, the file system used should also support resizing.

Recent versions of ext3, as well as the one we used in this chapter, support online resizing (resizing while mounted). ReiserFS is another example of a file system that supports resizing. In general, it's a good idea to check the manual for your file system to see how well it supports growing or shrinking and whether it can be done while mounted, if online resizing is a desired feature.

ext3 is used in the examples that follow. In our experience, ext3 file systems can be resized to a larger size while mounted with no problems, although resizing to a smaller size does require them to be unmounted. Use caution and make a backup before resizing file systems.

Another important consideration is the ability of the Xen guest to recognize the effects of the resizing of the underlying file system change. In recent versions of Xen, this has been demonstrated to be possible, but is tricky to set up. Refer to http://forums.xensource.com/message.jspa?messageID=8404 for more information. It is still safest to shut down the guest for the resizing process and then start it again after the process is complete. Listing 8.7 shows the commands to shut down and start the guest. Refer to Chapter 6, "Managing Unprivileged Domains," for more details on these commands. If downtime of the guest is an issue, it is possible to resize more aggressively, but it would be best to experiment on a test setup first. Expanding can be done if you have all the right support, such as a file system that supports it and a version of Xen that supports it. Shrinking is also possible, but fewer file systems support online resizing to a smaller size.

LISTING 8.7 Carefully Handling the Resizing of a DomU File System

```
[root@dom0]# xm shutdown -w guest1
<Do the resizing of the logical volume and file system here as shown below>
[root@dom0]# xm create -q guest1
```

Increasing the Size of a Volume

The first step in increasing the usable space in an LV is to extend it with the `lvextend` (logical volume extend) command. `lvextend` is part of the LVM2 Linux package and is used to extend or grow the size of an LV. Recall that a 4GB LV was created inside a 10GB VG. Now, the size of that LV could be increased to 5GB. Listing 8.8 shows how to use the `lvextend` command to extend a logical volume.

LISTING 8.8 Using `lvextend` to Extend a Logical Volume

```
[root@dom0]# lvextend -L 5G /dev/xen_vg/guest_partition_lvm
  Extending logical volume guest_partition_lvm to 5.00 GB
  Logical volume guest_partition_lvm successfully resized
[root@dom0]#
```

The next step is to resize the underlying file system to make use of the new space. To resize an ext3 file system, the `resize2fs` command is used. The `resize2fs` command is part of the e2fsprogs package and is used to resize ext2 and ext3 partitions. If a size is not passed to the `resize2fs` command, it automatically resizes to the size of the partition. Listing 8.9 shows the `resize2fs` command that would be used in this case so that the file system fills the LV. Notice that the resize is done online while the volume is mounted.

LISTING 8.9 Using `resize2fs` to Extend the Underlying File System

```
root@dom0]# resize2fs /dev/xen_vg/guest_partition_lvm
resize2fs 1.39 (29-May-2006)
Filesystem at /dev/xen_vg/guest_partition_lvm is mounted on /mnt/guest_partition_
lvm; on-line resizing required
Performing an on-line resize of /dev/xen_vg/guest_partition_lvm ➥
to 1310720 (4k) blocks.
The filesystem on /dev/xen_vg/guest_partition_lvm is now 1310720 blocks long.
[root@dom0]#
```

If the LV can be taken offline to resize it, the e2fsck command could be used to check the file system for errors before resizing it. e2fsck is also included in the e2f-sprogs package. Listing 8.10 shows an example of this.

LISTING 8.10 Using efsck to Check the File System for Errors

```
[root@dom0]# umount /dev/xen_vg/guest_partition_lvm
[root@dom0]# e2fsck /dev/xen_vg/guest_partition_lvm
e2fsck 1.39 (29-May-2006)
/dev/xen_vg/guest_partition_lvm: clean, 11475/655360 files, 105166/1310720 blocks
[root@dom0]#
```

Reducing the Size of a Volume

Next, we consider the case that more space is needed for another guest, and not all of the space allocated for the guest_partition_lvm LV is needed. The size of this LV can be reduced by basically reversing the extend process and changing the commands to extend the size of the volume and partition of the commands to reduce the size of the partition and volume. First, the file system is unmounted with the umount command, because reducing the size of the file system, unlike extending it, is not supported in ext3. Next, the size of the file system is reduced with the resize2fs command (this time with the new size of the partition as an argument). Finally, lvreduce, (logical volume reduce) a command included in the LVM2 package, is used to reduce the size of an LV. Notice that this is the opposite order in which we did the extend and resize, because we do not want to lose data on our file system. Listing 8.11 shows the umount and the file system check.

LISTING 8.11 Umounting and Checking the Logical Volume for Errors

```
[root@dom0]# umount /mnt/guest_partition_lvm/
[root@dom0]# e2fsck -f /dev/xen_vg/guest_partition_lvm
e2fsck 1.39 (29-May-2006)
Pass 1: Checking inodes, blocks, and sizes
Pass 2: Checking directory structure
Pass 3: Checking directory connectivity
Pass 4: Checking reference counts
Pass 5: Checking group summary information
/dev/xen_vg/guest_partition_lvm: 11475/655360 files (1.1% non-contiguous),
105166/1310720 blocks
root@dom:~# resize2fs  /dev/xen_vg/guest_partition_lvm 4G
resize2fs 1.39 (29-May-2006)
```

```
Resizing the filesystem on /dev/xen_vg/guest_partition_lvm to ➡
1048576 (4k) blocks.
The filesystem on /dev/xen_vg/guest_partition_lvm is now 1048576 blocks long.

[root@dom0]#
```

Listing 8.12 shows how to use the lvreduce command to shrink the size of the LV that contains the file system we shrunk in Listing 8.11. We use the -f option to force the operation; optionally you could leave it off and be prompted Do you really want to reduce the logical volume? [y/n]:.

LISTING 8.12 Using lvreduce to Shrink the Logical Volume

```
[root@dom0]# lvreduce -f -L 4G /dev/xen_vg/guest_partition_lvm
WARNING: Reducing active logical volume to 4.00 GB
  THIS MAY DESTROY YOUR DATA (filesystem etc.)
  Reducing logical volume guest_partition_lvm to 4.00 GB
  Logical volume guest_partition_lvm successfully resized
[root@dom0]#
```

At the time of this writing, although online resizing guest images to a bigger size is supported, it might still be tricky to setup Xen to support the change within the guest without rebooting the guest. Refer to http://forums.xensource.com/message.jspa?messageID=8404 for more information. Listing 8.13 shows the command to reboot a DomU from the Domain0 so that the DomU guest running on older versions of Xen can recognize the change to its disk. The xm reboot command should be issued after the changes to the volume have been made.

> **NOTE**
> Alternatively, you can use xm shutdown before the process of resizing, and then use xm create after the resizing process is complete. Refer to Chapter 6 for details of these xm commands.

LISTING 8.13 Using xm to Reboot the DomU Guest

```
<Do resizing of logical volume and file system here as shown above here>
[root@dom0]# xm reboot <guest name or id>
```

Image Snapshots Using Copy on Write

Copy on write (CoW) is a technique to support efficient sharing of a large object between two or more entities, such as processes or threads. It appears to each entity as though it has its own writeable copy of an object, such as a large file or address space. In reality, each entity has read-only access to the same shared object. If one of the entities writes to one of the blocks or pages that make up the object, that block is quickly duplicated, and the writer is given its own copy.

CoW is most efficient when sharing a large object that is changed rarely by the entities sharing it. Using CoW images when making DomU guests can make a lot of sense, both for reducing the amount of storage needed for similar guests (because guests can share parts of the file system that don't change) and also for a more efficient implementation of snapshots. There are many choices for implementing CoW images with Xen. Among these are using LVM snapshots, using the `blktap` interface for accessing disk, using network or cluster-based solutions, such as `CowNFS` or `parallax`, or a myriad of other solutions. In this section we look at one of the more common ways of using CoW images for DomU guests: LVM LV clones, also known as *writable persistent snapshots*. For more CoW options, refer to the Xen wiki at `http://wiki.` `xensource.com/xenwiki/COWHowTo`.

After LVM is set up and a guest partition or disk is using an LV, CoW clones can be created of LVM volumes. Be advised that this functionality was new as of version 2.6.8 of the Linux Kernel. The `guest_disk_partition` LV that was created earlier in this chapter in Listing 8.3 is used in the following clone examples. The first step is to ensure the `dm-snapshot` kernel module is loaded. Listing 8.14 shows the `modprobe` command to load the dm-snapshot module.

LISTING 8.14 Using `modprobe` to Load the Kernel Module Needed for LVM Snapshotting

```
[root@dom0]# modprobe dm-snapshot
[root@dom0]#
```

The next step is to create one or more CoW LVs that are snapshots (clones) of the `guest_partition_lvm` LV. In this example, two of them are created. Listing 8.15 shows the commands needed to create the LV clones.

LISTING 8.15 Using `lvcreate` to Create CoW Logical Volume Clones

```
[root@dom0]# lvcreate -s -L 1G -n clone1 /dev/xen_vg/guest_partition_lvm
  Logical volume "clone1" created
[root@dom0]# lvcreate -s -L 1G -n clone2 /dev/xen_vg/guest_partition_lvm
  Logical volume "clone2" created
[root@dom0]#
```

The result of the commands in Listing 8.15 is that two images now each appear to be a full image of `guest_partition_lvm` but are actually only a CoW image that stores the differences from the original, and the changes are only made when a clone is written to. Note that although the `guest_partition_lvm` LV could be written to, it should not be mounted or changed, because it is meant to be a reference or pristine image. The CoW images were created as 1GB, but they can be extended with the `lvextend` command as previously discussed.

There are a variety of advantages to using LVM, such as resizable partitions. Though LVM incrementally improves on the local disk storage methods available to Xen, it is not limited to just the devices physically connected to your Domain0 host. Network-attached storage devices can be used and managed through LVM. In some cases, the physical disk throughput has been saturated, or all physical disk capacity has been consumed, and one of the network-based storage systems supported by Xen would be more appropriate.

Network Image Storage Options

Several network-based storage mechanisms are good solutions for storing Xen guest system images. Having images on a network server or available on network-based storage can provide some nice features such as live migration (see Chapter 13, "Guest Save, Restore, and Live Migration") and increased flexibility over local disk images. For example, images mounted over the network can be shared by multiple guests, even across different physical Xen systems. Having the images in a central server can allow for easier backup and fail-over (running a guest on a different physical machine in the case of hardware failure).

However, when working over a network, some extra factors need to be taken into consideration, such as security of the network. For example, in some setups it might be possible for compromised guests or servers to access sensitive information on guests using network storage. Also, there are performance considerations such as how fast the network interconnect is and what level of performance degradation is experienced when an image is mounted over the network. Finally, accessing images over the network introduces another possible failure point.

In this section, we describe some of the network-based storage options and discuss some of their advantages and disadvantages. Specifically, we look at *iSCSI, ATA over Ethernet* (AoE), and the *Network File System* (NFS). There are many other network-based options, but these are some of the more commonly used for this purpose.

NFS and iSCSI use a network layer protocol for transport (for example, TCP). This means they could be used over a wide area network (WAN), but this is not generally recommended because they are intended for use on a local area network (LAN) with a high bandwidth interconnect. AoE, on the other hand, takes this one step further; it uses an Ethernet layer protocol for its transport, requiring that the client and server be on the same logical switch or subnet.

AoE is intended to be used when the client and server are under the same administrative control. Because no security is built into it, anyone on the same logical switch or subnet can access any AoE drives exported by the server. NFS and iSCSI do provide authentication mechanisms based on the client and user that is connecting. In our experience, AoE recovers and reacts more gracefully to temporary network outages than iSCSI or NFS. For example, it was able to continue an `fdisk -1` command listing from a drive that became available after the command was run.

Any of these network-based servers could be run from anywhere, but running either on a guest or on an external physical machine is recommended as opposed to on the Domain0 itself, because it is best practice to avoid unnecessary chances that could compromise the Domain0. See Chapter 11, "Securing a Xen System," for more security considerations.

iSCSI

iSCSI, which stands for *Internet Small Computer Systems Interface*, is a way of sharing data over the network. It is a transport protocol that connects SCSI drives, rather than mounted file system directories, on a server to a client over TCP/IP. The iSCSI client attaches a logical device over an Internet link and uses it as if it were a normal SCSI drive. An iSCSI server is not limited to exporting SCSI drives; non-SCSI disks can also be exported over iSCSI. After the client attaches the device, the client can treat the device just like a normal hard drive. The performance is good, because it scales with the bandwidth of the Ethernet link.

The server in an iSCSI setup is called a *target*. Several variants of iSCSI targets are available. Open source software iSCSI targets include the iSCSI Enterprise Target project and the Openfiler distribution. Commercial software iSCSI targets include Data-Core Software's SANsymphony and String Bean Software's WinTarget (acquired by Microsoft). There are also commercial hardware iSCSI targets such as many of IBM's DS family of storage servers and the PS Series architecture from EqualLogic, Inc.

The client in an iSCSI setup is called an *initiator*. There are software iSCSI initiators (such as the Cisco iSCSI Driver or the Open-iSCSI project) and hardware initiators (such as the iSCSI host bus adapters (HBAs) from Alacritech and Qlogic).

Server Setup in iSCSI

Many distributions, including Fedora and Ubuntu, have packages for an iSCSI target. The iSCSI target can also be built from source. Listing 8.16 shows how to install the iSCSI target.

LISTING 8.16 Installing `iscsitarget` from Source

```
#You will need the OpenSSL development libraries
[root@ubuntu-dom0]# apt-get install libssl-dev
OR
[root@fedora-dom0]# yum install openssl-devel

# download latest release from http://iscsitarget.sourceforge.net/
# At the time of this writing 0.4.15, ➡
so we use the following commands [output omitted]
tar zxf iscsitarget-0.4.15.tar.gz
cd iscsitarget-0.4.15/
make
make install
```

Another easy way to get a working iSCSI target is to download a virtual appliance for it. As of this writing, we couldn't find a Xen DomU guest configured as an iSCSI target available for download. However, we did find a VMware appliance that has the software from the open source iSCSI Enterprise Target project installed. We discussed in Chapter 5 how to convert VMware images to Xen guests.

The next step is to configure `iscitarget`. This step consists of making two simple changes to the `/etc/ietd.conf` file to get `iscsitarget` to export the drive that will be used. Listing 8.17 shows a simple example of our `/etc/ietd.conf` file. The changes made were to change the target name from `iqn.2001-04.com.example:` `storage.disk2.sys1.xyz` to `iqn.2007-10.com.mycompany:storage.disk2.` `data1.rack`, change `/dev/sdc` to `/dev/sdb`, and uncomment so that the device to export is the one that we have free (which, in our case, is `/dev/sdb`).

These are the only changes required to get a functional iSCSI server. For production use, you should change the target name on the first line of the Target stanza to reflect your organizational information because this name must be globally unique, as defined by the iSCSI standard.

A full description of the options are beyond the scope of this book. Some things that can be done through this config file include the addition of user-level security (which defaults to no security) and specifying the IO mode (which defaults to write access with write-through caching). Refer to the `ietd.conf` man page for more information.

LISTING 8.17 Simple `/etc/ietd.conf` iSCSI Target Configuration

```
# Note: need to change the target name
# Also, change /dev/sdb to the device to export
#Target iqn.2001-04.com.example:storage.disk2.sys1.xyz
Target iqn.2007-10.com.mycompany:storage.disk2.data1.rack1
    #Lun 0 Path=/dev/sdc,Type=fileio
    Lun 0 Path=/dev/sdb,Type=fileio
```

To start the iSCSI server, use the command in Listing 8.18. If you installed from a distribution package, the distribution might have different tools to start the init script for the iSCSI target server and different names for the iSCSI target server binary and init script.

LISTING 8.18 Starting the iSCSI Server

```
[root@dom0]# /etc/init.d/iscsi-target start
```

> **NOTE**
> For troubleshooting help, we recommend the `ietd` (iSCSI Enterprise Target Daemon) command. You can run it manually from the command line using `-d` for debuglevel and `-f` for foreground. Again, see the `ietd` man page for more information.

One common problem is that the iSCSI connections need to be allowed through the iSCSI server machine or guest's firewall. The default iSCSI target port is 3260, but this can be configured both from the `ietd.conf` file and also manually on the command line with the `-p` option. Finally, be sure to enable the `iscsi-target` service on boot, if desired. Refer to your distribution-specific documentation for details on how to start services at boot.

Client Setup in iSCSI

To set up the iSCSI client, also referred to as an *initiator*, it is necessary to install the appropriate iSCSI client tools. We had success installing the `open-iscsi` tools included in the `iscsi-initiator-utils` package in Fedora and included in the `open-iscsi` package in Ubuntu. If a package is not available for your distribution, you can install the iSCSI client from source by downloading it at `www.open-iscsi.org`. Listing 8.19 shows the commands for installing the iSCSI client from source.

LISTING 8.19 Installing `open-iscsi` from Source

```
[root@dom0]# wget http://www.open-iscsi.org/bits/open-iscsi-2.0-865.15.tar.gz
[root@dom0]# tar zxf open-iscsi-2.0-865.15.tar.gz
[root@dom0]# cd open-iscsi-2.0-865.15/
[root@dom0]# make
[root@dom0]# make install
```

To establish the connection from the client initiator to the server, the `iscsiadm` tool, which is part of the iSCSI client tools installed in Listing 8.19, is used. The `iscsiadm` tool communicates with the iscsid daemon to maintain iSCSI sessions. The `-m` option allows specification of the mode (discovery or node). In discovery mode, the iSCSI daemon probes the iSCSI target server for available exported targets. For the example in Listing 8.20, we can see that the target `iqn.2006-05.vm.iscsi:storage.sdb` is exported by the iSCSI target with `128.153.18.77`. We then use the node mode, specified with `-m node`, and the target can be attached by specifying the specified target name with the `-T` option, the `-p` for the server IP, and `-l` to log in. You can set up access permissions to particular targets from the iSCSI server configuration; refer to the previous discussion of `ietd.conf`.

LISTING 8.20 `iscsiadm` Commands to Detect and Log In to the iSCSI Target

```
[root@dom0]# iscsiadm -m discovery -t st -p 128.153.18.77
128.153.18.77:3260,1 iqn.2006-05.vm.iscsi:storage.sdb
[root@dom0]# iscsiadm -m node -T \
iqn.2006-05.vm.iscsi:storage.sdb -p  128.153.18.77 -l
[root@dom0]#
```

After successful login, the target is attached as an SCSI device (/dev/sdX) where by default x is the next available letter sd drive (that is, if you have an sda, the attached drive will be sdb). You can have more control of the naming of the attached devices using udev. The udev subsystem comes standard with most distributions and should be available from a package or from source. You can see www.kernel.org/pub/linux/utils/kernel/hotplug/udev.html for more information on udev.

When using udev, each time a device is connected/attached to the system, a udev device node is created for it. This is particularly useful in the iSCSI case because each time a device is connected, the /dev/sd* corresponding to it could be different (that is, sometimes it could show up as /dev/sdb, and other times as /dev/sdc, depending on what the next available SCSI device [sd] is), but with udev, there is a symbolic link to the corresponding sd* device made for each disk in /dev/disk/by-uuid, which uniquely identifies the device. Listing 8.21 shows the /dev/disk/by-uuid for the Domain0 that is acting as an iSCSI initiator and has the drive that was attached in Listing 8.20.

LISTING 8.21 udev disk by-uuid Device Listing

```
root@dom0 ls -l /dev/disk/by-uuid/
total 0
lrwxrwxrwx 1 root root 10 2007-07-07 11:16
➥3ab00238-a5cc-4329-9a7b-e9638ffa9a7b -> ../../sda1
lrwxrwxrwx 1 root root 10 2007-07-07 11:16
➥ d54098ac-5f51-4a67-a73d-33ac666691d2 -> ../../sdb1
```

Listing 8.22 shows the DomU configuration file that was used for this example iSCSI setup.

LISTING 8.22 An Example DomU Configuration File for iSCSI

```
kernel = "/boot/vmlinuz-2.6.16-xen"
ramdisk = "/boot/initrd.img-2.6.16.33-xen"
```

```
memory = 128
name = "iscsi_guest"
vif = [ '' ]
dhcp = "dhcp"
disk = ['phy:disk/by-uuid/d54098ac-5f51-4a67-a73d-33ac666691d2,xvda1,w']
```

> **NOTE**
> Because iSCSI devices are treated like block devices, having them mounted multiple times with write access is not recommended, as this is likely to cause file system corruption. For more information on the iSCSI Enterprise Target project, see http://iscsitarget.sourceforge.net/. For more information on the Open-iSCSI project, see www.open-iscsi.org/.

ATA over Ethernet (AoE)

The concept of ATA over Ethernet (AoE) is similar to that of iSCSI, but instead of exporting the device over a transport layer protocol, the device is exported over an Ethernet layer protocol. Generally, AoE delivers higher performance than iSCSI. Another benefit of AoE is that the setup is much simpler than iSCSI. To set up AoE, all that must be done is to install the appropriate kernel module and export a block device. The main drawbacks of AoE are that it works only on the same logical switch or subnet, and no security is built into the AoE protocol or server as compared to the client and user-specific access that iSCSI can support. The only security is the fact that the traffic is not routable (meaning, only exists on the same local subnet).

Server Setup in AoE

AoE, like other network-based storage solutions, has a server and a client component. The server component is called *Vblade*, which is a virtual EtherDrive Blade that exports block devices over a local ethernet. It models a physical device that has shelves and slots. So when you export a block device with the vblade command, you need to specify the shelf and the slot of a virtual EtherDrive.

The Vblade package comes with vbladed, which is a daemon version of vblade that logs its output to syslog instead of standard out, like the vblade binary does. Most distributions come with a package for Vblade, but it can also be built from source. Listing 8.23 shows the steps to install Vblade. The latest version of the Vblade package can be downloaded from http://sf.net/projects/aoetools/. More Vblade information can be found at http://sourceforge.net/projects/aoetools/.

LISTING 8.23 Building Vblade, the AoE Server Component, from Source

```
[root@aoe-server]# tar xzpf vblade-14.tgz
[root@aoe-server]# cd vblade-14/
[root@aoe-server]# make

[output omitted]

[root@aoe-server]# make install

[output omitted]
```

The first thing we do is use the `vblade` command to export a physical drive over AoE. Listing 8.24 shows this command and its output. In this example, a local disk is exported, but a file-based disk guest image could be exported in a similar manner. After it is verified that the `vblade` command is working similar to Listing 8.24, you can use Ctrl+C to quit. We use the `vbladed` command and track any errors with the system logger (that is, syslog). The usage of `vblade` is `vblade <shelf> <slot> <ethn> <device>`. So for the example shown in Listing 8.24, `vblade` uses `shelf 1`, `slot 1`, `eth0`, and `/dev/sda`. The slots and shelves refer to a logical numbering scheme based on a physical EtherDrive. For more information on the physical EtherDrive unit, visit `www.coraid.com` and `www.coraid.com/support/linux/`.

LISTING 8.24 Using `vblade` to Export a Physical Block Device

```
[root@aoe-server]# vblade 1 1 eth0 /dev/sda
octl returned 0
2147483648 bytes
pid 367: e1.1, 4194304 sectors
^C    <--- added for demonstration
```

We run the same command, this time with `vbladed`, as shown in Listing 8.25. The usage of `vbladed` is the same as `vblade`. `vbladed` calls an instance of `vblade`, runs it in the background, and sends output to the system logger.

LISTING 8.25 Using `vbladed` to Export a Physical Block Device

```
[root@aoe-server]# vbladed 1 1 eth0 /dev/sda
[root@aoe-server]#
```

vbladed runs in the background as a daemon with no output to standard out. That is all the setup you need on the server. For a production environment, you could use an initialization (init) script; check your distribution's documentation for details.

Client Setup in AoE

For the AoE client, you need to install the aoetools package and load the aoe module. The aoetools package is available for most distributions, but it can also be built from source. Listing 8.26 shows the steps to compile from source. You should first download the latest aoetools package from http://sf.net/projects/aoetools/.

LISTING 8.26 Compiling the AoE Client Tools from Source

```
[root@dom0]# tar xzf aoetools-21.tar.gz
[root@dom0]# cd aoetools-21/
[root@dom0]# make
[make output omitted]
[root@dom0]# make install
[make install output omitted]
[root@dom0]#
```

To load the aoe module, the modprobe command can be used as shown in Listing 8.27.

LISTING 8.27 Using modprobe to Load the aoe Module

```
[root@dom0]# modprobe aoe
[root@dom0]#
```

Now that aoetools is installed and the aoe module is loaded, aoe-stat can be run to display the AoE devices that are available. Listing 8.28 shows the AoE device status that was set up in Listing 8.25 by using the command aoe-stat.

LISTING 8.28 Using aoe-stat to List Available Devices

```
[root@dom0]# aoe-stat
    e1.1        2.147GB eth0 up
[root@dom0]#
```

For each AoE device, there will be a corresponding entry in /dev/etherd/, each of which appears to the AoE client, in this example the Domain0, as a block device. Listing 8.29 shows the directory listing for this example. The available AoE devices on the network automatically show up in /dev/etherd.

LISTING 8.29 Using `ls` to Get the Listing of Available AoE Block Devices

```
[root@dom0]# ls /dev/etherd/
e1.1
[root@dom0]#
```

You can now work with /dev/etherd/e1.1 just as if it were a normal block device. For example, you could partition it, format it, mount it, and populate it just as you would a physical drive. Partitions show up as the device name followed by the letter p, and then the partition number. Listing 8.30 shows an example listing after creating a partition on /dev/etherd/e1.1. When partitions are created on the AoE devices, they automatically show up in the /dev/etherd directory, with pN, where N is the partition number for the AoE device that was exported.

LISTING 8.30 Using `ls` to Get the Listing of Available AoE Block Devices (Now with a Partition)

```
[root@dom0]# ls /dev/etherd/
e1.1  e1.1p1
[root@dom0]#
```

After you have your guest image stored on /dev/etherd/e1.1p1 (just as you would store a guest image on /dev/hda1 or /dev/sda1), you can use a DomU guest configuration file similar to that shown in Listing 8.31. Alternatively, the same udev trick that was used in the iSCSI section can be used with AoE devices.

LISTING 8.31 DomU Guest Configuration File to Be Used with AoE Device

```
kernel = "/boot/vmlinuz-2.6.16-xen"
ramdisk = "/boot/initrd.img-2.6.16.33-xen"
memory = 128
name = "iscsi_guest"
vif = [ '' ]
dhcp = "dhcp"
disk = ['phy:etherd/e1.1p1,xvda1,w']
```

> **NOTE**
> Because AoE devices are treated like block devices, having them mounted multiple times with write access is not recommended, as this is likely to cause file system corruption.

NFS

Distributed file systems, such as AFS, NFS, and Samba, provide good support for sharing files across a network. They can also be used as a means to share files within Xen—for example, to store DomU root file systems or other files and directories. There is an important distinction between distributed file systems and the network attached storage solutions, such as iSCSI and AoE, discussed previously. In the distributed file systems, the files get mounted to the DomU, while in the network attached storage solutions, a block device is attached to the DomU. The advantage of mounting over a distributed file system, such as NFS, is that these file systems are designed to support multiple clients with write access at the same time. This is not the case with block devices because mounting the same partition with write access by multiple entities is a sure way to cause file system corruption.

Another good use for distributed file systems is when the server needs to periodically modify a file that will be used by one or more clients. This case is not easily handled with the network attached storage case, because the client cannot have the block device partition mounted with write access at the same time as the server (without the help of a distributed file system, of course).

The Network File System (NFS) originally developed by Sun in 1984 is one of the most mature and supported distributed file system options available. Despite its long history, however, it has been known to have some stability problems under heavy load when used as a root file system (even just in vanilla Linux).

Server Setup in NFS

Details of installing and running an NFS server are beyond the scope of this book. For more information, see http://nfs.sourceforge.net/nfs-howto/. Most modern distributions of Linux provide packages for an NFS server and install the dependent services as needed.

To configure your NFS server, you need to add a line to the /etc/exportfs file that gives the proper access to the share for the guest that will access it. Listing 8.32 shows an example of the /etc/exportfs file. The first entry in the line specifies the directory on the NFS server that is being exported. The second entry in the line specifies the IP address of the machine to which the data is exported; rw means read and write access, and sync means that write will happen synchronously or in real time and will not be batched. In our example, the export line allows a guest at the IP address 192.168.1.101 to mount the contents of /export/guest1 on the NFS server machine with read/write access (rw), synchronously (sync), and root is allowed to mount it (that is, root is not squashed) (no_root_squash).

LISTING 8.32 An Example /etc/exportfs File

```
/export/guest1      192.168.1.101 (rw,sync,no_root_squash)
```

If you want to export to multiple clients, you should have a line for each client. The lines could have different mount points and permissions. Writes from one machine can be seen by reads on the other. If they are going to be simultaneously writing the exact same files and directories, it is important to understand the NFS coherency model. Writes can be cached on the client for some time, and reads on that client will return the new data, but reads from other clients won't return the newly written data until it is written back to the server and any cached copies on other machines are refreshed.

When you make changes to the /etc/exportfs file, you should restart the NFS server so that it rereads it. This is typically done with the NFS server init script (usually found in /etc/init.d). Check the documentation for your distribution for the specifics.

Running an NFS server with the proper entry in /etc/exportfs takes care of the server side. Now on the client side, we need to configure the DomU guest to properly mount and use the data over NFS.

Client Setup in NFS

On most Linux systems, NFS support is built into the kernel, and you just need to use the standard mount command to access the exported files on the NFS server. (For more information on setting up the NFS client, see http://tldp.org/HOWTO/NFS-HOWTO/client.html). Listing 8.33 shows the command to mount the exported files from the server with configuration as in Listing 8.32. We will assume that the server's IP address is 192.168.1.100.

LISTING 8.33 Using mount to Mount the Files from the NFS Server

```
[root@nfs-client]# mount 192.168.1.100:/export/guest1 /mnt/data
[root@nfs-client]#
```

To mount the data automatically at boot, add the line as shown in Listing 8.34 to the /etc/fstab file. The first entry in the line is where to mount from (192.168.1.100:/

export/guest1), the next is the mount point (/mnt/data), the next is the file system type (nfs), the next is the options (rw) for read/write, the next field lets the dump command know whether the file system needs to be dumped, and the last field determines the order in which the file system will be mounted at boot time. For more information, see the fstab man page.

LISTING 8.34 fstab Line to Automatically Mount NFS Data at Boot

```
192.168.1.100:/export/guest1     /mnt/data     nfs     rw     0  0
```

Using NFS as Root File System

The difference between using NFS as a normal file server and using NFS as a root file system is straightforward in theory, but special care must be taken to use an NFS-mounted partition as the root file system. First, you need to have support for mounting the NFS root file system built into the client. This is typically not the default, so you will likely need to rebuild your kernel manually to add the support.

NOTE

Documentation for setting this up can be found at www.gentoo.org/doc/en/diskless-howto.xml. Another good reference for Debian-based systems is the article at www.debian-administration.org/articles/505.

After you have the configuration of the server and client working, you should populate a directory on the server machine with a root file system (that is, all the files needed for an installed operating system). You could extract a compressed file system image to populate it. For some more ideas on population methods, see Chapter 7.

Next, the DomU guest configuration file needs to have a few options for it to use the NFS server for its root file system. These are demonstrated in Listing 8.35.

LISTING 8.35 Example DomU Configuration File for Use with NFS

```
kernel = "/boot/vmlinuz-2.6.16-xen"
ramdisk = "/boot/initrd.img-2.6.16.33-xen"
memory = 128
name = "nfs_guest"
vif = [ '' ]
dhcp = "dhcp"
```

```
root=/dev/root
nfs_server= 192.168.1.101
nfs_root = /export/guest1_root
```

Comparing Network Storage Options

We have now seen several methods suitable for remotely attaching disks to support your DomU guests. In each case, you need to evaluate your network performance, reliability, security, and preexisting experience with the file system technologies.

In general, we find when sharing files that needed to written to one or more client DomUs and a server DomU, or one or more DomUs and the Domain0, that NFS is a more safe and reasonable solution than using iSCSI or AoE. However, using NFS as a root file system (that is, the root file system of a DomU) is more complicated than the iSCSI or AoE solutions.

Finally, in terms of security considerations, NFS requires a number of related network services (for example, portmap, mountd, and rpcd) and thus a number of open network ports on the server machine. One consideration is that each running network service does open up a potential avenue of attack for your system. iSCSI and AoE are stand-alone services and do not require these extra services to function. Table 8.1 summarizes the advantages and disadvantages of the different network-based storage options.

> **NOTE**
> Although Windows does have NFS clients available, if Windows DomU guest support is needed for sharing files for writing, SAMBA might be a better choice for the file server. Refer to www.samba.org for more information.

TABLE 8.1 Network-Based File Systems Suitable for Xen Guests

Network-Based Type	Advantages	Disadvantages
iSCSI	Looks like standard SCSI disk, scales with network bandwidth (TCP)	Overhead due to network layer
NFS	Easy setup, well-tested	Problems reported under heavy load, more services required, more ports open
AoE	Easy setup, low overhead	No security built in, not routable (link layer)

Guest Image Files

The most flexible way to store guest images is with image files. Files can then be stored using any of the storage options already discussed, including dedicated local partitions, LVM, or network-based storage. With the added flexibility, however, lower performance can be a trade-off.

In this section, we describe how you can use standard UNIX utilities to create your own guest system image files from scratch. In Chapter 5, we showed you that you can download and use prebuilt guest image files such as compressed tar files, disk images, and partition images. In this section we show you how to create all three of these types of image files yourself. First we show how you can make a compressed tar file. Then we will show how to make a file that you can treat as a hard disk and also how to make a file that you can treat like a partition. Recall that disk images contain partitions within them, and the partition images represent a single partition and contain a single file system. After basic disk or partition image files are prepared, they can be populated or filled with the files that make up the guest image. (Recall that this population process was the topic of Chapter 7; you should be able to use those methods on your custom built disk and partition images.)

Preparing Compressed tar Image Files

To create a tar image file, you need a root file system from which to create your tar image. This can be any file system that you want to back up or share. For this example, we use the root file system on the running Linux system.

Listing 8.36 shows an example of how to create a tar file of the root partition. This `tar` command creates a tar/gzip file named `linux-root.tgz` that contains the contents of the root—that is, "/"—partition. The c option tells `tar` that we are creating a tar file (as opposed to extracting one, which would be specified with an x option instead), the z option does a `gzip` compression, the p option tells `tar` to preserve the file system permissions, and the f option tells `tar` that we want to save into the file argument that follows. The first argument is the filename of the resulting tar file (because it must follow the f option), in this case `/linux-root.tar`. Next, we exclude the `proc` directory with the `--exclude` option, because /proc is populated automatically at boot by the kernel. Also, we exclude the tar file itself, because the tar file can't contain a copy of itself. Finally, the last argument is the root of the file system, indicated with the "/" character.

> **NOTE**
>
> You may also run across, or use yourself, the file extension `.tar.gz`, which is equivalent to `.tgz`. Optionally, you can leave out the z option to not use compression. In this case, you should also name your file appropriately. For example, your tar file with no compression should be named `linux-root.tar`. You could also use a `j` option instead of the z option to use bzip2 compression, which does more compression than gunzip. Be sure to name your file appropriately. In the bzip2 case, name your file `linux-root.tbz2` (equivalently `linux-root.tar.bz2`). Alternatively, you can use the compression tools, such as gunzip and bzip, to compress the tar file manually after the plain tar file has been created. Compression saves space, but you should remember that with any compression there is also the chance for file corruption. For more information and more advanced options, refer to the tar, gunzip, and bzip2 man pages.

LISTING 8.36 Using `tar` to Create a Compressed tar File

```
[root@linux]# tar -czpf /linux-root.tgz --exclude=/proc \
--exclude=/linux-root.tgz /
[root@linux]#
```

Recall that to use the tar file you need to extract it to the desired location; see the section "Downloading Compressed File System Images" in Chapter 5 for more details.

Preparing Disk Image Files

As described earlier in this chapter, you can also have your guest use a dedicated partition of a hard drive, an LV, or network-based storage; in those cases populating the partition, volume, or network-based storage is the same, but setting up the empty space is different. If you use a partition, volume, or network-based storage, you can later create an image file from any of them if you want to back up an image or share it with someone else. Image files are definitely more flexible and are best for sharing with others, but don't necessarily give as good of performance for normal runtime.

Typically, an operating system installer performs partitioning to the hard disk or disks inside the physical computer. The partitioning process typically involves breaking the disks into logically isolated segments called *hard disk partitions*. After the partitions are in place and formatted appropriately, the operating system can be installed (that is, extracted/copied) into one or more of the prepared partitions. A similar process is needed to create a virtual environment, a virtual disk or partition image file for example, in which to install a guest operating system to be used by a DomU guest. We now describe how you can make your own virtual disks and partitions that live in file systems stored on other physical partitions, LVs, or network-based storage.

Before we go into the details of creating disk and partition images, we begin with an overview of the process and then, in this section and the following sections, we elaborate on each step. To perform the initial step of creating a virtual disk image, we use the dd command. Then we use the losetup and fdisk commands to create virtual partitions within the virtual drive images, and use the kpartx command to make them available to the system. Next we format the partitions appropriately. We then use dd once again to create individual files that represent virtual partitions. The way we use dd in the disk and partition case is the same, but the way we work with the image file after using dd is different; disk image files are treated like disks (they get partitioned with fdisk), and partition image files are treated like partitions (they are formatted with mkfs). Then we use mkfs to format the partitions (both partitions within the disk image and partitions that are partition images themselves) with an appropriate file system. After the partitions (either real or virtual) are formatted with an appropriate file system, they are ready to populate.

To create a disk image file we first use dd to allocate the virtual space in a file; then we use fdisk to make virtual partitions.

Allocating Virtual Devices with dd

dd stands for *dump data* and is a utility used to copy and possibly convert to and from disks. When using files to store guest images, dd is a useful utility. Before jumping directly into using dd to create disk image files, we illustrate the basics of dd with a series of simpler examples.

The simplest way to use dd is to give it an input file (with the if=FILE option) and an output file (with the of=FILE option). For example, the command in Listing 8.37 copies the contents of file1 into file2 one block at a time, so both files contain hello, followed by a new line. In Listing 8.37, file1 is created by redirecting the output of the echo command into it. Then dd is used to copy the blocks of file1, the input file, into file2, the output file.

LISTING 8.37 Basic dd Usage

```
[user@dom0]$ echo hello > file1
[user@dom0]$ cat file 1
hello
```

```
[user@dom0]$ dd if=file1 of=file2
0+1 records in
0+1 records out
6 bytes (6 B) copied, 0.000103 seconds, 58.3 kB/s
[user@dom0]$ cat file2
hello
```

In this example, we could accomplish the same thing with the standard copy com-mand. However, dd is more powerful than the standard copy (cp) command because you can specify lower level details such as the block sizes and number of blocks to copy. When creating a disk image, these details are essential to producing files that look and feel like real block devices.

Let's take a closer look at dd by building up to a command that creates a file that we will use as a virtual disk image for a guest. First, let's add the block size (bs) option and see how that affects our dd command from Listing 8.37. In Listing 8.38, we add a block size of 3 bytes. Recall file1 contains the word hello followed by a new line; each of those characters is 1 byte for a total of 6. Therefore, dd reads two blocks (also called records) of size 3 bytes, one block at a time, until it reads the whole input file (file1) and writes it to the output file (file2). The block size in this example is set to 3 bytes; this is obviously not practical, but notice that now we have two blocks (or re-cords) that were read from file1, and the same two records were put into file2.

LISTING 8.38 Example Using dd with a Block Size Option

```
[user@dom0]$ dd if=file1 of=file2 bs=3
2+0 records in
2+0 records out
6 bytes (6 B) copied, 8.8e-05 seconds, 68.2 kB/s
1024 bytes (1.0 kB) copied, 0.000107 seconds, 9.6 MB/s
[user@dom0]$
```

Next, let's add the count option to our dd command in Listing 8.38. The count option tells dd how many blocks to copy. In Listing 8.39, we see that with a block size of 3 and a count of 1, dd copies one block, of the input file (file1) and puts it into the output file (file2), which results in the first 3 bytes of file1 being transferred into the first block of file2. The resulting file2 is exactly 3 bytes long and contains the first 3 bytes of file1 (that is, "hel"). The block size in this example is 3, and the count is set to 1. Notice that the resulting file2 is 3 bytes (the first 3-byte block of file1).

LISTING 8.39 An Example of dd with Block Size and Count Options

```
[user@dom0]$ dd if=file1 of=file2 bs=3 count=1
1+0 records in
1+0 records out
3 bytes (3 B) copied, 6.3e-05 seconds, 47.6 kB/s
[user@dom0] ls -lh file2
-rw-r--r-- 1 user group 3 2007-03-21 00:02 file2
[user@dom0]$ cat file2
hel[user@dom0]$
```

Now, let's add the seek option to the dd command of Listing 8.37. The seek option tells dd how many blocks to skip. So, with a seek of 2, the first two blocks of the output file are skipped and dd begins to write in the third block. file2 was left at 3 bytes after the last operation, so when it skips two blocks, it actually inserts a space of three empty bytes. In Listing 8.40, we see that with a seek option of two *blocks* (notice not bytes), dd reads the first block of the input file (file1) and puts it into the third block of the output file (file2). The resulting file2 is 9 bytes, where the last three bytes of file2 are the first three bytes of file1. The block size is 3 bytes, the count is 1, and the seek is 2 *blocks*. Notice that file2 is 9 bytes (the third block of file2 contains the first 3 bytes of file1).

LISTING 8.40 An Example of Using dd with Block Size, Count, and Seek Options

```
[user@dom0]$ dd if=file1 of=file2 bs=3 count=1 seek=2
1+0 records in
1+0 records out
3 bytes (3 B) copied, 5.1e-05 seconds, 58.8 kB/s
[user@dom0]$ ls -lh file2
-rw-r--r-- 1 user group 9 2007-03-21 00:13 file2
[user@dom0]$cat file2
hel    hel
[user@dom0]$
```

In the preallocated disk image case, the image file takes up all the space of the image file even if it is not all used by the guest. Now, let's put this all together to make a sparse disk image file (recall that with a sparse image, the space available is not taken up until it is used), as shown in Listing 8.41. The alternative to a sparse image is a preallocated disk image (see Listing 8.42 for an example). The trade-off between sparse and preallocated images is space/performance; sparse images take less space and require a little more overhead for allocation, while preallocated images take up more space with no allocation (of space) overhead. It is also important to note that creating a sparse image is nearly instantaneous regardless of the max size, while creating a preallocated image takes time proportional to the size of the image. Some users have noticed that sparse image files tend to fragment more easily, but your mileage might vary.

In Listing 8.41, the input file is /dev/zero, which is a special file that provides as many null characters as are read from it. The output file in this example is called guest_disk_sparse.img; this will be the disk image file for our example guest. The block size is set to 1k (or 1 kilobyte); this tells dd how much to read/write at a time. The seek is set to 4096k (or 4096 *1024 = 4194304 blocks); this tells dd how many blocks to skip before writing into the output file. Notice that this is how many blocks to seek (4096k = 4096*1024) and not where to seek to. Because block size is set to 1k (that is, 1024 bytes), the seek location is how many blocks to seek (4096k) multiplied by block size (1024). The count (or number) of blocks to write is set to 1. So the effect of this command is to write a single block of size 1k to the file guest_disk.img at the location approximately 4.1 gigabytes into the file (4.1 gigabytes because 1k * 4096k = 1 * 1024 * 4096 * 1024 is about 4.1 billion bytes or 4.1 gigabytes). This guest_disk.img file can now be used as a sparse disk image file, which means that space is allocated only as it is needed.

LISTING 8.41 Using dd to Create a Sparse Guest Disk Image File

```
[user@dom0]$ dd if=/dev/zero of=guest_disk_sparse.img ➥
bs=1k seek=4096k count=1
1+0 records in
1+0 records out
1024 bytes (1.0 kB) copied, 0.000107 seconds, 9.6 MB/s
[user@dom0]$ls -lh guest_disk_sparse.img
-rw-r--r--    1 user users        4.0G Jan 18 03:54 guest_disk_sparse.img
[user@dom0]$du -h guest_disk_sparse.img
12K     guest_disk_sparse.img
[user@dom0]$
```

In Listing 8.42, the input file is also /dev/zero. The output file is named guest_disk_allocated.img, the block size is 1020k, and the count is 4000. Notice that no seek option is specified. We don't want to seek into the virtual disk; we simply want to allocate the space, in this case 1024k*4000, which is 4GB. Also, block size has nothing to do with the file system block size. The block size used with dd simply tells dd how much to read/write at a time. The file system block size and the performance of the disk have nothing to do with this block size.

LISTING 8.42 Using dd to Create a Preallocated Guest Image File

```
[user@dom0]$ dd if=/dev/zero of=guest_disk_allocated.img bs=1024k count=4000
4000+0 records in
4000+0 records out
4194304000 bytes (4.2 GB) copied, 57.8639 seconds, 72.5 MB/s
[user@dom0]$ls -lh guest_disk_allocated.img
-rw-r--r--     1 user users        4.2G Jan 18 04:54 ➡
guest_disk_allocated.img
[user@dom0]$ du -h guest_disk_allocated.img
4.0G    guest_disk_allocated.img
[user@dom0]$
```

One of the main things to watch out for when using dd is to not accidentally use a physical device or hard drive as the output because it will overwrite its contents with the input file. There are cases where this is useful, but they are outside the scope of this book.

Setting Up and Controlling Virtual Devices with losetup

Now that we know how to create empty virtual disks, we need to make virtual partitions in them. Because this is not a real disk, we need to use some utilities to make our virtual disk look like a block device. The losetup command is used to set up and control loop devices. We use losetup to trick the system into using our disk image file as a normal block device so that we can use fdisk, in the next section, to make partitions on it.

The first step is to find a free loop device. Typically by default most distributions of Linux ship configured with only a small number of loopback devices. For those following along with your first example, you can probably just use an available one. The command to check for the next available loop device is the losetup command variant demonstrated in Listing 8.43. If you need more loopback devices, you need to increase the max_loop option for the loop kernel module (see the "Sample Problems" section in Chapter 6 for details).

LISTING 8.43 Using losetup to Find the Next Available Loopback Device and Associate It with the Guest Disk Image File

```
root@dom0# losetup -f
/dev/loop1
root@dom0# losetup /dev/loop1 guest_disk_sparse.img
root@dom0#
```

> **NOTE**
>
> Recall that in earlier versions of Xen, the guests that used file-based backed images were forced to use the loopback device. It was recommended to increase the number of loopback devices so that you wouldn't run out. If you are using the `file:/` for the guest image (in the guest configuration file), this uses the loopback devices. It is recommended to use the `tap:aio` interface instead.

Creating Partitions on the Virtual Disks with `fdisk`

Now that our virtual disk is attached to our system as if it was a real disk, we need to create one or more virtual partitions on it. The `fdisk` command is a partition table manipulator, that is used to create, delete, and modify partitions on a block device such as a hard drive. We show how to use `fdisk` to create partitions on our virtual hard disk image file in Listing 8.44. We create the first partition as a 512MB swap partition and used the rest of the drive as a Linux partition. You should be able to safely ignore the warnings at the end of the `fdisk` w (write) command, because this applies to physical partitions and not virtual ones. Recall that we used `fdisk` in Chapter 5 to do a similar task.

> **NOTE**
>
> For detailed instructions on using `fdisk`, see The Linux Documentation Project's `fdisk` section in the partitioning article at http://tldp.org/HOWTO/Partition/fdisk_partitioning.html. You might also be able to use GParted or QtParted for the partitioning steps. Refer to the References and Further Reading section for more information on these tools.

LISTING 8.44 Using `fdisk` to Create Partitions on Our Guest Disk Image File

```
root@dom0# fdisk /dev/loop1
Command (m for help): n
Command action
   e   extended
   p   primary partition (1-4)
p
Partition number (1-4): 1
First cylinder (1-522, default 1): 1
Last cylinder or +size or +sizeM or +sizeK (1-522, default ➥
     522): +512M
```

```
Command (m for help): n
Command action
   e    extended
   p    primary partition (1-4)
p
Partition number (1-4): 2
First cylinder (64-522, default 64): 64
Last cylinder or +size or +sizeM or +sizeK (64-522, default ➥
    522): 522

Command (m for help): p

Disk /dev/loop1: 4294 MB, 4294968320 bytes
255 heads, 63 sectors/track, 522 cylinders
Units = cylinders of 16065 * 512 = 8225280 bytes

      Device Boot     Start        End      Blocks   Id  System
/dev/loop1p1             1         63      506016   83  Linux
/dev/loop1p2            64        522    3686917+   83  Linux

Command (m for help): w
The partition table has been altered!

Calling ioctl() to re-read partition table.

WARNING: Re-reading the partition table failed ➥
with error 22: Invalid argument.
The kernel still uses the old table.
The new table will be used at the next reboot.
Syncing disks.
root@dom0#
```

Making Virtual Disk Partitions Available with kpartx

Finally, we use the kpartx tool to make the partitions available to the system. The kpartx command is a tool that is part of the multipath-tools package used to create device maps from partition tables. The multipath-tools require kernel support to operate correctly. If you get strange errors, you likely need to load the kernel module to support them. The kernel module that you need is dm-multipath. This module should be included with your distribution, but if not, you need to build the module for your running kernel. Check your distribution's documentation for more information on this process. You should be able to load the `dm-multipath` module with the `modprobe` command as shown in Listing 8.45.

LISTING 8.45 Using `modprobe` to Load `dm-multipath` Kernel Module

```
[root@dom0]# modprobe dm-multipath
[root@dom0]#
```

After we have the multipath-tools package installed and kernel module loaded, we can use `kpartx` to detect the partitions on our disk image. In Listing 8.46 we use `kpartx` to map the partitions within the disk image to the system as block devices. As you can see from the output of the `ls` command in Listing 8.46, the device nodes for the two partitions are created in `/dev/mapper` as `loop1p1` and `loop1p2`, respectively.

LISTING 8.46 Using `kpartx` to Associate the Partitions to Block Devices

```
[root@dom0]# kpartx -av /dev/loop1
add map loop1p1 : 0 3919797 linear /dev/loop1 63
add map loop1p2 : 0 3919860 linear /dev/loop1 3919860
[root@dom0]# ls /dev/mapper
control  loop1p1  loop1p2
[root@dom0]#
```

Now the disk partitions are ready to be formatted. We format them just as we did normal partitions. Listing 8.47 and Listing 8.48 show how to format our disk image partitions that we have been working with.

LISTING 8.47 Using `mkswap` to Format the Swap Partition within Our Disk Image

```
[root@dom0] # mkswap /dev/mapper/loop0p1
Setting up swapspace version 1, size = 518156 kB
no label, UUID=fd4315cb-b064-4e70-bf30-a38117884e5f
[root@dom0]#
```

LISTING 8.48 Using `mkfs.ext3` to Format the Partition within the Disk Image

```
[root@dom0]# mkfs.ext3 /dev/mapper/loop1p2
mke2fs 1.39 (29-May-2006)
Filesystem label=
OS type: Linux
Block size=4096 (log=2)
Fragment size=4096 (log=2)
```

```
245280 inodes, 489974 blocks
24498 blocks (5.00%) reserved for the super user
First data block=0
Maximum filesystem blocks=503316480
15 block groups
32768 blocks per group, 32768 fragments per group
16352 inodes per group
Superblock backups stored on blocks:
        32768, 98304, 163840, 229376, 294912

Writing inode tables: done
Creating journal (8192 blocks): done
Writing superblocks and filesystem accounting information: done

This filesystem will be automatically checked every 29 mounts or
180 days, whichever comes first.  Use tune2fs -c
➡or -i to override.
[root@dom0]#
```

Now that we have formatted the partitions, we can detach them with kpartx and then detach the disk image file using losetup as shown in Listing 8.49 .

LISTING 8.49 Using kpartx and losetup to Detach Partitions and Disk Image

```
[root@dom0]# kpartx -d /dev/loop1
[root@dom0]# losetup -d /dev/loop1
```

You can use the partitions within a disk image file as LVM partitions by first associating the disk image file with a loopback device, as we did in the losetup section previously in the chapter, and then using the kpartx tool. As before, we find the first available loop device (/dev/loop1) and associate the guest_disk_sparse.img to it.

After the partitions are mapped, you can use them just like you would normal partitions. In Listing 8.50, we use the LVM commands as we did in the LVM section earlier in this chapter.

LISTING 8.50 Using LVM Commands to Create a Logical Volume with the Partitions within the Disk Image (guest_disk_sparse.img)

```
[root@dom0]#  pvcreate /dev/mapper/loop7p1 /dev/mapper/loop7p2
  Physical volume "/dev/mapper/loop7p1" successfully created
  Physical volume "/dev/mapper/loop7p2" successfully created
[root@dom0]# vgcreate disk_vg /dev/mapper/loop7p1 ➡
/dev/mapper/loop7p2
```

```
  Volume group "disk_vg" successfully created
[root@dom0]#  lvcreate -n guest_partition -L 3G disk_vg
  Logical volume "guest_partition" created
[root@dom0]#
```

Preparing Guest Partition Image Files

Creating a guest disk partition image file is different from creating a disk image because the image file will be treated like a partition and not like an entire disk. This makes it easier to use the dd and mkfs tools to work with a single partition at a time. Recall that dd was explained in detail earlier in this chapter. Listing 8.51 shows the dd command, and Listing 8.52 shows the mkfs command.

LISTING 8.51 Using dd to Create a Sparse Guest Partition Image File

```
[user@dom0]$ dd if=/dev/zero of=guest_partition_sparse.img bs=1k seek=4096k \
count=1
1+0 records in
1+0 records out
1024 bytes (1.0 kB) copied, 0.000107 seconds, 9.6 MB/s
[user@dom0]$
```

One thing to take note of when using mkfs and the like is that it will warn you and prompt you to proceed when you are formatting a file that is not a block special device. For our example we pass the -F option to force it to format our image file.

LISTING 8.52 Using mkfs to Format a Guest Image File to ext3

```
[user@dom0]$ mkfs.ext3 -F guest_partition_sparse.img
mke2fs 1.39 (29-May-2006)
Filesystem label=
OS type: Linux
Block size=4096 (log=2)
Fragment size=4096 (log=2)
524288 inodes, 1048576 blocks
52428 blocks (5.00%) reserved for the super user
First data block=0
Maximum filesystem blocks=1073741824
32 block groups
32768 blocks per group, 32768 fragments per group
16384 inodes per group
```

```
Superblock backups stored on blocks:
        32768, 98304, 163840, 229376, 294912, 819200, 884736

Writing inode tables: done
Creating journal (32768 blocks): done
Writing superblocks and filesystem accounting information: done

This filesystem will be automatically checked every 32 mounts or
180 days, whichever comes first.  Use tune2fs -c or -i to override.
[user@dom0]$
```

Next, we create and use a disk partition image as swap. First, we set up a disk file as we did in Listing 8.51. The swap file we make will be about 512MB. You can modify this based on the amount of RAM your guest will use (a good rule of thumb that we borrow from working with real servers is equal amounts of swap and physical RAM for a desktop system, twice as much swap as physical RAM for a server) or based on the density of guests you want to achieve by using fast, cheap disks. As before, you may choose to make a sparse or preallocated image based on your disk space/performance needs. Listing 8.53 uses a sparse image file.

LISTING 8.53 Using dd to Create a Swap Image File

```
[user@dom0]$ dd if=/dev/zero of=swap_partition_sparse.img bs=1k \ seek=512k
count=1
1+0 records in
1+0 records out
1024 bytes (1.0 kB) copied, 0.000149 seconds, 6.9 MB/s
[user@dom0]$
```

Now that we have a swap partition image file, we can format it as a swap file using mkswap, as shown in Listing 8.54.

LISTING 8.54 Using mkswap to Format the Swap File

```
[user@dom0]$ mkswap swap_partition_sparse.img
Setting up swapspace version 1, size = 536866 kB
```

Now that we know how to format the disk and partition images, let's look at how we can mount them.

Mounting Disks and Partition Images

Before populating a disk or partition image, you first need to mount them to your file system, typically to your Domain0. In Chapter 7, we looked in detail at methods to populate guest images. We could apply those methods to the partition and disk images that we created earlier in this chapter. Many of the population methods discussed apply to mounted disk and partition images that you create manually.

Disk Images

Because disk image files are not block devices, they cannot be mounted with the standard mount command. Once again, we need to use the lomount command (as we did in Chapter 5) to mount the specific partition within the disk image. This is shown in Listing 8.55. When we used fdisk earlier in this chapter, we made the first partition swap and the second partition ext3, so we will mount the second partition. If we are working with a disk that we do not know the partition table structure of, we can use the fdisk command to list the partitions (see Listing 8.56 for an example). Notice that we mount the second partition with lomount, because this is our ext3 partition; the first partition is a swap partition.

LISTING 8.55 Mount the Guest Disk Image on the Loopback Device

```
[root@dom0]# mkdir -p /mnt/guest_image/
[root@dom0]# lomount -t ext3 -diskimage guest_disk_sparse.img -partition 2 /mnt/
guest_image
[root@dom0]#
```

Listing 8.56 shows the listing of the partitions in the disk image file. You can ignore the warning about cylinders because this is a file we are working with. (See the previous section on using losetup to associate an image file with a loopback device to get rid of this warning.) The fdisk output shows that guest_disk_sparse.img1 and guest_disk_sparse.img2 are devices, even though they are actually embedded in the file and not available directly by name. Again, if you need to work with these partitions as if they were real partitions, you can use losetup as demonstrated previously.

LISTING 8.56 List the Partitions in the Disk Image with fdisk

```
[root@dom0]# fdisk -l guest_disk_sparse.img
You must set cylinders.
You can do this from the extra functions menu.
```

```
Disk guest_disk_sparse.img: 0 MB, 0 bytes
255 heads, 63 sectors/track, 0 cylinders
Units = cylinders of 16065 * 512 = 8225280 bytes

Device                   Boot Start End    Blocks    Id  System
guest_disk_sparse.img1             1       63        506016   82  Linux swap
guest_disk_sparse.img2        64           522       3686917+ 83  Linux
[root@dom0]#
```

Partition Images

To mount the guest_partition_sparse.img file temporarily to a directory on the local system, we use mount with the loop option. Notice that if you mounted the disk image to the /mnt/guest_image mount point, you need to either unmount it (with the umount command as shown in Listing 8.57) or create a new mount point. Listing 8.58 shows the command to mount the guest partition image.

LISTING 8.57 If Mounted Already, Use umount to Unmount the Disk Image from /mnt/guest_image

```
[root@dom0]# umount /mnt/guest_image/
[root@dom0]#
```

LISTING 8.58 Mount the Guest Partition Image on the Loopback Device

```
[root@dom0]# mkdir -p /mnt/guest_image/
[root@dom0]# mount -o loop -t ext3 guest_partition_sparse.img  /mnt/guest_image
[root@dom0]#
```

We have now looked at several different DomU guest storage mechanisms. Table 8.2 shows a summary of the different types, listing some benefits and caveats.

TABLE 8.2 Strengths and Weaknesses of DomU Guest Storage Mechanisms

DomU Guest Type	Benefits	Caveats
File-based image	Flexibility, easy to share, easy to back up and archive. File can be stored on any of the other storage media listed in this table.	Decreased performance as compared with raw partition and logical volumes.

TABLE 8.2 continued

DomU Guest Type	Benefits	Caveats
Real Partition	High performance, easy setup. Enables you to convert existing installations in a straightforward way.	Can't fully use as normal partition once converted to Xen.
Logical Volume	Resizable, provides snapshot capabilities.	Recovery can be tricky, requires more initial configuration and setup.
Network-based (iSCSI, NFS, etc.)	Flexibility, allows for live migration.	Relies on speed of network interconnect, can be tricky to set up, NFS performance/reliability concerns.

Summary

This chapter showed how to configure a Xen DomU guest to be used in a wide variety of system image types, including a logical volume, a physical disk or partition, network-based file storage such as NFS, or disk image files. We also showed how to create your own file-based images. In Chapter 9, "Device Virtualization and Management," we focus on managing the devices given to the DomU guests.

References and Further Reading

"Accessing Data on a Guest Disk Image (`lomount` and `kpartx`). Fedora Wiki.
  `http://fedoraproject.org/wiki/FedoraXenQuickstartFC6#head-9c540`
  `8e750e8184aece3efe822be0ef6dd1871cd.`

"Booting Xen 3.0 Guests Using NFS." Debian Administration.
  `http://www.debian-administration.org/articles/505.`

"Converting a VMWare Image to Xen HVM." Ian Blenke Computer Engineer Blog.
  `http://ian.blenke.com/vmware/vmdk/xen/hvm/qemu/vmware_to_xen_`
  `hvm.html.`

"Creating a Customized Master Image for a Xen Virtual Server Manually." IBM Systems Software Information Center.
  `http://publib.boulder.ibm.com/infocenter/eserver/v1r2/index.`
  `jsp?topic=/eica7/eica7_creating_custom_image_xen_manually.htm.`

"Diskless Nodes with Gentoo." Gentoo Linux Documentation.
  `http://www.gentoo.org/doc/en/diskless-howto.xml.`

"Extending Xen* with Intel® Virtualization Technology." Intel Technology Journal.
http://www.intel.com/technology/itj/2006/v10i3/3-xen/9-references.htm.

Geambasu, Roxana and John P. John. "Study of Virtual Machine Performance over Network File Systems."
http://www.cs.washington.edu/homes/roxana/acads/projects/vmnfs/networkvm06.pdf.

"Gnome Partition Editor." (GParted) Gnome Welcome.
http://gparted.sourceforge.net/.

The iSCSI Enterprise Target.
http://iscsitarget.sourceforge.net/.

"iscsi-target." Virtual Appliance Marketplace.
http://www.vmware.com/vmtn/appliances/directory/217.

"Linux Partition HOWTO: Partitioning with fdisk." The Linux Documentation Project.
http://tldp.org/HOWTO/Partition/fdisk_partitioning.html.

"Logical Volume Management." Wikipedia.
http://en.wikipedia.org/wiki/Logical_volume_management.

"Logical Volume Manager (Linux)." Wikipedia.
http://en.wikipedia.org/wiki/Logical_Volume_Manager_%28Linux%29.

LVM HOWTO. The Linux Documentation Project.
http://tldp.org/HOWTO/LVM-HOWTO/.

"Open-iSCSI: RFC 3270 architecture and implementation." Open-iSCSI project.
http://www.open-iscsi.org/.

"A Simple Introduction to Working with LVM." Debian Administration.
http://www.debian-administration.org/articles/410.

"Using LVM-Backed VBDs." Xen Manual.
http://www.cl.cam.ac.uk/research/srg/netos/xen/readmes/user/user.html#SECTION03330000000000000000.

"Using the LVM utility system-config-lvm." Red Hat Documentation.
http://www.redhat.com/docs/manuals/enterprise/RHEL-5-manual/Deployment_Guide-en-US/s1-system-config-lvm.html.

"Using Parted."
http://www.gnu.org/software/parted/manual/html_chapter/parted_2.html.

"QtParted Homepage."
http://qtparted.sourceforge.net/.

"Setup to Do Online Resize of VM Using LVM." XenSource Support Forums.
http://forums.xensource.com/message.jspa?messageID=8404.

Virtual Machine Deployment Specification. VMCasting.
http://www.vmcasting.org/.

"VMDKImage: Migrate a VmWare Disk Image to XEN." Xen Wiki.
http://wiki.xensource.com/xenwiki/VMDKImage.

"Xen 3.0.x Limitations." Ian Blenke Computer Engineer Blog.
http://ian.blenke.com/xen/3.0/limitations/xen_limitations.html.

Chapter 9

Device Virtualization and Management

After mastering the basics of creating new guest domains, one of the next logical questions is how to enable your guest to use the various devices on the host computer. There is of course a tension between wanting guests to enjoy the full power and features of the devices present on a specific physical machine and wanting guests to remain portable across a wide variety of physical machines where the details of the underlying devices may be different. In this chapter, we discuss various approaches to device virtualization and management in Xen. We discuss Xen's basic approach to paravirtualization of devices as well as how major classes of devices, such as the disk and the network interface card, are abstracted. We discuss the role of full device emulation in Xen as well as simply assigning a device directly to a guest. We also discuss some of the ongoing work to virtualize more classes of devices in Xen and some additional options that exist for Hardware Virtual Machine (HVM) guests.

Device Virtualization

At the highest level, the choices for virtualizing devices parallel the choices for virtualizing the CPU. Full virtualization or emulation of devices would present each guest with the illusion of its own dedicated device with the same interface as a physical device. Paravirtualization of devices, on the other hand, would provide a simplified device interface to each guest. In this case, guests would realize the device had been modified to make it simpler to virtualize and would need to abide by the new interface.

Xen is known for its paravirtualized approach to CPU virtualization. Not surprisingly, Xen's primary model for device virtualization is also paravirtualization. However, there is a place for full virtualization or emulation of devices as well as the ability to grant one guest exclusive access to a device.

Paravirtualization of Devices

Xen's general approach to device management is to provide simplified, virtualized views of the underlying physical devices. A privileged domain, either Domain0 or a privileged driver domain, manages the actual device and then exports to all other guests a generic class of device that hides all the details or complexities of the specific physical device. For example, unprivileged domains have a device driver that uses generic commands to read or write disk blocks rather than a device driver that understands the low-level details of communicating with a specific physical disk.

Paravirtualization of devices is actually simpler to accomplish than paravirtualization of the CPU. Paravirtualization of the CPU requires changes to the kernel to use the new interfaces and simplified instruction sets. However, even an HVM guest can use the paravirtualized device model simply by installing a new device driver in the guest that understands the simplified device interface.

Unprivileged guests run a simplified device driver while a privileged domain with direct access to the device runs a device driver that understands the low-level details of the specific physical device. This division of labor is especially good for novel guest operating systems. One of the largest barriers to entry for a new operating system is the need to support device drivers for the most common devices and to quickly implement support for new devices. This paravirtualized model allows guest operating systems to implement only one device driver for each generic class of devices and then rely on the operating system in the privileged domain to have the device driver for the actual physical device. This makes it much easier to do operating system development and to quickly make a new operating system usable on a wider range of hardware.

Full Virtualization of Devices

In full virtualization, the unprivileged guest has the illusion that it is interacting with a dedicated device that is identical to the underlying physical device. This does not require the unprivileged guest to have a device driver that understands a simplified interface. However, it also does not provide the opportunity to have a single device driver that works with a large generic class of devices.

In full virtualization, a privileged domain would still be used to multiplex the physical device among multiple unprivileged guests, providing each with the illusion of exclusive access. Later in this chapter, we discuss how Qemu-dm can be used to provide such device emulation for HVM guests running on systems with virtualization extensions such as Intel-VT or AMD-V. There is also the possibility of specific hardware support for I/O virtualization, including smart devices that know how to interact with multiple guest domains directly, giving each the illusion of a dedicated device.

Full virtualization has the disadvantage that it is fundamentally less portable than the paravirtualized model. If you want to move unprivileged guests from one physical machine to another—either through live migration or static migration—the full virtualization model works only if both machines have identical devices. The paravirtualized model works as long as both machines have some form of each general class of device required by the guest.

No Virtualization

One last option in Xen is the ability to grant physical devices directly to an unprivileged domain. This can be viewed as no virtualization at all. However, if there is no support for virtualizing a particular device or if the highest possible performance is required, granting an unprivileged guest direct access to a device may be your only option. Of course, this means that no other domain will have access to the device and also leads to the same portability problems as with full virtualization.

Backends and Frontends

The basic architecture to facilitate paravirtualized device I/O is the backend/frontend architecture, illustrated in Figure 9.1. The backend driver runs in the privileged domain, and frontend drivers run in the unprivileged guests. In particular, the unprivileged guest issues a generic device request to its frontend driver. The frontend driver then communicates this request to the backend driver running in the privileged domain. The privileged domain then queues up the request and eventually issues the request to the actual underlying hardware.

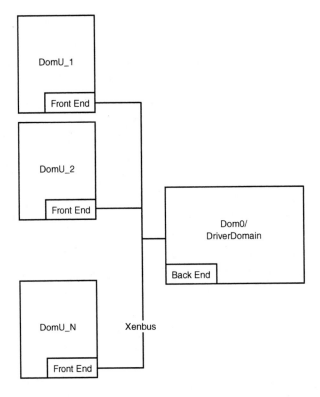

FIGURE 9.1 The split-driver model

The backend driver presents each frontend driver with the illusion of having its own copy of a generic device. In reality, it may be multiplexing the use of the device among many guest domains simultaneously. It is responsible for protecting the security and privacy of data between domains and for enforcing fair access and performance isolation.

Common backend/frontend pairs include netback/netfront drivers for network interface cards and blkback/blkfront drivers for block devices such as disks. Work has also been done on scsiback/scsifront and usbback/usbfront pairs, but support is not yet incorporated into the main Xen codebase.

The communication between the frontend and backend driver is done through system memory using XenBus, an architecture for shared event channels and producer/consumer ring buffers. XenBus tries to avoid costly data copies by simply mapping pages of memory from one domain to another. For example, to write data to disk or send data over the network, a buffer belonging to the unprivileged domain could be mapped into the privileged domain. Similarly, to read data from disk or receive data from the network, a buffer controlled by the privileged domain could be mapped into the unprivileged domain. Coordination of when to initiate I/O or when I/O is complete is done through shared events.

This communication is established by using XenStore to exchange the basic parameters needed to make the connection between frontend and backend drivers. When the frontend driver comes up, it uses XenStore to establish a pool of shared memory frames and an interdomain event channel for communications with the backend. After this connection is established, the frontend and backend place requests or responses into shared memory and send each other notifications on the event channel. This separation of notification from data transfer is efficient because it allows one notification to be used to transfer multiple data buffers and prevents unnecessary data copies.

XenStore both stores and provides visibility into the connections between backend drivers and frontend drivers in the system. We discussed some aspects of XenStore in Chapter 3, "The Xen Hypervisor." Here, we focus specifically on the parameters that relate to device management.

Backend Information in XenStore

In a domain's space in XenStore, the backend directory lists all the backend drivers hosted by this domain. Only Domain0 or driver domains host backend drivers. In the backend directory, there is a vbd directory for all virtual block devices (vbds) or blkback drivers exported. In the vbd directory, there is an entry for each domain running a frontend driver that is connected to that particular backend driver. Each such domain has a subdirectory named after its DomainID and finally within that directory is a subdirectory for the virtual device name.

The directory structure within the backend/vbd directory is backend/vbd/<domid>/<virtual-device where:

- `backend`—A directory containing all backends of the domain hosts
- `vbd`—A directory containing vbd backends
- `<domid>`—A directory containing vbd's for `domid`
- `<virtual-device>`—A directory for a particular virtual-device on `domid`

Each leaf directory within the `backend/vbd` tree contains a list of attributes of the device and of the connection between the backend driver and this particular frontend driver. Following is a list of such parameters:

- `frontend-id`—Domain ID for the domain running this frontend driver; also listed in the pathname of this parameter
- `frontend`—Path to the frontend domain
- `physical-device`—Device number of the backend device
- `sector-size`—Sector or block size of the physical backend device
- `sectors`—Number of sectors on the backend device
- `info`—Device information flags. 1=cdrom, 2=removable, 4=read-only
- `domain`—Name of the frontend domain
- `params`—Other parameters for the device
- `type`—Type of the device
- `dev`—Frontend virtual device as given by the user
- `node`—Backend device node; output from the block creation script
- `hotplug-status`—Connected or error; output from the block creation script
- `state`—Communication state across XenBus to the frontend (0=unknown, 1=initializing, 2=init. wait, 3=initialized, 4=connected, 5=closing, 6=closed)

Similarly, in the backend directory, there is a `vif` (virtual interface) directory for all virtual network devices or netback drivers exported. In the `vif` directory is an entry for each domain running a frontend driver that is connected to that particular backend driver. Each such domain has a subdirectory named after its DomainId and finally within that directory is a subdirectory for the `vif` number.

The directory structure within the `backend/vif` directory is `backend/vif/<domid>/<virtual-device` where:

- `backend`—A directory containing all backends of the domain hosts
- `vif`—A directory containing vif backends

- `<domid>`—A directory containing vif's for `domid`
- `<virtual-device>`—A directory for each vif

Each leaf directory within the `backend/vif` tree contains a list of attributes of the device and of the connection between the backend driver and this particular frontend driver. Some of these attributes, such as `frontend-id`, `frontend`, `domain`, `hotplug-status`, and `state` are exactly the same as in the `vbd` case. The new elements are `mac`, `bridge`, `handle`, and `script`. Following is a list of such parameters:

- `frontend-id`—DomainId for the domain running this frontend driver; also listed in the pathname of this parameter
- `frontend`—Path to the frontend domain
- `mac`—MAC address of the vif
- `bridge`—Bridge the vif is connected to
- `handle`—Handle of the vif
- `script`—Script used to start and stop the vif
- `domain`—Name of the frontend domain
- `hotplug-status`—Connected or error; output from the block creation script
- `state`—Communication state across XenBus to the frontend (0=unknown, 1=initializing, 2=init. wait, 3=initialized, 4=connected, 5=closing, 6=closed)

Frontend Information in XenStore

In a domain's space in XenStore, the device directory lists all the frontend drivers established for this domain. The `device/vbd` directory contains information on all the block device front drivers. Each blockfront device is listed by name as a leaf in the `device/vbd` directory and contains attributes linking it to the associated backend driver. The following is a list of these attributes:

- `virtual-device`—Domain ID for the domain running this frontend driver; also listed in the pathname of this parameter
- `device-type`—Device type ("disk," "cdrom," "floppy")
- `backend-id`—Domain ID of the backend
- `backend`—Path of the backend in the store (`/local/domain path`)
- `ring-ref`—Grant table reference for the block request ring queue

- `event-channel`—Event channel used for the block request ring queue
- `state`—Communication state across XenBus to the frontend (0=unknown, 1=initializing, 2=init. wait, 3=initialized, 4=connected, 5=closing, 6=closed)

Similarly, the `device/vif` directory contains information on all the network device front drivers. Each netfront device is listed by ID as a leaf in the `device/vif` directory and contains attributes linking it to the associated backend driver. The following is a list of these attributes:

- `backend-id`—Domain ID of the backend
- `mac`—MAC address of the vif
- `handle`—Internal vif handle
- `backend`—Path of the backend's store entry
- `tx-ring-ref`—Grant table reference for the transmission ring queue
- `rx-ring-ref`—Grant table reference for the receiving ring queue
- `event-channel`—Event channel used for the block request ring queue
- `state`—Communication state across XenBus to the frontend (0=unknown, 1=initializing, 2=init. wait, 3=initialized, 4=connected, 5=closing, 6=closed)

Granting Control of a PCI Device

For a domain other than Domain0 to directly control a physical device, the device must first be hidden from Domain0 and then control must be explicitly granted to another domain. Currently, there is support for hiding devices connected to the system through the Peripheral Component Interconnect (PCI) bus. Fortunately, many devices, such as network interface cards or SCSI controllers, are connected to the system in this way through either PCI expansion slots on the motherboard or integrated circuits fitted directly into the motherboard.

Identifying a PCI Device

The first step in hiding a device is learning the identifier of the device in the system. A device is commonly referred to by four numbers that specify the domain identifier, bus number, slot number, and function number by which the device is connected into the system. They are expressed in the format: `(<domain>:<bus>:<slot>.<function>)`. Here the term domain refers to a PCI domain and not a Xen domain.

The bus and slot numbers are two characters each, and the function number is one character. The domain number is four characters and is sometimes omitted for the default domain 0000. For example, (0000:01:02.3) refers to a device in the default domain 0000, bus 01, slot 02, and function 3. Note the preceding 0's in the domain, bus, and slot identifiers. Also note that the delimiter between the slot and function identifier is a period and not a colon.

On a Linux system, a good way to determine the correct identifier for a PCI device is using the utility lspci. lspci lists or displays information on all the PCI buses in the system and the devices connected to them. Listing 9.1 illustrates using the lspci utility to identify the Ethernet interfaces in the system. It shows two Ethernet controllers; one would be identified as (02:03.0), and the other as (02:03.1). In addition to using lspci, you can also examine information on the PCI devices contained in /proc/bus/pci directly.

LISTING 9.1 Using lspci

```
[root@dom0]# lspci | grep Ethernet
0000:02:03.0 Ethernet controller: Intel Corp. 82546EB ➥
    Gigabit Ethernet Controller (Copper) (rev 01)
0000:02:03.1 Ethernet controller: Intel Corp. 82546EB ➥
    Gigabit Ethernet Controller (Copper) (rev 01)
[root@dom0]#
```

Hiding a PCI Device from Domain0 at Boot

After you have the identifier for the device, the next step is to hide it from Domain0. One way to accomplish this is to add a pciback.hide kernel parameter to the module entry (if there are multiple module entries, add it to the module entry for the Domain0 kernel, not the one for the initial RAM disk) in the GRUB configuration file, typically grub.conf or menu.lst, for the Domain0 kernel. It may also be necessary to add the pciback.permissive option for drivers that need to write the registers on the PCI device itself. Listing 9.2 illustrates how to hide PCI devices from Domain0 at boot. Specifically, it shows a GRUB menu entry that hides two PCI devices, (02:03.0) and (0000:02:03.1), from Domain0. Notice that these are the same devices reported by lspci. One is identified with four numbers including the domain identifier, and the other is identified with only three numbers. The leading 0000 is the default and will be assumed if not specified.

LISTING 9.2 Hiding PCI Devices from Domain0 at Boot

```
title Xen 3.0 / XenLinux 2.6
  kernel /boot/xen-3.0.gz dom0_mem=262144
  module /boot/vmlinuz-2.6-xen0 root=/dev/sda4 ro ➥
console=tty0  pciback.permissive ➥
pciback.hide=(02:03.0)(0000:02:03.1)
```

To use this method of hiding the device from Domain0, pciback support must be compiled into the Domain0 kernel. When a device is successfully hidden from Domain0, you should see a message like the one in Listing 9.3 in /var/log/dmesg. You should also see the hidden PCI device in /sys/bus/pci/drivers/pciback.

LISTING 9.3 PCI Device Successfully Hidden

```
[user@dom0]$ cat /var/log/dmesg | grep pciback
[    1.154975] pciback 0000:02:03.1: seizing device ➥
      pciback.permissive

[user@dom0]$ ls /sys/bus/pci/drivers/pciback/
0000:02:03:1 new_id      permissive  remove_slot  unbind
bind            new_slot  quirks      slots
[user@dom0]$
```

> **NOTE**
>
> In Xen 2.0, hiding a PCI device used to be accomplished using the physdev_dom0_
> hide boot option. The pciback option replaces this in Xen 3.0.

Manually Unbinding/Binding a PCI Device at Runtime

Using the pciback.hide option at boot prevents Domain0 from binding a driver to a device at boot. It is also possible to unbind a device from its driver during runtime and bind it to the PCI backend using the PCI backend's sysfs directory (/sys/bus/pci/drivers/pciback). Listing 9.4 shows an example of unbinding a device from its network driver and binding it to the PCI backend. You can use this to give a device back to Domain0 if necessary.

LISTING 9.4 Manually Unbinding/Binding a PCI Device

```
[root@dom0]# echo -n 0000:02:03.0 > ➡
     /sys/bus/pci/drivers/3c905/unbind
[root@dom0]# echo -n 0000:02:03.0 > ➡
     /sys/bus/pci/drivers/pciback/new_slot
[root@dom0]# echo -n 0000:02:03.0 > ➡
     /sys/bus/pci/drivers/pciback/bindcat
[root@dom0]#
```

Granting a PCI Device to Another Domain

After a device has been hidden from Domain0, it can be granted directly to another domain. The simplest way to do this is to add a `pci` line in the other domain's guest configuration file. Listing 9.5 shows the configuration line used to grant two PCI devices, (`02:03.0`) and (`0000:02:03.1`), to a domain.

LISTING 9.5 `pci` Line in the Guest Configuration File

```
pci=['02:03.0','02:03.1']
```

For a configuration file in SXP format, PCI devices granted to a domain are specified as shown in Listing 9.6. Notice that the numbers are specified in hexadecimal with a leading 0x.

LISTING 9.6 SXP Format for Granting PCI Device

```
    (device (pci
        (dev (domain 0x0)(bus 0x2)(slot 0x3)(func 0x0)
        (dev (domain 0x0)(bus 0x2)(slot 0x3)(func 0x1)
    )
```

You could also accomplish the same thing with a command line parameter to `xm create` as shown in Listing 9.7. Notice that to pass in multiple devices the `pci` option is used multiple times. As the guest boots, you see several indications of the successful frontend configuration. The rest of the bootup messages have been removed for clarity.

LISTING 9.7 `pci` Parameter to `xm-create`

```
[root@dom0]# xm create NetDriverDomain pci=02:03.0 pci=02:03.1
[ 1856.386697] pcifront pci-0: Installing PCI frontend

[ 1856.386770] pcifront pci-0: Creating PCI Frontend Bus 0000:02
```

After the guest has booted, you can also run the `lspci` command in the guest to inspect the PCI state as shown in Listing 9.8.

LISTING 9.8 Using `lspci` to Inspect the Frontend Driver Configuration

```
[root@NetDriverDomain]# lspci
00:00.0 Bridge: nVidia Corporation MCP55 Ethernet (rev a2)
[root@NetDriverDomain]#
```

In the case of the network interface card that we transferred from Domain0 to the NetDriverDomain, we can also inspect its state with network-specific commands such as `ifconfig`. In Listing 9.9, we use `ifconfig` to check whether the MAC address of eth1 is the same as it was originally in Domain0. This is another confirmation that we have passed the physical network interface card properly between Domain0 and the NetDriverDomain. This of course requires noting the MAC address of the card in Domain0 before it is hidden.

LISTING 9.9 Using `ifconfig` to Inspect the MAC Address of a New Network Interface Card Passed from Domain0

```
[root@NetDriverDomain]# ifconfig -a
eth1      Link encap:Ethernet  HWaddr 00:1A:92:97:26:50

          inet addr:128.153.22.182  Bcast:128.153.23.255 ➥
     Mask:255.255.248.0

          UP BROADCAST RUNNING MULTICAST  MTU:1500  Metric:1

          RX packets:53 errors:0 dropped:0 overruns:0 frame:0

          TX packets:2 errors:0 dropped:0 overruns:0 carrier:0

          collisions:0 txqueuelen:1000

          RX bytes:7960 (7.7 KiB)  TX bytes:684 (684.0 b)
```

```
            Interrupt:23 Base address:0x2000
[root@NetDriverDomain]#
```

If you have any trouble with this process, one thing to double-check is that the PCI frontend functionality is compiled into the domain being granted control of the device. You can safely compile both PCI backend and frontend support into the same kernel.

Exclusive Device Access Versus Trusted Driver Domains

In the preceding section, we discussed how Domain0 can yield all control over a PCI device to another domain. There are two primary reasons to allow this. The goal may be to grant exclusive access to a device to a particular domain. Alternatively, there may still be a desire to share the device among multiple domains in the system, but the goal may be to offload the responsibility for device management from Domain0 onto a trusted driver domain. There are a number of advantages to trusted driver domains, and therefore we cover them in this chapter even though they are not fully supported in the most recent version of Xen.

Exclusive Device Access

After you've used the methods outlined in the previous section to grant control of a device to a particular domain, that domain is under no obligation to share it. This basically boils down to not virtualizing the device. That domain deals directly with the physical device as it would if it were not running in a virtual machine. The domain needs a device driver specific to the device and so this may not be an option for less popular operating systems. Also, the detailed knowledge of the physical device leads to portability problems.

Despite the problems, granting exclusive device access has definite advantages. First, it can deliver the highest performance access to the device. For example, if network performance is crucial to one of your domains, granting it a dedicated network interface card may be the right decision. It won't have to share the device with other domains, and it will avoid any overhead from device virtualization or emulation. Second, there are devices for which virtualization support does not yet exist. For these devices, granting the device directly to the domain that needs it the most may be the only option.

One thing that is important to realize, however, is that without hardware protection, a domain with direct physical access to a device can compromise other domains. For example, a domain could instruct the device to do a DMA into memory that belongs to another domain. In essence, a domain with direct physical access to a device must be considered part of the trusted computing base. If you don't trust all the software and security configuration in a domain, you are taking a risk by granting it direct physical access to a device.

One solution to this problem is hardware support in the form of an Input Output Memory Management Unit (IOMMU). An IOMMU, much like a traditional MMU, maps virtual addresses to physical addresses and so guarantees memory protection for other domains. Many hardware vendors including Intel, AMD, Sun, and IBM are producing IOMMU hardware. It seems likely that IOMMUs will become increasingly common. The main disadvantage is that the cost of translation can decrease performance and increase CPU utilization.

Trusted Driver Domains

A domain that is granted physical access to a device can choose not to share it with other domains (that is, retain exclusive device access). However, it is also possible for the domain to share the device with other domains by running a backend driver as with Domain0. The advantage of running in a separate driver domain is that any instability in the device driver will be isolated to the driver domain. If the driver domain crashes, requests in progress will likely be lost, but the driver domain can be restarted and I/O processing can continue. In contrast, instability in Domain0 impacts the stability of the entire system. Domain0 cannot simply be restarted. Given that device driver code traditionally has a higher percentage of bugs than the core operating system, moving the device driver to its own domain can significantly increase overall system stability. The main disadvantage to running the backend driver in a driver domain is increased complexity of configuration. There are more domains and more pieces in the trusted computing base to manage.

Without hardware protection, any driver with physical access to a device becomes part of the trusted computing base. Even with hardware protection, a driver domain must be considered part of the trusted computing base. All data sent to and from the device passes through the driver domain, and unprivileged domains that use that driver domain's services must trust it to keep its data protected from other unprivileged domains. It is easier to audit the security of a driver domain if you run only necessary software components. A driver domain should contain only the operating system, required device driver, and a minimal set of other software to directly support its role in the system. You could also imagine changing a general purpose domain into a driver domain simply by granting it direct physical access to a device and then exporting that device through a backend driver to other domains. However, this is not advisable.

Problems Using Trusted Driver Domains

In earlier versions of Xen, there was syntax in the configuration file for a domain to connect its frontend driver to a backend driver located in a domain other than Domain0. Listing 9.10 illustrates the configuration file syntax used to establish and use a backend driver in the domain, backendDomain.

LISTING 9.10 Configuration File Syntax for Designating a Backend Domain Other Than Domain0

```
In the configuration file for backendDomain:

#Setup a network backend
netif=1
#Setup a block device backend
blkif=1

In domains using the backend:

#Use a disk exported by backendDomain
disk=[phy:hda1, xvda,w,backendDomain]
#Use a network interface exported by backendDomain
vif=['backend=backendDomain']
```

If this syntax does not work on your system, another alternative may be to enter the configuration in XenStore manually. However, even with this method, there may be problems with attempts to do transitive page grant operations.

To begin, a good strategy is to set up a backend driver in Domain0 and a frontend driver communicating with it and then look in XenStore at all the attributes of the connection. This can serve as an example of the connection you want to establish with a new driver domain. After noting the full attributes, move the backend to a driver domain. For example, to point a blockfront driver at a backend driver in a driver domain other than Domain0, we could first set up a blockfront driver in Domain0 and a frontend driver in a DomU with ID X. We would then note the attributes of the backend/vbd and device/vbd directories in XenStore for Domain0 and domain X, respectively.

We could then grant the device to the trusted driver domain with ID Y following the procedure outlined previously in this chapter. Once we verify that the backend driver is indeed established in domain Y, we could edit the XenStore entries in both domain X and Y. Specifically, we could use XenStore-write to manually change the backend and backend-id attributes of the frontend connection (XenStore-write <Path to XenStore Entry> <value>). It is safest to do this while domains X and Y are both shut down.

When the editing is complete, restart the trusted driver domain, domain Y, and then domain X. When Domain X is started and the frontend driver comes up, it will use XenStore to set up a shared memory frame and an interdomain event channel for communications with the backend. You can check the ring-ref, event-channel, and state attributes after booting the frontend domain.

Device Emulation with QEMU-DM

We discussed the paravirtualized device model with frontend and backend drivers— either with the backend driver in Domain0 or a separate driver domain. We also saw how the same mechanisms used to grant physical device access to a driver domain can also be used to grant exclusive access to a device to one domain (that is, no virtualization). In this section, we discuss how to offer full virtualization of devices through QEMU's device emulation. In this model, multiple domains are given the illusion that they have exclusive access to a device that looks just like the underlying physical device. This is especially important for HVM domains. Although technically HVM domains could run special frontend device drivers, this is not typically done. Instead, HVM domains typically expect a set of virtual hardware realistic enough that it can use device drivers written for real physical devices.

QEMU is an open source machine emulator. It provides both CPU and device emulation. In fact, QEMU can itself be used for many of the same virtualization tasks as Xen. Xen relies extensively on code from QEMU for device emulation, especially for support of HVM guests. The QEMU device manager, called qemu-dm, is a service running as a backend in Domain0. The CPU emulator portion of QEMU is not used in Xen. To use services from qemu-dm in a Xen guest, the configuration file should contain the line:

```
device_model = '/usr/' + arch_libdir + '/xen/bin/qemu-dm'
```

In theory, any device currently supported by QEMU can be exposed to a guest through the qemu-dm backend driver. However, not all devices supported by QEMU are made available through the Xen guest configuration file. Currently, the following emulated devices can easily be made available: PIIX3 IDE hard drives, Cirrus Logic video cards, RTL8139 or NE2000 network cards, and various sound cards. Support for USB, PAE, ACPI, and APIC can also be enabled. Listing 9.11 shows a sample device section from an HVM guest's configuration file.

LISTING 9.11 A Sample Device Section on an HVM Guest's Configuration File

```
device_model = '/usr/' + arch_libdir + '/xen/bin/qemu-dm'

#nographic=0 # no graphics, only serial (do not enable for Windows guests) ➥
stdvga=0 # stdvga (cirrus logic model, default=0 disabled)
#pae=0    # HVM guest PAE support (default=0 disabled)
#acpi=0   # HVM guest ACPI support (default=0 disabled)
#apic=0   # HVM guest APIC support (default=0 disabled)
#usb=1    # USB support (devices may be specified through the
          # monitor window)
#usbdevice='mouse'   # normal/relative mouse
#usbdevice='tablet'  # tablet/absolute mouse


#----------------------MISC----------------------------------------------
#serial='pty'          # serial port re-direct to pty device,
                       # allows xm console or minicom to connect

#soundhw='sb16'        # sound card support (sb16, es1370, all;
                       # default none)
```

One commonly asked question is about using Windows in an HVM domain to run high-end 3D graphics applications such as games. The support for this is currently not very good. VMGL is one option; see the References and Future Reading section for more information. You could also use something like vnc or RemoteDesktop to access the desktop as discussed in Chapter 6, "Managing Unprivileged Domains." It may not give you experience you want, but it is an easy option to try. The real solution is IOMMU hardware and the corresponding software support. Currently, the graphics card expects the operating system to specify a range of physical memory for its use. However, when a guest operating system running in a virtual machine specifies a range of memory, it is not in those physical locations but is remapped by the hypervisor. An IOMMU would allow this mapping to be specified properly and securely.

Future Directions

In this section, we briefly describe ongoing work and trends in device management in Xen.

More Devices

Without device emulation like in QEMU, if you wander too far from disk and network, you have trouble. However, the flexibility to pass through additional device types continues to grow. A number of projects are actively exploring additional virtual device models. If you need support for a specific device and are willing to be adventurous, it may pay to consider software that has been developed for pvSCSI, virtual frame buffers, advanced display multiplexing support, usbback and usbfront drivers, scsiback and scsifront drivers, virtual SANS support, and drivers for fiberchannel and infiniband. Some links are given at the end of this chapter.

Smart Devices

One interesting possibility for the future may be virtualization aware devices, also called smart devices. Such devices would be aware that multiple VMs were accessing them and be able to maintain proper state for each VM. In some sense, this would push the functionality we described for backend drivers into the firmware of the device itself. In this case, the VMs would have a device driver for the actual physical device. There are a number of open questions surrounding smart devices, including how migration would be handled between physical machines that have different smart hardware.

Summary

Xen uses a split driver model in which a backend driver runs in the privileged domain and has access to the physical device while frontend drivers run in the unprivileged guests and pass generic requests to the privileged backend driver. We discussed this basic architecture as well as specific examples of the split device model for disks and network interface cards. We provided instructions for hiding PCI devices from Domain0 and granting them to other domains. We also discussed the advantages of trusted driver domains as well as some of the challenges with using them. We discussed how Xen also provides full virtualization of devices through QEMU's device emulation and how this is used to support HVM guests. Finally, we provided an overview of future directions in device virtualization in Xen.

References and Further Reading

Fraser, Keir, et al. "Safe Hardware Access with the Xen Virtual Machine Monitor." Proceedings of the 1st Workshop on Operating System and Architectural Support for the on Demand IT InfraStructure (OASIS). October 2004. Boston, MA.

> `http://www.cl.cam.ac.uk/research/srg/netos/papers/2004-oasis-ngio.pdf`

Virtual Frame buffer:

> `http://www.xensource.com/files/summit_3/Xenpvfb.pdf`
>
> `http://wiki.xensource.com/xenwiki/VirtualFramebuffer`

VMGL (Xen-GL): `http://www.cs.toronto.edu/~andreslc/xen-gl/`

> `http://xensource.com/files/xensummit_4/vmgl_Cavilla.pdf`

Blink (advanced display multiplexing for virtualized applications):

> `http://www.xensource.com/files/summit_3/GormHansenVirtFB.pdf`
>
> `http://lists.xensource.com/archives/html/xen-devel/2005-12/msg00234.html`

FibreChannel, VSANS:

> `http://www.xensource.com/files/summit_3/Emulex_NPIV.pdf`

Infiniband:

> `http://www.xensource.com/files/summit_3/xs0106_virtualizing_infiniband.pdf`

SCSI:

> `http://www.xensource.com/files/summit_3/xen-scsi-slides.pdf`

## Chapter 10

Network Configuration

Choosing a network configuration for your Xen guests is one of the most important aspects of administering a Xen system. Xen allows significant flexibility in network configuration. You can enable communication between Xen guests on the same machine as well as communication between a Xen guest and the global Internet. Guests can appear as distinct hosts on the physical machine's local network segment, or they can be placed behind a router or hidden behind a NAT gateway. Guests can even be restricted to no network access at all. Local virtual network segments can be created to enable guests to communicate privately among themselves without using the physical network. A driver domain can serve as a firewall, allowing subtle and powerful limits on the network access of guests, which can enhance the security of the overall system. This chapter will examine Xen networking options in detail. While some general networking experience is assumed, we have aimed to provide descriptions and instructions suitable for beginners.

Network Virtualization Overview

One of the basic roles of Xen is to share a physical network interface among multiple Xen guests, just as it shares the physical CPU among multiple guests. Logically, each DomU can have a virtual network interface card (NIC), and Xen multiplexes the outgoing packets from each DomU's virtual NIC onto the physical NIC. Similarly, Xen demultiplexes the incoming packets from the physical NIC onto each running DomU's virtual NIC. This can be done in three primary modes—bridging, routing, or network address translation (NAT).

On the other hand, virtual network interfaces do not require a physical network interface to function. You can create whole virtual network segments for communication between guest domains that result in no actual network transmissions. Guest domains can even have multiple network interfaces—some backed by physical interfaces and some that simply grant access to virtual network segments.

Another fundamental aspect of virtual networks is deciding the topology of the network. For example, all virtual guests can appear directly on the physical network segment. Alternatively, one domain can serve as a bridge, router, NAT gateway, or firewall for other domains. The administrator is free to build complex, multilevel virtual topologies inside a Xen system. However, in practice it is best not to introduce any more complexity than is necessary.

The administrator must also decide how IP addresses will be assigned to each virtual network interface. This depends heavily on the desired topology. Just as in the real world, after you have designed your virtual network topology, each network segment should have a subnet mask and network identifier to guide IP address assignment and routing. Network interfaces that are bridged to the outside world often get their IP addresses from an external DHCP server. Network interfaces on a virtual network segment could be assigned manually. It would even be possible to run a DHCP server in a virtual machine (VM) attached to a virtual network segment. As in the real world, virtual network configurations and topologies can have a big impact on the performance and security of your system. This chapter walks through the network configuration options, including how they can be set up using scripts, Xen configuration files, and also standard networking tools such as ifconfig, brtcl, ip, and so on. We defer the discussion of some tools most directly related to security, such as firewalls and `iptables`, until Chapter 11, "Securing a Xen System."

Designing a Virtual Network Topology

Because Xen can be used to create a wide variety of virtual network topologies, it is important to design your desired network topology before you begin to configure each guest properly. In this section, we recommend the following general steps for designing your network topology:

1. **Take an inventory of the physical devices in your machine.**

   The first step is to determine the number and type of physical network interfaces in the system. Laptops often have an Ethernet and wireless interface. Servers may have multiple Ethernet connections. We recommend that you ensure that all the network cards are working properly in Domain0 before attempting to share them with any guests.

2. **Decide on a sharing model for each physical device.**

   Decide for each physical NIC whether it will be shared with guest domains as a bridge, router, or NAT gateway. The decision will be influenced by the functionality and requirements of the guest domains running in your system. If you are not sure what to choose, we recommend a simple bridging configuration in which each guest domain appears directly on the physical network segment by sharing a single physical NIC.

   Other than the sharing model, a device can also be granted exclusively to one guest domain. Dedicated network devices can provide more secure, isolated, and better network traffic to the guest domain. If you have multiple physical network cards and some guest has a need for very high-performance or high-availability network I/O, a possible enhancement is to bond the NICs in the guest.

3. **Decide whether to create any purely virtual network segments.**

   A network segment is a subset network inside which the machines have the same subnetwork address and share the same physical media. Traffic on a virtual network segment will not be externally visible on a physical network segment. Similarly, it will not be visible to guest VMs that do not have a virtual interface on the segment. Thus, it provides a natural way to isolate the communication between guest domains.

It is recommended that each virtual network segment created have a functional purpose, such as to access an internal data share. Once created, the administrator can decide for each guest whether the guest needs access to the data share. If so, a virtual network interface would be created for the guest on that segment. You might choose not to even create an interface on that virtual network segment for guests running frequently attacked services such as Web servers or database servers. This would make it more difficult for attackers to compromise the Web server VM to reach the protected data share. Figure 10.1 illustrates an example of one such virtual network design.

4. **For each guest, determine the number of virtual network interfaces and whether each one connects to a physical network segment or a virtual one.**

   Finally, after we determine the driver domain's physical interfaces and the shared mode of the virtual network, we can record how many virtual network interfaces each guest domain needs and the role each interface plays. In Xen 3.0, guest domains can be configured to support up to three network interfaces without needing to be backed up by physical NIC.

5. **Determine how the MAC (Media Access Control) addresses and IP address will be assigned to each interface.**

   Data is delivered according to the IP and MAC addresses in the packet header. Therefore, each network interface, virtual or physical, needs its own MAC and IP address.

   The MAC address for each interface should be unique (at least on its local network). There are two ways to assign a MAC address to a virtual network interface: Xen-generated or user-specified. When we manually assign a MAC address to the virtual network interface, we should be aware that the network interfaces in the same network segment should have different MAC addresses. If you do not assign one manually, Xen generates one.

   IP addresses, as well as the local network subnet mask and default gateway, can be assigned dynamically via DHCP or manually. If the guest domains are routed to the Internet directly, we need to make sure we have enough global IPs for those virtual interfaces. If guest domains are in the same virtual network, their virtual interface should be configured with IP addresses (manually or using a local DHCP server) in the same subnet.

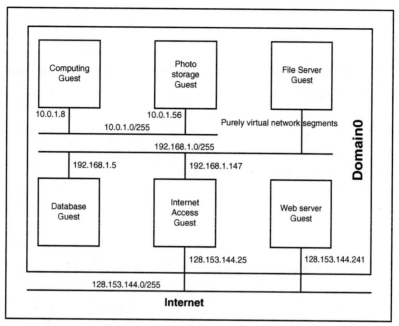

FIGURE 10.1 Some guest domains sit in a purely virtual network segment and communicate with other guest domains without contention with the Internet attacks.

6. Record the virtual network topology.

After you have completed all the previous steps, you should be able to draw a network diagram illustrating the connections between all the guest domains in your system and between guests and the outside world. Physical network administrators rely on diagrams like this to record the design of physical networks. As the administrator of a Xen system, you may have internal networks with similar complexities—different subnets, a set of externally accessible servers, a set of internally accessible servers, a firewall, and so on. Recording your design decisions in a network diagram helps you maintain the system as you add guests over time.

Bridging, Routing, and Network Address Translation

Xen provides three virtual network modes for guest domains to access the network through a physical device—bridging, routing, or network address translation (NAT). In bridging mode, the **virtual network interface** (vif) of guest domains is visible at the external Ethernet layer. In routing mode, the vif is not visible at the external Ethernet layer, but its IP address is externally visible. In NAT mode, the vif is not visible at the external Ethernet layer, nor does it have an external visible IP address.

A bridge relays the traffic between multiple network interfaces based on a MAC address independent of any higher-level protocol. A router forwards the packets at a higher layer based on an IP address (a machine's global network identifier) over the Internet. A NAT gateway translates between a single globally routable, external IP address and many local IP addresses that are not globally routable. This translation is possible by using a larger range of ports on the globally visible interface. A NAT gateway remaps a guest's IP and Port to Domain0's port. These choices will sound familiar to readers familiar with network configuration in general. Figure 10.2 illustrates the comparison.

In bridging mode, the brctl tool is used to create a software bridge interface in the driver domain. A physical network interface is then attached to the bridge. Xen guest domains' backend vifs can be attached to the software bridge interface at the time of domain creation using the guest domain's configuration file. When the bridge interface receives packets from the physical interface, it relays them to the different domains by their MAC addresses, making it seem that the domains receive the packets from the Ethernet. In bridging mode, guest domains appear "transparent" to the Ethernet.

When the driver domain is configured to be a router using the Linux iptables mechanism, all packets received by the physical network interface card (NIC) are processed by the driver domain's network IP layer. The driver domain looks up its IP table entries and then forwards the packets to its guest domains according to the destination IP addresses. In routing mode, the driver domain connects two different network segments together: the internal segment used by guest domains and the external segment connecting to the outside global Internet.

When the driver domain acts as a NAT gateway, the driver domain still acts as a router but furthermore maps a port number in its own IP address to a guest domain's IP address and port number. It works as a proxy, remapping the gateway's port to be a guest domain's IP and port and forwarding traffic to the guest domain. Guest domains' IP addresses are hidden behind the driver domain and invisible to the external Internet. In NAT mode, the driver domain hides guest domains in the internal private network segment from the external network segment.

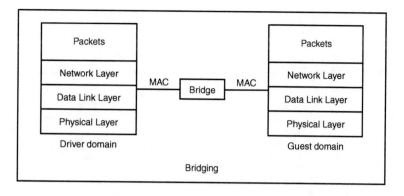

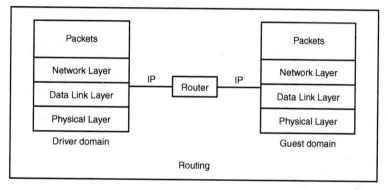

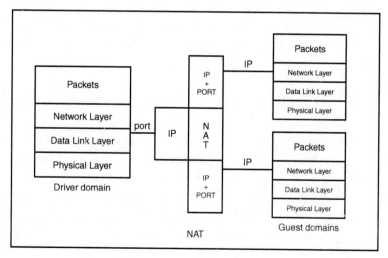

FIGURE 10.2   A bridge forwards the packet by MAC address at the link layer level, a router forwards the packets by IP address at the network layer, and a NAT gateway remaps a guest's IP and port to the driver domain's port at the network layer.

Generally, the sharing model for the physical interface is classified as either bridging or routing, and either can enable guest domains' access to the Internet. Table 10.1 illustrates the differences between these two sharing models.

TABLE 10.1 Comparing Between the Bridging and Routing Mode

Comparison Aspect	The Bridging Mode	The Routing Mode
ISO Layer	Data Link Layer	Network Layer
Identifier	MAC address	IP address
IP segments	Within a network segment	Connecting two different segments
IP assignment	Dynamic or Static	Static
Setup tools	Bridge-utils	Linux iptables
Data Filter	Bridge filter	IP filter
Isolation Properties	Well isolated from the driver domain	Hard to isolate from the driver domain
Configuration	Easy	A little complicated
Perceived Network Access	Ethernet	Internet

The bridging mode multiplexes and demultiplexes the packets by MAC addresses while the routing mode multiplexes and demultiplexes packets by IP addresses. While the Linux firewall provides the packet filter `iptables`, the Linux package `bridge-utils` also provides the Ethernet filter `ebtables`, enabling basic MAC filtering on the software bridge. With bridging mode enabled, we can further control and secure the network traffic with iptables configurations, enabling the IP packet firewall.

In Xen, the default configuration is bridging, which is usually the preferred configuration. Its architecture is more straightforward, and the configuration is simpler to apply.

In routing mode, the packets from guest domains are simply routed through the driver domain and sent onto the Ethernet, making it hard to isolate the packets from the driver domain or other guest domains. But in bridging mode, the driver domain's interfaces are imparted from the physical network interfaces. The software bridge works as a switch, connecting the physical interfaces with the domains' virtual interfaces. Multiple software bridges can be set up in a machine, with each physical interface attached to an individual bridge. Xen domains' virtual interfaces are flexible, to be attached to the bridges as configured. In this way it is easier to isolate and secure the domains.

It is also possible to dedicate a physical interface to just one domain, giving the guest direct access to the physical device. In this case, the driver domain is not involved in processing the guest network. The guest domain has exclusive access to the network. The network's effect from that physical interface on the driver domain is reduced to zero; meanwhile, the guest domain side has utilized the maximum network bandwidth of that physical interface. Normally, guest domains share the same network card with others. But if some guest domain has heavy network traffic, it is better to grant it an exclusive NIC to best isolate its traffic from other domains' and ensure its network services. Also, when we run some particular service, such as a DNS server or a Web server, it is common to designate a whole NIC to a guest domain. In this way, the guest domain behaves more as a physical machine and has the full control of the network. For further details and a concrete example, you can refer to Chapter 9, "Device Virtualization and Management."

Another solution for Xen to provide a high-availability or high-performance network is to bond two network interfaces in a guest. In this way, Xen guest's network capability can be greatly increased. One scenario is that the guest networking will still be available, even when one of the network cards is broken. When both network cards are working, the guest's network throughout is also raised. Bonding the network interfaces in the guest requires Xen virtual network driver support. Xen developers are still working on it and it is said that this feature will be included in the next Xen release. It is definitely worth keeping track of the development of Xen bonding NICs on the xen-devel mailing list.

Frontend and Backend Network Drivers and Naming

In Chapter 9, we discussed the frontend/backend model of device I/O. There is typically a pair of virtual interfaces (vifs) for each virtual network interface of a guest domain. The backend vif is the proxy of the guest domain in the driver domain, which delivers received packets to the guest domain and forwards guest packets to the network. The frontend vif is in the guest domain and appears to the guest as a typical network interface. The frontend vif is often of type veth or virtual Ethernet rather than eth, as is typical for a physical Ethernet interface. The backend vif in the driver domain passes the data to and from the backend vif with a shared buffer ring. Figure 10.3 explains the relationship of the frontend and backend interfaces for a guest domain.

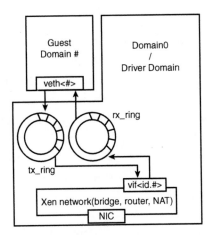

FIGURE 10.3 The backend vif of a guest domain in Domain0 or the driver domain is the proxy of its frontend vif in the guest domain.

When packets are sent to guest domains, the bridge or the router in the driver domain first receives the packets. It directs the packets to the proper guest domain's backend vif, and that backend vif puts the packets in the guest domain's frontend vif receiving buffer. The frontend vif inside the guest domain then processes the arrived packets as usual and delivers them up to the guest domain's application. When a guest domain sends packets to the Internet, the packets are sent to the frontend vif's sending buffer, and then the backend vif puts the packets from the vif's sending buffer into the bridge or router in the driver domain. The bridge or router then delivers it to the Internet.

Frontend interfaces exist in the guest domain as veth<#>, equivalent to the network interface in common physical machines. The backend virtual interfaces in the driver domain are notated by the format vif<id.#>. The id stands for the guest domain ID, and the vif number, #, indicates the corresponding order of the network interfaces inside the guest domain, which starts at 0. They are separated by dots. For example, vif1.0 refers to the zeroth network interface in the guest domain whose ID is 1. Each domain in a Xen system has a domainID. The privileged domain, Domain0, has domainID 0. Whenever a domU boots up, Xen assigns it a unique domainID as well. For further details, you can refer to Chapter 6, "Managing Unprivileged Domains."

In Domain0, backend vif0.0 is called the Xen loopback (or netloop) device. Its function is different from the guest domain's vif because the guest domain frontend vif passes the packets in the guest domain to its proxy backend in the driver domain (often Domain0). The Xen loopback device `vif0.0` exists only to enforce a data copy on the guest domain to the Domain0 path. The copy is desired because otherwise a packet sitting on the Domain0 receiving buffer would hold the guest domain's page containing the packet for an unbounded amount of time. There is no guarantee of when the user process will read the data and free the socket buffer.

> **NOTE**
> Herbert Xu has proposed a patch that removes the need for this loopback device. In the future, there may be no more Xen loop device in bridging mode.

Overview of Network Configuration in Xen

After you have designed a virtual network topology, it is time to implement your plan in Xen. In this section, we give a quick overview of this process and then later follow with sections covering the detailed steps for each sharing model.

High-Level Steps

The first step is to assign each physical device to a driver domain to manage it. Here whenever we mention a driver domain in this chapter, we refer to the domain who owns the physical network device. The simplest and most well tested configuration uses Domain0 as the driver domain. We recommend using Domain0 as the driver domain at least initially. Chapter 9 described in detail how to assign a device to a guest domain or driver domain. This can be Domain0, but there are advantages to placing the control in a separate privileged domain if possible.

The second step is to implement the sharing model chosen, whether bridging, routing, NAT, or dedicated. For firewalls, first set up the designed topology of the virtual network as described in this chapter, and then refer to Chapter 11 for firewall configuration information.

To implement the sharing model chosen, the following general configuration steps should be taken:

1. **Configure Xend to set up the sharing mode virtual network and run `xend` in Domain0.**

This is done through modifications in the Xend configuration file to choose the appropriate network configuration scripts. When `xend` starts, it configures the network according to the specified settings and scripts.

2. **Configure the network parameters in the guest configuration file and boot up a guest domain.**

   In the guest configuration file, you must also edit the network interface options to set the guest domain network interface's MAC address, IP address, and all other related network parameters. When the guest domain boots up, the pair of frontend and backend guest vifs are created for the domain.

3. **Configure the network interfaces inside the guest domain.**

   This includes setting the IP address, default gateway, and DNS server manually or by way of a DHCP service. The guest domain's frontend network interfaces must be consistent with the backend interface configurations in Step 2. It can be done by the graphical network configuration tool that most Linux distributions will provide

4. **Test the guest domains and the virtual network to ensure it is set up properly.**

   The tools `ifconfig`, `ping`, `ip`, and Ethereal/Wireshark can be helpful to verify or diagnose the setup of our virtual network topology, and to make sure that the bridge or router is properly forwarding packets to and from the guest.

Xend Configuration File

Xen has provided two types of scripts by default: network scripts and virtual network interface (vif) scripts. Network scripts are used to set up the virtual network in the driver domain when `xend` starts. vif scripts are used to bring up the guest virtual network interfaces when the guest boots up. Both of the default scripts are stored in the directory `/etc/xen/scripts`. Corresponding to Xen's three different virtual network modes, the default scripts are `network-bridge`, `vif-bridge`, `network-route`, `vif-route`, `network-nat`, and `vif-nat`.

The network scripts define and set up the networking environment or the network mode, and the vif scripts define and help to create and destroy the virtual interface behavior. When `xend` starts in Domain0, it calls the network script specified in the Xend configuration file to establish the corresponding virtual network. Bridging mode is the default configuration in the Xend configuration file. When Domain0 starts a new domain, it runs the vif script as specified by the Xend configuration file to bring up the backend virtual interface for this guest domain in the corresponding DriverDomain. The format for specifying a `network-script` and `vif-script` in the Xend configuration file is the following:

```
(network-script   scriptname)
(vif-script        scriptname)
```

As described in Chapter 6, the Xend configuration file's syntax is based on S-expression (SXP) format. The scriptname is the script filename that Xen will use when xend starts. As the common configuration file syntax, the lines starting with a # are comments. The script name can be `network-bridge`, `network-route`, `network-nat`, and `vif-bridge`, `vif-route`, `vif-nat`.

There are already sets of bridge options, route options, and NAT options predefined in the Xend configuration file. When you want to use one of the modes, just remove the # at the beginning of the line and then restart xend. Be sure to uncomment the two lines `network-script` and `vif-script` as a pair and comment all the rest of the network options to avoid conflicts.

Each script can take a number of arguments. When the scripts are using the arguments, the scriptname and the arguments should be quoted in single quotes, and the argument derivatives and the corresponding values should use the equal symbol to connect them. Different argument derivatives are separated by white spaces. The format will be as follows:

```
(network-script   'network-name  arg_derivative_1=value  argument_derivative_
2=value')
```

Following is a specific example:

```
(network-script   'network-bridge  netdev=eth1  vifnum=1')
```

The `netdev` argument specifies the hardware network device in Domain0. The `vifnum` argument specifies what the number of this vif should be. In this example, the script binds the physical network interface, `eth1`, to the setup bridge, and Domain0's second loopback device `vif0.1` will be combined to the bridge, too.

The scripts do not need to be in the default directory `/etc/xen/scripts`. The script can be put anywhere as long as the directory is specified in the option.

Following is a specific example by specifying the directory:

```
(network-script  '/opt/scripts/network-bridge')
```

More details on what arguments the default scripts can take are mentioned in later sections of this chapter.

Guest Domain's Configuration File

xend sets up the virtual network and provides the corresponding virtual interface available to guest domains. A guest domain's network interfaces are set up according to the guest domain's configuration file. The guest domain's configuration file determines how many virtual interfaces the guest domain has, which virtual bridge device the virtual interfaces attach to, what each virtual interface's MAC and IP address is, and how the virtual interface will get them. In a guest domain's configuration file, the following directives configure the guest domain's network interfaces: vif, nics, dhcp, netmask, and gateway. When neither the vif nor nics network directives is in the guest domain's configuration file, no network interface will be found inside the guest domain except the loopback interface, as if a machine has no network card plugged in.

vif

The vif directive is used to specify each virtual interface's IP and MAC address, indicating how many vifs the guest domain will have. vif configures a guest domain's network interfaces and has the richest options related to the backend vif. vif has the available options mac, ip, vifname, and type, which are all the possible parameters related to a guest domain's network interface, such as renaming the virtual interface and binding it to a bridge.

The vif options occur within square brackets "[]", and each of the guest domain's network interfaces is quoted by single quotation marks and separated by a comma. If multiple vifs are in a guest domain, it will be this way: vif = ['...','...','...',]. For each network interface, the options can be mac=xxxx, ip=xxxx, or bridge=xenbr#, and so on, and they are separated by a comma within the single quotation marks. If multiple vifs are assigned without specifying the vifname, the vif's name will be assigned in order by the sequential numbers.

Following are two example formats of vif:

```
vif = ['']
```

This guest domain has only one vif. All of the vif's configurations are within square brackets. It is empty inside the single quotation mark, indicating no specified network properties. When the option `mac` is not used in the directive, Xen automatically generates a MAC address to this vif. If the option `ip` is not used, DHCP service is the default way for the vif to obtain a dynamic IP. If the option `vifname` is not used, the default name will be `eth0`. If the directive `vif` does not appear in the configuration file, there will be no network interfaces in the guest domain. So the empty directive `vif` declares that the guest domain has a network interface.

```
vif = ['mac=xx:xx:xx:xx:xx:xx, ip=x.x.x.x, vifname=X, bridge=xenbr0',]
```

This guest domain also has only one vif. Here, there are four vif options separated by a comma, and they are all quoted inside the pair of single quotation marks. `xenbr0` is set up by the bridge network script, and the option `bridge=xenbr0` attaches this guest domain's vif to the bridge.

`nics`

The `nics` directive is a deprecated directive to specify how many interfaces the guest domain has. `nics` explicitly specifies how many network interfaces there will be in the guest domain and will be set up when the guest domain boots up. This directive is deprecated because the vif directive can also indicate how many network interfaces a guest domain will have. Xen 3.0 only supports up to three vifs for each guest domain. If the value of `nics` is inconsistent with the number indicated in the vif directive, the larger number of network interfaces will be created inside the guest domain. If we've configured `nics` once for a guest domain, and later change the `nics` value or remove this directive, we still need to go back to the guest domain and manually remove the interfaces inside the guest domain. Be careful when using this directive; it is easy to be confused and cause mistakes. This option is used in previous Xen versions. You can see it in the Xen manual 1.0. We recommend not using it any more to save the trouble. The `nics` value is an integer, and currently it is limited to no bigger than 3. Following is a format example of `nics`:

```
nics=1
```

> **NOTE**
> Xen users definitely want to have more interfaces in the guest domains. There have been proposals in the xen-devel list to change the limit value.

dhcp

The dhcp directive is an optional directive to specify whether to use the DHCP service to obtain an IP. Without the ip option mentioned in the vif directive or the ip directive in the guest configuration file, the guest domain's vif obtains the IP address by default from the DHCP service. So the value of the directive dhcp should be quoted with double quotation marks. Following is a format example of dhcp:

```
dhcp="dhcp"
```

netmask **and** gateway

The netmask and gateway directives are used to manually assign an IP to the guest domain when its IP is manually assigned. The netmask directive specifies the IP's subnet network. The gateway directive tells the guest domain which machine the packets should be forwarded to when a guest domain wants to send them over the Internet rather than in the intranet. It is important for routing.

These directives are the essential directives when manually configuring a guest domain's static IP. Following is the format example of the netmask and gateway options:

```
netmask="255.255.254.0"
gateway="128.153.144.1"
```

IP values should be surrounded by double quotation marks.

Later, in the network mode configuration guidance section, you will see more concrete examples of configuring the Xend and guest domain configuration files.

Details of Bridging Mode

In this section, we follow the high-level steps outlined in the previous section and provide a detailed low-level example of configuring a bridged network in Xen. As we've mentioned, a bridge is a link-layer device. It processes packets that contain source and destination MAC addresses, forwarding the packets to the destination host according to MAC address.

A Xen bridging virtual network works much like a hardware bridge device. Guest domains appear directly on the external Ethernet segment to which the driver domain is physically connected. Figure 10.4 illustrates the topology of Xen's guests in bridging mode. Xen's network bridge script uses `bridge-utils` to set up the software bridge in the Linux kernel.

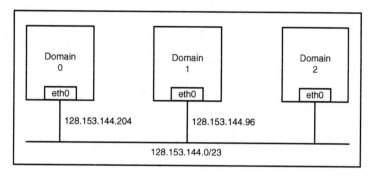

FIGURE 10.4 In bridging mode, guest domains are transparent to the Ethernet that the driver domain connects to.

In Xen bridging mode, a guest domain has a Xen-defined backend network interface connected to the bridge in the driver domain, and the common frontend network interface is installed inside the guest domain. When `xend` starts, the network script `network-bridge` brings up the virtual bridge interface, `xenbr0`. By default, the real physical interface `eth0` is changed to the name `peth0`, connecting to this bridge interface. Domain0's loopback device `veth0` is also brought up, its name is changed to `eth0,` and its backend virtual interface `vif0.0` is connected to the bridge interface. The pair of Domain0's virtual interface `eth0` and `vif0.0` are connected in a loopback fashion.

Bridging Configuration Example

Bridging is the default network architecture that Xen establishes for guest domains. In the Xend configuration file `/etc/xen/xend-config.sxp`, the default directives related to the virtual network are shown in Listing 10.1. Notice that the `network-bridge` and `vif-bridge` lines are the only ones uncommented.

LISTING 10.1 Xend Default Bridging Mode Configurations

```
(network-script network-bridge)
(vif-script vif-bridge)
# (network-script network-route)
# (vif-script vif-route)
# (network-script network-nat)
# (vif-script vif-nat)
```

The network script `network-bridge` is in the directory `/etc/xen/scripts`. It sets up the networking environment and uses the `bridge-utils` tool to set up the software bridge `xenbr0`. The vif script `vif-bridge` is also in the same directory as the network script. It sets up the backend vif for the guest domain when a guest domain boots up.

Before running the command `xm create` on a guest domain, we should first configure the guest domain's configuration file. Listing 10.2 shows an example of the directive related to the virtual network setup in a guest configuration file.

LISTING 10.2 An Example of a Guest Domain Default Bridging Mode Configurations

```
vif = ['mac=00:16:3e:45:e7:12, bridge=xenbr0']
```

When the guest domain is booting up, its virtual interface is assigned a user-specified MAC address and is connected to the bridge `xenbr0`. This directive specifies that the guest domain has one virtual network interface inside that domain, and its backend vif will be attached to the bridge `xenbr0`.

When Xen starts, using the command `ifconfig -a`, we can have a look at the network interfaces in the driver domain, in this case Domain0. Listing 10.3 shows this full output. This is a long list, and we walk you through it in detail. Table 10.2 lists the interfaces in the same order as they appear in Listing 10.3, along with a brief description of their purpose.

LISTING 10.3 The Driver Domain Bridging Interfaces

```
[user@Dom0]# ifconfig -a
eth0      Link encap:Ethernet  HWaddr 00:11:25:F6:15:22
          inet addr:128.153.144.204  Bcast:128.153.145.255      ➡
          Mask:255.255.254.0
          inet6 addr: fe80::211:25ff:fef6:1522/64 Scope:Link
          UP BROADCAST RUNNING MULTICAST  MTU:1500  Metric:1
          RX packets:66 errors:0 dropped:0 overruns:0 frame:0
          TX packets:30 errors:0 dropped:0 overruns:0 carrier:0
```

```
            collisions:0 txqueuelen:0
            RX bytes:10366 (10.1 KiB)  TX bytes:7878 (7.6 KiB)

lo          Link encap:Local Loopback
            inet addr:127.0.0.1  Mask:255.0.0.0
            inet6 addr: ::1/128 Scope:Host
            UP LOOPBACK RUNNING  MTU:16436  Metric:1
            RX packets:1448 errors:0 dropped:0 overruns:0 frame:0
            TX packets:1448 errors:0 dropped:0 overruns:0 carrier:0
            collisions:0 txqueuelen:0
            RX bytes:2314108 (2.2 MiB)  TX bytes:2314108 (2.2 MiB)

peth0       Link encap:Ethernet  HWaddr FE:FF:FF:FF:FF:FF
            inet6 addr: fe80::fcff:ffff:feff:ffff/64 Scope:Link
            UP BROADCAST RUNNING NOARP  MTU:1500  Metric:1
            RX packets:85 errors:0 dropped:0 overruns:0 frame:0
            TX packets:30 errors:0 dropped:0 overruns:0 carrier:0
            collisions:0 txqueuelen:1000
            RX bytes:11675 (11.4 KiB)  TX bytes:8046 (7.8 KiB)
            Interrupt:16

sit0        Link encap:IPv6-in-IPv4
            NOARP  MTU:1480  Metric:1
            RX packets:0 errors:0 dropped:0 overruns:0 frame:0
            TX packets:0 errors:0 dropped:0 overruns:0 carrier:0
            collisions:0 txqueuelen:0
            RX bytes:0 (0.0 b)  TX bytes:0 (0.0 b)

veth1       Link encap:Ethernet  HWaddr 00:00:00:00:00:00
            BROADCAST MULTICAST  MTU:1500  Metric:1
            RX packets:0 errors:0 dropped:0 overruns:0 frame:0
            TX packets:0 errors:0 dropped:0 overruns:0 carrier:0
            collisions:0 txqueuelen:0
            RX bytes:0 (0.0 b)  TX bytes:0 (0.0 b)

veth2       Link encap:Ethernet  HWaddr 00:00:00:00:00:00
            BROADCAST MULTICAST  MTU:1500  Metric:1
            RX packets:0 errors:0 dropped:0 overruns:0 frame:0
            TX packets:0 errors:0 dropped:0 overruns:0 carrier:0
            collisions:0 txqueuelen:0
            RX bytes:0 (0.0 b)  TX bytes:0 (0.0 b)
```

LISTING 10.3 continued

```
veth3     Link encap:Ethernet  HWaddr 00:00:00:00:00:00
          BROADCAST MULTICAST  MTU:1500  Metric:1
          RX packets:0 errors:0 dropped:0 overruns:0 frame:0
          TX packets:0 errors:0 dropped:0 overruns:0 carrier:0
          collisions:0 txqueuelen:0
          RX bytes:0 (0.0 b)  TX bytes:0 (0.0 b)

vif0.0    Link encap:Ethernet  HWaddr FE:FF:FF:FF:FF:FF
          inet6 addr: fe80::fcff:ffff:feff:ffff/64 Scope:Link
          UP BROADCAST RUNNING NOARP  MTU:1500  Metric:1
          RX packets:30 errors:0 dropped:0 overruns:0 frame:0
          TX packets:66 errors:0 dropped:0 overruns:0 carrier:0
          collisions:0 txqueuelen:0
          RX bytes:7878 (7.6 KiB)  TX bytes:10366 (10.1 KiB)

vif0.1    Link encap:Ethernet  HWaddr FE:FF:FF:FF:FF:FF
          BROADCAST MULTICAST  MTU:1500  Metric:1
          RX packets:0 errors:0 dropped:0 overruns:0 frame:0
          TX packets:0 errors:0 dropped:0 overruns:0 carrier:0
          collisions:0 txqueuelen:0
          RX bytes:0 (0.0 b)  TX bytes:0 (0.0 b)

vif0.2    Link encap:Ethernet  HWaddr FE:FF:FF:FF:FF:FF
          BROADCAST MULTICAST  MTU:1500  Metric:1
          RX packets:0 errors:0 dropped:0 overruns:0 frame:0
          TX packets:0 errors:0 dropped:0 overruns:0 carrier:0
          collisions:0 txqueuelen:0
          RX bytes:0 (0.0 b)  TX bytes:0 (0.0 b)

vif0.3    Link encap:Ethernet  HWaddr FE:FF:FF:FF:FF:FF
          BROADCAST MULTICAST  MTU:1500  Metric:1
          RX packets:0 errors:0 dropped:0 overruns:0 frame:0
          TX packets:0 errors:0 dropped:0 overruns:0 carrier:0
          collisions:0 txqueuelen:0
          RX bytes:0 (0.0 b)  TX bytes:0 (0.0 b)

vif1.0    Link encap:Ethernet  HWaddr FE:FF:FF:FF:FF:FF
          inet6 addr: fe80::fcff:ffff:feff:ffff/64 Scope:Link
          UP BROADCAST RUNNING NOARP  MTU:1500  Metric:1
          RX packets:41 errors:0 dropped:0 overruns:0 frame:0
          TX packets:50 errors:0 dropped:0 overruns:0 carrier:0
          collisions:0 txqueuelen:0
          RX bytes:5604 (5.4 KiB)  TX bytes:7725 (7.5 KiB)
```

```
xenbr0    Link encap:Ethernet   HWaddr FE:FF:FF:FF:FF:FF
          inet6 addr: fe80::200:ff:fe00:0/64 Scope:Link
          UP BROADCAST RUNNING NOARP  MTU:1500  Metric:1
          RX packets:97 errors:0 dropped:0 overruns:0 frame:0
          TX packets:0 errors:0 dropped:0 overruns:0 carrier:0
          collisions:0 txqueuelen:0
          RX bytes:16999 (16.6 KiB)  TX bytes:0 (0.0 b)
[user@Dom0]#
```

TABLE 10.2 Domain0 Network Interfaces

Interface Name	Purpose
eth0	Frontend network interface for driver domain with ID 0 (as in Domain0)
lo	Loopback interface for Domain0
peth0	Physical network interface
sit0	Proxy interface for tunneling from IPv6 over IPv4
veth1~veth3	3 unused frontend network interfaces for Domain0
vif0.0	Backend network interface for Domain0
vif0.1~veth0.3	The corresponding unused backend network interface for Domain0
vif1.0	Backend network interface for guest domain with ID 1
xenbr0	Bridge network interface

veth0 and vif0.0 are the pair of Domain0's network interfaces whose domain ID is 0. veth0 is renamed to be eth0. The xenbr0 interface is the software bridge interface set up in the driver domain. vif1.0 is the running guest domain's backend network interface. This guest domain's domain ID is 1, and it has only one network interface in this example.

We can see that peth0, xenbr0, vif0.0, and vif1.0 are sharing the same MAC address FE:FF:FF:FF:FF:FF, which is the Ethernet broadcast address. This indicates that the physical interface, the loopback device of Domain0, and the backend interfaces of guest domains are all broadcasting to the bridge interface xenbr0. When the physical network interface receives the packets, it sends them all directly to the bridge interface xenbr0. The software bridge determines which domain's backend interface to forward those packets to by the packets' MAC addresses. So, peth0 does not need to have an IP, only a MAC address. The physical interface's original IP has been imparted to eth0—the driver domain's virtual frontend interface. xenbr0 directs the packets either to eth0 or vif1.0 by their MAC addresses 00:11:25:F6:15:22 or 00:16:3e:45:e7:12. The guest domain's corresponding frontend virtual interface eth0 is installed inside the guest domain. From the DriverDomain's view, the eth0 in guest domain is vif1.0. Figure 10.5 shows a virtual device view of bridge mode.

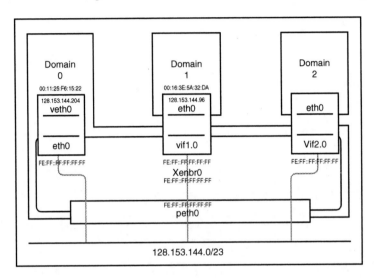

FIGURE 10.5 In bridging mode, the driver domain and the guest domains are all hooked to the Linux bridge. The bridge is responsible for delivering the packets to the domains by their MAC addresses.

Inside the guest domain, the network interfaces look the same as on a typical machine, as Listing 10.4 shows.

LISTING 10.4 The Guest Domain Network Interfaces

```
[user@DomU]# ifconfig -a
eth0    Link encap:Ethernet  HWaddr 00:16:3E:5A:32:DA
        inet addr:128.153.144.96  Bcast:128.153.145.255
        Mask:255.255.254.0
        inet6 addr: fe80::216:3eff:fe5a:32da/64 Scope:Link
        UP BROADCAST RUNNING MULTICAST  MTU:1500  Metric:1\
        RX packets:209 errors:0 dropped:0 overruns:0 frame:0
        TX packets:41 errors:0 dropped:0 overruns:0 carrier:0
        collisions:0 txqueuelen:1000
        RX bytes:33822 (33.0 KiB)  TX bytes:6178 (6.0 KiB)
```

```
lo        Link encap:Local Loopback
          inet addr:127.0.0.1  Mask:255.0.0.0
          inet6 addr: ::1/128 Scope:Host
          UP LOOPBACK RUNNING  MTU:16436  Metric:1
          RX packets:1217 errors:0 dropped:0 overruns:0 frame:0
          TX packets:1217 errors:0 dropped:0 overruns:0 carrier:0
          collisions:0 txqueuelen:0
          RX bytes:1820052 (1.7 MiB)  TX bytes:1820052 (1.7 MiB)

sit0      Link encap:IPv6-in-IPv4
          NOARP  MTU:1480  Metric:1
          RX packets:0 errors:0 dropped:0 overruns:0 frame:0
          TX packets:0 errors:0 dropped:0 overruns:0 carrier:0
          collisions:0 txqueuelen:0
          RX bytes:0 (0.0 b)  TX bytes:0 (0.0 b)
[user@DomU]#
```

In a guest domain, whether the Xen network is in bridging mode or routing mode, the network interface looks the same as it would in a non-virtualized machine.

Testing Results

First, we need to check that the guest domain connects to the Internet, so we use the `ping` command to ping an external website. The `ping` command sends ICMP requests to the destination IP address and receives ICMP replies. `ping` is the most commonly used command to examine whether two machines have a network connection. Listing 10.5 shows the ping results.

LISTING 10.5 The Guest Domain Pings www.google.com

```
[user@DomU]# ping www.google.com
PING www.l.google.com (64.233.161.147) 56(84) bytes of data.
64 bytes from od-in-f147.google.com (64.233.161.147):      ➥
               icmp_seq=1 ttl=243 time=16.9 ms
64 bytes from od-in-f147.google.com (64.233.161.147):      ➥
               icmp_seq=2 ttl=243 time=17.0 ms
64 bytes from od-in-f147.google.com (64.233.161.147):      ➥
               icmp_seq=3 ttl=243 time=21.1 ms

--- www.l.google.com ping statistics ---
3 packets transmitted, 3 received, 0% packet loss, time 2000ms
rtt min/avg/max/mdev = 16.920/18.381/21.155/1.965 ms
[user@DomU]#
```

From Listing 10.5, we can see that Google responds to each ICMP sent by the guest domain. TTL stands for Time To Live and sets a limit on the number of hops a packet can experience. In this case, it deducts from 255 to 243, which indicates it has passed through 12 routers or machines before arriving at the guest machine.

We use a remote machine 128.153.144.195 in the same subnet as the driver domain's IP address 128.153.144.204 to trace the routing path of the guest domain 128.153.144.96. The command tracert in the window displays the machines that the packet passes before the packet arrives at the destination address. Listing 10.6 shows the result.

LISTING 10.6 A Routing Trace from a Remote Machine in the Same Subnet

```
[@windows]# tracert 128.153.144.96
Tracing route to 128.153.144.96 over a maxium of 30 hops
1    3ms        1ms    1ms    128.153.144.96
Trace complete
[user@local]#
```

There is only one hop between our virtual machine and an external machine on the same subnet. In other words, the tracert output looks exactly as it would with a physical machine rather than a virtual machine even though the guest domain is running inside a virtual machine. In this case, Domain0 has the IP address 128.153.144.204, but there is no indication that Domain0 was involved in the tracert.

Next, we boot two guest domains in the bridging virtual network. When we use one guest domain to ping another, we use a network protocol analyzer, Ethereal or Wireshark, to take a packet trace on both the physical interface peth0 and the bridge interface xenbr0. (Ethereal or Wireshark is a powerful and useful network tool that can capture the packets on the network interfaces for troubleshooting, and analyze the network protocols and software.) One guest domain's IP is 128.153.144.96; the other is 128.153.144.97.

Figure 10.6 is the trace taken on the bridge interface xenbr0 by Ethereal, while Figure 10.7 is the trace taken on the physical interface peth0. We can tell from Figures 10.6 and 10.7 that the bridge interface directs the ICMP packets from one guest domain to the destination guest. We did see that the ICMP packets have been passed from one guest to another by the Xen bridge, but we didn't see any ICMP packets on the physical interface, which proves that the software bridge does not broadcast all the packets as a hub but works as a switch, delivering the packets to each specified domain.

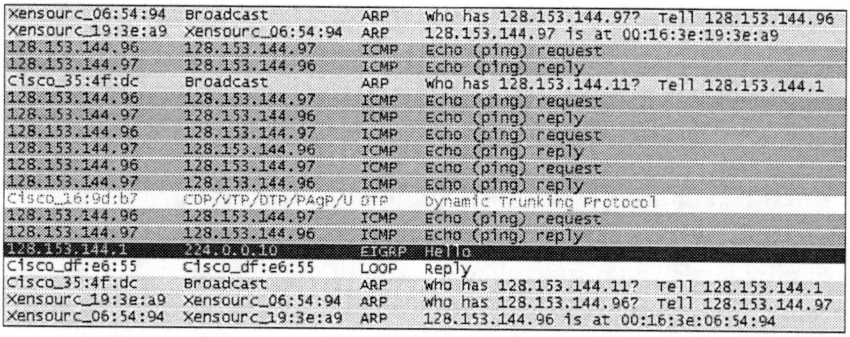

FIGURE 10.6 The software bridge directs the ICMP packets from one guest domain to another.

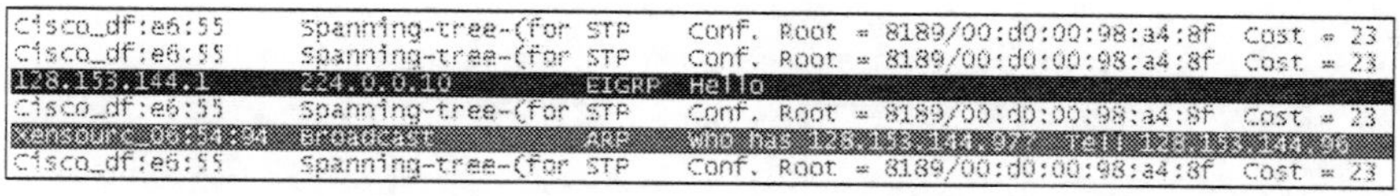

FIGURE 10.7 The physical network device does not deliver the packets from one guest domain to another in the same machine.

Finally, we can use the `brctl` command to display the bridge's information to check whether the guest domains have been hooked to the bridging virtual network. The `brctl` command, shown in Listing 10.7, is provided by the `bridge-utils` package.

LISTING 10.7 The Driver Domain Bridge Status

```
[user@Dom0]# brctl show
bridge name      bridge id            STP enabled    interfaces
xenbr0           8000.ffffffffffff    no             vif1.0
                                                     peth0
                                                     vif0.0
```

The bridge's name is `xenbr0`, and its MAC address is `FE:FF:FF:FF:FF:FF`. The guest domain's backend interface `vif1.0`, the driver domain's interface `vif0.0`, and the physical interface `peth0` are all connecting through the bridge `xenbr0`. The `xenbr0` interface is responsible for delivering packets to and from the appropriate interface according to MAC addresses.

Details of Routing Mode

In this section, we follow the high-level steps outlined in an earlier section and provide a detailed low-level example of configuring routing mode in Xen. As we've mentioned, a router is a network layer device above the link layer. It processes IP packets containing source and destination IP addresses, forwarding and routing the packets to the network segment nearer to the destination machine.

Xen's routing mode works much like a hardware router. Guest domains are routed to the Ethernet through the driver domain. With `ip_forwarding` enabled in `iptables` in the driver domain, it acts as a router, relaying guest domains' packets from one network segment onto the external network segment. Figure 10.8 demonstrates the topology of Xen routing mode.

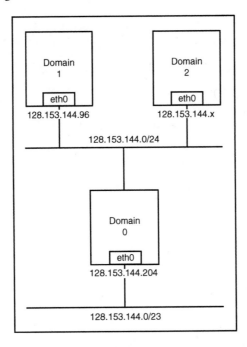

FIGURE 10.8 The guest domains are routed to the Ethernet through the driver domain. The driver domain acts as the gateway of the guest domains.

In routing mode, the guest domain sets the driver domain as its gateway. Whenever the guest domain tries to send its packets to the Internet, the packets are sent to the software router first. Then the driver domain routes these packets further to the Internet. On the other hand, when the backend vif of a guest domain receives packets from the software router, it puts the packets into the receiving buffers of its frontend interface. Then the guest domain receives the packet from its receiving buffer as it would with a physical network interface. The physical network interface in the driver domain is like one of the router's ports that connect to the outside network segment. The backend vifs of the guest domains that lie on the different network segments are like the other ports of the router.

Routing Configuration Example

First, in the Xend configuration file, we should comment the `network-bridge` and `vif-bridge` and uncomment the `network-route` and `vif-route`. The network directives, `network-script` and `vif-script`, are shown in Listing 10.8. Notice that the `network-route` and `vif-route` lines are the only ones uncommented.

LISTING 10.8 Xend Routing Mode Configurations

```
#  (network-script network-bridge)
#  (vif-script vif-bridge)
(network-script network-route)
(vif-script vif-route)
#(network-script network-nat)
#(vif-script vif-nat)
```

Additionally, several lines should be added to the script `/etc/xen/scripts/net-work-route`, as shown in Listing 10.9. In newer versions of Xen, it should already be fixed.

LISTING 10.9 To Fix the Xend `network-route` Script (if necessary)

```
echo 1 > /proc/sys/net/ipv4/ip_forward
echo 1 > /proc/sys/net/ipv4/conf/eth0/proxy_arp
```

The first line is the default line in the script, setting `ip_forwarding` in `iptables` so that the driver domain acts as a router.

The second line is added to fix the default `network-route` script. When `proxy_arp` is set, the router acts as the ARP proxy for the guest domain, answering an ARP request for the guest domain when the destination address is in another network segment. Notice that `eth0` on the second line is the current working network interface in the driver domain. You would change this if you were using a different interface for routing. If using the default `network-route` script without the second line, when the guest domain pings a running machine's IP, it will not receive any ICMP replies.

This problem can be clearly seen when using the network analyzer Ethereal to trace what happens to the ICMP request packets. For example, the pinged remote physical machine is 128.153.144.148, and its MAC address is 00:04:76:35:0a:72; the guest domain is 128.153.144.112, and its MAC address is 00:16:3e:06:54:94. First, we take a trace on the guest domain's virtual interface vif1.0. Figure 10.9 shows a screenshot of the Ethereal trace on the guest domain vif in routing mode.

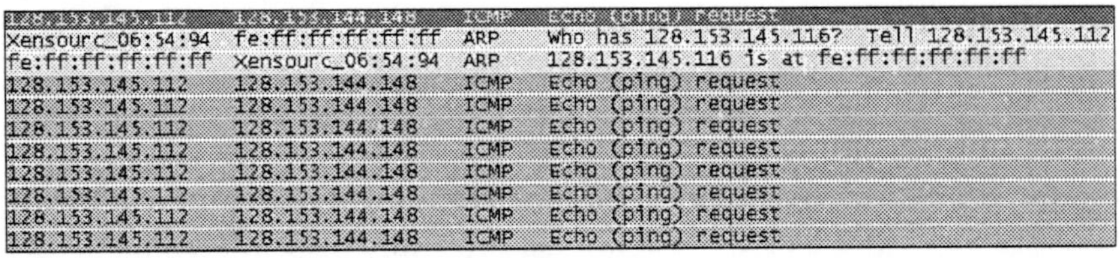

128.153.145.112	128.153.144.148	ICMP	Echo (ping) request
Xensourc_06:54:94	fe:ff:ff:ff:ff:ff	ARP	who has 128.153.145.116? Tell 128.153.145.112
fe:ff:ff:ff:ff:ff	Xensourc_06:54:94	ARP	128.153.145.116 is at fe:ff:ff:ff:ff:ff
128.153.145.112	128.153.144.148	ICMP	Echo (ping) request
128.153.145.112	128.153.144.148	ICMP	Echo (ping) request
128.153.145.112	128.153.144.148	ICMP	Echo (ping) request
128.153.145.112	128.153.144.148	ICMP	Echo (ping) request
128.153.145.112	128.153.144.148	ICMP	Echo (ping) request
128.153.145.112	128.153.144.148	ICMP	Echo (ping) request

FIGURE 10.9 The guest domain virtual interface sends ICMP requests but receives no replies.

The trace tells us that it does send out the ICMP requests but receives no responses. During the trace, there is an ARP conversation. ARP is the Address Resolution Protocol to map an IP address to its MAC address. The guest domain asks its backend virtual interface for the MAC address of a remote machine but receives the MAC address of the guest domain's backend virtual interface instead.

At the same time, we take a trace on the driver domain's eth0 to see what happened to that ICMP request packet, as shown in Figure 10.10.

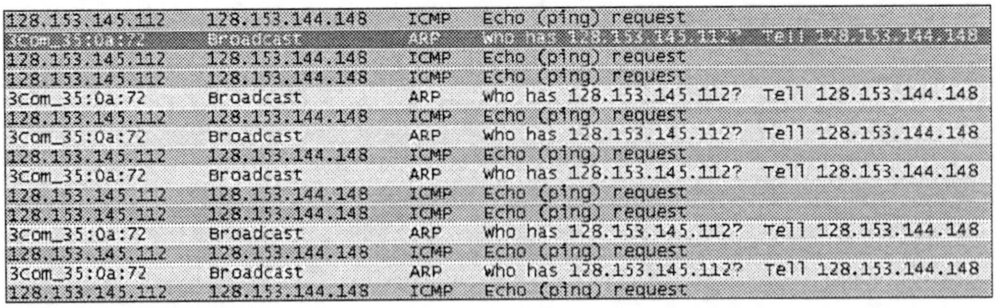

128.153.145.112	128.153.144.148	ICMP	Echo (ping) request
3Com_35:0a:72	Broadcast	ARP	who has 128.153.145.112? Tell 128.153.144.148
128.153.145.112	128.153.144.148	ICMP	Echo (ping) request
128.153.145.112	128.153.144.148	ICMP	Echo (ping) request
3Com_35:0a:72	Broadcast	ARP	who has 128.153.145.112? Tell 128.153.144.148
128.153.145.112	128.153.144.148	ICMP	Echo (ping) request
3Com_35:0a:72	Broadcast	ARP	who has 128.153.145.112? Tell 128.153.144.148
128.153.145.112	128.153.144.148	ICMP	Echo (ping) request
3Com_35:0a:72	Broadcast	ARP	who has 128.153.145.112? Tell 128.153.144.148
128.153.145.112	128.153.144.148	ICMP	Echo (ping) request
128.153.145.112	128.153.144.148	ICMP	Echo (ping) request
3Com_35:0a:72	Broadcast	ARP	who has 128.153.145.112? Tell 128.153.144.148
128.153.145.112	128.153.144.148	ICMP	Echo (ping) request
3Com_35:0a:72	Broadcast	ARP	who has 128.153.145.112? Tell 128.153.144.148
128.153.145.112	128.153.144.148	ICMP	Echo (ping) request

FIGURE 10.10 The destination machine could not obtain the requesting domain's MAC address.

We can tell that the requests reach the destination machine, but when the destination machine sends the ARP request and asks for the guest domain's MAC address, it receives no reply. This means the guest domain doesn't respond to the destination machine with its MAC address.

Finally, after we find and fix the problem by adding the second line in Listing 10.9, we can see that the guest domain receives the ICMP replies from the destination machine. Among the ICMP requests and replies, there is also an ARP conversation. This time it is the router who asks for the guest domain's MAC address. Having fixed the ARP problem, the guest domain can now communicate with the Internet. Figure 10.11 shows the trace taken on the guest domain.

```
fe:ff:ff:ff:ff:ff  xensourc_06:54:94  ARP   who has 128.153.145.112? Tell 128.153.145.111
xensourc_06:54:94  fe:ff:ff:ff:ff:ff  ARP   128.153.145.112 is at 00:16:3e:06:54:94
128.153.145.112    128.153.144.148    ICMP  Echo (ping) request
128.153.144.148    128.153.145.112    ICMP  Echo (ping) reply
128.153.145.112    128.153.144.148    ICMP  Echo (ping) request
128.153.144.148    128.153.145.112    ICMP  Echo (ping) reply
```

FIGURE 10.11 The guest domain successfully receives the ICMP replies from the destination machine.

Before starting the guest domain, we also need to configure its configuration file, which is a little more complicated than the bridging mode. Listing 10.10 shows a sample configuration of the directives related to the network interface setup.

LISTING 10.10 A Sample of a Guest Domain Routing Mode Configuration

```
vif = [ 'ip = 128.153.144.96' ]
NETMASK="255.255.255.0"
GATEWAY="128.153.144.204"
```

The IP address has to be defined twice. Both the vif and ip directives are the guest domain's IP. netmask is the same as the driver domain's netmask, and gateway is set as the driver domain's IP address. Consequently, all the packets that arrive at the physical interface will be forwarded to the driver domain according to the routing table. On the other hand, all the outgoing packets in guest domains will be forwarded to the gateway—the driver domain that will look up its routing table and direct the packets to the corresponding guest domain or to the Internet.

We also need to set up the netmask and gateway in the guest domain after a guest domain boots up. Inside the guest domain, configure the network interface the same as we did for the guest domain configuration file. Listing 10.11 displays the network interfaces inside the guest domain by using the ifconfig command.

LISTING 10.11 The Guest Domain Network Interfaces

```
[user@DomU]# ifconfig -a
eth0      Link encap:Ethernet  HWaddr 00:16:3E:5A:32:DA
          inet addr:128.153.144.96  Bcast:128.153.145.255    ➡
          Mask:255.255.255.0
```

```
          inet6 addr: fe80::216:3eff:fe5a:32da/64 Scope:Link
          UP BROADCAST RUNNING MULTICAST  MTU:1500  Metric:1
          RX packets:33 errors:0 dropped:0 overruns:0 frame:0
          TX packets:59 errors:0 dropped:0 overruns:0 carrier:0
          collisions:0 txqueuelen:1000
          RX bytes:6160 (6.0 KiB)  TX bytes:7650 (7.4 KiB)

lo        Link encap:Local Loopback
          inet addr:127.0.0.1  Mask:255.0.0.0
          inet6 addr: ::1/128 Scope:Host
          UP LOOPBACK RUNNING  MTU:16436  Metric:1
          RX packets:1409 errors:0 dropped:0 overruns:0 frame:0
          TX packets:1409 errors:0 dropped:0 overruns:0 carrier:0
          collisions:0 txqueuelen:0
          RX bytes:1966840 (1.8 MiB)  TX bytes:1966840 (1.8 MiB)

sit0      Link encap:IPv6-in-IPv4
          NOARP  MTU:1480  Metric:1
          RX packets:0 errors:0 dropped:0 overruns:0 frame:0
          TX packets:0 errors:0 dropped:0 overruns:0 carrier:0
          collisions:0 txqueuelen:0
          RX bytes:0 (0.0 b)  TX bytes:0 (0.0 b)
```

As we saw in the bridging mode example, the guest domain's network interface looks the same as for a regular physical machine.

Using the ifconfig command, we can also check the network interfaces of the driver domain in routing mode. It will look like that shown in Listing 10.12.

LISTING 10.12 The Driver Domain Routing Interfaces

```
[user@Dom0]# ifconfig -a
eth0      Link encap:Ethernet  HWaddr 00:11:25:F6:15:22
          inet addr:128.153.144.204  Bcast:128.153.145.255    ➡
          Mask:255.255.254.0
          inet6 addr: fe80::211:25ff:fef6:1522/64 Scope:Link
          UP BROADCAST RUNNING MULTICAST  MTU:1500  Metric:1
          RX packets:425 errors:0 dropped:0 overruns:0 frame:0
          TX packets:321 errors:0 dropped:0 overruns:0 carrier:0
          collisions:4 txqueuelen:1000
          RX bytes:175116 (171.0 KiB)  TX bytes:79088 (77.2 KiB)
          Interrupt:16

lo        Link encap:Local Loopback
```

```
          inet addr:127.0.0.1  Mask:255.0.0.0
          inet6 addr: ::1/128 Scope:Host
          UP LOOPBACK RUNNING  MTU:16436  Metric:1
          RX packets:1248 errors:0 dropped:0 overruns:0 frame:0
          TX packets:1248 errors:0 dropped:0 overruns:0 carrier:0
          collisions:0 txqueuelen:0
          RX bytes:2164056 (2.0 MiB)  TX bytes:2164056 (2.0 MiB)

sit0      Link encap:IPv6-in-IPv4
          NOARP  MTU:1480  Metric:1
          RX packets:0 errors:0 dropped:0 overruns:0 frame:0
          TX packets:0 errors:0 dropped:0 overruns:0 carrier:0
          collisions:0 txqueuelen:0
          RX bytes:0 (0.0 b)  TX bytes:0 (0.0 b)

veth0     Link encap:Ethernet  HWaddr 00:00:00:00:00:00
          BROADCAST MULTICAST  MTU:1500  Metric:1
          RX packets:0 errors:0 dropped:0 overruns:0 frame:0
          TX packets:0 errors:0 dropped:0 overruns:0 carrier:0
          collisions:0 txqueuelen:0
          RX bytes:0 (0.0 b)  TX bytes:0 (0.0 b)

veth1     Link encap:Ethernet  HWaddr 00:00:00:00:00:00
          BROADCAST MULTICAST  MTU:1500  Metric:1
          RX packets:0 errors:0 dropped:0 overruns:0 frame:0
          TX packets:0 errors:0 dropped:0 overruns:0 carrier:0
          collisions:0 txqueuelen:0
          RX bytes:0 (0.0 b)  TX bytes:0 (0.0 b)

veth2     Link encap:Ethernet  HWaddr 00:00:00:00:00:00
          BROADCAST MULTICAST  MTU:1500  Metric:1
          RX packets:0 errors:0 dropped:0 overruns:0 frame:0
          TX packets:0 errors:0 dropped:0 overruns:0 carrier:0
          collisions:0 txqueuelen:0
          RX bytes:0 (0.0 b)  TX bytes:0 (0.0 b)

veth3     Link encap:Ethernet  HWaddr 00:00:00:00:00:00
          BROADCAST MULTICAST  MTU:1500  Metric:1
          RX packets:0 errors:0 dropped:0 overruns:0 frame:0
          TX packets:0 errors:0 dropped:0 overruns:0 carrier:0
          collisions:0 txqueuelen:0
          RX bytes:0 (0.0 b)  TX bytes:0 (0.0 b)
```

```
vif0.0      Link encap:Ethernet   HWaddr FE:FF:FF:FF:FF:FF
            BROADCAST MULTICAST   MTU:1500   Metric:1
            RX packets:0 errors:0 dropped:0 overruns:0 frame:0
            TX packets:0 errors:0 dropped:0 overruns:0 carrier:0
            collisions:0 txqueuelen:0
            RX bytes:0 (0.0 b)   TX bytes:0 (0.0 b)

vif0.1      Link encap:Ethernet   HWaddr FE:FF:FF:FF:FF:FF
            BROADCAST MULTICAST   MTU:1500   Metric:1
            RX packets:0 errors:0 dropped:0 overruns:0 frame:0
            TX packets:0 errors:0 dropped:0 overruns:0 carrier:0
            collisions:0 txqueuelen:0
            RX bytes:0 (0.0 b)   TX bytes:0 (0.0 b)

vif0.2      Link encap:Ethernet   HWaddr FE:FF:FF:FF:FF:FF
            BROADCAST MULTICAST   MTU:1500   Metric:1
            RX packets:0 errors:0 dropped:0 overruns:0 frame:0
            TX packets:0 errors:0 dropped:0 overruns:0 carrier:0
            collisions:0 txqueuelen:0
            RX bytes:0 (0.0 b)   TX bytes:0 (0.0 b)

vif0.3      Link encap:Ethernet   HWaddr FE:FF:FF:FF:FF:FF
            BROADCAST MULTICAST   MTU:1500   Metric:1
            RX packets:0 errors:0 dropped:0 overruns:0 frame:0
            TX packets:0 errors:0 dropped:0 overruns:0 carrier:0
            collisions:0 txqueuelen:0
            RX bytes:0 (0.0 b)   TX bytes:0 (0.0 b)

vif1.0      Link encap:Ethernet   HWaddr FE:FF:FF:FF:FF:FF
            inetaddr:128.153.144.204   Bcast:128.153.144.204      ➥
            Mask:255.255.255.255
            inet6 addr: fe80::fcff:ffff:feff:ffff/64 Scope:Link
            UP BROADCAST RUNNING MULTICAST  MTU:1500  Metric:1
            RX packets:86 errors:0 dropped:0 overruns:0 frame:0
            TX packets:56 errors:0 dropped:0 overruns:0 carrier:0
            collisions:0 txqueuelen:0
            RX bytes:8726 (8.5 KiB)   TX bytes:8491 (8.2 KiB)
```

Recall that in bridging mode, eth0 is the alias of the driver domain's frontend interface veth0, peth0 is the physical network interface, and the guest domain's backend vif does not have IP addresses. However, from Listing 10.10 we can tell that in routing mode eth0 is the physical interface, the pair of veth0 and vif0.0 is unused, and no bridge interface xenbr0 is created. The driver domain owns eth0 and acts as a router, directing the packets to the guest domains. The guest domain's virtual backend interface has the same IP address as the driver domain's IP address, and its broadcast IP is the same as its IP address instead of a multicast IP address. By this setting, the packets are directly forwarded from the guest domain to the driver domain. Figure 10.12 shows a virtual device view of Xen routing mode.

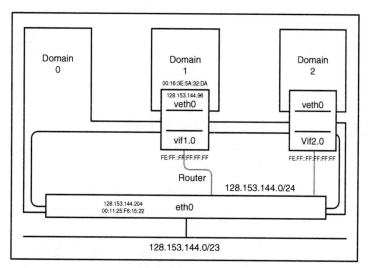

FIGURE 10.12 In routing mode, the driver domain behaves as the router, and the guest domains are all hooked to the Linux router. The router is responsible for delivering the packets to the domains by their IP addresses. The driver domain shares the physical interface with the router.

Testing Results

First, it is easy to check whether the guest domain has successfully connected to the Ethernet using the ping command to ping an external IP address (one of www.google.com's IP addresses), as shown in Listing 10.13.

LISTING 10.13 The Guest Domain pings Google

```
[user@DomU]# ping 64.233.161.104
PING 64.233.161.104 (64.233.161.104) 56(84) bytes of data.
64 bytes from 64.233.161.104: icmp_seq=1 ttl=242 time=17.4 ms
64 bytes from 64.233.161.104: icmp_seq=2 ttl=242 time=26.1 ms
64 bytes from 64.233.161.104: icmp_seq=3 ttl=242 time=37.8 ms

--- 64.233.161.104 ping statistics ---
3 packets transmitted, 3 received, 0% packet loss, time 2000ms
rtt min/avg/max/mdev = 17.457/27.153/37.897/8.377 ms
```

We can see that the guest domain successfully received the replies from 64.233.161.104. The TTL decreased from 255 to 242, which means it passes one more machine than in bridging mode. The decrease is because it also has to pass through the driver domain and asks the driver domain to relay the packet to the guest domain. While in bridging mode, the guest domain connects directly to the Ethernet.

Next, we need to further validate whether Xen is working as configured in the guest domain configuration file. We do this by examining the routing table entries, using the `route` command as shown in Listing 10.14. The -n option shows all the IP addresses in numerics instead of host names.

LISTING 10.14 The Driver Domain Routing Entries

```
[user@Dom0]# route -n
Kernel IP routing table
Destination      Gateway        Genmask          Flags Metric ➡
                      Ref    Use Iface
128.153.144.96  0.0.0.0        255.255.255.255 UH    0       ➡
                      0      0    vif1.0
128.153.144.0   0.0.0.0        255.255.255.0   U     0       ➡
                      0      0    eth0
169.254.0.0     0.0.0.0        255.255.0.0     U     0       ➡
                      0      0    eth0
0.0.0.0         128.153.144.1   0.0.0.0               UG    0       ➡
                      0      0    eth0
```

In the flags column of the routing table, U stands for "route is up," H stands for "target is a host," and G stands for "use gateway." From the first entry, we can tell that any packets sent to the host 128.153.144.96 will be sent to the guest domain's backend interface vif1.0, which will then pass it to the guest frontend. From the second entry, we can tell that for all the packets sent to a host in the subnet 128.153.144.0, it will send to the interface eth0 in the driver domain. The last entry means the packets sent to any other IPs will be forwarded to the outside through the driver domain's gateway 128.153.144.1. So whenever a packet comes in, Domain0 first looks up the routing table to see which interface to use. If the packets match the first rule, it sends the packet to the guest domain, or else it falls to the second rule; if it is not a guest domain's packets, it will reach the entry that specifies eth0 because the destination should be external in this case. In the third entry, the private "link local" block 169.254.0.0 is used when an interface tries to retrieve an IP address from a DHCP server that is not presented. (For more details, refer to IANA RFC 3330.)

Similar information can be obtained using the `ip` command, given in a different format, as shown in Listing 10.15. This gives us a good deal of information about the IP networks to which the machine is directly connected. The first line tells us that the router will select the IP 128.153.144.204 for a source address on the outgoing packets from the guest domain 128.153.144.96, whose corresponding interface is vif1.0. The rest has a similar outcome to that in Listing 10.14.

LISTING 10.15 The Driver Domain IP Routing Entries

```
[user@Dom0]# ip route show
128.153.144.96 dev vif1.0  scope link  src 128.153.144.204
128.153.144.0/24 dev eth0  proto kernel  scope link           ➡
                src 128.153.144.204
169.254.0.0/16 dev eth0  scope link
default via 128.153.144.1 dev eth0
```

Finally, we use a remote physical machine in the same subnet with the driver domain to ping the guest domain and check whether the guest domain is routing through the driver domain. Listing 10.16 shows the ping result.

LISTING 10.16 A Routing Trace from a Remote Machine

```
[user@windows]# tracert 128.153.144.96
Tracing route to 128.153.144.96 over a maximum of 30 hops
1    836ms        1ms    1ms    128.153.144.204
2    428          1ms    1ms    128.153.144.96
Trace complete
```

There is an additional hop relative to the bridging example. The Internet packets did pass through the driver domain 128.153.144.204 and then to the guest domain.

Details of NAT Mode

In this section, we follow the high-level steps outlined in an earlier section and provide a detailed low-level example of configuring a NAT in Xen. As we've mentioned, a NAT (network address translation) gateway works the same as in the routing mode. In addition, it maps a different port to each pair of internal IP address and port.

In Xen's virtual NAT mode, guest domains hide behind the driver domain as they would hide behind a physical NAT gateway. Behind the virtual NAT gateway, guest domains are within a private network, and each has its own private (not globally routable) IP address. However, outsiders on the Internet are not aware of the existence of the guest domains and are unable to contact them directly by their local IP addresses. The packets from that subnet all pass through the driver domain's IP on different ports.

Figure 10.13 shows Xen's NAT mode topology. The NAT gateway translates a packet arriving on a particular port to an internal guest domain and its appropriate application port. For example, if machine `10.0.0.11` behind the NAT gateway initiates a TCP connection from port 6789, the NAT gateway may change the outgoing packet to look like it is coming from IP address `128.153.145.111` port 9876. The NAT gateway would then make a note that any incoming traffic for port 9876 should be forwarded to `10.0.0.11` port 6789. This makes it possible for multiple hosts to share a single public IP address to access the Internet. It is also useful for securing the internal network from outsiders. Connections not initiated from behind the NAT gateway will be dropped because the NAT gateway will have no record of the proper translation.

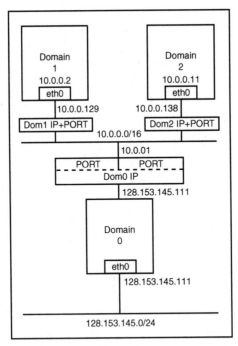

FIGURE 10.13 The guest domains hide behind the driver domain. The driver domain maps its own IP and port to the guest domain's Ethernet IP and port when the guest domains access the Internet.

Using one domain to serve a particular service is also more popular. We can also use NAT mode to map a server port, such as FTP(Port 21), HTTP(Port 80), and so on, to a particular domain, and direct external connections to a guest domain that hosts the specific service. This enables running and separating different services in different guests transparently to the external world, which still shares the same public IP but expands the computing capability of a specific service.

NAT Configuration Example

To set up the NAT mode, in the Xend configuration file make sure to comment the `network-script` and `vif-script` directives for the bridge and router setup and comment out the corresponding directive lines for `network-nat` and `vif-nat` scripts, as shown in Listing 10.17. Notice that the `network-nat` and `vif-nat` lines are the only ones uncommented.

LISTING 10.17 Xend NAT Mode Configuration

```
# (network-script network-bridge)
# (vif-script vif-bridge)
# (network-script network-route)
# (vif-script vif-route)
(network-script network-nat)
(vif-script vif-nat)
```

Xen's NAT script uses the private IP block `10.0.x.x/16` by default. An example of a guest domain's configuration file is shown in Listing 10.18.

LISTING 10.18 An Example of a Guest Domain NAT Configuration

```
vif = [ 'ip = 10.0.0.2', ]
NETMASK="255.0.0.0"
GATEWAY="10.0.0.1"
```

The difference in configuration for NAT mode from when we used routing mode is that we use a private network segment instead of having globally routable IP addresses. The guest domain's IP with the `0.x.x.x/24` range (that is, netmask of `255.0.0.0`) is a private IP address and is not reachable directly by the Internet. The guest's IP should be designated identically in both the `vif` and `ip` directives. In Listing 10.18, the IP is `10.0.0.2`, and the gateway is `10.0.0.1` by default.

Next, invoke `xm create` to create the guest domain. Inside the guest, configure the network interface to use the same IP as is configured in the guest's configuration file. The network interface in the guest domain should now resemble Listing 10.19.

LISTING 10.19 The Guest Domain NAT Interface

```
[user@DomU]# ifconfig -a
eth0     Link encap:Ethernet  HWaddr 00:16:3E:5A:32:DA
         inet addr:10.0.0.2  Bcast:10.255.255.255  Mask:255.0.0.0
         inet6 addr: fe80::216:3eff:fe5a:32da/64 Scope:Link
         UP BROADCAST RUNNING MULTICAST  MTU:1500  Metric:1
         RX packets:103 errors:0 dropped:0 overruns:0 frame:0
         TX packets:138 errors:0 dropped:0 overruns:0 carrier:0
         collisions:0 txqueuelen:1000
         RX bytes:13546 (13.2 KiB)  TX bytes:13968 (13.6 KiB)

lo       Link encap:Local Loopback
         inet addr:127.0.0.1  Mask:255.0.0.0
         inet6 addr: ::1/128 Scope:Host
         UP LOOPBACK RUNNING  MTU:16436  Metric:1
         RX packets:1272 errors:0 dropped:0 overruns:0 frame:0
         TX packets:1272 errors:0 dropped:0 overruns:0 carrier:0
         collisions:0 txqueuelen:0
         RX bytes:2953456 (2.8 MiB)  TX bytes:2953456 (2.8 MiB)

sit0     Link encap:IPv6-in-IPv4
         NOARP  MTU:1480  Metric:1
         RX packets:0 errors:0 dropped:0 overruns:0 frame:0
         TX packets:0 errors:0 dropped:0 overruns:0 carrier:0
         collisions:0 txqueuelen:0
         RX bytes:0 (0.0 b)  TX bytes:0 (0.0 b)
[user@DomU]#
```

The guest domain obtains an internal IP 10.0.0.2 and broadcasts to the entire subnet 10.0.0.0. In the driver domain, the network interface is shown in Listing 10.20.

LISTING 10.20 The Driver Domain NAT Interfaces

```
[user@dom0]# ifconfig -a
eth0    Link encap:Ethernet  HWaddr 00:11:25:F6:15:22
        inet addr:128.153.145.111  Bcast:128.153.145.255      ➠
        Mask:255.255.255.0
        inet6 addr: fe80::211:25ff:fef6:1522/64 Scope:Link
        UP BROADCAST RUNNING MULTICAST  MTU:1500  Metric:1
        RX packets:3948 errors:0 dropped:0 overruns:0 frame:0
        TX packets:692 errors:0 dropped:0 overruns:0 carrier:0
        collisions:39 txqueuelen:1000
        RX bytes:702026 (685.5 KiB)  TX bytes:228383          ➠
        (223.0 KiB)
        Interrupt:16
```

```
lo      Link encap:Local Loopback
        inet addr:127.0.0.1  Mask:255.0.0.0
        inet6 addr: ::1/128 Scope:Host
        UP LOOPBACK RUNNING  MTU:16436  Metric:1
        RX packets:81415 errors:0 dropped:0 overruns:0 frame:0
        TX packets:81415 errors:0 dropped:0 overruns:0 carrier:0
        collisions:0 txqueuelen:0
        RX bytes:756832064 (721.7 MiB)  TX bytes:756832064    ➡
        (721.7 MiB)


sit0    Link encap:IPv6-in-IPv4
        NOARP  MTU:1480  Metric:1
        RX packets:0 errors:0 dropped:0 overruns:0 frame:0
        TX packets:0 errors:0 dropped:0 overruns:0 carrier:0
        collisions:0 txqueuelen:0
        RX bytes:0 (0.0 b)  TX bytes:0 (0.0 b)


veth0   Link encap:Ethernet  HWaddr 00:00:00:00:00:00
        BROADCAST MULTICAST  MTU:1500  Metric:1
        RX packets:0 errors:0 dropped:0 overruns:0 frame:0
        TX packets:0 errors:0 dropped:0 overruns:0 carrier:0
        collisions:0 txqueuelen:0
        RX bytes:0 (0.0 b)  TX bytes:0 (0.0 b)


veth1   Link encap:Ethernet  HWaddr 00:00:00:00:00:00
        BROADCAST MULTICAST  MTU:1500  Metric:1
        RX packets:0 errors:0 dropped:0 overruns:0 frame:0
        TX packets:0 errors:0 dropped:0 overruns:0 carrier:0
        collisions:0 txqueuelen:0
        RX bytes:0 (0.0 b)  TX bytes:0 (0.0 b)


veth2   Link encap:Ethernet  HWaddr 00:00:00:00:00:00
        BROADCAST MULTICAST  MTU:1500  Metric:1
        RX packets:0 errors:0 dropped:0 overruns:0 frame:0
        TX packets:0 errors:0 dropped:0 overruns:0 carrier:0
        collisions:0 txqueuelen:0
        RX bytes:0 (0.0 b)  TX bytes:0 (0.0 b)


veth3   Link encap:Ethernet  HWaddr 00:00:00:00:00:00
        BROADCAST MULTICAST  MTU:1500  Metric:1
        RX packets:0 errors:0 dropped:0 overruns:0 frame:0
        TX packets:0 errors:0 dropped:0 overruns:0 carrier:0
        collisions:0 txqueuelen:0
        RX bytes:0 (0.0 b)  TX bytes:0 (0.0 b)
```

```
vif0.0 Link encap:Ethernet  HWaddr FE:FF:FF:FF:FF:FF
       BROADCAST MULTICAST  MTU:1500  Metric:1
       RX packets:0 errors:0 dropped:0 overruns:0 frame:0
       TX packets:0 errors:0 dropped:0 overruns:0 carrier:0
       collisions:0 txqueuelen:0
       RX bytes:0 (0.0 b)  TX bytes:0 (0.0 b)

vif0.1 Link encap:Ethernet  HWaddr FE:FF:FF:FF:FF:FF
       BROADCAST MULTICAST  MTU:1500  Metric:1
       RX packets:0 errors:0 dropped:0 overruns:0 frame:0
       TX packets:0 errors:0 dropped:0 overruns:0 carrier:0
       collisions:0 txqueuelen:0
       RX bytes:0 (0.0 b)  TX bytes:0 (0.0 b)

vif0.2 Link encap:Ethernet  HWaddr FE:FF:FF:FF:FF:FF
       BROADCAST MULTICAST  MTU:1500  Metric:1
       RX packets:0 errors:0 dropped:0 overruns:0 frame:0
       TX packets:0 errors:0 dropped:0 overruns:0 carrier:0
       collisions:0 txqueuelen:0
       RX bytes:0 (0.0 b)  TX bytes:0 (0.0 b)

vif0.3 Link encap:Ethernet  HWaddr FE:FF:FF:FF:FF:FF
       BROADCAST MULTICAST  MTU:1500  Metric:1
       RX packets:0 errors:0 dropped:0 overruns:0 frame:0
       TX packets:0 errors:0 dropped:0 overruns:0 carrier:0
       collisions:0 txqueuelen:0
       RX bytes:0 (0.0 b)  TX bytes:0 (0.0 b)

vif1.0 Link encap:Ethernet  HWaddr FE:FF:FF:FF:FF:FF
       inet addr:10.0.0.129  Bcast:0.0.0.0  Mask:255.255.255.255
       inet6 addr: fe80::fcff:ffff:feff:ffff/64 Scope:Link
       UP BROADCAST RUNNING MULTICAST  MTU:1500  Metric:1
       RX packets:128 errors:0 dropped:0 overruns:0 frame:0
       TX packets:93 errors:0 dropped:0 overruns:0 carrier:0
       collisions:0 txqueuelen:0
       RX bytes:0 (0.0 b)  TX bytes:0 (0.0 b)
[user@dom0]#
```

The network interfaces in NAT mode are similar to the routing mode, but the IP addresses are different. eth0 is the physical interface and has the driver domain's global IP, but the guest domain's backend interface vif1.0 obtains an internal virtual IP address of 10.0.0.129. The guest domain's netmask is 255.255.255.255, which indicates the subnet has only one IP, and the IP is 10.0.0.2. The backend vif's IP is the frontend vif's IP plus 127. This means the frontend guest IP ranges from 1 to 127 and the backend IP ranges from 128 to 254. Figure 10.14 illustrates a virtual driver view of Xen NAT mode.

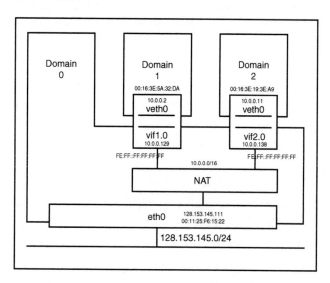

FIGURE 10.14 In NAT mode, the driver domain behaves as the NAT gateway and sets up the NAT iptables for the guest domains. The driver domain is responsible for mapping the packets to the guest domains' internal IP address and port.

Testing Results

Testing whether Xen works in NAT mode is a bit more complicated than bridging or routing modes. Here we set up two guest domains in the same virtual NAT network segment. When one guest domain pings another, we use the network protocol analyzer Ethereal to take the trace on the different interfaces. One trace is on the driver domain's physical interface, as seen in Figure 10.15, and the other is on the destination guest domain's vif, as seen in Figure 10.16.

```
128.153.144.207    224.0.0.252            UDP    Source port: 54239  Destination port: 5355
fe80::2980:4fc3:ce ff02::1:3              UDP    Source port: 54238  Destination port: 5355
128.153.144.207    224.0.0.252            UDP    Source port: 54239  Destination port: 5355
128.153.144.207    128.153.145.255        NBNS   Name query NB WAVES<00>
128.153.144.207    128.153.145.255        NBNS   Name query NB WAVES<20>
Cisco_df:dc        Broadcast              ARP    Who has 128.153.145.19?  Tell 128.153.145.1
128.153.144.207    128.153.145.255        NBNS   Name query NB WAVES<00>
128.153.144.207    128.153.145.255        NBNS   Name query NB WAVES<20>
Cisco_df:e6:55     Spanning-tree-(for     STP    Conf. Root = 8189/00:d0:00:98:a4:8f  Cost =
128.153.144.207    128.153.145.255        NBNS   Name query NB WAVES<00>
fe80::2980:4fc3:ce ff02::1:3              UDP    Source port: 54241  Destination port: 5355
128.153.144.207    224.0.0.252            UDP    Source port: 54242  Destination port: 5355
```

FIGURE 10.15 No ICMP packets on the driver domain's physical interface

10.0.0.11	10.0.0.2	ICMP	Echo (ping) request
Xensourc_06:54:94	Broadcast	ARP	who has 10.0.0.11? Tell 10.0.0.2
10.0.0.11	10.0.0.2	ICMP	Echo (ping) request
fe:ff:ff:ff:ff:ff	xensourc_06:54:94	ARP	10.0.0.11 is at fe:ff:ff:ff:ff:ff
10.0.0.2	10.0.0.11	ICMP	Echo (ping) reply
10.0.0.2	10.0.0.11	ICMP	Echo (ping) reply
10.0.0.11	10.0.0.2	ICMP	Echo (ping) request
10.0.0.2	10.0.0.11	ICMP	Echo (ping) reply
10.0.0.11	10.0.0.2	ICMP	Echo (ping) request
10.0.0.2	10.0.0.11	ICMP	Echo (ping) reply
10.0.0.11	10.0.0.2	ICMP	Echo (ping) request
10.0.0.2	10.0.0.11	ICMP	Echo (ping) reply

FIGURE 10.16 The destination guest domain replies to the ICMP requests.

As we can see, no ICMP packets are seen across the physical interface while they appear on the destination guest's interface, the same as the routing case. The guest domains' backend vifs are in a network segment different from the network segment that the physical interface sits in.

Next, we ping a remote destination machine 128.153.144.103 with a guest 10.0.0.11 and take the Ethereal traces on the guest domain's backend interface (see Figure 10.17), the driver domain's physical interface (see Figure 10.18), and the remote machine's physical interface (see Figure 10.19).

Xensourc_19:3e:a9	Broadcast	ARP	who has 10.0.0.1? Te#
fe:ff:ff:ff:ff:ff	xensourc_19:3e:a9	ARP	10.0.0.1 is at fe:ff:ff:f
10.0.0.11	128.153.144.103	ICMP	Echo (ping) request
128.153.144.103	10.0.0.11	ICMP	Echo (ping) reply
10.0.0.11	128.153.144.103	ICMP	Echo (ping) request
128.153.144.103	10.0.0.11	ICMP	Echo (ping) reply
10.0.0.11	128.153.144.103	ICMP	Echo (ping) request
128.153.144.103	10.0.0.11	ICMP	Echo (ping) reply

FIGURE 10.17 The guest domain sends its ICMP requests to the remote machine 128.153.144.103.

128.153.145.111	128.153.144.103	ICMP	Echo (ping) request
128.153.144.103	128.153.145.111	ICMP	Echo (ping) reply
128.153.145.111	128.153.144.103	ICMP	Echo (ping) request
128.153.144.103	128.153.145.111	ICMP	Echo (ping) reply
128.153.145.111	128.153.144.103	ICMP	Echo (ping) request
128.153.144.103	128.153.145.111	ICMP	Echo (ping) reply
128.153.145.111	128.153.144.103	ICMP	Echo (ping) request
128.153.144.103	128.153.145.111	ICMP	Echo (ping) reply
128.153.145.111	128.153.144.103	ICMP	Echo (ping) request
128.153.144.103	128.153.145.111	ICMP	Echo (ping) reply

FIGURE 10.18 The driver domain sends its ICMP requests to the remote machine 128.153.144.103.

128.153.145.111	128.153.144.103	ICMP	Echo (ping) request
128.153.144.103	128.153.145.111	ICMP	Echo (ping) reply
128.153.145.111	128.153.144.103	ICMP	Echo (ping) request
128.153.144.103	128.153.145.111	ICMP	Echo (ping) reply
128.153.145.111	128.153.144.103	ICMP	Echo (ping) request
128.153.144.103	128.153.145.111	ICMP	Echo (ping) reply

FIGURE 10.19 The remote machine replies to the driver domain's ICMP requests.

We can tell from the trace on the guest domain's backend interface that the internal private IP 10.0.0.11 tries to send the ICMP request to the global IP 128.153.144.103, and the packets are sent to the NAT gateway's internal private IP 10.0.0.1. But on the physical interface in driver domain, the guest domain's private IP has been replaced with the driver domain's global IP 128.153.145.111. On the remote machine, it appears that the driver domain requested the ICMP reply instead of the guest domain.

Using the ip route command, we can see what the routing entries in the driver domain look like, as seen in Listing 10.21. A route exists between the guest domain's backend vif 10.0.0.129 and its frontend vif 10.0.0.2.

LISTING 10.21 The Driver Domain NAT Routing Table

```
[user@Dom0]#ip route show
10.0.0.2 dev vif1.0  scope link  src 10.0.0.129
10.0.0.11 dev vif2.0  scope link  src 10.0.0.138
128.153.145.0/24 dev eth0  proto kernel  scope link  src ➡
128.153.145.111
169.254.0.0/16 dev eth0  scope link
default via 128.153.145.1 dev eth0
```

In the network-nat script, the iptable is configured using the iptables command shown in Listing 10.22. This command sets up the NAT table shown in Listing 10.23.

LISTING 10.22 The Command to Set Up the NAT Mode within the network-nat Script

```
iptables -t nat -A POSTROUTING -o eth0 -j MASQUERADE
```

LISTING 10.23 The Driver Domain's NAT Table

```
[user@Dom0]# iptables -L -t nat
Chain PREROUTING (policy ACCEPT)
target     prot opt source               destination

Chain POSTROUTING (policy ACCEPT)
target prot opt source                destination
MASQUERADE  all  --  anywhere             anywhere

Chain OUTPUT (policy ACCEPT)
Target     prot opt source               destination
[user@Dom0]#
```

Chain POSTROUTING and MASQUERADE in Listing 10.23 indicates that the internal private IP of all the packets will be masked with the eth0's external IP address as they are leaving the firewall.

Similarly, if we want to bind a specific service to a designated guest domain—for example, the guest domain 10.0.0.2 will handle all the Web service connections to balance the workload—then we can set up the Web server in the guest domain 10.0.0.2 and use the iptables command to forward all incoming requests for port 80 to the local IP address 10.0.0.2, as shown in Listing 10.24. This command directs all the packets of incoming Web requests to the address 10.0.0.2 by changing the destination IP address of the packets from the globally routable address of the NAT gateway (128.153.145.111) to 10.0.0.2. You can also use the same command as Listing 10.23 to verify the change has taken effect. For more details about the iptables command, you can refer to Chapter 11.

LISTING 10.24 The iptables Command to Direct a Service to a Guest Domain

```
[root@Dom0]# iptables -t nat -A PREROUTING -p tcp --dport 80 ➥
                    -i eth0 -j DNAT -t 10.0.0.2
```

Configuring Purely Virtual Network Segments

Bridging, routing, and NAT modes all enable guest domains to communicate with the global Internet. However, sometimes we may want to restrict a guest domain's communication to within the physical machine. This can be done with a purely virtual network segment, also referred to as a *host-only network*. It isolates guest domains from the outside network segment, enhances the security of the internal virtual network, and enables us to run tests within the internal network without using bandwidth on the physical network segment. For example, we can encapsulate a virus in a virtual machine and simulate an Internet connection among guest domains to analyze the virus's propagating patterns and methods. Using a purely virtual network is useful in this case because it won't release the virus.

There are two types of purely virtual networks: dummy0 interface and dummy bridge. One is to set up a fake network interface, dummy0, and its purely virtual network. Guest domains' specified virtual interfaces can be bound to this virtual network. Only the domains (the driver and the guests) can communicate with each other. The other type of purely virtual network sets up a virtual dummy bridge with only guest domains' vifs attached to it. In this scenario, the guest domains can communicate with each other only.

Configuring dummy0

dummy0 is a virtual interface that has the full functionality of a real physical network interface. We create dummy0 in the driver domain. There is essentially no difference between a physical network interface and dummy0 except that the physical interface has a physical device attached to it but dummy0 does not. Using dummy0, we set up the virtual network that is absolutely isolated from the Internet but allows the driver domain and the guest domains to communicate internally. Figure 10.20 shows a virtual device view of setting up Xen dummy0 interface.

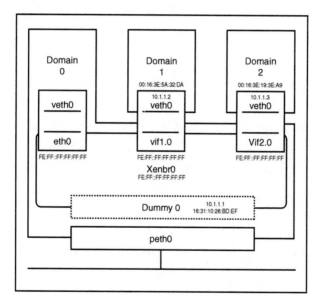

FIGURE 10.20 The vifs are hooked to Xen virtual network upon the dummy0.

To set up a dummy0 interface in the driver domain, follow these steps:

1. **Create a dummy0 interface in the driver domain.**

   The way to create a dummy0 interface may vary due to different Linux distributions. But the configuration parameters are similar. Here, we take Fedora/CentOS as an example. Create a new interface file: ifcfg-dummy0. Inside the file, configure it as shown in Listing 10.25.

LISTING 10.25 Configuration for dummy0 Interface in Fedora in File ifcfg-dummy0

```
DEVICE = dummy0
BOOTPROTO=none
ONBOOT=yes
USERCTL=no
IPV6INIT=no
PEERDNS=yes
TYPE=Ethernet
NETMASK=255.255.255.0
IPADDR=10.1.1.1
ARP=yes
```

In Listing 10.25, it specifies the new interface's name, which is dummy0, and its related network properties, such as that the IP address is 10.1.1.1 and the netmask is 255.255.255.0.

For the other distributions, we give some hints:

- In OpenSUSE, set the value of SETUPDUMMYDEV to yes in the file /etc/rc.config.
- In Ubuntu/Debian, add an interface in the file /etc/network/interfaces.
- In Gentoo, before compiling the kernel, choose Networking support-> Network device support ->Dummy net driver support to be [m].

Listing 10.26 shows two links that we must also add to the file /etc/modprobe. conf to load the dummy0 module when the driver domain boots.

LISTING 10.26 The dummy0 Module Entry

```
alias dummy0 dummy
options dummy numdummies=1
```

2. **Set up an internal bridging network based on dummy0.**

Set up the bridging mode virtual network and attach dummy0 to the virtual bridge xenbr0. In the Xend configuration file, specify the network device as dummy0 in the network-script directive, as shown in Listing 10.27. It will be combined with the virtual bridge xenbr0.

LISTING 10.27 Xend Configuration to Bind dummy0

```
(network-script 'network-bridge netdev=dummy0')
```

3. **Attach dummy0 to the guest domain's virtual interface.**

When configuring the guest domain's configuration file, attach the guest domain's virtual interface to the bridge in the vif directive as in the bridge mode. The vif parameter to attach the guest vif to the bridge in the guest configuration file is shown in Listing 10.28.

LISTING 10.28 The Guest Domain Configuration to Bind dummy0

```
vif=['bridge=xenbr0',]
```

Testing dummy0

This internal virtual network isolates the guest domains from the Internet because there is no physical interface attached to it. It is pingable between the driver domain and guest domains, and you can see its interface in the driver domain as shown in Listing 10.29.

LISTING 10.29 dummy0 Interface in the driver domain

```
dummy0    Link encap:Ethernet   HWaddr 16:31:10:26:BD:EF
          inet addr:10.1.1.1  Bcast:10.1.1.255  Mask:255.255.255.0
          inet6 addr: fe80::1431:10ff:fe26:bdef/64 Scope:Link
          UP BROADCAST RUNNING MULTICAST  MTU:1500  Metric:1
          RX packets:0 errors:0 dropped:0 overruns:0 frame:0
          TX packets:29 errors:0 dropped:0 overruns:0 carrier:0
          collisions:0 txqueuelen:0
          RX bytes:0 (0.0 b)   TX bytes:7738 (7.5 KiB)
```

Now it is clear that the dummy0 interface's IP is 10.1.1.1 as specified in Listing 10.25.

Configuring Dummy Bridge

The other kind of virtual network segment disconnects the driver domain from the guest domains. Guest domains are hooked to a dummy bridge interface. Figure 10.21 shows a virtual device view of setting up Xen's dummy bridge. Only the guest domains connect to each other. To do this, we need to set up a virtual bridge that only guest domains' virtual interfaces can connect to. This virtual network is an isolated network that keeps guest domains from interacting with the driver domain and the Internet.

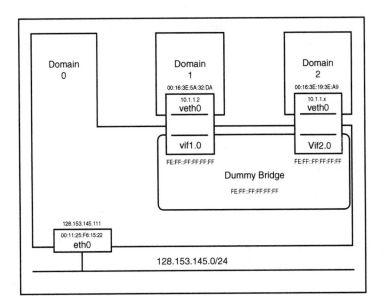

FIGURE 10.21 Guest domains are hooked to the dummy bridge interfaces.

To set up the dummy bridge, the following steps should be followed.

1. **Set up the virtual bridge by using the `brctl` command provided by the bridge-utils package. We can either put the commands shown in Listing 10.30 in our own script or just run them on the command line.**

LISTING 10.30 `xenbr1` Setup Command

```
brctl addbr xenbr1
brctl stp xenbr1 off
brctl setfd xenbr1 0
ip link set xenbr1 up
```

brctl's suboption `addbr` creates a logical bridge with the bridge name xenbr1. `stp` disables xenbr1's communication with the other bridges to avoid interference, `setfd` sets the bridge's listening and learning state time to be 0, and `ip link set` activates the dummy bridge. This change will not persist after reboot. If you want to maintain the configuration, it is better to put in a script that will run during boot up. You can refer to the `brctl` and `ip` man pages for more information.

2. **List the network interfaces in the driver domain, and a new bridge interface**
   xenbr1 shows up, as shown in Listing 10.31.

LISTING 10.31 The driver domain's Dummy Bridge Interface

```
xenbr1    Link encap:Ethernet   HWaddr 00:00:00:00:00:00
          inet6 addr: fe80::200:ff:fe00:0/64 Scope:Link
          UP BROADCAST RUNNING MULTICAST  MTU:1500  Metric:1
          RX packets:0 errors:0 dropped:0 overruns:0 frame:0
          TX packets:12 errors:0 dropped:0 overruns:0 carrier:0
          collisions:0 txqueuelen:0
          RX bytes:0 (0.0 b)  TX bytes:3656 (3.5 KiB)
```

Up to now, we have seen the bridging interfaces in three different cases: One is
set up by xend in bridging mode, another is set up on the dummy0, and the other
one is manually setting up the dummy bridge. The script network-bridge generally attaches a physical device peth0, the driver domain's backend virtual interface
vif0.0, to the bridge. The guest domains' vifs can be configured and attached to
the bridge by the vif-bridge script. So in Xen, default bridging mode, the Internet, the driver domain, and the attached guest domains can communicate with each
other. But because dummy0 has no connection to the Internet, the bridge interface with
dummy0 attached enables the communications between only the driver domain and
guest domains. Furthermore, when we set up the bridge manually, it is a bare bridge,
and only the guest domains' interfaces will be configured and attached to it. This leads
to the communications between only guest domains.

3. **In the guest domain's configuration file, attach the guest domain's virtual**
   interface to the dummy bridge xenbr1 in the driver domain, as shown in
   Listing 10.32.

LISTING 10.32 Setting the Guest Domain's vif Directive to the Dummy Bridge

```
vif = ['mac=00:16:3e:45:e7:12, bridge=xenbr1']
```

The difference from the default configuration is that the bridge option is assigned
to the dummy bridge xenbr1 instead of the bridge xenbr0 that Xen's default script
sets up.

Testing Dummy Bridge

After the guest domain is booted, the dummy bridge's interface as seen in the driver domain looks like that shown in Listing 10.33. The output is excerpted from the ifconfig command.

LISTING 10.33 The Dummy Bridge Interface in the driver domain After the Guest Domain Boots

```
xenbr1     Link encap:Ethernet  HWaddr FE:FF:FF:FF:FF:FF
           inet6 addr: fe80::200:ff:fe00:0/64 Scope:Link
           UP BROADCAST RUNNING NOARP  MTU:1500  Metric:1
           RX packets:29 errors:0 dropped:0 overruns:0 frame:0
           TX packets:0 errors:0 dropped:0 overruns:0 carrier:0
           collisions:0 txqueuelen:0
           RX bytes:7332 (7.1 KiB)  TX bytes:0 (0.0 b)
```

The dummy bridge xenbr1's MAC address has changed from 00:00:00:00:00:00 to FE:FF:FF:FF:FF:FF. This indicates that the dummy bridge works. The MAC address FE:FF:FF:FF:FF:FF is a valid local scope individual MAC address. You can refer to the local scope individual MAC address information.

We set up two guest domains to test whether the dummy bridge works. Both of the guest domains' configuration files attach their vifs to the dummy bridge xenbr1. Inside the guest domains, we configure their private network IPs to be 10.1.2.3 and 10.1.2.4. When the guest domains boot up, the guest domains' backend vifs in the driver domain look like those shown in Listing 10.34. The output is taken from the output of the ifconfig command.

LISTING 10.34 The Guest Domains' vifs Bound to the Dummy Bridge

```
vif1.0     Link encap:Ethernet  HWaddr FE:FF:FF:FF:FF:FF
           inet6 addr: fe80::fcff:ffff:feff:ffff/64 Scope:Link
           UP BROADCAST RUNNING NOARP  MTU:1500  Metric:1
           RX packets:149 errors:0 dropped:0 overruns:0 frame:0
           TX packets:102 errors:0 dropped:0 overruns:0 carrier:0
           collisions:0 txqueuelen:0
           RX bytes:8880 (8.6 KiB)  TX bytes:9371 (9.1 KiB)
vif2.0     Link encap:Ethernet  HWaddr FE:FF:FF:FF:FF:FF
           inet6 addr: fe80::fcff:ffff:feff:ffff/64 Scope:Link
           UP BROADCAST RUNNING NOARP  MTU:1500  Metric:1
           RX packets:102 errors:0 dropped:0 overruns:0 frame:0
           TX packets:46 errors:0 dropped:0 overruns:0 carrier:0
           collisions:0 txqueuelen:0
           RX bytes:7943 (7.7 KiB)  TX bytes:2208 (2.1 KiB)
```

When each guest domain pings the other guest domain's IP, both have echoes. When either of them pings the driver domain's IP 128.153.144.205, the driver domain is unreachable.

In the driver domain, if we ping to the guest domain's IP 10.1.2.3 or 10.1.2.4, neither is reachable.

Assigning MAC Addresses to Virtual Network Interfaces

Whether a virtual interface is mapped to a physical interface or not, one fundamental aspect of configuring a virtual network interface is assigning it a MAC address. A unique MAC address allows for proper addressing of network traffic at the lowest level. Physical network interface cards are given unique MAC addresses by their manufacturers. Each virtual network interface must also have a unique MAC address (unique at least on that local network). In Xen, there are two ways of assigning a MAC address to a virtual network interface in a guest domain: generated or specified.

MAC Addresses

A MAC address is used to identify the interface in the physically connected Ethernet. Normally, a MAC address is globally unique and burned in the network card's ROM by the NIC manufacturers. However, in practice, a MAC address need only be unique on the actual local network segment to which it is attached. The MAC address is used so that network packets can be delivered from one interface to another within the network segment. If two machines on the same LAN have the same MAC address, it causes confusion as multiple machines act on packets intended for only one of them.

A MAC addresses is 48 bits long and is typically represented as six octets, separated by colons. The first three octets indicate the identity of the entity that manufactured that network interface card. This prefix is issued by the IEEE to the manufacturer, and the other three octets are assigned by the manufacturer. Virtual network interface cards do not, of course, have a manufacturer as such. However, Xen generates a MAC address for a guest domain as 00:16:3E:xx:xx:xx. (Similarly, VMware assigns a MAC address to any guest image as 00:05:69:xx:xx:xx.) By looking for the 00:16:3E prefix, we can tell whether it is a Xen guest domain's virtual NIC or a real physical vendor NIC.

Two important bits really matter when assigning a MAC address. They are the first and second least significant bits of the second leftmost byte in a MAC address, bit B7 and B8, shown in Figure 10.22. When the bit B7 is set to 0, this MAC address is a manufacturer-assigned MAC address. If the bit B8 is set to 1, it is a multicast MAC address. For example, FF:FF:FF:FF:FF:FF is a broadcast MAC address that will be received by all the machines in the Ethernet while FE:FF:FF:FF:FF:FF is a local unicast MAC address, which is used in the Xen network. So a user-specified MAC address should at least be a unicast MAC address. To learn more about MAC address assignment, refer to the standard IEEE 802-2001.

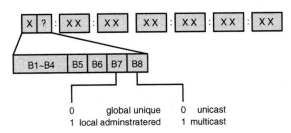

FIGURE 10.22 B7 indicates that the MAC address is global or local; B8 indicates whether unicast or multicast.

Specifying or Generating a MAC Address for a Guest Domain

Xen allows users to specify a MAC address for a guest domain. Usually if users want to change a machine's MAC address, we need to use certain tools to erase the MAC address that the manufacturer has burned in the network card and burn a new MAC address into it. Virtualization permits users to assign any MAC address that they want for the guest domain without dealing with the hardware. However, be careful that the MAC address does not conflict with any other physical MAC address or any guest domain's MAC address on the same local network, or the guest domain will get all, some, or none of the packets. It is recommended to let Xen generate it unless you know what you are doing. One exception is if the same MAC address is generated for two guests on two different Xen systems attached to the same physical network segment. This is extremely unlikely, however. The user-defined MAC address should be specified in the guest domain's configuration file. Inside the vif directive, assign the user-defined MAC address to the option mac.

Following is one format example:

```
vif=[ 'mac=xx:xx:xx:xx:xx:xx', ]
```

This guest domain has one vif, and its MAC address is xx:xx:xx:xx:xx:xx. When the guest domain boots, we can see that the MAC address appears on the frontend vif inside the guest domain.

If a MAC address is not mentioned in a guest domain's configuration file, when the guest domain is booting, Xen automatically generates a MAC address, which looks like 00:16:3E:xx:xx:xx, for the guest domain's virtual interface. Automatically generating a MAC address by Xen ensures that you do not accidentally assign the same MAC address to different guests on the same machine by, for example, forgetting to edit a guest configuration file that was copied from another guest to create a new one. If you have no idea which MAC address a guest domain network interface should have, or don't prefer a specific MAC address to a guest domain, allowing Xen to generate the MAC address for you is a good idea.

Assigning IP Addresses

Unlike MAC addresses, IP addresses depend on where the guest domains lie in the network topology. IP addresses are used to route through the Internet and look for a path to a destination. Before booting up the guest domains, we need to consider the following questions: Will the guest domain get its IP from an external DHCP server, do we need to manually assign the guest domain an IP, or will the guest domain get its IP from an internal DHCP server in Domain0?

As in bridging mode, the guest domain interacts with the driver domain at the Data Link layer, lower than the IP layer, so how the guest domain in bridging mode obtains an IP address depends on how it is decided inside the guest domain. The driver domain simply delivers the packets to the outside at the Data Link layer.

In routing mode, the driver domain is responsible for relaying the packets at the IP layer for the guest domain. The driver domain and the guest domain share the same network segment, so it is more like pseudo-bridging. It is better for the guest domain to manually assign the IP. If the guest domain in routing mode hopes to use DHCP instead, the dhcrelay tool, which is the Dynamic Host Configuration Protocol Relay Agent, may be helpful for the guest domain to obtain an IP from the external DHCP. For more details, please refer to the man page dhcrelay.

In the NAT mode, the guest domain takes advantage of the private segment IP and hides from the outside. Therefore, it is impossible for the guest to obtain the IP from the external DHCP server. However, the guest domain can obtain the IP from a DHCP server set up inside the driver domain. We do not recommend setting up an internal DHCP server in bridging or routing mode when an external DHCP server already exists. Your local server would conflict with the external DHCP server, and which server actually assigns each IP would depend on which one answers first, leading to unexpected results.

Next, we need to know what kind of IP the guest domain needs. IP addresses are classified into three types according to their functionalities: *global unique IP*, *private IP*, and *broadcast IP*. Global IP can be reached by any machine on the Internet and is unique in the world. Private IP can only be used in the internal network and cannot be routed to by machines over the Internet. Broadcast IP is used to broadcast to multiple machines in the same subnetwork instead of only one destination, and thus cannot be assigned to a guest domain. There are three blocks of private IPs:

- The Class A block `10.0.0.0~10.255.255.255`
- The Class B block `192.168.0.0~192.168.255.255`
- The Class C block `172.16.0.0~172.31.255.255`

The `10.0.0.0` address space, or simply `10/8`, is a single class A private network; `172.16/12` contains 16 contiguous class B networks; and `192.168/16` contains 256 contiguous class C networks. For further details, please refer to the IETF/RFC1918 standard; its link is provided in the References and Further Reading section.

By knowing how we should get an IP for a guest domain and what kind of IP the guest domain should have, we can go on to configure the guest domain's vif and assign an appropriate IP either by an external DHCP server, by manually assigning it, or by an internal DHCP server.

Using an External DHCP Server to Obtain an IP for a Guest Domain

Most ISPs provide DHCP services that automatically hand out an IP address to a booting host over UDP (ports 67 and 68). When Xen works in bridging mode, guest domains appear transparent on the Ethernet and can interact with the local network's DHCP server and obtain its unique `ip`, `netmask`, and `gateway` for the frontend vif.

The configuration steps are:

1. Configure the guest domain's configuration file and add the directive `dhcp="dhcp"` on a new line, but don't specify an IP address in the vif directive.
2. Make sure the DHCP client is running inside the guest domain and configure it to automatically obtain an IP for the network interface.

Manually Assigning an IP to a Guest Domain

We can also manually assign a static IP to the network interface for a guest domain instead of dynamically assigning it. In Xen's routing mode, the guest domain's gateway should be configured to be the driver domain's IP, so it needs manual IP configuration. In bridging mode, we can also manually configure a static IP for the guest domain so that each time the guest domain is brought up it will have the same IP, provided that the configured static IP is not used by any other machines in the Internet.

There are also two steps to configure a guest domain's static IP when Xen is in routing mode: configure both the frontend and backend vif. The frontend vif is configured in the guest domain's configuration file, and the backend vif is configured inside the guest domain.

1. In the guest domain's configuration file, remove the directive `dhcp="dhcp"`. Add two directives, `netmask="x.x.x.x"` and `gateway="x.x.x.x"`, and add the corresponding `ip` option `ip=x.x.x.x` to the vif directive.

   If Xen works in bridging mode, the configuration step can directly jump to the second step.

2. Also configure the same IP, netmask, and gateway parameters inside the running guest domain, disabling the DHCP client service.

Each Linux distribution network interface uses a different configuration file:

- In Fedora, the network configuration file is `/etc/sysconfig/network-scripts/ifcfg-eth#`.

- In Ubuntu, it is `/etc/network/interfaces`.

- In Gentoo, it is `/etc/conf.d/net`.

- In openSUSE, it is `/etc/{hosts, networks, route.conf}`.

- In Solaris, it is `/etc/{hosts, defaultgateway, defaultrouter}`.

> **NOTE**
> The backend vif and the frontend vif should be configured consistently, or the guest domain's network won't function. Should there be a mismatch, the packet from the guest domain cannot be delivered correctly to the driver domain.

Using an Internal DHCP Server to Obtain an IP for a Guest Domain

If no external DHCP server exists, we can set up an internal DHCP to assign IPs to guest domains in bridging mode, which works similarly to the external DHCP server. In NAT mode, however, using the internal DHCP server for guest domains to obtain IP is a little complex and different.

First we need to set up a DHCP server in the driver domain. The DHCP server in the driver domain should be configured properly and run to allocate the IPs with the network segment where the driver domain lies. When the NAT script runs, it modifies the DHCP server configuration to be able to allocate the private IPs between `10.0.0.0` to `10.0.255.255`.

Second, we need to configure the guest domain's configuration file. To do this, we should remove any `ip` option in the `vif` directive, remove the `netmask` and `gate-way` directives, and add `dhcp="dhcp"`. When the guest domain boots up, the driver domain's DHCP server will assign the `ip 10.0.x.1` to the guest domain's backend vif.

Third, inside the running guest domain, we need to manually assign the static IP to the frontend interface. The frontend vif's IP can be calculated out to be `"x.x.x.(x+127)"` if the internal DHCP server assigns `x.x.x.x` to the backend vif. The netmask is `255.255.0.0`, and the gateway is always `10.0.0.1` by default.

In this chapter we have briefly introduced the setup of virtual network bridging, routing, and NAT in Xen and the network configuration to a guest domain. Next, we deal with the case of multiple interfaces. Obviously the configuration will be more complex and advanced. A classic application is the firewall setup for guest domains, which is explained in detail in Chapter 11.

Handling Multiple Network Interfaces in a Domain

When a machine has multiple network interfaces, each network interface may own a different network segment, and each one may have its own functionalities: either public IP or private IP; either wire or wireless; either Internet or intranet, and so on. When a driver domain has multiple physical interfaces, we need to set up the appropriate virtual network for them. When a guest domain needs multiple virtual interfaces, we need to set up the right number of virtual interfaces for the guest domain and configure each virtual interface correctly to the virtual network.

Handling Multiple Network Interfaces in a driver domain

In the driver domain, the virtual network is set up by scripts and configured by the Xend configuration file in `/etc/xen/xend-config.sxp`. Xen provides the scripts `network-bridge` and `vif-bridge`; `network-route` and `vif-route`; `network-nat` and `vif-nat`. These are used to set up the corresponding virtual network for a single virtual interface. When we need to set up multiple virtual networks, we can either write our own script to call the default scripts in `/etc/xen/scripts`, or write our own scripts to set up the customized network.

The usage format of the scripts is represented in Listing 10.35.

LISTING 10.35 Usage of the Scripts

```
network-bridge (start|stop|status) [vifnum=VAL] [bridge=VAL]
               [netdev=VAL] [antiproof=VAL]
network-route (start|stop|status) [netdev=VAL] [antispoof=VAL]
network-nat (start|stop|status) [netdev=VAL] [antispoof=VAL] ➡
            [dhcp=VAL]
options:
vifnum        The number of Virtual interface in Dom0 to use
bridge        The bridge to use (default xenbr${vifnum}),      ➡
              specially for bridge virtual network
netdev        The interface to add to the bridge/route/NAT     ➡
              (default eth${vifnum}).
antispoof     Whether to use iptables to prevent spoofing      ➡
              default no).
phcp          Whether to alter the local DHCP configuration    ➡
              (default no)
VAL           the corresponding value for each options,
              either number or interface name or yes/no
```

An example of such a user-defined script, my-own-script, can be written like that shown in Listing 10.36 and put in the directory /etc/xen/scripts.

LISTING 10.36 Multiple Virtual Network Script Named as my-own-script

```
#!/bin/sh
dir=$(dirname "$0")
"$dir/network-bridge" start vifnum=0 netdev=eth0 bridge=xenbr0
"$dir/network-bridge" start vifnum=1 netdev=eth1 bridge=xenbr1
```

This script is a shell script, placed in the directory /etc/xen/scripts. The line dir=$(dirname "$0") gets the network-script's relative directory. So xend can find the default script network-bridge and run it to bring up a bridge for each physical device.

In the Xend configuration file, put the script my-own-script into the network-script directive. If any arguments need to be passed into your script, single quotation marks should be placed around your script and its arguments in the network directive, such as 'network-nat dhcp=yes'. If the script is not in the /etc/xen/scripts directory, the absolute path should be given out in the network directive such as '/root/home/my-own-script'. In the preceding case, xend sets up a corresponding bridge for each virtual network and attaches a bridge to each physical interface. eth0's virtual network bridge interface is xenbr0, and eth1's virtual network bridge interface is xenbr1.

When we write our own script to set up the customized network, we need to know whether the vif is working on the link layer or the network layer. If it is the link layer, we should use the vif-bridge script for the guest domain's vif, while we should use the vif-route or vif-nat script if it is the network layer.

Handling Multiple Network Interfaces in a Guest Domain

In the guest domain, network interfaces can be set up in two ways: Using the configuration file before booting up the guest domain, or dynamically adding a network interface using the xm command when the guest domain is running.

Configure Multiple vifs to a Guest Domain

Having configured the vif directive in the guest domain's configuration file, Xen brings up the corresponding network interfaces in the guest domain when booting up. Each pair of single quotation marks stands for a new network interface in the guest domain and is separated by a comma. The specification of each network interface is defined within the pair of quotation marks for its MAC address, IP address, network type, and so on.

Following are two format examples:

```
vif=['', '',]
```

This is the simplest way to configure two vifs to a guest domain. The vifs' MAC addresses are generated by Xen, and their IP addresses are determined by the guest domain itself.

```
vif=['mac=x:x:x:x:x:x:x, bridge=xenbr0','mac=x:x:x:x:x:x:x, bridge=xenbr1',]
```

This configuration specifies two network interfaces in the guest domain. One is eth0, assigned a user-defined MAC address and attached to the virtual network xenbr0. The other is eth1, assigned a user-specified MAC address and attached to the virtual network xenbr1.

Configure a Running Guest Domain with the Command xm

xm is the command that manages the Xen guest domains. It provides the subcommand that can dynamically set up new network devices to the running guest domain. xm can list information about the guest domain network devices, create a new network device, or remove a network device. These subcommands can dynamically create or remove network devices in the guest domain while a guest domain's configuration file sets up the guest domain's network interface statically. Table 10.3 lists the xm network subcommands.

TABLE 10.3 xm Network Options

Subcommand	Options	Description
network-list <Domain/Domain_id>		List all the network interfaces of a guest domain specified either by the domain's ID or name.
	-L --long	List the interfaces in the XML format.
network-attach <Domain>		Create a new vif to the guest domain with MAC address Xen generated.
	mac=<mac>	Assign a MAC address to the new network interface.
	ip=<ip>	Assign an IP address to the new network interface.
	bridge=<bridge>	Attach the network interface to the bridge.
	vifname=<name>	Give the new vif an alias.
	script=<script>	Create the vif using the script vif-bridge, vif-network, or vif-nat.
network-detach Domain dev_id		Remove the specified network interface from the guest domain. dev_id refers to the sequential number of the vif in the guest domain. This subcommand is broken.

The xm network-list command can tell us all the guest domain's vif parameters, which is helpful in diagnosing the network device. Listing 10.37 shows an example.

LISTING 10.37 An Example of the Command xm network-list with L Option

```
[root@Dom0]#xm network-list  -l DomU
(0
    ((backend-id 0)
        (mac 00:16:3e:5a:32:da)
        (handle 0)
        (state 4)
        (backend /local/domain/0/backend/vif/2/0)
        (tx-ring-ref 521)
        (rx-ring-ref 522)
        (event-channel 9)
        (request-rx-copy 0)
        (feature-rx-notify 1)
        (feature-sg 1)
        (feature-gso-tcpv4 1)
    )
)
```

The command xm network-list displays all the virtual device information of a guest domain stored in the XenStore space. The information is quoted by parentheses. Inside the outermost parenthesis is the virtual network device index number 0. The block next to the virtual network device index contains all the related information such as its MAC address 00:16:3e:5a:32:da, its backend name vif2.0, and so on. Table 10.4 explains each item's meaning.

The xm network-attach command can dynamically load a pair of virtual frontend and backend interfaces to the specified guest domain when the guest domain is running instead of configuring it before booting up. We can see that one more Ethernet interface appears inside the guest domain, and a corresponding vif appears in the driver domain. Listing 10.38 shows an example.

LISTING 10.38 An Example of the Command xm network-attach

```
[root@Dom0]#xm network-attach DomU --script=vif-bridge
[root@Dom0]#ifconfig
vif1.1    Link encap:Ethernet  HWaddr FE:FF:FF:FF:FF:FF
          inet6 addr: fe80::fcff:ffff:feff:ffff/64 Scope:Link
          UP BROADCAST RUNNING NOARP  MTU:1500  Metric:1
          RX packets:0 errors:0 dropped:0 overruns:0 frame:0
          TX packets:45 errors:0 dropped:442 overruns:0 carrier:0
          collisions:0 txqueuelen:0
          RX bytes:0 (0.0 b)  TX bytes:6107 (5.9 KiB)
[root@Dom0]#
```

In the guest domain, we can also see that a new network interface is brought up. As the xm network-attach subcommand has a bug, the fourth vif setup will fail without any notice because only three network interfaces are allowed. Listing 10.39 shows an example. The solution to detach the dynamically setup vif is to shut down the guest domain. Then the dynamic configuration will be gone. At next reboot, we will have to reconfigure it again.

LISTING 10.39 An Example of the Subcommands xm network-attach and network-list

```
[root@Dom0]# xm network-attach DomU
[root@Dom0]# xm network-attach DomU
[root@Dom0]# xm network-attach DomU
[root@Dom0]# xm network-attach DomU
[root@Dom0]# xm network-list U
Idx BE     MAC Addr.     handle state evt-ch tx-/rx-ring-ref ➡
BE-path
```

```
0   0   00:16:3e:5a:32:da    0    4    9    521  /522   ➡
/local/domain/0/backend/vif/2/0
1   0   00:16:3e:1e:cc:a7    1    4    10   1035 /1036  ➡
/local/domain/0/backend/vif/2/1
2   0   00:16:3e:27:59:9c    2    4    11   1549 /1550  ➡
/local/domain/0/backend/vif/2/2
3   0   00:16:3e:5a:32:dd    3    6    -1   -1   /1     ➡
/local/domain/0/backend/vif/2/3
[root@Dom0]#
```

We can tell that the fourth vif fails because of its negative values of evt-ch and tx-/rx-ring-ref. The fourth vif won't work. Table 10.4 lists the XenStore information about the vif frontend device for the domain.

TABLE 10.4 Network-List Information Items

Information Items	Description
Idx	The vif index number in the guests domain
BE	BackEnd domain
MAC Addr.	The MAC address assigned to the vif
handle	The vif number
state	The communication state across XenBus to the backend
	0=unknown, 1=initializing, 2=init or wait, 3=initialzed, 4=connected, 5=closing, 6=closed
evt-ch	The event channel abbreviation used for the two ring queues
tx-/rx-ring-ref	The grand table reference for the transmission/receiving ring queue
BE-path	The vif backend directory path in XenStore

For further details on the explanation of XenStore, refer to Chapter 3, "The Xen Hypervisor."

vnet—Domain Virtual Network

VPN (Virtual Private Network) is an important network architecture that provides confidential communication in a public network. Physical machines from different locations are connected and virtualized to be in the same private network with the communications encrypted. Xen also provides a similar feature for the guest domains in different driver domains. Virtual network (vnet) connects the guest domains from different network segments and emulates to be as if in the same virtual network segment.

Besides enhancing the secure communications between guest domains in different domains over the Internet, vnet also supports consolidating whole networks into Xen. It provides a network illusion that the guest domains in different domains are in a local private virtual network, isolating the virtual networks from each other. vnet establishes an adaptive inter-VM virtual network. This approach lends itself to grid computing, distributed or parallel applications.

vnet is based on the bridging virtual network. The virtual Ethernet traffic between the domains in vnet is tunneled inside IP packets over the public network. vnet is an optional component to Xen's virtual network infrastructure. By default, it is not shipped along with Xen packages. At the time this book was written, it is necessary to download the Xen source code and compile this optional support yourself. In general, there have been problems with vnet. At present, it is poorly documented, except for the Xen Users' Manual. It seems that vnet is not fully complete and tested yet. In the following section, we give only a simple idea of how to install and run vnet according to the Xen Users' Manual.

Installing vnet

vnet can be installed in two ways: as a Linux kernel module or as a user space daemon in the driver domain.

Following are the steps you'll need to take to install vnet:

1. **Download the newest Xen source code on the xen.org Web page.**

2. **Enter Xen source code and go to the directory `tools/vnet`. The detailed instructions are in the text file `00INSTALL`.**

   Before compiling and installing vnet, make sure the Xen kernel has already included the cryptographic algorithms such as MD, SHA, DES, and so on, and the IPsec and VLAN options.

   IPsec is a set of protocols by IETF for securing Internet protocol communications. For more details, look at the IETF rfc2401 at the link www.ietf.org/rfc/rfc2401.txt. VLAN is a virtual LAN (Local Area Network) defined in the IEEE 802.1Q specification referred to in the link www.ieee802.org/1/pages/802.1Q.html.

3. Using the **make** and **make install** commands, the module **vnet_module.ko** will be created in the **tools/vnet/vnet-module/** or the user space daemon **varpd** will be created in the **tools/vnet/vnetd**.

Running vnet

After vnet is installed into Xen, we can use the command vn in the directory /usr/ sbin to manually install the module, or the script network-vnet in the directory / etc/xen/scripts to install the vnet module by xend. Also, some vnet example configuration files are copied to the directory /etc/xen: vnet97.sxp, vnet98.sxp and vnet99.sxp. The encryption of the communication is optional. Inside the vnet configuration file, the encryption can be configured and enabled.

The steps to run vnet are to load the vnet module, configure vnet, and then create vnet. We discuss each of these steps in greater detail in the following sections.

Load the vnet Module

To load the vnet module, manually run the vn insmod command before xend starts. You can also use xend to load the module. You configure the Xend configuration file /etc/xen/xend-config.sxp, comment out the network-bridge script, and add a new line for the vnet script, as shown in Listing 10.40.

LISTING 10.40 Xend vnet Configuration

```
#(network-script network-bridge)
  (network-script network-vnet)
```

The network-vnet script calls another script, vnet-insert, which installs the module and calls the script network-bridge.

Configure vnet

We need to first configure vnet in the .sxp file, which contains the format shown in Listing 10.41.

LISTING 10.41 Format of vnet Configuration in the xendsxp File

```
(vnet      id         <vnetid>)
           (bridge    <bridge>)
           (vnetif    <vnet_interface>)
           (security  <level>))
```

You can see each directive's configuration in Table 10.5.

TABLE 10.5 vnet Configuration Directives

Suboption	Arguments	Description
id	vnetid	vnetid is to identify the vnet.
		vnetid is a 128-bit identifier: (ffff:ffff:ffff:ffff:ffff:ffff:ffff:ffff)
		Or a short form looks like ffff, which means
		(0:0:0:0:0:0:0:ffff); 0 is not allowed and 1 is reserved.
bridge	<bridge>	Define the vnet bridge name:
		vnet will be a bridge-mode network, the virtual machines are contained in the vnet by attaching vif to this bridge.
vnetif	<vnet_interface>	Define the vif name of vnet; it is optional. Translate the vnet packets over the network.
security	<level>	Packets encryption level:
		None—no encryption of the packets over the vnet.
		Auth—authenticate required.
		Conf—authenticate and packets encrypted.

Listing 10.42 shows an example of the vnet configuration file.

LISTING 10.42 An Example of the Xend Configuration File—vnet2007.sxp

```
(vnet (id 2007) (bridge vb2007) (security none))
```

This example defines a vnet whose ID is 2007 bridge name is vb2007, and no authentication or packet is encryption required.

Create vnet

The xm command provides subcommands to create vnet. The command line xm vnet-create vnet2007.sxp creates vnet according to the configuration in the file vnet2007.sxp. Table 10.6 shows other vnet-related xm subcommands.

TABLE 10.6 xm vnet Subcommands

Subcommand	Options	Description
vnet-create	<Xend_config>	Set up vnet
vnet-delete	<vnet_id>	Delete the specific running vnet
vnet-list		Display the information of all the vnets in use

For more details on vnet, look at the documents in the directory `tools/vnet/doc` and in Xen's Users' Manual at the link `www.cl.cam.ac.uk/research/srg/netos/xen/readmes/user/user.html`.

Summary

As we have seen in this chapter, there are many ways to successfully construct the virtual network for guest domains: either connecting them to the Internet, hiding them behind a NAT gateway, or securing their communications in an isolated, purely virtual network segment. Through virtual network Xen setup, the guest domains can communicate with the other domains or machines on the Internet. In Chapter 11, we further discuss how to secure these communications as well as other security precautions needed for production Xen deployments.

References and Further Reading

"An Attempt to Explain Xen Networking." Xen Users Mailing List.
    `http://lists.xensource.com/archives/html/xen-users/2006-02/msg00030.html`.
"Dynamic Host Configuration Protocol." Wikipedia.
    `http://en.wikipedia.org/wiki/Dynamic_Host_Configuration_Protocol`.
IEEE Standard 802-2001.
    `http://standards.ieee.org/getieee802/download/802-2001.pdf`.
"IP Address." Wikipedia.
    `http://en.wikipedia.org/wiki/IP_address`.
Linux Command: brctl.
    `http://www.linuxcommand.org/man_pages/brctl8.html`.
Linux Command: iptables.
    `http://www.linuxcommand.org/man_pages/iptables8.html`.

Linux Command: route.
   http://www.linuxcommand.org/man_pages/route8.html.
"MAC Address." Wikipedia.
   http://en.wikipedia.org/wiki/MAC_address.
MAC Address Vendor Search.
   http://standards.ieee.org/regauth/oui/index.shtml.
Matthews, Jeanna N. et al. "Data Protection and Rapid Recovery from Attack with a Virtual Private File Server."
   http://people.clarkson.edu/~jnm/publications/cnis2005.pdf.
"Network Address Translation." Wikipedia.
   http://en.wikipedia.org/wiki/Network_address_translation.
"Network Configuration." Xen Users' Manual Xen v3.0.
   http://www.cl.cam.ac.uk/research/srg/netos/xen/readmes/user/
   user.html.
"network-route and vif-route Setup Help." Xen Users Mailing List.
http://lists.xensource.com/archives/html/xen-users/2006-03/
msg00725.html.
"OSI and TCP/IP Layering Differences." TCP/IP Model. Wikipedia.
   http://en.wikipediaorg/wiki/TCP/IP_model#Layers_in_the_
   TCP.2FIP_model.
RFC1918: Address Allocation for Private Internets.
   http://www.ietf.org/rfc/rfc1918.txt.
"Using Multiple Network Cards in XEN 3.0." Debian Administration.
   http://www.debian-administration.org/articles/470.
"Virtual Private Network." Wikipedia.
   http://en.wikipedia.org/wiki/VPN.
"Xen Networking." Xen Wiki.
   http://wiki.xensource.com/xenwiki/ XenNetworking.

Chapter 11

Securing a Xen System

When administering a physical machine, one of the most important tasks is securing the system. This can take many forms, including applying the most recent patches, closing all unnecessary ports, and auditing for unusual or suspicious behavior. These activities are just as important when you run the same software in a virtual machine. In addition, running systems in Xen introduces new opportunities and challenges in security. As a trusted layer below the operating virtual machines, Xen can provide additional tools to monitor and secure the virtual systems. On the other hand, because Xen is a trusted layer below the virtual machines, any compromise to either Xen itself or the trusted Domain0 could cause problems to all guest VMs. In this chapter, we cover both securing Xen itself and using Xen to increase the security of the unprivileged guest virtual machines running on the system.

Structuring Your System for Security

There are a number of fundamental choices you can make in structuring your Xen system for increased security. In this section, we describe some of these choices, including separating functionality into special purpose virtual machines and creating virtual network segments.

Special Purpose Virtual Machines

Special purpose virtual machines are a great way to increase security by limiting the resources they have access to or by limiting what other machines they are given access to. Running device drivers in DriverDomains or creating a special domain for a World Wide Web (www) server are both examples of creating a special purpose domain to increase the security of your system by isolating their tasks.

An administrator can tailor the use of special virtual machines to match the security level of software and data that resides on that system. For example, the public Web server should not also be the network share where all the confidential documents and finances for a company reside. The public Web server should be isolated in its own virtual machine away from sensitive data that is meant only to be shared inside the company. The security levels of these two tasks differ and so should their virtual machines.

This is not to say that all applications or servers should be their own virtual machine, but rather that they should be grouped according to their security threat. Creating a virtual machine for each service becomes a resource intensive and potentially wasteful endeavor. To illustrate the idea of separating tasks according to their security level, we continue with the previous example. Suppose the company wanted to add a spam filter. This spam filter server could easily live with the www server because the principle behind both is to share their information with the rest of the Internet. The information sent to or received from the Internet facing servers is there to be shared with the world, while the principle behind the company's network share is to provide a confidential central storage area with very limited access. The guiding idea in separating tasks by their security threats is to give as little access as possible.

Creating Virtual Network Segments

Separating network access can also greatly reduce the threat placed on an administrator's servers. Continuing with the previous example, the external, Internet facing, public Web server virtual machine should not even sit on the same network connections as confidential or internal virtual machines (VMs). Xen affords us this ability as described in Chapter 10, "Network Configuration." We can give the Web server a VM as an interface with a globally routable IP address on the public network segment and create a virtual network segment for all the internal VMs. We could then have a firewall or NAT VM with an interface on both network segments.

Xen also has the capability to completely isolate the VMs from the public network. For example, we could place the file share VM on a second virtual network segment without a firewall or NAT. Any internal VM that required both Internet access and access to the internal file share would then have two virtual network interfaces—one on the isolated file share network and one on the internal firewalled segment. Similarly, internal-only VMs such as a data mining VM or payroll VM could be assigned to the isolated VM segment. Xen provides this type of strong network isolation.

Securing the Privileged Domain

If the privileged domain, Domain0, is compromised, then so are all the unprivileged domains, DomUs. For this reason it is vitally important that the Domain0 operating system be well secured or "hardened" against attack. The smaller and simpler you can keep Domain0 by removing unessential software and features, the easier it will be to secure the system. Every feature you remove from Domain0 is one less feature that can be used in an attack on the system.

Removing Software and Services

A strong concept while securing a system is to strictly limit the software installed and running on the system. Removing unnecessary software and services includes moving all services not essential for guest management out of Domain0 and into guest VMs. Any service running in Domain0 represents a possible entry point for an attack.

The list of installed software can be intimidating, from the kernel of the OS, to the user space programs, system services, network services, configuration files that save the data, and so on. Large distributions such as Red Hat have a large number of programs installed in them to provide a more robust and feature-rich experience for the end user.

A standard Fedora 6 install can have as many 2,365 executables in the path alone. Few administrators could identify all these programs, much less keep them all patched according to the newest security warnings or monitor whether any have been modified. This is why limiting the number of components involved is a key concept. The fewer items involved, the easier it will be to detect problems and maintain the system. Having fewer items installed leads to fewer tools that an attacker has to work with on your system.

We recommend starting with a bare-bones install and then further examining any installed package to determine whether it is truly needed.

Limiting Remote Access

Removing software for network services is especially important because they are the primary entry point for attackers. Moving network services such as anonymous ftp and World Wide Web servers into unprivileged domains helps ensure that if a service is compromised, the damage is limited to a single VM. Of course, if the attacker gains control of a DomU, it can use that domain as a launching pad for other attacks. Therefore, limiting the access of domains running network services to the rest of the system is also important. Similarly, monitoring the outgoing network access of these domains is important in detecting a compromise. Through some simple planning of backups, a compromised VM can be restored quickly and then patched to help prevent further intrusions.

Any remaining open network port on Domain0 should be treated as a possible entry point and point of attack. You may even want to consider allowing console-only access to Domain0. However, you have to gauge this against the necessity or convenience of being able to administer the system for a given environment. In some environments, console access may simply not be possible. Of course, individual guest domains could still be remotely accessible even if remote administration of Domain0 is disabled.

One powerful tool for auditing open ports is netstat. netstat is a command line tool that displays information on network connections currently on the computer. This information ranges from UNIX style ports to the standard TCP and UDP ports to the interfaces themselves. netstat has many options, from displaying statistics on interfaces to displaying the routing table to currently open sockets. We limit our discussion here to auditing the open ports for security reasons. Our objective is to list the currently open ports so we know what the current status is. For more information on all of netstat's options and capabilities, refer to the netstat manual page.

We now use a netstat example to list our open ports. Because netstat can display so much information to us at once, we need to refine our requests. We start with just ongoing TCP connections. As shown in Listing 11.1, this is accomplished by simply typing netstat -t, where the -t flag is for the currently active TCP connections.

LISTING 11.1 Netstat List of Active TCP Ports

```
[root@dom0]# netstat -t
Active Internet connections (w/o servers)
Proto Recv-Q Send-Q Local Address        Foreign Address        ➡
          State
tcp       0      0 172.16.2.34:60295                             ➡
          65-116-55-163.dia.stati:ssh ESTABLISHED                ➡
tcp       0      0 ::ffff:172.16.2.34:ssh
    mobile-yapibzla:4824        ESTABLISHED
[root@dom0]#
```

From this output we can see two TCP connections that are currently in the ESTAB-LISHED state. Both are SSH connections—one inbound and one outbound. The first line shows an outbound SSH connection from this machine, 172.16.2.34, to the external IP address, 65.116.55.163. The port numbers for each end of the connection are also shown after the IP address (IPAddress:port). On the local machine, ephemeral port 60295 is used, and on the external machine the SSH port (22) is used. As shown here, netstat will often substitute the commonly used name of the port for the port number so it is easier to understand. The second connection is an incoming SSH connection from a computer named "mobile-yapibzla" on their ephemeral port 4824 that is connecting to our local machine, 172.16.2.34, on our SSH port.

Listing 11.1 shows all ongoing TCP connections, but we also want to see any open ports that are waiting for a connection. This would be the case if, for example, we were running a Web site from our localhost, but no one is currently connected. netstat allows you to add another flag to the command line that allows us to see sockets that have not yet been established. This is done with the flag a added to our command, which makes our new command netstat -ta. Running this command in our example gives us the output found in Listing 11.2.

LISTING 11.2 Netstat List of Active TCP Ports

```
[root@dom0]# netstat -ta
Active Internet connections (servers and established)
Proto Recv-Q Send-Q Local Address        Foreign Address  ➡
          State
```

```
tcp       0       0 *:815                        *:*          ➡
                        LISTEN
tcp       0       0 *:sunrpc                     *:*          ➡
                        LISTEN
tcp       0       0 localhost.localdomain:ipp    *:*          ➡
                        LISTEN
tcp       0       0 localhost.localdomain:smtp   *:*          ➡
                        LISTEN
tcp       0       0 172.16.2.17:60295                         ➡
             65-116-55-163.dia.stati:ssh ESTABLISHED
tcp       0       0 *:ssh                        *:*          ➡
                        LISTEN
tcp       0       0 localhost.localdomain:ipp    *:*          ➡
                        LISTEN
tcp       0       0 ::ffff:172.16.2.17:ssh                    ➡
         mobile-yapibzla:4824        ESTABLISHED
[root@dom0]#
```

This output from netstat displays the same information as before—one SSH session outbound and one SSH session inbound—but now also includes sockets that are in the LISTEN state. These are open ports waiting for incoming connections.

For ports in the LISTEN state, the local address column indicates which connections would be allowed. Some ports are open only for localhost, as denoted by the local address being localhost.localdomain, as is the case with the smtp and ipp lines in Listing 11.2. Other connections are open to any address, which is denoted by a wild card of *.

Listing 11.3 shows three ports open to the outside world—one on port 815, another on sunrpc's port of 111, and finally the SSH port of 22. These are services that should be considered for removal or relocation to a VM, if possible. For example, to close the SSH port, you would kill the sshd process running on the machine and remove it from the startup configuration to prevent it from being started when the machine is rebooted.

However, TCP is only half the story. The complementary command can be done with UDP by switching the flag t to a u. To view both UDP and TCP at the same time, simply add both the t and the u to the command line. Keeping the a flag for all states of the ports makes our new command netstat -tua to display all sockets for TCP and then all UDP sockets.

LISTING 11.3 Netstat List of Active TCP Ports

```
[root@dom0]# netstat -tua
Active Internet connections (servers and established)
Proto Recv-Q Send-Q Local Address          Foreign Address  ➡
              State
tcp        0      0 *:815                   *:*              ➡
              LISTEN
tcp        0      0 *:sunrpc                *:*              ➡
              LISTEN
tcp        0      0 localhost.localdomain:ipp  *:*           ➡
              LISTEN
tcp        0      0 localhost.localdomain:smtp  *:*          ➡
              LISTEN
tcp        0      0 172.16.2.17:60295                        ➡
       65-116-55-163.dia.stati:ssh ESTABLISHED
tcp        0      0 *:ssh                   *:*              ➡
              LISTEN
tcp        0      0 localhost.localdomain:ipp  *:*           ➡
              LISTEN
udp        0      0 *:filenet-tms           *:*
udp        0      0 *:809                   *:*
udp        0      0 *:812                   *:*
udp        0      0 *:bootpc                *:*
udp        0      0 *:mdns                  *:*
udp        0      0 *:sunrpc                *:*
udp        0      0 *:ipp                   *:*
udp        0      0 172.16.2.17:ntp         *:*
udp        0      0 localhost.localdomain:ntp  *:*
udp        0      0 *:ntp                   *:*
udp        0      0 *:filenet-rpc           *:*
udp        0      0 *:mdns                  *:*
udp        0      0 fe80::fcff:ffff:fef:ntp  *:*
udp        0      0 fe80::20c:29ff:fe0a:ntp  *:*
udp        0      0 localhost.localdomain:ntp  *:*
udp        0      0 *:ntp                   *:*
[root@dom0]#
```

From this example we can see the same TCP open ports as before. However, there are quite a few open UDP ports including NTP and MDNS. These are services that you should consider removing from Domain0.

The Internet Assigned Numbers Authority (IANA) maintains a list of well-known port numbers that you can consult to help identify the common purpose of open ports. This list is available at www.iana.org/assignments/port-numbers.

Limiting the Local Users

We also recommend limiting user access to Domain0. Only the administrator of the machine should be able to log in. Multiuser systems, such as Linux, have had several local user exploits. Limiting local users to an unprivileged domain when possible can limit any such breaches.

Depending on the security needs, it may be prudent to disable root from logging in directly. Using su could still allow an administrator to assume the root account once logged in. It is also possible to disable the root account from logging in interactively and using the sudo command to execute commands with root rights without needing to assume the root account on a regular basis.

Move Device Drivers into DriverDomains

One of the most vulnerable pieces of an operating system is its device drivers. Device drivers are not typically written by core kernel developers but instead by the device manufacturers or some third party interested in running that device on a given operating system. Therefore, the quality of device driver code varies widely. Device drivers are also less tested than core kernel code because the percentage of users running a particular device is lower than the total number of people running the operating system. Overall, studies have found a much higher rate of bugs or vulnerabilities in device drivers. Nevertheless, they typically run as fully privileged kernel code.

Moving device drivers into a separate DriverDomain can be an important step in securing your system. As discussed in Chapter 9, "Device Virtualization and Management," DriverDomains control access to a physical device and run the device driver code. This effectively isolates a potentially unstable or vulnerable driver. Consider what happens if a device driver running in Domain0 fails to release a lock. The whole system can stop and wait for that lock to be released, resulting in Domain0 halting forever. If a device driver running in a DriverDomain fails, that domain can be stopped and restarted. It can cause problems for guest VMs with outstanding I/Os, but there is a much greater chance of recovering the system and in particular without affecting VMs not using that device.

Firewall and Network Monitors

Xen's network structure not only gives us great flexibility but also allows us to watch all activity to all VMs with ease. This is possible when Domain0 has access to the physical network interfaces and forms a natural checkpoint for network traffic. This allows us to watch the traffic using a network monitor such as `Snort` and still be able to stop all incoming packets to Domain0 at the door using a firewall such as netfilter's `iptables` for Linux-based Domain0s or `ipf` for UNIX-based Domain0s. The next section explains how to use `iptables` in Domain0 to limit all network traffic destined for it; then the following section discusses `Snort`.

Running a Firewall with `iptables`

The network connection is one of the main inlets for attacking a machine. Limiting the exposure of the network should be on the mind of every administrator. However, physically disconnecting the network cable (an airgap) is not normally acceptable; a firewall, such as `iptables` under Linux or `ipfilter` under Solaris and BSD, is normally employed. These firewall rules and ideas can be applied to the privileged domain or in any of the unprivileged domains.

`iptables` Overview

Netfilter's iptables is a framework that allows for software control over network packets. The iptables project uses both a kernel side element and a user space element. The kernel side element does the work of accepting, altering, or rejecting the network packets. The user space element provides the capability to easily alter the rules of accepting, rejecting, and altering.

Iptables is structured internally as a simple table, which allows for simple, easy to understand rules. Each rule accepts or denies a particular type of network packet. The rules are applied in order, and the action specified by the first matching rule is applied. A common practice is to list a set of network traffic to be allowed followed by a final rule that denies everything else. It is important for the "deny all" rule to be last; because all packets match this rule, any other configuration lines will be effectively ignored.

The iptables project has a much loftier goal of providing a robust framework that allows for complex network control from quality of service policy to controlled network address translating routers. Our goals for this chapter are much simpler. We start with a simple deny everything rule and then add a few exceptions for basic management. If you want to know more about IP tables, we recommend one of the books listed at the end of this chapter for further reading.

iptables Configuration

Because iptables is comprised of both a kernel side and a user space side, obtaining iptables can be slightly confusing. Luckily, however, most distributions come with iptables already installed, including Fedora, CentOS, and SUSE. Gentoo, however, requires that you build the necessary modules for the kernel and emerge the user space tools.

Under UNIX brands, including Solaris and the BSD family, it is more common to find the utility IPFilter or ipf. Refer to the individual documentation for your UNIX brand for complete details.

Should your Domain0 distribution not have iptables installed and not have it available via its package management system, there are two simple items you need to install.

The kernel configuration requires, at a minimum, the CONFIG_NETFILTER option either built-in or as a module. If you build it as a module, be sure to add the module to the list of modules loaded at bootup. Depending on your plan and how advanced you want to make iptables, other options in the kernel might be required, especially for network address translation and IP-based filtering.

After finishing the kernel part, the user space tools, which contain the iptables program itself, can be found from the project's Web site at www.netfilter.org. After extracting the tarball containing the latest ipfilter package, locate the INSTALL file in the top level of the directory. This file gives detailed instructions and releases any specific actions that are needed. It also contains a list of known common problems and their solutions. Making the tool requires only two simple make commands, as shown in Listing 11.4.

LISTING 11.4 Building iptables

```
[root@dom0]# make KERNEL_DIR=/path/to/your/kernel/sources
[output omitted]
[root@dom0]# make install KERNEL_DIR=/path/to/your/kernel/sources
```

Now with the iptables program installed, the next step is to plan the appropriate rules for your network. As you learned in Chapter 10, a good, well-thought-out network design can save you a lot of time and problems. Figure 11.1 shows a simple network. Knowing where to limit network access makes the process of understanding and using `iptables` much simpler.

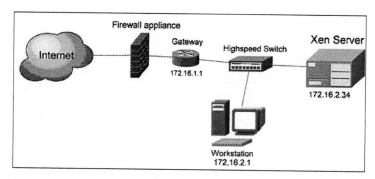

FIGURE 11.1 Network diagram representing a simple network

One last configuration issue to attend to is the location of the files that `iptables` will use to store its rules in between system boots. This location is often distribution specific, and you should consult the documentation for your choice of Domain0. The standard location for Red Hat Fedora, for example, is to store this information in the file `/etc/sysconfig/iptables`. With OpenSUSE, the default location is in `/etc/sysconfig/SuSEfirewall2`.

An `iptables` Example

First we create a simple rule to allow for SSH connections to our Domain0. Remember that we will add the most important rule of "deny all" last so that our "accept" rules are evaluated first. For our example, we will say that our Domain0 host is at 172.16.2.34, and our client computer that we want to allow to connect to Domain0 resides at 172.16.2.1. SSH uses port 22 and the TCP protocol. Most information about which port and which transport layer a protocol uses is publicly available on the Internet. We add our allow rule by using the `iptables` command as shown in Listing 11.5.

LISTING 11.5 Adding `iptable` Rules

```
[root@dom0]# iptables -A INPUT -s 172.16.2.1 -d 172.16.2.34➥
    -p tcp -dport 22 -j ACCEPT
```

Now let's dissect this command to more fully understand it.

The first argument, `-A INPUT`, is to tell `iptables` that we want to append a rule to the chain called `INPUT`. By default there are three chains: `INPUT`, `OUTPUT`, and `FORWORD`. A chain itself is nothing more than a collection of rules. The chains are each evaluated based on their intended destination. The `INPUT` chain is invoked when the packet is destined for the firewall's addresses. The `OUTPUT` rule chain is invoked when a packet is originating from the firewall. Finally, the `FORWORD` chain is evaluated when the destination is not the computer running `IPtables` but rather an address behind it.

The second argument, `-s 172.16.2.1`, is the source destination. This rule matches only from the IP address of 172.16.2.1. If the IP address that is trying to connect to us is something else, it moves on to the next rule. To specify all addresses, you can simply leave off the `-s` argument.

The third argument, `-d 172.16.2.34`, is our Domain0 IP address. This is where the incoming packet has to be heading to match this rule. Again, to specify any address, leave off the `-d` argument. This may be useful to reject any packets coming from a known bad host, no matter where they may be destined.

The fourth argument, `-p tcp`, is the protocol. `iptables` has the capability to specify a rule for `TCP`, `UDP`, `ICMP`, or `ALL` protocols.

The fifth argument, `-dport 22`, is the destination port on our Domain0 that the incoming connection is trying to contact. In SSH's case, it is 22. In a normal Web server's case it is 80. In Xen, relocation requests are done over port 8002.

The last argument, `-j ACCEPT`, is a jump to the accept state. So this packet passes all the rest of the rules and moves on. The `-j` argument is the jump to an action; in our case, we accept the packet. Different situations may require different actions. Other actions `iptables` can take are `LOG`, which sends the packet information to the syslog daemon on the computer and continues to process the packet; `DROP`, which simply destroys the packet and moves on to the next packet to be processed; and `REJECT`, which is similar to `DROP` except it sends an error packet back to the host that informs the sender that the packet was blocked. `REJECT` has the benefit of sending the information that the packet was not received but has the problem of taking more network resources. A malicious attacker could abuse this by sending known `REJECT` packets, causing your `iptables` to fill the network with `REJECT` messages. Another pair of actions is `DNAT` and `SNAT`, which both rewrite an IP address of the packet. `SNAT` rewrites the address that sent the packet while `DNAT` rewrites the address that the packet is destined for. One final action a rule is allowed to take is `MASQUERADE`, which is used to do source network address translation by using the `iptables` host's address.

To recap, the rule shown in Listing 11.5 allows a computer at 172.16.2.1 using the SSH protocol to connect to our Domain0 on 172.16.2.34. Now that we understand how to append rules, we need to understand how to remove them should we make a mistake or have a change in the network. There are two ways to remove an individual rule. The first method is to count the number of the rule in the listing and use the -D argument, as shown in Listing 11.6.

The example command in Listing 11.6 deletes the third rule in the INPUT chain. In some complex rule sets, counting can be time consuming.

LISTING 11.6 Removing an iptable Rule by Number

```
[root@dom0]# iptables -D INPUT 3
```

A second method for removing a rule is to mirror the command that would have been used to create it; just replace the -A flag with a -D flag. This can save you time in complex rule sets because it is not important where the rule sits but rather if it matches. To use this on the example SSH rule in Listing 11.5, we would duplicate the rule but changing the append flag to a delete flag. This can be seen in Listing 11.7.

LISTING 11.7 Removing an iptable Rule by Type

```
[root@dom0]# iptables -D INPUT -s 172.16.2.1 -d 172.16.2.34 \
    -p tcp -dport 22 -j ACCEPT
```

To view all rules in their current state or to see whether the rule is truly deleted, call iptables with -L command as shown in Listing 11.8.

LISTING 11.8 Listing iptable Rules

```
[root@dom0]# iptables -L
[output omitted]
```

If however, your end objective is to remove all rules and begin anew, iptables has a flush command, shown in Listing 11.9.

LISTING 11.9 Removing all iptable Rules

```
[root@dom0]# iptables --flush
```

This flush command should be used with caution because it does remove all rules.

Armed with all this background in iptables, we now create a simple set of commands that will set up our Domain0 firewall. For our example in Listing 11.10, we will say that our Domain0 lives at the IP address 172.16.2.34, everything on the private subnet 172.16.x.x is friendly, and we will accept connections from it. Everything else is assumed to be hostile.

LISTING 11.10 Simple iptable Rule Set

```
[root@dom0]# iptables -- flush
[root@dom0]# iptables -A INPUT -s 172.16.0.0/12 -d 172.16.2.34 \
    -p tcp -dport 22 -j ACCEPT
[root@dom0]# iptables -A INPUT -s 172.16.0.0/12 -d 172.16.2.34 \
    -p tcp -dport 8002 -j ACCEPT
[root@dom0]# iptables -A INPUT -d 172.16.2.34 -j REJECT
```

This provides us local SSH access and local Xen relocation. Everything else trying to connect is rejected. This example allows for Xen migration from our trusted LAN of 172.16.0.0/12, but if you're not planning on enabling Xen migration, this feature should be disabled and the rule removed from iptables.

A default policy of denying everything should be any administrator's starting point; from there open ports as they are required. To allow Xen relocation, for example, enable TCP connections on port 8002. Stated a different way, disabling communications on port 8002 will prevent Xen migrations. However, it is best practice to limit the address range that can connect to this port to the range of trusted IP address.

Even with the capability to deny access based on the sender's IP address, this still leaves us open to attack from sources using IP spoofing, and we do not yet have a mechanism that will warn us of an intrusion.

IP spoofing is when an attacker fakes the source address of network packets. The attackers may have different reasons for this, from Denial of Service (DoS) attacks to Man in the Middle attacks. To limit your susceptibility to IP spoofing, an administrator can take several simple steps. First is to program network routers on the perimeter of the private network to reject addresses that originate from outside the private network with a private network source address. Another action is to move to protocols that do not use source address authentication. An example is to move from the remote shell protocol to a safer protocol such as SSH.

Even with all the proper measures taken, there is still the possibility of being compromised. Having a system in place that watches for statistical anomalies and performs pattern-matching for known attack methods can alert us when an attack has been or is currently being attempted. For this we need an Intrusion Detection System (IDS), and Linux, Solaris, and the BSDs have a good lightweight IDS program named Snort.

Snort

Snort is a powerful, open source, and highly configurable network IDS for Linux, UNIX, and Microsoft Windows. Snort has four key capabilities:

- Watch and log packets coming over the wire in real time
- Inspect payloads and detect more complex attacks such as buffer overflow and stealth scans
- Work as a full-fledged IDS
- Integrate with `iptables` to provide inline intrusion detection

Snort, like `iptables`, is a large and impressive product in its own right. We only cover a small amount here in this chapter. Snort's widespread use has made it commonplace in industry and easy to find support for.

Obtaining Snort

Snort is freely available from `www.snort.org` and through most major distributions. If Snort is not found in your distribution package management system, then building it from source is relatively painless. First you need to download and install the pcap library as shown in Listing 11.11. The pcap library is found at `www.tcpdump.org`.

LISTING 11.11 Downloading and Building pcap

```
[root@dom0]# wget http://www.tcpdump.org/release/libpcap-0.9.5.tar.gz
[root@dom0]# tar -xpzf libpcap-0.9.5.tar.gz
[root@dom0]# cd libpcap-0.9.5
[root@dom0]#./configure
[root@dom0]# make
[root@dom0]# make install
```

Now that we have pcap installed, we can install Snort using the standard method of config, make, and make install as shown in Listing 11.12.

LISTING 11.12 Downloading and Building Snort

```
[root@dom0]# wget http://www.snort.org/dl/current/snort-2.6.1.3.tar.gz
[output omitted]
[root@dom0]# tar -xpzf snort-2.6.1.3.tar.gz
[root@dom0]# cd snort-2.6.1.3
[root@dom0]#./configure
[output omitted]
[root@dom0]# make
[output omitted]
[root@dom0]# make install
```

Snort and Network Intrusion Detection Mode

Snort has many options and configurations, the scope of which is beyond this chapter, but fortunately, setting up an initial intrusion detection system is easy.

The configuration files that dictate Snort's behavior are located, in a standard install, in the /etc/snort directory, with the main file being /etc/snort/snort. conf. The snort.conf has many configuration options, but each is reasonably well documented within the file as well as being explained in the documentation on the official Web site, www.snort.org.

By default, Snort comes with a reasonable set of rules preconfigured in the snort. conf file. You can also write your own rules in the configuration file. Several books and numerous online resources on creating custom rules are available.

To see Snort in action, all we have to type is snort -dl /var/log/snort. This command tells Snort to run and log its activity to the /var/log/snort directory as shown in Listing 11.13. After several seconds, we can press Ctrl+C to exit Snort and look at the statistics at the end.

LISTING 11.13 Running Snort

```
[root@dom0]# snort -dl /var/log/snort
Running in packet logging mode
Log directory = /var/log/snort

        --== Initializing Snort ==--
Initializing Output Plugins!
Var 'any_ADDRESS' defined, value len = 15 chars,        ➥
     value = 0.0.0.0/0.0.0.0
```

```
Var 'lo_ADDRESS' defined, value len = 19 chars,        ⇥
      value = 127.0.0.0/255.0.0.0
Verifying Preprocessor Configurations!
***
*** interface device lookup found: peth0
***

Initializing Network Interface peth0
OpenPcap() device peth0 network lookup:
        peth0: no IPv4 address assigned
Decoding Ethernet on interface peth0

        --== Initialization Complete ==--

   ,,_      -*> Snort! <*-
  o"  )~    Version 2.6.1.1 (Build 30)
   ''''     By Martin Roesch & The Snort Team:
            http://www.snort.org/team.html
            (C) Copyright 1998-2006 Sourcefire Inc., et al.

Not Using PCAP_FRAMES

(................)


*** Caught Int-Signal


================================================================================

Snort received 111 packets
    Analyzed: 54(48.649%)
    Dropped: 0(0.000%)
    Outstanding: 57(51.351%)
================================================================================
Breakdown by protocol:
    TCP: 8           (14.815%)
    UDP: 20          (37.037%)
   ICMP: 8           (14.815%)
    ARP: 11          (20.370%)
  EAPOL: 0           (0.000%)
   IPv6: 0           (0.000%)
ETHLOOP: 0           (0.000%)
```

```
   IPX: 0            (0.000%)
  FRAG: 0            (0.000%)
 OTHER: 7            (12.963%)
DISCARD: 0           (0.000%)
===============================================================================
Action Stats:
ALERTS: 0
LOGGED: 54
PASSED: 0
===============================================================================
Snort exiting
[root@dom0]#
```

In Listing 11.13, Snort analyzed 54 packets and raised 0 alerts. Alerts are raised when one of the rules Snort is watching for is violated. The logs are in tcpdump's binary format. This is done for greater speed so that Snort can keep up with network traffic. No alerts were raised because it was run on a safe network using only the default rule set that came with Snort. Snorts' web site, www.snort.org, contains more details on how to customize your rule set to your expected network traffic and is an excellent recourse for Snort documentation.

Mandatory Access Control with sHype and Xen Security Modules

To this point, we have focused primarily on structuring your Xen system to prevent and monitor for attacks from outside. It is also important to consider enforcing security within a Xen system. While there are many advantages to co-locating many VM on the same physical machine, it also introduces the possibility of undesired interactions between the VMs, especially in the case of VMs owned by mutually untrusting entities.

Although unprivileged domains cannot directly access another unprivileged domain because of Xen's isolation, it is possible for malicious VMs to gather covert information about other VMs. For example, if two VMs share a virtual network segment, they could snoop each other's network traffic. Similarly, VMs may be able to observe the pattern of each other's disk activity. They may even be assigned memory pages or disk blocks once owned by another. A VM without performance isolation might be able to issue a Denial of Service attack by attempting to consume all available physical resources.

One solution to this problem is to never run VMs with different security needs on the same physical machine. However, this is not always feasible or desirable. For example, consider a large virtual hosting environment in which VMs are migrated between physical machines for load balancing or in preparation for hardware maintenance. VMs could belong to many different companies, including some direct competitors that never want their VMs co-located. Similarly, individuals working on government or military applications may want to run both secure applications and commodity applications without maintaining multiple physical machines. In these environments, the ability to securely enforce mandatory access control between VMs running on the same physical machine is essential.

In this section, we describe the support for mandatory access controls between VMs in Xen.

sHype

One of the first security modules created to allow for mandatory access control (MAC) of the VMs in Xen was developed by IBM Research. It is called the *Secure Hypervisor Access Control Module* or, more commonly, *sHype/ACM*. sHype extensions to Xen allow for both the VMs and their resources to be labeled. Once labeled, a policy can be set that dictates which VMs and resources are allowed to run or be accessed at any given time.

sHype has its roots in IBM research as a secure hypervisor or VM manager. IBM used the insight gained from many years of using and developing VMs to form the sHype project to supply security for other, non-IBM hypervisors such as Xen. The sHype project itself covers a large range of security aspects from role-based access, mandatory access control (MAC), and virtual TPM support.

Role-Based Access Control (RBAC) is an approach to grant rights based on the role of the user or computer rather than on the individual user directly. So a person may have the role of administrator and be a member of that group while another user may be of the sales group. The rights and abilities come from the membership in the group and are assigned directly to the user.

This differs from MAC, in which the system security policy directly grants or denies the rights based on the sensitivity of the labeled item. Two items may have two different labels, and an administrator may have access to one but not the other depending on his label. Despite having full administrator rights everywhere else, if his label does not match, access is denied.

Currently only MAC has made it into the Xen stable sources with an ongoing effort for virtual TPM support.

Adding sHype to Xen

To add sHype to Xen 3.2, you need to download the latest source code from Xen's Web site, www.xen.org/download, and extract it into a directory using tar as shown in Listing 11.14.

LISTING 11.14 Obtaining the Xen Source

```
[root@dom0]# wget http://bits.xensource.com/oss-xen/release/ \
3.2.0/src.tgz/xen-3.2.0-src.tgz
[output omitted]
[root@dom0]# tar -xpzf xen-3.2.0-src.tgz
[root@dom0]# cd xen-3.2.0-src
```

Next we need to edit the top-level configuration file. Because Xen is a large and complex project, all the MAC functionality has been grouped together within the Xen Access Control Module (ACM). Find the file in the top directory of Xen's source code named Config.mk. Open this file in a text editor, find the line that contains the switches to enable mandatory access, and change it from n to y as shown in Listing 11.15. The letter must be lowercase for the build process to understand it.

LISTING 11.15 Switching Config.mk Values On

```
ACM_SECURITY ?= y
XSM_ENABLE ?= y
```

Having set these two values in the Config.mk file as shown in Listing 11.15, we can now compile and install/reinstall Xen. If you already have Xen installed and work on this system, building the target xen and the target tools should be sufficient. However, for the sake of completeness and to help eliminate the possibility of errors from mismatching Xen and Domain0 kernel settings, we will allow Xen to build its entire project. Listing 11.16 shows the commands to build the entire project.

LISTING 11.16 Building Mandatory Access Control

```
[root@dom0]# make world
[output omitted]
[root@dom0]# make install
```

Now we have built in the sHype extensions of Xen. To check to make sure that our settings and build were successful, we can execute a `which` command on the program named `xensec_ezpolicy` as shown in Listing 11.17. If the program is not found, check the `Config.mk` file to make sure your settings are correct and watch the Xen build for errors.

LISTING 11.17 Checking That the Xen Build Was Successful

```
[root@dom0]# which xensec_ezpolicy
/usr/sbin/xensec_ezpolicy
[root@dom0]#
```

Next we need to configure the policies that dictate its behavior. Having the ability to enforce a policy without a policy does us little good.

Configuring an sHype Policy

Policies are configured from a simple XML file. Before embarking on configuring this file, we consider the security layout of the organization to design a function policy. We use an example of a hosting provider that has three customers. For the sake of illustrating the example, we'll say the customers are CompetitorA, CompetitorB, and NonCompetitor. Both CompetitorA and CompetitorB have the technical knowledge and compete in the same markets as each other. It is conceivable that one VM owned by either CompetitorB or CompetitorA could disrupt the VMs from the other company. To prevent these knowledgeable enemies from interacting, we disallow these two VMs from running on the same physical machine. This is an item for a Chinese Wall policy. NonCompetitor is in an entirely different market and has little to no interest in either CompetitorB or CompetitorA. But just because they do not have an interest in each other does not mean that their VMs should cooperate. This relationship should be expressed as a Simple Type Enforcement policy.

With our objective clearly laid out, let's construct our XML policy file by using a special Python program that is bundled with Xen called `xensec_ezpolicy`. This Python program makes use of wxGTK python extensions that may not be installed in your distribution by default but can be found easily through most distributions' package management systems.

When the program initially starts, we are presented with a simplistic interface that allows us to get straight to the business of creating our organizations. We go ahead and create our three organizations, CompetitorA, CompetitorB, and NonCompetitor, as seen in Figure 11.2.

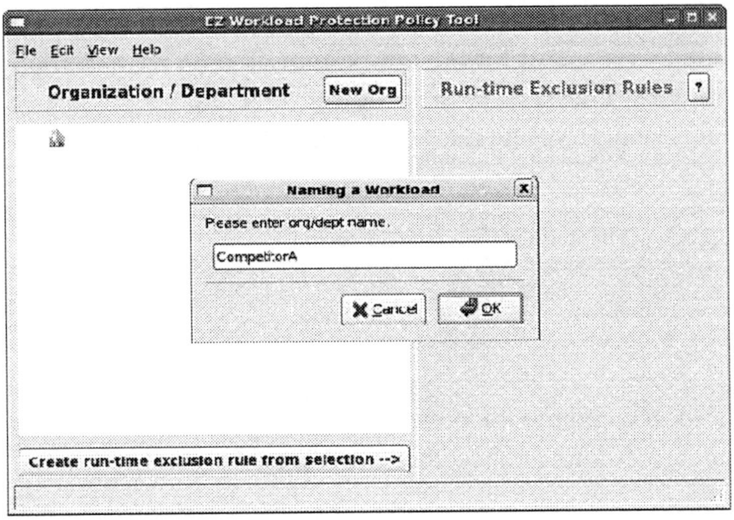

FIGURE 11.2 Entering a name for a workload

All organizations are automatically set to Simple Type Enforcement among each other. To add a Chinese Wall policy, select the two problem VMs of CompetitorA and CompetitorB and click the Create Run-time Exclusion Rule from Selection button. It asks for a name of the rule, as seen in Figure 11.3. The name for the policy is there for easing the administration over a large number of policies. We now see a new runtime exclusion rule added on the right half of the window as illustrated in Figure 11.4.

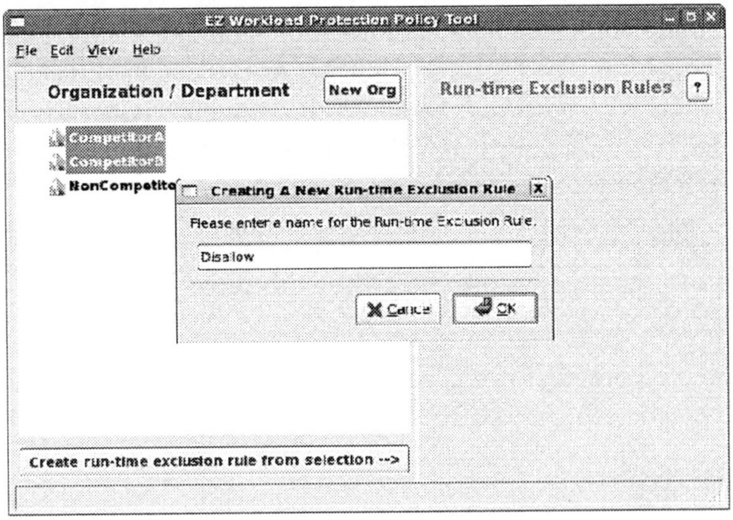

FIGURE 11.3 Creating a new runtime exclusion rule

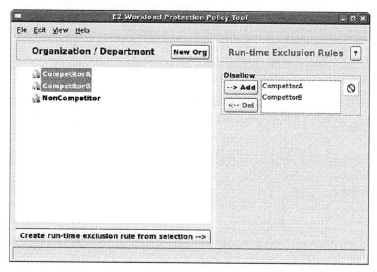

FIGURE 11.4 Entering runtime exclusion rules for competitors

Having completed our security policy, we select Save as Xen ACM Security Policy and give it a name of CompetitorAB. This saves our file in the default location of `/etc/xen/acm-security/policies`. If that directory does not exist, you'll receive an error. Simply create the directory and save the layout again. The file itself will be named `CompetitorAB-security_policy.xml`. The first part of the filename is what we typed into `xensec_ezpolicy`, and the second half is the directory it resides in. Stated a different way, you can find the file `CompetitorAB-security_policy.xml` in the "security\policies" directory.

Now that we have created our XML file, let's examine the first part of it as shown in Listing 11.18.

LISTING 11.18 Excerpt from the Policy XML File

```
<?xml version="1.0" encoding="UTF-8"?>
<!-- Auto-generated by ezPolicy        -->
<SecurityPolicyDefinition xmlns="http://www.ibm.com" xmlns:xsi="http://www.
w3.org/2001/XMLSchema-instance" xsi:schemaLocation="http://www.ibm.com ../
    ../security_policy.xsd ">
  <PolicyHeader>
     <PolicyName>/example.xml</PolicyName>
     <Date>Tue Feb 16 19:02:49 2007</Date>
  </PolicyHeader>
```

```
<SimpleTypeEnforcement>
    <SimpleTypeEnforcementTypes>
        <Type>SystemManagement</Type>
        <Type> CompetitorA </Type>
        <Type> CompetitorB </Type>
        <Type>NonCompetitor</Type>
    </SimpleTypeEnforcementTypes>
</SimpleTypeEnforcement>

<ChineseWall priority="PrimaryPolicyComponent">
    <ChineseWallTypes>
        <Type>SystemManagement</Type>
        <Type> CompetitorA </Type>
        <Type> CompetitorB </Type>
        <Type>NonCompetitor</Type>
    </ChineseWallTypes>

    <ConflictSets>
        <Conflict name="Disallow">
            <Type> CompetitorA </Type>
            <Type> CompetitorB </Type>
        </Conflict>
    </ConflictSets>
</ChineseWall>
```

One item that you might notice listed in the XML that was not in the policy creation tool is the `SystemManagement` type. This is your trusted domain, Domain0. Also notice that that all organizations are listed in the Chinese Wall element. These are the valid types for defining conflict sets found in the next block of the XML. These conflict sets are the rules for preventing VMs from executing on the same physical hardware. Execution of the `xm create` command on the second VM while the other VM in the rule set is running will fail, returning an error saying "Error: (1, 'Operation not permitted')." Migration of VMs that are not labeled or that are labeled with conflicting types will also be denied. So if CompetitorA was running and CompetitorB tried a live migration, Xen would deny it.

Now that we have created our XML, we need to turn the XML into a binary representation that we can load at boot time. To accomplish this, we will use another tool bundled with Xen called xensec_xml2bin. Listing 11.19 shows how to use this tool.

LISTING 11.19 Creating a Binary File from XML

```
[root@dom0]# xensec_xml2bin CompetitorAB
arg=CompetitorAB
Validating policy file /etc/xen/acm-security/policies/          ➡
    CompetitorAB-security_policy.xml...
XML Schema /etc/xen/acm-security/policies/                      ➡
    security_policy.xsd valid.
Creating ssid mappings ...
Policy Reference name (Url): CompetitorAB
Creating label mappings ...
Max chwall labels:   5
Max chwall-types:    4
Max chwall-ssids:    5
Max ste labels:      9
Max ste-types:       4
Max ste-ssids:       9
[root@dom0]#
```

This generates a binary file, `CompetitorAB.bin`, in the same directory as the XML file, `/etc/xen/acm-security/policies`. We can now load this binary file into Xen at boot time so that Xen can enforce the policy from the start of execution. To accomplish this task we just need to copy our new `CompetitorAB.bin` file into the boot directory next to Xen as shown in Listing 11.20.

LISTING 11.20 Copying the Binary File to the Boot Directory

```
[root@dom0]# cp /etc/xen/acm-security/policies/CompetitorAB.bin   ➡
    /boot/CompetitorAB.bin
```

Now we need to tell Xen to read the file at boot, which amounts to nothing more than adding a simple line to the `grub.conf` file as shown in Listing 11.21. We need to add another module command to the Xen menu item, such as `module /boot/CompetitorAB.bin`.

LISTING 11.21 GRUB Configuration with Binary Policy File

```
title Kernel-2.6.18.2-34-xen
 root (hd0,4)
 kernel /boot/xen.gz
 module /boot/vmlinuz-2.6.18.2-34-xen root=/dev/sda5          ➡
     vga=0x317 resume=/dev/sda2 splash=silent showopts
 module /boot/initrd-2.6.18.2-34-xen
 module /boot/CompetitorAB.bin
```

After accomplishing this, Xen needs a reboot to load the newly compiled Xen with mandatory access control and our policies. When Domain0 starts again, we can perform another few simple checks to ensure that our changes so far have taken hold. First thing we will do is simply list the currently running VMs using the xm command like normal, but adding the flag -label as shown in Listing 11.22.

LISTING 11.22 Copying the Binary File to the Boot Directory

```
[root@dom0]# xm list --label
Name             ID Mem(MiB) VCPUs State   Time(s) Label
Domain-0          0    464      2 r-----   264.0            ACM:example:➡
SystemManagement
[root@dom0]#
```

Another column is listed at the end of the normal output that gives its label. If the mandatory access control extensions are not in Xen, the default value in the field is INACTIVE; if they are correct, the label on Domain0 is SystemManagement as we expected from our XML file.

The second method to make sure Xen is using the mandatory access extensions and our policy file is to check the output of Xen's messages while booting. This is done simply by using the xm command with the dmesg subcommand as shown in Listing 11.23.

LISTING 11.23 Excerpt from Xen dmesg Showing ACM Is On

```
(XEN) Brought up 2 CPUs
(XEN) Machine check exception polling timer started.
(XEN) acm_set_policy_reference: Activating policy CompetitorAB
(XEN) acm_init: Enforcing CHINESE WALL AND SIMPLE TYPE ENFORCEMENT boot policy.
(XEN) *** LOADING DOMAIN 0 ***
```

Next we need to label our resources and VMs for them to start. All access control is done using these labels. The VM's name or any other characteristics are not evaluated. Only Domain0 can label machines or resources, which is another reason why Domain0 access should be limited. By default, a domain is not labeled and therefore is denied the ability to start. If you use the xm command, you can see the result as shown in Listing 11.24.

LISTING 11.24 Domain Denied without a Label

```
[root@dom0]# xm create CompetitorA
Using config file "/etc/xen/CompetitorA".
```

```
  kernel: /boot/vmlinuz-2.6.16.smp.NoPAE.x86.i686.Xen.domU
  initrd: /boot/initrd-2.6.16.smp.NoPAE.x86.i686.Xen.domU.img
   CompetitorA: DENIED
   --> Domain not labeled
Checking resources: (skipped)
Error: Security Configuration prevents domain from starting
```

To label our machines, we use the xm command. The configuration file for the VMs must have a kernel line or xm gives an error. The syntax for the command is as follows: xm addlabel {Label} dom {Config file}. In our example shown in Listing 11.25, the config file happens to be the same name as the label.

LISTING 11.25 Labeling the VMs

```
[root@dom0]# xm addlabel CompetitorA dom CompetitorA
[root@dom0]# xm addlabel CompetitorB dom CompetitorB
[root@dom0]# xm addlabel NonCompetitor dom NonCompetitor
```

This command adds a line, as shown in Listing 11.26, to the bottom of the configuration file to label it and identify which policy is running it.

LISTING 11.26 Label inside the Configuration File

```
access_control = ['policy=CompetitorAB,label=CompetitorA']
```

We still have one more piece to label before a machine can run on our system, and that is the resources. Listing 11.27 shows how we label the resources.

LISTING 11.27 Labeling the Resources of a VM

```
[root@dom0]# xm addlabel CompetitorA res file:
    /svr/xen/CompetitorA/Webserver_disk.img
[root@dom0]# xm addlabel CompetitorB res file:
    /svr/xen/CompetitorB /Webserver_disk.img
[root@dom0]# xm addlabel NonCompetitor res file:
    /svr/xen/NonCompetitor/Webserver_disk.img
```

Now that all the domains and their resources have their respective labels, we can once again start running VMs. To ensure that the policy is being obeyed, we start all three VMs in order. We should see CompetitorA start, CompetitorB be denied, and NonCompetitor start. The procedures are shown in Listing 11.28.

LISTING 11.28 Letting Access Control Do Its Work

```
[root@dom0]# xm create CompetitorA
Using config file "./CompetitorA".
Going to boot Example Linux release 1.0.5 (2.6.16.smp.NoPAE.x86.i686.Xen.domU)
  kernel: /boot/vmlinuz-2.6.16.smp.NoPAE.x86.i686.Xen.domU
  initrd: /boot/initrd-2.6.16.smp.NoPAE.x86.i686.Xen.domU.img
Started domain CompetitorA
[1]+  Done

[root@dom0]# xm create CompetitorB
Using config file "./CompetitorB".
Going to boot Example Linux release 1.0.5 (2.6.16.smp.NoPAE.x86.i686.Xen.domU)
  kernel: /boot/vmlinuz-2.6.16.smp.NoPAE.x86.i686.Xen.domU
  initrd: /boot/initrd-2.6.16.smp.NoPAE.x86.i686.Xen.domU.img
Error: (1, 'Operation not permitted')

[root@dom0]# xm create NonCompetitor
Using config file "./NonCompetitor".
Going to boot Example Linux release 1.0.5 (2.6.16.smp.NoPAE.x86.i686.Xen.domU)
  kernel: /boot/vmlinuz-2.6.16.smp.NoPAE.x86.i686.Xen.domU
  initrd: /boot/initrd-2.6.16.smp.NoPAE.x86.i686.Xen.domU.img
Started domain NonCompetitor
[root@dom0]#
```

Indeed, this is exactly the behavior we wanted. While CompetitorA is running, CompetitorB is not allowed to run. This has no effect on NonCompetitor.

Xen Security Modules (XSM)

In addition to the sHype/XSM, a more generic security framework for Xen has been implemented by the National Information Assurance Research Laboratory within the National Security Agency (NSA). This is the same group responsible for developing Security Enhanced Linux (SELinux), and in fact the XSM implementation was derived from the Linux Security Modules (LSM) from SELinux.

XSM is a security framework that allows custom security modules to be downloaded. In the language of XSM, the sHype/ACM work would be one possible security module. The XSM framework allows security model-specific code to be removed from the main Xen hypervisor in exchange for general security interfaces that can be used to set any desired policy.

Another significant difference between the XSM work and the sHype/ACM work is an emphasis on decomposing Domain0. As mentioned earlier in this chapter, one important key to securing a Xen system is making Domain0 as small and bulletproof as possible. The XSM work takes this even further by systematically identifying all the privileges currently granted to Domain0 and allowing these privileges to be granted to different domains. Much like we have seen device drivers moved into privileged DriverDomains, XSM enables granting separate rights, such as the ability to create new domains or the ability to configure the physical hardware, to different privileged domains besides a single Domain0.

Currently, three XSM modules are implemented: a dummy default module, the sHype/ACM module based on the IBM work, and a Flask module implemented by NSA. The Flask module will seem familiar to those already using SELinux. Its capabilities include Multi-Level and Multi-Category Security (MLS/MCS) as well as Role-Based Access Control and Type Enforcement (RBAC/TE). In Multi-Level Security, the multiple-levels are traditionally named Top Secret, Secret, Classified, and Unclassified. Even within a level such as Top Secret, there may be the need to further decompose access by specific project or job function. For example, in a commercial environment, there might be a category for each nondisclosure agreement signed with another company, with access granted on a need-to-know basis even within the highest security level. Role Based Access Control organizes users into groups or roles and assigns a set of authorizations to each role. As users change roles within an organization, old access rights for their previous roles can be easily revoked, and new access rights for their new role can be added simply. Type Enforcement defines low-level types of objects, the set of accesses that are possible to those objects, and the auditing performed on each access. The Type Enforcement policy directly specifies access, and all other policies build on top of it.

For installations interested in a secure deployment of Xen, Xen together with SELinux makes a strong combination. Excellent documentation on SELinux is available at www.nsa.gov/selinux/.

DomU Security

After considering attacks from outside and attacks from other DomUs, we turn our attention to the security of individual unprivileged domains.

In general, security of unprivileged domains should be handled as if they were physical, stand-alone computers in their own right. You should keep the software and operating system up to date and watch for security warnings on software you are running. An administrator would also be wise to learn about and leverage all existing security capabilities of the operating system residing on an unprivileged domain such as

SELinux for Linux guests, as well as use chroot environments or jails to run troubled applications. It is also important to make well-informed decisions when choosing a particular service to run. For example, you might want to choose a mail transport agent implementation that is known for its security over one with a history of problems. Depending on the data contained in the VM, more extreme measures may be in order that will decrease the performance of the overall machine. Such examples are encrypting the entire secondary memory with an encryption algorithm such as Blowfish or AES. This can be done easily in Linux through the use of the device mapper crypto target. Another extreme measure is to enable alternate security measures in the Linux kernel such as stack randomization. More general guest security is beyond the scope of this book, but many excellent security references are available.

Running VMs Only When Needed

Xen affords administrators another availability option that is usually not as realistic with physical machines, and that is running them only when needed. It would normally not be realistic to shut down a server at the end of the business day and restart it at the beginning of the next. However, with Xen, the process can be scripted, allowing the administrators to take sensitive servers down when no one should access them.

Backing Up Virtual Machine Images

One of the great advantages of running a VM is the ability to easily backup the device or file that resides on Domain0 that holds the contents of the unprivileged domains. Keeping current backups is a good idea to help limit the time to return to a known good state after a compromise.

One important idea to remember after a VM is compromised and a backup is restored is to patch the backup to prevent a future problem. If the attack and compromise were automated, such as a worm or some other fast-moving method, making use of Xen's extended networking capabilities may help bring the backup online and on the Internet to get patches without exposing the VM to infection again until it's ready.

Another interesting security aspect of using backups and restores of VMs is the ability to study certain security threats. The full image of a compromised guest can be saved for later forensic analysis. You can also keep a deliberately unpatched VM and continue to reinfect it. This can help you study different methods to prevent the infection and learn about its propagation.

Dangers of VM Backup and Restore

Backing up VM images can also introduce new and challenging security problems because backup VMs are often not fully patched. For example, in rolling back to an earlier VM image, patches applied since the last checkpoint could be removed. In general, it can be tempting to keep many rarely used VMs around for special purposes. Often VMs like this are not kept patched.

This can result in a constant flux of computers that appear online for a short while and then disappear for prolonged periods of time, making it difficult to maintain a network perimeter. For example, it can be difficult to fully eradicate a virus when old VMs can reappear and reintroduce the vulnerability back into a network. Having a large number of short-lived machines on the network can also make it difficult to track down the owner or source of offending machines.

Another problem with rolling back to a previous VM image is that a once deleted file could be unintentionally restored if the VM is rolled back to a prior known good restore point because of a crash or some other problem. Similarly, rolling back a VM can allow it to reuse information such as one-time encryption keys that have already been observed by an attacker.

Users can also cause network resource collision by suspending and then resuming their VMs. This is possible because the virtual machine will take a resource, say an IP address from the DHCP server, and then it is suspended. Sometime later, after the DHCP server has expired that lease and granted it to another computer, the VM may be restored and begin using that address, resulting in two machines with the same address on the network.

Addressing these challenges requires new administration strategies, such as including dormant VMs in the active effort that the administrator is already doing for the physical machines, or policies that require users to boot unauthorized VMs in an isolated virtual network segment. Special MAC address allocation strategies could be used to distinguish VMs from physical machines, and naming conventions that identify the owner of the VM could be employed.

Summary

In this chapter, we saw how to protect our privileged Domain0 from both standard attacks and attacks from within the VM itself. We also explored using the principle of granting the least privileges possible to guide us through security decisions on whether to separate tasks into different VMs or to organize your virtual network connections.

We also explored securing the unprivileged domains using more classical security methods that would be deployed on a physical computer. Appendix B has a complete list of commands for xm, including the security-related items in Xen.

References and Further Reading

Garfinkel, Tal and Mendel Rosenblum. "When Virtual Is Harder Than Real: Security Challenges in Virtual Machine Based Computing Environments." Stanford University Department of Computer Science.
> `http://www.stanford.edu/~talg/papers/HOTOS05/virtual-harder-`
> `hotos05.pdf.`

`iptables` Project Home Page. Netfilter Web site.
> `http://www.netfilter.org/projects/iptables/index.html.`

"Linux Firewalls Using iptables." Linux Home Networking.
> `http://www.linuxhomenetworking.com/wiki/index.php/Quick_HOWTO_`
> `:_Ch14_:_Linux_Firewalls_Using_iptables.`

"Red Hat Virtualization." Red Hat Documentation.
> `http://www.redaht.com/docs/manuals/enterprise/RHEL-5-manual/`
> `Virtualization-en-US/index.html.`

Sailer, Reiner et al. "Building a MAC-based Security Architecture for the Xen Opensource Hypervisor." Paper on mandatory access control in Xen.
> `http://www.acsac.org/2005/abstracts/171.html.`

Secure Hypervisor (sHype) Home Page.
> `http://www.research.ibm.com/secure_systems_department/projects/`
> `hypervisor/index.html.`

"Security Enhanced Linux." National Security Agency—Central Security Service Web site.
> `http://www.nsa.gov/selinux.`

"The su Command."
> `http://www.bellevuelinux.org/su.html.`

Xen Users' Manual.
> `http://www.cl.cam.ac.uk/research/srg/netos/xen/readmes/user/`
> `user.html.`

Deitel, Harvey M. "An introduction to operating systems," revisited first edition (1984). Addison Wesley, 673.

Rash, Michael. "Linux Firewalls: Attack Detection and Response with iptables, psad, and fwsnort." No Starch Press. 2007.

Chapter 12

Managing Guest Resources

You should now be comfortable with creating and managing guest images, including using different types of images as well as distributing different devices and resources to the guests. In this chapter, we cover some of the more advanced aspects of guest resource management. First we present tools for acquiring information that will be useful for assessing how resources are currently shared among guests. Then we move onto guest memory management, VCPU management including the VCPU scheduler, and finally end with IO schedulers. We include a discussion of Xen guest isolation characteristics, paying particular attention to handling of severe resource consumption in one guest so that other guests remain stable.

Accessing Information about Guests and the Hypervisor

In Chapter 6, "Managing Unprivileged Domains," we introduced xm list, a simple command for getting the status of running guest domains. A number of similar tools are available that provide access to detailed information about guests as well as the hypervisor—xm info, xm dmesg, xm log, xm top, and xm uptime. These tools lend themselves to tasks such as debugging odd behavior, getting a better understanding of what's going on under the hood, auditing the security of the system, and observing the impact of recent administrative actions.

xm info

The xm info utility provides a convenient command for grabbing systemwide and hardware information such as number of physical CPUs, hostname, and version of the hypervisor. Much of this information is not typically available from inside a guest, Domain0 or otherwise, because they see only virtualized devices and not the physical hardware. This information can be essential for performance analysis purposes. We start with an example of the xm info command being run as shown in Listing 12.1.

The rows in Listing 12.1 are gathered from three main sources: general system information, hardware specifications, and Xen-specific information. We cover each section in turn.

LISTING 12.1 An Example of xm info

```
[root@dom0]# xm info
host              : xenserver
release           : 2.6.16.33-xen0
version           : #7 SMP Wed Jan 24 14:29:29 EST 2007
machine           : i686
nr_cpus           : 4
nr_nodes          : 1
sockets_per_node  : 2
cores_per_socket  : 1
threads_per_core  : 2
cpu_mhz           : 2800
```

```
hw_caps                  : bfebfbff:20000000:00000000:    ➭
     00000180:0000641d:00000000:00000001
total_memory             : 3071
free_memory              : 0
xen_major                : 3
xen_minor                : 0
xen_extra                : .4-1
xen_caps                 : xen-3.0-x86_32
xen_pagesize             : 4096
platform_params          : virt_start=0xfc000000
xen_changeset            : unavailable
cc_compiler              : gcc version 4.1.2 20060928    ➭
     (prerelease) (Ubuntu 4.1.1-13ubuntu5
cc_compile_by            : root
cc_compile_domain        :
cc_compile_date          : Tue Jan 23 10:43:24 EST 2007
xend_config_format       : 3
[root@dom0]#
```

The first four attributes displayed are taken from the uname function and mostly relate to the privileged guest domain's kernel.

- **host**—The hostname of the system. This is not necessarily the DNS hostname the router assigned to the computer, but the local hostname usually displayed with the command prompt. Xen does not check whether the local hostname is the same as the DNS hostname.

- **release**—The Domain0 kernel's release number.

- **version**—The date that Domain0's kernel was compiled.

- **machine**—The platform the Domain0 kernel was built for. In the case of x86 architectures, such as i686 and i386, this attribute is not necessarily the precise hardware platform but is definitely compatible with the underlying hardware.

The next nine attributes displayed are all hardware specifications.

- **nr_cpus**—The number of logical CPUs present in the system. The number of logical CPUs in a system is the maximum number of threads that can be run simultaneously on all physical CPUs combined. Physical CPUs refers to the actual processors on the motherboard. Multiple threads can be run on each CPU due to either hyperthreading or multiple cores.

- **nr_nodes**—Number of NUMA cells. NUMA stands for Non-Uniform Memory Access and is a way of associating a specific processor to a specific portion of memory located physically closer to that processor for quicker access and some interesting features. If a computer's motherboard does not support NUMA, this value is set to 1 as is the case in Listing 12.1. If NUMA was supported this number would be greater than 1. The number of NUMA cells does not affect the total number of logical CPUS, only the distribution of work on those CPUs.

- **sockets_per_node**—Number of CPU sockets per NUMA cell. A socket is the physical location on which a processor sits. Only sockets that house a processor and are being used are recognized and counted as a socket.

- **cores_per_socket**—CPU cores per CPU socket. Today multicore processors are common. Each core acts like a separate CPU while sharing the caches. Thus each separate core acts as an independent logical CPU.

- **threads_per_core**—Whether single or multicore, a processor can also be enabled with hyperthreading technology. Due to the nature of the technology, each separate core may have hyperthreading capabilities, and therefore each core will be seen as two separate cores, or two logical CPUs.

- **cpu_mhz**—This is the maximum clock speed of each processor.

- **hw_caps**—Stands for hardware capabilities and is a bit vector representing the CPU flags also normally available in /proc/cpuinfo. These flags tell the operating system whether things such as Physical Address Extension (PAE) are available. The corresponding flags from cpuinfo for this particular machine are shown in Listing 12.2 and are much more readable than a bit vector. If you need to figure out whether your machine supports a feature such as PAE, look to this file.

LISTING 12.2 CPU Flags in /proc/cpuinfo

```
[root@dom0]# grep flags /proc/cpuinfo
flags           : fpu tsc msr pae mce cx8 apic mtrr mca cmov ➥
    pat pse36 clflush dts acpi mmx fxsr sse sse2 ss ht tm    ➥
    pbe lm constant_tsc pni monitor ds_cpl cid cx16 xtpr lahf_lm
[root@dom0]#
```

- **total_memory**—The total amount of RAM available, used and unused.

- **free_memory**—The amount of RAM not used by either guests or the Xen hypervisor. This memory is claimable if a guest requests more memory.

The rest of the attributes are Xen specific.

- **xen_major**—The first number in a Xen release number. This number represents a major turning point in the development of Xen. In this book we are only using Xen 3, which was a large improvement on Xen 2.

- **xen_minor**—The middle number in a Xen release number. This number represents additions of smaller features and fixes of major bugs while keeping the direction of the product to be represented by the xen_major number.

- **xen_extra**—The third and last number in a Xen release number. This represents minor changes such as bug fixes. The higher the extra number is, the more stable it should be compared to earlier versions.

- **xen_caps**—This contains the Xen hypervisor version, which currently would be either 2.0 or 3.0. It also specifies whether this is on an x86 or some other platform such as ppc, and whether it is built for 32-bit or 64-bit. Finally, a "p" would indicate that the hypervisor is Physical Address Translation or PAE enabled. It is called xen_caps because the Xen kernel version defines some of the capabilities of Xen.

- **xen_pagesize**—Size of blocks of data read from a block device, such as a hard drive, into main memory represented in bytes. This number doesn't really change except between 64-bit and 32-bit machines where the size of a page is 65536 bytes and 4096 bytes, respectively.

- **platform_params**—The Xen hypervisor reserves some amount of space at the top of virtual memory. This parameter shows the address at which the hypervisor turns over memory to the guests. Above this address, the hypervisor reigns. The value of this cut-off point depends on the amount of virtual memory available to the guest and is influenced by whether the system is 64-bit or 32-bit and whether it has PAE.

- **xen_changeset**—The mercurial revision number. This number is useful only if you compiled Xen from source code that was downloaded from the Xen mercurial version control server.

- **cc_compiler**—The compiler version of the hypervisor is important if you are planning on compiling modules or new guest kernels. The compiler version of a module and a kernel should be the same. If a module was not compiled correctly, you get a message similar to Listing 12.3 when trying to load the module using insmod.

LISTING 12.3 Module Load Errors

```
[root@dom0]# insmod ./ath/ath_pci.ko
insmod: error inserting './ath/ath_pci.ko': -1 Invalid module format
dom0# modinfo ./ath/ath_pci.ko
filename:       ./ath/ath_pci.ko
author:         Errno Consulting, Sam Leffler
description:    Support for Atheros 802.11 wireless LAN cards.
version:        0.9.2
license:        Dual BSD/GPL
vermagic:       2.6.18-1.2798.fc6 SMP mod_unload 586 REGPARM 4KSTACKS gcc-3.4
<entry continues, but is irrelevant for what we're discussing>
[root@dom0]#
```

The error received when trying to load the module in Listing 12.3, from the first command, is not very descriptive. However, compare the kernel and compiler version in the vermagic (a truncated form of version magic) line of Listing 12.3 (2.6.18-1.2798. fc6 and gcc 3.4), with the kernel and compiler versions given previously in Listing 12.1 (2.6.16.33-xen0 and gcc 4.1.2). vermagic is the kernel version and compiler that the module was compiled for. We can see that the kernel versions match in major and minor number (2.6), but one is 2.6.18 and one is 2.6.16. Also, one is compiled with gcc 3.4 and the other with gcc 4.1.2. In this case, the problem is the incorrect gcc version. The problem can be resolved by recompiling the module after switching the gcc version.

- **cc_compile_by**—The user that compiled the kernel.
- **cc_compile_domain**—An identifying marker, possibly the DNS hostname, of the user who compiled the kernel. If you compile your own kernel, you might not see anything displayed here.
- **cc_compile_date**—The date and time the kernel was compiled.

The last attribute is actually Xend specific.

- **xend_config_format**—This value is hard coded in the source code for xm info. It is used to represent certain features and formats supported by the current Xen version.

xm dmesg

The Xen hypervisor prints its own system messages independent of any guest's kernel. At the beginning of powering on a Xen server, right before booting Domain0, messages are printed prefixed with (XEN). This signifies a message from the hypervisor. The xm dmesg command is used to display just these hypervisor-specific messages, whereas the Linux dmesg command displays the Domain0's kernel messages as well as the hypervisor's messages.

For convenience, we view only the beginning and end of an example Xen dmesg output as shown in Listing 12.4.

LISTING 12.4 An Example of xm dmesg

```
[root@dom0]# xm dmesg

  __    __           ___   __ _   _       _
  \ \/ /__ _ __     |__ / / _ \| | | |   / |
   \  // _ \ '_ \     |_ \| | | | | | |_ __| |
   /  \  __/ | | |    ___) | |_| |  _| _|__| |
  /_/\_\___|_| |_|   |____(_)___(_) |_|     |_|

http://www.cl.cam.ac.uk/netos/xen
University of Cambridge Computer Laboratory

Xen version 3.0.4-1 (root@) (gcc version 4.1.2 20060928  ➥
    (prerelease) (Ubuntu 4.1.1-13ubuntu5)) Tue Jan 23 10:43:24 EST 2007
Latest ChangeSet: unavailable

(XEN) Command line: /xen-3.0.gz console=vga
(XEN) Physical RAM map:
(XEN)  0000000000000000 - 000000000009d400 (usable)
(XEN)  000000000009d400 - 00000000000a0000 (reserved)

<dmesg output removed here>

(XEN)  ENTRY ADDRESS: c0100000
(XEN) Dom0 has maximum 4 VCPUs
```

```
(XEN) Scrubbing Free RAM: .done.
(XEN) Xen trace buffers: disabled
(XEN) Std. Loglevel: Errors and warnings
(XEN) Guest Loglevel: Nothing(Rate-limited: Errors and warnings)
(XEN) Xen is relinquishing VGA console.
(XEN) *** Serial input -> DOM0                              ➤
(type 'CTRL-a' three times to switch input to Xen).
[root@dom0]#
```

With the `--clear` option, it's possible to clear the hypervisor's message buffer, as shown in Listing 12.5.

LISTING 12.5 Clearing xm dmesg Log

```
[root@dom0]# xm dmesg --clear
[root@dom0]# xm dmesg

[root@dom0]#
```

The buffer has been cleared so nothing is displayed the second time of running xm dmesg. There isn't much reason for doing this because the message buffer is circular; it will never run out of memory but instead overwrites older data.

xm log

There exist a few different logging constructs in Xen that report to three files: xend.log, xend-debug.log, and xen-hotplug.log, all contained in /var/log/xen/ by default. The log file names and locations can be changed either through /etc/xen/xend-config.sxp or their respective scripts. Listing 12.6 shows how to change the log file's location. The xend.log location is commented out, and a new location is specified for xend.log.

LISTING 12.6 Xend Log Configuration

```
#(logfile /var/log/xen/xend.log)
(logfile /xendlog/xend.log)
```

It's possible to set the logging level desired for xend.log. If you browse the Xen logs you will notice that most of the messages are DEBUG messages. These aren't always necessary and in some cases you may not want the clutter. To change the debug level, you must edit a line in xend-config.sxp that looks like Listing 12.7. The possible logging levels with severity in increasing order are DEBUG, INFO, WARNING, ERROR, and CRITICAL.

Messages to xend.log are usually only printed when an administrator executes a command on a guest, like starting, pausing, or shutting down guests. The amount of messages on the DEBUG level will not affect performance of the Xen system.

DEBUG messages contain information on the status of a current operation and the parameters that are passed to commands.

INFO mostly logs what commands the administrator has executed along with what virtual devices have been created and destroyed.

WARNING messages indicate that something irregular happened and may be a problem.

ERROR messages are printed when something is broken, like a guest was started unsuccessfully or other situations where Xen did not behave how the user requested.

A CRITICAL message means the entire Xen system may be broken, rather than a single guest or operation. You should never see a CRITICAL log message.

Unless you are developing guest images and testing if they are created successfully, the WARNING log level should suffice. On the other hand, if you aren't sure which logs you will need, the grep command can parse only the level of messages you want from the log.

LISTING 12.7 Loglevel Configuration

```
#(loglevel DEBUG)
(loglevel INFO)
```

The purpose and use of each log file is as follows:

- **xend.log**—Records actions of xm and programs that interact with Xend, and this is the file that xm log will print.

- **xend-debug.log**—When a script or program encounters a bug or some fault of the code, the output is printed to xend-debug.log. Look at this file if the xend.log file doesn't offer enough information when trying to fix a problem.

- **xen-hotplug.log**—Records errors that have to do with connecting or accessing devices such as vifs, virtual bridges, hard drives, and so on. The default location of this log file is the same as the other two, /var/log/xen. However, you can change where the log is saved by modifying a single line in /etc/xen/scripts/xen-hotplug-common.sh. The directory path in the line that looks like exec 2>>/var/log/xen/xen-hotplug.log should be changed to the location you want to print the log.

xm top

Similar to the top command in Linux, the xm top command runs an interactive ncurses program that displays all running guests in a formatted table with statistics on how they are using resources. xm top actually runs the program xentop, but the xm command in general can be more convenient because you only have to remember a single command. xentop is useful for forming a quick picture of what the system is doing at a given point in time and watching how certain actions affect the Xen system. Figure 12.1 shows what a typical instance of xentop looks like.

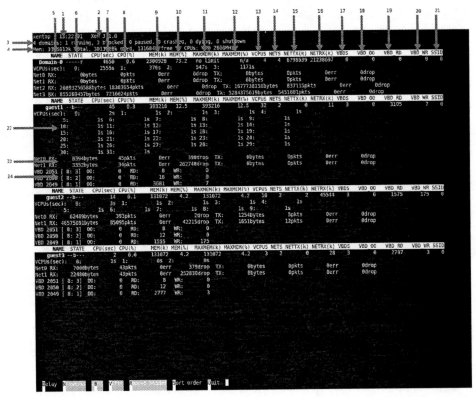

FIGURE 12.1 A screenshot of the xentop command showing running statistics on Domain0 as well as two other guest virtual machines

xentop displays a dynamic, changing list of statistics on all running Xen guests. This includes information otherwise difficult to obtain, such as percentage of CPU usage and percentage of memory usage per domain. The screenshot in Figure 12.1 has different elements numbered identifying its description in the following list:

1—Current wall clock time.

2—Xen version running.

3—The total number of domains followed by a tally of which domains are in which states. For a description of what the states mean, see the discussion of xm list in Chapter 6.

4—The total amount of physical memory, memory being used, and free memory.

5—The name of each domain in alphabetical order.

6—The state as would be printed in xm list.

7—The amount of time spent running on a CPU, as would be printed in xm list.

8—Current CPU usage presented as a percentage of total CPU potential in the system. Thus, if there's two CPUs, each is considered 50 percent of the total potential.

9—Amount of memory allocated to the domain. Covered later in this chapter.

10—Percentage of total system memory allocated to the guest domain.

11—Maximum amount of memory a domain may possess. Covered later in this chapter.

12—Maximum amount of memory a domain may possess presented as a percentage of total system memory.

13—Number of VCPUs owned by a guest domain whether they be active or inactive.

14—Number of network devices owned by a guest domain.

15—Amount of network traffic in kilobits that is leaving a domain through any interface it owns.

16—Amount of network traffic in kilobits that is entering a domain through any interface it owns.

17—Amount of VBDs forwarded to the domain.

18—The number of OO (Out of) requests for a block device. There are a number of kernel threads that work to satisfy read and write requests to VBDs. Sometimes a kernel thread is told by a scheduler that there are requests to satisfy, but no requests are found in the queue of requests. Thus, the kernel thread is out of requests. When the OO request counter is high, it is a sign that the physical block device cannot keep up with the guest's IO demand. When the OO request counter is low, the physical block device is sufficient for the current IO workload.

19—Number of read requests for any block device.

20—Number of write operations for any block device.

21—Used with labels and security issues covered in Chapter 11, "Securing a Xen System." SSID stands for service set identifier.

22—VCPUs the guest has, even if not currently in use, and a total of how many seconds each VCPU has spent executing on a logical CPU.

23—Network interfaces the guest is aware of and statistics on RX and TX.

24—Virtual Block Devices owned by the guest are shown as well as read and write statistics.

You can manipulate a lot of this data in several ways through command line arguments and hotkeys in the application. The Q key, for example, quits the application. The hotkey commands are shown at the bottom left of the xentop ncurses window shown in Figure 12.1.

The following list describes the keys that are used to interact with xentop after it's running. Many of these commands can also be passed to xentop on the command line when starting the program.

D—Sets the amount of seconds before the program queries for an update of all information.

N—Toggles the network interface statistics from being shown as in item 23 in the preceding list. This may also be set on the command line with the --networks option.

B—Toggles rows of data showing which virtual block devices are attached to which guest domains. This may also be set on the command line with the -x or --vbds option.

V—Toggles rows of data, showing which VCPUs are attached to which guest domains. This may also be set on the command line with the --vcpus option.

R—Toggles the VCPU statistics from being shown as in item 22 preceding. This may also be set on the command-line with the –repeat-header option.

S—Information is initially sorted in alphabetical order by name, but with this command, switches to sorting the data by each column.

Q—Quits the program.

Arrows—Scrolls through the table of guests. Scrolling is used when you have a lot of guest domains currently running.

The most typical reason for using `xm top` is looking for the guests that are using the most of some resource, like network bandwidth, processor time, or main memory. Another common usage is examining the effects of a DomU configuration change before and after the change takes place.

`xm uptime`

The classic Linux `uptime` command shows how long the current machine has been running since it was last booted. On a Xen machine in Domain0, `xm uptime` shows how long all the guests have been running since each of them was created. Listing 12.8 shows an example. This is not the same as the CPU time shown in the `xm list` command. `uptime` is independent of how much time a guest has been executing on any CPU.

LISTING 12.8 An Example of `xm uptime`

```
[root@dom0]# xm uptime
Name                        ID Uptime
Domain-0                     0 21 days,   3:08:08
generic-guest               19  6 days,   5:43:32
redhat-guest                27  1:16:57
ubuntu-guest                 1 21 days,   0:50:45
gentoo-guest                 4 21 days,   0:38:12
[root@dom0]#
```

Allocating Guest Memory

Memory is one of the resources that must be shared by all guests. Xen reserves a portion of memory at the beginning of the virtual memory address space for the hypervisor. (You may remember reading about this with the `platform_params` field at the beginning of this chapter.) The rest of the virtual memory is given to Domain0 and DomUs. This section describes some of the limitations and controls available for shared memory.

In Xen, as in most modern operating systems, physical memory is shared via a virtual memory abstraction. This provides security by making it impossible for separate guests or processes to even name each other's memory, let alone access it without hypervisor or operating system support. It also provides convenience by handling the paging to and from disk that provides programmers with the illusion of more usable memory than physically exists. Of course, this illusion can only be preserved so far. If processes on the machine are simultaneously and actively using more memory than exists, the performance of the entire system will slow to a crawl at disk speeds rather than DRAM access times.

To help prevent this performance problem and to protect well-behaved guests from a memory-guzzling guest, Xen enforces a limit on the amount of memory that can be consumed by each guest. During creation, a guest is designated a portion of memory logically separated from the memory space of other guests. The default amount of memory assigned is 256MB, but a different amount may be specified with memory=, a guest configuration parameter.

As a safety and security precaution, a limit to the amount of memory a guest may have is set in place. This limit is by default the initial allocation of memory to the guest or may be set in the configuration file with maxmem=. After creation, a guest's maximum allowed memory can be changed with the xm mem-max command, though changing maxmem above what it started at will not allow for any more memory because memory hot plugging is not implemented in Linux yet. However, decreasing maxmem and increasing it to the memory it started with after decreasing will work. Notice that the configuration file parameter is maxmem but the command line xm subcommand is mem-max.

For Domain0 there is also the ability to set a minimum amount of memory through the xend-config.sxp file. The line that contains this parameter looks like (dom0-min-mem 256). There currently is not a tool to set a minimum for unprivileged guests, but they do have a default minimum of 1MB. Be careful to not make a guest's memory allocation too low as this can cause the guest to become unstable. For example, in a Linux guest, this may trigger the Out Of Memory (OOM) killer. An OOM killer destroys processes to fit within the available memory constraint. The OOM killer tries to pick the least harmful way to free up more memory. The general guideline for picking processes to destroy is to select the process that has done the least amount of work, is using the most amount of memory, the least amount of processes possible, as well as other factors. Regardless, having processes automatically killed by the kernel is not a fun experience.

The strategy Xen offers for memory management is an excellent protective measure against misbehaving guests. In this case, misbehaving guests refers to guest domains hogging memory. Later in this chapter as well as Appendix E, "Xen Performance Evaluation," we discuss misbehaving guests in regards to other system resources.

Because a guest by default will not automatically request more memory, a misbehaving guest can never steal memory from another guest, though this may not be the case if you implement your own automatic memory manager. Thus, if a guest's process gets out of hand with memory usage, rendering the system inoperable, all other guests will see no performance degradation. However, in the case that Domain0 is the misbehaving guest, all guests are impacted because the other guests' vbd and vif drivers rely on corresponding backend drivers in Domain0. For this reason, it's generally a good idea to use Domain0 only for Xen administration and to not run any services beyond what is absolutely required, which was covered in Chapter 11.

Shadow Page Tables

Shadow page table memory is another type of memory that can be managed. A *page* is a block of data copied to main memory from a block device such as a hard drive, and a page table keeps track of which pages are currently in main memory. Guest domains maintain their own page tables, and the hypervisor translates these guest page tables into the real page tables to make the appropriate changes to files. This allows for easier porting of operating systems to Xen because less intrusive changes have to be made to the guest kernel.

The default amount of shadow memory is 8MB but may be set otherwise through the creation configuration file option `shadow_memory=`. The more main memory a guest has, the more pages it will potentially be accessing. Thus, some Xen developers (in `/etc/xen/xmexample`) recommend 2KB of shadow memory per MB of domain memory and a few MB of shadow memory per VCPU. In general, we do not recommend modifying the amount of shadow memory without a clear justification.

> **NOTE**
> Shadow page tables cause a significant performance hit. For this reason, hardware manufacturers, such as Intel and AMD, are developing ways to store these on chip. For more detail on this see `http://softwarecommunity.intel.com/articles/eng/1640.htm` and `http://www.amd.com/us-en/assets/content_type/white_papers_and_tech_docs/34434.pdf`.

Balloon Driver

Linux supports hardware and logical memory hotswapping, but the technique used can be complicated and was not available when Xen was first designed. However, the Xen balloon driver offers a unique and simpler alternative to hot plugging memory.

Rather than changing the amount of main memory addressed by the guest kernel, the balloon driver takes or gives memory pages to the guest operating system. That is, the balloon driver will consume memory in a guest and allow the hypervisor to allocate it elsewhere. The guest kernel still believes the balloon driver has that memory and is not aware that it is probably being used by another guest. If a guest needs more memory, the balloon driver will request memory from the hypervisor, then give it back to the kernel. This comes with a consequence; the guest starts with the maximum amount of memory, maxmem, it will ever be allowed to use.

When a user in Domain0 changes the memory allocated to a guest, the new memory request is written to an attribute stored in the XenStore file system. The attribute is target and represents the amount of memory Domain0 last requested the guest to have, not necessarily how much memory the guest has. The guest waits for a change in the target attribute and once changed, it will request the given amount through a hypercall to the hypervisor.

When a user changes the memory allocated to a guest from within the guest, a hypercall is made to the hypervisor to make the request without notifying Domain0. That is, the guest balloon driver only reads from XenStore but does not write to it. This has the effect of Domain0 being unaware of the change and not knowing the real amount of memory being used by the guest.

> **NOTE**
> For more information on how the Xen balloon driver works, read the paper "Resizing Memory with Balloons and Hotplug" in the Ottawa Linux Symposium Proceedings from 2006. This article can be found at www.linuxsymposium.org/2006/**hotplug**_slides.pdf.

From the user's perspective, interaction with the balloon driver from the guest's side of things is accomplished through a proc interface. A single file prints current memory statistics and accepts numbers from the user, possibly through the echo command, as memory requests. Listing 12.9 shows the proc interface to the balloon driver from a guest's perspective.

LISTING 12.9 Balloon Driver Status

```
[user@domU]$ cat /proc/xen/balloon
Current allocation:     64512 kB
Requested target:       64512 kB
Low-mem balloon:         5376 kB
High-mem balloon:           0 kB
Driver pages:            1268 kB
```

```
Xen hard limit:              ??? kB
[user@domU]$
```

The following list describes each row of information contained in Listing 12.9.

- **Current allocation**—Refers to the amount of memory that has already been given to the domain, and that the domain should know of.
- **Requested target**—The total amount of memory the guest has asked Domain0 for but does not necessarily have.

Unless you are involved with kernel device driver development, you shouldn't be concerned with `low-mem balloon`, `high-mem balloon`, and `driver pages`.

- **Low-mem balloon**—The portion of memory that the guest kernel can map in its kernel space directly. Faster to access than `high-mem`. The `low-mem balloon` value is how much the collection of `low-mem` can be expanded. The same goes for the `high-mem balloon` value. Together, the `low-mem` and `high-mem` values are the total amount of memory that may be added to the guest past what has already been allocated.
- **Driver pages**—A count of the number of pages that have been reserved for kernel device drivers running in the guest. Device drivers are allowed to reserve portions of memory from the allocated portion of memory in a guest.
- **Xen hard limit**—All question marks when the guest is under its maximum allowed memory. If the guest has requested above its maximum allowed memory, `xen hard limit` displays that limit.

If a user desired an automatic policy for memory management, one could be written without much trouble. A few components would be needed. A script would have to be installed into each guest that has automatic memory management. This script would watch the memory use of the guest through a command, such as free, and echo higher or lower requests for memory to the balloon driver proc interface. Examples of echoing a memory amount to the balloon driver from the guest operating system are shown later in this section.

Hardware-based Virtual Machines (HVMs) don't have to run the same drivers as the paravirtualized guests. Without the balloon driver, HVM guests are restricted to whatever memory they are allotted during creation. Fortunately, the balloon driver was modified to also work with HVM guests and in this case, memory management should work the same as paravirtualized guests.

> **NOTE**
> For a much more detailed discussion of the difference between paravirtualized and hardware virtualized memory in guests, read "Extending Xen* with Intel Virtualization Technology" in the *Intel Technology Journal*. The article can be found at `http://download.intel.com/technology/itj/2006/v10i3/v10-i3-art03.pdf`.

Improving Stability with Swap Space

As is true for even nonvirtualized computers, a good safety precaution is to have a swap partition set up in any guests that use a lot of memory. A swap space serves as a failsafe in the case that all or most of the available main memory is used. Pages of memory are moved to this swap space as temporary storage so there is room in main memory for new information to be stored. If a guest runs out of memory, and it does not have a swap device, then it will probably freeze and be unrecoverable. The malfunctioning guest may use a lot of CPU time as a consequence. Though this will not affect other guests, because of Xen's CPU scheduler, covered later, leaving a misbehaving guest running could waste a lot of energy and make the processor hot. When this happens, the domain will not be recoverable through offering it more memory because the failing guest doesn't have enough free CPU cycles to run its balloon driver for memory hot plugging. However, this protection comes with a price. In practice, memory accesses to swap run very slowly. This inefficiency is called *thrashing*, where the CPU is constantly swapping out pages and reading new data into main memory instead of processing the data. Realize that if two guests are contained on the same hard drive, the thrashing of one guest could affect the other by slowing down IO.

Managing the Allocation of Guest Memory

So far the nature of memory in Xen has been covered. Now a couple xm commands are presented that allow for ballooning memory.

xm mem-set

The command responsible for allocating and deallocating memory to a guest is xm mem-set. To start, we show the result of creating a guest with more memory than is currently free. Second, we show an example of setting the memory of a running guest higher when mem-max was not set for the domain on creation. We also show what happens with Domain0 memory during creation of a guest. Finally, we show how memory requests through the balloon driver work when sufficient memory is already freed to satisfy the request.

When there is not enough free memory to satisfy the memory requirement of a guest's creation, Domain0 will surrender any extra memory above its minimum memory limit to satisfy the request. So Domain0 deallocates its own memory to satisfy other guests. If this switch of memory doesn't satisfy the entire request, the guest is given less than it requested but is still created.

Listing 12.10 first shows the memory allocated to Domain0 and then shows the memory allocation after creating a guess with 1GB of memory.

LISTING 12.10 Memory Allocation Before and After Guest Creation

```
[root@dom0]# xm list
Name                           ID Mem(MiB) VCPUs State  Time(s)
Domain-0                       0     8092     4 r-----   158.5
[root@dom0]# xm create /etc/xen/domU.cfg mem=1024
[root@dom0]# xm list
Name                           ID Mem(MiB) VCPUs State  Time(s)
Domain-0                       0     7077     4 r-----   160.9
generic-guest                  1     1024     1 -b----     0.2
[root@dom0]#
```

We start with 1GB of free memory to show that there is enough memory to satisfy a request of 100MB. Listing 12.11 reflects this fact with the xm info command.

LISTING 12.11 An Example to Show Free Memory Information

```
[root@dom0]# xm info | grep free
free_memory            : 1024
[root@dom0]#
```

When we created our guest used in Listing 12.10, we didn't explicitly set a mem-max value. Thus, the default value is whatever the memory allocation was to start. If the guest requests anymore memory, it is denied, and the Xen hard limit warning is triggered. The initial amount of memory is 64MB. The request is recorded, but the hard limit warning is triggered, and no memory is given. The hard limit warning we speak of is the Xen hard limit line that shows 64512kB. If the warning was not triggered, the number would have remained as three question marks: "???".

Listing 12.12 shows an example of attempting to increase a guest's memory allocation when maxmem is not set. Notice that we are running commands from DomU and Domain0. The xm list command can be run only from Domain0, and we print the contents of /proc/xen/balloon to show the conditions inside the guest we are trying to change.

LISTING 12.12 Increase Memory When maxmem Has Not Been Set

```
[root@dom0]# xm list generic-guest
Name                     ID    Mem VCPUs      State    Time(s)
generic-guest             4    64    1        r-----    65.2
<Here we switch to the guest console>
[user@domU]$ cat /proc/xen/balloon
Current allocation:     64512 kB
Requested target:       64512 kB
Low-mem balloon:         5376 kB
High-mem balloon:           0 kB
Driver pages:            1268 kB
Xen hard limit:           ??? kB
<Back to Domain0>
[root@dom0]# xm mem-set generic-guest 100
<Here we switch to the guest console>
[user@domU]$ cat /proc/xen/balloon
Current allocation:     64512 kB
Requested target:      102400 kB
Low-mem balloon:         5376 kB
High-mem balloon:           0 kB
Driver pages:            1272 kB
Xen hard limit:         64512 kB
<Back to Domain0>
[root@dom0]# xm list generic-guest
Name                     ID    Mem VCPUs      State    Time(s)
generic-guest             4    64    1        r-----    78.3
[root@dom0]#
```

Now we show what a domain acts like when the configuration variable maxmem is set, in Listing 12.13. The domain is started with maxmem=256.

LISTING 12.13 Increasing Memory When maxmem Is Set

```
[root@dom0]# xm list generic-guest
Name                     ID    Mem VCPUs      State    Time(s)
generic-guest             5    64    1        r-----   191.4
[user@domU]$ cat /proc/xen/balloon
Current allocation:     65536 kB
Requested target:       65536 kB
```

```
Low-mem balloon:       198144 kB
High-mem balloon:           0 kB
Driver pages:            1024 kB
Xen hard limit:           ??? kB
[root@dom0]# xm mem-set generic-guest 256
[user@domU]$ cat /proc/xen/balloon
Current allocation:    262144 kB
Requested target:      262144 kB
Low-mem balloon:         1536 kB
High-mem balloon:           0 kB
Driver pages:            1024 kB
Xen hard limit:           ??? kB
[root@dom0]# xm list generic-guest
Name                      ID    Mem VCPUs      State   Time(s)
generic-guest              2    256     1      r-----    387.0
[root@dom0]#
```

The extra memory given to the guest is subtracted from the `low-mem balloon` value, and if maximum memory was high enough to make `high-mem` necessary, that would be subtracted too.

xm mem-max

The mem-max command in Xen is somewhat limited at the moment. Though it can increase or decrease the maximum memory parameter of domains on-the-fly, increasing the value above what it equaled during creation does not allow more memory. This is the problem of not being able to hotswap memory, which we discussed earlier.

Thus, we show an example of setting mem-max lower in Listing 12.14, continued from Listing 12.13.

LISTING 12.14 An Example of xm mem-max

```
[root@dom0]# xm mem-max generic-guest 256
[user@domU]$ cat /proc/xen/balloon
Current allocation:    262144 kB
Requested target:      262144 kB
Low-mem balloon:         1536 kB
High-mem balloon:           0 kB
Driver pages:            1024 kB
Xen hard limit:        262144 kB
[user@domU]$
```

Managing Guest Virtual CPUs

One of the most critical factors in critiquing system performance is CPU utilization. This involves the priorities processes are given to use processors as well as the scheduling of processes. In this section, we cover an interesting feature in Xen that allows for restricting which CPU's guests may run on or even giving a guest an entire CPU to itself to isolate it one step further from other guests. In the next section, we cover the scheduling of guests.

Comparing Virtual, Logical, and Physical Processors

Processors in Xen are virtualized so that they may be shared between many guests, and up to 32 virtual CPUs (VCPUs) may be given to any single guest. The number of VCPUS allowed in a single guest is not limited by the number of physical CPUs; there is a hard limit of 32. This hard limit is linked to an implementation detail—in particular, the number of bits stored in a long integer on 32-bit machines. The same limit was kept for 64-bit kernels.

There is no difference between the actual physical processor model and what is perceived in virtual guests with their virtual processors. The difference is that a virtual processor may not have all the cores of the real processor, but the virtual processor still functions with the same instruction set. If a virtual processor could pretend to be a different physical processor, this would be emulation and not virtualization.

In addition to virtual CPUs, there are also logical CPUs. Logical CPUs represent the total number of threads of execution that can simultaneously take place at any particular instance. The total number of logical CPUs determines how many VCPUs can be scheduled and running at any single point in time. If there are more VCPUs than logical CPUs, the VCPUs wait for other VCPUs to relinquish control of the logical CPU. Counting the number of logical CPUs in a Xen machine can be done with the rows in xm info labeled nr_cpus, nr_nodes, sockets_per_node, cores_per_socket, and threads_per_core. For a description of these xm info fields, see the "xm info" section at the beginning of this chapter.

The way the logical CPUs are numbered is important as well. Based on the numeration explained in the "xm info" section, logical CPUs are divided into a tree. The tree starts with NUMA cells if it's a NUMA machine, then the sockets or physical CPUs, then the number of cores in each processor, and finally the number of threads of execution each core is capable of. Figure 12.2 shows a possible numbering scheme for a NUMA machine, and Figure 12.3 shows a scheme for a UMA machine.

NUMA Cell 1				NUMA Cell 2			
Socket 1		Socket 2		Socket 3		Socket 4	
Core 1	Core 2	Core 3	Core 4	Core 5	Core 6	Core 7	Core 8
Core 1	Core 2	Core 3	Core 4	Core 5	Core 6	Core 7	Core 8
vcpu 1	vcpu 2	vcpu 3	vcpu 4	vcpu 5	vcpu 6	vcpu 7	vcpu 8

FIGURE 12.2 Logical CPU numbering in a dual processor, single core, hyperthreading NUMA machine

UMA			
Socket 1		Socket 2	
Core 1		Core 2	
Thread 1	Thread 2	Thread 3	Thread 4
vcpu 1	vcpu 2	vcpu 3	vcpu 4

FIGURE 12.3 Logical CPU numbering in a dual processor, single core, hyperthreading UMA machine

The virtual CPU(s) that are given to domains aren't initially tied to any specific CPU. Based on the CPU scheduler, which is covered later in this chapter, VCPUs run on whichever CPUs are free. However, there are tools in place to activate/deactivate VCPUs as well as restrict them to running on a specific processor, which is called *pinning*.

The number of VCPUs to be given to a guest, not logical CPUs, can be set on creation with the vcpus= parameter. A warning is given if the number is below 1 or above 32. Though VCPU hot plugging is implemented and functional, it is not possible to add more VCPUs than what a guest is created with. Thus, you can only decrease and increase the number of VCPUs to a maximum of the number the guest started with. The number of VCPUs a guest has equates to the number of processes that can be executed simultaneously given enough logical CPUs.

A lot of the isolation offered by Xen for CPU usage between guests is due to the VCPU scheduler and not VCPU management. The VCPU scheduler is covered in the next section.

HVM VCPU Management

An HVM guest runs most instructions on the CPU without help from the hypervisor. However, certain instructions are still required to be intercepted by the hypervisor as well as some interrupts and page faults. By running more commands directly rather than going through the hypervisor, there is the hope of a speed up. As a consequence, HVM guests are not capable of hot swapping VCPUs. HVM guests are allocated a certain amount at creation time, and that is the number they are stuck with.

> **NOTE**
> For a much more detailed discussion on the difference between paravirtualized and hardware virtualized VCPUs in guests, read "Extending Xen* with Intel Virtualization Technology" in the *Intel Technology Journal*. The article can be found at http://download.intel.com/technology/itj/2006/v10i3/v10-i3-art03.pdf.

VCPU Subcommands

Now the three xm subcommands used for VCPU management are discussed. These commands can list information about VCPUs, make certain VCPUs run on certain physical CPUs, and increase or decrease the amount of VCPUs a guest is granted.

xm vcpu-list

xm vcpu-list displays which guests have which VCPUs and which CPUs each VCPU runs on. The state of each VCPU is shown as well.

In Listing 12.15 we have generic-guest with 10 VCPUs. The VCPUs of generic-guest are assigned to CPUs based on the load of the CPUs. These assignments are likely to change as the processing load of the Xen system changes.

LISTING 12.15 Listing Virtual CPUs Assigned to and Virtual CPUs of Guests

```
[root@dom0]#xm vcpu-list
Name               ID   VCPU   CPU State   Time(s) CPU Affinity
Domain-0           0    0      2   -b-      772.6 any cpu
Domain-0           0    1      1   -b-      347.4 any cpu
Domain-0           0    2      3   -b-      243.2 any cpu
Domain-0           0    3      1   r--      135.4 any cpu
apache-serv        5    0      3   -b-      273.0 any cpu
fedora-img         4    0      2   -b-      192.7 any cpu
mirror             3    0      1   -b-      704.0 any cpu
generic-guest      12   0      0   -b-        8.2 any cpu
generic-guest      12   1      0   -b-        2.7 any cpu
generic-guest      12   2      3   -b-        0.2 any cpu
generic-guest      12   3      3   -b-        0.1 any cpu
generic-guest      12   4      2   -b-        0.1 any cpu
```

```
generic-guest          12      5      1     -b-        0.1 any cpu
generic-guest          12      6      3     -b-        0.2 any cpu
generic-guest          12      7      1     -b-        0.3 any cpu
generic-guest          12      8      2     -b-        0.1 any cpu
generic-guest          12      9      0     -b-        0.2 any cpu
[root@dom0]#
```

xm vcpu-set

When VCPUs are activated or deactivated, it is handled by hot plug within the guest such as the xm mem-set command. This is a capability that the Xen guest kernel must support, which comes by default in the kernels Xen uses.

Listing 12.16 is an example of the command in Domain0 used to change the number of VCPUs allocated to a guest and the corresponding system message printed in the guest operating system. First, we change the number of VCPUs of generic-guest to one, which means the guest no longer has to deal with SMP issues. The message returned, "Disabling SMP...", marks the change in the kernel. When we add seven more VCPUs to the domain, a message is printed saying that CPUs are being initialized. After initialization, the VCPUs are used just like normal.

LISTING 12.16 An Example of Using xm vcpu-set

```
[root@dom0]#xm vcpu-set generic-guest 1
[user@domU]$ Disabling SMP...
[root@dom0]#xm vcpu-set generic-guest 8
[user@domU]$ Initializing CPU#3
Initializing CPU#2
Initializing CPU#5
Initializing CPU#7
Initializing CPU#1
Initializing CPU#6
Initializing CPU#4
[root@dom0]#xm vcpu-set generic-guest 20
[root@dom0]#
```

Also, if we try to give a guest more VCPUs than it was initialized with on creation, the minimum amount of VCPUs are given to the domain, meaning the smaller value of the VCPU's argument or the number of logical CPUs in the system. No error message is printed, as in Listing 12.16.

`xm vcpu-pin`

`xm vcpu-pin` bridges the connection between virtual and physical CPUs. Virtual CPUs can be pinned to a physical CPU so that all operations run on that particular VCPU will be on that particular physical CPU. Listing 12.17 shows the `vcpu-pin` command in action with the same setup as in Listing 12.15. The first argument is the domain ID that owns the VCPU. The second argument is the virtual CPU number. The third argument is the physical CPU number to pin the VCPU to, or "all" to allow the VCPU to run on any physical processor.

LISTING 12.17 An Example of `xm vcpu-pin`

```
[root@dom0]# xm vcpu-pin 0 1 3
[root@dom0]# xm vcpu-list 0
Name              ID   VCPU   CPU  State   Time(s)  CPU Affinity
Domain-0          0    0      2    -b-     772.7    any cpu
Domain-0          0    1      3    -b-     347.5    3
Domain-0          0    2      3    -b-     243.4    any cpu
Domain-0          0    3      1    -b-     135.1    any cpu
[root@dom0]#
```

When to Manually Administer VCPUs

If you have a specific set of applications you'd like to run in a few guests, tuning/restricting your CPU usage would be an intelligent idea. You can restrict a guest that is less CPU-intensive by giving it one or fewer VCPUs while enabling a CPU-intensive guest with more VCPUs. Regardless of your decision, the following advice should be considered.

If you are planning on having a substantial number of guests running, we recommend sticking with the default settings for VCPUs. The only place that VCPU pinning may be advantageous is to restrict a CPU to run only for Domain0. Each guest relies on the services Domain0 offers to some degree, and enough guests can put a significant demand on Domain0 depending on the type of work they're doing—especially heavy I/O. Thus assigning Domain0 its own CPU can be advantageous for overall system performance.

Assigning more VCPUs to a guest than there are logical CPUs in the computer is generally not a good idea. The extra VCPUs will not be able to run simultaneously with the rest and may adversely impact performance by adding extra overhead.

To learn how to administer restrictions on the use and load of VCPUs, see the following section on scheduling.

Tuning the Hypervisor Scheduler

To understand how the hypervisor scheduler works, let's first explain what a normal operating system process scheduler does. This allows us to compare the two. The job of a process scheduler that can be found in any operating system's kernel is to cycle through "running" processes one at a time, or more than one at a time in the case of symmetric multiprocessors, and execute their instructions on a CPU. The policy of the scheduler dictates which process will run next and for how long. In Xen, guests are assigned VCPUs that are not attached to any specific CPU by default and therefore use their own process schedulers to execute processes on VCPUs. The VCPU scheduler in the Xen hypervisor decides which VCPU from which guest will run on which real CPU for how long.

In Xen 2.0, a few different schedulers were available, but some of them were removed in Xen 3.0 to be replaced by the credit scheduler. The credit scheduler is the default scheduler while the earliest deadline first (sEDF) scheduler is deprecated and planned for removal. We cover only the credit scheduler as this is planned to be the sole scheduler in the future.

The credit scheduler's main goal is to balance VCPU work over all the logical VCPUs, called *load balancing*, and to restrict the performance hit a misbehaving or CPU-intensive guest could have on any other guest, called *performance isolation*. Fortunately, the credit scheduler reaches better performance than its predecessors while maintaining a simpler interface for tweaking compared to previous schedulers.

Weight and Cap

On creation, each guest is assigned two numbers, a weight and a cap. A *weight* affects the amount of time a guest may have compared to other guests, in effect creating a ratio. A guest with a weight of 512 will have twice as much CPU time as a guest with 256. And if these were the only two guests on the Xen system, the guest with 512 would have two-thirds of the total CPU time (512 / (512 + 256)) and the guest with 256 would have the remaining 1/3 of the total CPU time (256 / (512 + 256)). The weight must be in the range of 1 to 65535, and the default is 256.

A *cap* is essentially a ceiling on the percentage of CPU time a domain may utilize. The value is a percent where 50 represents half of a CPU (50%), 100 represents a single

CPU (100%), and 200 represents two CPUs (200%). The default cap is set to 0, which equates to no limit. If a cap allows a guest to use more CPUs than exist in the system, the guest in effect has no limit.

Weight and cap are all a user needs to modify the performance of the scheduler. However, when we modify these variables in combination with VCPU pinning, discussed in the previous section, more CPU usage restrictions are possible. If a guest is pinned to a particular CPU, its weight gives it time only on that single CPU. Assuming other guests do not have pinned VCPUs, the scheduler balances all guests so that the pinned guest is granted more time on its chosen CPU.

The weight and cap of a guest decide the amount of CPU the guest may use. Using these values, VCPUs are put into queues, one queue per CPU, with a priority. The priority is either "over" or "under" depending on whether the VCPU used its allotted CPU time. They are given credits to spend on execution, which represents a VCPU's allotted time. Once a VCPU executes, it loses credits. When a VCPU spends credits, its priority will eventually reach "under" and be put in the queue behind VCPUs with "over" priority.

For most purposes, the credit scheduler settings could probably be left as the defaults. Only special cases, where you know exactly what you will be running, would warrant adjusting the cap and weight of a VCPU.

Protection from Misbehaving Guests

The credit scheduler offers the most isolation between guests compared to previous schedulers. The default behavior of the credit scheduler is to load balance VCPUs across physical CPUs. With the default cap and weight settings for each guest, if a guest starts using CPU cycles excessively it will not be able to interfere with the others. For example, if there are eight guests and one of them goes haywire, the offending guest will use most of the CPU capacity until other guests want to use more of the CPU. If all eight guests were to try working at their maximum capacity, they would each get one-eighth of the CPU time.

This protection is disrupted if a user changes the cap and weight settings. These settings could increase or decrease the protection provided. If a guest is given a smaller weight, that guest will be able to affect others less and be affected by the CPU use of other guests more. The opposite is true if the weight is increased. If the cap is changed from 0 to another value, the guest will be limited in the amount of CPU it's ever allowed to use. This would obviously increase protection, but the credit scheduler is already good at load balancing.

Using the Credit Scheduler Command

The command xm sched-credit accepts three options for accessing the credit scheduler. First is an option for displaying the scheduling information of a single guest. Second is an option to change the weight of a guest. Third is an option to change the cap.

Listing 12.18 shows the default values of a guest. The -d option chooses the guest domain to view, and if there are no more options, the default behavior is to print the scheduler values of a guest. If all domains were left to the default settings, each guest would have no limit to the amount of CPU it could utilize while sharing CPUs equally with other guests when there isn't enough CPU to totally satisfy all guests.

LISTING 12.18 An Example Displaying xm sched-credit Default Settings

```
[root@dom0]# xm sched-credit -d generic-guest
{'cap': 0, 'weight': 256}
[root@dom0]#
```

In the Listing 12.19, we change the weight to 500 with the -w option. Remember, this value doesn't mean anything without comparison to the weight of other domains. In any case, generic-guest now has more CPU time than before.

LISTING 12.19 An Example of Setting xm sched-credit Weight

```
[root@dom0]# xm sched-credit -d generic-guest -w 500
[root@dom0]# xm sched-credit -d generic-guest
{'cap': 0, 'weight': 500}
[root@dom0]#
```

The cap of a guest can be changed with the command in Listing 12.20. The guest is being given a maximum CPU usage of 50 percent of one CPU with the -c option.

LISTING 12.20 An Example of Setting xm sched-credit CPU Percentage (Cap)

```
[root@dom0]# xm sched-credit -d generic-guest -c 50
[root@dom0]# xm sched-credit -d generic-guest
{'cap': 50, 'weight': 500}
[root@dom0]#
```

It is also possible to set the weight and cap during creation of a guest through the creation configuration file. Listing 12.21 shows examples of the parameters that must be set.

LISTING 12.21 Set Cap and Weight in Guest Configuration File

```
cpu_cap=1000
cpu_weight=459
```

Choosing a Guest IO Scheduler

There are also schedulers for IO operations in Linux. These schedulers are not Xen specific, but the fact that multiple guests may share block devices potentially makes this parameter even more important. There are four IO schedulers in Xen: noop, deadline, anticipatory, and complete fair queuing. We explain the basic idea behind and the strengths of each scheduler.

Noop Scheduler

This scheduler is a simple implementation in that it only implements request merging. *Request merging* is the process of finding duplicate requests and servicing those requests only once.

Though this scheduler is simple, it still has its uses. Some high-end IO controllers have scheduling built into them. In these cases the noop scheduler, which imposes minimal policy on IO, may offer the best performance. Another benefit of noop is the decreased overhead involved in making requests to a storage device. The total amount of CPU cycles used to service a request is significantly decreased. However, if no hardware scheduler is built into storage, the number of IO requests serviced per minute will be far lower than using other schedulers.

Deadline Scheduler

This scheduler adds a queue so that it can sort the order of IO requests. It implements request merging, one-way elevator, and a deadline for each request. An *elevator* is an algorithm to sort requests in ascending or descending order. The term *elevator* is used because the problem is similar to that of moving an elevator most efficiently.

A write operation in Linux returns immediately, and programs don't block on them, so deadline favors reads by making their deadlines shorter than writes. This is a significant difference if you are mainly reading or writing to storage.

Anticipatory Scheduler (as)

The anticipatory algorithm is similar to deadline; it implements request merging, a one-way elevator, and deadlines. The main difference is when a request times out and the anticipatory scheduler decides to fulfill the request. When this happens, the scheduler waits a period of time to see whether another request from a nearby location will be received. If not, it returns to the usual list and acts exactly like the deadline scheduler.

If for some reason there are many single requests scattered across the drive, this scheduler would probably perform poorly. On average, however, it is considered faster than both deadline and noop. It's been recommended that this scheduler be used on small systems with low IO capabilities.

Complete Fair Queuing Scheduler (cfq)

Unless a Linux distribution changes it in the kernels it offers, this is the default IO scheduler. The goal is to achieve fair sharing of IO bandwidth. First, each process has an IO queue of its own, and each queue gets a portion of the IO time slice based on its IO priority. These process-specific queues can have request merging and elevator-style sorting. The IO priority is decided by the Linux process scheduler. Then the IO requests are batched into fewer queues, one for each IO priority level. These IO priority queues are not process specific. At this point, merging and elevator-style sorting can take place on the priority queues. If a process has time in its time slice, it is allowed to idle in order to wait for closer IO requests. This is essentially the same thing as the anticipatory scheduler.

This scheduler offers the best performance for the widest range of applications. It's also considered best for mid- to large-size servers with many processors and many storage devices. If you are unsure of which scheduler to use or you are not worried about achieving the most optimal IO performance, cfq is a safe bet.

Using IO Schedulers

To check which "elevator" or IO scheduler you are using, try one of the commands in Listing 12.22. The first command may not work if too many system messages were printed and the beginning of the buffer was overwritten. However, the dmesg command tells you what the default IO scheduler is. The second command doesn't necessarily tell you what the default IO scheduler is for all devices, but it does tell you the IO scheduler being used for a specific device. The hda in the second command can be replaced with whatever device is connected and recognized on the system.

LISTING 12.22 Display IO Scheduler Informaiton

```
[root@linux]# dmesg | grep "io scheduler"
io scheduler noop registered
io scheduler anticipatory registered
io scheduler deadline registered
io scheduler cfq registered (default)
[root@linux]# cat /sys/block/hda/queue/scheduler
noop anticipatory deadline [cfq]
[root@linux]#
```

To change the default IO scheduler, all you have to do is add a parameter to your guest's kernel command line, be it Domain0 or a DomU. However, if you change it for a guest, you normally do not have direct access to the kernel command line. So for Domain0, an example GRUB configuration for changing the scheduler to anticipatory is displayed in Listing 12.23. The four options are noop, as, deadline, and cfq.

LISTING 12.23 Change IO Scheduler in Guest's Kernel Command Line

```
title Fedora w/ Xen 4.0.4-1
    kernel /xen.gz root_mem=512M
    module /vmlinuz-2.6.16.33-xen ro root=/dev/hda1 elevator=as
    module /initrd-2.6.16.33-xen
```

For a guest domain, `elevator=as` would be added to its configuration file.

You may also be able to change this during runtime, which makes testing much more convenient. Listing 12.24 shows how. To change to any of the schedulers, use the names displayed in the scheduler file.

LISTING 12.24 Changing the IO Scheduler at Runtime

```
[root@linux]# echo "anticipatory" >/sys/block/hda/queue/scheduler
[root@linux]# cat /sys/block/hda/queue/scheduler
noop [anticipatory] deadline cfq
[root@linux]#
```

Notice the `hda` in the chain of directory. If you change the scheduler in this fashion, you will only be changing it for that particular IO device. If you change the default scheduler through the kernel command line, you change the default scheduler for all IO devices that will be detected.

This is a relatively easy way to switch IO schedulers. It's recommended that you make a set of tests that mimic the sort of operations you will be making your system perform and compare the results of those tests for every IO scheduler. There are no clear guidelines as to which scheduler is best for which applications and tasks; each user situation is unique. Thus, lots of testing is the only way to optimal IO performance.

Summary

You should now be familiar with what resources are available for distribution to guests and how those resources can be monitored and distributed. We showed how to get information on the physical hardware such as memory and processors as well as the virtual equivalents for each guest. In addition, we showed ways to restrict or change the use of these resources such as pinning VCPUs to physical CPUs and ballooning guest memory dynamically. With this knowledge, more advanced configurations and debugging opportunities are possible. Appendix B, "The xm Command," contains a reference of the xm commands that were used in this section.

In Chapter 13, "Guest Save, Restore, and Live Migration," we cover three interesting features available in Xen. These features allow for the state of a running guest to be saved on one physical machine and restored to become the same running guest on another physical machine. Furthermore, live migration allows for this movement from one physical machine to another without stopping the guest.

References and Further Reading

Archived Xen Developer's Mailing List.
> `http://sourceforge.net/mailarchive/forum.php?forum_name=xen-devel.`

Chisnall, David. The Definitive Guide to the Xen Hypervisor. Amazon.com.
> `http://www.amazon.com/Definitive-Hypervisor-Prentice-Software-Development/dp/013234971X.`

"Credit-Based CPU Scheduler." Xen Wiki.
> `http://wiki.xensource.com/xenwiki/CreditScheduler.`

"Extending Xen* with Intel® Virtualization Technology." Intel Technology Journal.
> `http://download.intel.com/technology/itj/2006/v10i3/v10-i3-art03.pdf.`

Love, Robert. "Kernel Korner - I/O Schedulers." Linux Journal.
> `http://www.linuxjournal.com/article/6931.`

Matthews, Jeanna N. et al. "Quantifying the Performance Isolation Properties of Virtualization Systems." Clarkson University.
> `http://people.clarkson.edu/~jnm/publications/isolation_ExpCS_`
> `FINALSUBMISSION.pdf`.

Pratt, Stephen. "Workload Dependent Performance Evaluation of the Linux 2.6 I/O Schedulers." Proceedings of the Ottowa Linux Symposium 2004, vol 2.
> `http://www.linuxsymposium.org/proceedings/LinuxSymposium2004_`
> `V2.pdf`.

Schopp, J. H. et al. "Resizing Memory with Balloons and Hotplug." Proceedings of the Ottowa Linux Symposium 2006 vol 2.
> `http://www.linuxsymposium.org/2006/linuxsymposium_procv2.pdf`.

Shakshober, D. John. "Choosing an I/O Scheduler for Red Hat® Enterprise Linux® 4 and the 2.6 Kernel." Red Hat Magazine.
> `http://www.redhat.com/magazine/008jun05/features/schedulers/`.

Xen 2.0 and 3.0 User Manual. University of Cambridge.
> `http://www.cl.cam.ac.uk/research/srg/netos/xen/documentation.`
> `html`.

XEN: Benchmarks
> `http://www.bullopensource.org/xen/benchs.html`.

## Chapter 13

Guest Save, Restore, and Live Migration

In this chapter, we begin by exploring Xen's capability to easily checkpoint the state of a guest domain to disk for quick restoration at a later time. We continue by exploring how Xen makes the migration of guest domains a simple and powerful administrative task. We discuss cold static migration, warm static migration, and live migration of guests, along with the prerequisites and benefits of each.

Representing the State of a Virtual Machine

At the heart of any migration is the ability to fully represent the state of a guest. When a guest virtual machine is completely shut down, this is trivial. An inactive Xen guest is completely defined by its file system image(s), configuration file, and its operating system kernel. Clearly, a guest could be cloned or even moved to another physical machine by making copies of these files. Backup of a guest can be accomplished in this way.

A guest that is active in execution, on the other hand, is a more complicated matter. While a guest is running, saving its state additionally involves creating a snapshot of its memory, device I/O states, open network connections, and the contents of its virtual CPU registers. Xen can save this state information to disk or transfer it over the network, which allows for both backup and migration of VMs.

This idea of saving the state of a running guest is similar to the hibernation feature on many personal computers, which is especially popular among laptop users. In hibernation, a system's state is checkpointed and saved to disk so that the system can park the hard drive heads, power down, and resume its previous state next time it is powered up. Laptop users sometimes rely on this feature to temporarily suspend the state of the machine when moving from place to place, or for conserving battery power when the laptop is not being used. In the case of a virtual machine monitor like Xen, a similar facility can be used to checkpoint states to facilitate rollback in the event a guest fails, or to save the state of a guest past the shutdown of the physical machine on which it is running.

Xen provides a domain save and restore facility to handle the suspension of guest VMs to checkpoint files, operated by the `xm save` and `xm restore` commands. When a guest is saved to disk it is suspended, and its resources are deallocated. As in the case of hibernate, ongoing network connections are not preserved.

With the `xm migrate` command, Xen supports warm static migration (regular migration), where a running guest is temporarily suspended and then relocated to another physical host, as well as live migration, where a guest may be relocated from one host to another seamlessly, without dropping ongoing network connections and with little client perceptible delay. Live migration is particularly useful when bringing down a physical machine for maintenance. In this case, guests can be relocated to a new physical machine in preparation for the maintenance without a disruption in service. The ability to relocate a guest is also useful for load balancing guests and their resource consumption.

In this chapter, we discuss the uses of xm save, xm restore, and xm migrate in detail.

Basic Guest Domain Save and Restore

Xen makes it possible to suspend a guest domain, save its state to a file, and resume that state later through its domain save and restore facility. Figure 13.1 illustrates the process of saving a guest's state to disk. As with hibernation, when a domain's state is saved on disk, it is suspended, and network connections to and from that guest are interrupted (due to TCP timeouts).

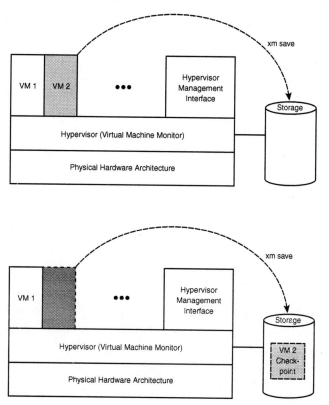

FIGURE 13.1 Xen provides an easy-to-use facility for hibernating guests to checkpoint files, to be restored at a later point in time.

xm save

Saving a guest VM's state first suspends that guest VM and then dumps its state information to disk. The guest VM will not continue to execute until it is restored, much like in the case of hibernation.

Listing 13.1 shows the syntax of this command.

LISTING 13.1 Usage of xm save

```
xm save domain filename
```

When performing an xm save, an administrator supplies a filename argument to specify where the serialized state of the guest VM should be written. This file is colloquially called a *checkpoint file*. This does not erase any previously saved checkpoints. You are free to save as many distinct checkpoints as you want. Thus it is possible to archive a collection of different running states for a particular guest domain.

Either a guest domain ID number or domain name may be supplied as the domain argument. After running this command, Xen suspends the state of the guest-specified domain to the specified file, and the domain no longer executes on the host. Thus it is impossible to save the state of Domain0 in this fashion because the Xen Domain0 must remain operational as the control interface between the administrator and Xen.

In Listing 13.2, we show the output of xm list running in Domain0. The output shown illustrates we are running a guest domain named TestGuest that has 64MB of RAM allocated to it.

LISTING 13.2 Domains Running on Domain0 (Before Checkpointing)

```
[root@dom0]# xm list
Name                      ID Mem(MiB) VCPUs State    Time(s)
Domain-0                   0      511     2 r-----    1306.0
TestGuest                  1       63     1 -b----       4.5
[root@dom0]#
```

To save TestGuest's state, the corresponding ID number needs to be noted and passed as an argument to the xm save command. In Listing 13.2 we see that the ID that corresponds with TestGuest is 1, and an example suspension using the checkpoint file name TestGuest.checkpt is shown in Listing 13.3.

LISTING 13.3 Checkpointing a Guest's State Using xm save

```
[root@dom0]# xm save 1 TestGuest.checkpt
[root@dom0]#
```

Note that replacing 1 with TestGuest as an argument to xm save also works. We know that the state of TestGuest has successfully finished saving when it is no longer listed as residing on Domain0, which we check by invoking xm list as shown in Listing 13.4. The xm save command does not return immediately, but instead returns after checkpointing is complete.

LISTING 13.4 Domains Running on Domain0 (After Checkpointing)

```
[root@dom0]# xm list
Name                       ID Mem(MiB) VCPUs State   Time(s)
Domain-0                    0      511     2 r-----   1411.8
[root@dom0]#
```

We can observe that our checkpoint file now exists in the present working directory and determine its size by issuing the ls -la command as shown in Listing 13.5. The ls -lah command may instead be used to view file sizes that are more human readable.

LISTING 13.5 Checkpoint File

```
[root@dom0]# ls -la
-rwxr-xr-x 1 root root 67266796 Feb  6 03:54 TestGuest.checkpt
[root@dom0]#
```

Now that TestGuest has been suspended, is no longer executing, and has been saved to a state file, we have successfully used Xen's domain save facility. Note that if there is not enough disk space to save the checkpoint file, the guest remains running and the xm save command fails with a generic error message.

A checkpoint contains the contents of the entire memory state of the guest. Thus, the time required to save the guest's state is proportional to the amount of memory allocated for the guest. The size of the checkpoint file is also approximately the same as the amount of memory allocated to the guest VM, plus a small amount of extra disk space to store additional state information.

Listing 13.6 shows the output of xm list for a system with three sample guests—one with 64 megabytes, one with 128 megabytes, and one with 256 megabytes of RAM allocated. Table 13.1 shows the size of the checkpoint file and the total time taken to save each of these guests. In all three cases, the checkpoint file is slightly larger than the amount of memory allocated to the guest. It is also clear that the time taken to complete the save grows with the an increase in amount of allocated memory. The actual time taken to save the guest's state varies with the speed of the underlying file system and the hardware used to store the checkpoint file.

LISTING 13.6 Domains Running on Domain0 with Varying Memory Allocations

```
[root@dom0_Host1]# xm list
Name                     ID  Mem(MiB) VCPUs State   Time(s)
Domain-0                  0      511    2 r-----   1306.0
Guest64MB                 7       63    1 -b----      3.1
Guest128MB                8      127    1 -b----      2.8
Guest256MB                9      255    1 -b----      2.1
[root@dom0_Host1]#
```

TABLE 13.1 Checkpoint File Size and Time Proportions

Actual Guest RAM Allocation (MB)	File Size On Disk (MB)	Time to Save Guest State (sec)
65.5	67.1	0.859
130.8	134.5	2.426
261.9	268.7	4.802

xm restore

Restoring a guest domain from a state file is initiated by the xm restore command. Listing 13.7 shows the syntax of this command.

LISTING 13.7 Usage of xm restore

```
xm restore filename
```

On the execution of this command, Xen restores the state of the guest located in the specified filename. The numerical domain ID of a guest domain is not preserved through save and restore, so no consideration needs to be taken to avoid an ID conflict—a unique ID is automatically assigned when restoring a guest from a checkpoint file.

On Domain0, we currently have a state file for a domain in the present working directory, observed by issuing the ls command, as shown in Listing 13.8.

LISTING 13.8 Checkpoint File

```
[root@dom0]# ls
TestGuest.checkpt
[root@dom0]#
```

Note that no guest domains are currently residing on Domain0, by invoking `xm list`, as we do in Listing 13.9.

LISTING 13.9 Domains Running on Domain0 (Before Restoration)

```
[root@dom0]# xm list
Name                       ID Mem(MiB) VCPUs State   Time(s)
Domain-0                    0     511      2 r-----   1702.2
[root@dom0]#
```

To restore the domain from our checkpoint file, we issue the `xm restore` command with its checkpoint's file name as an argument, as in Listing 13.10.

LISTING 13.10 Restoring a Guest's State Using `xm restore`

```
[root@dom0]# xm restore TestGuest.checkpt
[root@dom0]#
```

We know that restoration is complete when we can observe TestGuest residing on Domain0, by invoking `xm list`, shown in Listing 13.11. The `xm restore` command will not return until restoration is complete. Once TestGuest is restored from a state file, it continues executing where it left off at the time it was suspended, though network connections are likely to have timed out.

LISTING 13.11 Domains Running on Domain0 (After Restoration)

```
[root@dom0]# xm list
Name                       ID Mem(MiB) VCPUs State   Time(s)
Domain-0                    0     511      2 r-----   1795.9
TestGuest                   2      63      1 -b----      0.4
[root@dom0]#
```

Xen's domain save and restore facility has several potential uses. For example, the ability to restore from checkpoints may potentially be used in developing a rapid crash recovery procedure, where a guest is restored to a default state much faster than rebooting. Similarly, it is also useful while debugging or testing changes to a system, by allowing an administrator to save quickly restorable checkpoints that can be reverted to in the event of a failure. Quick installs cannot be performed simply by providing such an image because checkpoint files do not contain a guest's file system contents; instead, quick installs and zero setup installations would require an image of a guest's file system, and optionally a checkpoint file, if it is desired to ship the installation with the guest being in a particular execution state.

Possible Save and Restore Errors

Listing 13.12 shows the error that occurs when there is not enough disk space to store the checkpoint file of a guest at the location of the path specified by the user. You should free up space or specify a different path to store the checkpoint file to fix this problem. If you specify a checkpoint file name that is the same as an existing file name, `xm save` overwrites the existing file without warning.

LISTING 13.12 Error: xm_save failed

```
[root@dom0]# xm save TestGuest TestGuest.checkpt
Error: /usr/lib64/xen/bin/xc_save 46 82 0 0 0 failed
Usage: xc save <Domain> <CheckpointFile>

Save a domain state to restore later.
[root@dom0]#
```

The error shown in Listing 13.13 can occur under several circumstances. This message commonly occurs when the domain contained in the checkpoint file you specified is already running. The message may also occur if the checkpoint file you specified is corrupt or invalid, or in situations where there is not enough RAM on the host system to restore the guest contained in the checkpoint file you specified.

LISTING 13.13 Error: Restore failed

```
[root@dom0]# xm restore TestGuest.checkpt
Error: Restore failed
Usage: xm restore <CheckpointFile>

Restore a domain from a saved state.
[root@dom0]#
```

Listing 13.14 shows a different type of restore error. This occurs when the checkpoint file is inaccessible, which happens if the checkpoint file you specified does not exist, is inaccessible due to permissions, or cannot be read due to device error.

LISTING 13.14 Error Message When `xm restore` Is Unable to Read File

```
[root@dom0]# xm restore TestGuest.checkpt
Error: xm restore: Unable to read file /root/TestGuest.checkpt
[root@dom0]#
```

Types of Guest Relocation

The ability to easily move a guest operating system across the network from one physical host to another can be useful for a number of different administrative tasks such as load balancing or dealing with scheduled maintenance. Xen provides integrated relocation, or migration, support as illustrated in Figure 13.2. It helps manage the process of preparing, transporting, and resuming guests from one nearby host to another.

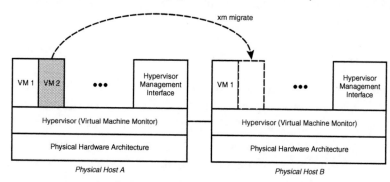

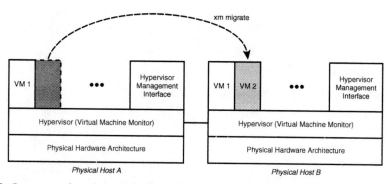

FIGURE 13.2 Guests may be relocated (migrated) between different Xen servers for various administrative purposes.

For comparison purposes, we begin our discussion about guest relocation by intro-ducing the concept of cold static relocation, in which an administrator manually copies all the files that define a guest to a different machine, and executes xm create to start the guest at its new location. We then discuss Xen's integrated migration facility, which automates two major paradigms of guest relocation over a network—warm static mi-gration and live migration. For warm static migration (also called regular migration), a guest is suspended on its source host, all relevant state information is transferred to its destination host, and the guest is resumed on its destination host after its state and memory have been safely relocated. This process is effectively the same as checkpoint-ing a guest, manually copying the checkpoint file to another host, and restoring the guest on the new host. Warm static migration does not preserve ongoing network con-nections and does expose client visible downtime; for live migration, however, a guest is transferred without being suspended, and its services and connections are not only preserved but continue effectively uninterrupted.

Cold Static Relocation

Cold static relocation is accomplished manually without the help of Xen's integrated migration facility. Understanding the elements of this manual process aids in a better understanding of and an appreciation for the xm migrate command.

A halted guest may be relocated between two hosts by ensuring that its configura-tion file appears on and its file systems are available to both hosts. There are two ways of accomplishing this goal. The first occurs when both hosts share underlying storage (network attached storage). The second method involves manually copying the con-figuration file and file systems from the host to the target hardware. In the latter case, manual copying might take a long time because a guest's file systems might be very large. The transfer of a guest's file systems and configuration file by manual means might occur, for instance, through the use of optical media or FTP/SFTP. A much simpler option is to store the guest's file systems on network-attached storage, which makes copying unnecessary to make the guest's file systems available on both the source and destination hosts.

A running guest might also be relocated using this method, but must first be sus-pended to a checkpoint file. A guest domain may be checkpointed using the xm save command. Once suspended, a guest may be relocated by ensuring its file systems, checkpoint file, and configuration file are accessible on the destination host. When two physical hosts share the same underlying storage, this is equivalent to what xm migrate does for our next type of relocation, warm static migration.

Warm static migration could also be performed by manual copying methods if the two physical hosts did not share the storage systems on which all the needed files were stored. Once these three components are available on the desired destination host, the guest may be reactivated using the xm restore command.

Be advised that invoking xm create for the same guest domain on two different hosts at once has serious ramifications. Although the configuration file and operating system kernel would remain undamaged, multiple guests manipulating the same storage directly would likely lead to file system corruption.

Warm Static (Regular) Migration

Warm static migration, or regular migration, of a guest domain is the combined process of pausing the execution of that guest's processes on its original host, transferring its memory and processes from its origin host to a destination host, and resuming its execution on the destination host. Warm static migration enables a domain to be migrated from one physical host to another, only temporarily pausing its execution, without requiring it to be shut down and restarted. This is illustrated in Figure 13.3. Xen provides fast and simple integrated facility for performing regular migration of guest domains between hosts for load balancing, transferring from old to new hardware, or bringing physical hosts down for maintenance while adopting their guests on other hosts.

Migration requires a guest's memory contents to be transferred, I/O transactions temporarily quiesced, CPU register states transferred, and network connections rerouted and resumed on the destination host. Xen does not currently support the automatic mirroring of a guest's file systems between different hosts, nor does it automatically transfer a guest's file systems, because the act of copying an entire root file system is often too cumbersome to instantaneously transfer during migration. As a result, if a Xen user wants to use Xen's integrated migration support, it is currently necessary to configure guests to access their file systems over network shares that are equally available to both the source and destination host. In regular migration, a guest domain is suspended to easily handle the transfer of guest memory pages that would be continuously changing if the guest was otherwise allowed to continue to run. Suspending the guest also satisfies the need to quiesce I/O.

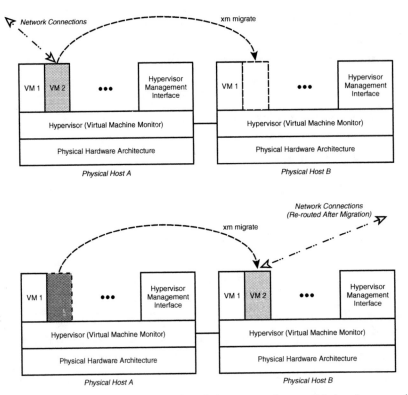

FIGURE 13.3 In warm static migration, a guest domain is temporarily suspended on its source host prior to relocation and resumed on its destination host after its memory contents have been transferred.

Live Migration

The mere ability to migrate a guest domain from one physical host to another is beneficial, but performing migration by temporarily suspending and then restoring a guest's state is not suitable in all applications. This process of migration can incur outages that are perceptible to system users. These sorts of outages are typically on the order of seconds or minutes, depending on the network infrastructure and the amount of memory a guest is allocated. Warm static or regular migration is not applicable for use in situations where in-use guests must be relocated without their services experiencing downtime; instead, in such situations, the ability to migrate a guest while maintaining its current state, operation, and network connections is desired.

Xen's third form of relocation, live migration, enables a domain to be migrated while it is in operation and without the interruption of its services or connections, as illustrated in Figure 13.4. Live migration of a guest is the act of seamlessly moving its execution to the new physical host, including redirecting established and future network connections away from its original and to its new location.

Live migration is considerably more complicated than regular migration primarily because the state of the guest is changing while it is being copied. This requires an iterative process of copying the state, checking to see what has changed in the meantime, and then copying what has changed.

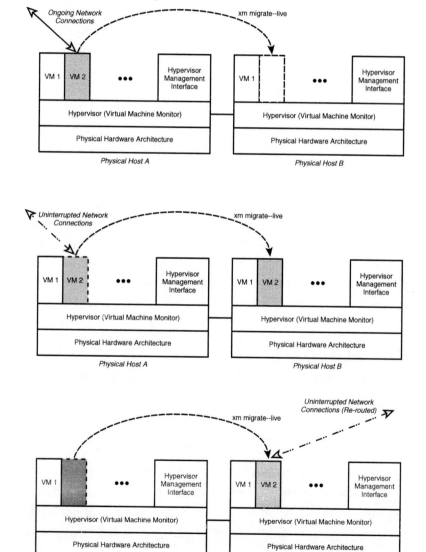

FIGURE 13.4 In live migration, a guest domain continues to execute and remains available throughout relocation, and client connections to its services go uninterrupted.

Making memory that belongs to an active guest available on a different host system is difficult because processes that are executing and memory pages that are swapped to and from disk consistently alter the contents of memory and consistently make attempted copies out-of-date. Like regular migration of a guest, Xen's live migration must also transfer and restore CPU register states, quiesce I/O transactions, and reroute and resume network connectivity on the destination host; however, in live migration, these events must occur in a way and over a small enough duration that there is no perceptible downtime of the guest's services. Additionally, like regular migration, a guest's file systems must be network-accessible to both the source and destination hosts.

The implementation of Xen's live migration involves the novel use of an iterative multipass algorithm that transfers the virtual machine guest memory in successive steps. After the source VM and the destination VM first negotiate to ensure resources are sufficient on the receiving machine, an initial pass over the guest's memory is performed with each page being transferred to the destination. On each successive iteration, only the guest memory that has been dirtied in the interim is sent. This process is executed until either the remaining number of dirty guest pages is sufficiently small enough that the remaining pages can be transmitted quickly or the number of dirty pages remaining to transfer in each pass is not decreasing. At that point, the system is actually quiesced and the final state sent to the new host and the transfer of control to the new physical machine completed. In most cases, this final step can be accomplished so quickly that there is no client perceptible delay and ongoing network connections are preserved.

Preparing for xm migrate

To support regular and live migration, a Xen configuration must include the following:

- Two or more physical hosts with xend configured to listen for relocation requests
- Hosts that are members of the same layer-2 network
- A storage server that is accessible by guests on both the source and destination hosts, which provides network access to guests' root and all other file systems
- A configuration file for each guest on both the source and destination hosts
- Sufficient resources on the destination host to support the arrival of guests
- The same version of Xen running on both the source and destination hosts

In the subsections that follow, we cover each of these steps in detail.

Configuring `xend`

To enable relocation (migration) support between hosts we must first edit their `xend` configuration files. In `/etc/xen/xend-config.sxp` on each host (or `/etc/xen/xend.conf`, depending on your system), remove the comment character ("#") from the beginning of each of the following lines if necessary (note that these lines might not immediately follow one another), as illustrated in Listing 13.15.

LISTING 13.15 An Example `/etc/xen/xend-config.sxp` Prior to Enabling Relocation Support

```
#(xend-relocation-server no)
#(xend-relocation-port 8002)
#(xend-relocation-address '')
#(xend-relocation-hosts-allow '')
```

On the `xend-relocation-server` line, ensure the value is set to yes. This enables `xend` to listen for relocation requests from other hosts so that it can receive the relocated guests. These lines should now read as shown in Listing 13.16.

LISTING 13.16 An Example `/etc/xen/xend-config.sxp` After Enabling Relocation Support

```
(xend-relocation-server yes)
(xend-relocation-port 8002)
(xend-relocation-address '')
(xend-relocation-hosts-allow '')
```

The second and third lines specify the port and address that `xend` should listen on for incoming migration requests. You may change the `xend-relocation-port` or leave it the default, port 8002. Leaving the `xend-relocation-address` field blank between the single quotes configures `xend` to listen on all addresses and interfaces. The fourth line may be used to restrict access to migration on a particular host to only certain hosts. Leaving this field blank allows all hosts with network access to the relocation port and address on which `xend` is listening to negotiate migration. Leaving these fields blank suffices for testing purposes but may not provide a desirable level of security in production systems. A better idea is to specify a list of hosts that should be allowed to negotiate migration with a particular host, and/or create a separate, secure network for guest migration. Of course for tighter security, a good idea is to configure both.

It is imperative for the relocation service to be accessible only by trusted systems and for live migration to be performed only across a trusted network. It is important to perform migration across a trusted network because when migrated, the contents of a guest's memory are transferred from the source to destination hosts in a raw, unencrypted form. The memory contents might contain sensitive data and can be intercepted on a shared network by other hosts capable of scanning the migration traffic. Additionally, allowing unrestricted access to the relocation service on a host could allow an attacker to send fraudulent guest domain data to that host, and possibly hijack or impair system and network resources. Whenever possible, the `xend-relocation-address` should be set on the source and destination hosts to the address of an interface that is connected to an isolated administrative network, where migration can occur in an environment that is not shared with untrusted hosts (or the Internet). Ideally, the transmission medium should be high speed for best results. Having an isolated network for migration and listening for relocation requests only on that network adds natural security to a Xen configuration by physically preventing untrusted hosts from accessing the relocation port or spying on a migrating guest's memory contents. Please see Chapter 11, "Securing a Xen System," for more tips on hardening your Xen configuration.

To have xend's relocation service listen only on one address, specify the address in the xend configuration file. For example, if the address 10.10.3.21 is bound to a network interface available to Domain0, the setting illustrated in Listing 13.17 causes xend's relocation service to only listen for relocation requests sent to 10.10.3.21. This configuration feature helps secure a host's relocation service if undesired hosts are blocked from making connections to the specified address, either by firewall rules or by being bound to a network interface connected to a separate administrative network.

LISTING 13.17 An Example of xend Bound to a Relocation Address

```
(xend-relocation-address '10.10.3.21')
```

The format for specifying a restricted set of allowed hosts to connect to the relocation service is a list of regular expressions, separated by spaces, that specify hosts that are to be accepted. For instance, the example in Listing 13.18 would cause a particular host to only listen to migration requests from itself and hosts within the our-network. mil domain. Host IP addresses may also be listed in this line. Restricting access to the relocation service by only certain hosts can also be achieved through good firewall practices, either in addition to or instead of setting `xend-relocation-hosts-allow`. Any host that matches any one of the regular expressions listed in this field will be allowed to negotiate migration with the local host.

LISTING 13.18 An Example of Restricting Allowed Source Hosts

```
(xend-relocation-hosts-allow '^localhost$                 ➡
     ^.*\.our-network\.mil$')
```

For our sample configuration, we want our hosts Domain0_Host1 (10.0.0.1) and Domain0_Host2 (10.0.0.2) to accept relocation requests only from themselves and each other, but, unfortunately, our hosts do not have separate real or virtual network interfaces on a separate network just to be used for relocation. Remember that this host setup can be less secure than having a separate network and interface for guest relocation, and can decrease network performance. Our sample xend configuration file for Domain0_Host1, contained in Listing 13.19, shows xend configured only to accept migration requests from its own host and Domain0_Host2.

LISTING 13.19 A Sample xend Configuration File for Domain0_Host1

```
# dom0_Host1 (10.0.0.1)
# Xend Configuration File
#

# = Basic Configuration =
(xend-unix-server yes)
(xend-unix-path /var/lib/xend/xend-socket)


# =*= Relocation Configuration =*=
(xend-relocation-server yes)  # Enable guest domain relocation
(xend-relocation-port 8002)                               ➡
     # Port xend listens on for relocation requests
(xend-relocation-address '')
     # Interface to listen for reloc requests [ALL]       ➡
(xend-relocation-hosts-allow '^localhost$                 ➡
     ^localhost\\.localdomain$ 10.0.0.2')
     # Hosts that are allowed to                          ➡
     send guests to this host [only 10.0.0.2!]


# = Network Configuration =
(network-script network-bridge)
(vif-script vif-bridge)

# = Resource Configuration =
(dom0-min-mem 256)
(dom0-cpus 0)
```

Likewise, our sample `xend` configuration file for Domain0_Host2, with `xend` configured only to accept migration requests from its host and Domain0_Host1, is contained in Listing 13.20.

LISTING 13.20 A Sample `xend` Configuration File for Domain0_Host2

```
# dom0_Host2 (10.0.0.2)
# Xend Configuration File
#

# = Basic Configuration =
(xend-unix-server yes)
(xend-unix-path /var/lib/xend/xend-socket)


# =*= Relocation Configuration =*=
(xend-relocation-server yes)  # Enable guest domain relocation
(xend-relocation-port 8002)                                      ➥
    # Port xend listens on for relocation requests
(xend-relocation-address '')                                     ➥
    # Interface to listen for reloc requests [ALL]
(xend-relocation-hosts-allow '^localhost$                        ➥
    ^localhost\\.localdomain$ 10.0.0.1')
    # Hosts that are allowed to                                  ➥
    send guests to this host [only 10.0.0.1!]


# = Network Configuration =
(network-script network-bridge)
(vif-script vif-bridge)

# = Resource Configuration =
(dom0-min-mem 256)
(dom0-cpus 0)
```

Proximity of Sources and Destinations on the Network

For guest migration to be possible, the source and destination hosts need to be members of the same layer-2 network and the same IP subnet. This is because Xen needs to maintain the same environment for a guest's services before and after migration, including the same IP and MAC addresses. A guest's IP and MAC addresses are transferred with that guest so that its network services remain accessible to other hosts once its migration completes.

Packet redirection to a new host is generally accomplished through Address Resolution Protocol (ARP), a protocol already familiar with networking hardware. If the source and destination hosts are located on different subnets, connections have to be redirected to the distant destination host in a more complicated way—for example, through the use of tunneling on Domain0, "Mobile-IP," dynamic DNS, or reconnection at the application level. In addition to the administrative complexity these proposed methods would create, they would also cause undesirable effects such as increasing overhead, latency, and even bandwidth usage if tunneling is used. Due to issues such as these, at the time of this publication, Xen does not provide an integrated capability to migrate guests between hosts that are not on the same layer-2 network and IP subnet. Solutions such as IP tunneling in Domain0 must be manually configured as needed. In many scenarios, the need for geographically-isolated source and destination hosts coincides with the need to be able to shift all dependency away from the source location; as such, tunneling is not viable because it depends on the source location to be able to maintain resources at its end of the tunnel.

Network-Accessible Storage

Recall that the migration support for Xen guests requires guest root file systems located on some form of mutually shared storage. Xen does not yet provide a facility for the automatic mirroring of local storage volumes at the Domain0 level, though work is currently being done to explore such possibilities. It is therefore necessary for each guest that is to be migrated to have its file system(s) mapped to network shares because the local devices available to a guest's original host will not be available locally on its destination host following migration.

There are several approaches to making a guest's files network accessible, including NFS, iSCSI, AoE, GNBD, and many others. Services such as iSCSI, ATA-over-Ethernet, and GNBD share access to volume block devices over the network, whereas services such as NFS share access to portions of a file system. See Chapter 8, "Storing Guest Images," for details on configuring a suitable network storage service such as the one mentioned in this section.

Guest Domain Configuration

We configure our guest's virtual block device, storing its root file system to be mapped to an ATA-over-Ethernet (AoE) shared volume. You may choose whichever network storage service is most convenient for your own needs on your premises. First, we set up the AoE initiator (client) on both of our hosts. Then we create an LVM volume group and volumes on our AoE share to serve as our sample guest's root and swap logical partitions. We define a virtual disk in the guest configuration file that points to our shared block device and also use pygrub as a bootloader.

Both the source and destination Xen hosts need a configuration file for guests that are to be migrated, which will be the same for our hosts because all of our guest's virtual block devices will be accessible identically on both the source and destination hosts. We name this sample guest TestGuest, and Listing 13.21 shows the configuration in /etc/xen/TestGuest that is identical on both hosts. If a network block storage service is to be used but LVM is not, configure the disk line so that it points directly to the device on Domain0 that corresponds to the appropriate network block device (located in the /dev/ tree).

LISTING 13.21 A Sample /etc/xen/TestGuest with LVM and ATA-over-Ethernet on Both
                Domain0 Hosts

```
name = "TestGuest"
memory = "64"
disk = [ 'phy:/dev/VolumeGroup0/TestGuest-volume,xvda,w' ]
vif = [ 'mac=00:16:3e:55:9d:b0, bridge=xenbr0' ]
nographic=1
uuid = "cc0029f5-10a1-e6d0-3c92-19b0ea021f21"
bootloader="/usr/bin/pygrub"
vcpus=1
on_reboot    = 'restart'
on_crash     = 'restart'
```

The configuration shown in Listing 13.21 works for network storage services that export entire block devices; however, because NFS exports a file system and not a form of raw access to block devices, configuring a guest to have an NFS-shared root file system is slightly different. The main difference is that the guest configuration file will not define a virtual block device pointing to a shared block device, but instead will have an NFS server configured that stores the guest's root file system. An NFS root on TestGuest may be set up by the configuration in /etc/xen/TestGuest on both hosts, shown in Listing 13.22.

LISTING 13.22 A Sample of /etc/xen/TestGuest with NFS on Both Domain0 Hosts

```
name = "TestGuest"
memory = "64"
vif = [ 'mac=00:16:3e:55:9d:b0, bridge=xenbr0' ]
nographic = 1
uuid = "cc0029f5-10a1-e6d0-3c92-19b0ea021f21"
bootloader = "/usr/bin/pygrub"
vcpus = 1
root = "/dev/nfs"
nfs_server = '10.0.0.40'                # Address of our NFS server
nfs_root = '/XenGuestRoots/TestGuest'              ➥
     # Path on server of TestGuest's root
on_reboot    = 'restart'
on_crash     = 'restart'
```

Version and Physical Resource Requirements

In addition to both the source and destination hosts needing to run the same version of Xen to allow for migration, the destination host also must have sufficient resources available to it in order to support the arrival of a guest. The destination host must have access to memory that is unallocated to either Domain0 or other domains to handle the arriving guest, and the minimum amount of memory needed equals the amount of memory allotted to the guest on the source host, plus an additional 8MB of temporary storage.

Experience with xm migrate

Xen's internal relocation facility supports both warm static migration and live migration. It is available through the xm migrate command.

xm migrate

This command minimally takes the domain ID (or domain name) of the guest that is to be migrated and the destination host to which it is to be migrated to as its first and second arguments, respectively. If a domain with the same numerical domain ID exists on the destination host, migration still occurs, but the guest is assigned a different domain ID on the destination host. Listing 13.23 shows the syntax of the command.

LISTING 13.23 Usage of `xm migrate`

```
xm migrate domain_id destination_host [-l|--live] [-r|--resource rate]
```

`xm migrate` supports two optional arguments: `--live` and `--resource`. The `--live` argument specifies live migration as the form of migration to be performed. If `--live` is not used, regular migration will be the type of migration performed. To reduce network saturation, the optional `--resource` argument, followed by a `rate` in megabits per second, may be used to specify the rate of data transfer during migration. The `--resource` argument is generally unnecessary when using a private network dedicated for migrations to be performed, and it is best to avoid supplying it whenever possible to ensure optimal throughput; however, if a single network or even a single network interface on a host shares both migration and normal guest network traffic, it may be wise to supply this argument to reduce the network saturation so that connections to and from guests are not affected as dramatically.

Xen's relocation facility, as interfaced through the `xm migrate` command, makes guest relocation a simple task. We demonstrate the usage of the `xm migrate` command for performing both regular migration and live migration.

Using `xm migrate` for Warm Static Migration

In this section, we perform a warm static (regular) migration of a guest domain. The Domain0_Host1 system is currently running one guest domain, TestGuest, as seen by invoking `xm list` at a console on Domain0_Host1 and as shown in Listing 13.24.

LISTING 13.24 Domains Running on Domain0_Host1

```
[root@dom0_Host1# xm list
Name                          ID Mem(MiB) VCPUs State    Time(s)
Domain-0                       0      511     2 r-----    5010.6
TestGuest                      1       63     1 -b----      15.3
[root@dom0_Host1]#
```

The guest domain TestGuest is the guest to be relocated using warm static migration, from Domain0_Host1 to Domain0_Host2. TestGuest (10.0.0.5) is currently accessible from a separate workstation on our network, which we reveal using the `ping` command in Listing 13.25.

LISTING 13.25 Demonstrating Remote Accessibility Using `ping`

```
[root@Other_Workstation]# ping TestGuest
PING TestGuest (10.0.0.5) 56(84) bytes of data.
64 bytes from TestGuest 10.0.0.5: icmp_seq=1 ttl=64 time=2.48 ms
64 bytes from TestGuest 10.0.0.5: icmp_seq=1 ttl=64 time=2.31 ms
64 bytes from TestGuest 10.0.0.5: icmp_seq=1 ttl=64 time=2.98 ms
64 bytes from TestGuest 10.0.0.5: icmp_seq=1 ttl=64 time=2.77 ms
[root@Other_Workstation]#
```

Next, to perform a warm static migration of our sample guest from its current host Domain0_Host1 to its destination host Domain0_Host2 (10.0.0.2), we run the xm migrate command at a console on Domain0_Host1, illustrated in Listing 13.26.

LISTING 13.26 Performing a Warm Static Migration Using xm `migrate`

```
[root@dom0_Host1]# xm migrate 1 10.0.0.2
[root@dom0_Host1]#
```

After the migration is complete, TestGuest executes on Domain0_Host2. You can check that it has finished successfully and is currently residing on Domain0_Host2 by running xm list in a terminal on Domain0_Host2, as illustrated in Listing 13.27.

LISTING 13.27 Domains Running on Domain0_Host2

```
[root@dom0_Host2]# xm list
Name                     ID Mem(MiB) VCPUs State   Time(s)
Domain-0                  0     511     2 r-----    710.1
TestGuest                 4      63     1 -b----     16.2
[root@dom0_Host2]#
```

To demonstrate that the guest is still accessible with its same IP address and hostname after the migration, we repeat our ping from our generic workstation on the network, as shown in Listing 13.28.

LISTING 13.28 Demonstrating Remote Accessibility at Same IP Address after Warm Static Migration

```
[root@Other_Workstation]# ping TestGuest
PING TestGuest (10.0.0.5) 56(84) bytes of data.
64 bytes from TestGuest 10.0.0.5: icmp_seq=1 ttl=64 time=2.99 ms
64 bytes from TestGuest 10.0.0.5: icmp_seq=2 ttl=64 time=2.27 ms
64 bytes from TestGuest 10.0.0.5: icmp_seq=3 ttl=64 time=2.53 ms
64 bytes from TestGuest 10.0.0.5: icmp_seq=4 ttl=64 time=2.43 ms
[root@Other_Workstation]#
```

The domain is still accessible on the network the same way it was prior to migration.

Using xm migrate for Live Migration

Now we demonstrate how to perform a live migration of a guest domain. First, let's examine our guest domain, TestGuest, residing on Domain0_Host1. To do so, we invoke xm list, as in Listing 13.29.

LISTING 13.29 Domains Running on Domain0_Host1

```
[root@dom0_Host1]# xm list
Name                      ID Mem(MiB) VCPUs State   Time(s)
Domain-0                   0      511     2 r-----   7170.6
TestGuest                  1       63     1 -b----     15.1
[root@dom0_Host1]#
```

Here, we see that TestGuest is residing on Domain0_Host1. The guest domain TestGuest is the guest we will once again migrate, only this time we will perform a live migration. We previously installed the Apache HTTP Web server on our sample guest in preparation for this example, and it is publishing a directory containing a large-sized file. To demonstrate the persistence of connections with our guest during and after live migration, we commence the downloading of a large file from a separate workstation on our network, as shown in Figure 13.5. We observe the status of our download after performing a live migration of our guest to confirm that connections to our guest's services remain uninterrupted throughout the process. We also present a test consisting of constant pings to illustrate the temporary increase in latency during migration when accessing the guest over the network.

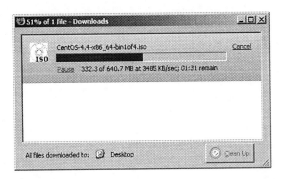

FIGURE 13.5 A connection from another computer on our network is established with our guest domain, and the guest begins serving us a large file.

Next, we request live migration of our sample guest from its current host, Domain0_Host1, to its destination host, Domain0_Host2 (10.0.0.2), to occur through the xm interface. We do this by invoking xm migrate on its source host, Domain0_Host1, as shown in Listing 13.30.

LISTING 13.30 Performing a Live Migration Using xm migrate --live

```
[root@dom0_Host1]# xm migrate --live 1 10.0.0.2
[root@dom0_Host1]#
```

After the migration is complete, TestGuest will reside completely on Domain0_Host2. You can check that it has finished successfully and is currently residing on Domain0_Host2 by running xm list in a terminal on Domain0_Host2, which is illustrated in Listing 13.31.

LISTING 13.31 Domains Running on Domain0_Host2

```
[root@dom0_Host2]# xm list
Name                    ID Mem(MiB) VCPUs State   Time(s)
Domain-0                 0      511     2 r-----   4314.2
TestGuest                6       63     1 -b----     17.4
[root@dom0_Host2]#
```

To confirm that live migration did not disrupt any connections to our sample guest domain, we observe our download on the client workstation as shown in Figure 13.6.

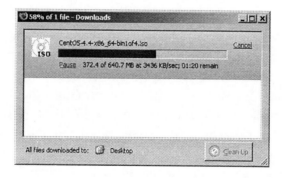

FIGURE 13.6 The connection to our guest domain remains uninterrupted during and after migration.

Although the download rate of the file we were downloading decreased during migration, our connection was not dropped. From the client's perspective, the guest domain remained completely accessible during and after its transfer to Domain0_Host2.

During this example, we ran the ping utility on a separate workstation to illustrate the increase in latency experienced during live migration. We set up this test to perform constant pings before, during, and after TestGuest (10.0.0.5) was live migrated from Domain0_Host1 to Domain0_Host2. Listing 13.32 shows the results of the ping command.

LISTING 13.32 Guest Latency During Live Migration

```
[root@Other_Workstation ~]# ping TestGuest
PING TestGuest (10.0.0.5) 56(84) bytes of data.
64 bytes from TestGuest (10.0.0.5): icmp_seq=1 ttl=64 time=2.29 ms
64 bytes from TestGuest (10.0.0.5): icmp_seq=2 ttl=64 time=1.06 ms
64 bytes from TestGuest (10.0.0.5): icmp_seq=3 ttl=64 time=1.07 ms
64 bytes from TestGuest (10.0.0.5): icmp_seq=4 ttl=64 time=1.05 ms
64 bytes from TestGuest (10.0.0.5): icmp_seq=5 ttl=64 time=5.77 ms
64 bytes from TestGuest (10.0.0.5): icmp_seq=7 ttl=64 time=6.13 ms
64 bytes from TestGuest (10.0.0.5): icmp_seq=8 ttl=64 time=4.06 ms
64 bytes from TestGuest (10.0.0.5): icmp_seq=9 ttl=64 time=1.08 ms
64 bytes from TestGuest (10.0.0.5): icmp_seq=10 ttl=64 time=1.09 ms
64 bytes from TestGuest (10.0.0.5): icmp_seq=11 ttl=64 time=1.08 ms
64 bytes from TestGuest (10.0.0.5): icmp_seq=12 ttl=64 time=1.11 ms
[root@Other_Workstation ~]#
```

With Xen's approach for performing live migration, the guest domain is unreachable typically for only 50ms. Due to the brevity of its networking quiescence, the guest domain should have no apparent downtime from the perspective of client computers connected to that guest. Interruption of active connections should not occur because the time the guest domain is unavailable resembles the effects of an otherwise temporary surge in network latency. Even when migrating a computer gaming server, where high latencies often obviously affect application performance in an obvious way to users, this effective latency generally goes unnoticed (as seen in the famous demonstration of the live migration of a Quake game server while players are connected to it and participating in the game). Imperceptibility is what makes the illusion of live migration work.

Possible Migration Errors

Migration, though a fun demo, is more important when the capability is actually need-ed. In fact, for production systems, migration is something that should not be taken lightly. It is important to consider the level of computing power and other resources available when planning to migrate additional guests to a host. An easy mistake is to saturate all available hosts with guests when load balancing, and then at a later time attempt to migrate guests from one heavily loaded host to another that lacks the avail-able resources to keep up with the demand. It is key to remember that if a host cannot normally support a particular guest due to resource limitations, it is not a viable des-tination host for the migration of that guest. Thus some planning of your migration infrastructure and contingency migration plans are in order.

In situations where systems are under extreme load, and where a noticeable and unacceptable decrease in performance might result from migrating a guest from one busy host to another, it is wise to have extra guests on the same hosts, and instead try to mix guests with different types of loads in a way that minimizes competition for the same resources of hosts.

The problem shown in Listing 13.33 can be encountered when:

- The destination host does not have enough memory to complete migration and now the guest domain is in a nonfunctioning zombie state.

- The xm migrate command is terminated prematurely on the source host.

LISTING 13.33 "Zombie-migrating" Guest Listed

```
[root@dom0_Host1]# xm list
Name                        ID Mem(MiB) VCPUs State   Time(s)
Domain-0                     0      191     2 r-----  49980.3
Zombie-migrating-TestGuest  14      256     1 ---s-d   1421.6
[root@dom0_Host1]#
```

Unfortunately, at the time of this writing, if this situation is encountered, the zombie guest cannot be destroyed, and the host needs to be restarted to alleviate this problem. A possible workaround for the zombie's memory consumption is to use xm mem-set to lower the memory allocated to the zombie to the minimum allowed amount (1MB).

Summary

In this chapter, we explored Xen's integrated facilities for guest domain checkpointing and migration that make these tasks trivial and useful for system administration. Xen makes saving and restoring guest domain states to disk possible through the easy-to-use xm save and xm restore commands. The ability to checkpoint guests makes it possible to pause and resume guest execution at a later date, roll back guest states for faster-than-rebooting crash recovery, and crudely transport guests between hosts.

Xen's integrated support for migration makes relocating guests between distinct physical hosts much more intuitive than manual means of relocating a guest image. Migration is performed with the xm migrate command, optionally with the --live argument for live migration. Live migration is particularly useful for crash avoidance, load balancing, and bringing down hosts for maintenance without interrupting the operation of important virtual machines.

References and Further Reading

Clark, Christopher et al. "Live Migration of Virtual Machines."
http://www.cl.cam.ac.uk/research/srg/netos/papers/2005-migration-nsdi-pre.pdf.

Virijevich, Paul. "Live Migration of Xen Domains." Linux.com.
http://www.linux.com/articles/55773.

Xen Users' Manual, Xen v3.0.
http://www.cl.cam.ac.uk/research/srg/netos/xen/readmes/user/user.html.

## Chapter 14

An Overview of Xen Enterprise Management Tools

This chapter focuses on tools and support for running Xen in an enterprise environment. The main purpose of these tools is to provide a GUI interface to simplify the process of guest creation and provisioning. Most tools also provide management consoles for controlling and monitoring currently running guests. Many tools provide support for managing multiple physical hosts and their virtual guests, including support for migration of guests between machines. Many tools provide support for administering many virtual guests in a uniform manner, such as user account management or package management support. Some tools are specific to Xen while others can be used with other virtualization systems as well. We begin with an overview of the programmatic interfaces to the Xen hypervisor, around which system management tools such as this can be built. We then survey Enterprise Xen products and Xen management software. Specifically, we examine XenEnterprise, XenServer, and XenExpress from XenSource; Virtualization Manager from IBM; Virt-Manager from Red Hat; Enomalism from Enomaly; and XenMan from the ConVirt Project.

Programmatic Interfaces to the Xen Hypervisor

Before jumping into a survey of management tools for Xen systems, we describe the interfaces on which all of these management tools are built. Some interfaces are unique to Xen, but increasingly the Xen hypervisor is being modified to support a standard set of interfaces that can be used by other virtualization systems as well. This trend recognizes that the tasks involved in managing a set of virtual machines is similar regardless of whether the underlying virtualization system is Xen, VMware, QEMU, KVM, or any other system. Some systems may support unique features, but the basic functions of creating new VMs, allocating resources to VMs, starting or stopping VMs, and querying the status of VMs remain constant. Many other features are similar not only throughout virtualization systems, but also to managing a large cluster of physical machines. Standard interfaces allow software developers who invest in cluster management and virtualization management systems to deploy their software with a wide variety of underlying technologies. Standard interfaces also allow system administrators who invest in deploying and understanding the subtleties of certain management software to continue use even if they switch virtualization technologies.

Libvirt

The libvirt C toolkit (`http://libvirt.org`) provides a higher-level management interface for tools and applications. The goal of libvirt is to provide all the operations needed to manage guests or domains running on a single physical node. The libvirt library does not provide high-level multinode management features such as load balancing. Instead, libvirt provides lower-level features that enterprise-level cluster management software can use to build high-level multinode management features.

The libvirt toolkit supplies a stable interface that isolates upper-level software from changes in the underlying virtualization environment. In fact, libvirt is designed to be usable by any virtualization environment. Each virtualization environment would implement the libvirt interface on which the upper layer tools rely.

On a Xen system, the implementation of libvirt would make use of XenStore, Xen hypervisor calls, or a connection to Xend through an interface such as RPC.

Xen-CIM

The Common Information Model (CIM) is a set of standards designed to enable interoperability of tools for system management with systems from many vendors. It enables customers to run heterogeneous clusters or data centers in which each piece interacts with other pieces through standard interfaces rather than locking customers into a single vertical stack of solutions from one vendor. It also allows vendors to focus on what they do best rather than requiring them to write custom management tools.

An organization called the Distributed Management Task Force (DMTF) oversees the standardization of CIM models, protocols, documents, usage, and certification. Within DMTF, working groups focus on a number of areas, including virtualization and cluster management. The Open Source Xen-CIM project is working to produce the first implementation of the Open Standard DMTF System Virtualization model. Enterprise-level cluster management solutions, including tools originally written for outer virtualization systems, can use the CIM as the integration interface.

Xen API

The Xen API is an XML-RPC protocol for remote and local management of Xen-based systems. In addition to the XML-RPC calls, there are bindings to the XML-RPC interface for Python, C, and Java. The Xen API includes interfaces for starting, pausing, suspending, resuming, rebooting, and shutting down virtual machines. It passes back useful error messages that can be used in handling errors. It also includes an interface for requesting statistics and metrics on the system.

Both libvirt and Xen-CIM can use an interface to xend called the Xen Management API, or Xen API. The libvirt library and Xen-CIM both export to high-level applications and tools a stable, standard, non-Xen specific interface on which they can rely. Xen API exports to layers such as libvirt and Xen-CIM a lower-level Xen specific interface on which they can build. The Xen API can also be used to remotely manage Xen-based systems, even without enterprise-level cluster management solutions.

This can be enabled as xen-api-server in the xend configuration file.

Legacy Interfaces to Xend

There are a number of other interfaces to xend that have been implemented and used over time. The new Xen API should in time replace these other interfaces, but they are worth knowing about. Xend can listen for HTTP style requests typically on port 8000. This is referred to as xend-http-server in the xend configuration file. Similarly, xend can listen on a UNIX domain socket, typically /var/lib/xend/xend-socket. This is specified as xend-unix-server in the xend configuration file. The most direct predecessor of the Xen API interface is the XML-RPC server interface, enabled with xend-unix-xmlrpc-server in the xend configuration file. All these interfaces have the same goal—to provide a programmatic interface to xend that would enable higher-level management tools besides xm as well as enabling remote management of Xen guests.

Citrix XenServer Enterprise, Standard, and XenExpress Editions

The Citrix XenServer Product Group (formerly XenSource) plays a dual role of leading the open source Xen community and producing value-added enterprise solutions based on Xen technology. They offer three primary products—Citrix XenServer Enterprise, Citrix XenServer Standard, and Citrix XenServer Express. Express Edition is a free starter package supporting both Windows and Linux guests. It offers the Xen Single Server Management console. Standard includes native 64-bit hypervisor support and XenCenter Administrative Console with MultiServer Management and is fully supported by Citrix. Enterprise is the highest-end solution and supports flexible management of an aggregated pool of computer and storage resources. It offers Xen-Motion Live Migration support and the Xen Administrator Console with MultiServer and MultiPool Management.

Figure 14.1 and Figure 14.2 show screenshots of the cross-platform XenSource Administrative Console that was offered by XenSource before it was acquired by Citrix. It supported quick and easy creation of new guests from CD/DVDs, ISOs, or other install sources. It also supported the cloning of existing guests. It allowed the performance of each guest as well as the system as a whole to be easily monitored and enabled for dynamic adjustments in resource allocation as well as the ability to create, suspend, and resume guests.

A demo of Citrix Xen Server and its XenCenter Administrative Console is available at `www.citrixxenserver.com/Pages/XenEnterprise_Demo.aspx`.

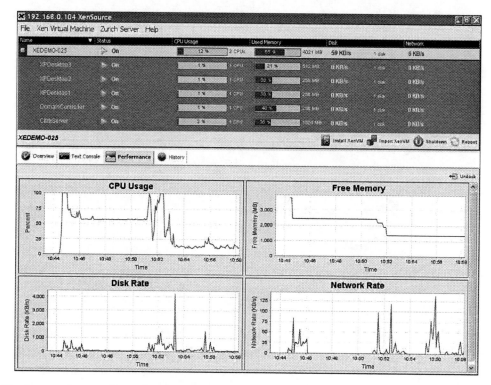

FIGURE 14.1 The original XenSource Administrative Console

As home to the founders and key developers of Xen, the Citrix XenServer Product Group is a trusted source of high-performance, easy-to-deploy Xen solutions. Using open source solutions, you can deploy an unlimited number of Xen guests of any type. However, using the XenServer products can dramatically simplify the process and give access to definitive technical support for Xen.

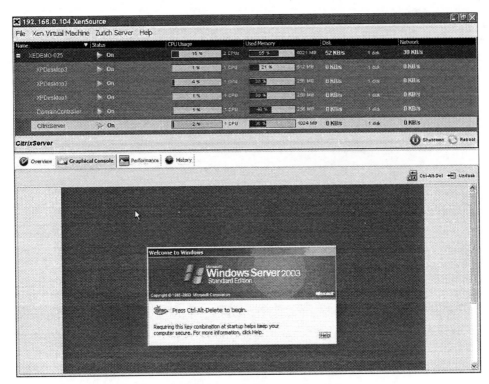

FIGURE 14.2 XenSource provides a graphical console for access to guests.

> **Note**
> For more information about XenServer products, Citrix XenServer product overview is an excellent resource. See also:
>
>   http://www.citrixxenserver.com/products/Pages/XenEnterprise.aspx
>   http://www.citrixxenserver.com/products/Pages/XenServer.aspx
>   http://www.citrixxenserver.com/products/Pages/XenExpress.aspx

Virtual Iron

Virtual Iron is another company offering full enterprise-class virtualization solutions. Founded in 2003, Virtual Iron originally used its own operating system, but in 2006 switched to using the Xen hypervisor underneath its own layer of management software. Virtual Iron offers server consolidation products for both Windows and Linux guests. Its focus has been on fully virtualized, unmodified HVM guests rather than on paravirtualized guests. Virtual Iron competes directly with VMware. An often repeated point regarding Virtual Iron is its ability to provide a comparable solution to VMware's ESX Server product at approximately one-fifth the cost.

One component of Virtual Iron's management software is an administrative console called Virtualization Manager. It has many of the same features as the XenSource Administrative Console but generally is more polished. While XenSource is a clear authority on the underlying hypervisor, Virtual Iron had a several-year head start on the administrative tools it originally used with its own operating system.

Virtual Iron Virtual Manager is a Web-based graphical user interface. Figure 14.3 shows a sample screenshot. It supports monitoring of guest performance and resource consumption as well as dynamic resource adjustment (called LiveCapacity). It also offers a number of advanced features including LiveRecovery to support failover and LiveMigrate to support live migration of virtual machines.

The Virtual Iron platform also includes Virtualization Services, a layer of software that includes support for virtual storage and network connectivity, virtual server resource management, server logical partitioning, high performance drivers, and hot plug CPU and memory management. The Virtualization Services software is open source, released under the GPL.

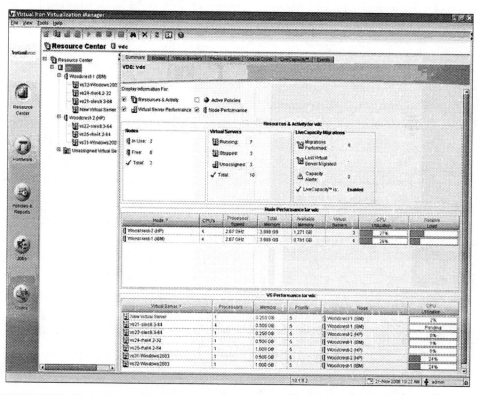

FIGURE 14.3 The Virtual Iron Virtualization Manager offers a full-featured administrative console.

Virtual Iron offers three primary editions of its software. The Enterprise Edition offers full support for virtualization of multiple physical servers. The Professional Edition, available for no charge via download, is limited to management of a single physical machine. The Community Edition supports the Xen development community and includes the Virtual Iron Open Source Virtualization Services Stack.

IBM Virtualization Manager

An alternative management console, also called Virtualization Manager, is available from IBM, the company where virtualization first started. If you are running IBM servers in your environment, you are likely familiar with an integrated suite of system management tools called IBM Director. IBM Virtualization Manager is an extension of IBM Director that enables users to manage virtual machines and their associated resources. In particular, IBM Virtualization Manager supports discovery, visualization, and management of a collection of systems from a single console. If you are already using IBM Director, IBM Virtualization Manager can provide a natural and easy-to-use extension of your current environment, which allows you to effectively manage Xen guests.

Unlike the XenSource Administrative Console, IBM Virtualization Manager is not exclusive to Xen. It supports different virtualization systems from a variety of vendors including IBM Hardware Management Consoles (HMC), VMware, Microsoft Virtual Server, as well as Xen through the CIM standard we described earlier in this chapter. If you are using multiple virtualization systems in your environment or you are transitioning from one virtualization system to another, then the ability to manage everything with one tool can be a powerful advantage.

The extension can provide views such as topology maps and health information for your virtualized environments. The topology map is useful for viewing the relationships between virtual and physical resources.

The machines to be managed require IBM Director Core Services and the Virtualization Manager Xen CIM Provider. The managed systems also require disk space for the Xen guest images. A prerequisite to using the Create Virtual Server Wizard is to create an image to be used when the virtual server is created. It is recommended that there be 2GB on the /var file system (for a Xen master image), with an additional 2GB available disk capacity for each Xen instance to be created by IBM Virtualization Manager.

IBM Virtualization Manager leverages IBM's long-standing expertise in virtualization and managing virtual machines. Like IBM Director, IBM Virtualization Manager is a fully supported enterprise-grade product available from IBM and is free for use on IBM hardware platforms. Distributions officially supported with IBM Virtualization Manager are SUSE Linux Enterprise Server 10 for x86, EMT64, and AMD64.

> **Note**
> For information about IBM Director and the Virtualization Manager extension see http://www-03.ibm.com/systems/management/director/about/
> http://www-03.ibm.com/systems/management/director/extensions/vm.html.

Enomalism

Enomalism is another interesting open source (LGPL) management tool for use with Xen virtual machines. It is predominantly developed by the Canadian consultancy company Enomaly, based in Toronto. Enomalism has a number of interesting features not found in many other administrative tools. These features make Enomalism well-worth considering, depending on your usage model.

Enomalism allows updates of application software packages to be distributed to many virtual machines via a process called *VMcasting*. VMcasting allows package updates to be distributed via RSS feeds to the guests. This allows system administrators to automate the process of installing, configuring, removing, or upgrading selected software packages.

Enomalism supports the Enomalism Virtual Appliance (EVA) transport format. Essentially EVA is a type of packaging format. Such an EVA package might be a total Web serving solution comprising Web server and database, all of which are preconfigured and ready to run. A single EVA package can contain a plurality of virtual machines. It is important to note that EVA is not the same as the VMware disk format or the Microsoft Virtual Disk format.

Enomalism enables centralized user account management with LDAP. Specifically, guest virtual machines are configured so that system administrators do not have to manually administer users' accounts on their virtual machines. Using the Enomalism LDAP directory, you can configure numerous preferences regarding who can manage and use specific domains, or provision new virtual machines.

Enomalism offers a firewall management interface through which individual per-VM firewall rules can be set. Enomalism also integrates many other useful and advanced features such as partition management, guest migration functionality, and support for manipulating logical volume groups.

Enomalism is a Web-based application that uses Asynchronous JavaScript and XML (AJAX). The Web functionality can be handy when you need to work on machines remotely, or do not have access to a local Xen management server. Enomalism also exports an API so that that users can program custom virtual machine control features into their own Web applications.

The Enomalism guest creation and provisioning process is simple and straightforward. You first select an image from any of the prebuilt images at your disposal. Figure 14.4 illustrates that selecting a virtual machine to import can be as simple as clicking a radio button on the Enomalism interface.

Figure 14.4 and Figure 14.5 illustrate the process of selecting and downloading a virtual machine image. After the image is downloaded, create a new virtual machine based on that image by choosing the destination Domain0 and a name for the new guest.

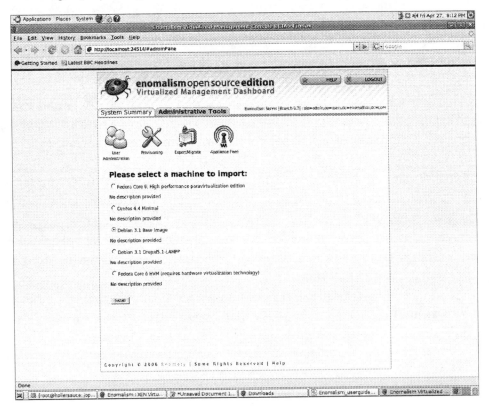

FIGURE 14.4 Selecting a machine image is as simple as clicking a radio button.

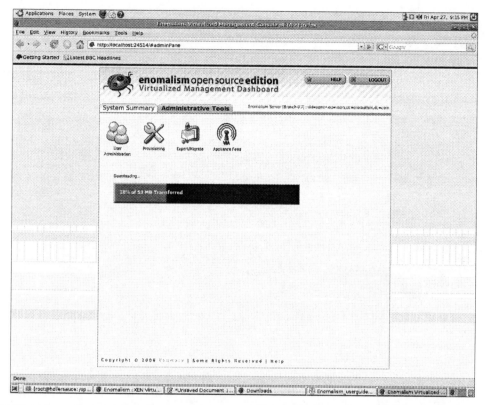

FIGURE 14.5   Creating a new guest based on a downloaded image is also simple with Enomalism.

In our experience, installing and using the open source version of Enomalism can be complicated. We recommend considering the enterprise edition and Enomaly's Xen consulting service if your budget allows.

virt-manager

Another popular tool for managing Xen virtual machines is the Virtual Machine Manager or virt-manager, developed by Red Hat. virt-manager is an open source application released under the terms of the GPL. Virt-manger offers similar functionality to the XenSource Administrative Console in a package that is easy to integrate with an existing Linux environment.

Virt-manager, like the other management tools we've discussed, offers graphs of guest performance and resource utilization for monitoring the health of your system and an easy-to-use graphical tool for guest configuration and management. It allows you to easily configure and alter resource allocation and virtual hardware. It also includes an embedded VNC client to view a full graphical console to the guest domain. Figure 14.6 illustrates using the Hardware tab of virt-manager to view and configure the resources allocated to a guest. Figure 14.7 illustrates using the Overview tab of virt-manager to monitor the current status of a guest.

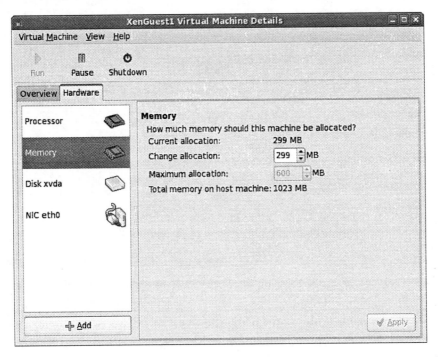

FIGURE 14.6 The Hardware tab can be used to view and configure the resources of a virtual machine.

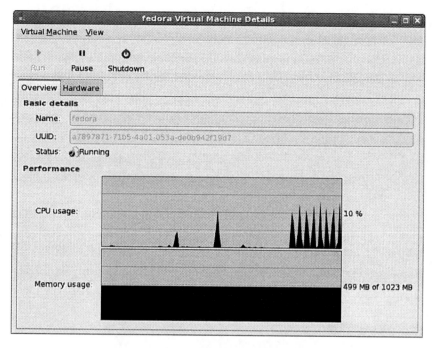

FIGURE 14.7 The Overview tab has a performance monitor showing CPU and memory consumption over time, as well as the current state of the virtual machine.

Like IBM Virtualization Manager, virt-manager can be used to manage guests in different virtualization systems. While IBM Virtualization Manager uses CIM, virt-manager uses libvirt as an abstraction layer to the underlying virtual machine technology. Libvirt currently has support for KVM and QEMU guests as well as Xen guests. Support for other guests might be added in time.

Virt-manager provides a way to control libvirt-supported virtual networks for your guests and allows you to select the virtual network to be connected to your guest. It also has a rather handy graphical user interface for adding virtual block devices (VBDs) as well as virtual networking interface connections (VNICs). These VBD and VNIC definitions can be dynamically added or removed to inactive guests, or altered at runtime for active machines. It is also worth mentioning that Network Satellite, also from Red Hat, can be used to create and manage virtualized Xen hosts. For more details, refer to the white paper found at `www.redhat.com/f/pdf/whitepapers/ Satellite500-VirtStepbyStep-Whitepaper.pdf`.

Virt-manager is not just for RHEL or Fedora. Other distributions already include virt-manager as part of their default distribution. SUSE has support in SLED and OpenSUSE. CentOS also has support for virt-manager as a default package.

One reason you might opt to use virt-manager is if you are currently running an Enterprise Linux distribution like RHEL or SLES in your environment. In this situation, you may not be interested in a base install of XenEnterprise because it would install directly on your physical machine, replacing your commercially-supported distribution. In this case, it is recommended that you use your preexisting vendor support for the distribution-recommended virtualization management tools unless you have strong reason to do otherwise.

Other users who do not have a distribution-supported package or those who want a newer version than the packaged offering can build virt-manager easily from source. virt-manager is written in the Python scripting language using GTK+ and Glade libraries. The installation process is the common autotools compilation procedure. Simply unpack the archive package, run the configure script, and invoke the usual make file build process, as shown in Listing 14.1.

LISTING 14.1 virt-manager Compilation Procedure

```
[root@dom0]# gunzip -c virt-manager-xxx.tar.gz | tar xvf -
[output omitted]
[root@dom0]# cd virt-manager-xxxx
[root@dom0]# ./configure --prefix=/path/to/install/root
[output omitted]
[root@dom0]# make
[output omitted]
[root@dom0]# make install
```

The dependencies of virt-manager are listed on the virt-manager Web site and vary from release to release. The major libraries it depends on are Python (for the application logic), pygtk for graphical interaction via the Python language, and libvirt for the virtual machine control interfaces. See the details on the download page for more information.

After your virt-manager installation is complete, you can typically launch it by using the virt-manager command line, or by selecting Applications, System Tools, and finally Virtual Machine Manager from the menu. Listing 14.2 shows the Help menu for the command line. Additionally, after your virt-manager is installed, you can use the virtual machine installation command line tool, virtinst, to easily provision your guest operating system instances. Virt-manager even expresses some of its API via the freedesktop.org DBus specification. This allows you to implement custom applications to interact with virt-manager to provide additional integration points.

LISTING 14.2 Command Line Options for virt-manager

```
[root@dom0]# virt-manager --help
usage: virt-manager.py [options]

options:
  -h, --help               show this help message and exit
  -c URI, --connect=URI

                           Connect to hypervisor at URI
  --no-dbus                Disable DBus service for controlling UI
```

Virt-manager is a powerful tool and is shipping with many distributions by default. Because of this and its open source license, virt-manager has a low barrier of entry. We found virt-manager to be an excellent tool and highly recommend it.

> **NOTE**
> Many additional screenshots of virt-manager are available online at:
>
> http://virt-manager.et.redhat.com/screenshots.html
> http://virt-manager.et.redhat.com/screenshots/install.html

XenMan

The final management tool we examine in this chapter is XenMan. It is a product of the ConVirt Project. The ConVirt Project, short for Controlling Virtual Systems, is an open source project specifically targeted at solving the frustrations and management problems surrounding virtualization environments. XenMan is the administration console of the project and is distributed under the GPL license.

In our experience, XenMan is solid and easy to use. It also looks arguably more polished than virt-manager and is just as easy to download, compile, and use free of charge. However, there is official support for virt-manager through Red Hat. XenMan is also specifically designed for Xen.

XenMan is a graphical life cycle management tool designed to be easy to use while still being feature-complete. XenMan supports features such as starting and stopping machines as well as provisioning new virtual machines.

XenMan is an open source project hosted on Source Forge (`http://xenman.sourceforge.net/`). Source Forge is a Web site dedicated to hosting open source projects of all kinds. Source Forge does not require any authorization or registration to download from. XenMan maintains packages for two distributions, OpenSUSE and Fedora Core, in addition to the source tarball. All three are available from the Source Forge site. Other packages are contributed by the community and include Ubuntu, Debian, and Gentoo.

Installing XenMan with its prebuilt RPM packages is simple, as shown in Listing 14.3. It does have a dependency of python-paramiko available in most distributions' package management systems such as yum for Fedora or YaST for SUSE.

LISTING 14.3 XenMan Binary Package Installation Instructions

```
[root@dom0]# rpm -U xenman-0.6.1.fedora.noarch.rpm
[root@dom0]#
```

Installing from source is also straightforward. Simply download the tarball, extract it, and follow the directions found in the README.install file as shown in Listing 14.4.

LISTING 14.4 XenMan Source Derived Installation Instructions

```
[root@dom0]# tar -xpzf xenman-0.6.tar.gz
[root@dom0]# cd xenman-0.6
[root@dom0]# sh ./distros/suse/configure_defaults-suse.sh
[root@dom0]# sh ./mk_image_store
[root@dom0]# chmod 0755 ./xenman
```

To test your install, simply attempt to run XenMan from the command line as shown in Listing 14.5.

LISTING 14.5 Running XenMan

```
[root@dom0]# xenman
[root@dom0]#
```

When you first start the program, you are presented with a summary page that allows you to quickly assess the state of the server and what guests are running as well as the servers to which you are connected. Figure 14.8 shows the initial dashboard view of XenMan at startup. The spinners on the left show the virtual machines available to this XenMan instance. The Image Store shows the template guests available for the creation of new virtual machine instances.

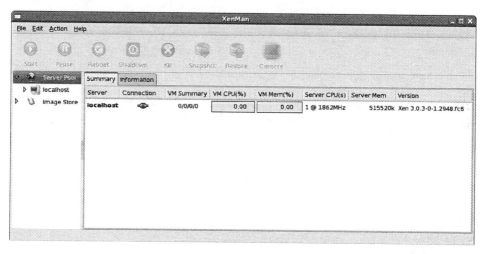

FIGURE 14.8 XenMan has a summary page that provides a quick overview of the running guests.

XenMan has two main areas on the left—one to see which servers have which virtual machines and their status, as well as a provisioning area. The provisioning area allows you to easily create new virtual machines. By default, XenMan has three predefined options. First is a Fedora paravirtualized install that is downloaded from the Internet. Second is a Linux CD install that creates an HVM that boots from a Linux CD. The third option is to create an HVM for use with Microsoft Windows. Figure 14.9 shows the general provisioning screen for a Fedora guest. Many options are specified on this screen. These options allow you to tweak the fundamental options for your virtual machine deployment.

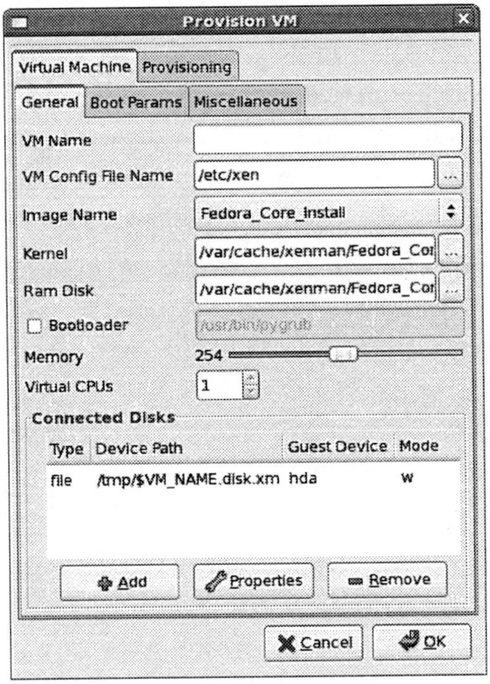

FIGURE 14.9 Fedora provisioning with XenMan

After provisioning a new machine, Xenman creates the necessary files for each machine—that is, Xen configuration file, and disk file. It also displays a summary of the machine's configuration. Figure 14.10 shows a newly created Fedora virtual machine. It is shown under the localhost Server Pool. The Summary and Information tabs on the right provide details about our new guest. Note the machine is in the stopped state by default.

XenMan allows you all the same options on an already existing machine by simply opening the Xen configuration file for that virtual machine. XenMan also provides most of the same command line functionality that you can get from the xm command but through a nice user interface, such as start, pause, reboot, shutdown, kill, snapshot, resume, and access to the console.

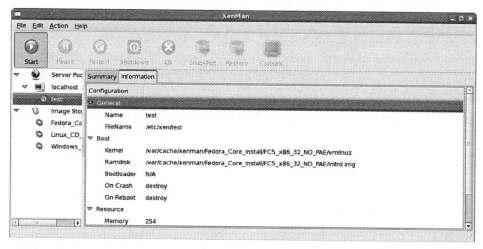

FIGURE 14.10 XenMan allows the configuration of a created guest to be examined.

Figure 14.11 illustrates the running of a virtual machine in XenMan. Note the check mark showing the running state. The other guests on this particular XenMan listing are in the stopped state. The panel on the right shows the console output of the running virtual machine.

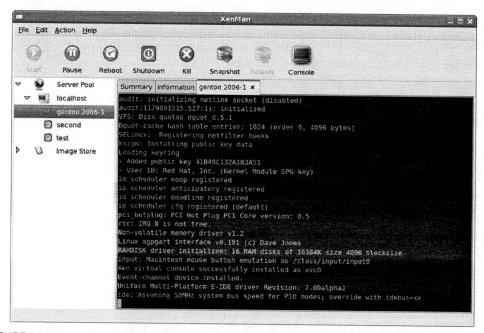

FIGURE 14.11 XenMan shows the state of all guests (running or stopped).

XenMan is a well-behaved administration tool that accomplishes the problems it set out to solve. It greatly reduces the problem of administering Xen servers. Its user interface is easy to understand, even for a first-time user. Its install is simple, and an administrator can be up and running within minutes. XenMan is a continuing project that is currently working on adding migration to its impressive list of features as well as adding more package support of more platforms. Overall, XenMan is a great, simple, open source administration console for the most common tasks associated with Xen.

Managing Multiple Systems

Individuals investigating the use of Xen guests in production enterprise environments often have questions about the best methodology for maintaining and updating those guests. A good general rule of thumb is that once a virtual machine has a network connection, it can be managed using most of the same tools used to manage physical machines. For example, some management tools have support for heartbeat monitoring to detect problems with service and to restart it. These same tools can be used to monitor services running in a virtual machine. Similarly, we discussed how Enomalism has some special support for updating guests via VMcasting.

Other than this, the best way to maintain virtual machines is typically to use the same tools available for maintaining physical machines of the same type. For example, if you are running a SUSE-based guest, YaST Online Update or Novell Zenworks should be the tool you choose. If the distribution you are using is Debian-based, continue using the normal apt-get based software update tools that are out there. The same is true for Gentoo and Portage. For Red Hat-based distributions, you can chose to enable a local yum server or use a tool such as Red Hat Network for your update tasks.

Summary

Choosing enterprise management tools for Xen can be complicated. As always, it depends heavily on your existing environment and what you are already familiar with using. Also, the feature set of the management tools varies substantially. All have basic functionality for guest creation and provisioning, but beyond that it can be a patchwork quilt of interesting features. No one tool supports all environments, and no one tool has all the features you might want. The tools also vary substantially in price and level of support. However, for anyone managing Xen in a production environment, it is well worth considering these tools that definitely make creating and managing Xen guests easier.

References and Further Reading

"Citrix XenServer Demo."
http://www.citrixxenserver.com/Pages/XenEnterprise_Demo.aspx.

"Citrix XenServer Enterprise Edition."
http://www.citrixxenserver.com/products/Pages/XenEnterprise.aspx.

"Citrix XenServer Express Edition."
http://www.citrixxenserver.com/products/Pages/XenExpress.aspx.

"Citrix XenServer v4 Overview."
http://www.citrixxenserver.com/products/Pages/myproducts.aspx.

"Citrix XenServer Standard Edition."
http://www.citrixxenserver.com/products/Pages/XenServer.aspx.

Enomalism XEN Virtualized Server Management Console.
http://www.enomalism.com/.

"IBM Director Extensions: Virtualization Manager." IBM Web Site.
http://www-03.ibm.com/systems/management/director/extensions/vm.html.

Virtual Iron Home Page.
http://www.virtualiron.com/.

"Virtual Machine Manager: Home."
http://virt-manager.org/.

"Virtual Machine Manager: Installation Wizard Screenshots."
http://virt-manager.et.redhat.com/screenshots/install.html.

"Virtual Machine Manager: Screenshots."
http://virt-manager.et.redhat.com/screenshots.html.

"Welcome to ConVirt." Information about XenMan - Open Source Virtualization Management.
http://xenman.sourceforge.net/.

Xen API: The Xen API Project. Xen Wiki.
http://wiki.xensource.com/xenwiki/XenApi.

Appendix A

Resources

Xen is still very much a moving target. It is under active development, and substantial aspects of its architecture are evolving. Many details of Xen are documented only in the code itself. This appendix highlights helpful resources for getting additional information and for tracking the inevitable changes in Xen. We highlight a few of the main sources of good information about Xen; there are of course many others, including excellent articles or blogs from early Xen adopters. As with most topics, your curiosity and a good search engine will take you a long way.

Xen Community

The first stop for anyone serious about learning more about Xen should be the Xen Community site hosted at http://xen.org (formerly http://www.xen-source.com/xen/ as shown in Figure A.1).

It links directly to many of the other resources we cover in this appendix, including the Xen Wiki, the Xen mailing lists, the source code for Xen, and notes from Xen Summit meetings, where major directions in Xen architecture are presented and discussed.

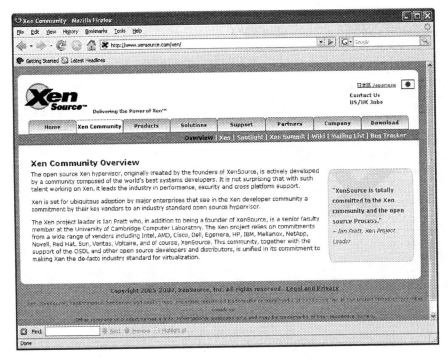

FIGURE A.1 The Xen Community Overview page is a good place to start.

XenWiki

The XenWiki, at `http://wiki.xensource.com/xenwiki/` (shown in Figure A.2), contains a wealth of information including documentation on everything from installing Xen, to debugging problems with Xen, to guides for contributing to Xen development. It also contains pointers to Xen-related products and services such as Xen-based hosting companies, consultants specializing in Xen, and third-party administrative tools.

> **NOTE**
> A word of warning: Some of the material in the XenWiki is out of date and no longer accurate. It is worth noting the date on any page of material. The main XenWiki page also has a choice to view the most recent changes. This is a good way to get a sense for what material is under active development.

Substantially more information contained in the XenWiki is suggested from the links on the main page. Therefore, we recommend browsing the TitleIndex option to get a more complete list of the material in the XenWiki.

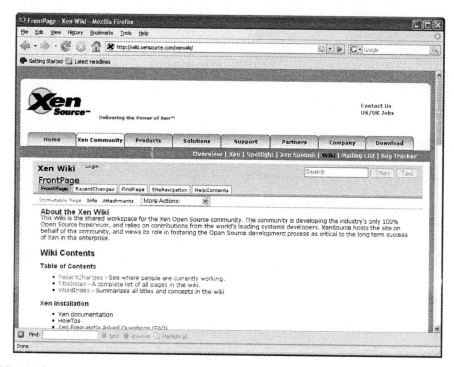

FIGURE A.2 The XenWiki is a rich source of online documentation.

Xen Mailing Lists and Bug Reporting

Another important step for those interested in learning more about Xen is joining one or more of the various Xen mailing lists at `http://lists.xensource.com` (shown in Figure A.3). There are a variety of typical lists including xen-announce for announcements, xen-users for questions about installing and running, and xen-devel for Xen developers. There are also a good number of specialty lists for groups developing specific aspects of Xen. In addition, several coordination lists for discussion of merges or announcements of change sets are listed.

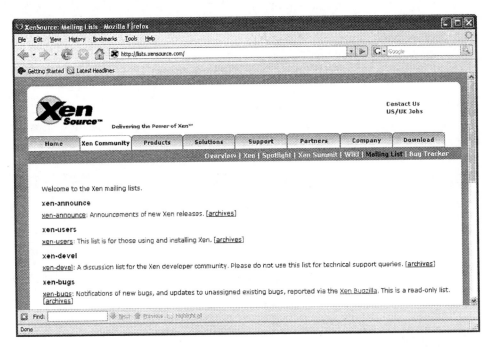

FIGURE A.3   Consider joining some of the Xen mailing lists to keep up on the most recent developments.

There is also a read-only list, xen-bugs, which is generated by defect reports entered in Xen's Bugzilla repository at `http://bugzilla.xensource.com/bugzilla/index.cgi` (shown in Figure A.4). You can search for the status of existing bug reports. You can also report new bugs if you create an account by registering your name and e-mail address.

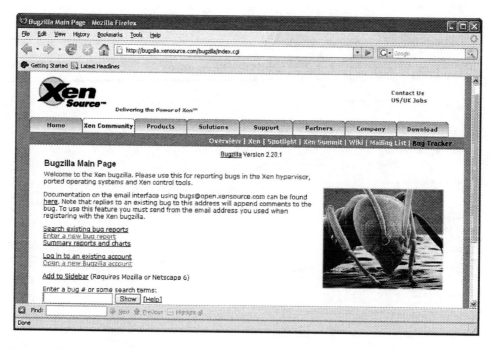

FIGURE A.4 If you are having a problem with Xen, check the Bugzilla repository to see whether others have encountered the same problem, and if not, consider reporting it.

Xen Summits

If you are interested in tracking upcoming changes in Xen, one of the best resources is the notes section from Xen Summit meetings at www.xen.org/xensummit/ (shown in Figure A.5). Xen Summits are opportunities for the Xen development community to meet face-to-face to discuss new ideas and plans for upcoming additions to Xen. Slides from presentations at the Xen Summits are typically archived on the Web.

Development resources for the open source Xen project come from a wide variety of sources, and this is reflected in the attendance and presentations at the Xen Summits. Representatives from XenSource (Citrix XenServer Product Group), including founders of the Xen Project and developers of core components of xend, cover information on the Xen roadmap and plans for feature integration. There are presentations on major development projects from companies such as IBM, Sun, SGI, Samsung, Red Hat, Novell, Intel, AMD, HP, Fujitsu, and many others. Academic and governmental contributors also attend and present results of their work.

It is important to realize that some of the work presented at the Xen Summits represent prototype features being developed and tested by individual groups. Much of it will not be immediately available in typical Xen installations, and some of it will never be incorporated into the stable release versions of Xen. Nevertheless, the slides from presentations at Xen Summits do provide a good preview of how Xen is evolving.

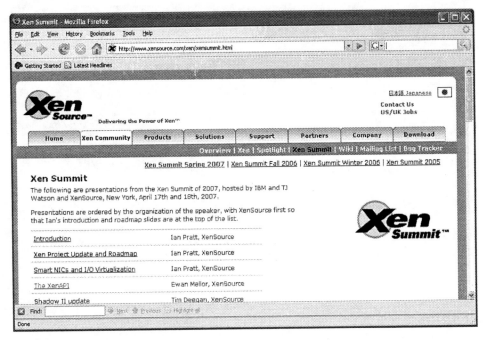

FIGURE A.5 Attending a Xen Summit is a great way to meet people doing active Xen development.

Xen Source Code

As with any rapidly evolving project, documentation for some details exists only in the source code. Therefore, consulting the XenSource code is an option that advanced Xen users and administrators might want to consider.

The place to start for access to the XenSource code is at `http://xenbits.xen-source.com/` (shown in Figure A.6). There you find a number of different versions of the XenSource code including the stable or testing versions of important releases (for example, xen-2.0 or xen-3.0), as well as testing versions of more recent numbered releases (for example, xen-3.1). The development version including all the most recent changes is also available as xen-unstable.

Each release is available as a Mercurial repository. Mercurial is a popular source control system (often abbreviated with "hg" the chemical symbol for mercury). If you are not familiar with Mercurial, there are step-by-step tutorials for installation and use at `www.selenic.com/mercurial/wiki/index.cgi/Tutorial`. There is also an excellent tutorial on using Mercurial specifically with Xen available at `www.cl.cam. ac.uk/research/srg/netos/xen/readmes/hg-cheatsheet.txt`.

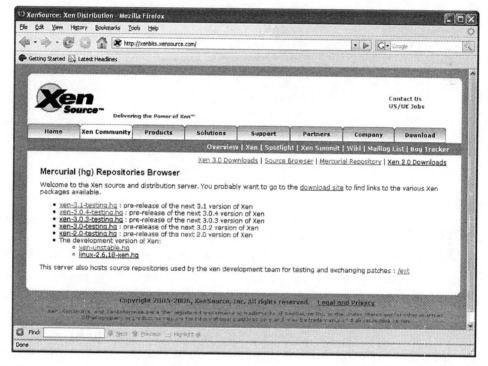

FIGURE A.6 If you want to build Xen from source or do some Xen development, the Xen Mercurial (hg) Repository is the place to start.

You can also browse the Xen code online at `http://lxr.xensource.com/lxr/ source` (shown in Figure A.7). This does not give you the same flexibility to choose which version of the XenSource code to examine, but is a quick way to get started without installing Mercurial or downloading the full repository.

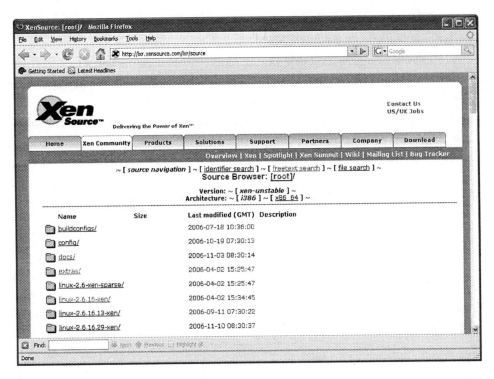

FIGURE A.7 If you just want to read some details in the XenSource code, viewing it online with the Xen-Source browser might be easier than downloading the entire source tree.

However you choose to browse the code, you might want some navigational advice from the root directory of the main XenSource tree. Many of the portions of Xen most visible to users are located in the tools subdirectory. For example, xm (written in Python) can be found in tools/python/xen/xm. Similarly, the xend source is in tools/python/xen/xend. Under tools, there are also directories for pygrub, xenstore, vnet, and many other topics covered in this book. The code for the Xen hypervisor itself is found in the main Xen subdirectory. Patches to the Linux source code that are necessary for Xen are located in the various Linux subdirectories. Some documentation can be found throughout the source tree, for example, in the main docs subdirectory or the tools/examples directory.

Academic Papers and Conferences

Another place to look for information about Xen is in various academic papers and conferences (academic and otherwise). Xen began as a research project at the

University of Cambridge, and the original Xen Project Web site at `http://www.cl.cam.ac.uk/research/srg/netos/xen/` (shown in Figure A.8) contains many useful links including to the Xen User's Manual at `http://www.cl.cam.ac.uk/research/srg/netos/xen/readmes/user/user.html`. Some information in the original Xen site is now out-of-date, and some links off the page such as the FAQ link connect directly to pages maintained by XenSource.

One particularly useful link for identifying academic papers about Xen is the Architecture link off the main page. It leads to a list of papers and presentations about the original design of Xen including the seminal paper on Xen, "Xen and the Art of Virtualization," published in 2003. Work on Xen has appeared in a number of conferences and workshops such as the Symposium on Operating Systems Principles (SOSP), the USENIX Annual Technical Conference, the International Conference on Architectural Support for Programming Languages and Operating Systems (ASPLOS), the Symposium on Networked Systems Design and Implementation (NSDI), the Ottawa Linux Symposium (OLS), and LinuxWorld.

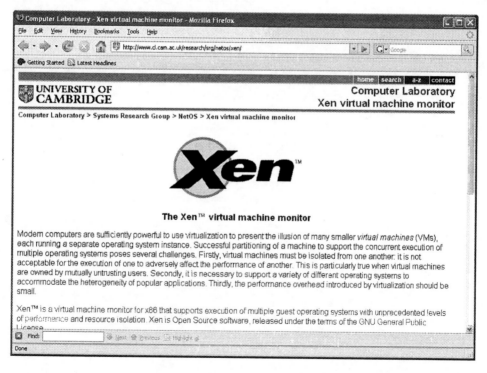

FIGURE A.8 The University of Cambridge Xen Project Web site is an excellent reference.

Distribution-Specific Resources

Depending on what operating system or distribution you are running, there might also be a wealth of information specific to running Xen in your particular environment. Table A.1 contains a partial list of distribution-specific Xen resources to get you started.

TABLE A.1 Distribution-Specific Xen Resources

Operating System/Distribution	Xen Resources
Red Hat/Fedora Linux	http://fedoraproject.org/wiki/Tools/Xen http://www.redhat.com/mailman/listinfo/ fedora-xen
SUSE Linux	http://en.opensuse.org/Xen http://www.suse.de/~garloff/linux/xen/
Debian Linux	http://wiki.debian.org/Xen
Ubuntu Linux	https://help.ubuntu.com/community/Xen
Gentoo Linux	http://gentoo-wiki.com/HOWTO_Xen_and_Gentoo
Solaris	http://opensolaris.org/os/community/xen/ http://mail.opensolaris.org/mailman/listinfo/ xen-discuss
NetBSD	http://www.netbsd.org/ports/xen/

The xm Command

xm is the Xen command to administer Xen guest domains. It can manage devices, activate or deactivate guest domains, and retrieve information on domain configuration or status. The xm command uses the following format:

```
xm subcommand [ options] < arguments>
[…]: an optional argument;
<…>: a required argument
```

In Tables B.1 through B.9, the notation "domain" is used to represent the domain name, and "domain-id" is used to represent a domain's numeric identity number.

The xm subcommands are listed by category, and each subcommand's options are listed alphabetically. When looking up some related topic, it is better to search by category; while if looking up some specific command, searching alphabetically is a better choice. For more details on the xm command, see the xm man page.

TABLE B.1 General Subcommand

Subcommand	Options	Description
`xm help`		List all the possible xm subcommands for reference.
	`-help/-h` `<subcommand>`	Display the specific subcommand's help information.

TABLE B.2 Block Device-Related Subcommands

Subcommand	Options	Description
`xm block-list <domain>` `[options]`	`--long`	Display the virtual block devices in a domain. Display in the XML simplified format.

`xm block-attach`
 `<domain> <Backdev>`
 `<Frontdev> <Mode>`
		Add a new virtual block device to the domain.

`xm block-detach`
 `<domain> <devID>`
 `[options]`
	`--force/-f`	Remove a virtual block device from the domain.
		
		 Enforce to remove the virtual block device.

`xm vtpm-list [options]`		Display all the virtual Trusted Platform Module devices.
	`--long`	Display in the XML simplified format.

TABLE B.3 Domain Related-Subcommands

Subcommand	Options	Description
`xm domid <domain name>`		Display the domain name's corresponding ID.
`xm domname <domain id>`		Display the domain ID's corresponding name.
`xm dump-core <domain>` `[filename] [options]`		Dump a guest domain's core file to /var/xen/dump or to a specified filename.
	`--crash/-C`	Force the guest domain to terminate after dumping the core file.
`xm dry-run` `<guest config file>`		Validate the resource access of a domain's configuration file.
`xm top`		Display a dynamic real-time view of running domains.
`xm uptime [options]` `<domain>`	`-s`	Display a domain's uptime. Current time in simple format.

TABLE B.4 DomU-Related Subcommands*

Subcommand	Options	Description
xm list [options] [domain]		List Xen domain's ID, status, and resource information.
	--long/-l	List domains' status by the options in a guest domain's configuration file.
	--label	Additionally display the domain's security label.
xm create [options] <guest config file> [configuration options]		Boot up the guest domain according to the guest domain configuration file.
	--path=directory list separated by colon	Set the search path for the guest domain's configuration file.
	--dryrun/-n	Validate the run of a guest domain and display the domain's configuration result.
	--pause/-p	The guest domain will be in pause state after booting up.
	--console_ autoconnect/-c	The terminal will connect to the guest domain console after booting up.
xm shutdown [options] <domain>		Shut down the specified guest domain.
	-w	The guest domain is terminated after the services in the guest domains have been nicely shut down.
	-a	Shut down all domains.
xm reboot [options] <domain>		Reboot the guest domain.
	-w	Wait for all the services in the guest domain to be nicely closed and then reboot.
	-a	Reboot all the domains.
xm destroy <domain>		Force to terminate the guest domain.
xm pause <domain>		Change a running guest domain to be in the pause state.
xm unpause <domain>		Change a paused guest domain back to be in the running state.
xm console <domain>		Connect to the guest domain.
xm sysrp <domain> <magic sysrq letter>		Send a magic system request signal to the guest domain.

*The DomU-related subcommands are all about the Xen guest domain's status.

TABLE B.5 Network-Related Subcommands*

Subcommand	Options	Description
xm network-list [options] <domain>		Display the information of network interfaces in the guest domain.
	--long/-l	Display the information in the SXP format.
xm network-attach <domain> [--script=<script>] [--ip=<ip>] [--mac=<mac>]		Add a specific network interface to the guest domain.
xm network-detach <domain> <devID> [options]		Remove a specific network interface from the guest domain.
	--force/-f	Enforce to remove a specific network interface.

*The network related subcommands are all about dynamically operating on virtual network interfaces in the guest domain.

TABLE B.6 Resource Management-Related Subcommands

Subcommand	Options	Description
xm mem-max <domain> <memory value>		Set the domain's maximum memory usage.
xm mem-set <domain> <memory value>		Dynamically set the current domain's memory. usage.
xm sched-credit -d <domain> [options]		Set the weight or upper limit of CPU usage for a domain.
	--domain=guest domain/-d domain	Specify the domain to set the CPU usage parameter.
	--weight=integer value/-w integer value	Specify the weight value of a guest domain's CPU usage.
	--cap=integer value/-c integer value	Specify the upper limit of a guest domain that can use CPU.
xm sched-sedf <domain> [options]		Set the SEDF scheduler parameters for a domain.
	--period=ms/-p ms	Set the accounting period of a domain.
	--slice=ms/-s ms	Set the maximum time slice for a domain.
	--latency=ms/-l ms	Set the latency limit to support I/O intensive and real-time cases.
	--extra=flag/-e flag	Set the flag so that overrun of a domain will be allowed.
	--weight=float value -w float value	Another way of setting --period or --slice.

Subcommand	Options	Description
`xm vcpu-list [domain]`		Display the VCPU assignment for each domain.
`xm vcpu-pin <domain> <vcpu> <cpus>`		Set a CPU set for a VCPU of a specific domain.
`xm vcpu-set <domain> <vcpus>`		Set the VCPU set for a domain.

TABLE B.7 Security-Related Subcommands

Subcommand	Options	Description
`xm labels [policy] [type=dom|res|any]`		Display the labels of a specified type and policy.
`xm addlabel <label> [dom <configuration file>|res <resource>] <policy>`		Either add a label by a domain's configuration file or a global resource label file with the specified policy.
`xm getlabel <dom <configuration file>| res <resource>>`		Display the label by a domain or resource.
`xm rmlabel <dom <configuration file>| res <resource>>`		Remove a label from the domain's configuration file or a global resource label file.
`xm makepolicy <policy>`		Set a new policy and create a policy file `.bin` or `.map`.
`xm loadpolicy <policy binary file>`		Load a policy binary file into the running hypervisor.
`xm cfgbootpolicy <policy> [kernel version]`		Configure to boot with a specified policy by adding module option in the Xen `grub.conf`.
`xm dumppolicy`		Display the current policy information from the hypervisor.
`xm resources`		Display each resource label information from the global resource label file.

TABLE B.8 Vnet-Related Subcommands

Subcommand	Options	Description
`xm vnet-list [options]`		List the current virtual network.
	`--long/-l`	Display the Vnet in the SXP format.
`xm vnet-create <vnet configuration file>`		Create the Vnet by the Vnet configuration file.
`xm vnet-delete <vnetID>`		Delete a Vnet from the current running Vnet list.

TABLE B.9 Xend-Related Subcommands

Subcommand	Options	Description
`xm log`		Display the xend log file.
`xm dmesg [options]`		Display the xend bootup message.
	`--clear/-c`	Clear the message buffer after dmesging.
`xm info`		Display the Xen system information.
`xm serve`		Invoke remote XMLPRC over ssh.

Appendix C

Xend Configuration Parameters

xend is Xen's control daemon. It is responsible for domain related tasks, such as creation, shutdown, and migration of domains. The xend configuration file is used to specify the behavior of xend.

In Tables C.1 through C.5, the notation "..." is used to represent what the user needs to fill in. The appropriate value or the corresponding script is provided in the Default Value column.

Possible parameters are listed by category.

TABLE C.1 Log-Related Parameters

Parameters	Default Value	Description
`(logfile   …  )`	`/var/log/xen/xend.log`	Specify the logfile's path and filename.
`(loglevel   …  )`	`DEBUG`	Log the message according to the specified level. The options for values are `DEBUG`, `ERROR`, `INFO`, `CRITICAL`, and `WARNING`.

TABLE C.2 Server-Related Parameters

Parameters	Default Value	Description
`(xend-address … )`	`' '`	Listen on the HTTP connection IP.
`(xend-http-server …)`	`yes | no`	Start up the xend HTTP server, use `http://ip:port/xend` to browser the hypervisor.
`(xend-port … )`	`8000`	Set the xend HTTP server IP port.
`(xend-tcp-xmlrpc-server …  )`	`yes | no`	Start up the HTTP server defined in xml-rpc protocol.
`(xend-unix-path … )`	`/var/lib/xend/ xend-socket`	Specify the UNIX domain socket that is used for the UNIX domain server to output data.
`(xend-unix-xmlrpc-server   … )`	`yes | no`	Start up the UNIX domain socket server defined in xml-rpc protocol.

TABLE C.3 Migration-Related Parameters

Parameters	Default Value	Description
`(external-migration-tool …)`	' '	Use a script to migrate guest's external device, such as disk image or a virtual TPM.
`(xend-relocation-address … )`	' '	Listen on that address for the migration connection.
`(xend-relocation-hosts-allow … )`	' '	Listen on the domain name or the IP that matches the regular expressions.
`(xend-relocation-port … )`	8002	Specify the relocation server port used for migration.
`(xend-relocation-server … )`	yes | no	Start up the relocation server for cross-machine migration.

TABLE C.4 Network-Related Parameters

Parameters	Default Value	Description
`(network-script … )`	`network-bridge`	Set the script that set up the networking environment.
`(vif-script … )`	`vif-bridge`	Set the virtual interface type that will be used as backend.

TABLE C.5 Domain-Related Parameters

Parameters	Default Value	Description
`(console-limit … )`	1024	Configure the console server's buffer size for each domain.
`(dom0-cpus … )`	0	Set the number of CPUs that Domain0 can use.
`(dom0-min-mem … )`	256	Set the minimum reserved memory size for Domain0.
`(enable-dump … )`	yes | no	Configure to core dump of guest domains when crashed.
`(vnc-listen … )`	127.0.0.1	Set VNC server IP to listen on.
`(vncpasswd … )`	' '	Set VNC console default password on HVM domain.

Appendix D

Guest Configuration Parameters

A guest configuration file is used by xm to start running the Xen guest. The parameters in a guest configuration file are in the Python format. Tables D.1 through D.8 list the guest configuration parameters by category. The parameters use the following format:

```
parameter item = <value type>
... inside <value type, ...>: omitting the rest possible similar value types
```

TABLE D.1 Boot Parameters

Parameter Format	Description
bootloader= '<bootloader_path/pygrub>'	Specify the boot loader program that will be used by the DomU during the boot process.
extra=<integer value>	Customize the environment and boot to the run level.
kernel=/boot_path/xen_kernel"	Specify the kernel image path and filename.

TABLE D.1 continued

Parameter Format	Description
`memory= <integer value>`	Set the guest domain's memory usage size.
`name=<guest domain name>`	Set the guest domain name.
`ramdisk=/ramdisk_path/ ramdisk_file`	Optionally specify the ramdisk file location.
`uuid=<128-bit Hexdecimal>"`	Set a universal unique identifier for the guest domain.

TABLE D.2 LVM Parameters

Parameter Format	Description
`disk=['dev_type_in_dom0:/path _to_dir,dev_type_in_domU, access_mode', '…']`	Define the disk devices that the guest domain can or may access.
	The device type in Domain0 can be `tap:aio`, `phy`, `file`; the access mode can be `r`, `w`.
`root="/root_device_path/root _device_type"`	Root partition kernel parameter.

TABLE D.3 NFS Parameters

Parameter Format	Description
`nfs_root='/fullpath_to_root_ directory'`	Set the nfs root directory.
`nfs_server='IP dotted decimal'`	Set the nfs server IP.

TABLE D.4 CPU Parameters

Parameter Format	Description
cpus="integer, ..."	Set the CPUs that the guest domain can access.
vcpus=integer value	Set the number of virtual CPUs that can be used.

TABLE D.5 TPM Parameters

Parameter Format	Description
vtpm=['instance=integer value, backend=integer value']	Set the trusted platform module.

TABLE D.6 PCI Parameters

Parameter Format	Description
pci = ['domain:bus:slot.func', '...']	Pass a PCI device to the guest domain.

TABLE D.7 Network Parameters

Parameter Format	Description
dhcp="dhcp|yes|no"	Set the mode how the guest domain obtains its IP.
gateway="IP dotted decimal"	Set IP for the guest domain's gateway.
hostname="string"	Set the guest domain hostname over the network.
netmask=" IP dotted decimal"	Set the network mask for the IP.
vif=['mac=12-digit hexdecimal, ip=dotted hexdecimal, bridge=devicename', '...']	Set the guest domain's virtual network interfaces.

TABLE D.8 Domain Behavior Parameters

Parameter Format	Description
`on_crash='behavior mode'`	Set the behavior mode when the guest domain crashes. Behavior mode can be one of `destroy`, `restart`, `rename-restart`, `preserve`.
`on_poweroff='behavior mode'`	Set the behavior mode when the guest domain is powered off.
`on_reboot='behavior mode'`	Set the behavior mode when the guest domain reboots.

Appendix E

Xen Performance Evaluation

The Clarkson University group has long been dedicated to Xen research. When Xen was first released, the Clarkson group carried out a repeated research effort on Xen to compare and validate Xen's performance. This repeated research helped provide credibility to the Xen project and helped the project gain recognition in both academia and industry. The group later focused on virtualization's isolation properties, when they compared the performance isolation properties of Xen with other virtualization systems. This isolation research has given good guidance to the virtualization industries. For further details, you can refer to the published papers as follows:

- "Xen and the Art of Repeated Research," B. Clark, T. Deshane, E. Dow, S. Evanchik, M. Finlayson, J. Herne, J. N. Matthews, Proceedings of the USENIX 2004 Annual Technical Conference, June 2004. Downloadable at `http://www.usenix.org/events/usenix04/tech/freenix/full_papers/clark/clark.pdf`.

- "Quantifying the Performance Isolation Properties of Virtualization Systems," J. Matthews, W. Hu, M. Hapuarachchi, T. Deshane, D. Dimatos, G. Hamilton, M. McCabe, J. Owens, ExpCS 07, June 2007. Downloadable at `http://www.usenix.org/events/expcs07/papers/6-matthews.pdf`.

In this appendix, we summarize the results from these papers and add an additional section on network performance testing.

Xen Performance Measurements

The paper "Xen and the Art of Repeated Research" from FREENIX05 repeats and extends experiments described in the paper "Xen and the Art of Virtualization" by Barham et al. from SOSP-03. Results quantify the overhead of Xen relative to base Linux and the degradation experienced when running multiple virtual guests on the same physical machine. (The degree to which these results still hold for the latest versions of Xen is unknown.) Specifically, the paper answers a number of questions including

- Could the results from the SOSP-03 Xen paper be reproduced?
- Could Xen be realistically used for virtual Web hosting with multiple VMs per machine?
- Do you need a $2,500 Dell Xeon server to run Xen effectively or will a three-year-old x86 do the job?
- How does a virtual machine monitor on commodity PCs compare to a virtual machine monitor on a mainframe?

Repeatability of the Xen Team's Results

Our first task was to convince ourselves that we could successfully reproduce the results presented in "Xen and the Art of Virtualization." The paper itself contains clear details on their test machine—a Dell 2650 dual processor 2.4GHz Xeon server with 2GB of RAM, a Broadcom Tigon 3 Gigabit Ethernet NIC, and a single Hitachi DK32EJ 146GB 10K RPM SCSI disk.

We had little trouble acquiring a matching system. We ordered a machine matching these specifications from Dell for approximately $2,000. If we had been repeating older research, reproducing an acceptable hardware platform might have been a significant challenge.

The only significant difference in our system was the SCSI controller. Their controller had been a 160MB/sec DELL PERC RAID 3Di, and ours was a 320MB/sec Adaptec 29320 aic79xx. Thus our first hurdle was the need to port the driver for our SCSI controller to Xen. The Xen team was extremely helpful in this process and in the end we contributed this driver (and several others) back into the Xen source base.

Our second hurdle was assembling and running all the benchmarks used in the Xen paper including OSDB, dbench, lmbench, ttcp, SPEC INT CPU 2000, and SPEC-web99. (The Xen team was helpful in providing details on the parameters they used for each test and even providing some of their testing scripts.) We generalized and extended their scripts into a test suite that would help save others this step in the future.

In our experiments, we replaced CPU-intensive SPECINT 2000 with FourInARow, an integer-intensive program from freebench.org. We wrote our own replacement for the Web server benchmark, SPECweb99, using Apache JMeter.

Our final hurdle was that our initial measurements showed much lower performance for native Linux than the original paper. In comparing the details of our configuration with the Xen team, we discovered that performance is much higher with SMP support disabled.

With those hurdles behind us, we successfully reproduced measurements from the original Xen paper, comparing the performance of XenoLinux and UML to native Linux.

We then added error bars to illustrate standard deviation where we ran at least five tests of each benchmark. OSDB on UML gave errors in the majority of runs. We received only one score for OSDB-IR and no scores for OSDB-OLTP from all our experiments. We were missing some measurements for UML. We investigated further, but were unable to determine a cause.

Reporting standard deviation adds important information about the reliability of a reported score. The standard deviation of most benchmarks is less than 1 percent. dbench has a standard deviation of 14 percent and 18 percent for native Linux and XenoLinux, respectively.

In our experiments, the relative performance of XenoLinux and UML compared to native Linux was nearly identical to the performance reported in the original paper as shown in Figures E.1 and E.2. Our CPU-intensive and Web server benchmarks were not directly comparable to SPEC INT and SPECweb99, but accomplished a similar purpose and demonstrate similar relative performance.

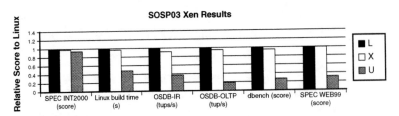

FIGURE E.1 Relative performance of native Linux (L), XenoLinux (X), and U-ser-mode Linux (UML) from Figure 3 of the original "Xen and the Art of Virtualization" paper minus the data on VMware Workstation

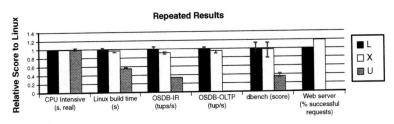

FIGURE E.2 Relative performance results of native Linux (L), XenoLinux (X), and User-mode Linux (U) from performing similar experiments. The native Linux results are disabled in all experiments with SMP.

Finally, we were ready to answer our first question: Could we reproduce the results from the SOSP-03 Xen paper? We have mentioned a few caveats, but overall the answer was yes. We could reproduce the comparison of XenoLinux and native Linux to within a few percentage points on nearly identical hardware.

Xen and Virtual Web Hosting

One of the stated goals of Xen is to enable applications such as server consolidation. In comparing Xen to Denali, the Xen paper page 2 states "Denali is designed to support thousands of virtual machines running network services which are small-scale and unpopular. In contrast, Xen is intended to scale to approximately 100 virtual machines running industry standard applications and services."

We set out to evaluate the suitability of Xen for virtual Web hosting. Specifically, we wanted to determine how many usable guests could be supported for the purpose of hosting a Web server.

The original Xen paper includes a figure showing the performance of 128 guests each running CPU Intensive SPEC INT2000. We hoped to begin by showing the performance of 128 guests each running a Web server benchmark. However, when we went to configure our Dell Xeon server for this experiment, we ran into certain resource limitations. First, as stated in the paper, the hypervisor does not support paging among guests to enforce resource isolation. Therefore, each guest must have a dedicated region of memory. For the 128-guest SPEC INT experiment, they used 15MB for each guest, reserving 80MB for the hypervisor and Domain0. This amount—15MB—is not sufficient for an industry standard Web server. Second, the Xen team used raw disk partitions for each of the 128 guests. The Linux kernel supports only 15 total partitions per SCSI disk. Getting around this limit requires patching the kernel (as the Xen team did) or using a virtualized disk subsystem. We tried the virtualized disk subsystem in the Xen 1.0 source tree without success.

If we were to increase the memory allocated per guest from 15MB to a more typical memory size of 128MB, we could accommodate only 15 guests plus Domain0. To support 100 guests at 128MB per guest would require more than 12GB of memory. At 64MB per guest, 100 guests would require more than 6GB of memory. In our Xeon server, the most memory we can support is 4GB.

> **NOTE**
> Instead of using SPECweb99 to measure Web server performance, we wrote a replacement for it using Apache JMeter. JMeter is a flexible framework for testing functionality and performance of Web applications under load. We instrumented JMeter to follow the same distribution of requests and placed the proper static and dynamic content on each server as under the experiment in SPECweb99. More information including our JMeter test plans and documentation is available at www.clarkson.edu/class/cs644/xen.

Figure E.3 reports our results for 1 to 16 concurrent servers. We reported results for native Linux both with SMP enabled and disabled. For Xen, we allocated 98MB for each guest in addition to Domain0. Our results in Figure E.3 show that native Linux with SMP enabled retains high performance even with 16 concurrent Web server processes under high load significantly higher than SPECweb99. XenoLinux drops off steadily as more guests are added. Linux with SMP disabled is shown for completeness.

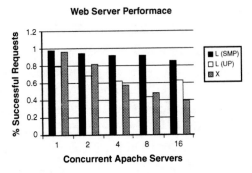

FIGURE E.3 Comparing the Web server's performance for native Linux with SMP enabled, native Linux with SMP disabled, and XenoLinux by scaling the concurrent guests

Thus, we were ready to answer our second question: Could we realistically use Xen for virtual Web hosting? We found Xen to be quite stable and could easily imagine using it for 16 moderately loaded servers. However, we would not expect to be able to support 100 guests running industry standard applications.

Comparing XenoLinux to Native Linux on Older PC Hardware

We wondered how Xen would perform on an older PC rather than a new Xeon server. So in addition to running on a 2.4GHz dual processor server, we ran our tests on a P3 1GHz processor with 512MB of PC133 memory with 10/100 3COM (3c905C-TX/TX-M Ethernet card) and a 40GB Western Digital WDC WD400BB-75AUA1 hard drive.

In Figure E.4, we first show the performance of Xen and native Linux on this older PC platform relative to native Linux on the Xeon server. Clearly, raw performance is less on the older PC. Figure E.5 shows the relative performance of Xen to native Linux on the older platform to the relative performance of Xen to native Linux on the faster platform. On average, Xen is only 3.5% slower relative to native Linux on the older PC.

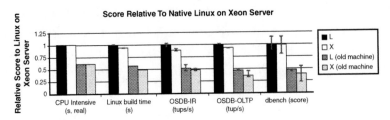

FIGURE E.4 Similar experimental results on the old machine compared relatively to the performance on the new Xeon server

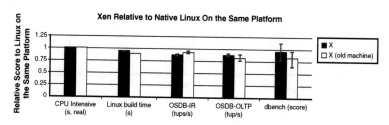

FIGURE E.5 The same results on the old machines, but compared relative to the Xen paper's performance of Xen to native Linux on the same platform

Although the relative overhead is nearly the same on both systems, one disadvantage of the older PC is that we will be able to create fewer guests. For example, while we are able to create 16 guests with 128MB of memory each on the Xeon server, we can create only 3 such guests plus Domain0 on the older PC.

Thus, we were ready to answer our third question: Do you need $2,500 Dell Xeon server to run Xen effectively or will a three-year-old x86 do the job? No, an older PC can efficiently run Xen, but only with a small number of guests. Of course, newer machines would be required for HVM support.

Xen on x86 Versus IBM zServer

Virtualization for the x86 might be relatively new, but it has been around for more than 30 years on IBM mainframes. It is natural to question how multiple Linux guests with Xen on x86 compare to multiple Linux guests on an IBM mainframe designed specifically to support virtualization. This is especially relevant given the following posting from Keir Fraser of the Xen team to the Linux Kernel Mailing List: "In fact, one of our main aims is to provide zseries-style virtualization on x86 hardware!"

We tested on an IBM Server z800 model 2066-0LF with 1 processor and 8GB of memory. The zServer was connected to an ESS800 Enterprise Storage System via Ficon with two channel paths from one Ficon card. This machine was valued at more than $200,000. Our zServer was an entry-level model. The single CPU executed a dummy instruction every other cycle; a software upgrade was required to remove this feature.

Figure E.6 compares performance on the zServer to native Linux and Xen on both the new Xeon server and the old PC. On the zServer, we ran Linux guests with the 2.4.21 kernel just as in our x86 native Linux and Xen tests. For the zServer, it is specifically 2.4.21-1.1931.2.399.ent #1 SMP. We found that Xen on the Xeon server significantly outperforms the zServer on these benchmarks.

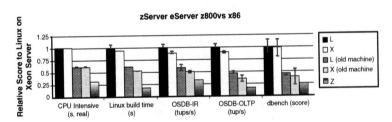

FIGURE E.6 The performance results on zSeries Linux guests relative to native Linux on the Xeon server; Xen on the Xeon server as well as native Linux and Xen on the older PC are also shown for comparison.

At first, we were surprised by these results. Results presented by IBM in "Linux on zSeries Performance Update" by Thoss show comparable performance for a modern z900 with 1 CPU. Figure E.7 presents a graph similar to one in the zSeries paper showing the performance of dbench on our zServer, our Xeon server, and our older x86. As in the zSeries paper, throughput for a one CPU zServer does not rise above 150MB/sec. However, we show a more significant degradation for more than 15 concurrent clients.

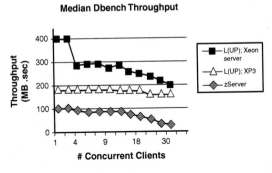

FIGURE E.7 Throughput reported by dbench compared for 1 to 24 concurrent clients for native Linux on a Xeon server, native Linux on an older PC, and Linux on the zServer

This comparison of our results to the zSeries paper leads us to believe that no simple software configuration enhancements will improve performance on our zServer, and that our figures although generated on an older model were comparable to more recent offerings from IBM. The zSeries paper also gave dbench scores for zServers with 4, 8, and 16 processors. Their results indicate that performance would be significantly better for a zServer with multiple processors. For example, it reports around 1000MB/sec for a 16 CPU z900.

In Figure E.8, we add measurements using our Web server benchmark of the zServer with 1 to 16 Linux guests to the data that was presented in Figure E.3. Xen on the Xeon server and the zServer perform similarly, with the zServer performing better than Xen at 2, 4, and 16 guests, but worse at 1 and 8 guests.

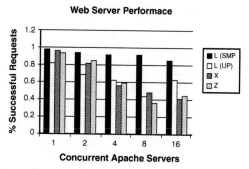

Web Server Performace

FIGURE E.8 The Web server's performance on the zServer compared among native Linux with SMP enabled, native Linux with SMP disabled, and XenoLinux on a Xeon server

Thus, we were ready to answer our fourth question: How does a virtual machine monitor on commodity PCs compare to a virtual machine monitor on a mainframe? At least on our low-end zServer, Xen on x86 performed better for most workloads we examined. For a $2,500 machine to do so well compared to a machine valued at more than $200,000 is impressive!

Performance Isolation in Xen

Performance isolation is the degree to which each virtual machine is insulated or protected from the resource demands of the other virtual machines on the same hardware. It is an important aspect to indicate how well a virtualization system can protect or isolate one guest virtual machine in it from another, especially in an untrusting commercial hosting environment.

Performance isolation might vary due to the presence of the different resource consumption in a misbehaving virtual machine. Knowing the performance degradation in the good guest machines due to different resource categories is important for other virtualization providers and customers of commercial hosting services to decide how to choose the virtualization systems. We categorize a virtual machine's resources into five kinds: CPU, Memory, Processes, Disk Bandwidth, and Network Bandwidth. An application running in one virtual machine can turn out to be a malicious resource exhauster, such as a CPU eater, fork bomb, memory hog, and so on.

In our paper "Quantifying the Performance Isolation Properties of Virtualization Systems" from ExpCS 07, we evaluated the impact on the other well-behaving virtual guests while one misbehaving virtual machine is running one malicious resource consumer. To carry out these experiments, we designed five intensive resource consumer applications, whose design specification is listed in Table E.1.

TABLE E.1 Intensive Resource Stress Application Specification

Intensive Resource Consumption	Specification
Memory intensive	Loops constantly allocating and touching memory without freeing it
Fork bomb	Loops creating new child processes
CPU intensive	Tight loop containing integer arithmetic operations
Disk intensive	Running 10 threads of IOzone each running an alternating read and write pattern
Network intensive (transmitter)	4 threads each constantly sending 60KB sized packets over UDP to external receivers
Network Intensive (Receiver)	4 threads which each constantly read 60KB packets over UDP from external senders

These intensive resource-consuming applications have been grouped as a suite of isolation stress test benchmarks for Performance Isolation Evaluation. They are open source and can be downloaded at www.clarkson.edu/class/cs644/isolation/.

These experiments were run on a single IBM ThinkCentre that ran four virtual machine guests. This physical machine contained a Pentium 4 Processor, 1GB of memory, and a gigabit Ethernet card, while each virtual guest running inside it was granted 128MB of memory and fair-share CPU cycles. An Apache Web server was running in each VM as the common service. We use the Web server benchmark SPECweb to evaluate the Web service quality in the well-behaving VMs (only running Apache Web server) and one misbehaving VM (running Apache Web server and one kind of intensive resource consumer application).

The Web server benchmark SPECweb reported the QoS results in percentage. We calculate the service quality degradation by averaging the well-behaving VM's Good QoS percentage and subtracting them by 100%. In some cases, the Web service was so badly affected and could not provide any service that the SPECweb could not report any results. We used DNR (Do Not Report) to indicate this condition.

In these experiments, their performance isolation properties varied due to different resource consumptions in the misbehaving VM, as shown in Table E.2. For each experiment, we reported the percent degradation in good response rate for both the misbehaving VM and the average for the three well-behaving VMs.

TABLE E.2 Performance Isolation Evaluation on Xen (Xen 3.0)

Resource Consumption	Well-Behaving	Misbehaving
Memory	0.03	DNR
Fork	0.04	DNR
CPU	0.01	0
DISK IO	1.67	11.53
Network Receiving	0	0.33
Network Transmitting	0.04	0.03

Table E.2 illustrates the importance of considering multiple types of "misbehavior" when evaluating the performance isolation properties of a virtualization system. If we looked only at the CPU intensive resource experiment results, our conclusion would have been different than if we had considered the disk and network intensive experiments, or the memory intensive and fork bomb experiments.

In the presence of an intensive CPU stress application running in the misbehaving VM, Xen performed well on this experiment—even in the misbehaving VM. We verified that the CPU load on the misbehaving VM did rise to nearly 100%. We suspected that the normal OS CPU scheduling algorithms were already sufficient to allow the Web server sufficient CPU time. In the memory case, SPECweb in the Xen's misbehaving VM could not report results at all due to the VM running out of memory, but all other well-behaving guests continued to report nearly 100% good results. When the fork bomb ran in the guest, the misbehaving VM presented no results, but the other three well-behaving containers continued to report nearly 100% good response time. When IOzone benchmark ran in the guest, Xen reports a mixed situation. The misbehaving VM saw a degradation of 12%, and the other three VMs were also impacted, showing an average degradation of 1% to 2%. In the network receiving experiment, the misbehaving virtual machine acted as the packet receiver and continuously received packets from an external malicious physical machine. The results showed that the well-behaving VMs had no degradation and the misbehaving VMs showed a slight, but repeatable, degradation of less than 1%. In the network transmitting experiment, the misbehaving virtual machine acted as the packet sender, sending packets to an external physical machine. The misbehaving and well-behaving VMs in Xen were both similarly affected with a very slight degradation of 0.03% to 0.04%.

Overall, the results in Table E.2 indicate that Xen protects the well-behaving VMs. The average degradation for the disk intensive case is the worst at 1.67%. One thing that this table highlights, however, is a slight but consistent degradation on most experiments. More comparisons among VMware Workstation, OpenVZ, and Solaris containers are presented in the original paper.

Performance of Xen Virtual Network and Real Network

Here we discuss an experiment that we conducted to evaluate the network latency introduced by the different modes of the Xen virtual network. We hope that it will be a good reference to help Xen administrators decide how to choose a Xen network setup.

In Xen, xend establishes a virtual network by setting up a soft bridge or soft router in the driver domain. Similar to a hardware bridge in the Ethernet, the soft bridge connects the guest domain transparently to the driver domain's network segment. Similar to a hardware router in the Internet, the soft router connects the virtual network's segment to the Ethernet network segment.

The experiments were taken between two different ThinkCentre machines on the same physical Ethernet. The test machines are Pentium 4 processor, 1GB Memory, and 1 gigabyte network card. We use the ping command to statistically record the network latency. The comparisons were between the two physical machines, two Domain0s, and two guest domains. Each of these three pairs are compared on a physical network, virtual bridging network, and virtual routing network. Following are the experiments we took:

- A physical machine pings itself, as the baseline of the loopback; The Domain0 pings itself.
- The guest domain pings itself.
- The guest domain pings the Domain0 in the same machine.
- Domain0 pings another machine's Domain0 in bridging mode as the baseline of two machines' communication; one Domain0 pings another Domain0 in routing mode; a guest domain in one machine pings a guest domain in another machine.
- One physical machine pings another Domain0 in bridging mode as the baseline for one Xen machine's communicating with a non-Xen machine; one physical machine pings another Domain0 in routing mode; one physical machine pings another guest domain.
- One physical machine pings another physical machine.

In our experiments, the first physical machine or Domain0's IP address was 128.153.145.111, while the second physical machine or Domain0's IP address was 128.153.145.116. The guest domain with IP address 128.153.145.112 is in the first physical machine while another guest domain 128.153.145.113 is in the second physical machine. When using a 100Mb hardware switch, the cables connecting two machines should be as short as possible. In each experiment, we take it three times, record the latter two, and take their average as the final result demonstrated in Table E.3. We discard the first result, considering the discrepancy by setting up the DNS lookup cache for the first time and the clean sending and receiving buffer.

TABLE E.3 Performance Comparison Between With and Without Virtual Network

Experiment No.	Pinging Domain	Pinged Domain	Baseline/ Testing	Echoing Average
1	Loopback in a physical machine		Baseline	0.0215
2	Bridged loopback in Domain0			0.029
3	Routed loopback in Domain0			0.028
4	Bridged guest domain in the same machine	Bridged Domain0 in the same machine		0.1615
5	Routed guest domain in the same machine	Routed Domain0 in the same machine		0.1055
6	Bridged guest domain in the same machine	Bridged guest domain in the same machine		0.183
7	Routed guest domain in the same machine	Routed guest domain in the same machine		0.2865
8	Bridged Domain0	Bridged Domain0	Baseline	0.959
9	Routed Domain0	Routed Domain0		0.935
10	Bridged guest domain	Bridged guest domain		1.1595
11	Routed guest domain	Routed guest domain		1.148
12	Physical machine	Bridged Domain0	Baseline	1.541
13	Physical machine	Bridged guest domain		1.094
14	Physical machine	Routed Domain0		0.8955
15	Physical machine	Routed guest domain		0.920
16	Physical machine	Physical machine		1.832

Generally, from experiments 1-7 and experiments 8-16, we can tell that the communication within the virtual network took much less time than the communication across the real network because it saved the cable latency.

In one machine, overhead introduced by the Domain0's loopback compared to the physical machine's loopback was more than 30%. But regardless of whether Xen is configured in bridging mode or in routing mode, the overheads were almost the same.

Compared to the loopback of a physical machine, a guest domain pinging its own Domain0 introduces almost five times the overhead. That's mostly due to the overhead through the Xen virtual network. The packets either pass through a soft bridge or a soft router. The mechanism to pass the packets from the backend interface of the guest domain to the frontend interface is similar to the loopback. So the overhead is introduced by the bridge or router's forwarding. We found that the virtual routing had introduced more overhead than the virtual bridging.

However, when the guest domain pings another guest domain in the same virtual network (in the same physical machine), the routing mode introduces more overhead than the bridging mode. That's probably because the router operates at a higher layer than the bridge.

When a domain pings a remote domain in another physical machine, the bridging mode and the routing mode do not have distinguishing differences. But obviously, pinging a guest domain introduces more overhead than pinging Domain0.

Finally, when Xen domain in bridging mode pings a physical machine, the guest domain has better performance than Domain0 in the same machine. In routing mode, the guest domain has almost the same performance as Domain0 in the same machine, which is reasonable because the bridge treats Domain0 and the guest domains equivalently when connected over the local Ethernet. The guest domain has less workload than the Domain0 when accessing the Internet. So the guest domain's network performance is better than Domain0. However, in routing mode, Domain0 is the gateway of the guest domain, and all the packets of the guest domain that get sent out to the Internet have to go through Domain0 first.

Summary

In this appendix, we collected a set of experiments to quantify the performance characteristics of Xen including performance, performance isolation, and network performance. You might want to consider running similar experiments on your exact hardware and specific version of Xen. However, we hope our measurements and experiment descriptions help guide you in choosing the number and mixture of Xen guests to deploy and the network configurations to choose.

Index

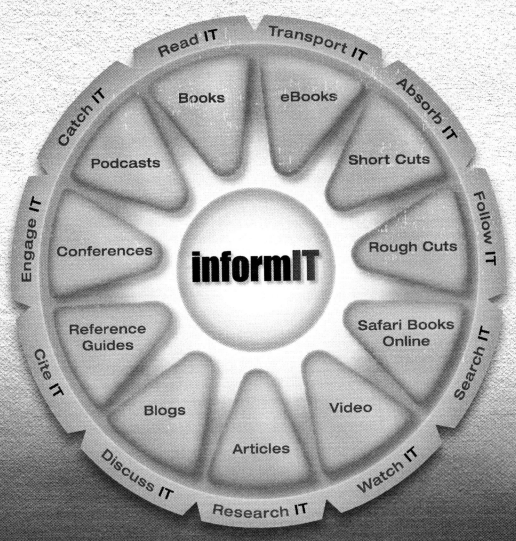

Safari Library
Subscribe Now!
http://safari.informit.com/library

Safari's entire technology collection is now available with no restrictions. Imagine the value of being able to search and access thousands of books, videos and articles from leading technology authors whenever you wish.

EXPLORE TOPICS MORE FULLY

Gain a more robust understanding of related issues by using Safari as your research tool. With Safari Library you can leverage the knowledge of the world's technology gurus. For one flat monthly fee, you'll have unrestricted access to a reference collection offered nowhere else in the world -- all at your fingertips.

With a Safari Library subscription you'll get the following premium services:

- **Immediate access to the newest, cutting-edge books** - Approximately 80 new titles are added per month in conjunction with, or in advance of, their print publication.

- **Chapter downloads** - Download five chapters per month so you can work offline when you need to.

- **Rough Cuts** - A service that provides online access to pre-published information on advanced technologies updated as the author writes the book. You can also download Rough Cuts for offline reference.

- **Videos** - Premier design and development videos from training and e-learning expert lynda.com and other publishers you trust.

- **Cut and paste code** - Cut and paste code directly from Safari. Save time. Eliminate errors.

- **Save up to 35% on print books** - Safari Subscribers receive a discount of up to 35% on publishers' print books.

Safari Books Online

Addison Wesley · Cisco Press · Microsoft Press · Peachpit Press · Redbooks · AdobePress · FT Press FINANCIAL TIMES · New Riders · PRENTICE HALL · Wharton School Publishing · SAMS · ALPHA · lynda.com · O'REILLY · QUE · IBM Press

ALSO AVAILABLE FROM PRENTICE HALL

The Definitive Guide to the Xen Hypervisor

David Chisnall

Foreword by Ian Pratt, Xen Project Leader, VP Advanced Technology, Citrix Systems

Print book ISBN—9780132349710

Also available in PDF, Sony Reader, and Kindle eBook formats, and in Safari Books Online.

This book is a comprehensive handbook on the inner workings of XenSource's powerful open source paravirtualization solution. From architecture to kernel internals, author David Chisnall exposes key code components and shows you how the technology works, providing the essential information you need to fully harness and exploit the Xen hypervisor to develop cost-effective, high-performance Linux and Windows virtual environments.